Time Out

Edinburgh

timeout.com/edinburgh

Published by Time Out Guides Ltd, a wholly owned subsidiary of Time Out Group Ltd.
Time Out and the Time Out logo are trademarks of Time Out Group Ltd.

© Time Out Group Ltd 2006
Previous editions 1998, 2000, 2002, 2004.

10 9 8 7 6 5 4 3 2 1

This edition first published in Great Britain in 2006 by Ebury Publishing
Ebury Publishing is a division of The Random House Group Ltd,
20 Vauxhall Bridge Road, London SW1V 2SA

Random House Australia Pty Limited 20 Alfred Street, Milsons Point, Sydney, New South Wales 2061, Australia
Random House New Zealand Limited 18 Poland Road, Glenfield, Auckland 10, New Zealand
Random House South Africa (Pty) Limited Isle of Houghton, Corner Boundary
Road & Carse O'Gowrie, Houghton 2198, South Africa

Random House UK Limited Reg. No. 954009

Distributed in USA by Publishers Group West
1700 Fourth Street, Berkeley, California 94710

Distributed in Canada by Publishers Group Canada
250A Carlton Street, Toronto, Ontario M5A 2L1

For further distribution details, see www.timeout.com

ISBN
To 31 December 2006: 1-904978-66-5
From 1 January 2007: 9781904978664

A CIP catalogue record for this book is available from the British Library

Colour reprographics by Wyndeham Icon, 3 & 4 Maverton Road, London E3 2JE

Printed and bound in Germany by Appl

Papers used by Ebury Publishing are natural, recyclable products made from wood grown in sustainable forests

Barclay Church. *See p124.*

Time Out Guides Limited
Universal House
251 Tottenham Court Road
London W1T 7AB
Tel + 44 (0)20 7813 3000
Fax + 44 (0)20 7813 6001
Email guides@timeout.com
www.timeout.com

Editorial
Editor Will Fulford-Jones
Deputy Editor Elizabeth Winding
Consultant Editor Keith Davidson
Listings Editor Rebekah McVitie
Proofreader Patrick Mulkern
Indexer Jackie Brind

Editorial/Managing Director Peter Fiennes
Series Editor Ruth Jarvis
Deputy Series Editor Lesley McCave
Business Manager Gareth Garner
Guides Co-ordinator Holly Pick
Accountant Kemi Olufuwa

Design
Art Director Scott Moore
Art Editor Pinelope Kourmouzoglou
Senior Designer Josephine Spencer
Graphic Designer Henry Elphick
Digital Imaging Dan Conway
Ad Make-up Jenni Prichard

Picture Desk
Picture Editor Jael Marschner
Deputy Picture Editor Tracey Kerrigan
Picture Researcher Helen McFarland

Advertising
Sales Director Mark Phillips
International Sales Manager Ross Canadé
International Sales Executive Simon Davies
Advertising Sales (Edinburgh) Christie Dessy
Advertising Assistant Kate Staddon

Marketing
Group Marketing Director John Luck
Marketing Manager Yvonne Poon
Marketing & Publicity Manager, US Rosella Albanese

Production
Group Production Director Mark Lamond
Production Manager Brendan McKeown
Production Coordinator Caroline Bradford

Time Out Group
Chairman Tony Elliott
Managing Director Mike Hardwick
Financial Director Richard Waterlow
TO Magazine Ltd MD David Pepper
Group General Manager/Director Nichola Coulthard
TO Communications Ltd MD David Pepper
Group Art Director John Oakey
Group IT Director Simon Chappell

Contributors
Introduction Will Fulford-Jones. **History** Will Fulford-Jones (*Murders most horrid* Kaye McAlpine; *Going under* Christine Ure).
Edinburgh Today Keith Davidson (*Present imperfect* Mark Robertson, *additional material* Keith Davidson). **Architecture**
Keith Davidson. **Literary Edinburgh** Isla Leaver-Yap (*Down and dirty* Kaye McAlpine). **Festival Edinburgh** Robin Lee
(*My Edinburgh* Jason Hall). **Where to Stay** Ian Sclater (*So spa, so good* Keith Davidson). **Sightseeing: Introduction**
Will Fulford-Jones. **Old Town** Kaye McAlpine (*Enter the labyrinth* Isla Leaver-Yap). **New Town** Kaye McAlpine (*In memoriam*
Ian Sclater, *additional material* Will Fulford-Jones). **Stockbridge** Kaye McAlpine. **Calton Hill & Broughton** Mark Fisher.
Arthur's Seat & Duddingston Keith Davidson, Will Fulford-Jones, Ian Sclater. **South Edinburgh** Keith Davidson (*Pedal power*
Mark Fisher). **West Edinburgh** Keith Davidson. **Leith & the Coast** Keith Davidson. **Restaurants** Keith Davidson (*My Edinburgh*
Jason Hall). **Pubs & Bars** Keith Davidson (*My Edinburgh* Jason Hall). **Shops & Services** Louisa Pearson (*My Edinburgh*,
Walk: Pick up a picnic Jason Hall). **Festivals & Events** Will Fulford-Jones. **Children** Kaye McAlpine. **Comedy** Jason Hall
(*You're having a laugh* Keith Davidson). **Film** Jason Hall. **Galleries** Isla Leaver-Yap. **Gay & Lesbian** Robin Lee. **Music**
Mark Robertson (*My Edinburgh* Jason Hall). **Nightclubs** Dave Pollock. **Sport & Fitness** Keith Davidson. **Theatre & Dance**
Mark Fisher. **Trips Out of Town: Getting Started** Will Fulford-Jones. **Glasgow** *Sightseeing* Neil Scott (*Death on the rock*
Will Fulford-Jones); *Eat, Drink, Shop* Keith Davidson, Louisa Pearson; *Arts & Entertainment* Mark Fisher, Will Fulford-Jones,
Dave Pollock, Mark Robertson, Neil Scott (*Festivals & events* Neil Scott; *Which side are you on?* Will Fulford-Jones); *Where
to Stay* Keith Davidson, Will Fulford-Jones; *Directory* Will Fulford-Jones. **Around Edinburgh** Keith Davidson, Mark Fisher,
Will Fulford-Jones (*Unearthly garden of delights* Ian Sclater). **Directory** Will Fulford-Jones.

Maps JS Graphics (john@jsgraphics.co.uk).

Photography Olivia Rutherford, except: page 12 Private Collection, The Stapleton Collection/The Bridgeman Art Library;
page 15 Private Collection, Agnew's, London, UK/The Bridgeman Art Library; page 16 TopFoto/Fotomas; page 19 Gustavo
Tomsich/Corbis; page 20 Topham Picturepoint, TopFoto.co.uk; pages 107, 113, 122 Muir Vidler; page 110 Alys Tomlinson;
page 190 Tim Porter; page 222 Christina MacDougall; page 244 Manuel Harlan; page 245 Pete Dibdin; page 251
the Glasgow School of Art 1990; page 277 Richard Campbell. The following images were provided by the featured
establishment/artist: pages 45, 167, 183, 219, 230.

The Editor would like to thank Dan Lerner and Helen Pidd, Philip and Debbie Martin at Pilrig House, Haftor Medbøe, and all
contributors to previous editions of *Time Out Edinburgh*, whose work forms the basis for parts of this book.

Contents

Scott Monument.
See p102.

Introduction

The Scots are a famously patriotic bunch, as proud of their nation as the day is long. However, while residents of cities such as Glasgow never tire of talking up their towns and their country, Edinburghers are rather calmer: plainly glad of their origins, but in no particular hurry to shout about them from the rooftops. Such reticence sits comfortably with the city as a whole, which attracts visitors not by bellowing a list of its virtues at them through a megaphone but with a quiet, politely phrased invitation. Even the tatty tartan souvenir shops that line the Royal Mile seem careful not to disrupt the illusion that this is a city entirely out of time.

With only a few conspicuous exceptions (the lad-packed bars of Lothian Road, the clumsy redevelopments on Princes Street), central Edinburgh carries itself with a serene, stately dignity. The architecture in the New Town is solemn, measured, sometimes imperious, but the buildings in the less regimented Old Town also retain a tangible grace. The parks are expansive and, in some cases, quite grand; the sun-worshippers within them are careful to keep themselves covered. Even the traffic, both pedestrian and vehicular, seems to move at a restrained pace. Big-city bustle is largely absent.

Edinburgh derives much of this character from its history, which at times threatens to overwhelm it. The tourist industry is almost entirely predicated on the past: an ancient church here, a ghost tour there, and, towering above the town, the grand old castle. With the exception of those who travel here on business (the town's day-to-day economy is driven by its resident financial institutions) and those who head here in August to take in the chaotic array of cultural festivals, few visit Edinburgh for its present and future.

And yet, at last, the town seems keen to approach the 21st century. Neighbouring Glasgow (covered in detail elsewhere in this book) remains a more culturally vibrant city, but the last decade has seen Edinburgh redefine itself: with high-end restaurants, chic hotels and, most conspicuously, a slew of unashamedly modern new buildings, from the controversial Scottish Parliament complex by Holyroodhouse to a seemingly limitless programme of residential construction in Leith. The city's much-loved past remains in place: the grand monuments, the cosy pubs, the hulking old volcano. But there's also a good deal more to see. Pretty soon, you feel, even the locals might begin to get excited.

ABOUT TIME OUT CITY GUIDES

This is the fifth edition of *Time Out Edinburgh*, one of an expanding series of around 50 Time Out guides produced by the people behind the successful listings magazines in London, New York, Chicago and other cities around the globe. Our guides are all written by resident experts who have striven to provide you with all the most up-to-date information you'll need to explore the city or read up on its background, whether you're a local or a first-time visitor.

THE LOWDOWN ON THE LISTINGS

Above all, we've tried to make this book as useful as possible. Addresses, phone numbers, websites, public transport information, opening times, admission prices and credit card details are all included in the listings, as are details of selected other services and facilities. However, businesses can change their arrangements at any time. Before you go out of your way, we strongly advise you to phone ahead to check opening times and other particulars. While every effort and care has

been made to ensure the accuracy of the information contained in this guide, the publishers cannot accept responsibility for any errors it may contain.

PRICES AND PAYMENT

We have noted where shops, hotels, restaurants, theatres and other venues accept the following credit cards: American Express (AmEx), Diners Club (DC), MasterCard (MC) and Visa (V). Some will also accept other credit cards such as JCB or Discover, travellers' cheques issued by a major financial institution, and debit cards such as Switch or Delta.

The prices we've listed in this guide should be treated as guidelines, not gospel. Fluctuating exchange rates and inflation can cause prices to change rapidly, especially in shops and restaurants. If prices vary wildly from those we've quoted, ask whether there's a good reason, and please email to let us know. We aim to give the best and most up-to-date advice, so we always want to know if you've been badly treated or overcharged.

THE LIE OF THE LAND

Although the street layout can be confusing, especially in the Old Town, Edinburgh's compact size helps make it a relatively straightforward place to negotiate. To make both book and city easier to navigate, we've divided Edinburgh into areas and assigned each one a chapter in our Sightseeing section. The same area names are also used in business addresses throughout the guide. Although these area designations are a simplification of the city's geography, we hope they'll help you to understand its layout. An overview map on pages 322-323 illustrates these areas. In the listings, we've also included postcodes for any venues to which you may need to write.

Every listing in the book also contains details of the bus routes that serve it. Edinburgh's bus system, operated by Lothian Buses is extensive and efficient, with some central destinations served by as many as 20 different routes. For details on the public transport system, *see pp296-297*.

The back of this book also contains street maps for central Edinburgh (and Glasgow), on which are pinpointed the locations of the hotels (❶), restaurants and cafés (❶), and pubs and bars (❶) featured in the guide. The majority of businesses in the book are located in the area covered by these maps; where this is the case, we've included a grid reference.

TELEPHONE NUMBERS

The area code for Edinburgh and its environs is 0131. All telephone numbers in this guide take this code unless otherwise stated. For more on telephones and codes, *see pp305-306*.

ESSENTIAL INFORMATION

For all the practical information you might need for visiting Edinburgh, including visa, customs and immigration information, details of the local transport network, a listing of emergency numbers and a selection of useful websites, please turn to the Directory at the back of the book (*see pp296-309*).

LET US KNOW WHAT YOU THINK

We hope you enjoy *Time Out Edinburgh*, and we'd like to know what you think of it. We welcome tips for places that you consider we should include in future editions, and appreciate your feedback of our choices. Please email us at guides@timeout.com.

There is an online version of this book, along with guides to over 100 international cities, at **www.timeout.com**.

Time Out
Travel Guides

Worldwide

All our guides are
written by a team of
local experts with a
unique and stylish
insider perspective.
We offer essential tips,
trusted advice and
honest reviews for
everything you need
to know in the city.

Over 50 destinations
available at all good
bookshops and at
timeout.com/shop

YOU KNOW WHO YOU ARE.

EDINBURGH
20 GEORGE STREET • 44-131-260-3000
HARDROCK.COM

In Context

Scottish Parliament. *See pp27-29.*

Edinburgh, as mapped by Joris Hoefnagel in the 16th century.

History

The Rock of all ages.

Approach Edinburgh from any direction and the horizon will be dominated by Edinburgh Castle, welded to its basalt outcrop. Catching the rays of the westering sun, visible from halfway to Glasgow and from the opposite shores of Fife, here is a natural fortress whose occupants, secure on their dizzying heights, could survey the flowing waters of the Firth of Forth and watch for raiders approaching in the distance. It was on this natural vantage point that Edinburgh began: first with the fortress on the rock, and eventually with the city that flowed down the castle's ridge, spilling northwards across the intervening valley to the New Town and beyond.

Edinburgh's dramatic setting is the result of a landscape shaped by fire and ice. Over 300 million years ago, volcanoes spewed molten lava across desolate landscapes to form the hills of the city. Creeping northwards across the globe as the continents played their slow game of marriage and divorce, Scotland vanished under vast rivers of grinding, groaning ice,

which carved out a mountainous landscape across it. With the disappearance of the final Ice Age glaciers some 15,000 years ago, the stage was set for the emergence of this most visually striking of cities.

IN THE BEGINNING

It's not known when people first began to colonise the area that became Edinburgh, but traces of human occupation go back more than ten millennia. Rewind 5,000 years and you'd have seen hunter-gatherers foraging along the Water of Leith; go back just three millennia and you would have witnessed the introduction of farming (evidence of which can still be detected in the terraces on the flanks of Arthur's Seat). The hills of Edinburgh bear the signs of early fortification and hut settlements; when dredged in the 18th century, the waters of Duddingston Loch revealed caches of Bronze Age weapons.

It's unknown whether or not the Romans occupied the Castle Rock, although from their fort at Inveresk, five miles away, they would have had a fine view of its imposing bulk. However, it is known to have been a stronghold for Celtic tribes such as the Gododdin. King Mynyddog ruled from the rock at the start of the seventh century; it was he and his people who named it Dun Eidyn, meaning 'hill fort'.

In AD 638, southern Scotland was conquered by the Northumbrians, who built on the rock and Anglicised its name to Edinburgh. (Contrary to popular belief, the name does not derive from the phrase 'Edwin's Burgh'.) But in the middle of the tenth century the MacAlpin kings repelled the Northumbrians southwards. When, in 1018, Malcolm II defeated them at Carham, the rock and the area surrounding it became Scottish.

THE FIRST CASTLE

It was Malcolm III, on the throne from 1058-93, great-grandson of Malcolm II (who reigned from 1005-34), who established the first known castle on the hill. Also known as 'Canmore' ('big head' or 'great leader'), Malcolm is best remembered for his appearance in Shakespeare's *Macbeth* and for his marriage to Margaret, the Saxon princess who, fleeing the arrival of the Normans to England, arrived on the shores of the Forth in 1070 and wed the king. Margaret proved a pious but energetic queen: in between producing nine children, she played a central role in the introduction of Roman Catholicism to Scotland, founded a priory at Dunfermline in Fife, established a ferry service for pilgrims across the Forth and even, it is said, worked several miracles. Having learned of the death of her husband and son in a raid at Alnwick, Margaret died in the royal residence on the Rock in 1093. The oldest extant building on the Rock, the 12th-century St Margaret's Chapel, is dedicated to her.

After a brief period when Malcolm's brother Donald sat on the throne in a joint rule with his nephew Edmund, three of Malcolm and Margaret's six sons went on to rule Scotland. Of these, it was David, the youngest, who had the greatest impact. During his reign, from 1124-53, he established religious foundations throughout Scotland. Edinburgh folklore has it that David was hunting one day when he was knocked from his horse and attacked by a stag, only to be saved when a cross (or 'rood') appeared in his hand. His gratitude to God found a lasting monument in the shape of Holyrood Abbey, which he founded in 1128 with the help of some construction-savvy Augustinian friars. The Gothic ruins of the Abbey can still be seen in the grounds of Holyroodhouse.

Religion, though, was by no means David's only concern. During his three decades on the throne, he established a royal mint in Edinburgh, introduced feudalism to Scotland and established the first royal burghs (towns granted special charters to hold markets and fairs). Edinburgh was one such burgh, although the now-vanished Borders town of Roxburgh and the currently English Berwick then had greater status.

GETTING MY RELIGION

When Holyrood Abbey was completed in 1141, a number of Augustinian monks were brought from St Andrews to fill it. The lower half of what is now the Royal Mile became known as the Canongate, a separate burgh named for the canons at Holyrood; separated from the city of Edinburgh by the defensive Netherbow Port, it didn't officially become part of Edinburgh until 1856.

The Palace of Holyroodhouse wasn't built until 1498, but with the Abbey in place, Edinburgh began to creep down the spine of the volcanic ridge from the Castle Rock. The houses of the city's burgesses faced on to the High Street; behind them, long gardens rolled downwards, their lower walls used as part of the city defences. Parallel to the Canongate, the deep valley of the Cowgate developed into an entrance through which cattle were herded to market; the newly arrived Black Friars (Dominicans) established a friary at its eastern end in 1230. With a succession of religious orders arriving in town (the Dominicans were followed by the Franciscans, or Grey Friars, in 1429), Edinburgh became an ecclesiastical centre of some importance.

The other main religious building in the settlement was the Church of St Giles, today's High Kirk of St Giles. Historians have found mention of a church in Edinburgh as early as 845, but the building that is believed to have once stood on the site of St Giles's was replaced by Alexander I in 1120. The church was formally dedicated by Bishop David de Bernham of St Andrews in 1243.

BRUCIE BONUS

While riding his horse along the coast one stormy night in 1286, Scotland's King Alexander III fell to his death over a cliff at Kinghorn. Alexander left no living children to inherit his title; his young granddaughter, the so-called 'Maid of Norway', died before she could be brought to the throne. With his demise began a long and sombre chapter in Scotland's history of warfare with England.

Repeatedly ravaged by English armies, Scotland nevertheless managed to secure its independence after Robert the Bruce's victory at Bannockburn in 1314. The Treaty of Edinburgh was signed in 1328, ending hostilities between the two kingdoms.

The following year, Bruce granted Edinburgh the status of royal burgh, giving its burgesses important fiscal privileges.

However, Bruce died mere months later. David II, his son and successor, was only five years old when he ascended to the throne, a position of weakness that left the kingdom vulnerable to renewed strikes by the English. Edward III attacked first in 1333; and then, nine years after David's death in 1371, Richard II followed suit, besieging the castle and burning both the Canongate and St Giles.

'By the time Mary, Queen of Scots returned from France, politics was dominated by religious unrest.'

David II had died without having produced an heir, and was succeeded by Robert II, the son of Walter the Steward and Robert the Bruce's daughter, Marjorie. Through this dynastic marriage, Robert II was able to start a dynasty of his own: the House of Stewart. It was during this period that Edinburgh emerged as Scotland's most populous burgh, a position it was to hold for the next 400 years.

A DRAMATIC DYNASTY

The Stewarts proved to be dynastically tenacious, and went on to rule Scotland for three centuries. As individuals, however, they were somewhat short-lived; this was a period of lawlessness that saw successive kings murdered or killed in battle, the throne then passing to children who were too young to rule in their own right. This succession of Stewart child-kings in turn left Scotland vulnerable to the machinations of rival court factions. The family also, as we shall see, proved somewhat unimaginative in their choice of baby names.

James I (1406-37) tried to curb the power of the nobles, but himself became a victim of their power struggles and was murdered at Blackfriars in Perth in 1437. His six-year-old son was hastily crowned James II by his mother at Holyrood Abbey, but his turbulent reign ended with by now obligatory abruptness in 1460 when he was killed by an exploding cannon while besieging the English occupiers of Roxburgh Castle.

It was during James II's time on the throne that the Old Town began to take shape. The Grassmarket and the Cowgate started to form more fully, though development to the south and north was made difficult by natural features such as the Craig Burn, which was dammed in the mid 15th century for defensive purposes, and became the Nor' Loch. The town's first defensive

wall was built around this time: called the King's Wall, it ran eastwards from halfway down the south side of the Castle Rock, above the Grassmarket and the Cowgate, to the Netherbow, then dipped down to the Nor' Loch. As the town crept along the spine of the ridge, the familiar herringbone pattern of narrow closes and wynds began to emerge. It's still visible in places today, but in medieval times, the closes would have been muddy, steep, slippery and covered in ordure from both people and animals. The worst part of all this? Soap was not manufactured in Edinburgh until 1554.

The principal landmarks in the medieval city were the Castle, the Lawnmarket, the High Kirk of St Giles, the Mercat Cross and the Tolbooth, on the south side of the High Street. The last of these was, as its name would suggest, a booth where tolls were paid. Later, a prison was added; by the 15th century, both the Scottish Parliament and the Court of Session had begun to meet there.

Like his father and his grandfather, James III (1460-88) inherited the throne as a child, at a time when his kingdom was riven by warring factions and power struggles. His mother, Mary of Gueldres, demanded that Parliament (then sitting in the Castle) name her regent; all the while, the young king was at the bottom of the hill in Holyrood Abbey with the Bishop of St Andrews. The precarious situation caused the Edinburgh mob to riot, the first recorded glimpse of the volatile and well-organised body that would cause havoc at regular intervals over the next few centuries.

Despite the turbulence, the Cowgate emerged as the town's fashionable quarter during James's reign, the French writer Froissart remarking on its fine aristocratic mansions, gardens and orchards. From around 1485, dwellings were also built in the Canongate: while the walled city was growing overcrowded, these new houses boasted both spacious rooms and back gardens. But the lack of a defensive wall left the area open to attack, and the Abbey itself was regularly sacked and looted by a host of interlopers.

Commerce was also flourishing. As the only major town with a port between the Tweed and the Forth, Edinburgh was ideally placed to capitalise on foreign trade opportunities; between 1320 and 1450, for example, wool exports boomed. But when, in 1469, the town ceased to be ruled by the merchant burgesses, it became a self-electing corporation. Cloth sellers, beggars and fishwives plied their trade from booths around St Giles on the High Street; their stalls eventually became permanent fixtures.

In 1477, James III chartered markets to be held in the Grassmarket, partly to alleviate the congestion caused by traders on the High

Holyrood Abbey. *See p13*.

Street. He granted the citizens of Edinburgh the Blue Blanket just five years later, a symbol of the independence of the municipality, its right to levy customs at the port of Leith, and the exclusive rights of the town's craftsmen.

There was an ulterior motive behind for James's kindness to Edinburgh. In 1479, at the behest of his Flemish astrologer, he imprisoned his two brothers. One, the Earl of Mar, had died in the Canongate Tolbooth, but the other, the Duke of Albany, had escaped from the castle by drugging his jailers, and promptly fled to France. When the English attempted to put Albany on the throne, James mustered an army to face them, but a group of disgruntled Scottish nobles took the opportunity to imprison James in the Castle. The English, under the command of the future Richard III, entered the Tolbooth and demanded that James be released into Richard's hands. But the Edinburgh mob rioted, and Albany realised that his brother still had popular support. James kept the throne.

WRITING THE WRONGS

Although he was just 15 years old at the time of his coronation, James IV immediately set about enhancing the status and reputation of his crown and his kingdom. An educated man, whose reign coincided with the end of the medieval age, James is often described as the 'Renaissance prince'. His extensive architectural programme saw the construction of the Great Halls of Stirling and Edinburgh castles and the addition of a gold-tipped crown spire to St Giles Cathedral, but it was far from his only legacy: he also founded the Scottish navy.

The arts also benefited from James's enthusiasm. The first Scottish printing press opened in 1507 at the foot of Blackfriars Wynd, the narrow street that led from the High Street to the Dominican Friary. Founded by Walter Chapman and Andro Myllar, it published books on government and law along with works by two of Scotland's greatest poets, William Dunbar and Robert Henryson.

The first selection of Dunbar's work to be published, in 1508, offers a snapshot of life in the town. In one vitriolic passage, Dunbar attacks the city fathers for their tight-fisted attitudes; in another, which carries currency to this day, he outlines the differences between Edinburgh's rich and poor. Following in his footsteps, the likes of James Hogg and Robert Louis Stevenson have found mileage in the idea that behind Edinburgh's elegant façade lurks something demonic.

SCOTLAND 2, ENGLAND 2

Holyrood witnessed an occasion of some grandeur on 8 August 1503, when James IV married Henry VII's 12-year-old daughter, Margaret Tudor. The events that followed were considerably less splendid. As part of the marriage settlement, James had signed the Treaty of Perpetual Peace with England, but

Murders most horrid

Edinburgh's history is defined by grisly death, its landscape dotted with grim reminders of those who died in less than fortunate circumstances. Few boast grimmer histories than the **Grassmarket**, one of Edinburgh's chief execution sites. A Covenanter memorial on the raised ground next to the zebra crossing marks the spot where the gallows once stood. However, it wasn't just Covenanters who died here: dozens of people had the life choked out of them at the end of the hangman's noose. In this light, the name of the Last Drop pub takes on a new meaning; next to it is Maggie Dickson's, named for a woman ('Half-Hangit Maggie') who survived her execution. It's hardly surprising that the area is said to be haunted by a man with rope burns around his neck.

Captain John Porteous was one of many who died here, but not at the gallows. Porteous, Captain of the City Guard, had broken up a riot that followed the hanging of smuggler Andrew Wilson by ordering his troops to fire at will, wounding or killing more than 30 people. Found guilty of murder, Porteous

was sentenced to death in 1736, but when news came through that he was to be reprieved, a furious mob liberated him from prison, dragged him to the Grassmarket and strung him up from a dyer's pole (*pictured left*).

The **High Street** also had its share of dramatic executions, including that of William Burke on 28 January 1829 (*see p23*). Thousands came to watch him kick out his last at the Lawnmarket. By all accounts, the day was like a public holiday: although many wanted him 'burked' or strangled by hand, the crowd's roar when he was hanged could be heard in the New Town.

Down in **Parliament Square**, next to St Giles, Robert Johnstone suffered the indignity of being hanged twice in a single day. Found guilty of robbery, the 23-year-old Johnstone was hanged on 30 December 1818, but the gallows failed, commonly seen as evidence of divine intervention. The crowd, who wanted him released, attacked the magistrates, cut Johnstone down and bore him off, hotly pursued by police constables. A tug-of-war began, with the unconscious Johnstone as the rope. The police won, whereupon Johnstone was revived, taken back to the gallows and – bloodied, disorientated and bareheaded – hanged once more. The whole episode took eight hours.

The **Mercat Cross** now stands at Parliament Square, but it used to be further down the High Street, nearer Old Fishmarket Close and the Fringe Office; you can see the outline in cobbles. The Covenanting James Graham, fifth Earl and first Marquis of Montrose, was executed here in 1650. Dressed in white gloves and fluttering ribbons, he was said to look more like a bridegroom than a felon. After being hanged, his body was quartered: his head was stuck on the tollbooth, while his limbs went to Stirling, Perth, Glasgow and Aberdeen. After the Reformation, his remains were buried in St Giles.

Montrose died a traitor's death, high treason insofar as that he stood against the king. However, petty treason – acts of violence or murder against your father, master or husband – could also reap a dreadful punishment, and few were more terrible than that suffered by Robert Weir. Apprehended in 1604 for the murder four years earlier of the Laird of Warriston, for whom he had worked as a servant, Weir was one of only a few people in Scotland ever to be broken on the wheel, his bones smashed one by one with the cutting edge of a plough. Weir was left to die a slow and agonising death; records show that after 24 hours at the Mercat Cross, Weir (plus wheel) was transported to the scene of his crime near Warriston.

Weir was not the only person implicated in the murder: Jean Livingstone, the Laird's wife, and several other servants were also executed for the crime, just four days after it took place. Livingstone's serving women were strangled and then burned on Castlehill, close to the spot where today stands the Witches' Memorial (*pictured below*). The lady herself was beheaded at the Maiden, Edinburgh's guillotine (now on display at the Museum of Scotland), at the Girth Cross of Holyrood.

it signally failed to live up to its name. Only a decade after the accord, the French persuaded James to attack England, and the two countries went to war once more.

In 1513, James IV led his army into Northumberland. Despite their numerical superiority, the Battle of Flodden was a disaster for the Scots: 10,000 were killed, among them the king himself. In Edinburgh, disbelief at the defeat turned to panic when it was realised the English might press north and attack the city. Work on the Flodden Wall began, though the attack never materialised. Still visible in parts today, it had six entry points; when it was eventually completed in 1560, it formed the town's boundary for a further two centuries.

The life and death of James's son James V, who ascended to the throne in 1513 at the age of one, continued the dynastic turmoil but added to it a religious element. When James died in 1542, it was thought that stability could be ensured by marrying off his six-day-old daughter – the future Mary, Queen of Scots. But to whom? The Scots were split between those who wanted a French alliance (Cardinal Beaton and Mary's mother, Mary of Guise, among them) and those who preferred an English match.

Henry VIII of England sent the Earl of Hertford's army to Scotland to 'persuade' the Scots that a marriage to his son, Edward, was preferable. After landing at Leith in the early summer in 1544, Hertford went on to loot both the Abbey and the Palace of Holyroodhouse in an episode that has come to be known as the 'rough wooing'. Hertford's 10,000-strong forces then stormed the Netherbow, but were repulsed.

Three years later, though, in September 1547, the English returned with an army commanded by the Duke of Somerset. The Battle of Pinkie Cleuch was fought at Musselburgh, just outside the town, between the insurgent English and the defensive Scots. The Scots lost and were chased back to the gates, but the castle was held; after French and Dutch reinforcements arrived in Leith the following year, the English were finally repelled and the port was reinforced to prevent further invasion. At the age of five, Mary was sent to live in France; by the time she returned, Scottish politics was dominated by religious unrest.

MARRIAGE AND MURDER

The Reformation Parliament declared Protestantism to be Scotland's official religion in 1560, and John Knox became the leader of the Reformed Church. The faction that had previously been pro-French and pro-Mary now also became pro-Catholic, while the Protestant forces rallied against them. Knox hated Mary, and the period between her arrival at Leith from

France in August 1561 and her abdication in 1567 saw much friction between the Catholic monarchy and the Protestant church.

Mary married Henry Darnley, a cousin, in 1565. Darnley was a grandchild of Margaret Tudor, which made Elizabeth I even more suspicious of their claims on the English throne. Darnley was also a shameless manipulator: it has been suggested that the brutal assassination at Holyrood in 1566 of David Rizzio, Mary's favoured Italian secretary, was engineered by him in an attempt to cause Mary to miscarry, and perhaps even kill her, leaving the throne vacant for his assumption.

The couple's relationship became increasingly fractious until, in 1567, Darnley's house was blown up with him inside. While no proof of Mary's involvement ever emerged, suspicions fell upon Lord Bothwell, one of her most loyal supporters. When the pair subsequently married, public opinion turned violently against the Queen. Forced to abdicate in favour of her infant son, the future James VI, Mary escaped from imprisonment at Loch Leven Castle, only to have her army defeated near Glasgow. She took refuge in England, spending 19 years as the prisoner of Elizabeth I before her execution in 1587.

THE WISEST FOOL IN CHRISTENDOM

Born in a tiny room in Edinburgh castle, James VI (1567-1625) was brought up by Protestant tutors, alienated from his mother, and subject to several kidnapping attempts as a child. By the time he assumed the reins of government, he had grown into a suspicious and wary man. His reign was a permanent headache, thanks to tussles with the economy, the nobles and, above all, the Church.

James VI's long-term ambition was to inherit the English crown from the childless Elizabeth I. Elizabeth, meanwhile, was reluctant to formally recognise 'that false Scotch urchin' as her heir. However, on her death in 1603, Sir Robert Carey galloped up from London to Holyrood in an incredible 36 hours to announce that James VI of Scotland was now James I of England. James, once described as 'the wisest fool in Christendom', left for London to be crowned king, an event known as 'the Union of the Crowns'. He promised to return to Scotland every three years, but it was 16 years before Scotland saw its monarch again.

The years following James's departure were characterised by social unrest, religious turmoil and a loss of national identity, as Scotland came to terms with absentee rule. One particularly unpleasant legacy left by James was the regular witch hunts, held until 1670. Suspected witches were tried first by immersion in the Nor' Loch;

those who managed to escape drowning were then burned at the stake. In all, some 300 women died in this fashion.

But despite the difficulties faced by the country as a whole, the first years of the 17th century were not unprofitable for Edinburgh. Local merchants thrived, with goldsmiths, watchmakers and bookbinders all flourishing in Parliament Square, and the University of Edinburgh, founded in 1582 as the Tounis College, continued to grow. Early 17th-century building work bears testament to the town's prosperity: the east wing of the Castle was rebuilt by Sir James Mason, Parliament House was begun in 1632 (the Scottish Parliament was, by then, resident in the city), and, a year later, Holyroodhouse was extended.

MERRY MONARCHS

James died in 1625 and was succeeded by his son, Charles I, who was crowned King of Scots in 1633. Charles made it his mission to impose uniformity throughout the kingdom, but his attempt to force bishops on the Presbyterian Church met with strong resistance. A riot broke out in St Giles in 1637, with an old cabbage seller by the name of Jenny Geddes throwing her stool at Dean Hanna, shouting, 'Dost thou say mass in my lug?' The Bishop of Edinburgh mounted the pulpit in an attempt to calm the crowd, but the riot spread into the streets.

As a result of this perceived assault on their freedoms, a document called the National Covenant was drawn up in order to assert the Scots' rights to both spiritual and civil liberty. On the last day of February 1638, it was read from the pulpit of Greyfriars Kirk; over the next two days, a host of lairds and burgesses came to sign it. Thus began the turmoil of the Covenanting Wars, which were to continue into the reign of Charles II.

Edinburgh suffered horribly during the troubles that ensued. Trade dropped off dramatically and, in 1644, plague killed a fifth of the population. Although Edinbugh's sanitation didn't improve – it wasn't until 1687 that Parliament decreed that the council should provide 20 carts to remove refuse – it remained a lively place to be. Golf was played in virtually any open space, archery was practised by many locals, and the young men of the town were apt to use their pistols to shoot fowl from their windows. The Kirk, for its part, was forever berating the townspeople for spending Sundays in ale houses.

A map drawn in 1647 shows a bewildering number of closes running off the High Street and down through the Cowgate, with St Giles and the old burying ground behind. Edinburgh spread a little beyond the Flodden Wall in 1617

Mary, Queen of Scots. *See p18.*

when High Riggs was bought by the town, and further areas were added in 1639 – notably Calton Hill and the Pleasance, to the north and south of the Canongate.

> **'The misery of civil war was exacerbated by wretched living conditions and a series of terrible harvests.'**

Charles had been distracted from events in Edinburgh by the outbreak of civil war in England. Although Edinburgh Castle was held by forces loyal to the King, the rule of the Covenant held sway elsewhere in the town. By 1649, Oliver Cromwell had assumed power in England; on 30 January, Charles I was executed at Whitehall in London. The Scots were outraged that their Parliament had not been consulted – after all, Charles had been their king too – but six days later proclaimed Charles II king of Scotland, on the condition he accepted the Covenanters' demands.

Charles refused, and instead asked the Marquis of Montrose, who had been loyal to his father, to conquer Scotland for him. However, Montrose was defeated and captured by the Covenanters, brought to Edinburgh and, on 21 May 1650, executed. Cromwell's response was to invade, defeating the Scots under General Leslie at the Battle of Dunbar on 3 September 1650; 3,000 Scottish soldiers died in battle, while a further 10,000 were taken prisoner.

RESTORATION, RESTORATION

Although Cromwell's government and the Scots' Presbyterian Church shared the same values, Cromwell's Scottish occupation proved increasingly unpopular, thanks in no small part to the swingeing taxes he imposed for the maintenance of his army. Charles II's return to the throne after Cromwell's death in 1658, an event that became known as the Restoration, was therefore greeted with relief.

It didn't last. When Charles II reneged on acts made in favour of Covenanters, discontent simmered once again. After the Covenanters won a crucial victory at the Battle of Drumclog in 1679, Charles sent the Duke of Monmouth to crush them, which he did at the Battle of Bothwell Brig later that year. In a period since nicknamed 'the Killing Time', the survivors were marched to Greyfriars Kirkyard in Edinburgh and imprisoned for five months with little food, shelter or water. Many died or were executed; several hundred others were sent as slaves to Barbados.

James VII of Scotland (simultaneously James II of England) ascended the thrones of both countries on the death of his brother Charles in 1685, but his Catholicism made him unpopular. The Dukes of Argyll and Monmouth tried and failed to unseat him. But when James finally fathered a male heir, a group of English noblemen sought to replace him with William of Orange, a Protestant, and his wife Mary (James's daughter). James fled to France and the protection of Louis XIV.

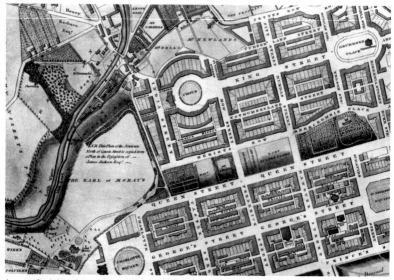
James Craig's 18th-century plans for Edinburgh's **New Town**. *See p21.*

AN END TO AN OLD SONG

Many in Edinburgh and in the Scottish Parliament were delighted by William's ascension to the throne; some even burned effigies of the Pope on hearing the news of his landing. However, supporters of James VII, named 'Jacobites' after the Latin for James (*Jacobus*), mounted resistance to the new regime almost as soon as their leader had gone into exile. The misery of civil war was exacerbated by wretched living conditions, a series of terrible harvests, and an English war with France that had a serious impact on trade. Then, in 1698, the so-called Darien Scheme, designed to establish a trading colony in Central America, virtually bankrupted the nation. At this news, the citizens finally cracked, storming the Tolbooth and setting fire to the Cowgate.

The collapse of the scheme strengthened the hand of those who promoted a union of the Scottish and Westminster parliaments. After much discussion, argument and lavish bribery, the Act of Union became law in January 1707, with the dissolution of the Scots Parliament following three months later. When Lord Seafield, the Lord High Chancellor of Scotland, was presented with the act for royal assent, he is reported to have touched it with his sceptre and said: 'There's an end of an auld sang'. It would be nearly 300 years before the Scottish Parliament sat again.

THE AGE OF IMPROVEMENT

The 18th century is known in Edinburgh as the 'Age of Improvement'. The phrase refers to the massive building programme that was implemented in the 1760s, but also to the influence of the Enlightenment – the spirit of intellectual inquiry that flourished in the 18th century – among the lawyers, academics and churchmen of the city. Edinburgh was buzzing with the words of men such as the philosopher David Hume, geologist James Hutton and economist Adam Smith, author of *The Wealth of Nations*.

Social and cultural improvements arrived apace. The year 1725 saw Lord Provost George Drummond draw up plans for a new medical school; four years later, the city's first infirmary opened at Robertson's Close, receiving a Royal Charter in 1736. The number of students at the university doubled between 1763 and 1783, the year the Royal Society of Edinburgh was founded; by 1821, it had quadrupled. Able to support two newspapers as early as 1720, this was a cultured town: the formation of a school of design in 1760 pre-dated London's Royal Academy by eight years.

However, at the start of the 18th century the city's geography was still profoundly medieval in its nature; a cramped, towering whole clinging grimly on to the hillside. By and large, the old city walls still formed the town boundaries, so as the population grew to well over 50,000 during the 18th century, the only way to build was up. This resulted in the 'lands'; six-, seven-, and even eight-storey buildings that were prone to collapse. Something needed to be done, but what?

REBELLION AND ENLIGHTENMENT

Gradually, southern Scottish cities such as Edinburgh and Glasgow came to realise that their union with Great Britain offered beneficial opportunities for commerce and trade. Edinburgh was initially seduced by the glamour of Charles Edward Stuart, better known as Bonnie Prince Charlie: he 'took' the city in 1745 with the assistance of a number of Highland clans, before heading southwards in an attempt to claim the British throne. However, the sympathies of the townspeople ultimately remained Hanoverian.

Shortly after Stuart's last fateful stand at Culloden, the city embarked on an incredibly ambitious building programme: the expansion of Edinburgh across the valley north of the castle. The scheme was influenced by the appalling living conditions in the plague- and epidemic-prone Old Town, but it also had a political motivation: to demonstrate to the world that Edinburgh was a civilised, cultured European city.

The competition to design the New Town was won in 1766 by a 22-year-old architect named James Craig. His plan was simple, elegant and harmonious, consisting chiefly of three main streets (Princes, George and Queen) positioned between two imposing squares.

> **'Visitors are often unaware that the city's handsome centre is ringed by poorly resourced housing schemes.'**

But work on the development had begun long before Craig won the commission. The Nor' Loch was drained in the early 1760s; then, in 1763, work on the North Bridge, built to span the valley separating the old and new parts of the city, started in earnest. The two million cartloads of earth dug from the foundations of the New Town formed the basis for the Mound, begun in 1781 but not completed until 1830.

Going under

Ever since James IV awarded a charter to the Barber Surgeons of Edinburgh in 1567, the city has been an important centre of medical research. It's a tradition that continues to this day, with a number of biotech firms and research labs based in and around the city (including the Roslin Institute, responsible for cloning Dolly the sheep), but which found arguably its most important pioneer just over 150 years ago.

Until the mid 19th century, the only relief from the pains of surgery was a stiff drink or a session of hypnosis. Appalled by the suffering he witnessed while working as the Professor of Midwifery at the University of Edinburgh, Dr James Young Simpson resolved to find a means of making operations and childbirth safer and less traumatic. By 1847, he had found what he believed to be the ideal method: chloroform.

The conservative medical profession viewed Simpson's findings with suspicion, but he wasn't deterred. Intent on demonstrating chloroform's effectiveness and safety, he invited colleagues to dinner at his Queen Street house. There, abandoning the Victorian tradition of passing the port after dinner, he casually passed the ether instead.

Finding themselves abandoned in the drawing room, Mrs Simpson and the other ladies hastened to the dining room and found all three doctors sprawled asleep and snoring at the table. His point was proven.

Simpson faced more opposition from the (all-male) clergy, who decreed that painless childbirth went against the Biblical commandment that women should 'bring forth children in sorrow'. Simpson, every woman's hero, countered this by reminding the churchmen that when creating Eve 'from Adam's rib', God first considerately rendered Adam unconscious.

Support for anaesthesia eventually came from an exalted, if unexpected, quarter. Queen Victoria, already a mother of seven and the wiser for it, would not be deterred from enlisting chloroform in giving birth to her eighth. The safe arrival of Prince Leopold in 1853 proved the endorsement Simpson needed, especially when the grateful Queen created him baronet, the first ever appointed for medical services. One of Dr Simpson's first non-royal patients to give birth with the help of chloroform was so delighted that she saddled her unfortunate daughter with the name Anaesthesia.

Around the same time, Edinburgh also pushed southwards: George Square was laid out in 1766, and a new college for the university was built in 1789 at the old Kirk O'Fields. But it was the New Town that proved most popular: around 7,000 people were living there by 1792, including many rich lawyers and merchants. The result of the wealthier classes moving northwards was that a social apartheid of sorts formed, the notion of a city with two faces surfacing once more. The contrast between the respectable gentility of the New Town and the squalid low-life of the Old Town, with its cock-fighting dens, oyster taverns and brothels, became a recurring theme that even 21st-century Edinburgh has found hard to shift.

The duality of life in 18th-century Edinburgh is perfectly reflected in the tale of Deacon William Brodie. A respected craftsman and councillor by day, Brodie spent his nights drinking, gambling and whoring around the Old Town. Having racked up immense debts in the process, Brodie was forced to turn to thieving in a bid to better balance his income and his expenditure. When his double life was uncovered, he fled to Amsterdam, but was eventually captured and hanged in 1788 from gallows he himself had helped design. His story eventually inspired Robert Louis Stevenson to pen *The Strange Case of Dr Jekyll and Mr Hyde*.

GREAT SCOTT

The rise of the New Town virtually parallels the increased influence of Edinburgh-born Sir Walter Scott (1771-1832), a titan of the late 18th and early 19th centuries. Scott's character and interests were largely influenced by time spent as a child in the Borders, where he had been sent to recuperate from the polio that would leave him with a permanent limp. The romance of Borders legends and ballads enthralled the imaginative child, and the collection of similar stories from all parts of Scotland became a life-long passion.

After an education at the Royal High School and the Law Faculty of the University, Scott embarked on a legal career that would eventually see him become Deputy Sheriff of Selkirk and Principal Clerk to the Court of Session in Edinburgh, while simultaneously finding great acclaim as a writer. But while his literary and legal works are rightly famed, his wider influence should not be underestimated: his tireless efforts almost single-handedly awakened the world to the romantic potential of Scotland, and paved the way for its rehabilitation after the Jacobite debacle. It was thanks to Scott's enthusiasm and perseverance that the long-lost 'Honours of Scotland' – the crown, sceptre and sword of state – were uncovered from their hiding place in Edinburgh Castle and put on public display. He was also responsible for the first visit to Scotland of a British monarch since the reign of Charles II, when, in 1822, he persuaded George IV to visit the capital of 'North Britain'.

So well had Scott succeeded in restoring Highland traditions that lowland Edinburgh was awash with tartan for the King's visit (kilts, the dress of the Highland rebels, had been banned after Culloden). Even portly George appeared before his subjects swathed in tartan, albeit with the precautionary addition of pink

The **Heart of Midlothian** marks the site of the **Tolbooth**, destroyed in 1817.

silk tights to shield the Royal knees from impious gazes. One Edinburgh lady remarked that since the Scots had so few opportunities to admire the Royal personage, it was just as well the King revealed so much of it during his visit.

VICTORIAN EDINBURGH

Edinburgh added a number of notable features to its townscape in the first three decades of the 19th century, among them Waterloo Bridge in the east and Melville Street in the west. However, not every construction project ended in success; or, for that matter, ended at all. Begun in 1822, William Playfair's National Monument to honour the dead of the Napoleonic Wars was never completed but never destroyed: the Parthenon-like structure, long ago dubbed 'Scotland's Disgrace', stands on Calton Hill to this day, a reminder that Scotland was once again losing its way. Power was in held by London and the intellectual activity of the Enlightenment was declining. Edinburgh's glory days were behind it.

Regardless of this, the city underwent a third period of expansion during the Victorian era, when suburbs such as Marchmont, Morningside and Bruntsfield were erected. The city that had become two-part when the New Town was built found itself with still more faces, each with its own character. The solid Victorian suburbs were peopled by the growing middle classes; the grand New Town remained the area of choice for lawyers and judges; and the teeming Old Town became a slum.

The building frenzy was matched by the missionary zeal of the Free Kirk, which came into being when 474 ministers seceded from the Church to form a breakaway organisation in May 1843 (the 'Disruption'). The occasion was the General Assembly, the grievance was the right of congregations to choose their own minister, and the scene of the split was the Church of St Andrew and St George on George Street. The dissenting churchmen marched down Hanover Street to Tanfield Hall in Canonmills; 'No spectacle since the Revolution,' noted Lord Cockburn in his journal, 'reminded one so forcibly of the Covenanters.' The split wasn't resolved until 1929.

Through it all, the population of greater Edinburgh spiralled, growing from 100,000 at the start of the 19th century to 320,000 by 1881. One of the reasons for the dramatic increase was the influx of people from Ireland and the Scottish highlands; displaced by the Clearances, they moved to the city in search of work. Among them were William Burke and William Hare, a pair of Irish labourers who came to work on the Union Canal to the west of the city, but eventually abandoned digging ditches in favour

of a more lucrative trade supplying corpses to the University's Anatomy School. Burke and Hare infamously spurned the established – if somewhat unsavoury – practice of digging up recently buried bodies in favour of providing fresh ones, unfortunate by-products of a killing spree the pair carried out from their lodgings in the West Port, just off the Grassmarket. Convicted of 16 murders in 1829, Burke was hanged on the evidence of his turncoat partner. A pocketbook made from his skin is still on display in the somewhat grisly medical museum at Surgeon's Hall on South Bridge.

With the increase in population came unemployment. Riots in 1812 and 1818 were both blamed on poor economic conditions; by the 1830s, outbreaks of cholera and typhoid had decimated the Old Town. The misery was compounded in 1824 when a fire destroyed much of the High Street, leading to the formation of the world's first municipal fire service.

A study conducted by Dr George Bell in the 1850s found that 159 of the Old Town's closes lacked drainage and fresh water. Bell also bemoaned the alcoholism endemic among the Old Town's inhabitants; a decade or so earlier, a separate study undertaken by a young doctor named William Tait had found by that the area contained an impressive 200 brothels. Attempts were made to restore the neighbourhood, particularly by William Chambers (Lord Provost from 1865-69), but it was on a downward spiral that was to continue into the 20th century.

When the neglected Paisley Close on the High Street collapsed in 1861, killing 35 people, public outrage caused the Town Council to agree to the adoption of proper health and safety regulations. Dr Henry Littlejohn was appointed as the first Medical Officer of Health in Scotland. Littlejohn's report on sanitary conditions in Edinburgh coincided with the election of the philanthropic publisher William Chambers as Lord Provost, resulting in the improvement scheme of 1866 that cleared some of the congested slums of the Old Town and created new streets such as St Mary's and Blackfriars, both of which provided housing for artisans.

FASTER THAN WITCHES

The Victorian era was also defined by technological advances, particularly in the fields of transport and medicine. In the early 1600s, London was 13 days away by coach; towards the end of the century, the journey could be done in a 'mere' four days. But with the advent of the age of steam, travel became far easier, to the benefit of all concerned.

Between 1845 and 1846, rail tunnels were built between Haymarket and Waverley Stations, through the south flank of Calton

Hill and under the Mound. Trains travelling through them brought tourists and travellers straight into the heart of the city, where they would emerge to face the Castle, the Gothic bulk of the Scott Monument (begun in 1840), the galleries at the foot of the Mound and the splendour of the Princes Street Gardens. A century and a half later, it's still the best way to arrive in the city. The first public train ran between London and Edinburgh in 1850; just 12 years later, the famous *Flying Scotsman* did the run in only ten-and-a-half hours. In 1890 the completion of the Forth Bridge, hailed as the eighth wonder of the world, linked the city with towns beyond the Forth, while a network of suburban lines facilitated Edinburgh's expansion into outlying villages.

And yet for all Edinburgh's optimistic expansion, Glasgow had begun to assume increasing importance in Scotland by the end of the Victorian era. The two international festivals held in Glasgow in 1888 and 1901 far outshone the one staged at the Meadows in Edinburgh in 1886; at the same time, Glaswegians such as designer Charles Rennie Mackintosh were creating an artistic and architectural legacy that is still revered today. As the historian and journalist Allan Massie has pointed out, Edinburgh at the end of the 19th century was just the biggest small town in Scotland.

THE 20TH CENTURY

The history of the first half of the 20th century was dominated by the two world wars. Scots made up ten per cent of British recruitment in the Great War, with 25 per cent of the Scottish male population marching off to war. Long lists of the many who did not return can be seen on Lorimer's Scottish National War Memorial at the Castle.

Although a Zeppelin raid in 1916 caused damage in Leith (and also, with ironic accuracy, scored a direct hit on the German Church at Bellevue), Edinburgh itself suffered very few direct attacks in the first war. The city's lack of heavy industry meant it also escaped the worst ravages of the Depression in the 1930s, and athough it was a peripheral victim of the first air raid of World War II in October 1939, when the Luftwaffe attacked Royal Navy cruisers off Inchgarvie in the Forth, it also was spared the worst of the aerial attacks during the conflict. Still, Edinburgh already had plenty on its plate.

Although few buildings of any great architectural repute were added during the 20th century, the shape of the city continued to morph. The suburbs went on creeping outwards, but buildings were in general more likely to be pulled down than put up. At last, the city fathers (and private contractors) finally got to grips with the decaying Old Town, upgrading the city's infrastructure while simultaneously moving the population to outlying areas such as Niddrie and Craigmillar. Even today, visitors to Edinburgh are often left unaware that the city's undeniably handsome centre is ringed by poorly resourced housing schemes, a number of which have fallen victim to shocking urban decay.

END OF THE MILLENNIUM

Many of Edinburgh's traditional industries, among them publishing, declined during the 20th century. However, the addition of two new universities (Heriot Watt and Napier) helped to boost the city's already strong academic reputation, and the city has also become one of Europe's top financial centres, specialising in banking, fund management and insurance. As in the rest of Scotland, the tourist industry continues to be vital to the local economy.

The city's most notable cultural phenomenon of the 20th century was the establishment of the Edinburgh International Festival in 1947. The opening event featured music from the Vienna Philharmonic Orchestra, ballet from Sadler's Wells and theatre from the Old Vic. Just as crucial, though, were the eight theatre companies that, excluded from the official programme, staged shows in smaller venues. Others followed suit in subsequent years, and the ebullient, ever-expanding Fringe began to make a reputation all of its own.

A decade or two before the festival was launched, Edinburgh saw a brief cultural flowering known as the 'Scottish Renaissance', centred around writers and artists such as Hugh MacDiarmid, James Bridie, Edwin Muir, Naomi Mitchison, Lewis Grassic Gibbon and Neil M Gunn. Something of that feel returned during the 1990s, thanks to the presence of a few vibrant publishing houses, such as Canongate, and the international success of Irvine Welsh's *Trainspotting*. The novel brought some realism to the city's image by throwing the spotlight on its ills, chiefly the heroin epidemic that swept through it in the 1980s.

But the event that history may come to regard as the century's most significant came right at its close, with the partial devolution of Scotland and the establishment of a Scottish Parliament in the capital. With the forging of a new political identity, Edinburgh today is looking to its capital city status, rather than its striking physical landscape, to define itself anew.

▶ For more on **Edinburgh Castle**, see p80.
▶ For more on **Charles Rennie Macintosh** and his Glaswegian legacy, see p257.

Key events

c1-c300AD The rock is the fortress of Votadini, tribal allies of Romans.
c300-c700 The rock becomes the stronghold of the Gododdin, a British tribe.
638 Northumbrians take over southern Scotland.
c950 The Northumbrians are defeated by Kenneth MacAlpin.
1018 The Battle of Carham; Malcolm II drives Northumbrians from Lothian.
1070 Malcolm Canmore marries Margaret. The first castle is built on Castle Rock.
1093 Malcolm III is killed; Margaret dies.
1084-1153 David I reigns, during which he founds the Augustinian Priory at Holyrood.
1243 High Kirk of St Giles is consecrated.
1286 Alexander III is killed. Scotland is invaded by Edward I of England.
1314 Thomas Randolph retakes Edinburgh Castle from English occupation.
1329 Robert the Bruce gives the Royal Charter to Edinburgh.
1333 Berwick falls to the English.
1349 The Black Death arrives, with further epidemics in 1362 and 1379. Around a third of the Scottish population die of the plague.
1477 James III charters a livestock market in Grassmarket.
1488-1513 James IV reigns, during which the Great Hall is built at the Castle and the Royal Palace of Holyroodhouse is begun.
1513 The Scots are defeated at Flodden, and James IV is killed. Flodden Wall is built.
1542 Mary, Queen of Scots inherits the throne from James V. Holyroodhouse and the Abbey are attacked in the 'Rough Wooing'.
1560 John Knox declares Protestantism the official religion of Scotland.
1561-67 Mary returns from France to rule.
1565 Mary marries Henry Darnley.
1566 Mary's secretary, David Rizzio, is murdered at Holyroodhouse. Mary gives birth to the future James VI at Edinburgh Castle.
1582 Edinburgh University is founded.
1603 James VI accedes to the English throne as James I; the Court moves to London.
1638 The National Covenant is signed in Greyfriars Kirkyard.
1639 Parliament House is completed; it is the seat of the Scots Parliament until 1707.
1650 The Marquis of Montrose is executed at Mercat Cross.
1681 James Dalrymple publishes *Institutions of the Law of Scotland*.

1695 The Bank of Scotland is established.
1699 The Darien Scheme collapses.
1707 The Act of Union; Parliament moves to Westminster.
1726 The city's last witch-burning is held.
1727 The Royal Bank of Scotland is founded.
1736 The Porteous Riots take place.
1767 Construction of the New Town begins.
1771 The *Encyclopaedia Britannica* is published by William Smellie. Walter Scott is born in College Wynd.
1784 The last execution in the Grassmarket.
1787 An Edinburgh edition of Robert Burns' poems is published.
1817 *Blackwood's Magazine* and the *Scotsman* are founded.
1824 The Great Fire destroys much of the High Street and results in the formation of world's first municipal fire brigade. The Botanic Garden is established at Inverleith.
1836 Work on Waverley Station begins.
1843 The church is split by the Disruption.
1847 Alexander Graham Bell, inventor of the telephone, is born in South Charlotte Street.
1864 Edinburgh's last public hanging.
1871 The first international rugby match is played at Raeburn Park.
1874 Heart of Midlothian FC is founded.
1875 Hibernian FC is founded.
1890 The Forth Rail Bridge opens.
1895 Electric street lighting is introduced.
1903 Edinburgh Zoo opens.
1925 Murrayfield Stadium opens.
1947 The first Edinburgh International Festival is staged.
1964 Heriot-Watt University is founded.
1996 The Stone of Destiny returns to Edinburgh Castle.
1997 Scotland votes in favour of establishing a Scottish Parliament.
1998 The Royal Yacht *Britannia* is berthed permanently at Leith.
1999 The Scottish Parliament starts to meet once more.
2000 Donald Dewar, the first ever First Minister of Scotland, dies.
2002 Fire destroys a block of the Old Town on the Cowgate.
2004 The new Scottish Parliament Building at Holyrood is opened by the Queen.
2005 An estimated 225,000 join the Make Poverty History march.
2006 Smoking is banned in all enclosed public spaces.

WARM RECEPTION
EDINBURGH STYLE..

One thing you're sure of when you check into the new **smartcityhostel** in Edinburgh is a warm reception. **smartcityhostel** Edinburgh is a new style of hostel designed for the young and adventurous so, no matter if you are travelling or arriving you can be confident of a warm welcome.

smartcityhostel is 5 star standard hostel which means a hotel style experience at hostel prices. You can eat, sleep, drink. chill out, have fun - all in-house. You can also take advantage of the great location and see the sights or take in the nightlife - in fact anything you want to do and be sure of somewhere warm and safe to crash out.

Booking Hotline 0870 892 3000
Book online www.smartcityhostels.com

smartcityhostels EDI
EDINBURGH
THE ULTIMATE URBAN RESORT EXPERIENCE

50 Blackfriars Street, Old Town, Edinburgh, EH1 1NE T: 0870 892 3000
e:info@smartcityhostels.com   www.smartcityhostels.com

Scottish Parliament.

Edinburgh Today

Be careful what you wish for…

Under Tony Blair, Labour rode to power at the 1997 UK general election promising devolution for Scotland. Following a long-awaited referendum later the same year, in which three-quarters of those voting approved the idea, the wheels were set in motion. Elections were held in May 1999, and the new Scottish Parliament was convened for the first time around a month later. So far, so good. But even leaving aside the controversy surrounding the construction of the Scottish Parliament complex (see p28 **Present imperfect**), things haven't gone altogether smoothly.

Scotland relinquished control of its own affairs all the way back in 1707, the date of the Act of Union with England. For the best part of three centuries, decisions affecting the country were made in London; Scotland's very idea of itself, the one that defines the culture for both locals and visitors, was largely formed while

the country was piggy-backing on the greater imperial and post-imperial adventures of the United Kingdom. During the 19th and 20th centuries, the country enjoyed all the appurtenances of nationhood with few of the responsibilities, while its long and engaging history – nowhere better exemplified than Edinburgh – drew eyes back rather than forward. Some have suggested that all these factors contributed to a national mythology formed from nothing better than slogans penned for souvenir tea towels: 'Here's tae us, wha's like us, damn few, and they're a' deid.'

PROVINCIAL POLITICS

For many years, Scotland existed quite happily within the UK framework. The clamour for a greater degree of self-determination began to build only in the last few decades: founded in 1934, the Scottish National Party won

Present imperfect

It's sometimes said that truly profound works of art should anger as many people as they delight. By that logic, the building housing the **Scottish Parliament** (**photo p27**) has been a roaring success. The site chosen in early 1998 for the development was suitably dramatic, poised between the Old Town, Arthur's Seat and the historic royal residence of Holyroodhouse, and its construction was always going to be a high-profile undertaking. However, few anticipated just how contentious it would eventually become.

Catalan architect Enric Miralles was chosen from of a field of hundreds to design the historic building. Like Donald Dewar, the original Scottish First Minister, he never witnessed the project come to fruition: Miralles died of a brain tumour in July 2000, three months before Dewar died of a brain haemorrhage following open heart surgery. The premature deaths of the two men meant that neither saw the completed structure, but it also followed that they weren't around for much of the controversy that surrounded its construction. Project management failures, spiralling costs (the original estimate of £40 million proved to be roughly £400 million short) and lengthy delays became the focus of national discussion about the new parliament, overshadowing the actual business of politics. The Queen finally opened the building on 9 October 2004, seven years after devolution was finally approved and three full years behind schedule.

Visitors to Edinburgh generally like the leaf-shaped building, as peculiar as it is beautiful, and architecture critics have also been kind: the building won the Stirling Prize, Britain's most prestigious architecture award, in 2005. The majority of Scots, though, have so far been less convinced, grumbling about everything from the building's perceived lack of Scottishness (granted, bamboo door fronts, upturned boat-shaped skylights and grass on the roof aren't quintessentially Edinburghian features) to its apparent flimsiness: when a beam in the roof collapsed and caused the temporary closure of the debating chamber in 2006, several commentators didn't even bother attempting to disguise their glee. The schadenfreude in some quarters was almost overwhelming.

Indeed, ask around town, and locals may tell you that the Scottish Parliament was a monumental waste of taxpayers' money, a poorly-managed project that was far too grand and overblown. They're sentiments that chime nicely with traditional Caledonian thrift and disdain for ostentation. But reading between the lines, it's hard not to tally these grumbles with a general nervousness about the building's purpose, and a worry that, perhaps, this devolution thing isn't all it's cracked up to be.

its first seat in the Houses of Parliament as recently as 1967. The hectoring tones of Margaret Thatcher and the subsequent dramatic divergence between Labour-voting Scotland and Conservative-voting England during the 1980s and early '90s strengthened the nationalists' resolve to get their own way.

But once devolution was granted, then what? Where were the conceptual tools that would allow contemporary Scots to understand their present and their future? They'd arguably started to fall into disuse when James VI left for London to become James I of Great Britain in 1603, and were definitely abandoned after the Union. The wailing and gnashing of teeth over Holyrood's construction can be seen as the manifestation of a deeper collective anxiety: the advent of devolution held a mirror up to a nation that could no longer hide from itself by claiming unwanted subsidiary status. Scotland is a country of just five million people, subsumed within a larger nation state that itself is part of the European Union. Outside more prosperous areas such as central Edinburgh, endemic problems of poverty and poor health endure.

Scots won't vote for full separation from the UK, so the Scottish Parliament is, necessarily, a somewhat watered-down affair. While Holyrood concerns itself with issues such as health and education, all the big national and international debates – defence, foreign policy, the economy – are held at Westminster. As such, heavyweight Scottish politicians still head for London, tainting the northern chamber with a hint of provincialism.

When proportional representation granted factional fringe parties such as the Scottish Socialists a foot in the Holyrood door, it began to dawn on Scots that their MSPs were representative of the people in the strictest sense. In a parallel 'eureka!' moment, it also became clearer that for all its claims to distinction, modern Scotland was created in dialogue with England. It's little wonder that the parliament building became a useful target for people's frustrations. That said, the associated anguish raised far more interesting questions. If the symbols of nationalism don't really matter, what does? And what happens next in Edinburgh?

FOLLOW THE MONEY

A recent report on the state of the Edinburgh economy put its growth rate from 2000 to 2004 above many sizeable American and European cities, among them London, Paris, Boston, Amsterdam and Dublin. The Scottish capital may not be the biggest metropolis in the world, nor the richest, but it is one of the most buoyant. The leisure and entertainment sectors are booming, and employment rates are high. So, too, are property prices: within the last decade, the cost of a modest apartment near the city centre has more than tripled. New housing developments are going up on every spare scrap of land, including the waterfront from Leith to Granton.

> ## 'Finally, Scots are facing up to the responsibilities of running a country, though it's proving harder than simply claiming to be one.'

In the towns and districts around Edinburgh, a plethora of old and new industries – information technology, telecommunications, chemicals, medical engineering – have helped drive the economic growth. And in the city itself, several long-standing legal, financial and administrative institutions have flourished. The Royal Bank of Scotland, HBOS (the result of a merger between Halifax and Bank of Scotland) and Standard Life have headed the *Scotsman*'s annual list of the country's top companies in recent years; all have head offices in the city and employ huge numbers of people. The city also remains an important European fund management centre, with more than £300 billion of other people's savings tended from its offices and computer terminals.

The tourist industry has long been a huge money-spinner for the city; with the increased presence and popularity of budget airlines, more and more visitors are flocking to it. At the last count, Edinburgh's various August festivals (the International Festival, the Festival Fringe and an assortment of other events; for all, *see pp41-50*) supported nearly 4,000 jobs and brought the city an annual

income of £184 million. The year-round attractions of Edinburgh Castle, the Palace of Holyroodhouse, the Royal Yacht *Britannia*, the Royal Mile and the like generate even more: close to £1.7 billion, all told.

Given the state of the city's economy, it's unsurprising that so many people want to live here, further turning up the heat on the local property boom. One recent study suggested that around 25 per cent of Edinburgh residents come from other towns in Scotland, nearly 20 per cent hail from elsewhere in the UK, and as many as ten per cent arrived here from outside the British Isles. Evidence of this can be found in Leith: for some years favoured by young Spaniards, the area has seen a huge influx of Poles since the expansion of the EU in 2004.

USE YOUR ILLUSION

On 1 July 1999, Edinburgh hosted a celebration for Scotland's new-found devolved status. Concorde flew low over the city and Garbage headlined a gig in Princes Street Gardens. After an apt preamble about the native tendency for gloomy prognostications from lead singer and local girl Shirley Manson, the band launched into 'Only Happy When it Rains'.

Looking around the city now, the signs are generally good. The economy, as mentioned above, is in good shape, and the creation of a devolved legislature has brought power closer to the people. Finally, Scots are facing up to the responsibilities of running a country, though it's proving much harder than simply claiming to be one. The locals have an opportunity to decide what it really means to be Scottish in the 21st century, and how the country can move forward accordingly.

However, Manson hit the nail on the head when she spoke of the streak of pessimism that runs through the national character. An entire generation has grown up against a backdrop of prosperity – hitting the style bars of Edinburgh's West End and George Street after work, living in new apartments, enjoying healthy salaries – but not everyone thinks the party will go on forever. For one thing, in peripheral housing estates around the city and elsewhere in Scotland, it never really started. The cussed Edinburgh voters who kept casting their ballot for pro-devolution parties in the 1980s and early 1990s know that what global capitalism can bring, it can also take away; it's best not to take anything for granted.

▶ For details on how to visit the **Scottish Parliament**, *see p95*.
▶ For more on **new buildings in Edinburgh**, *see pp33-35*.

All change in **Leith**. See p35.

Architecture

A new wave of designers are building to last in Edinburgh.

Its magnificent setting and history of intellectual and artistic endeavour have often, famously, led to Edinburgh being described as the 'Athens of the North'. A 'dream of a great genius', wrote one 1820s visitor; while Mary Shelley had the narrator of *Frankenstein* comment on 'the beauty and regularity of the New Town of Edinburgh, its romantic castle and its environs, the most delightful in the world…' For the visitor interested in architecture, Edinburgh's array of great buildings, constructed over the last 800 years, is endlessly rewarding.

Topographically, the city has been dealt a spectacular hand. The Pentland Hills lie to the south and a coastal plain stretches north and east to the Firth of Forth, while Arthur's Seat and Castle Rock, along with Calton Hill and the Salisbury Crags, lend geographical drama. This setting has helped shape a city of two distinct characters: the architectural chaos of the Old Town looks across to the regularity of the New Town, a triumph of classical formality played out in a gridiron of well-disciplined streets. In 1995, UNESCO designated the Old Town and New Town a World Heritage Site, an honour that underlines the city's knack for seducing its visitors.

EARLY DAYS

Under the ambitious rule of the Malcolm III, the first in a long line of Scottish kings to emerge from the House of Canmore, Edinburgh's Castle Rock emerged as a fortified stronghold: today's **Edinburgh Castle** (*see p81*). Named for Malcolm's wife, **St Margaret's Chapel** is the earliest architectural survivor from those times. Built around 1120, the small stone building has a chevron-decorated chancel arch. The expanding settlement was declared a royal burgh in 1125 AD; three years later, **Holyrood Abbey** (*see p94*) was founded. Linear development gradually linked Holyrood to the Castle Rock, defining the well-trodden route of today's **Royal Mile**.

Architecturally, little remains from Edinburgh's infant years. Instability and limited funds meant that few structures were built of stone: most of the houses were instead crudely constructed from wattle and post, covered in clay for insulation and thatched with straw, rushes or heather. Their lifespan was no more than a couple of decades, even assuming they escaped the fires that were a common occurrence during the frequent raids by the English. Of the handful of medieval stone structures still standing in Edinburgh, St Giles (today's **High Kirk of St Giles** on the Royal Mile; *see p88*) dates from the 12th century, but only fragments of the original building remain: the church was extensively remodelled in the late 14th century, when Gothic transepts and chapels were added.

As its national stature grew during the reign of James III (1460-88), Edinburgh witnessed a surge in confidence and building activity. Holyrood Abbey became a royal residence and was expanded, leading to the 1498 addition of the **Palace of Holyroodhouse** (*see p94*). Edinburgh Castle was augmented by Crown Square and its baronial Great Hall, topped with a hammerbeam roof.

Money was also pumped into houses of worship, Trinity College Church perhaps most notable among them. The building has long since been demolished, but its magnificent altarpiece, by Hugo van der Goes, was preserved, and is now on display in the **National Gallery of Scotland** (*see p103*). Similar grand gestures resulted in a distinctive crown steeple being added to the central tower of St Giles around 1500; the resulting structure became a template for the numerous crown steeples built in subsequent years on churches across Scotland.

LIVING ARRANGEMENTS

Narrow lanes, known locally as wynds and closes, developed like ribs from the spine of the Royal Mile during medieval times. Simultaneously, many existing houses had extra storeys tacked on to them, often haphazardly, in addition to jutting windows and a confusion of roof levels. **John Knox's House** (c1490) is one of the few remaining examples (*see p90*), but it is a relatively restrained one: some timber-framed structures protruded as far as seven feet into the street.

Eventually, building regulations began to rein in the property speculators. But even as far back as the 15th century, local architects were experimenting with new ideas in a bid to solve a housing shortage crisis brought on by the city's rising population. The rocky and uneven terrain of the Old Town, combined with the ancient 'feu' system of land tenure (which granted leases in perpetuity), made horizontal development problematic. Expansion was thus forced upwards, leading to the birth of the tenement: dwellings stacked in storeys, linked by a common stairwell.

Daringly exploiting the ridge of the Old Town, tenements frequently bridged different levels down the side of the slope, making them some of the tallest domestic buildings in Europe at the time. Standing cheek by jowl along the Royal Mile, the sandstone or harled (a mix of small stones and lime plaster) tenements had more in common with the architecture of northern Europe than that of England. The five-storey **Gladstone's Land** (c1620-30; *see p84*) retains the once commonplace street arcade and an oak-panelled interior.

With the upper Royal Mile awash with merchants, its lower reaches soon became the location of choice for the nobility, their mansions flanking the approach to the Palace of Holyroodhouse. **Moray House** (c1628, with its pyramid-topped gate piers, and the vast **Queensberry House** (c1634; *see p92*), now part of the new Scottish Parliament complex (*see p95*), are the grandest of the buildings that survive. Around this time, buildings regulators began introducing measures intended to reduce the risk of fire: a law in the 1620s stipulated that all buildings must have tile or slate roofs, and a 1674 edict forced developers to give their properties stone façades.

The Palace itself was rebuilt in the 1670s with a triumphant blend of Scottish and European influences, creating a thickset façade with turreted towers fronting an inner courtyard lined with classical arcades. New wealth brought along in its well-heeled wake a new **Parliament House**; built next to St Giles in 1637, its presence added weight to Edinburgh's role as Scotland's capital. The building was given a classical overhaul in the early 19th century.

Elsewhere, the city flaunted its internationalism, exemplified by its easy (if rather tardy) handling of the Renaissance 'palace' style in the grandly ornamented **George Heriot's School** (1628), south of the Royal Mile. Churches were constantly being built along the Royal Mile, among them John Mylne's handsome **Tron Kirk** (1663, today the Old Town Information Centre; *see p89*) and the aristocratic and Dutch-looking **Canongate Kirk** (1688; *see p91*), with its delicate, curving gables.

TIME FOR A MAKEOVER

The 1707 Act of Union with England provoked an identity crisis for Edinburgh, and some dubbed the city 'a widowed metropolis'. But the capital, not given to extended periods of mourning, soon came to see architecture as an essential way of asserting its character.

The collapse in 1751 of a Royal Mile tenement highlighted the old-fashioned and run-down state of the Old Town and the need for 'modern' living quarters. George Drummond, the city's Lord Provost, drew up proposals the following year to expand Edinburgh, creating the grandiose **Exchange** (now the City Chambers) on the Royal Mile and, in 1765, the **North Bridge**. The bridge, the first to cross Nor' Loch, offered easy access towards the port of Leith and, importantly, to a swathe of redundant land to the north of the Old Town. This was to become the site of the 'new towns', collectively known as today's New Town.

'Edinburgh doesn't lack new buildings, but it's wary of creative departures.'

Conceived as Edinburgh's 'civilised' face, the first **New Town**, designed in 1766 by James Craig, was built to a regimented layout. Influenced by the growing Europe-wide fascination with classical civilisation, Edinburgh's new architecture adopted proportion and grandeur as its hallmarks. One leading practitioner of the style was Robert Adam, who designed the residential enclave of **Charlotte Square** (from 1792) as a grand full-stop to the west end of George Street. **General Register House** (c1788; *see p102*), on the axis of North Bridge, is another example of Adam's well-mannered classicism, its cupolas and pedimented portico a gracious retort to the haphazard gables of the Old Town.

CLASSICAL REINVENTION
By the early 1800s, architecture had taken on an increasingly crucial role in expressing the city's newly cultivated identity. Edinburgh had been dubbed the 'Athens of the North' as early as 1762; though the nickname still raises eyebrows, the city's topography made the analogy plausible. What's more, Edinburgh liked the idea of being an intellectual 'Athenian' metropolis, especially compared with the imperial 'Roman' English capital of London. As the Scottish Enlightenment held sway, architect William Playfair provided a stone and mortar representation of Calton Hill's status as Edinburgh's Acropolis with his **City Observatory** (1818; *see p116*), a cruciform mini-temple capped by a dome.

The Observatory stands next to another Playfair construction, one of the city's most controversial buildings. Begun in 1826 to commemorate the Napoleonic Wars, the Parthenon-inspired **National Monument** (*see p116*) is built around 12 huge columns, set on a vast stepped plinth in an attempt at classical allusions. However, a funding crisis meant the structure was never completed; ever since, it has laboured under the nickname 'Edinburgh's Disgrace'. The monument later formed a visual link to Thomas Hamilton's

Royal High School (1825) on the lower slopes of Calton Hill. Described as the 'noblest monument of the Scottish Greek revival', the structure was neo-classicism at its most authoritative, with a central 'temple' flanked by grand pavilions.

Playfair's work can be seen elsewhere in the city. Even after the funding debacle that put paid to his plans for the National Monument he remained a busy man, producing further classical expression in the forms of the **Royal Scottish Academy** (1823, *see p104*) and the **National Gallery of Scotland** (1850, *see p103*), a monumental, temple-inspired duo on the Mound, parading an army of columns and classical trimmings.

SCOTTISH BARONIAL: TRIUMPH OF THE FICTIONAL
George IV visited Edinburgh in 1822, dressed in pink stockings and a kilt. His sartorial advisor was Sir Walter Scott, author and campaigner for the 'tartanisation' of Scotland. Scott's campaign bore fruit in brick and stone, when the 1827 Improvement Act advised that new buildings and those in need of a facelift should adopt the 'Old Scot' style. Turrets, crenellations and crows' feet elbowed their way past Doric columns and back into the city's architecture; **Cockburn Street**, the first vehicular link between the Royal Mile and what is today Waverley Station, is a determined example of the style.

Elsewhere, several new public buildings masqueraded as rural piles airlifted from the Scottish Highlands. The old **Royal Infirmary** (1870; *see p96*), to the south of the Royal Mile, sports a central clock-tower and an array of turrets. **Fettes College** (1865-70), north of the New Town, is an exuberant intermarriage of Highland baronial seat and French chateau. Its construction inspired JK Rowling when she was dreaming up Hogwarts School of Witchcraft and Wizardry.

This growing adventurousness soon gave way to architectural promiscuity. The city's well-off institutions showed confident but sometimes florid excess, with a pick-and-mix approach to building style. The headquarters of **Bank of Scotland**, grandly posed on the precipice of the Mound, were given a neo-baroque makeover. The **British Linen Bank** on St Andrew's Square, now owned by Bank of Scotland, instead opted for the Renaissance palazzo look, its Corinthian columns topped by six colossal statues.

The Gothic revival also made its mark. Augustus Pugin, the master of the decorated pinnacle and soaring spire, designed the **Highland Tolbooth** (1844) below Castle

Moray House, among the grandest 17th-century buildings still standing. *See p31.*

Esplanade; today, it's the Hub (*see p83*), headquarters of the Edinburgh International Festival. But the finest line in romantic Gothic came in the shape of George Meikle Kemp's **Scott Monument** (1844; *see p103*) on Princes Street, a fitting memorial to the man who reinvented Scotland's medieval past.

PRETTY VACANT

Little disturbed by industrialisation, late 19th-century Edinburgh saw no huge bursts of construction; in the 20th century, the impetus to build was further anaesthetised by two world wars. Clean-cut 1930s modernism made scant impression, save for the robustly authoritarian government edifice **St Andrew's House** (1937-39; *see p115*) on the lower reaches of Calton Hill. Designed by Thomas Tait, with an imposing, symmetrical façade, it's a true architectural heavyweight.

With upwardly mobile residents siphoned off to the New Town, a large part of the Old Town had, by the Victorian era, developed into an overcrowded slum. As early as 1892, influential urban planner Sir Patrick Geddes, who inspired the revamp of Ramsay Gardens just below Castle Esplanade, had proposed seeding the area with members of the university as a means of adding to its intellectual weight, but his plan was not adopted.

Instead, in the years before and after World War II, Edinburgh's residents were encouraged to decamp to a series of council-built satellite townships on the periphery of the city, first among them the Craigmillar Estate. This social

engineering, achieved through town planning, was a crude mirror of the earlier and socially exclusive New Town. However, through it all, the fate of the crumbling Old Town remained in the balance.

In 1949, as part of a scheme drawn up by influential town planner Patrick Abercrombie, slum tenements and the rather grander George Square were demolished to create space for a new university campus. The sacrifice of George Square, its buildings replaced by unpopular 1960s-style architecture, sent a rallying call to the preservation troops, and much of the Old Town was saved as a result. But other parts of the city suffered through explosions of 1960s brutalism: the ugly, block-like **St James Centre**, just off Princes Street, is perhaps the most conspicuous example. The subsequent backlash sent city planners retreating into an ultra-cautious approach. Accusations of architectural timidity reached their height in 1989, when a prime redundant site on the Royal Mile was given over to the Scandic Crown Hotel (now the **Radisson SAS Hotel**; *see p55*), constructed in a Disneyfied, imitation-Old Town style.

A few modern buildings did sneak past the planning department, most notably around the **Exchange**, the city's new financial quarter to the west side of Lothian Road. Terry Farrell's **Edinburgh International Conference Centre** (1995) on Morrison Street forms the nucleus of the area, with big-name companies inhabiting the surrounding office blocks.

Small is beautiful

Glasgow has the Armadillo, London has the Gherkin, and Dublin has the Spire, soaring 120 metres over O'Connell Street. Edinburgh, with its World Heritage Site status inhibiting such grand gestures in both the Old and New Towns, has nothing that compares. A number of large-scale commercial and residential projects are at various stages of development, but the 'wow' factor is largely absent.

The most interesting contemporary architecture to have been erected in Edinburgh in recent years has, on the whole, been much more low-key, insinuating itself quietly into its surroundings. In Holyrood, the controversial Parliament building has been the centre of attention, but poke around in the lanes between Holyrood Road and the Royal Mile and you'll find the **Scottish Poetry Library** (see p95) in Crichton's Close. Created by Malcolm Fraser Architects and attractively clad in blue glazed tiles, it was winner of Channel 4's Building of the Year competition in 2000.

A couple of notable – if very different – institutions have been improved in recent

years by the addition of new buildings. In the west of the city, the spacious, calming **Families Reception Centre** at Saughton Prison netted architect Gareth Hoskins a regional award from RIBA in 2001. On Napier University's Craiglockhart campus, meanwhile, sits the **Egg** (2004), a lecture theatre with space station aesthetics designed by the Building Design Partnership.

In the residential sector, Edinburgh has of late been developing a taste for loft living and other more unusual styles of home. Perhaps the most impressive building in the latter category is **Barlas House**, a wholly modern townhouse slotted into the Georgian environs of Hart Street, in Broughton. The building, completed in 2002, earned up-and-coming architecture firm Zone a housing award from the Saltire Society, set up in the 1930s to encourage Scots to be more interested in their own culture and creativity. Two years later, Richard Murphy Architects also won a Saltire Society gong for its sleek conjoined blocks at the foot of **Old Fishmarket Close** (*pictured*). Tall, white and wood-clad on their upper storeys, they're extremely handsome, but the real marvel is how they were squeezed into such a tight spot. The ground floor of one block is home to Shaws Bistro & International Tapas Bar; see p147.

While architects are quietly granted licence to experiment with architectural forms on small lanes and university campuses, building on the Royal Mile usually inspires rather more controversy. That didn't stop Malcolm Fraser Architects taking on the challenge of converting the old Netherbow Theatre into the **Scottish Storytelling Centre** (see p90), incorporating the adjacent and historic John Knox House Museum into the project. The building, which opened in spring 2006, includes a modest but instantly attractive street-facing tower that houses Edinburgh's old city bell. It looks perfectly modern, but is also very much at home in its Old Town surroundings, and even pulls off the trick of complementing the 15th century structure next door. It may not demand attention, but it certainly rewards interest.

The central parabolic sweep of the **Scottish Widows Building** (1998) on Morrison Street, while hardly the stuff of no-holds-barred invention, offers the only bold design gesture in the whole precinct.

VOICE OF THE PEOPLE
It can be hard to coax the residents of Edinburgh into sharing their opinions on contemporary architecture, but absolutely everyone has a view about one key building:

the **Scottish Parliament** at Holyrood (see p95). A textbook example of poor project management, it was dogged by controversy and ill fortune from start to finish. The building was first discussed in 1997, but its original budget of £40 million seemed to be plucked from the air by a government spokesman.

By 1999, there was a site, a plan, an architect (celebrated Catalan Enric Miralles), and an increased budget of £109 million. Partly inspired by the hull shapes of some small upturned boats he saw in Northumberland, Miralles' vision was far from conservative, but we'll never know precisely how it would have developed: he died in summer 2000 at the age of just 44. The political driving force behind the project, First Minister Donald Dewar, passed away little more than three months later.

As the early years of the 21st century ticked by, the building became a grim national joke, and its potential architectural merit was eclipsed by more pressing concerns: how long was this going to take, and how much would it eventually cost? The answer was five years and £431 million, more than ten times the original think-of-a-number budget. But even with costs having soared into the stratosphere, the completed building was by no means immune from embarrassment: when a beam came loose in the main debating chamber in 2006, politicians were evacuated for two months while the problem was resolved.

Up close, the building's exterior can seem overly detailed and fussy, but it's far more impressive from a distance. For the best perspective, take a walk over Salisbury Crags and look down on the whole site, which also includes Michael Hopkins', vast, tent-like **Our Dynamic Earth** (1999; see p92). The other stand-out building in the vicinity is the **Tun** (2002), a mix of offices and retail space created from the bones of a former brewery building. Designed by Allan Murray Architects, it offers a funky challenge to the desperate blandness of the *Scotsman* newspaper offices across the way.

21ST-CENTURY EDINBURGH

Most of the architectural action in recent times has been focused on Leith, which has changed immensely during the last decade or so and continues to morph. The enormous **Scottish Executive** at Victoria Quay (1996) was a precursor to the **Ocean Terminal** shopping mall, designed by Sir Terence Conran (2001, see p187), but they're both mere dots on the landscape when compared with the scheme envisioned for Edinburgh Forthside. The plans call for housing and other amenities to be built all the way from Leith docks in the east to Granton harbour in the west,

a massive investment stretching along more than two miles of waterfront.

Most of the development along the water will be residential, the economic buoyancy of the city in recent years having led to a housing boom that has seen modern apartments thrown up on virtually every spare scrap of land. One of the most high-profile constructions is **Quartermile**, set on the 19 acres of the old Royal Infirmary site between the Meadows and Lauriston Place (just a quarter of a mile, hence the name, from the Castle). The first homes are scheduled for completion in 2007.

Edinburgh itself certainly doesn't lack new buildings, but it remains wary of big, creative departures, particularly in the city centre. An architectural history spanning nearly 900 years tends to focus minds back rather than forward. Planning errors from the 1960s have lodged in folk memory, and the recent Scottish Parliament saga hardly disposed anyone towards outlandish design.

Such conservatism makes the **Museum of Scotland** (1998; see p99) all the more precious. Situated next to the grand Victorian edifice of the **Royal Museum** (see p99), the Benson and Forsyth-designed building pays homage to its location with references to traditional Scottish forms and to the great curve of the Half Moon Battery of Edinburgh Castle. Architecturally it is a notable success, but it seems unlikely that the city centre will be blessed with any other new buildings of a similarly imaginative scope.

That said, a couple of upcoming developments hold plenty of promise. Located on a Cowgate site destroyed by fire in 2002, **SoCo** will comprise a new arts centre, a hotel and a healthy portion of private housing; it's hoped that the complex will be completed by 2009. But while SoCo is ambitious, Allan Murray's plans for **Caltongate**, centred around the former New Street bus depot between the Royal Mile and Calton Road, are positively daring. As part of the plan, Murray wants to demolish some still occupied tenements on the Royal Mile and replace them with a glass-fronted hotel; offices, a conference centre and private housing would sit in the area behind it.

Predictably, Murray's scheme ran straight into a slew of objections. Smaller projects get past the regulators with relative ease (see p34 **Small is beautiful**), but when it comes to massive developments, Edinburgh continues to have trouble marrying old and new.

▶ For more on **Old Town**, see pp76-99.
▶ For more on **New Town**, see pp100-108.
▶ For more on **Leith**, see pp131-136.

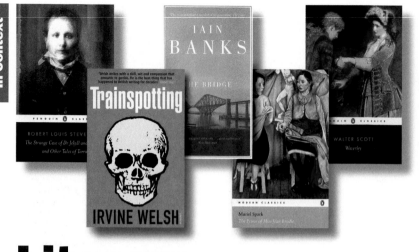

Literary Edinburgh

A city with tales to tell.

'This profusion of eccentricities, this dream in masonry and living rock, is not a drop-scene in a theatre, but a city in the world of every-day reality.'
— Robert Louis Stevenson,
Edinburgh: Picturesque Notes

Stevenson's 1878 musings on the character of his home town sits just as well with an analysis of its wayward literary past. From erudite enlightenment in the genteel manner of Sir Walter Scott's *Waverley* to the truculent patter of Irvine Welsh's *Trainspotting*, the fiction spawned by the Scottish capital has traversed both the grandeur and the gutter with equal relish.

While some of the capital's scribes have hurled themselves into the city's netherworlds with rare and committed abandon, others have sought to cover up the malaise of poverty and marginalisation with the kind of quiet civility for which the city has long been renowned. Alongside the idealised myth of the Scottish literary tradition has run a simultaneous eagerness to avoid discussing some of the city's harsher realities. For over 150 years, Scott and the poet Robert Burns have remained the stalwart figureheads of the romantic and tourist-friendly tropes of Scottishness, shot through with lilac hues of heather and heroic scenery. The highbrow status of literature in Edinburgh rests upon the recollections of a decidedly selective memory.

ARRIVALS AND DEPARTURES

During the late 18th and 19th centuries, Edinburgh's bookselling and publishing industries rivalled those of London, as the city busily preened itself in the wake of the success of its biggest national export: the Scottish Enlightenment. Yet the city responsible for publishing the first *Encyclopaedia Britannica* was by no means one big culture club. The smart drawing rooms of the New Town, favoured by those connected to Edinburgh's publishing industries, stood in stark contrast to the dank closes and squalid alleys of the working-class (and still-shambolic) Old Town.

The most influential literary figure of this period – and perhaps in Scottish history – was **Sir Walter Scott**, who combined a soaraway legal career with a prolific sideline as a writer. Scott's blockbuster poems and novels introduced readers to the hitherto neglected landscape and heritage of the Scottish Borders and Highlands: epic poems such as *The Lay of the Last Minstrel* and *The Lady of the Lake*, and novels such as *The Heart of Midlothian* and *Rob Roy,* communicated the writer's deep knowledge of and love for his Scottish heritage to the literary world of the early 19th century.

One writer who adapted well to the two-faced nature of Edinburgh in the late 18th century was poet **Robert Burns**, a regular visitor to the city. On the one hand, he enjoyed charming polite society in opulent Georgian villas following the success of his Kilmarnock poems in 1786; on the other, he wasn't averse to indulging in the licentiousness of the public inns. But it was left to **Robert Louis Stevenson** to pass comment on the city's curious duplicity in *The Strange Case of Doctor Jekyll and Mr Hyde*: although the book is purportedly set in London, the topography it depicts is undeniably that of Edinburgh, with its veneer of bourgeois propriety casually bordering on impoverished slums.

Jekyll and Hyde scavenges its plot from the tale of Deacon Brodie, a wealthy Edinburgh cabinet-maker by day but a thief by night, who ended up hanged on gallows he himself had designed. However, the tale also recalls the infamous Edinburgh murderers William Burke and William Hare, who suffocated the incapacitated and elderly before selling their bodies as specimens for use on the university's dissecting tables. Sixteen bodies later, Hare saved himself from the noose by incriminating his partner, who was hanged for his crimes in January 1829. In an epilogue perhaps too appalling even for fiction, Burke's skin was then tanned and fashioned into purses and pocketbooks. His skeleton still sits in the Edinburgh Medical School; for depriving his victims of a burial, he suffers the same fate still. Against such a coarse backdrop of real-life violence, *Jekyll and Hyde*'s Manichean tension between enlightened science and inexplicable savagery smacks of wry local satire, with a fitting taste for the gothic that is alive in the city's literature even today.

Like many of the city's locals during the 19th century, Stevenson had a love-hate relationship with Edinburgh, finally abandoning its keen winds for the sunnier climes of Western Samoa in the 1890s. National treasure **Muriel Spark** also left the capital, although not before taking inspiration from James Gillespie's High School,

her alma mater, while devising the setting for her novel *The Prime of Miss Jean Brodie*. Spark's old school still sits near the leafy surrounds of respectable Morningside, but the book's shrewd take on Edinburgh's tempestuous religious history and schism between Calvinism and Catholicism takes its backdrop from the Tolbooth, St Giles Cathedral, and, of course, John Knox's house on the High Street. Indeed, the book's title character remarks upon her own lineage back to her cabinet-making namesake.

Edinburgh's uncommon literary talents and its even rarer topography have also pricked the interest of visiting writers. **George Eliot**, **Daniel Defoe**, and **William Makepeace Thackeray** all spent time here, while **Mary Shelley** gave the city a rather unflattering cameo in *Frankenstein*. Although **William Wordsworth** dropped in on Sir Walter Scott, the *Edinburgh Review* of the time had little praise for the emerging poet. Wordsworth and his sister Dorothy spent a couple of nights at the Grassmarket's White Hart Inn; **Thomas de Quincey**, author of the celebrated *Confessions of an English Opium Eater*, went one better and moved here from London in 1826. Residing in a variety of addresses across town, partly in an effort to evade his creditors, the novelist died in the city in 1859 and was buried in St Cuthbert's graveyard, at the bottom of Lothian Road.

NATIONAL PRIDE

The city's shape-shifting literary style is due in part to the problematic negotiations of its many identities, since it is a tradition unevenly built upon three languages: English, Scots and Gaelic. From the Union of the Crowns in 1603 and the subsequent shift in the dynamics of power between Scotland and London, through to the failure to secure a Scottish referendum in 1979, and even the comedown that followed the formation of the Scottish Parliament in 1999, the literature of the city has moved with the often volatile rise and ebb of nationalism.

Scottish literature also has enduring links with the legal world, with a preponderance of lawyers and judges among its leading lights. **James Boswell**, Sir Walter Scott, Robert Louis Stevenson, **Henry Cockburn** and **Francis Jeffrey**, the first editor of the *Edinburgh Review*, were all scholars of law before they were writers. Even the *Review*'s motto carried judicial weight: *'judex damnatur ubi nocens absolvitur'* or 'the judge is condemned when the guilty is acquitted'. The *Review* was one of the most influential magazines of the 1800s before closing in 1929; four decades after its demise, its name was

Down and dirty

WILLIAM DUNBAR
Selected Poems
EDITED WITH AN INTRODUCTION BY HARRIET HARVEY WOOD

If you thought that **Irvine Welsh** was the first writer to lay bare Edinburgh's less salubrious characteristics, think again. The *Trainspotting* author is just one in a long line of poets, writers and free thinkers to expound some less than complimentary opinions and observations about the city and its environs. Characters such as Renton, Sick Boy and Begbie aren't the exceptions: for five centuries, they've been the literary norm.

The High Street has been a particular target for writers down the years, as what should have been an elegant causeway between two seats of power has rarely been anything of the sort. As far back as the 1500s, its failings provoked a colourful tirade from **William Dunbar**, priest, legal clerk and the court poet of James IV, who complained about the 'fensum flytings of defame' (abuse shouted in the streets) and had concerns about beggars: 'all honest folk thai do molest,' he wrote, accusatorily.

Dunbar's real problem, though, was the smell; as he lamented, 'May nane pas throw your principall gaittis/For stink of haddockis and of scattis'. The aroma was compounded at the Tron by food – 'cokill and wilk [cockles and whelks]/Pansches [tripe], pudingis of Jok and Jame' – but also by the stench arising from Nor Loch, now the site of Princes Street Gardens but then a dumping-ground for waste and even corpses. Around the city, passers-by ran the risk of being splattered with waste as it was hurled from the windows with a cry of 'gardiloo!' (from the French *gardez l'eau*). The tenements, luckenbooth shopfronts and stalls appalled the writer:

'Your stinkand stull that standis dirk
Haldis the lycht fra your parroche kirk;
Your foirstairis makis your houses mirk
Lyk na cuntray bot heir at hame.'
– Dunbar, *To the Merchants of Edinburgh*

Some 200 years later, not much had changed: the gloomy lands and closes still stood, the Cowgate was a teetering mass of slums, and drinking *howfs*, brothels and market stalls stood cheek by jowl with the kirk and the law. Still, some poets embraced it. **Allan Ramsay** (1686-1758) happily reminisced about lock-ins at Lucky Wood's tavern on the Canongate ('To the sma hours

recycled to launch a new publication, which continues to print the work of authors local, national and international.

> **'A far cry from Muriel Spark's decorous aspersions, Irvine Welsh's Edinburghers bawl their complaints in the legendarily impenetrable Scottish vernacular.'**

The University of Edinburgh has educated many notable writers: among them are **JM Barrie**, best known for his ever-young creation Peter Pan, and **Sir Arthur Conan Doyle**, who took inspiration from his professor, Dr Joseph Bell, as he went about devising the character of Sherlock Holmes. More recently, **Alexander McCall Smith**, author of the *No.1 Ladies'* *Detective Agency* series, studied at the university and went on to become a professor in medical law at the institution. Even after shifting thousands of books on both sides of the Atlantic, it's a job he continues to maintain to this day.

THE MODERN WORLD

Despite McCall Smith's success, the city's two most notable contemporary novelists are arguably **JK Rowling** and **Ian Rankin**, a pair of writers who embrace the city's taste for the gothic in very different ways. Rowling's Harry Potter books have done much to colour the imaginations of youngsters attending Fettes College, on which Hogwarts may or may not have been partly modelled, but has also provided a not unwelcome fillip to the city's café culture. Rowling, famously, began sketching out her books in local coffeehouses; unsurprisingly, a host of Old Town establishments have since laid claim to being the birthplace of her first novel, *Harry Potter and the Philosopher's Stone*.

we aft sat still/Nick'd round our toasts and snishing mill'), and even wrote an elegy to local madam Lucky Spence, in which she offers her girls some blunt advice:

'When he's asleep, then dive and catch
His ready cash, his rings or watch;
And gin he likes to light his match
                    at your spunk-box,
Ne'er stand to let the fumbling wratch
                    een take the pox'
– Ramsay, Lucky Spence's Last Advice

The pox to which Spence refers is almost certainly gonorrhoea, known locally as 'Canongate breeks'. Local man of letters **James Boswell** surely contracted it at least once in Edinburgh, given that he endured in the region of 20 bouts.

While the anonymous author of the Ranger's Impartial List of the Ladies of Pleasure in Edinburgh (published c.1775) detailed the addresses and talents of the city's prostitutes ('She has a certain knack at her business superior to most others'), he fails to vouchsafe their health. No matter: you could take your pick from Mrs Agnew's at the Netherbow, Miss Forsyth's in Marlin's Wynd (the remains of which can be seen inside the Tron), Miss Tibby Nairn's in Fowles's Close and others. The author promised a second volume, but no booklet is thought to have been published. Presumably the strain of the research became too much.

Robert Fergusson, who was born in Cap and Feather Close off the High Street in 1750 and died in Edinburgh's Bedlam only 24 years later, wrote exhuberant poems packed with vivid imagery. His poem 'Auld Reekie' stands testament to 18th-century life, but Dunbar would have despaired: the stinks from the Nor Loch and the food markets are still there, and so is the gardiloo...

'Then with an inundation big as
The burn beneath the Nor Loch brig is
They kindly shower Edina's roses
To quicken and regale our noses...

'Gillespie's Snuff should prime the nose
Of her that to the market goes
If they wad like to shun the smells
That buoy up frae markest cells;
Whare wames o' paunches sav'ry scent
To nostril gi'e great discontent.'
                    – Fergusson, Auld Reekie

Born exactly a century later, **Robert Louis Stevenson** once wrote: 'I believe Fergusson lives in me'. Stevenson haunted the howfs of the Old Town, drinking in both atmosphere and alcohol. As a child, he had been frightened by the creaking door of a cupboard made by the infamous Deacon William Brodie. As a young man, in those dives, he saw the type of characters that appear in Treasure Island and The Strange Case of Doctor Jekyll and Mr Hyde, the latter inspired by Brodie himself.

Rankin's series of bestsellers exposes the tartan noir of the town and its less touristy vistas, as Detective Inspector Rebus passes through Edinburgh's brothels, bars and banks with a world-weary demeanour. Rankin, born in Fife but resident in Edinburgh since his days at the university, has built a veritable industry from unassuming beginnings: his crime novels have been adapted for TV and translated into more than 27 different languages, and form the basis for online quizzes, fan gatherings and even tours of the city.

While Rankin's life is now an extremely comfortable one, Rebus continues to tread his fearless path through the perils of Edinburgh's iniquitous side-streets and housing schemes; some purely fictitious, but others very much based on reality. But one delight shared by both the detective and his maker is the Oxford Bar on Young Street in the New Town. A literary landmark since the days of Sydney

Goodsir Smith, a regular during the 1950s, the bar has long been a favourite both with Rankin and his most famous invention.

Iain Banks lives just outside Edinburgh, but the city and its environs regularly crop up in his work or even inspire it: Complicity, Whit and The Bridge all carry with them shades of the city. Banks may not enjoy the blockbuster sales of Rowling (or even, for that matter, Rankin), but his novels and epic space operas (The Algebraist, Excession) have carved him an important place in the local literary pantheon.

But the novelist who most radically changed the outside world's view of contemporary Scots literature was Leith-born **Irvine Welsh**, another in a long line of writers keen to expose an urban underbelly that the city fathers would far rather conceal. In novels such as The Acid House and Trainspotting, Welsh writes of a town guilty of self-gentrification and of pushing its predominantly working-class inhabitants into

Further reading

If you're keen to discover more about the city's local writing heritage, your first stop should be Edinburgh's **Central Lending Library**, located on the George IV Bridge (242 8000, www.edinburgh.gov.uk/libraries, *see p84*) and open every day except Sunday. It might seem a bit of a maze when you first walk through the doors, mastered only by seasoned veterans and the librarians themselves, but it's not as cluttered as it appears. The Edinburgh Room, on the floor below the entrance level, houses over 100,000 items pertaining to the city, perfect if you like your town history verbose and very particular. Opposite is the **National Library of Scotland** (*see p85*), open to the public as a reference library – although you'll need to show an appropriate form of ID to get your hands on a short-term reader's ticket (623 3700, www.nls.uk).

The other main resource for those wanting to further investigate local writing is the **Scottish Poetry Library** (*see p95*) tucked away just off the High Street (5 Crichton's Close, Old Town, 557 2876, www.spl.org.uk) and open six days a week. Founded in 1984, the library boasts an impressive array of books, videos and audio recordings, both historical and contemporary; its trilingual website (in English, Scots and Gaelic) contains a searchable database of its stock. Admission and borrowing is free, though proof of address is needed for the latter.

Close by here sits Edinburgh's newest writing resource. Built on the site of the old Netherbow Arts Centre and opened in summer 2006, the **Scottish Storytelling Centre** (43-45 High Street, Old Town, 556 9579, www.scottishstorytellingcentre.co.uk, *see p90*) is the first purpose-built complex of its type in the world. Insisting that stories aren't just for children, the centre's staff host spoken-word and dramatic performances in the theatre all year round, as well as regular workshop events for all ages. For more informal banter, there's also a great café.

The biggest of several annual literary events held in the city is, inevitably, the **Edinburgh International Book Festival**. The event is one of the highlights of August's cultural overload, bringing together guests of immense eminence (Edward Said, Salman Rushdie, Margaret Atwood) with renowned Scottish authors (AL Kennedy, Liz Lochhead, James Kelman) for a series of talks, readings and discussions. Visit www.edbookfest.co.uk for programme details; *see also pp41-50*.

The other big annual literary shindig held here is the **Festival of Scottish Writing** (www.edinburgh.gov.uk), staged at various venues throughout the city every May. Organised in conjunction with Edinburgh City Libraries, the festival invites a host of poets, novelists and non-fiction writers from all over Scotland to give readings and performances, which include a number of events aimed at children. Most of the talks and events are free, though some are ticketed: check online for full details.

For details of Edinburgh's **Writers' Museum** in the Old Town, *see p85*. For the town's best bookshops, *see pp188-189*.

an outer ring of 'problem' housing schemes. He should know: having grown up in one of them, Muirhouse, he later took a job at Edinburgh City Council's housing department. Welsh was also one of only a few local writers willing to talk about the fact that Edinburgh's heroin trade led to it becoming the HIV capital of Europe during the 1980s and '90s, and his cast of fitba' casuals and subcultural dropouts speak of the city in far less adulatory tones than most. A far cry from Muriel Spark's decorous aspersions, lovingly voiced in a clipped Morningside accent, Welsh's Edinburghers are afflicted by privation, AIDS and drug addiction, and bawl their complaints in the legendarily impenetrable Scottish vernacular.

The prose of Scott, Spark, Rowling, Rankin and even Welsh earned Edinburgh the title of UNESCO's first City of Literature in 2004,

and the presence of two major annual book festivals on the city's cultural calendar (for both, *see above* **Further reading**) has been of further benefit to the boom of literary tourism in the capital. With an abundance of endearingly haphazard second-hand bookshops, numerous bars bearing the names of famous local novels and authors, literary pub crawls around the Old Town and even a museum devoted to local scribes, the city has leapt at the chance to articulate and exploit its literary flair. We can only hope that the writers the city celebrates continue to expose the corners it doesn't want you to see.

> ▶ For a list of **notable books about Edinburgh**, *see p309*.

Festival Edinburgh

Everyone's welcome at the planet's biggest
arts celebration.

For most of the year, Edinburgh is a relaxed,
reasonably sedate city, revelling in the
benefits of its capital status while enjoying the
calm that comes with a population of less than
half a million residents. But come August, it's all
change. The population doubles, the atmosphere
becomes almost continental, and the grey stone
façades burst into colour. It's the largest arts
celebration in the world, drawing performers
from Uppsala to Uluru and all points in between.

Not everyone is enamoured with this
dramatic shift in the city's character. Many
locals, who prefer the rather slower pace of life
that rolls along over the other 11 months of the
year, jump ship and rent out their properties to
visitors for massive fees. Other residents simply
stay and grumble. However, they're very much

in the minority: for most, the festivals together
comprise the highlight of the city's cultural
calendar. Unique is an overused word, but it
absolutely applies here. Taking in everything
from high-budget opera to low-concept DJ
nights, literary discussions in the New Town
to tightrope walkers on the Royal Mile, August
in Edinburgh is like no place else on earth.

The array of performers is extraordinary;
truly, all human life is here. Legions of
internationally renowned writers, artists
and performers descend on the city. Famous
cinematic faces arrive to revive their careers
or pay homage to the movies that made them,
and the usually busy London comedy circuit
virtually closes for a month. But Edinburgh
also fills with rank amateurs on a wing and

a prayer, making one last tilt at fame and fortune before the money runs out. You may have to stand in line for three hours to get into the latest hot-ticket show, or you may be the only person in the audience. You might be moved to tears by dramatic theatre and sent into paroxysms of laughter by a stand-up comic. Or, of course, vice versa. Whatever you see, though, you're unlikely to forget the experience.

About the Festivals

The **Edinburgh International Festival** (EIF) began in 1947 with the express aim of providing war-torn Europe with a focus for the very best in new drama, music and the visual arts. The organisers hoped the festival would unite the continent's culture, while the great festivals of Salzburg and Munich found their feet again in the aftermath of World War II. To say that they achieved their ambitions is akin to suggesting that the Scottish weather can be a little changeable. Over the last 60 years the EIF – and its various offshoots and specialist competitors – has come to define the city in the eyes of many travellers.

The EIF has naturally evolved down the years, and the biggest change in recent years has been the retirement of Director Sir Brian McMaster after 15 years at the helm. McMaster retired after the 2006 event and handed the reins to Jonathan Mills, an Australian composer and the former director of the Melbourne

Festival. On appointment, Mills said, 'I am both excited and humbled to be offered the opportunity to build on the twin traditions of excellence and innovation established by this wonderful event'. Some commentators have suggested that he only got the exciting and humbling opportunity because other, better-qualified candidates couldn't be persuaded to take it on, but Mills will be judged by his programming. Watch this space.

The traditional primacy of the EIF has meant that August's events are often simply referred to as 'the festival', but it's important to recognise that there are a huge bundle of administratively separate jamborees taking place at the same time. Chief among them is **Edinburgh Festival Fringe**, which began in decidedly modest circumstances in 1947 when eight companies not invited to the EIF decided to hold their own 'unofficial' performances during the event. The anarchic, chaotic event dwarfs its grander rival these days: around 2,000 shows were staged here in 2006. The Fringe broke away from the EIF in 1998, and now commences a week earlier than its rival.

The Fringe differs from all Edinburgh's other festivals, and virtually all cultural festivals in Europe, in that there is absolutely no quality control. Anyone can put on a show, provided they can hire a venue, find accommodation and live on fresh air and dreams for a month or so. The only thing that most acts have in common is their willingness to pay £300-odd to the

The heady heights of showbiz.

Festival Fringe Society in order to guarantee a listing in the Fringe Programme, a sprawling 250-page brochure that emerges each June.

The Fringe attracts a bewildering, heady array of aspiring young talent, consummate crowd-pleasers, once-in-a-lifetime amateurs and old pros looking for a career boost. But don't be fooled by the sheen of amateurism: the Fringe is now a well-oiled machine. Comedy and theatre are the mainstays, but dance, music, and, to a lesser degree, visual art all feature in the programme. Venues vary wildly, from the holy triumvirate of the Pleasance, the Gilded Balloon and the Assembly Rooms to, in 2005, a double-decker bus, a mock World War II bunker and a knitwear shop. The only rule is that there are no rules.

The **Edinburgh International Film Festival** also arrived in 1947, after the Edinburgh Film Guild grew somewhat piqued that the International Festival had omitted film from its remit. It's since become an important date in the industry calendar, but is also a popular event among the cinemagoing public, who get to see a wide selection of flicks long before their UK release dates.

Three years after the Film Festival arrived, a decidedly different event made its bow: the **Edinburgh Military Tattoo**, a soldiers' parade of music, dance and athleticism. It's grown into the single most popular event in the city each August, selling over 200,000 tickets each year, and inspires what many believe are the world's longest queues. The Tattoo is currently held on the Castle Esplanade, but there are plans to move it to a new, purpose-built arena in Princes Street Gardens on the site of the dilapidated Ross Bandstand.

As the city attracted greater and greater crowds, other festivals sprang up, hoping for a piece of the action. Held a week before the Fringe, the **Edinburgh Jazz & Blues Festival** began in 1979. The **Edinburgh International Book Festival** was launched four years later and is now the largest event of its type in the world. In 2004, around 30 galleries established the low-key **Edinburgh Art Festival**. A year or so earlier, the first ever **Festival of Politics** was staged, inspired by the opening of the Scottish Parliament. Two events are aimed at locals: the **Edinburgh Mela**, a two-day outdoor event that celebrates Asian culture in the city with performances, food stalls, children's activities and a bazaar, and the politically minded **Edinburgh People's Festival**, which aims to 'bring the arts to the ignored indigenous communities' by staging shows in the city's more deprived areas. And two events are private industry jamborees: the **Edinburgh International Television**

Festival, founded in 1976, and the **Edinburgh Interactive Entertainment Festival**, which does at least open its doors to the public for brief demonstrations of upcoming video games.

Comedy

Although the **Edinburgh People's Festival** usually contains a small comedic component, those in search of laughs need look no further than the **Fringe** programme: almost 400 comedy shows were staged as part of the event in 2005. Although stand-up is no longer as fashionable as it once was, the Fringe continues to grow, with a massive array of comics relocating from all corners of the globe each

Special events

Festival Cavalcade
www.edinburghcavalcade.com.
Dates 5 Aug 2007; 3 Aug 2008.
The Edinburgh Festival opens with a two-hour afternoon parade of noise and colour through the centre of town. Trailed by the cast of the Military Tattoo, floats lead the way down Princes Street, bobbing with the casts of plays and shows eager to dazzle spectators into buying a ticket.

Fringe Sunday
www.edfringe.com. **Dates** 12 Aug 2007; 10 Aug 2008.
On the second Sunday of the Fringe, the Meadows (*see p124*) plays host to a showcase of the talent performing at the festival that year, essentially serving as a free sample of the enchanting variety that characterises the Fringe. Street performers, displays and stalls add to the mix as 15,000 people turn up and participate in the largest, most vibrant garden party of the summer.

International Festival Fireworks Concert
www.eif.co.uk. **Dates** 2 Sept 2007; 31 Aug 2008.
The International Festival's closing concert in Princes Street Gardens is accompanied by some spectacular explosions lighting up the night sky above the castle. The concert is ticketed and always sold out, but the fireworks are free and best viewed from North Bridge, Princes Street or Salisbury Crags. Some 225,000 revellers watched the 40-minute extravaganza in 2005.

year in the hope of landing an agent, securing a major touring contract, signing a TV deal and – almost as an afterthought, it sometimes feels – making the paying punters laugh.

The popularity of the Fringe as a comedic career-maker can be traced back to 1960, when Oxbridge revue *Beyond the Fringe* made its debut at the event before going on to extended runs in the West End and on Broadway and kickstarting the careers of Peter Cook, Dudley Moore, Jonathan Miller and Alan Bennett in the process. In truth, the show wasn't especially well received when it played in the Scottish capital, but the fact that it began on the Fringe inspired many other comics and ensembles to head north during August to try their luck.

That said, it wasn't until the 1980s that the Fringe's reputation as a hotbed of new comedy really began to translate into mainstream success. Launched in 1981, the Perrier Award was set up to draw attention to what its judges believed to be the best comedy and/or cabaret show on the Fringe. The inaugural winner was a Cambridge University revue that starred Stephen Fry, Hugh Laurie, Emma Thompson and Tony Slattery, all unknown at the time.

Many of the acts who won the gong in the early and mid 1980s have since faded from view. However, the roll call of winners and nominees in the late '80s and early '90s really established the award's cachet. Jeremy Hardy, who won in 1988, is still a familiar face on British TV (and an even more familiar voice to listeners of BBC Radio 4); 1990 winner Sean Hughes landed a high-profile TV contract on the back of his triumph; and Frank Skinner (1991), Steve Coogan (1992) and Lee Evans (1993) remain three of the biggest – and best-paid – names in British comedy.

It's this golden age, and its seemingly concomitant guarantee of national fame, that arguably still drives the Fringe's comedy component. After all, what else could possibly persuade hordes of hard-up comics to spend August haemorraging most of the cash they've earned over the other 11 months of the year on usually futile attempts to crack the big time? Competition is insanely fierce, but the chance that the show you bring to the Fringe could be Your Big Break is, for most aspiring funnymen, simply too tempting to pass up.

The largest comedy gathering in the world is also, for its performers, the most gruelling. Most major comedy festivals last for no more than a week, and generally consist of one-off showcases at which acts have to make crowds laugh for a mere 20 minutes. Edinburgh demands more. Although a few big-name comics fly in for short and often extremely lucrative theatrical engagements, those on the lower rungs of the ladder commonly take to the stage six days a week for a gruelling three-week stretch. Aided by their existing reputations (and a knockout agent), a lucky few land evening slots at prestigious venues. Others are quickly forced to resign themselves to the fact that, if the sun comes out, their daily 3.10pm slot in a scruffy pub cellar may not sell out. Indeed, they may be the only person in the room.

If they're not too dispirited, exhausted or drunk, a handful of comics each year get the opportunity to play the **Late & Live** show at the **Gilded Balloon**, a bearpit of a comedy club that starts at 1am every night. Unlike most laugh-ins, the set-up welcomes boozed-up hecklers and positively encourages audiences to waylay the four performers, who each have half an hour to fill. A good showing here can make a comic's career; more often, it breaks them, at least until the next day, when they have to head back to their regular gig and start again.

The primary comedy venues on the Fringe are the **Assembly Rooms**, the **Pleasance**, the Gilded Balloon and the **Underbelly**; each produces their own brochure, in addition to the Bible-like free Fringe guide available all over the city. Still, don't limit yourself: comics play in a multitude of smaller locations around the city. It's all something of a lottery, but every lottery has a winner… doesn't it?

Film & TV

The **Edinburgh International Film Festival** started life as a gala celebration of documentaries, but now presents a mix of new features and shorts, animated flicks and factual programming, retrospectives and revivals. Director John Huston described it in 1972 as 'the only film festival worth a damn'; although it's since been overtaken in prominence by Cannes and Sundance, it remains an important date in the cinema calendar. There's a strong industry presence at the events – official delegates are immediately recognisable by their ever-present half-full wine glasses and all-black outfits – but there are also plenty of tickets available to regular punters.

The Film Festival is sometimes referred to as a 'hoover festival', picking up the best movies from the international festivals over the preceding 12 months and giving them UK premières. A strong hand guides the selections: the organisers choose a Directors' Showcase each year, and the Rosebud section for first- and second-time directors has assumed great importance since it was introduced in 1995.

Adventurous cinema-goers can expect to see the future hits of intelligent cinema up to a year before they take their bow at the box office: *Tsotsi*, *Hero* and *The Motorcycle Diaries* all played here well ahead of their eventual UK release dates. Alongside them, of course, are a number of movies that will vanish without trace. Blockbusters are few and far between, but short films and animations feature prominently. Documentaries have come back into fashion recently, following the success of *Fahrenheit 9/11* and *Super Size Me*; a new award for the best documentary was introduced in 2006. Every year *The List* Surprise Movie plays to an unprepared audience; the last three choices have been *Spirited Away*, *The Life and Death*

of *Peter Sellers* and *Lords of Dogtown*. Alongside the screenings are a range of talks and discussions featuring cast, crew and critics.

Media folks are past masters at navel-gazing, and nowhere are their talents more apparent than at the weekend-long **Edinburgh International Television Festival**. Here, the focus is on lectures, discussions and debates about the past, present and future of the idiot box. It's an industry-only event, the importance of which is later amplified by the excessive coverage it receives from those who forked out the £400 delegate fee to attend.

My Edinburgh Ginnie Atkinson

An Edinburgher through and through, Ginnie Atkinson worked as assistant press officer for the Edinburgh International Film Festival (EIFF) while studying at Edinburgh College of Art. After a brief spell in London, she came home to work in theatre, education, broadcast facilities and production before returning to EIFF; she's been its Managing Director since 1994.

'I love the scale of the city and the fact that there's a castle in the middle of it; its history and the fact that it has long been the seat of learning and invention. It seems to be a place where people reflect upon the wonders of life.

'My favourite places in Edinburgh are the **Canongate** (*see p91*) – the secret places off its spine are varied and fabulous – and the **Pentland Hills** (*see p286*). But the real hidden gem is probably the **Royal Botanic Garden** (*see p111*). The fact that few visitors venture that far makes it a real find, a haven of alternative culture. And peaceful, too.

'Just being in Edinburgh during Festival time is phenomenal. The energy and the stamina for partying and celebration is hardly a secret: there is a tangible optimism and the city seems to be quite uninhibited, so the atmosphere is unique... even if you are working all the time. Festival goers are up for it, in whatever way 'it' might happen to them. It's pretty much all about risk, and no one is really seeking a safe haven. You have to remain open-minded; make sure you try to buy a ticket for something that's a hot tip and for something you might otherwise steer clear of. Those are the two extremes of experience: one involves queueing and the other involves surprise.

'If I only had a single weekend to spend in Edinburgh at Festival time, I'd head straight for whatever films were screening as part of the EIFF retrospective, because the chance to see them is so rare. It's fairly easy to find a really good film to see. I'd also try to find a genuinely funny stand-up.

'Edinburgh in general – and the festival in particular – is a fantastic place for starting a romance, whether lifelong or a quick fling. It's an uninhibited and often inebriated place; together, they add up to circumstances that dictate that "if you can't do it now, you never will". I'm sure there are thousands of people who have experienced this; other than that, I'm saying nothing...'

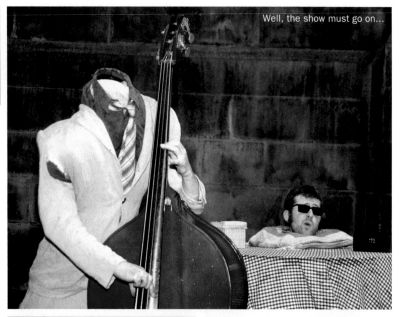
Well, the show must go on...

Literature & debate

Pitching its well-appointed marquees in the gardens of Robert Adam-designed Charlotte Square, the **Edinburgh International Book Festival** is a cultured haven that carefully sets itself apart from the chaotic festival throngs in the Old Town. Compared with its competitors, the event moves at an almost genteel pace, fuelled not by deep-fried pizza and Tennent's Extra but by dry white and canapés.

The Book Festival's programme comprises a range of talks, readings and discussions, grouped into broad themes that change each year. The festival's organisers appear keen to encourage participation: debates are an increasingly prominent part of the programme, as are events for children, who can romp safely in the enclosed gardens. Aspiring writers are encouraged to join one of several writers' workshops, and to visit the writers' retreat hidden among the trees.

Most authors make only a single appearance at the event, but the truly stellar – or the truly tenacious – may show up several times during the two-week programme. Big names in recent years have included Ian Rankin, Zadie Smith, Richard Dawkins, Harold Pinter, Seamus Heaney and Doris Lessing. The event has become more and more politically minded in recent years. Alongside the expected slew of novelists, poets and critics, Rageh Omaar, Tony Benn and Gordon Brown all appeared in 2006, lending the event a cutting edge.

Those interested in current events should also investigate the four-day, unrelated **Festival of Politics**. Launched only a few years ago and held at the Scottish Parliament building, the festival includes an array of talks, debates and discussions (the opening event in 2006 featured Sir Sean Connery in conversation with the parliament's Presiding Officer George Reid). Admission to most events is free to the public.

Music

Edinburgh is an old-fashioned city in many respects, not least of which is its range of music programming during August's festivals. Though a few daring types have attempted to bring rock and pop to the fore (more of which in a moment), classical music and opera still dominate.

Alongside theatre and dance, classical music is one of the cornerstones of the **Edinburgh International Festival**. The Usher Hall stages concerts more or less nightly during the event, sometimes hosting several performances during the same evening. Programming, split roughly 50-50 between orchestral concerts and chamber recitals, tends to be fairly conservative: the headline events at the EIF in 2006 were performances of the complete symphonic cycles of Beethoven and Bruckner. Still, standards are generally high. Around half a dozen opera performances are also staged during August; the **Fireworks Concert** in Princes Street Gardens (*see p43*) draws a close to proceedings with suitable pomp and circumstance.

There's also a surprising amount of classical music on offer at the **Fringe**, much of it very worthwhile. Young musicians dominate, generally performing in one-off concerts or short-run recital series. The Festival of British Young Orchestras takes place annually as part of the programme and is usually worth a look, as are the free daily lunchtime shows at **St Mary's Cathedral** (*see p229*).

The rest of the Fringe's musical programme is an anything-goes jumble that takes in everything from traditional Scottish folk to wink-wink cabaret, from the scary (free jazz) to the positively petrifying ('Howard Jones – the Acoustic Nights'). After many years rock music finally appears to have got a firm foothold here; it's all thanks to Scotland's biggest brewer, who bankroll the **T on the Fringe** event (www.tonthefringe.com). It's something of a moot point whether any gig in an athletics stadium – where Snow Patrol played in 2006 – can be said to sit on the fringe of anything. But never mind. Rock fans should also check out the **Underbelly**, which has expanded its music programming during the fringe in recent years. And in the week leading up to the Tattoo, the 7,500-capacity Castle Esplanade arena has hosted the likes of Rod Stewart and Tom Jones.

Although you won't find their details in any official programme, the town's clubs and music venues take full advantage of the influx of hedonists and book big-name DJs during August. Sessions often last until 5am, when clubbers emerge blinking into the dawn. Promoters are keen to attract festival goers, but few book DJs far enough ahead to get into the Fringe brochure. Check flyers and *The List* for details on what's going on while you're in town.

The **Edinburgh Jazz & Blues Festival** can get a little lost in all these crazy goings-on, perhaps partly because it begins a week before the Fringe. However, while its programme is chiefly populated by local musicians, it does draw the occasional big name: Dionne Warwick, Wynton Marsalis and Jools Holland have all performed here. More or less every strand of jazz is covered at the event, with concerts staged throughout the day and night.

Theatre & dance

Those of a theatrical bent should investigate the programmes of both the **Edinburgh International Festival** and the **Fringe**.

The latter undoubtedly offers plenty of variety, but the quality control is considerably more audience-friendly at the former.

The roster of theatre and dance at the EIF is small, grand and expensive to stage. Recently, works by Shakespeare, pieces by modern Scottish writers and an assortment of drama from around the world have made up the lion's share of the programme, with productions – most of them at the King's Theatre or the Royal Lyceum – gradually growing more challenging under the watch of Brian McMaster. Not coincidentally, this event's casual broadening of the event's remit coincided with an array of ticket-discounting schemes which helped increase attendance among the young and less well-off. While you might find acclaimed international acts making their UK debuts as part of the Festival, you won't see brand-new acts breaking through into the big time; the EIF generally leaves that to its pals on the Fringe.

The variety of theatre and dance on the Fringe is baffling, dazzling and, at times, off-putting. Everybody from amateurish private school ensembles to well-known American troupes come to the party, performing everything from classic Edwardian costume drama to sexually explicit modern ballet. Shock and controversy are touchstones; the more attention a show receives, the more tickets it sells. Never mind the quality; feel the width.

Among the venues, the **Traverse** (*see p246*) prides itself on staging cutting-edge drama, and is perhaps the beating heart of Fringe theatre. *Gagarin Way*, *The People Next Door* and *Outlying Islands* all started here, and its bar is the hangout for many a luvvie.

Further Information

With so much to see in such a short space of time, planning your August itinerary can be a daunting prospect. The chaotic, spontaneous vibe is all part of the experience, but a little forward planning is crucial if you're to get the best out of it.

First and foremost: try and approach the festivals with some measure of organisation. Military precision isn't essential, but it certainly helps: unless you're in an improv troupe, it's best not to turn up and make it up as you go along. Have a look at the programme(s) before you arrive in Edinburgh, and keep your ear to the ground. By all means rock up ticketless and let nature take its inexorable course, but don't come crying to us when the only show you can get into is the Aberystwyth Amateur Dramatics Society's production of *Carousel*. In Welsh.

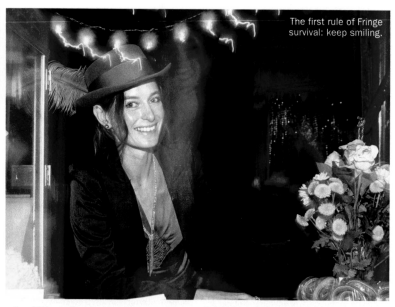

The first rule of Fringe survival: keep smiling.

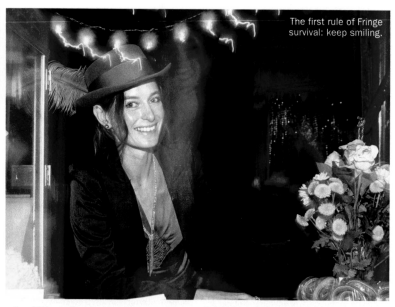

In addition to its printed programme, each festival has its own website at which you can find out what's on and book tickets for future events. Perhaps the most useful online resource, though, is **www.edinburghfestivals.co.uk**, which contains a searchable database listing what's on across all the major festivals. The catch-all set-up makes it that much easier to plan your schedule.

So, how do you go about sorting the diamonds from the rough? Well, this is the one time of the year when press coverage really counts. Ignore the publicity stunts and read the reviews instead. Although cost-cutting in recent years has lowered the quality of its reviews, the daily festivals supplement published by the *Scotsman* newspaper is well worth a look. Arguably the most reliable reviews are found in the *Guardian*; the *Edinburgh Evening News* and the *Herald* also offer daily criticism of what's on. The *Scotsman* and the *Herald* award, respectively, Fringe Firsts and Angel Awards to new plays, comedies, concerts and films that have particularly impressed their critics; tickets for these immediately start selling like the proverbial hot cakes. And then there's *The List* (*see p303*), which offers extensive coverage of the festivals; usually published fortnightly, it comes out every Thursday during August.

Several free festival newspapers, usually staffed by young writers and aspirant culture vultures, litter bars and cafés during August.

Containing news, reviews, interviews, features, listings and scurrilous gossip, they make up in enthusiasm what they lack in professionalism. *Three Weeks* is the longest established of this breed; the *Skinny* is also worth a peek. And then, of course, there's good old-fashioned word of mouth, which can be more reliable than the combined mental resources of the media corps. Don't be shy: pitch in and ask those folks sitting a few seats away if they've seen anything good or – just as crucially – if they've spent good money on any absolute stinkers.

Perhaps your greatest difficulty when planning a visit to Edinburgh in August, and almost certainly your greatest expense, will be your accommodation. Prices for virtually all kinds of lodgings soar during the summer, and get booked up months in advance. In addition to the various types of accommodation detailed on *pp52-72*, a number of flats, apartments and houses come on to the market in August for short-term lets, their owners having escaped the madness of the festivals and gone on a holiday of their own. For a list of agencies, *see pp70-71*. The Fringe website also has a message board on which offers of accommodation are posted.

Booking tickets

In theory, booking tickets for the various August festivals should be an utter nightmare. There are literally thousands of performances held here during the course of the month, from grand-scale concerts in the grounds of Edinburgh Castle to fringe gigs staged in the back seat of a car, and the overload ought to result in chaos at the various box offices. However, credit is due to the festivals' organisers: whether you'd rather purchase online, by phone, via mail or in person, buying tickets for shows at most of the festivals is generally very straightforward.

The easiest way to book tickets before arriving in Edinburgh is by going online. All the major festivals now take internet bookings; in most cases, you can choose either to have your tickets sent to you or collect them from the relevant festival's box office when you arrive. Once you're in town, you're best off booking either by phone or at one of the walk-up box offices: the Fringe has an office on the High Street, the Film Festival sells passes for all its events through the Filmhouse, and tickets for the Edinburgh International Festival, the

Festival of Politics and the Jazz & Blues Festival are all available from the Hub. For full details, *see p50* **Festivals directory**.

If you're planning to jump between festivals, as most visitors do, some advance booking will definitely be necessary. Many events staged as part of the Book Festival, Film Festival and Edinburgh International Festival are one-offs, and those featuring big names do tend to sell out ahead of time. Many comedy and theatre shows on the Fringe run for far longer, in some cases nightly over a three-week period, which means you may have less trouble picking up tickets when you arrive. Others, though, run for only limited periods (in some cases, only a single night); often you'd do well to book ahead.

Those heading north purely to take in the Fringe may want to consider heading up there early. On the first weekend, punters can buy two tickets for the price of one for most shows, a godsend for the financially stretched. The caveat, of course, is that some of the shows

What it costs

Edinburgh Art Festival

Prices generally follow regular museum and gallery admission rates.

Edinburgh Festival Fringe

Pick a number... Tickets for the majority of day-in-day-out comedy and theatre shows, and to low-key musical events, cost between £6 and £10. Admission to short-run or one-off shows by big-name stand-ups, and to gigs by well-known bands as part of T on the Fringe, are often around the £15-£20 mark. However, there are plenty of exceptions to these rules of thumb: you may even get into some shows for free.

Edinburgh Interactive Entertainment Festival

Games screenings, the sole portion of the event open to the public, are free.

Edinburgh International Book Festival

Tickets for most events cost between £5 and £10, with a few freebies dotted around the calendar.

Edinburgh International Festival

As you might expect, opera tickets are the most expensive, starting at around £7 but running to £60 (or, for gala performances, as much as £85). Tickets for classical concerts, dance performances and theatre

events generally start around £7 and rise to anywhere between £25 and £40 depending on the event. Look out, though, for the Lloyds TSB series of concerts, at which all tickets are priced at £10.

Edinburgh International Film Festival

Tickets for the majority of films will cost around £7.50, with a discount of 33 per cent for concessions.

Edinburgh Jazz & Blues Festival

Tickets for the majority of concerts are between £6 and £12. A few big names charge up to £20 or even £25, but there are also a number of free shows.

Edinburgh Mela

The festival itself is free, but entrance to the headline shows in the main marquee is usually around £10.

Edinburgh Military Tattoo

Prices in 2006 began at £11 and went all the way up to £36 for the best seats.

Edinburgh People's Festival

Tickets for paid-for events are usually less than £5.

Festival of Politics

Most events are free; tickets for the handful of paid-for events are around £5.

aren't yet running on all cylinders: many are essentially at 'preview' stage and are more than a little ragged around the edges. Alternatively, head for the Fringe's new innovation: the **Half Price Hut**, on the corner of Waverley Bridge and Princes Street. Open 11am to 9pm daily throughout the Fringe, the hut offers 50 per cent discounts on tickets to many of that day's shows. And it's also worth hanging around the main comedy and theatre venues in the early evening to catch excited promoters handing out free tickets for shows that are selling poorly in an attempt to conjure up an audience.

Festivals directory

Edinburgh Art Festival
Venue: various museums & galleries. Information: www.edinburghartfestival.org. **Tickets** pre-sale not necessary. **Dates** 6wks, late July-early Sept (exact 2007 & 2008 dates tbc).

Edinburgh Festival Fringe
Venue: various venues. Information & tickets: Fringe Office, 180 High Street, Old Town, EH1 1QS (information 226 0026/box office 226 0000/ www.edfringe.com). **Tickets** *Online, phone, in-person & postal bookings from mid June. Box office mid June-July noon-3pm Mon-Sat; mid-late July 10am-6pm daily; early Aug-end festival 10am-9pm daily. Phone bookings mid June-July 10am-6pm Mon-Sat; mid-late July 10am-6pm daily; early Aug-end festival 9am-9pm daily.* **Dates** 5-27 Aug 2007; 3-25 Aug 2008.

Edinburgh Interactive Entertainment Festival
Venue: various venues. Information & tickets: 01462 456780/www.eief.co.uk. **Tickets** pre-sale via website. **Dates** 2-3 days, late Aug (exact 2007 & 2008 dates tbc).

Edinburgh International Book Festival
Venue: Charlotte Square Gardens, New Town. Information & tickets: year-round office at 137 Dundee Street, Edinburgh, EH11 1BG; pre-sales at Waterstone's, 83 George Street, EH2 2ES (information 228 5444/box office 0845 373 5888/www.edbookfest.co.uk). **Tickets** *Online & postal bookings from mid June. Phone & in-person bookings mth before festival 9.30am-5.30pm Mon-Sat; during festival 9.30am-8.30pm daily.* **Dates** 11-27 Aug 2007; 16 Aug-1 Sept 2008.

Edinburgh International Festival
Venue: various venues. Information & tickets: The Hub, Castlehill, Old Town, EH1 2NE (administration 473 2099/box office 473 2000/www.eif.co.uk). **Tickets** *Online, phone, in-person & postal bookings from early April. Box office mid Apr-late July 10am-5pm Mon-Sat; late July-end festival 9am-7.30pm Mon-Sat, 10am-7.30pm Sun.* **Dates** 12 Aug-2 Sept 2007; 10-31 Aug 2008.

Edinburgh International Film Festival
Venue: various cinemas & theatres. Information & tickets: Filmhouse, 88 Lothian Road, Old Town, EH3 9BZ (information 229 2550/administration 228 4051/box office 623 8030/www.edfilmfest.org.uk). **Tickets** *Online, phone & in-person bookings from mid July.* **Dates** 15-26 Aug 2007; exact 2008 dates tbc.

Edinburgh International Television Festival
Venue: Edinburgh International Conference Centre. Information & tickets: 117 Farringdon Road, London EC1R 3BX (020 7278 9515/www. mgeitf.co.uk). **Tickets** *Online, phone & postal bookings from early in the yr.* **Dates** 24-26 Aug 2007; 22-24 Aug 2008.

Edinburgh Jazz & Blues Festival
Venue: various venues. Information & tickets: year-round office at 29 St Stephen Street, New Town, EH3 5AN; pre-sales at the Hub, Castlehill, Old Town, EH1 2NE (information 467 5200/box office 473 2000/www.edinburghjazzfestival.co.uk). **Tickets** *Online, phone, in-person & postal bookings from mid June. Box office mid Apr-late July 10am-5pm Mon-Sat; late July-end festival 9am-7.30pm Mon-Sat, 10am-7.30pm Sun.* **Dates** 27 July-5 Aug 2007; exact 2008 dates tbc.

Edinburgh Mela
Venue: Pilrig Park, Leith. Information: Queen Margaret University College, Guthrie Wright Building (Room 40), Clerwood Terrace, EH12 8TS (339 3583/www.edinburgh-mela.co.uk). **Tickets** pre-sale not necessary. **Dates** 1-2 Sep 2007; exact 2008 dates tbc.

Edinburgh Military Tattoo
Venue: Castle Esplanade, Old Town. Information & tickets: 32-34 Market Street, Old Town, EH1 1QB (0870 755 5118/www.edintattoo.co.uk). **Tickets** *Information Sept-July 10am-4.30pm Mon-Fri; Aug 10am-9pm Mon-Fri, 10am-7.30pm Sat, 10am-4.30pm Sun. Online, phone, in-person & postal bookings from early Dec. Box office mid Dec-end festival 10am-4.30pm Mon-Fri.* **Dates** 3-25 Aug 2007; 1-23 Aug 2008.

Edinburgh People's Festival
Venue: various venues. Information & tickets: Communication Workers Union, 15 Brunswick Street, EH7 5JB (556 8869/www.edinburgh peoplesfestival.org.uk). **Tickets** *Phone bookings from June.* **Dates** 1wk, early Aug (exact 2007 & 2008 dates tbc).

Festival of Politics
Venue, information & tickets: Scottish Parliament, Holyrood, EH99 1SP (348 5000/www.festivalof politics.org.uk. **Tickets** pre-sale only for selected events, from the Scottish Parliament or the Hub, Castlehill, Old Town, EH1 2NE. *Box office mid Apr-late July 10am-5pm Mon-Sat; late July-end festival 9am-7.30pm Mon-Sat, 10am-7.30pm Sun.* **Dates** 4 days, late Aug (exact 2007 & 2008 dates tbc).

Where to Stay

Where to Stay   52

Features

Swallow Albany. *See p61*.

Where to Stay

Visitors to the city are spoilt for choice, but early booking is essential...

In the not so dim and distant past, Edinburgh used to explode into life like a Roman candle during the International Festival and Fringe, before fizzling out just as quickly and allowing the locals to reclaim their city. But the last decade or so has seen Edinburgh transformed into a year-round destination, which in turn has created a buoyant demand for accomodation across a range of budgets. Tartan carpets and thistle-patterned wallpaper are becoming things of the past; new investment, particularly from a clutch of ambitious, home-grown hoteliers, has challenged the old-stagers to raise their games.

At the upper end of the market, the **Hilton Caledonian** and the **Balmoral** remain bastions of tradition and good old-fashioned extravagance. Their day is far from past; indeed, both have benefited from multi-million-pound cash injections in recent years. But since the sleek, chic **Malmaison** opened in 1994, hoteliers have worked towards more modern luxury. **Rick's** has grown into a hugely successful bar, restaurant and ten-room boutique hotel; hopes are high for the **Hudson** and the **Tigerlily**, both of which opened in 2006.

At the cheaper end of the spectrum, chain hotels continue to play a vital part in providing budget options for the city's visitors. While few possess much character, many of them occupy prime locations in the centre of town. For a bit more local flavour, try one of the more modestly priced independents: the **Ailsa Craig Hotel**, for instance, offers the chance to stay in a converted Georgian townhouse, while the **Claremont** offers impressive views over Arthur's Seat and the Forth.

New hotels have been springing up regularly over the last few years, and several new developments are in the pipeline. Monaco-based Ken McCulloch, who built and sold the Malmaison hotel chain before forming Dakota Hotels (www.dakotahotels.co.uk), is to open a 127-room venture in South Queensferry in March 2007. A major hotel is set to be built on the site of the former railway goods yard at Morrison Street, and there's talk of a new five-star hotel in the Caltongate development, currently taking shape in the centre of the city alongside Waverley Station. Keep your eyes peeled and your options open.

PRICES AND SERVICES

Hotels in this chapter have been arranged by area and placed into four price bands: Deluxe, Expensive, Moderate and Budget. Room rates given include VAT. However, note that prices vary wildly. If you're planning to visit in the run-up to Hogmanay or during August (*see p208*), or if your stay coincides with a rugby international (*see p239*) or a major conference, you may end up paying a premium for your room. Book as early as possible.

The flipside is that bargain deals are increasingly commonplace – particularly from October to April, when rates can drop by more than 50 per cent. Significant savings can also sometimes be made if you're prepared to wait until the last minute before booking: most clued-up hoteliers would rather sell their beds at a discount than leave them empty. This applies even to smarter hotels: they may command top rates from business travellers

---

The best Hotels

For old-school luxury
Howard (*see p60*); Scotsman (*see p53*); Witchery by the Castle (*see p55*).

For new-school style
Hudson (*see p61*); Le Monde (*see p61*); Tigerlily (*see p61*).

For a bargain break
Edinburgh Central SYHA Hostel (*see p67*); Links Hotel (*see p70*); student accommodation (*see p71*).

For a room with a view
George (*see p59*); Paramount Carlton (*see p55*); Parliament House (*see p65*).

For a little bit extra
The eponymous restaurant at Channings (*see p64 & p155*); the bar at Malmaison (*see p184 & p184*); One Spa at the Sheraton Grand (*see p72 & p203*).

> ❶ Blue numbers given in this chapter correspond to the location of each hotel on the street maps. *See pp324-336.*

Witchery by the Castle. See p55.

from Monday to Thursday, but they rely on more budget-conscious leisure travellers at weekends, so you may be able to strike a deal.

If you arrive in town without having pre-booked your hotel, it may be worth getting in touch with the **Edinburgh & Lothians Tourist Board** (*see p306*). Staff can make reservations for hotels across the city direct from its office for a small booking fee.

We've listed a selection of services for each hotel at the bottom of each review, covering everything from the in-room entertainment options to the availability and cost of parking facilities (always call to check the situation if you're travelling by car). A number of hotels and hostels offer high-speed internet facilities: 'wireless' denotes those that offer a wireless connection throughout; 'DSL' is used for hotels where a high-speed connection is available only via a cable; and 'shared terminal' refers to a computer in the hotel's lobby or business centre.

Many hotels have disabled access and specially adapted rooms: the Edinburgh & Lothians Tourist Board can provide a list. Other advice is available from **Edinburgh City Council** and **Grapevine**; for both, *see p300*. Smokers should call ahead to check whether the hotel has smoking rooms: following on from the 2006 law banning smoking in enclosed public places, many hotels are now completely non-smoking.

HOSTEL ACCOMMODATION

Rates for hostel accommodation are given per person per night unless stated otherwise. The independent hostels do get very busy:

try to book ahead if at all possible. If you intend to stay out late, it's worth remembering to check curfews when making your booking.

Those looking to travel around the country should contact the **Scottish Youth Hostel Association (SYHA)**, which runs a number of hostels in Scotland. Standard membership costs £8; it's not required for a stay in an SYHA property, but non-members will be charged an extra £1 a night, and are ineligible for other SYHA benefits. You can join online or when you check in to any SYHA hostel. For bookings across Scotland, call 0870 155 3255; for general enquiries, call 01786 891400. There's plenty of information at www.syha.org.uk.

Old Town

Deluxe

Scotsman

20 North Bridge, EH1 1YT (556 5565/fax 652 3652/www.thescotsmanhotel.co.uk). Nicolson Street–North Bridge buses. **Rates** £200-£350 double; £380-£1,500 suite. **Credit** AmEx, DC, MC, V. **Map** p330 H7, p336 F3 ❶

The 2001 facelift given to this building, the former offices of the *Scotsman* (the onetime reception area is now the buzzing North Bridge Brasserie), pre-served and restored its original Edwardian features, from the elaborate cornicing and marble floors to the walnut panelling and stained-glass windows. More modern luxuries include the state-of-the-art Escape Health Club, the über-chic Cowshed Spa (*see p64* **So spa, so good**), a 16m stainless steel pool and the Vermilion restaurant (*see p148*), located at the foot of the opulent marble staircase. Each room is

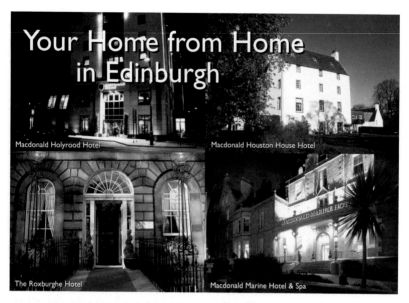

individually decorated with estate tweeds and original art, and has a well-stocked wine bar and a privacy hatch for delivering room service. The corner turret rooms house giant step-up baths.

Bar. Business centre. Concierge. Disabled-adapted rooms. Gym. High-speed internet (shared terminal, wireless). Parking (limited; £20). Pool. Restaurant. Room service. Spa.

Witchery by the Castle

352 Castlehill, EH1 2NF (225 5613/fax 220 4392/ www.thewitchery.com). Bus 35/Nicolson Street–North Bridge buses. **Rates** £295 suite. **Credit** AmEx, DC, MC, V. **Map** p330 G7, p336 D4 ❷

Taking its name from the witches once burned at the stake nearby (a well on the Castle Esplanade marks the spot), the historic, romantic and charismatic Witchery is not so much a hotel as a restaurant with a few suites attached. The suites, some with kitchens attached, are located in two buildings straddling the Royal Mile: two in the 16th-century building in Boswell's Court, and five in the more 17th-century dwelling off Sempill's Court. Each one is dark, theatrically Gothic and lavishly furnished with antiques, sumptuous leather and velvet upholstery, claw-foot Victorian baths and grand, carved wooden beds. Often imitated but never bettered, the Witchery is *the* place to indulge yourself if you have the means, and if they have a room. **Photo** *p53.*

Restaurant. Room service.

Expensive

Apex International & Apex City

31-35 Grassmarket, EH1 2HS (300 3456/fax 220 5345/www.apexhotels.co.uk). Bus 2, 23, 27, 41, 42. **Rates** £135-£180 double. **Credit** AmEx, DC, MC, V. **Map** p330 G8, p336 C4 ❸

The Apex International's 2002 transformation from bland mid-market residence to sleek designer spot still holds steady. With black rubberised floors, brown leather furnishings, American cherrywood panelling and shiny chrome fittings, it epitomises mainstream contemporary style. All the rooms are decorated identically; add-on gadgetry includes Playstations, DVD and CD players and interactive TVs. Superior rooms and rooftop restaurant Heights boast stunning views of the castle; Japanese-inspired Yu Spa takes care of your health and beauty needs.

Yards away sits the Apex City (61 Grassmarket, 243 3456), an even sleeker sister hotel. Inside, all is contemporary, chic and stylish (without, mercifully, being too precious). The rooms are laid out in four 'zones' (for sleeping, working, relaxing and bathing); walk-in power showers, separate from the bath, are a nice bonus. The street-facing Agua bar-restaurant is great for people-watching, but you can also use the restaurants and the spa at the Apex International and charge the bill to your room.

Bar. Business centre. Concierge. Disabled-adapted rooms. Gym. High-speed internet (shared terminal, wireless). Parking (limited; free). Pool. Restaurants (2). Room service. Spa.

MacDonald Holyrood Hotel

81 Holyrood Road, EH8 8AU (0870 194 2106/ fax 550 4545/www.macdonaldhotels.co.uk/holyrood). Bus 35, 36. **Rates** £99-£230 double/twin; £149-£280 suite. **Credit** AmEx, DC, MC, V. **Map** p331 K7 ❹

Located across the street from the *Scotsman* offices and a caber's toss from the new Scottish Parliament, the Holyrood, perhaps unsurprisingly, was built with the business traveller in mind. (That said, it's also close to the Royal Mile, Our Dynamic Earth and Arthur's Seat.) The rooms are furnished with maple wood and splashes of Harris tweed, and equipped with heated mirrors to banish the post-shower haze. There's an impressive restaurant, a well-equipped gym and a 14m pool, and, on the Club Floor, a private butler to attend to your every whim.

Bar. Business centre. Concierge. Disabled-adapted rooms. Gym. High-speed internet (shared terminal, wireless). Parking (£15). Pool. Restaurant. Room service. Spa.

Paramount Carlton

North Bridge, EH1 1SD (472 3000/fax 556 2691/ www.paramount-hotels.co.uk). Nicolson Street–North Bridge buses. **Rates** £90-£160 single; £100-£250 double. **Credit** AmEx, DC, MC, V. **Map** p331 J7, p336 F3 ❺

The block-long Carlton offers fine views of the city from every room, something that even its five-star competitors can't match. A dramatic and long-overdue renovation has transformed its previously tired appearance, and guests are now greeted by a grand reception with contemporary lighting, pale marble flooring and an imposing staircase. The rooms have also all been revamped, although the style is comfortable rather than cutting-edge.

Bar. Business centre. Concierge. Disabled-adapted rooms. Gym. High-speed internet (shared terminal, wireless). Parking (£18). Pool. Restaurant. Room service. Spa.

Radisson SAS Hotel

80 High Street, Royal Mile, EH1 1TH (557 9797/ fax 557 9789/www.radissonsas.com). Bus 35/ Nicolson Street–North Bridge buses. **Rates** £95-£230 double; call for suite prices. **Credit** AmEx, DC, MC, V. **Map** p331 J7, p336 F4 ❻

Constructed in the late 1980s, its faux-Gothic façade designed to blend with its historic neighbours (judge for yourselves whether it succeeds), this outpost of the Radisson chain has been transformed by a £5-million refurb at the hands of award-winning Glasgow design firm Graven Images. The interior style is clean-cut, sleek and monochromatic, albeit with subtle contemporary Scottish motifs. Just off the main entrance, the newly opened Itchycoo bar-restaurant aims for a Manhattan feel, with an island bar, stainless steel and black surrounds and huge 3D photographic portraits of 20th-century icons (Warhol, Picasso et al) by Edinburgh actor/artist Bob Kingdom. Another bonus: ample parking space.

Bar. Concierge. Disabled-adapted rooms. Gym. High-speed internet (shared terminal, wireless). Parking (£7). Pool. Restaurant. Room service. Spa.

Past masters

Given that Edinburgh is so overwhelmed by its history, it makes sense that a number of the city's hotels enjoyed previous lives before welcoming tourists through their doors. Many hotels are housed in plain old residential properties, converted into public lodgings throughout the last half-century or so. Others, though, have a more engaging story to tell.

Some hotels make a virtue of their history, with the **Scotsman** (*see p53*) chief among them. The sandstone premises were the headquarters of the *Scotsman* newspaper for almost a century: a gym takes up the floor once occupied by the paper's huge printing presses, while the former reception area now houses the North Bridge Brasserie. Savour your walk down the staircase to Vermilion, the hotel's grand restaurant: in the old days all but the most senior staff were forbidden to set foot on its marble splendour.

For all its romantic, decadent appeal, much of the **Witchery by the Castle** (*see p55*) once formed part of the assembly hall of the Church of Scotland, and the sumptuous Old

Rectory suite was the rectory of the nearby church until just a decade ago. And then there's the **Glasshouse** (*see p65*), a sleek paean to 21st-century luxury hidden behind the carefully preserved Victorian sandstone façade of the Lady Glenorchy Church.

Prestonfield (*see p68*; **photo** *left*) also has a religious connection, albeit more tangential. The original building on the site was owned by staunch Catholics, and was burned down by students as part of an anti-Catholic protest in 1681. Sir William Bruce, who had recently completed the Royal Palace of Holyroodhouse, designed the extravagantly baroque manor house that replaced it. In 2004, Lord Watson of Invergowrie, then the MSP for Glasgow Cathcart, tried to emulate the 17th-century students' example by setting the hotel's curtains alight upon being refused service at the bar. He was jailed for attempted arson.

The Edwardian townhouse now occupied by **Channings** hotel (*see p64*) was formerly home to polar explorer Sir Ernest Shackleton, who lived there from 1904 after being named Secretary of the Royal Scottish Geographical Society. The hotel is always on the lookout for Shackleton memorabilia with which to decorate the rooms. Conversely, the **Hudson** (*see p61*) bears no traces of its former life: it was a busy post office before the Royal Mail closed it down.

The elegant **Bonham** (*see p59*) has a varied history. A medical practice up until 1951, it was then sold to Edinburgh University and operated as a women-only hall of residence. Guests are said to include former students, who delight in coming back with partners and flouting the rules they had to follow in their student days. But the hotel with perhaps the liveliest history is the **Malmaison** (*see p72*) up in Leith. Built in 1833, it began life as a seaman's mission, the first port of call for men just off the ships at the nearby docks. However, it was also, at one time, reputed to house one of Edinburgh's better bordellos.

Moderate

Bank Hotel

1 South Bridge, EH1 1LL (556 9940/fax 558 1362/ www.festival-inns.co.uk). Nicolson Street–North Bridge buses. **Rates** £70-£120 double; £90-£140 suite. **Credit** AmEx, MC, V. **Map** p331 J7, p336 F4 ❼
Nine rooms situated above Logie Baird's Bar, a popular post-work hangout, accessed via a hidden

doorway at the rear. The mood is determinedly Caledonian, with wood panelling and dark tartan furnishings. Each bedroom is themed around a famous Scot: the James Young Simpson room, named for the pioneer of anaesthetics, has anatomical sketches, while the Thomas Telford room, in honour of the builder of bridges and aqueducts, is dominated by a black four-poster construction over the bed. *Bar. Room service.*

Jurys Inn

43 Jeffrey Street, EH1 1DG (200 3300/fax 200 0400/http://edinburghhotels.jurysdoyle.com). Nicolson Street–North Bridge buses. **Rates** £61-£167 double/ twin. **Credit** AmEx, DC, MC, V. **Map** p331 J7 ❽

If it looks like an old office block, that's because it used to be an old office block. However, while the hotel itself isn't anything out of the ordinary, the location is a tourist's dream, sitting within minutes of the Royal Mile, Princes Street and the New Town. You probably won't want to spend much time here, but neither will you waste any time getting out to do some serious sightseeing.

Bar. Business centre. Disabled-adapted rooms. High-speed internet (DSL, shared terminal, wireless). Pool. Restaurant.

Tailors Hall

139 Cowgate, EH1 1JS (622 6801/fax 622 6818/ www.festival-inns.co.uk). Nicolson Street–North Bridge buses. **Rates** £50-£90 single; £80-£140 double/twin; £100-£160 triple. **Credit** AmEx, MC, V. **Map** p330 H7, p336 E4 ❾

Smack in the middle of the Old Town, right on the historic Cowgate, this 17th-century building directly overlooks the courtyard of the Three Sisters bar, which, in summer especially, is one of the busiest central hangouts by both day and night. (Tip: if you plan to get at least some shut-eye, ask for a room in the quieter new wing.) The interior is thoroughly modern, and while rooms vary greatly in size and shape, they're all clean and comfortable. A lively spot, to put it mildly.

Bar. High-speed internet (wireless). Restaurant. Room service.

Budget

Ibis Edinburgh Centre

6 Hunter Square, EH1 1QW (240 7000/fax 240 7007/www.ibishotel.com). Nicolson Street–North Bridge buses. **Rates** £55-£77 single/double. **Credit** AmEx, DC, MC, V. **Map** p330 H7, p336 F4 ❿

The Ibis chain has a reputation for efficiency and good value and a tendency towards thoroughly bland anonymity. Its sole Edinburgh operation lives up (and down) to all three characteristics: you know exactly what you're going to get, even if you won't really remember much about it. Pricing aside, the best bit is the central location, just a few steps away from the Royal Mile.

Bar. Disabled-adapted rooms. High-speed internet (DSL, wireless).

Travelodge

33 St Mary's Street, EH1 1TA (0870 191 1637/fax 557 3681/www.travelodge.co.uk). Bus 35/Nicolson Street–North Bridge buses. **Rates** £60-£110 single/ double. **Credit** AmEx, DC, MC, V. **Map** p331 J7 ⓫

The review of the Ibis directly above could virtually double up for the Travelodge, since the same perks (keen value, clean reliability) and caveats (it looks as if it was designed by committee somewhere outside

Slough) apply here. Once again the location is key: it's in the heart of the Old Town, roughly halfway between Arthur's Seat and Edinburgh Castle.

Bar. Disabled-adapted rooms. High-speed internet (DSL). Parking (limited; £5). Restaurant.

Hostels

Brodies Backpackers *93 High Street, EH1 1TB (556 6770/www.brodieshostels.co.uk). Bus 35/ Nicolson Street–North Bridge buses.* **Open** *Reception 7am-midnight daily. No curfew.* **Rates** £10-£18 dorm bed; £44-£54 double. **Credit** MC, V. **Map** p331 J7 ⓬

Budget Backpackers *37-39 Cowgate, EH1 1JR (226 6351/www.budgetbackpackers.com). Nicolson Street–North Bridge buses.* **Open** *Reception 24hrs. No curfew.* **Rates** £10-£16 dorm bed; £16-£25 double. **Credit** MC, V. **Map** p330 H8, p336 D4 ⓭

Castle Rock Hostel *15 Johnston Terrace, EH1 2PW (225 9666/fax 226 5078/www.scotlands-top-hostels.com). Bus 2, 23, 27, 41, 42.* **Open** *Reception 24hrs. No curfew.* **Rates** £12.50-£15 dorm bed; call for double prices. **Credit** AmEx, DC, MC, V. **Map** p330 G8, p336 G4 ⓮

Edinburgh Backpackers Hostel *65 Cockburn Street, EH1 1BU (reception 220 1717/fax 226 5162/reservations 220 2200/reservations fax 477 4636/www.hoppo.com). Bus 35/Nicolson Street– North Bridge buses.* **Open** *Reception 24hrs. No curfew.* **Rates** from £14 dorm bed. **Credit** MC, V. **Map** p330 H7, p336 F3 ⓯

Edinburgh Metro SYHA Hostel *11 Robertson's Close, Cowgate, EH1 1LY (hostel 0870 004 1115/ central bookings 0870 155 3255/www.syha.org.uk). Nicolson Street–North Bridge buses.* **Open** *Reception 7am-11.30pm daily. No curfew.* **Rates** £15-£23 single, plus membership. **Credit** MC, V. **Map** p331 J7, p336 F4 ⓰

High Street Hostel *9 Blackfriars Street, EH1 1NE (557 3984/fax 556 2981/www.macbackpackers.com). Bus 35/Nicolson Street–North Bridge buses.* **Open** *Reception 24hrs. No curfew.* **Rates** £13-£17 dorm bed. **Credit** AmEx, DC, MC, V. **Map** p331 J7, p336 F4 ⓱

Royal Mile Backpackers *105 High Street, EH1 1SG (557 6120/fax 556 3999/www.scotlands-top-hostels.com). Bus 35/Nicolson Street–North Bridge buses.* **Open** *Reception 7am-3am daily. No curfew.* **Rates** £12.50-£14 dorm bed. **Credit** AmEx, MC, V. **Map** p331 J7 ⓲

New Town

Deluxe

Balmoral

1 Princes Street, EH2 2EQ (556 2414/fax 557 3747/ www.thebalmoralhotel.com). Nicolson Street–North Bridge buses or Princes Street buses. **Rates** £270-£470 single/double; £590-£1,500 suite. **Credit** AmEx, DC, MC, V. **Map** p326/p330 H6, p336 F2 ⓳

A kilted doorman will welcome you to 'Scotland's most famous address', where the trappings are everything you'd expect from a five-star hotel: marble floors, crystal chandeliers and service that's

always attentive but rarely intrusive. The emphasis in the 180 rooms is on cool, earthy colours and geometric shapes. Exterior rooms offer panoramic views, while the quieter interior rooms overlook the chandeliered Palm Court, where a famous afternoon tea is served in serene spendour before the space morphs into the Bollinger Bar at Palm Court (see p149). Hadrian's Brasserie does a fair imitation of cosmopolitan Milan, but the real jewel is the Michelin-starred Number One (see p153).
Bars (2). Business centre. Concierge. Disabled-adapted rooms. Gym. High-speed internet (shared terminal, wireless). Parking (£20) Pool. Restaurants (2). Room service. Spa.

Expensive

Bonham
35 Drumsheugh Gardens, EH3 7RN (226 6050/ reservations 623 9300/fax 623 9306/www.the bonham.com). Bus 13, 19, 37, 41, 47. **Rates** £75-£145 single; £99-£245 double; £150-£350 suite. **Credit** AmEx, DC, MC, V. **Map** p329 C7 ⑳
A townhouse exterior gives way to a contemporary blend of comfortable, light and (happily) not very Starck minimalism within. The elaborately carved, wood-panelled reception area, with original telephone booths bookending the entrance, is particularly welcoming. Neutral colours, with some bright splashes and art deco furniture in the public areas, complement the soaring ceilings and cornices of the original Victorian building. Many of the 48 individually decorated rooms feature original art by local students. The restaurant (see p151) is another perk, especially

with the occasional offer making it far more affordable (tables of four can enjoy a three-course weekend lunch with two bottles of wine for just £65 per table). Popular with style-conscious visitors.
High-speed internet (DSL, wireless). Parking (limited; free). Restaurant. Room service.

Edinburgh Residence
7 Rothesay Terrace, EH3 7RY (623 9304/fax 226 3381/www.theedinburghresidence.com). Bus 13. **Rates** £135-£395 suite. **Credit** AmEx, DC, MC, V. **Map** p329 C7 ㉑
Like the Howard, its sister property (see p60), the Edinburgh Residence is identifiable only by a discreet gold plaque. Inside, the reception area is beautifully traditional, with dark red furnishings, wood panelling, a grandfather clock and a reverent atmosphere. The three categories of suites (Town House, Grand and Classic) vary in size and facilities, but all have idiosyncrasies: the Town House suites feature bookcases that conceal fold-down beds, while some Classic rooms have separate exits on to Rothesay Terrace. There's no bar or restaurant, but meals are served in the suites, and guests can socialise in the Drawing Room, which has a self-serve honesty bar.
Concierge. Disabled-adapted rooms. High-speed internet (shared terminal, wireless). Parking (limited; free). Room service.

George
19-21 George Street, EH2 2PB (0131 225 1251/ fax 226 5644/www.principal-hotels.com). Princes Street buses. **Rates** £89-£179 single; £199-£249 double; £299-£499 suite. **Credit** AmEx, DC, MC, V. **Map** p326/p330 G6, p336 D1 ㉒

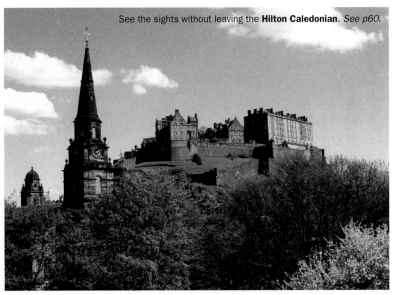

See the sights without leaving the **Hilton Caledonian**. *See p60.*

If the Balmoral and Caledonian are the king and queen of the city's hotels, the George is the princess. The grande dame is looking much fresher these days after to an extensive refurbishment: Carvers, the restaurant, remains one of the grandest old style hotel eateries in the country, but the hotel's reception area is now less fussily appointed, a stylish café-bar (Tempus) has been added, and all 116 rooms in the Contemporary (formerly plain old 'East') Wing have had a complete makeover. The north-facing deluxe doubles on floors five to seven boast eye-popping 180-degree views of the Forth shore and Fife, while those facing west offer views of the castle. The heather-coloured walls, subtly checked throws and floral print cushions create a contemporary Scottish look that won't date any time soon.
Bar. Business centre. Concierge. Disabled-adapted rooms. High-speed internet (DSL, wireless). Restaurants (2). Room service.

Hilton Caledonian

4 Princes Street, EH1 2AB (222 8888/fax 222 8889/ www.hilton.com/caledonian). Princes Street buses. **Rates** £130-£295 single; £175-£380 double. **Credit** AmEx, DC, MC, V. **Map** p330 E7, p336 A2 ㉓
At the west end of Princes Street, the Caledonian's imposing red sandstone façade has made the hotel an Edinburgh landmark. Once in danger of losing her lustre, she's been restored to her former glory thanks to a 125-room, multi-million-pound refurbishment that included a makeover of the two-floor Living Well leisure club. Nevertheless, the Caley steadfastly refuses to follow any current design trends, instead retaining a sense of a bygone era

throughout: huge arched corridors lead past broad staircases, lit by towering stained glass windows. A high standard of service has made the hotel a favourite with luminaries from Nelson Mandela to Sean Connery, who calls it home when he's in town. Elegant, opulent and even ostentatious. **Photo** *p59.*
Bars (2). Business centre. Concierge. Disabled-adapted rooms. Gym. High-speed internet (DSL, shared terminal, wireless). Parking (limited; £9.50). Pool. Restaurants (2). Room service. Spa.

Howard

34 Great King Street, EH3 6QH (557 3500/ reservations 274 7402/fax 557 6515/www.the howard.com). Bus 13, 23, 27. **Rates** £75-£145 single; £105-£295 double/twin; £185-£395 suite. **Credit** AmEx, DC, MC, V. **Map** p326 F4 ㉔
Only the brass plaque on the front door reveals the identity of this terraced townhouse. Built in 1829, the Howard is a perfect example of how to successfully combine Georgian style with modern luxury. The breakfast room, with its sumptuous arrangement of red Victorian chairs, overlooks elegant Great King Street; you can almost hear the hansom cabs' horses clip-clopping by. The terraced suites in the basement have their own separate entrances and are particularly popular with honeymooning couples. Large bathrooms with state-of-the-art showers and roll-top baths are luxurious bonuses. Service is exemplary; a butler checks in guests in the lavishly decorated drawing room.
Concierge. Disabled-adapted rooms. High-speed internet (shared terminal, wireless). Parking (limited; free). Restaurant. Room service.

Royal Scots Club class. *See p61.*

Le Monde

16 George Street, EH2 2PF (270 3900/fax 270 3901/www.lemondehotel.co.uk). Princes Street buses. **Rates** £245 double; £295 suite. **Credit** AmEx, DC, MC, V. **Map** p326/p330 G6, p336 D1 ㉕
Part of a new £12-million entertainment complex in a former office building, Le Monde is unlike any other hotel in Edinburgh. The theme, as the name suggests, is the world: 17 of the 18 suites are dedicated to different destinations, with the 18th modelled on the waterworld of Atlantis. Tokyo is serene, with beautiful, framed kimonos on the walls and *Lost in Translation* in the DVD player; New York is done out like a Manhattan loft; and Reykjavik features cool blue walls, a huge chunk of volcanic rock and lampstands like blocks of ice. The fun continues in the bathrooms, with plasma screens and waterproof remotes. If you fancy a change of scenery, the hotel encourages guests to flit from city to city during their stay (subject to availability). Escapist fun.
Bars (3). Concierge. Disabled-adapted rooms. High-speed internet (wireless). Restaurant. Room service.

Roxburghe

38 Charlotte Square, EH2 4HG (240 5500/fax 240 5555/www.roxburghe-hotel.co.uk). Princes Street buses. **Rates** £75-£145 single; £99-£245 double; £150-£250 suite. **Credit** AmEx, DC, MC, V. **Map** p330 E7, p336 A1 ㉖
The Roxburghe's exterior remains faithful to Robert Adam's Georgian design, but its interior has been transformed into an almost seamless blend of 19th-century elegance and 21st-century style. Huge leather armchairs sit invitingly on the beechwood floors in the lobby, and the open courtyard in the centre is a hive of activity during the Edinburgh International Book Festival in Charlotte Square across the street: patrons wander back here to take high tea. Some of the rooms in the back extension are a little featureless, but views of Edinburgh Castle from the higher floors do much to compensate.
Bar. Business centre. Concierge. Disabled-adapted rooms. Gym. High-speed internet (DSL, shared terminal, wireless). Parking (£15). Pool. Restaurant. Room service. Spa.

Royal Scots Club

29-30 Abercromby Place, EH3 6QE (556 4270/ fax 558 3769/www.royalscotsclub.com). Bus 13, 23, 27. **Rates** £105-£200 double. **Credit** AmEx, DC, MC, V. **Map** p326 G5 ㉗
A gentlemen's club vibe is still very much in evidence on entering this classic Georgian townhouse, just a short walk from Princes Street. Founded in 1919 as a tribute to those who fell in the Great War, the Royal Scots Club today exudes a strong sense of history and a palpable air of tranquillity. The modernised rooms have been tastefully furnished in a traditional style; some have four-poster beds and fine views towards the Firth of Forth. Classic features abound, most eye-catchingly in the shape of the real fire in the lounge. **Photo** *p60.*
Bar. Gym. High-speed internet (DSL, wireless). Restaurant. Room service.

Swallow Albany

39-43 Albany Street, EH1 3QY (556 0397/fax 557 6633/www.swallowhotels.com). Playhouse buses. **Rates** £85-£110 single; £145-£270 double. **Credit** AmEx, MC, V. **Map** p326 H5 ㉘
Tucked away in a corner of the New Town and converted from three Georgian townhouse, the Albany is a discreet spot, albeit one priced a little higher than its rather basic facilities suggest it should be. It's now owned by Maidstone-based Swallow Hotels, whose recent Scottish acquisitions have made it the largest hotel brand north of the border; they also operate two hotels just by the West End, Greens (24 Eglinton Crescent, EH12 5BY, 337 1565) and Thistle Court (5 Hampton Terrace, EH12 5JD, 313 5500), and Stockbridge's Learmonth Hotel (18-20 Learmonth Terrace, EH4 2JH, 343 2671). **Photo** *p63.*

Tigerlily

125 George Street, EH2 4JN, (225 5005/fax 225 7046/www.tigerlilyedinburgh.co.uk). Princes Street buses. **Rates** £175 double; £245-£295 suite. **Credit** AmEx, DC, MC, V. **Map** p326/p330 E6, p336 B1 ㉙
This sumptuous and ambitious new hotel, restaurant/cocktail bar and nightclub complex is located in a five-storey townhouse building. Each of the 33 bedrooms and suites is decorated differently, but all combine classic and contemporary influences, smooth and textured surfaces and, as the hotel's name suggests, masculine and feminine appeal. In the main stairwell, giant disco balls splash the walls with their sparkle; every window has a row of red pin-point lights along the ledge, giving the building a soft glow when viewed from outside. The oak door to each room has an engraved silver tigerlily motif and a leather-bound handle; leather pulls open the wardrobes and cabinets. Two knock-out, spacious suites overlooking George Street are dominated by huge, canopied beds.
Bars (2). Concierge. Disabled-adapted rooms. High-speed internet (wireless). Restaurant. Room service.

Moderate

Hudson

9-11 Hope Street, EH2 4EL (247 7000/fax 247 7001/www.thehudsonhotel.co.uk). Princes Street buses. **Rates** £90 single; £100-£150 double. **Credit** AmEx, MC, V. **Map** p330 E7, p336 A1 ㉚
The newly opened Hudson brings a contemporary edge to the Georgian building in which it's housed, just off Princes Street. Targeting a tech-savvy clientele looking for quality and style without the price tag, it's had £7m worth of urban style poured into it. A café is unconventionally located in the reception area; there's a bar and a nightclub downstairs (all the male bar staff wear black business kilts). The rooms have a New York loft apartment feel, done out in masculine browns, beiges and dark reds with walnut panelling and plasma-screen TVs. The beds are generously-proportioned, with Egyptian cotton sheets and sumptuous pillows. The marble-floored

bathrooms are stocked with luxury toiletries by Molton Brown, who provide discount vouchers for their nearby shop on George Street.

Bars (2). Disabled-adapted rooms. High-speed internet (DSL, wireless). Restaurant. Room service.

Old Waverley

43 Princes Street, EH2 2BY (556 4648/fax 557 6316/www.oldwaverley.co.uk). Princes Street buses. **Rates** £129 single; £169 double/twin; £195 triple/family. **Credit** AmEx, DC, MC, V. **Map** p326/p330 H6, p336 E2 ③①

Dating back to 1848, the Old Waverley is one of the capital's oldest hotels. A multi-million-pound renovation has recently restored the sparkle to what had become a somewhat faded spot. While maintaining a traditional feel, all of the rooms have been stylishly refitted. The south-facing rooms boast outstanding views of the castle and Old Town; as do Cranstons restaurant and the Abbotsford Room bar, where sitting over an early evening drink and surveying the panorama is a real treat.

Bar. High-speed internet (wireless). Restaurant. Room service.

Rick's

55a Frederick Street, EH2 1HL (622 7800/ www.rickedinburgh.co.uk). Princes Street buses. **Rates** £130 double. **Credit** AmEx, MC, V. **Map** p326/p330 F6, p336 C1 ③②

Nightlife is high on the agenda at Rick's. A bar (see *p177*) and restaurant with ten boutique rooms attached, it's been one of Edinburgh's top 'in' places

since its inception in 1998. The New Town location is handy for nightlife, but you might find it tough to head out at all: the mammoth beds, complete with walnut headboards and cream angora blankets, demand to be lounged on, while a tempting room service menu could further sabotage your plans. A very decent option indeed, especially for the price.

Bar. High-speed internet (wireless). Restaurant. Room service.

Budget

Frederick House

42 Frederick Street, EH2 1EX (226 1999/fax 624 7064/www.townhousehotels.co.uk). Princes Street buses. **Rates** £35-£90 single; £50-£140 double. **Credit** AmEx, MC, V. **Map** p326/p330 F6, p336 C1 ③③

This listed building has been transformed from offices into five floors of bedrooms in patterned greens, golds and reds. The best rooms are at the front of the hotel, while the Skyline suite has views across the Firth of Forth. It's run by the same group as the Ailsa Craig and Greenside hotels (*see p67*).

High-speed internet (DSL, wireless). Parking.

Hostels

Belford Backpackers *6-8 Douglas Gardens, EH4 3DA (220 2200/fax 477 4636/www.hoppo.com). Princes Street buses.* **Open** *Reception* 24hrs daily. No curfew. **Rates** £14-£19 dorm bed. **Credit** MC, V. **Map** p329 B7 ③④

Georgian splendour at the **Swallow Albany**. *See p61.*

So spa, so good

Time was when travellers would be happy with a roof, a bed, a Corby trouser press and perhaps a bacon sandwich in the morning. Happily, that time has long since past. Visitors to UK cities have learned to expect a lot more from their hotels: increasingly impressive restaurants and ever more stylish bars, certainly, but also other amenities, with fitness centres and spas perhaps top of the list. A new generation of super-sleek hotel spas arrived in the city in 2001, in an attempt by hoteliers both to attract more travellers to their operations and to tap the local market.

The 16-metre stainless steel pool at the **Scotsman**'s Escape fitness centre (*see p53*) is the epitome of understated urban chic. Expect some serious pampering at the hotel's Cowshed spa (also found in London, at Babington House in Somerset and at Soho House in New York), but without the po-faced approach found at many luxury spas: an

aromatherapy massage is dubbed the Pampered Cow, while a massage for pregnant women is the Blooming Cow. (Men are welcome, but the Cowshed knows its market.)

Such levity would seem out of place at the Terry Farrell-designed One Spa, by the **Sheraton Grand** (*see p72*; **photo left**). The cool glass frontage and colourful blue and green blinds make it stand out from its other neighbours, and put it in a different league from the Sheraton's own banal 1980s façade. The spa's most memorable feature is the outdoor rooftop hydropool, although the impressive list of treatments and facilities takes in everything from simple Swedish massages to a hammam bathing area.

Such hot competition meant that the **Balmoral** (*see p57*) more or less had to take the plunge, installing a basement spa as part of a rolling refurbishment that was finally completed in 2004. It was an immediate hit. Yu Spa at the **Apex International** (*see p55*) is another good choice, though it's open only to hotel residents. Otherwise, you'll need to head out of town to find other spas of a similar standard: to Oshi, at the **Langs Hotel** in Glasgow, or to **Stobo Castle** in the Borders (Stobo, Peeblesshire, 01721 725300, www.stobocastle.co.uk), a tranquil modern spa accommodated in a 200-year-old castle around 30 miles south of Edinburgh.

Caledonian Backpackers *3 Queensferry Street, EH2 4PA (226 2939/fax 226 2939/ www.caledonianbackpackers.net). Princes Street buses.* **Open** *Reception* 24hrs daily. No curfew. **Rates** £11-£22 dorm bed. **Credit** MC, V. **Map** p329 D7 ㉟

Princes Street East Backpackers
5 West Register Street, EH2 2AA (556 6894/ fax 557 3236/www.edinburghbackpackers.com). Nicolson Street–North Bridge buses or Princes Street buses. **Open** *Reception* 24hrs daily. No curfew. **Rates** £11-£15 dorm bed; £30-£40 double. **Credit** MC, V. **Map** p326/p330 H6, p336 A2 ㊱

Stockbridge

Expensive

Channings

15 South Learmonth Gardens, EH4 1EZ (315 2226/ reservations 623 9302/fax 332 9631/www.channings. co.uk). Bus 19, 37, 41, 47. **Rates** £80-£140 single; £110-£185 double; £130-£275 suite. **Credit** AmEx, MC, V. **Map** p325 B4 ㊲

Channings recently converted ten attic rooms into five spacious junior suites, their decor inspired by the fact that polar explorer Sir Ernest Shackleton lived here

a century ago. Portholes now run along the corridors, and you can sit in the bath (in what must be some of the biggest bathrooms in the city) and admire a huge blow-up print of Shackleton's ship, *Endurance*, battling through the snowy wastes. The other rooms are equally crisp and handsome. Downstairs sits the eponymous restaurant (*see p155*); a bar menu is also available. The hotel is part of the Town House group, which also owns the Bonham (*see p59*), the Howard (*see p60*) and the Edinburgh Residence (*see p59*).
Bar. Business centre. Concierge. High-speed internet (wireless). Parking. Restaurant. Room service.

Budget

Inverleith Hotel

5 Inverleith Terrace, EH3 5NS (556 2745/www. inverleithhotel.co.uk). Bus 8, 17, 23, 27. **Rates** £39-£55 single; £59-£119 double; £69-£119 triple/family. **Credit** MC, V. **Map** p326 E2 ⓺
This old-fashioned hotel is set in a Victorian townhouse next to the Royal Botanic Garden. Rooms at the rear are compact but exude warmth and homeliness, with thick bedspreads and luxurious furnishings. Try to nab the grandest room, which overlooks the Botanics and has a four-poster bed. The hotel also lets out a self-catering apartment in New Town with room for up to seven guests; rates start at £89 per night.
Bar. High-speed internet (wireless). Room service.

Calton Hill & Broughton

Expensive

Glasshouse

2 Greenside Place, EH1 3AA (525 8200/fax 525 8205/www.theetoncollection.com). Playhouse buses. **Rates** £150-£230 double; £250-375 suite. **Credit** AmEx, MC, V. **Map** p327 J5 ⓸

The clue is in the name of this hotel, behind the façade of the former Lady Glenorchy church at the foot of Calton Hill. Floor-to-ceiling windows in every room offer impressive views over the two-acre, lavender-scented roof garden or the city skyline; even the bathrooms are glass (with screening, naturally). The clean, modern lines throughout make for a stylish boutique hotel, but it's not been over-designed: the rooms here feel cultured and classy. It's just a stone's throw (no, don't!) from the commotion of the capital, but once inside you'll feel a million miles away from it all.
Bar. Concierge. Disabled-adapted rooms. High-speed internet (DSL, wireless). Room service.

Parliament House

15 Calton Hill, EH1 3BJ (478 4000/fax 478 4001/ www.parliamenthouse-hotel.co.uk). Playhouse buses. **Credit** AmEx, DC, MC, V. **Map** p327/p331 J6 ⓸
The Parliament House hotel is comprised of three buildings: a Georgian frontage, a Jacobean side building and the rear section, a mere architectural pup at just over a century old. The hotel was refurbished in 2005, giving it a more contemporary look throughout; its rather grandiose name belies a welcoming residence. Rooms vary in both size and outlook; some are cavernous, with views of Arthur's Seat and the Old Town, while others are of cosier dimensions, and look out over Leith and the Firth of Forth. The MPs' Bistro provides a colourful and roomy dining space.
Bar. Disabled-adapted rooms. High-speed internet (wireless). Restaurant. Room service.

Royal Terrace

18 Royal Terrace, EH7 5AQ (557 3222/fax 557 5334/www.theroyalterracehotel.co.uk). Playhouse buses. **Rates** £115 single; £175 double/twin; £240-£270 suite. **Credit** AmEx, DC, MC, V. **Map** p327 K5 ⓸

Borough. *See p68.*

P R E S T O N F I E L
"So extravagant it's like walking onto the set of some flamboyant costume drama."
Condé Nast Traveller
www.prestonfield.com

Royal Terrace (the street, not just the hotel) was designed in 1822 by William Playfair, whose many contributions to Edinburgh's cityscape include nearby Regent Terrace, the Royal Scottish Academy and the National Gallery. After a decade of under-investment, the Royal Terrace (just the hotel, not the street) has benefited from a facelift. The rooms on the third floor and patio floor have been refurbished (top-floor rooms are small, due to the sloped attic ceilings), and all of the public areas have been newly upgraded, with the restaurant doubling in size. The tartan carpets and floral wallpaper have made way for a more contemporary look, but the Georgian opulence is still echoed in the chandeliers, cornices and overall grandeur. The garden, with its life-size chess board and fountain, is popular in summer.
Bar. Concierge. Gym. High-speed internet (wireless). Pool. Restaurant. Room service.

Moderate

Holiday Inn Express

Picardy Place, EH1 3JT (558 2300/fax 558 2323/ www.hieedinburgh.co.uk). Playhouse buses. **Rates** £110-£130 single/double. **Credit** AmEx, MC, V. **Map** p327 J5
As with most hotels in the Holiday Inn Express chain, this Picardy Place operation offers convenient, good-value accommodation without too much character. There are six floors of clean, uncomplicated rooms (complete with wireless internet access), plus a popular in-house bar. Continental breakfast is included in the rates. There are other branches in Leith (*see p72*), on Queensferry Road (No.107, EH4 3HL, 0870 400 9025) and on Corstorphine Road (No.132, EH12 6UA, 0870 400 9026).
Bar. Business centre. Disabled-adapted rooms. High-speed internet (DSL, wireless). Parking (limited).

Budget

Ailsa Craig Hotel

24 Royal Terrace, EH7 5AH (556 1022/fax 556 6055/www.townhousehotels.co.uk). Playhouse buses. **Rates** £35-£75 single; £60-£150 double. **Credit** AmEx, DC, MC, V. **Map** p327 K5
Like its sister hotel the **Greenside**, just along the street at No.9 (557 0022), Ailsa Craig boasts big, clean rooms that have retained their original Georgian features. Though they're a bit on the basic side, some have views towards the Forth, and all enjoy the quiet of this residential crescent. With families in mind, some of the rooms are kitted out with five beds. The public areas also retain a traditional character and unassuming comfort.
Bar. High-speed internet (wireless).

Balfour Guest House

90-92 Pilrig Street, EH6 5AY (554 2106/fax 554 3887). Bus 7, 10, 11, 12, 14, 16, 22, 25, 49. **Rates** £30 single; £50 double. **Credit** MC, V. **Map** p327 K1

Warm hospitality, a central location, free parking (for those with cars) and a minibus to ferry around visitors (for those without) make this a popular choice for groups. There's a dining room in the basement; packed lunches are available on request.
Bar. High-speed internet (wireless).

Claremont

14-15 Claremont Crescent, EH7 4HX (556 1487/ fax 556 7077/www.claremont-hotel.co.uk). Bus 8. **Rates** £30-£40 single; £56-£70 double. **Credit** AmEx, MC, V. **Map** p326 H2
Located on a leafy crescent in Broughton, the Claremont comprises two huge Georgian houses knocked into one. The rooms won't win any design awards, but they are clean and spacious, with views of Arthur's Seat or the Forth. There are occasional special events in the public bar.
Bar. Parking (free).

Hostels

Edinburgh Central SYHA Hostel *9 Haddington Place, Calton Hill & Broughton (0870 155 3255/ www.syha.org.uk). Bus 7, 10, 12, 14, 16, 22, 25, 49.* **Open** call for details. No curfew. **Rates** £15-£24, plus membership. **Credit** MC, V. **Map** p327 J4

Get to the **Point**.
See p69.

Alternative accommodation

In addition to its various hotels and hostels, the best of which are listed throughout this chapter, Edinburgh offers a variety of other accommodation options, including campsites and caravan parks, private apartments and seasonal lets. Keep an eye out for good deals: prices can vary wildly from property to property. And remember: venturing just a few streets outside the city centre may mean stumbling upon better-value accommodation.

Camping & caravanning

Edinburgh Caravan Club Site
35-37 Marine Drive, EH4 5EN (312 6874/ fax 336 4269/www.caravanclub.co.uk). Bus 16, 27, 28, 29. **Rates** *Members £4.50-£7.50 pitch, plus £4-£5.30/adult, £1.50-£2.20/child.* **Credit** MC, V.

Mortonhall Caravan Park
38 Mortonhall Gate, Frogston Road, EH16 6TJ (664 1533/fax 664 5387/www. meadowhead.co.uk/mortonhall). Bus 11, 32, 52. **Rates** *£10-£23 pitch & 2 adults, plus £1.50/additional adult.* **Credit** MC, V.

Private lettings

Hotel accommodation makes sense if you're here for just a few nights' stay, but it can be a somewhat restrictive and pricey option for longer visits. If you're planning to hang around for a bit longer, one sensible alternative is to rent an apartment. Some

are fully serviced; others are self-catering and, therefore, usually cheaper. Many have minimum-let periods: a few nights, a week or even as much as a month. Bookings are generally taken online. During the various August festivals and in the run-up to Hogmanay, the short lettings market is predictably busy and prices inflate dramatically with demand; book as early as possible to ensure the widest choice of accommodation (and, for that matter, the best value).

If something longer-term is required and you're on a budget, flatshares can be a comfortable option. Look in the *Scotsman*'s accommodation section on a Thursday for available rooms. *The List* also publishes a selection of flatshare ads on a fortnightly basis. Most flatshares are bound by a six-month lease, but a few ads do crop up for week- or month-long lets. For an extensive online selection of longer-term lets, the **Edinburgh Solicitors' Property Centre** (www.espc.co.uk) has a variety of flatshare and flat rental ads.

Self-catering accommodation

Self-catering apartments are designed chiefly for short-term lets, whether for holidaymakers, for business travellers or, in August, for the innumerable performers and spectators who descend on the city for the various festivals that take place

South Edinburgh

Deluxe

Prestonfield
Priestfield Road, Prestonfield, EH16 5UT (225 7800/fax 668 3976/www.prestonfield.com). Bus 2, 14, 30. **Rates** *£175-£255 double; £250-£295 suite.* **Credit** AmEx, DC, MC, V.
Like its sister, the Witchery (*see p55*), Prestonfield has blossomed under the ownership of restaurateur James Thomson. Set in parkland on the edge of Arthur's Seat, the building dates back to 1687; much of the old character remains, from the winding, tree-lined drive to the ornate cornicing, but the opulent antique furniture and imported upholstery adds some European flavour. Rooms, whether in the main building or a modern extension to the rear, are decorated in keeping with the sumptuous splendour of

the public areas, a combination of Jacobean manor and continental chateau; modern comforts such as plasma-screen TVs sit alongside splendid antique pieces. Don't be surprised to see the odd peacock or Highland cow sauntering past: it's all part of the incomparable experience.
Bar. Business centre. Concierge. Disabled-adapted rooms. High-speed internet (wireless) Parking (free). Restaurant. Room service.

Moderate

Borough
72-80 Causewayside, EH9 1PY (668 2255/ fax 667 6622/www.boroughhotel.com). Bus 42. **Rates** *£80-£125 double; £105-£190 family room.* **Credit** AmEx, MC, V. **Map** p331 K11 ⑰
Considering the location on one of the busiest routes in and out of the city, the rooms at this stylish boutique hotel are surprisingly serene. Beechwood

throughout the month. Myriad properties are available, from modern developments to historic houses such as **Gladstone's Flat**, run by the National Trust of Scotland, and **Pilrig House**, a converted Regency townhouse with its own gate on to Pilrig Park. Prices are generally affordable, and get keener the longer you stay.

Properties vary in size as well as style. The largest of the **Swanston Cottages** sleeps up to eight people, making it extremely good value. While we've listed nightly rates, most properties operate a minimum-stay rule, although this can be as few as three days.

Ardmor Apartment

3 Gayfield Street, Calton Hill & Broughton, EH1 3NR; 28 Scotland Street, New Town, EH3 6PX (554 4944/www.ardmorapartments. com). Gayfield Street: Playhouse buses. Scotland Street: bus 8, 13, 17, 36. **Rates** £95-£140/night. **No credit cards.** **Map** p326 G4 & p327 J4.

Gladstone's Flat

477b Lawnmarket, Old Town, EH1 2NT (243 9331/www.nts.org.uk). Bus 2, 23, 27, 41, 42. **Rates** £21.50-£65/night. **Credit** MC, V. Bus 2, 23, 27, 41, 42.

Pilrig House

30/3 Pilrig House Close, Leith, EH6 5RF (554 4794/www.pilrighouseapartment.co.uk). Bus 11, 36. **Rates** £80-£140/night. **No credit cards.**

Royal Mile Apartment

Four locations: Old Town (2), Calton Hill & Broughton (2) (554 1301/www.edinburgh royalmile.co.uk). Various buses. **Rates** £80-£225/night. **Credit** MC, V.

Royal Mile Mansions

Flat 43, Royal Mile Mansions, 50 North Bridge, EH1 1QN (669 3771/www. apartmentscentral.co.uk). Nicolson Street– North Bridge buses **Rates** £46-£93/night. **Credit** MC, V. **Map** p331 J7.

Swanston Cottages

Six holiday cottages at Swanston Farm, six miles south of Edinburgh (445 5744/ www.swanston.co.uk). No bus. **Rates** £50-£105/night. **Credit** AmEx, MC, V.

Serviced accommodation

This alternative to short-term self-catered accommodation combines the luxury of hotel service with the privacy and freedom of your own apartment. However, it can come at quite a price. As with self-catering accommodation above, we've listed nightly rates, but many properties operate a minimum-stay policy.

Apartment Service

Six locations: Old Town (2), New Town (2), South Edinburgh, West Edinburgh (020 8944 1444/fax 020 8944 6744/www.apartment service.com). Various buses. **Rates** £55-£160/night. **Credit** AmEx, MC, V.

▶

panelling and bold blocks of colour are used to sumptuous effect, and no expense has been spared on the bathrooms: finishes are slick and contemporary, with monsoon-like showers and even rubber ducks. Downstairs sits a spacious, retro-tinged bar and a moderately priced, glowingly reviewed restaurant (*see p163*). A contemporary, snug base, with the city centre a brisk 15-minute walk away. **Photo** *p65.* *Bar. Concierge. High-speed internet (wireless). Restaurant. Room service.*

Novotel Edinburgh Centre

80 Lauriston Place, EH3 9DE (656 3500/fax 656 3510/www.accor-hotels.com). Bus 1, 2, 10, 11, 15, 15A, 16, 17, 23, 24, 27, 34, 35, 45. **Rates** £69-£209 double. **Credit** AmEx, DC, MC, V. **Map** p330 F9 ⓐ
Edinburgh isn't exactly packed with comfortable, affordable accommodation; any moderately priced addition to its list of hotel options is welcome, even when it arrives in the city as an identikit package. Typical of the likeable, mid-market Novotel company, this operation offers good sized rooms furnished in a contemporary, minimalist style. *Bar. Concierge. Disabled-adapted rooms. Gym. High-speed internet (DSL, shared terminal, wireless). Parking (limited; free). Pool. Restaurant. Room service.*

Point

34 Bread Street, EH3 9AF (221 5555/fax 221 9929/ www.point-hotel.co.uk). Bus 1, 2, 10, 11, 15, 15A, 16, 17, 23, 24, 27, 34, 35, 45. **Rates** £80-£155 double/twin; £125-£350 suite. **Credit** AmEx, MC, V. **Map** p330 E8 ⓐ
In a bid to keep up with the Joneses across town, the Point recently completed a light refurbishment of all 140 bedrooms (most of which afford excellent views of the castle) and softened its formerly minimalist look. The reception area, once akin to the lobby of a modern office block, is far more welcoming, though the clean lines, sweeping curved walls and blocks of

Alternative accommodation (continued)

Calton Apartments
44 Annandale Street, Calton Hill & Broughton, EH7 4AW (556 3221/fax 557 0022/www.townhousehotels.co.uk). Bus 7, 10, 12, 14, 16, 22, 25, 49. **Rates** £50-£260/night. **Credit** AmEx, MC, V. **Map** p327 J3.

Canon Court Apartments
20 Canonmills, New Town, EH3 5LH (474 7000/fax 4747001/www.canoncourt.co.uk). Bus 8, 17, 23, 27, 36. **Rates** £89-£170/night. **Credit** AmEx, MC, V. **Map** p326 F3.

Kew Apartments
1 Kew Terrace, West Edinburgh, EH12 5JE (313 0700/fax 313 0747/www.kewhouse.com). Bus 12, 26, 31. **Open** 8am-10pm daily. **Rates** £100-£180/night. **Credit** AmEx, MC, V.

No.5 Self-Catering Apartments
3 Abercorn Terrace, Portobello, EH15 2DD (tel/fax 669 1044/www.numberfive.com). Bus 12, 15, 15A, 26, 32, 42, 49. **Rates** £13-£64/night. **Credit** AmEx, MC, V.

Serviced Apartments Company
Six locations: New Town (2), Calton Hill & Broughton, South Edinburgh, West Edinburgh (2) (0845 122 0405/fax 0117 974 5939/www.sacoapartments.co.uk). Various buses. **Rates** £70-£190/night. **Credit** AmEx, MC, V.

West End Apartments
2 Learmonth Terrace, Stockbridge, EH4 1PQ (332 0717/fax 226 6512/www.edinburghapartments.biz). Bus 24, 29, 42. **Rates** £35-£65/night. **No credit cards.** **Map** p325 B4.

Lettings agencies & websites

The agencies and websites listed below all offer a variety of self-catered accommodation around the city, ranging from luxurious family houses to more basic and affordable apartments. Some properties are let out for as little as a week at a time; others required minimum terms of a month or even longer. **Festival Beds** differs from the other firms listed in that it deals not in self-catered apartments but in B&B accommodation, and rents properties out only during August (the other companies detailed below all operate year-round).

Note that while we have provided address information where available, not all letting agencies accept visitors. Always call ahead if you're thinking of popping in.

Apartments in Edinburgh
12 Regent Terrace, EH7 5BN (556 8309/fax 478 0251/www.apartmentsinedinburgh.com).

Clouds
26 Forth Street, EH1 3LH (550 3808/www.clouds.co.uk).

soft colour continue to give a feeling of futuristic fluidity. The white bedrooms have an understated simplicity, Egyptian cotton bedspreads splashed with burgundy cushions. The ground floor restaurant serves mainly modish European dishes with a local flavour, while the glass-fronted Monboddo bar is a magnet for the cocktail crowd. **Photo** *p67.*
Bar. Business centre. Disabled-adapted rooms. High-speed internet (DSL, wireless). Restaurant. Room service.

Salisbury Green
Pollock Halls, 18 Holyrood Park Road, EH16 5AY (651 2001/fax 667 7271/www.salisburygreen.co.uk). Bus 2. 14. 30. 33. **Rates** £54-£89 single; £59-£134 double/twin. **Credit** MC, V. **Map** p331 M11 ㊿
This 2006 newcomer boasts an unusual location in the grounds of a halls of residence complex belonging to the University of Edinburgh. Built as a merchant's home in 1748, it's the oldest building on site, and the atmosphere still smacks of the country house it once was before the city encroached. Although it has been tastefully refurbished, its protected status means that it has retained many original features, such as detailed wooden surrounds and refreshingly irregular room layouts. Some rooms have extra features, such as a sunken bath or a reading area tucked snugly into a turret, while others hint at their past with marble fireplaces, beams or carved bookshelves. Guests can use the two bars elsewhere on the site.
Concierge. Disabled-adapted rooms. High-speed internet (wireless in public areas). Parking (limited, free).

Budget

Links Hotel
4 Alvanley Terrace, EH9 1DU (229 3834/fax 228 9173/www.festival-inns.co.uk). Bus 11, 15, 15A, 16, 17, 23, 45. **Rates** £75 single; £95 double. **Credit** AmEx, MC, V. **Map** p330 F11 (51)

Edinburgh Holiday Flats
www.edinburghholidayflats.com.

Factotum
63 Dublin Street, New Town, EH3 6NS
(0845 119 6000/fax 0845 119 6010/
www.factotum.co.uk).

Festival Beds
225 1101/fax 225 2724/
www.festivalbeds.co.uk.

Festival Flats
3 Linkylea Cottages, Gifford, East Lothian,
EH41 4PE (01620 810620/fax 01620
810619/www.festivalflats.net).

Glen House Apartments
101 Lauriston Place, EH3 9JB (228 4043/fax
228 4046/www.edinburgh-apartments.co.uk).

Mackay's Agency
30 Frederick Street, New Town, EH2 2JR
(225 3539/fax 226 5284/www.mackays-
self-catering.co.uk).

Student accommodation

The city's universities let out their halls
of residence during academic vacations.
The University of Edinburgh alone has some
2,000 rooms available during summer; at the
Pollock Halls, many rooms face Arthur's Seat,
giving them some of the best views of any
university accommodation in the country.

Some halls are a bus ride away from the
centre of town, but prices are often keen and
the rooms provide a useful form of clean and
basic accommodation for visitors to the city.

Edinburgh Conference Centre
Heriot-Watt University, Riccarton Campus,
Riccarton, EH14 4AS (451 3669/
fax 451 3199/www.eccscotland.com).
Bus 25, 34, 45. **Rates** B&B £37.50-£55.
Credit MC, V.

Napier University Student Accommodation Office
219 Colinton Road, South Edinburgh,
EH14 4DJ (455 3738/fax 455 3739/
www.napier.ac.uk/accommodation).
Bus 10, 27, 45. **Rates** B&B £85-£125.
Credit MC, V.

Queen Margaret University College
Hospitality Services Department, Clerwood
Terrace, Corstorphine, EH12 8TS (317 3317/
fax 317 3313/www.qmuc.ac.uk). Bus 1, 21,
26, 32. **Rates** B&B £27-£50. **Credit** MC, V.

University of Edinburgh Accommodation Service
18 Holyrood Park Road, South Edinburgh,
EH16 5AY (667 1971/fax 667 0330/
www.accom.ed.ac.uk). Bus 2, 14, 30,
33. **Rates** £32-£104. **Credit** MC, V.
Map p331 M10.

Spread over three adjacent townhouses, the Links'
26 rooms are now bright and modern, thanks to an
extensive redecoration effort. On the ground floor is
a popular sports bar, kitted out with multiple high-
definition TVs; in spring and summer the crowd
spills out on to the patio overlooking Bruntsfield
Links (see p240). The atmosphere is lively and good-
humoured, but peace and quiet are a premium, particularly in the front-facing bedrooms. Located close
to the green expanses of the Meadows and the
student-packed suburb of Marchmont, the hotel is a
ten-minute bus ride away from the city centre. Rates
include a full Scottish breakfast, served in the bar.
Bar. Room service.

Minto Hotel
*16-18 Minto Street, EH9 1RQ (668 1234/fax 662
4870/www.edinburghmintohotel.co.uk). Nicolson
Street–North Bridge buses.* **Rates** £30-£60
single; £60-£105 double; £95-£125 family room.
Credit AmEx, MC, V.

The Minto provides a cheap stopover for groups;
there's often a wedding or party taking place in the
hotel's function suite. While the establishment falls
into the basic-but-comfortable category, the warm
welcome keeps the regulars flocking back.
*Bar. High-speed internet (wireless). Parking (free).
Restaurant. Room service.*

Premier Travel Inn
*82 Lauriston Place, EH3 9HZ (0870 990 6610/
fax 0870 990 6611/www.premiertravelinn.com).
Bus 1, 2, 10, 11, 15, 15A, 16, 17, 23, 24, 27, 34,
35, 45.* **Rates** £57-£77 double/family room.
Credit AmEx, DC, MC, V. **Map** p330 F9 ⑤②
There's not a great deal of charisma visible at this
outpost of the increasingly ubiquitous chain, but no
matter: the rooms are clean and comfortable, and the
location convenient. Other Premier Travel Inns are
dotted around the city; check the website for details.
*Bar. Disabled-adapted rooms. High-speed
internet (wireless).*

West Edinburgh

Expensive

Sheraton Grand

1 Festival Square, Lothian Road, EH3 9SR (229 9131/fax 228 4510/www.sheraton.com). Bus 1, 2, 10, 11, 15, 15A, 16, 17, 23, 24, 27, 34, 35, 45. **Rates** £105-£260 single; £105-£300 double; £400-£900 suite. **Credit** AmEx, DC, MC, V. **Map** p329 D8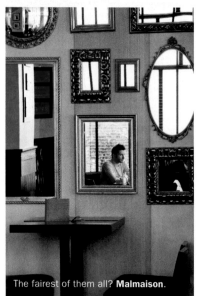

It might be located in the heart of Edinburgh's new financial district, but the Sheraton Grand's USP is its leisure facilities. Chief among them is the One Spa, one of Europe's best city spas (*see p64* **So spa, so good**): lie on an ergonomic bed by the rooftop hydropool or book yourself a beautifying treatment. All rooms are equipped with Sheraton's amazingly comfortable Sweet Sleeper beds. Four restaurants – the beautifully refurbished Grill Room, the brasserie-style Terrace and two Italian-themed Santini options (*see p164*) – cater to most tastes.

Bar. Business centre. Concierge. Disabled-adapted rooms. Gym. High-speed internet (shared terminal, wireless). Parking (£8). Pool. Restaurants (4). Room service. Spa.

Moderate

Dunstane House

4 West Coates, Haymarket, EH12 5JQ (337 6169/ fax 337 6060/www.dunstane-hotel-edinburgh.co.uk). Bus 12, 26, 31, 38. **Rates** £59-£85 single; £98-£190 double. **Credit** AmEx, MC, V.

Built as a mansion in 1852, Dunstane House became a hotel in 1969. Orkney-born owners Shirley and Derek Mowat have lent an Orcadian theme to Skerries restaurant and the Stane Bar. The traditional decor of the public rooms is complemented by a quaint country feel in the bedrooms, where floral bedspreads and decorative wallpaper in autumnal colours are cosy without straining the eyes. In summer, the patio tables in the front gardens offer excellent views.

Bar. Disabled-adapted rooms. High-speed internet (wireless). Parking (free). Restaurant. Room service.

Original Raj

6 West Coates, Haymarket, EH12 5JG (346 1333/ www.rajempire.com). Bus 12, 26, 31, 38. **Rates** £35-£60 single; £60-£120 double. **Credit** MC, V.

Facilities are a bit basic at this 17-room B&B, but the Indian theme more than compensates. Each room features warm colours, hand-made furniture shipped in from Jaipur and a canopy bed, all good for bringing out the inner hippy. There are many other B&B-style hotels in this part of town, but this is the stand-out. Look for the elephant in the garden.

Leith & the coast

Moderate

Holiday Inn Express

Britannia Way, Ocean Drive, EH6 6JJ (555 4422/ fax 555 4646/www.hiex-edinburgh.com). Bus 1, 10, 16, 22, 35, 36. **Rates** £79-£120 double/twin. **Credit** AmEx, DC, MC, V. **Map** p324 X2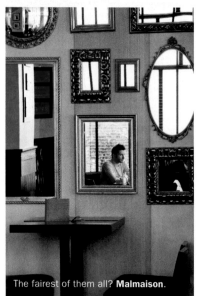

Guests at the Holiday Inn Express enjoy views of the Royal Yacht *Britannia* (*see p135*); Ocean Terminal is also close at hand. There's rather less to say about the accommodation itself, which has all the pros and cons of most purpose-built hotels run by corporate giants. For more Holiday Inns, *see p67*.

Bar. Business centre. Disabled-adapted rooms. High-speed internet (wireless). Parking (free).

Malmaison

1 Tower Place, EH6 7DB (468 5000/fax 468 5002/ www.malmaison.com). Bus 1, 10, 16, 22, 35, 36. **Rates** £135-£155 double; £195-£255 suite. **Credit** AmEx, DC, MC, V. **Map** p324 Y2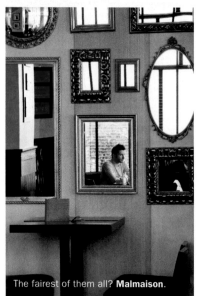

The conversion of this former seaman's mission, the first operation in the Malmaison chain, set new standards for Edinburgh's hotel trade and helped push along the resurgence of Leith. Behind the turreted, castle-like façade, the rooms have recently been renovated in quietly stylish fashion; among them is the penthouse Arthur's Suite, with views of Arthur's Seat from the bed and bathtub, and the Port of Leith four-poster room, from which you can see the harbour. The leather-banquetted, candlelit brasserie serves up uncomplicated, French-influenced food, while the adjacent café-bar (*see p184*) is a destination watering hole for local media types and apparatchiks from the Scottish Executive.

Bar. Disabled-adapted rooms. Gym. High-speed internet (wireless). Parking (free). Restaurant. Room service.

The fairest of them all? **Malmaison**.

Sightseeing

Features

Maps

Barclay Church. *See p124.*

Introduction

Welcome to Edinburgh.

St Bernard's Well in Stockbridge.

The eventual arrival of the Scottish Parliament, the development of a shiny new financial district, the construction of several new museum buildings and the ongoing regeneration of Leith have all, in their ways, helped haul it into the 21st century. However, at least for the casual sightseer visiting the city, Edinburgh remains dominated by its past. Soaring high-rise structures are conspicuous by their absence. With only a couple of exceptions, the most imposing and impressive buildings here are also the oldest: staunch, fearsome and April-grey. The popular image of Edinburgh is far from an outdated cliché.

Famously set among seven hills, Edinburgh remains very much in tune with its natural surroundings. Suburban villages such as Stockbridge and Duddingston, and even towns such as Leith, have been gradually incorporated into the main body of the city, but their distinct characters remain intact. For a picture-perfect overview of the city, head to the top of Arthur's Seat. However, the best way to experience Edinburgh at ground level is to get lost in its maze of bridges, crescents and wynds. There's something of interest on almost every street.

ORIENTATION

The best way to negotiate your way around central Edinburgh is to pay almost no attention to the street names. Instead, navigate according to the compass points in relation to the three major landmarks: **Arthur's Seat**, **Edinburgh Castle** and **Calton Hill**. Major streets change names constantly: the Royal Mile labours under four identities (Castlehill, Lawnmarket, High Street and Canongate) in 1,600 cobbled metres; crossing it, North Bridge becomes South Bridge becomes Nicolson Street becomes Clerk Street, and so on. It can be a little confusing.

The best place to start any tour of the city is the **Old Town** (*see pp76-99*), the original settlement of medieval Edinburgh that remains dominated by the glowering silhouette of Edinburgh Castle. It's bound to the north and west by Princes Street Gardens, and to the south and east by the remains of the Flodden Wall (which goes up to the Pleasance).

North of the castle sits the **New Town** (*see pp100-108*), a succession of magnificently regular 18th-century planned developments that stretch from Princes Street down the hill towards the Forth, and end, unofficially, at the Water of

Leith. The area's approximate boundaries are **Calton Hill** (*see pp114-117*), identifiable by the telescope-shaped Nelson Monument and the pillars of the National Monument, and the triple towers of St Mary's Episcopal Cathedral. As Edinburgh expanded, the New Town reached the leafy village of **Stockbridge** (*see pp109-113*) and the less regimented developments of the Raeburn Estate, the Dean Village and the Royal Botanic Garden. North-east of the city centre sits the port of **Leith** (*see pp131-136*): a district in its own right, it's flanked by the fishing village of Newhaven to the west and the seaside town of Portobello to the east.

To the south-east, **Arthur's Seat** (*see pp118-122*) dominates the skyline, with the tiny village of Duddingston tucked behind it. **South Edinburgh** (*see pp123-125*) stretches inland from the Meadows up towards the Pentland Hills, taking in the so-called villages of Bruntsfield and Marchmont, Craigmillar Castle in Little France, and the Royal Observatory on Blackford Hill. **West Edinburgh** (*see pp126-129*) goes from Lothian Road and the New Town out towards the airport and encompasses the Union Canal, the new financial district, the Zoo and the old Roman port of Cramond.

Sightseeing tours

Bus tours

If walking around Edinburgh gets too much, and the number of hills make that a fairly likely eventuality, you can take a bus tour of the city with a variety of different companies. There's not a lot to choose between them, though buses are conducted on vintage buses. All tours depart regularly from Waverley Bridge, and booking isn't usually required. Tours take about an hour; tickets allow passengers to alight or rejoin the tour at any point over a 24-hour period. Times below are approximate: call for full details. For the Edinburgh Literary Bus Tour, which runs during summer, check the website for the **Edinburgh Literary Pub Tour** (*see below*).

City Sightseeing *220 0770/www.edinburghtour. com.* **Tours** *Summer* every 20mins, 9.30am-7pm daily. *Spring, autumn* every 20mins, 9.30am-5pm daily. *Winter* every 30mins, 10am-4pm daily. **Meeting point** Waverley Bridge; check online for other stops on route. **Tickets** £9; £3-£8 concessions; free under-5s; £20 family. **Credit** MC, V.
MacTours *556 2244/www.mactours.co.uk.* **Tours** *Summer* every 20mins, 9.30am-7pm daily. *Spring, autumn* every 20mins, 9.30am-5.30pm daily. *Winter* every 20mins, 10am-4pm daily. **Meeting point** Waverley Bridge; check online for other stops on route. **Tickets** £9; £3-£8 concessions; free under-5s; £20 family. **Credit** MC, V.

Walking tours

Along with the city's plethora of ghost tours (for a full list, *see p98* **Things that go bump in the night**), a couple of literary tours merit mention. The **Edinburgh Literary Pub Tour** takes in a variety of writers, from Burns through to Welsh, while **Rebustours** concentrates on the books of Ian Rankin. Booking is recommended for the former and necessary for the latter.

Edinburgh Literary Pub Tour *226 6665/ www.edinburghliterarypubtour.co.uk.* **Tours** *June-Sept* 7.30pm daily. *Apr, May, Oct* 7.30pm Thur-Sun. *Nov-Mar* 7.30pm Fri. **Meeting point** Beehive Inn, Grassmarket. **Tickets** £7; £6 concessions. **Credit** MC, V (advance bookings).
Rebustours *553 7473/www.rebustours.com.* **Tours** 2.30pm, days vary. **Meeting point** *Body Politic, Hidden Edinburgh* Royal Oak, Infirmary Street. *Edinburgh Glimpsed Anew* Stockbridge Bookshop, 26 NW Circus Place. **Tickets** £10; £9 concessions. **Credit** MC, V (advance bookings).

The best Sights

Arthur's Seat
You versus the volcano. *See p118.*

Calton Hill
Old Edinburgh at its most haunting. *See p116.*

Closes in the Old Town
Small but perfectly formed. *See p86* **Enter the labyrinth.**

Edinburgh Castle
No mere tourist trap. *See p80.*

Modern Leith
Changing by the day. *See p131.*

Museum of Scotland
Stories galore, both local and national. *See p99.*

Princes Street Gardens
Bring a book. *See p101.*

Royal Botanic Garden
A green party out in Stockbridge. *See p111.*

Scottish Parliament
Democracy in action. *See p95.*

Scottish Storytelling Centre & John Knox House
Old and new under one roof. *See p90.*

The Old Town

Where it all began.

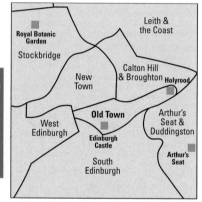

Leith &
the Coast

Royal Botanic
Garden

Stockbridge

New
Town

Calton Hill
& Broughton Holyrood

Old Town

West
Edinburgh

Arthur's
Seat &
Duddingston

Edinburgh
Castle

Arthur's
Seat

South
Edinburgh

Viewed from the air – or, more easily, on any one of the copies of 17th- and 18th-century maps you can buy around town – the Old Town resembles some ancient leviathan, running from the castle down to Holyrood. The Royal Mile is its undulating spine, while the ribs of the beast splay out to the north and south, taking in both major thoroughfares and tiny passageways. On the ground, this translates into a compact, sloping walk that takes in more historic attractions and key sites than any pocket of land in Scotland. Politics, religions, lives and loves were forged, betrayed and destroyed in among the closes, pends, wynds, tunnels and vennels of the Old Town.

Beside George Heriot's School (*see p97*) and at the east end of the Cowgate (*see p96*), stand the remnants of the **Flodden Wall**. Built by citizens as a precautionary measure after the disastrous defeat of the Scots at Flodden in 1513, it protected stretches of Edinburgh from much feared English depredations. To the north, where Waverley Station and Princes Street Gardens now sit, the town was protected by the Nor' Loch. The wall ran from the eastern bounds of the loch, up and over the Royal Mile, continuing south up the Pleasance and west along what's now Drummond Street, then on to Teviot Place and north past Heriot's and the West Port to the Castle Rock.

If you're not from Scotland, or even if you are, signposting in the Old Town can seem bizarre. Bear in mind that a close is a narrow

alleyway that usually opens up into a courtyard of some sort (check out Trunk Close or Lady Stair's Close, and read the Scottish poetry extracts carved into the flagstones); a wynd is a narrow winding lane leading off the main thoroughfare (go into the Tron and you can see Marlin's Wynd, a roadway that was lost to the city years ago, *see p89*); a pend is a narrow, covered entryway to the backcourt of a block of houses; and a vennel is simply a narrow alley. For more on these entrancing little strips, *see p86* **Enter the labyrinth**.

Narrow is the key word when it comes to the Old Town. The older buildings are easy to spot from the way they are crammed together; Edinburgh's citizenry of old built upwards, not outwards. The population lived in teetering tenements, the poor eking out an existence in the basements and attics while the more genteel classes lived in comfort on the mid-level floors. At one point in the city's history, the poverty-stricken and socially excluded existed in dank dwellings in the dark vaults and caverns found below South Bridge.

With money, life could be comfortable, if not overly ostentatious. Even the better houses were sparsely furnished, but were at least prettified by painted rafters and wall tapestries. Studded doors kept any dangers on the outside; inside the floors were strewn with aromatic grasses. The latter must have felt like a necessity in summer: sanitation here was dire. The Nor' Loch and the Burgh Loch (now the **Meadows**, *see p124*) were dumping grounds for waste of all kinds, while householders got rid of slops by heaving them out of the windows on to the street below with a warning cry of 'Gardy loo!'. The churchyards' ground levels were rapidly rising, thanks to the numbers of the dead, and a steady stream of animals were herded through the **Cowgate**, to be sold in the **Grassmarket** and butchered at the **Fleshmarket**. It's no wonder that one visitor likened Edinburgh to a comb: filthy at the teeth, but with some clean parts in between.

Within these few square miles, the population grew. Typhus was rife and, inevitably, plague struck; by the end of the 16th century, it had wiped out a third of the population. Edinburgh recovered, and numbers began to soar once more, but fires then took a heavy toll, adding to the coal-fired fug that hung over the city and giving rise to the nickname Auld Reekie.

Royal Mile. *See p78.*

Sightseeing

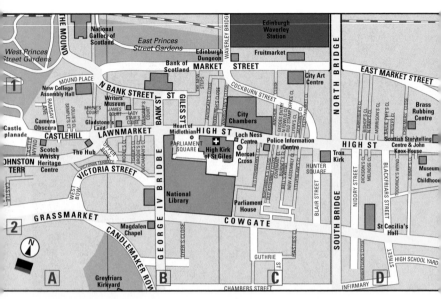

In 1754, four tenements of Carrubbers Close, and the 15 families within, were taken by fire, while the blaze of 1824 toppled the spire of the Tron Kirk. The more recent Old Town blaze of December 2002 was one of the city's most disastrous in terms of the property it destroyed, but consolation came with the fact that nobody lost their life.

Further down the Royal Mile is a memorial to the disaster of 24 November 1861, when the 250-year-old tenements at 99 and 103 High Street collapsed without warning, killing 35 inhabitants. As the debris was searched for the dead and injured, a boy's voice was heard calling 'Heave awa lads, I'm no deid yet!'. A more Anglicised version of his cry can be found carved above the entry to Paisley's Close.

Although the planning for town expansion began in 1752, and the initial building of the New Town started in the late 18th century, it wasn't until the middle of the 19th century that the cramped environs of the Old Town really became too much for the population, and 'the Great Flitting' to the New Town began. The Old Town still has a lower population than the New Town these days, and a more commercial feel, with much of that commerce centred around the tourist industry. It's hardly surprising: the Old Town is like a huge open-air museum, with around 900 years of architecture on show.

The Royal Mile is bookended by such extremes. At its western end, high on the forbidding Castle Rock, sits **Edinburgh Castle**; here you'll find St Margaret's Chapel, the oldest extant building in Edinburgh. And at its eastern extremity, at the foot of the Canongate and next to the imposing Palace of Holyroodhouse, sits the hugely controversial **Scottish Parliament** building, completed only a few years ago. Nearby, where a brewery and a gasworks once stood, there is a rash of other contemporary buildings, housing **Our Dynamic Earth** (see p92), the Holyrood Hotel, offices for the *Scotsman* newspaper, studios for the BBC, and some glass and chrome-filled bars.

The Old Town was linked to the New Town by way of North Bridge and a huge earthwork: the **Mound**, which meanders down from the Lawnmarket and High Street, bisecting Princes Street Gardens. Links to the suburbs and villages to the south of the city were created by means of two further bridges: George IV Bridge, where you can find several libraries and a multitude of trendy bars and restaurants, and South Bridge. The latter doesn't really look like a bridge at all; it's made up of concealed arches and vaulted foundations, some of which were made more obvious following the 2002 fire.

The Royal Mile

Running from the edge of the castle grounds to the **Palace of Holyroodhouse**, the Royal Mile often changes its identity. At various points, the street is called Castlehill, Lawnmarket, the High Street and the Canongate, although the latter

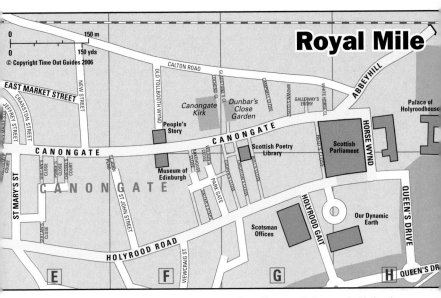

two predominate along much of its length: just over a modern mile. Kings and queens have ridden and driven from the castle to the palace and back, battles have been fought up and down its length, and men have been hanged and women burned upon it. It's more sedate these days, at least for 11 months of the year.

The street itself is busy with tourist foot-traffic most of the time; unsurprising, since many of Edinburgh's main attractions sit on or near it. It's flanked on both sides by around 60 closes and wynds (see p86 **Enter the labyrinth**), home to tightly packed clusters of residential tenements, pubs, restaurants and cafés. These super-skinny streets also provide the eerie setting for many of Edinburgh's popular ghost tours (see p98); don't be scared by loitering 'jumper-ooters' at night.

The Royal Mile, between George IV Bridge and the Tron, becomes the focal point of the **Edinburgh Festival Fringe** (see p42) during August, as hundreds of street performers, souvenir-hawkers and desperate thespians descend upon it to sell their wares. Members of the public not paying complete attention to their surroundings may find themselves enlisted as the unwitting star (or victim) of an amateur juggling act, or the reluctant paperweight for thousands of fliers and free newspapers (see p79). The street is also popular year-round with buskers, especially pipers piping pibroch, reels, airs and regular renditions of 'Flower of Scotland'. No decision has yet been made

on what will eventually become the National Anthem of Scotland, but this old tune has certainly been adopted with great enthusiasm by fans of the national rugby and football teams.

Castlehill

The Royal Mile begins at **Castlehill**, home – naturally enough – of **Edinburgh Castle** (see p81). The castle stands on the towering basalt hunk of Castle Rock; one of Edinburgh's extinct volcanos, it stands 435 feet (130 metres) tall and has long provided Edinburghers with a vantage point over the city and its environs. The rock has been inhabited by humans since at least the ninth century BC; over the ages, a succession of wooden and stone fortifications were built on the site, although most of the buildings visible today date from the 18th and 19th centuries.

The castle was a royal residence until the Lang Siege of 1571-3, when supporters of Mary, Queen of Scots were bombarded by troops led by James Douglas. At the time, Douglas was the Regent Morton and governed on behalf of Mary's son, the infant King James VI of Scotland (James I of England). The royal home was then moved to the **Palace of Holyroodhouse** at the other end of the Mile, and the castle was extensively refurbished and heavily fortified.

The castle was last involved in battle in 1745, when its cannons were used to repel the invading forces of the Young Pretender, Charles Edward Stuart. Better known as 'Bonnie Prince

Charlie', he was the son of the deposed Catholic monarch King James VII (of Scotland) and II (of England). However, a burst of shellfire does still echo from the castle's walls six times a week; for more, *see p83* **The world at one**.

The approach to the castle runs through the Esplanade, where the world-famous and almost invariably sold-out **Edinburgh Military Tattoo** (*see p43*) has been held every August since 1950. When the Tattoo's temporary seating is not in place, the castle's imposing Half Moon Battery dominates the Esplanade. Built after the Lang Siege to defend the eastern side of the stronghold (the other sides are protected by sheer cliffs), it provided the basis for the castle's massive artillery strength. Behind it on the left are the palace apartments, now one of the castle's museums. A small gate at the eastern end of the north side of the Esplanade leads down winding paths to Princes Street Gardens.

The view from the Esplanade's southern parapet looks out over the suburbs of Edinburgh as far as the Pentland Hills; the northern aspect leads the eye over the New Town and across the Firth of Forth to Fife. Various military memorials on the Esplanade serve as sombre remembrance to the many Scottish soldiers killed in action overseas. Also here is the tomb of Ensign Charles Ewart, who single-handedly captured the standard of the famous French Invincibles at the Battle of Waterloo. His memory is further celebrated in the name of a pub a little way down to the east (521 Lawnmarket, 225 7440).

Look out, too, for the **Witches' Memorial**, a lasting epitaph to a dreadful historical trend Edinburgh shares with much of Europe. Although it's often said to date to the Middle Ages, witch-burning was actually a popular sport of Renaissance and Enlightenment man, and was a paranoid passion of James VI. This bronze, wall-mounted relief marks the spot where over 300 women were burned as witches between 1479 and 1722. It's little comfort to learn that in Scotland, the victims were usually strangled before the fire was lit.

On the extreme left, as you face away from the castle, stands **Ramsay Gardens**, an irregular complex of romantic baronial buildings bristling with spiral staircases and overhangs. Constructed around the poet Allan Ramsay's octagonal 'goose-pie' house, the buildings were erected (for the most part) in the late 19th century in a bid to lure the upper classes back to the Old Town. Today, all of them in private hands, they're some of the city's most desirable and expensive real estate. The low, flat building next to them is much less attractive, but originally performed an

important function: as the Castlehill reservoir, built in 1851, it supplied water to Princes Street. It now houses the **Edinburgh Old Town Weaving Company** (*see p83*).

Edinburgh's oldest official tourist attraction, the **Camera Obscura** (*see below*), stands next door in a striking black and white tower. Best visited on clear days, it's akin to an 18th-century CCTV system. Nearby **Cannonball House** is so named because of the two cannonballs lodged about halfway up the west gable end wall. They're said to have marked the level to which water piped from Comiston Springs in the Pentland Hills would rise, thereby proving that it could be used to feed the Castlehill reservoir.

Opposite is the **Scotch Whisky Heritage Centre** (*see p84*), which occupies a former school building. Regular tours offer insight into the history of whisky-making; there's also an extremely well-stocked shop (with samples) and an educational amusement ride. Just a few metres away, where Castlehill meets the top of Johnston Terrace, stands a grand building by James Graham and Augustus Pugin, the latter famed for designing London's Houses of Parliament. Completed in 1844 as the Victoria Hall, it later become the Tolbooth St John's Kirk, complete with a towering 240-foot (75-metre) Gothic spire. The church was reopened by the Edinburgh International Festival in 1999 as its headquarters; it's now known as the **Hub** (*see p83*), and has a rather nice café (*see p144*).

Camera Obscura & the World of Illusion

Castlehill (226 3709/www.camera-obscura.co.uk). Bus 23, 27, 41, 42, 45. **Open** *July, Aug 9.30am-7.30pm daily. Apr-Jun, Sep, Oct 9.30am-6pm daily. Nov-Mar 10am-5pm daily.* **Admission** *£6.45; £4.15-£5.15 concessions.* **Credit** *MC, V.* **Map** *p78 A1, p330 G7, p336 D4.*

Created by the optician Maria Short in the 1850s, the Camera Obscura is a system of mirrors that projects a periscope image of the city on to a white disc in the centre of a small darkened room. Major landmarks are pointed out by the guides as they pan the lens across the city. While it's certainly no longer as thrilling as it must have been in Victorian times, the camera is an authentic working example of an historic visitor attraction. More impressive to the modern tourist is the set of powerful telescopes on the roof, which offer superb views across the city. Once you've spied on Edinburghers going about their business, you'll really begin to notice the CCTV cameras on the city's streetcorners.

Before you reach the camera, you'll pass through three floors of exhibits, including holographs, pin-hole cameras, morphing machines and other visual and interactive technology. Kids love the distorting mirrors on the building's exterior; if you don't want to pay to go inside, these can be enjoyed for free.

Edinburgh Castle

Castlehill (inquiries 668 8800/ticket office 225 9846/
www.historic-scotland.gov.uk). Bus 23, 27, 41, 42,
45. **Open** (last entry 45 mins before closing) *Apr-*
Sept 9.30am-6pm daily. *Oct-Mar* 9.30am-5pm daily.
Admission £10.30; £4.50-£8.50 concessions.
Credit MC, V. **Map** p330 F7, p336 C3.

Military barracks, prison, royal residence, murder
scene, birthplace of kings and queens... Edinburgh
Castle has served a variety of purposes during the
centuries it has stood high above the city. While its
lofty position was employed to military advantage
in years gone by, it's now extremely useful as a nav-
igational guide if you get lost in the surrounding
warren of streets and closes. However, most visitors
chiefly use it as the city's main tourist attraction.

Built upon centuries of older stone structures, the
castle now comprises of a collection of buildings
housed within the protective enclave of the battery
walls (the other sides are protected by the sheer drop
of the basalt cliffs). Many of the buildings were constructed and altered over several centuries, which can
prove confusing for visitors. For example, although
the **Great Hall** was originally built in 1511 under the
instruction of James IV, almost everything there
today, from the Gothic entrance screen and panelling
to the fireplace and flooring, dates from an extensive
restoration that began in 1886. The main exception is
the incredibly ornate hammerbeam roof, one of the
foremost architectural treasures within the castle.

The oldest extant building is **St Margaret's
Chapel**. Dating from the 12th-century reign of
David I, it fell out of use in the 16th century and was

employed as a gunpowder store for years. Its
intended use was rediscovered in 1845, and it was
restored to a serene simplicity. **David's Tower** –
or, rather, the ruins of it – is another remnant of early
royal constructions, although most of what can
be seen in the dank vaults dates from rebuilding
after the Lang Seige. The **Royal Palace** in Crown
Square (originally the Palace Yard) requires far less
imagination to visualise its regal history. The
redoubtable Mary of Guise, mother to Mary, Queen
of Scots, died here in 1560, while Mary herself gave
birth to James VI in the birthing chamber, a small,
panelled room. The last sovereign to sleep within
this royal residence was Charles I in 1633.

The **Honours of Scotland Exhibition** is
housed within the Royal Palace, in the first floor's
Crown Room. Alongside the Crown (commissioned
in 1540 by James V from Edinburgh goldsmith
John Mossman), the Sceptre (presented to James IV
by Pope Alexander VI around 1494) and the Sword
of State (presented to James IV by Pope Julius II in
1507), you can see the Stone of Destiny (aka the
Stone of Scone), on which Scottish kings were
crowned for centuries. Or, at least, you can see what
staff believe to be the Stone of Destiny. In 1950, four
Scots students swiped the Stone from Westminster
Abbey, where it had sat since Edward I removed it
from Scone Abbey in 1296. And then, three months
later, a similar stone turned up outside Arbroath
Abbey, and was taken back to London. That stone
was eventually returned to Scotland in 1996, but
opinion is split as to its legitimacy.

Edinburgh Castle.

As you'd expect, the castle is steeped in military history, but is also still a military barracks. It's currently home to the Royal Scots and Royal Scots Dragoon Guards (Carabiniers & Greys), which, like the other Scottish regiments, were subsumed into the Royal Regiment of Scotland in 2006. The two regiments each have their own museum at the castle, which also houses the **National War Museum of Scotland**. It charts four centuries of Scottish involvement in wars in a humbling and largely objective way.

A still more sombre military note is sounded by the imposing **Scottish National War Memorial** on Crown Square. Designed in 1924 by Sir Robert Lorimer and opened in 1927 by the Prince of Wales (later Edward VIII), it's a shrine to Scotland's war dead. (If you're at the castle solely to visit the memorial, you don't need to pay the entrance fee.) Below Crown Square are the castle vaults, where you'll find an effective reconstruction of the conditions endured by prisoners of war from successive skirmishes with France in the 18th and 19th centuries, and the American War of Independence.

The buildings are the main attractions at the castle, but it's worth keeping your eyes peeled for more ephemeral bits and pieces: the Dog Cemetery on the Upper Ward, the graffiti scrawled by Napoleonic and American POWs (and their banknote forgery equipment), the 'Laird's Lug' spying device in the Great Hall, and Mons Meg, the huge six-ton cannon that stands next to St Margaret's Chapel. Representing the height of technological advancement in her time, she was presented to James II in 1457 and last fired in 1681, when her barrel burst. While you're enjoying the views or scaring yourself with a peep over the sheer drops, spare a thought for Sir Thomas Randolph and his men, who scaled the northern precipice in 1314 in order to wrest the castle from the English.

The most illuminating way of exploring the castle is with one of the audio guides (available in six languages; £3 adults, £1-£2 for concessions). There's a café and a restaurant within the castle, as well as plenty of toilets. The gift shop's offerings cover all bases, from tartan tat and pocket-money treats to toys, shirts and full-size replica weaponry. Disabled visitors should note that a wheelchair-accessible courtesy vehicle runs from the Esplanade to the upper reaches of the castle.

Edinburgh Old Town Weaving Company & Geoffrey (Tailor) Tartan Weaving Mill

555 Castlehill (226 1555/www.tartanweavingmill. co.uk). Bus 23, 27, 41, 42, 45. **Open** *Exhibition* 9am-5.30pm daily. *Shop* 9am-5.30pm Mon-Sat; 10am-5.30pm Sun. **Admission** free. **Map** p78 A1, p330 G7, p336 D3.

Behind the extensive tartan-stacked shop, visitors can see the various processes that go into producing Scotland's national dress. Experienced workers attend the noisy working looms, the output of which is sold at the front of the shop. Attractions include a 'from sheep to shop' tartan guide, and a chance to handle the threads before the high-powered looms work their magic. You can even get all garbed up and have your photo taken for tartan posterity, as well as checking out your clan history.

Hub

348 Castlehill (473 2000/www.thehub-edinburgh. com). Bus 23, 27, 41, 42, 45. **Open** *Shop & café* 9.30am-6pm Mon, Sun; 9.30am-10pm Tue-Sat. *Ticket office* 10am-5pm Mon-Fri. *Festival office* Apr-July 10am-5pm Mon-Sat. Aug 9am-7.30pm Mon-Sat; 10am-7.30pm Sun. **Admission** free. **Credit** AmEx, MC, V, **Map** p78 A1, p330 G7, p336 D4.

The Grade A-listed Tolbooth St John's Kirk started life as the Victoria Hall for the Established Church General Assembly in 1844, following the religious 'Disruption' of the previous year (*see p23*). After it was bought by the Edinburgh International Festival in the late 1990s, it was renamed the Hub and extensively refurbished; a fantastic mix of Victorian Gothic and contemporary style, it's a prime example of how architectural approaches of different eras can be sympathetically blended. The bold colour

Sightseeing

The world at one

Contrary to popular belief, the gunfire that emanates from Edinburgh Castle each lunchtime isn't a tribute to its military history. The tradition arose in the 19th century as an aid to sailors out in Leith Harbour, and an echo of the time ball atop Nelson's Monument on Calton Hill. Starting in 1861, the ball was raised and then dropped at precisely 1pm to allow seamen to check their chronometers were set correctly. Unfortunately, the ball was often shrouded in fog, and it was decided that a cannon should be fired simultaneously. That way, if sailors couldn't see the signal, they could at least hear it.

Technology has moved on a little since then, but the tradition continues. At 1pm daily (except Sundays), a burst of shellfire booms from a 105mm field gun on the castle walls, terrifying unprepared tourists while simultaneously amusing the locals. Since the death in 2005 of local hero Tom McKay (aka 'Tam the Gun'), who performed the task for 27 years, the task has been shared by various bombardiers. McKay's long service was commemorated by the 2006 arrival of a memorial bench close to the gun; if you think your eardrums can take the noise, it affords a good close-up view of the action.

scheme of the Assembly Hall upstairs, said to adhere to architect Augustus Pugin's original palette, is particularly noteworthy. The rich red stairwell is decorated with some 200 plaster statues by Jill Watson, representing people who have performed in the EIF over the years. It's open to the public as an information point, a ticket office and a café (see p144); if the weather's good, action spills out on to a terrace.

Scotch Whisky Heritage Centre

354 Castlehill (220 0441/www.whisky-heritage.co.uk). Bus 23, 27, 41, 42, 45. **Open** *Apr-Sept* 9.30am-6.30pm daily. *Oct-Mar* 10am-5pm daily. Last tour 1hr before closing. **Admission** £8.95; £4.75-£6.75 concessions; £19.95 family. **Credit** AmEx, MC, V. **Map** p78 A1, p330 G7, p336 D4.

The shop alone makes this tourist-orientated whisky centre worth a visit. The huge selection of blends and malts, some popular and some obscure, includes one of only 83 bottles of 50-year-old Balvenie Cask 191 ever produced. The catch? It costs six grand.

However, the hour-long tour remains the main attraction. Visitors are guided through a series of displays, exhibitions and finally a theme-park style ride, which together chart the history of whisky production since the 15th century. Scotland's national drink is shown in all its constituent parts, with the tastes, smells and noises of its production cleverly intertwined in an educational (if light-hearted) sensory journey. If you're over 18, the cover charge includes a dram, designed in part to entice drinkers down to the pleasant, well-stocked bar below the exhibition.

Lawnmarket & George IV Bridge

Stretching between the Hub and George IV Bridge, the **Lawnmarket** draws its name not from a grassy history, but from the fine linen cloth called 'lawn' that was once sold here. The street is now dotted with pubs and souvenir shops, but isn't without its appeal, especially once you get off the main drag and explore some of the closes that lead off it.

Perhaps the Lawnmarket's most handsome building is **Gladstone's Land** (see right), a well-maintained example of a plush 17th-century townhouse. There's another fine building from the same era just down nearby Lady Stair's Close. Robert Burns stayed in Lady Stair's House on his first visit to Edinburgh; appropriately, it now holds the **Writers' Museum** (see p85), which celebrates the work of Burns, Sir Walter Scott and Robert Louis Stevenson. This area is now known as Makars' Court, from 'makar', the Scots word for poet. Quotations in Scots, Gaelic and English, from 17 Scottish writers of note, are engraved on paving stones approaching the museum. Nearby **James's Court** was once home to James Boswell, biographer of Samuel Johnson; it's now best visited for a restorative pint in the cosy **Jolly Judge** pub (225 2669).

Bank Street, which winds around to the left before becoming the **Mound**, is home to the grand **Bank of Scotland** head office, which recently enjoyed a major refurbishment. The bank itself merged with the Halifax in 2001 to become HBOS, one of the UK's top banking institutions. Designed in the 1860s along classical lines but embellished with baroque flourishes, its building has a gold statue-topped roof which is a highlight of Edinburgh's central skyline. The **HboS Museum on the Mound** inside (see p85) offers a history of banking. The Mound continues down to Princes Street, Edinburgh's busiest thoroughfare (see p101).

Opened in 1834 to complement the parallel South Bridge, **George IV Bridge** heads south from the Lawnmarket and crosses the Cowgate. Walking across the bridge, a trio of libraries dominate: the **National Library of Scotland**, the **Central Library** (incorporating the Children's Library) and the **Music Library**. The tone is lowered by the ugly, boarded-up office buildings, although they are due to be demolished. Numerous bars and cafés dot the length of the bridge; continuing south will eventually lead you to the famous **Greyfriars Kirk** (see p97).

Central Library

George IV Bridge (242 8020/www.edinburgh.gov.uk/libraries). Bus 23, 27, 41, 42, 45. **Open** 10am-8pm Mon-Thur; 10am-5pm Fri; 9am-1pm Sat. **Admission** free. **Map** p78 B2, p330 H7, p336 D4.

The headquarters of Edinburgh's library service was built in 1870 and today houses the Edinburgh Room, the Scottish Department, and reference, fiction and lending libraries. The Edinburgh Room contains over 100,000 items pertaining to the city, from newspaper cuttings to historical prints. It's a reference library only, but some of its items are available on loan from the Scottish Department below it.

An adjacent building houses the Central Children's Library and the Music Library. The latter has an extensive selection of sheet music, biographies and CDs from all genres. You have to be a local resident to borrow items, but all are welcome to browse.

Gladstone's Land

477b Lawnmarket (226 5856). Bus 23, 27, 41, 42, 45. **Open** *Apr-Oct* 10am-5pm daily. Closed Nov-Mar. **Admission** £5; £4 concessions; £10-£14 family. **Credit** MC, V. **Map** p78 B1, p330 G7, p336 D3.

Built in 1550 and extensively rebuilt 70 years later by Merchant Burgess Thomas Gledstanes (an ancestor of prime minister William Gladstone), Gladstone's Land is a typical example of the lands (tenements) that once lined the Royal Mile, right down to the high-level entry to the dwelling up a flight of narrow stairs. The National Trust for Scotland maintains the property in the 17th-century style of its former owner; room reconstructions include a bedchamber, complete with painted

Sightseeing

wooden ceilings and an ornately carved bed, while the inevitable gift shop is found in the restored 'luckenbooth' premises below.

HBOS Museum on the Mound

Bank of Scotland Head Office, The Mound (529 1288/www.bankofscotland.co.uk). Bus 23, 27, 41, 42, 45. **Open** 10am-5pm Tue-Fri; 1-5pm Sat, Sun. **Admission** free. **Map** p78 B1, p330 H7, p336 E3.

Reopened in September 2006, the HBOS Museum on the Mound is one of only three banking museums in the UK. Showcasing a unique collection of artefacts and memorabilia, it has a mix of static and interactive displays to keep visitors entertained. There's a section on forgers and forging, plus a gallery dedicated to the history of the Mound headquarters, set in context alongside the development of the city.

The bank itself was founded by the Parliament of Scotland back in 1695, and is one of the few institutions created by it to have survived. To this day it continues to issue its own banknotes, all of which are legal tender throughout the UK.

National Library of Scotland

George IV Bridge (226 4531/www.nls.uk). Bus 23, 27, 41, 42, 45. **Open** hrs vary by room and season; call or check online for details. **Admission** free. **Map** p78 B2, p330 H7, p336 E4.

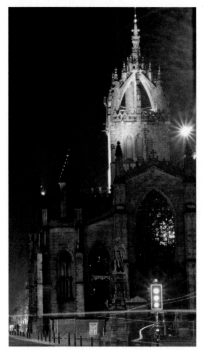

High Kirk of St Giles. *See p88.*

Founded as recently as 1925 (its functions were previously fulfilled by the Faculty of Advocates Library at Parliament House), the NLS is one of the UK's deposit libraries, entitled to request a copy of every printed item published in the UK and Ireland. It contains eight million printed books, 1.6 million maps and 100,000 journals, newspapers and magazines, available to view for research purposes here and in the Causewayside Building to those 'requiring material not readily available elsewhere'. Admission is by ticket only, for which ID is required. During the summer and autumn the Exhibition Hall beyond the main door houses small but intriguing exhibitions pertaining to Scottish printing and writing.

Writers' Museum

Lady Stair's House, Makars' Court, Lawnmarket (529 4901/www.cac.org.uk). Bus 23, 27, 41, 42, 45. **Open** *Aug* 10am-5pm Mon-Sat; noon-5pm Sun. *Sept-July* 10am-5pm Mon-Sat. **Admission** free. **Map** p78 B1, p330 G7, p336 D3.

The only original dwelling of Lady Stair's Close still standing, Lady Stair's House is remarkable for its sharp turnpike staircases and maze-like layout. Built by William Gray in 1622, it was given to the City of Edinburgh in 1907, and now contains curiosities and memorabilia relating to three of Scotland's most celebrated writers: Sir Walter Scott, Robert Burns and Robert Louis Stevenson. Glass cases are filled with early editions of their works, complemented by models of the writers themselves with appropriate voiceover tapes. Also on display is a selection of personal effects, including a chessboard and a large ornate pipe once belonging to Scott and one of Burns' snuffboxes. A small corner of the building contains a selection of the authors' works and comfy chairs in which to curl up and read them. There's also a 'trip step' staircase – a 17th-century burglar alarm – in situ. The museum's permanent displays are supplemented by a programme of temporary exhibitions on other Scottish writers, including contemporary authors.

High Street, west of the Bridges

Just below the crossroads between George IV Bridge, the Mound and the Royal Mile, the **High Street** broadens for a short while with a sense of ordered elegance brought about by Georgian and Victorian planning. A 1997 statue of Edinburgh-born philosopher and historian David Hume, a hugely influential figure in the Scottish Enlightenment, watches over proceedings. While modern, the bronze is fashioned on classical lines, lending its subject a pedagogic gravitas. Three innocuous brass bricks laid into the opposite pavement mark the site of the city's last public hanging: on 21 June 1864, murderer George Bruce was put to death in front of 20,000 people. The public hangman was engaged on other duties at the time, so another prisoner obliged.

Enter the labryinth

Its one-way streets, labyrinthine topography and devious parking restrictions mean that Edinburgh is best traversed on foot. And nowhere is better suited to pedestrian exploration than the Old Town, thanks to the array of narrow lanes, wynds, stairs, courts and closes that cut across the various levels of the High Street and feed off into the depths of the city.

These cramped, narrow streets originally slipped between Edinburgh's tenements, accommodating taverns and shops and housing thousands of the city's residents. Their floors were once dirt tracks, with the emphasis on the word 'dirt': all Edinburghers were legally permitted to throw their daily waste out on to the closes. The closes heaved with people; in 1774 it was recorded that they housed more people per square metre than anywhere else in Europe. As a result epidemics were rife, from the spread of bubonic plague in the 17th century to cholera 200 years later.

Living conditions remained dire right up until the early 1900s. Indeed, many of the original closes remain condemned these days, boarded off as either council-owned or private property. However, plenty do remain open, and the ability to negotiate them successfully tends to be what separates the seasoned locals from the visitors.

Starting from the top of the Lawnmarket at castle level, the **Castle Wynd Steps** will take you right to the bottom of the Grassmarket, while **James's Court**, **Lady Stair's Close** and **Wardrop's Close** all lead in the opposite direction, between the Lawnmarket and the top of the Mound. These latter three closes are a particularly rewarding find, with the **Writers' Museum** (see p85) on one side and the **Jolly Judge** pub (see p84) on the other.

Directly opposite Lady Stair's Close is the less inviting **Fisher's Close**, which heads down on to Victoria Terrace and then, a few steps later, on to Victoria Street. Although Fisher's Close is occasionally pockmarked with graffiti and awash in what seem to be authentically 18th-century fragrances, streets like it are generally safe, even in the evening; things that go bump in the night tend to be those rolling down Lothian Road or Cowgate at chucking-out time. However, common sense might dictate that you avoid walking alone through a winding narrow lane in the dead of night.

On the south side of Lawnmarket, opposite Gladstone's Land (see p84), run two other closes with interesting histories. Leading into two courtyards, **Riddle's Close** was where philosopher David Hume wrote his *Political Discourses*. Nearby **Brodie's Close** was home to the rather less savoury Deacon Brodie, a respectable member of Edinburgh society who led a double life as a burglar. He was put to death outside St Giles on gallows he had designed himself, an irony remembered in the plaque on the wall of **Deacon Brodie's Tavern** (435 Lawnmarket, 225 6531).

With the exception of a few dead-ends, all the closes along the High Street either feed on to the parallel artery that runs at a lower level – the Cowgate and Grassmarket – or run down towards Princes Street. In the centre of the High Street are **Advocate's**, **Roxburgh's** and **Warriston's Closes**, which bring you to the foot of Cockburn Street. In the 15th century, these tributaries would have taken you down to the Nor' Loch, created as part of the city's defences but eventually a breeding ground for the plague. The water was finally drained in 1817 to make way for the New Town, and the closes are now a handy route to the considerably more pleasant **Princes Street Gardens**.

This section of the Royal Mile, east of George IV Bridge but west of the North and South Bridges, is an unarguably impressive part of town. The stretch is dominated by the suitably imposing **High Kirk of St Giles**, where Scottish Reformer John Knox once preached and where, in 1639, stallholder Jenny Geddes is reputed to have hurled her three-legged creepie stool at the Dean of Edinburgh as he read from the Anglican Book of Common Prayer, which was viewed by many post-Reformation Scots

as being a deal too close to Catholicism. 'Deil colic the wame o' ye, fause thief,' she cried, adding 'Daur ye say Mass in my lug?'

In the 15th century the area outside St Giles was crammed with shops and 'luckenbooths' (lockable stalls). Now **Parliament Square**, it is empty save for the occasional ambling tourist. **Parliament House** runs along the back of the square; its plush Parliament Hall is worth a visit. Home to the Scottish Parliament in the 17th century, it's now used by lawyers

Perhaps the most infamous of all the Old Town alleys was lost for well over two centuries. As part of efforts to gentrify the Old Town in 1753, the grand Royal Exchange (now the City Chambers) was built over part of **Mary King's Close**, the lower floors of which acted as the new building's foundations. The construction was a conscious effort literally to bury the memories of disease, starvation and desperation that lurked in the close, which was quarantined during the plague that struck in 1645. It's said that the whole street was blocked up and its inhabitants left to die; it's now reputed to be one of the most haunted places in Scotland. Forgotten for years, the underground lane was re-opened to the public in 2003 and is now open for tours (*see p98* **Things that go bump in the night**). It's undoubtedly the most authentic preservation of the old alleyways.

If you're in a hurry to catch a train, **Fleshmarket Close** cuts through from the High Street, across Cockburn Street and right down to Market Street, where a side entrance to Waverley Station sits at the bottom of the close steps. Further down the High Street towards Holyrood, you'll find **Carruber's Close**, once home to the theatre of literary great Allan Ramsay. However, magistrates gave it the final curtain only one year after its opening in 1736. Before this short-lived thespian invasion, the close was a refuge for Jacobites in the late 1600s.

Walk past the Tolbooth and turn left after Canongate Kirk, and you'll find a rather inconspicuous lane that leads to **Dunbar's Close**, perhaps the most rewarding of all the city's closes. At the end is a tranquil garden, with ornamental flower beds and manicured hedges; it's laid out in a 17th-century style, but was created less than 30 years ago by the Mushroom Trust, a local charity.

The garden affords fine views of the old Royal High School, which looks set to become the National Photography Centre for Scotland in future years.

Nearby, **Lochend, Little Lochend** and **Campbell's Closes** all lead on to Calton Road, while picturesque **White Horse Close**, named in honour of Queen Mary's palfrey horse, formed part of the Royal Mews in the 1700s. Nowadays the old inn building on the close is let as self-catered accommodation. Further up, on the other side is **Crichton's Close**; although not as lavish as its regal counterpart, it leads on to Holyrood Road and is home to the unassuming Scottish Poetry Library (*see p40*).

discussing cases from the adjoining District Court, Court of Session and High Court. It's not unusual to find solicitors marching up and down Parliament Hall, usually in pairs, engaged in earnest discussion about cases on which they're working. The area was once St Giles's churchyard, which explains why John Knox's grave can be found in the middle of a car park.

In front of St Giles, in Parliament Square, is the **Heart of Midlothian**, a heart shape set into the cobblestones of the street that marks the spot where Edinburgh's Tolbooth prison stood (not to be confused with the Canongate Tolbooth, which still survives). Built as a town hall, the Tolbooth became a multifunctional civic building and was used by the Scottish Parliament in the 16th and 17th centuries, until Charles I demanded that a new parliamentary building be constructed. It continued to house the HQ of the city guard (those 'black banditti' caricatured by the poet Robert Fergusson, *see p39*), who often displayed the severed heads of executed criminals outside the prison. After the building was finally demolished in 1817, its stones went to build the sewerage system of Fettes Row in the New Town. However, the long-held habit of spitting on the Heart of Midlothian, begun by the criminal fraternity when the land was still held the Tolbooth, is still upheld by locals.

To the east of the kirk you'll find the **Mercat Cross** (literally, 'market cross'), identifiable by the white unicorn holding a Saltire flag at the top of its turret. Reconstructed in the 19th century, the cross originally stood at the top of Old Fishmarket Close; the site is marked on the pavement with a pattern of bricks. Among the many unfortunates executed here was James Graham, the dashing, reckless Marquis of Montrose; Graham had returned from exile to avenge the death of Charles I, but was betrayed and captured before being hanged, drawn and quartered here in 1650. Nearby in Parliament Square sits the **Loch Ness Discovery Centre** (*see below*); just along the High Street is the **Police Information Centre** (*see p89*) and the **Edinburgh Festival Fringe** office (*see p83*), which sells tickets and souvenirs.

Across the High Street from St Giles are the **City Chambers**, where the city council sits. Completed in 1761 and one of the first truly Georgian buildings in Edinburgh, the premises were originally part of the Royal Exchange. However, when it failed to thrive (traders still preferred to do their business in the open air at the Mercat Cross), the city council moved into the building in 1811. The chambers were built on top of three closes; the most famous, **Mary King's Close**, is today a spooky museum accessible only as part of a tour (*see p98* **Things that go bump in the night**).

High Kirk of St Giles

High Street (225 4363/visitor services 225 9442). Bus 23, 27, 35, 41, 42, 45/Nicolson Street–North Bridge buses. **Open** *Apr-Sept* 9am-7pm Mon-Sat. *Oct-Mar* 9am-5pm Mon-Sat. Call for service times. **Admission** free; donations welcome. **Map** p78 B1, p330 H7, p336 E4.

There has been a church on the site of St Giles since 854. Nothing remains of the earliest structures, but the four pillars that

A violent past: the **Mercat Cross**.

surround the Holy Table in the centre have stood firm since around 1120, surviving the desecration of marauding armies during the Reformation in the 16th century. The kirk was considerably refurbished in the 19th century and much of what can be seen today dates from this period. Pedants should note that the fabric of the building itself is referred to as St Giles, while the church itself is known as the High Kirk of Edinburgh.

John Knox became minister here in 1560, 12 years before his death. This was a tumultuous time for religion in Scotland, with Edinburgh – and Knox – very much at the heart of the Scottish Reformation. The kirk has changed status many times through the years, and today is often referred to as a cathedral even though it has only had two bishops in its history. Charles I first designated it a cathedral in 1633, but it retained the tag after the bishops were banished in the Glorious Revolution of 1688. As a Presbyterian place of worship, it cannot technically be considered a cathedral at all.

Inside, a great vaulted ceiling shelters a medieval interior dominated by the banners and plaques of Scottish regiments. The main entrance takes visitors past the West Porch screen, originally designed as a royal pew for Queen Victoria. Newer features include the 1911 Thistle Chapel, an intricately decorated chamber built in honour of a chivalric order named the Knights of the Thistle. The intimate panelled room was designed by Robert Lorimer, who also designed the Scottish War Memorial at Edinburgh Castle (*see p82*). Installed in 1992, the organ is an even more recent addition, and features a glass back that reveals its workings.

Numerous memorials and statues pay tribute to the likes of Knox, Robert Louis Stevenson and even Jenny Geddes, but perhaps the most notable feature of the interior is its magnificent stained glass windows. Constructed in the workshops of William Morris, the richly-hued Edward Burne Jones window is designed to be enhanced by the western light it catches. The dazzling West Window, dedicated to Robert Burns by Icelandic artist Leifur Breidfjord in 1984, is also noteworthy, while Douglas Strachan's North Window is a blaze of rich, cold colours and swirling designs. **Photo** *p85*.

Loch Ness Discovery Centre

1 Parliament Square, Royal Mile (225 2290/www. 3dlochness.com). Bus 23, 27, 35, 41, 42, 45/Nicolson Street–North Bridge buses. **Open** *July, Aug* 9.30am-8pm daily. *Sept-June* 9.30am-6pm daily. **Admission** £4.95; £3.50-£4 concessions; £14.95 family. **Credit** MC, V. **Map** p78 C1, p330 H7, p336 E4.

No, Loch Ness hasn't been piped down to Edinburgh in order that tourists needn't bother making the long journey north. Based on the work of Loch Ness expert Adrian Shine, the Discovery Centre houses a multilingual exploration of the facts and myths that surround this most infamous body of water. Enjoy the 3D displays and decide for yourself whether Nessie really could exist.

Police Information Centre

188 High Street (226 6966/www.lbp.police.uk). Bus 23, 27, 35, 41, 42, 45/Nicolson Street–North Bridge buses. **Open** *May-Aug* 10am-10pm daily. *Mar, Apr, Sept, Oct* 10am-8pm daily. *Nov-Feb* 10am-6pm daily. **Admission** free. **Map** p78 C1, p330 H7, p336 E4.
You name it, Edinburgh has a museum for it. Staffed by friendly coppers (indeed, it's a working police office), this small room has information on almost every aspect of policing in Edinburgh both past and present. Historic exhibits include a macabre business-card holder made from the cured skin of infamous grave-robber William Burke (*see p23*). During the Festival, the Lothian and Borders Police Pipe Band marches along Princes Street at 11am each weekday morning; some of the pipers head here afterwards and play for around 30 minutes.

Cockburn Street, Market Street & the Bridges

Cockburn Street has long been the city centre's home of alternative culture, permanently ornamented by skiving youths loitering outside the record shops (*see p205*) and clothing stores. Two galleries (**Collective** and the **Stills Gallery**; *see p221 and p222*) add a little variety to the street. Astute art-hounds may care to continue down to the bottom of Cockburn Street, turn right on to **Market Street**, and continue past the **Edinburgh Dungeon** (*see right*) to the excellent **Fruitmarket Gallery** and the **City Art Centre** (*see p221*). During August, Market Street is lined with people queuing for Tattoo tickets; the event's offices, open year-round, are next to the Dungeon.

Back up on the High Street, the **Tron Kirk** sits almost opposite the junction with Cockburn Street. Built in the 17th century, the church now houses the **Old Town Information Centre** (*see right*). Just behind here is Hunter Square, a favoured haunt of Edinburgh's homeless fraternity. Some of them can be a little aggressive, so use caution.

At the traffic lights, the High Street is cut in two by **North Bridge** and **South Bridge**. Collectively known as 'the **Bridges**', they were built to provide access to the south of the city, and hastened expansion into the New Town in the late 18th century. Although South Bridge looks like a continuous street, it's actually supported by 19 massive arches, only one of which is visible.

Looking up North Bridge towards the New Town, the last building on the left of North Bridge formerly housed the offices of the *Scotsman* newspaper. Purpose-built for the company in 1905, the rugged, iconic edifice was vacated by the company 94 years later, since when it has been transformed into an impressive luxury hotel (*see p53*). At the front of the building, an enclosed spiral staircase provides a short cut down to Market Street and Waverley Station. The dank stairway has been the setting for foul murder in several Edinburgh-set detective thrillers, and an entirely credible one at that. Unless you enjoy the stench of stale urine, you may want to take the long way around.

Edinburgh Dungeon

31 Market Street (240 1000/www.thedungeons.com). Princes Street buses. **Open** *Apr-Oct* 10am-5pm daily. *Nov-Mar* 11am-4pm daily. **Admission** £11.95; £7.95-£9.95 concessions; £37.75 family. **Credit** AmEx, MC, V. **Map** p78 C1, p330 H7, p336 E3.
If you like your history packed with facts, this might not be for you. However, if raw flesh, disease, murder, exaggerated pantomime mayhem and the pornography of violence are more your bag, then a trip to the Edinburgh Dungeon – run by the folks behind the similar operation in London – is an entertaining way to find out about Scotland's murky past. Exhibits focus on local horrors, from the plague-ridden streets and brutal judicial executions to the murderous trade of Burke and Hare. There are all sorts of diabolical torture instruments on show, and a reconstruction of the cave that was home to notorious (and, quite possibly, wholly mythical) 14th-century cannibal Sawney Bean. Costumed guides do their utmost to scare you through the place.

Tron Kirk & Old Town Information Centre

Tron Kirk, High Street (225 8408). Bus 35/Nicolson Street–North Bridge buses. **Open** *July, Aug* 10am-7pm daily. *May-June* 11am-5pm daily. *Sept-Apr* noon-5pm daily. **Admission** free. **Map** p78 C2, p331 J7, p336 F4.
Housed in a grand old church that survived both the development of South Bridge in 1785 and the Great Conflagration of 1824, this information centre is curiously short on actual information. It does, however, contain a shop selling tickets to city attractions, plus a bizarre array of souvenirs, ranging from 'see you Jimmy' hats to nodding skulls. The main attraction is the reclaimed underground remains of Marlin's Wynd, an early 16th-century street that was razed and built over in around 1636.

High Street, east of the Bridges

Beyond the traffic lights, just behind the Bank Hotel, **Niddry Street** dips steeply down towards the Cowgate. Behind its shabby walls, which have been done up to represent 19th-century Edinburgh in at least one BBC drama, is a warren of cellars built into the arches of South Bridge. These subterranean expanses are atmospheric places, brought to life through a number of guided tours (*see p98*). **Nicol Edwards** (556 8642), touted as the city's most haunted pub, is found here, as is the **Medieval**

Torture Museum, which displays instruments of torture used on suspected witches in Germany during the Middle Ages. It's currently accessible with a ticket to an **Auld Reekie** tour (*see p98*).

A little way down the High Street, past the slightly cack-handed Radisson SAS Hotel (*see p55*) and hostel-heavy **Blackfriars Street**, sits the slightly façade of the **Museum of Childhood** (*see below*), the first museum of its type in the world. Children who favour a more hands-on experience may prefer the **Brass Rubbing Centre**, located just opposite on Chalmers Close (*see below*). Down from here is the new **Scottish Storytelling Centre** (*see right*), which incorporates **John Knox House**.

If you've time, nip down **Trunk Close**, just behind the Storytelling Centre. If you're in luck, the gate will be open and you can access a small landscaped garden, one of the many little treasures that lurk behind the gloomy entrances of the city's closes. Another of them, nearby **Tweeddale Court**, holds one of only a few surviving stretches of the old city wall. The Netherbow, the eastern city gate, used to stand at roughly this point on the High Street.

Brass Rubbing Centre

Trinity Apse, Chalmers Close, High Street (556 4364/www.cac.org.uk). Bus 35, 36/Nicolson Street– North Bridge buses. **Open** *Aug* 10am-5pm Mon-Sat; noon-5pm Sun. *Apr-Sept* 10am-5pm Mon-Sat. Closed Oct-Mar. **Admission** free. **Map** p78 D1, p331 J7.

The Brass Rubbing Centre is housed in an atmospheric location: the apse that is the only surviving remnant of the Gothic Trinity College Church, founded in 1460. The centre demonstrates that although brass-rubbing might be a good kids' activity, it also can have an artistic side, particularly when Celtic knots are involved. Cheery, friendly staff and good schematic guides show how it's done.

Museum of Childhood

42 High Street (529 4142/www.cac.org.uk). Bus 35, 36/Nicolson Street–North Bridge buses. **Open** 10am-5pm Mon-Sat; noon-5pm Sun. **Admission** free. **Credit** *Shop* MC, V. **Map** p78 D2, p331 J7.

This popular attraction was founded in 1955 by local councillor Patrick Murray, who made sure that visitors understood the difference between a museum of childhood and a museum for children. The extensive collection of toys and childhood mementos stretches back decades, to when lead soldiers and china-headed dolls were state-of-the-art toys, but also runs through to the era of Barbie and Ken.

In truth, while grins of recognition are usually spread wide across the faces of kids-at-heart of all ages, older generations may enjoy their trip down memory lane far more than pre-teens. While there are hundreds of bygone toys on display, many displaying a level of craftsmanship absent on today's

shelves, there's a distinct lack of the kind of inter-activity that 21st-century kids are growing up to expect from museums. That said, a few early automaton boxes – the Haunted House, Sweeney Todd et al – do provide entertainment. Much of the museum evokes a rose-tinted impression of bygone innocence, but the stark image of a child-sized World War II gas mask is a powerful reminder that not everything was idyllic in the old days. There's a small shop at the entrance; check online for details of occasional guest exhibitions.

Scottish Storytelling Centre & John Knox House

43 High Street (556 9579/www.scottishstorytelling centre.co.uk). Bus 35, 36/Nicolson Street–North Bridge buses. **Open** *July, Aug* 10am-6pm Mon-Sat; noon-6pm Sun. *Sept-June* 10am-6pm Mon-Sat. **Admission** *Scotland's Stories* free, *John Knox House: Inside History* £3; £1-£2.50 concessions. **Credit** MC, V, not in café. **Map** p78 D2, p331 J7.

After extensive refurbishment and interior reconstruction, the Scottish Storytelling Centre reopened its doors in June 2006. Through the unassuming doorway and past a bright café selling organic and homemade food, a light, airy space holds a free permanent exhibition entitled Scotland's Stories. Aimed at all ages, it contains an interactive wall that serves as an introduction to all kinds of Scottish tradition and literature; it's full of mini tableaux behind doors, and touchy-feely boxes for the littl'uns. There's also a sound and vision display on Robert Louis Stevenson, and networked access to storytelling events throughout Scotland. The fully refurbished theatre has been acoustically designed around the needs of the unaccompanied human voice, but the wall can be swung out into the exhibition space to provide a more intimate area for storytelling.

The entrance also provides access to **John Knox House**, which boasts an engagingly eccentric history. The building was saved from demolition in 1830 out of reverence for the belief that it was the last home of Knox, the founder of Scottish Presbyterianism. However, there's little conclusive evidence that he ever lived here, and the house is instead believed to have been the home of goldsmith James Mossman; certainly, it's Mossman's initials, along with those of wife Mariota Arres, that can be seen on the lintel above the entrance. The museum covers its tracks by offering biographical insights on both Mossman and Knox.

There are myriad treasures in its rooms, leading off a turnpike stair complete with a trip-step and doors with false locks to foil intruders. Look out for the Tower of Destiny, with its gruesomely jolly representations of the final moments of Knox, Mossman, Mary, Queen of Scots and Sir William Kirkcaldy of Grange, who defended Edinburgh Castle against the enemies of Mary. And do take time to admire the exterior of the building, with its first-floor entry door, lintel stone, and the exhortation 'Luf God abufe al and yi nychtbur as yi self'.

Our Dynamic Earth. *See p92.*

The Canongate

The **Canongate** takes its name from the route used by Augustinian canons, who arrived at Holyrood Abbey in 1141, to reach the gates of Edinburgh. Situated outside the old city walls, it was separate from Edinburgh until as recently as 1856, with the Netherbow Port marking the spot where one burgh ended and the other began. It's a mostly residential area these days, but it's dotted with fascinating museums and independent shops offering everything from occult paraphernalia to bagpipes.

Instantly recognisable by its clock, its bell tower and its outside stairway, the **Canongate Tolbooth** was built in 1592, and later served as a council chamber, a police station and a prison. It now serves as the **People's Story** (*see p95*), a lively interpretation of working-class life in Edinburgh through the centuries.

Opposite sits the **Museum of Edinburgh** (*see p92*), which offers fascinating insights into the other end of the social spectrum. It's contained within Huntly House, three timber-framed houses that were joined into one in 1570, surmounted by three overhanging white-painted gables of a kind that were once common in the Old Town. Under Huntly House, **Bakehouse Close** leads to the offices of the

Architecture+Design Scotland (formerly the Royal Fine Art Commission for Scotland), a national body responsible for promoting high standards of planning and architectural design. Its newly refurbished building is worth a peek.

The bell-shaped Dutch design of **Canongate Kirk** stands out from the tenement buildings on the Royal Mile. Its construction was ordered in 1688 to accommodate the displaced congregation of Holyrood Abbey, after James VII turned the Abbey into a royal chapel for the use of the Knights of the Thistle. It remains Edinburgh's official military church; the royal family often worship here when they're staying in the Palace of Holyroodhouse.

Canongate Kirkyard offers excellent views over Calton Hill, and is the resting place for some well-known figures (*see p93*). Among them are Robert Burns' muse Clarinda, further commemorated by a tea-room (*see p141*) a little further down. Just the right side of twee, it's a sedate place to relax over a nice cup of tea. Poetry by Burns, and many other poets through the ages, can be found at the **Scottish Poetry Library** down Crichton's Close (*see p40*). Few locals know of **Dunbar's Close Garden**, found at the end of an unassuming close on the north side of the Canongate, but it's definitely worth a peek (*see p86* **Enter the labyrinth**).

Further east along Canongate sit some hugely attractive houses, most obviously the two well-kept, gleaming white edifices of **Canongate Manse** and **Whitefoord House**. The latter is now a residence for Scottish war veterans. **White Horse Close** is also very pretty; the gabled building at the end was once a coaching inn, and the departure point for the stage coach to London. It was called into service in 1745 as the officers' quarters of Prince Charles Edward Stuart's army.

At the bottom of the Royal Mile is the **Palace of Holyroodhouse**, one of the Queen's official residences. From a distance, the building appears perfectly symmetrical, but on closer inspection, it becomes clear that the left tower is much older than the right. The palace was damaged considerably by Cromwell's forces, who accidentally burned down the south wing. However, it was restored in the reign of Charles II and lovingly decorated by Queen Victoria, whose influence can still be seen today during the guided audio tours that run when the royals aren't in residence. The purpose of the strange, squat building just inside the fence by the main road is unknown: it might have been a bathhouse, or perhaps a doocot (where 'doos', or pigeons, nest). The palace has played an integral role in Scottish history. Most recently, it was here that the Queen appointed the late Donald Dewar as First Minister in 1999, just as the Scottish Parliament met for its first session of modern times.

The grounds of the palace contain the ruins of **Holyrood Abbey**, founded by David I in 1128 and irrevocably linked with the Scottish monarchy. James II, born in the abbey lodgings, was married there, as were James III, James IV and Mary, Queen of Scots. James V and Charles I were crowned there; David II, James II, James V and Lord Darnley were all buried within its walls. It suffered extensive attacks throughout the centuries, motivated by politics and religion: it was sacked by Edward II in 1322, damaged in 1544 and again in 1570 (with the loss of the choir and transepts) and violated yet further by a mob of Presbyterian vandals in 1688. It was finally abandoned in 1768.

Close by Holyrood sits Enric Miralles' **Scottish Parliament** complex, controversial from the outset but now gradually settling into its neighbourhood. The complex features an array of distinctive buildings made from glass, concrete and wood, but also takes in the restored and refurbished original buildings, among them the 17th-century, Grade A-listed Queensberry House. The second Duke of Queensberry returned home here in 1707 after attempting to placate crowds opposed to the dissolution of the Scottish parliament. After a hard day at the

office, he probably was none too pleased to find that his lunatic son had escaped his guards and had spitted and roasted the kitchen boy. The oven he used still exists, though the building is now used as parliamentary offices.

The Scottish Parliament is just one of several new constructions on Holyrood Road. Close by are the offices of the *Scotsman*, the modern glass façade of the Tun (home to BBC Scotland, the Commission for Racial Equality and the British Council, among others) and the exclusive **MacDonald Holyrood Hotel** (*see p55*). And just next to the Parliament buildings sits **Our Dynamic Earth** (*see below*); despite having drawn comparisons with London's Millennium Dome, both for its appearance and theme, it's largely seen as a success.

Amid all this investment and development, the **Dumbiedykes** estate stands out a mile. Located just off Holyrood Road (the flats have spectacular views looking out on to Salisbury Crags), it's one of Edinburgh's poorest estates, an area of desperate poverty that's remained tucked away in the centre of the capital while other, similar neighbourhoods were constructed in the far-flung peripheries of the city. Major redevelopment is now under way, but it's still best avoided at night.

Museum of Edinburgh

Huntly House, 142-146 Canongate (529 4143/ www.cac.org.uk). Bus 35, 36. **Open** *Aug* 10am-5pm Mon-Sat; noon-5pm Sun. *Sept-July* 10am-5pm Mon-Sat. **Admission** free. **Map** p79 F2, p331 K7.
While the People's Story across the road is a tribute to hardship and to Edinburgh's redoubtable working class folk, the Museum of Edinburgh is a shrine to the burgesses and the patrician classes. Housed in Huntly House, three original tenements dating from 1570, the displays are fabulously eclectic: Roman coins, Victorian silverware, a piece of the shaft of the original Mercat Cross, even the collar and bowl of Greyfriars Bobby. The original version of the National Covenant of 1638 is housed here; some of its signatures are in blood. Staffing constraints mean that access is occasionally limited, but even there's still plenty to see even when only one of the two floors is open.

Our Dynamic Earth

Holyrood Road (550 7800/www.dynamicearth.co.uk). Bus 35, 36. **Open** *July, Aug* 10am-6pm daily. *Apr-June, Sept, Oct* 10am-5pm daily. *Nov-Mar* 10am-5pm Wed-Sun. Last entry 70mins before closing. **Admission** £8.95 adult; £1.50-£6.50 concessions; £19-£37.50 family. **Credit** MC, V. **Map** p79 H2, p331 L7.
Our Dynamic Earth is located near the former home of Edinburgh-born James Hutton, the so-called 'Father of Geology'. It's anyone's guess what he'd make of its ultra-modern, tent-like exterior, but he'd surely approve of its educational aims: to take

Walking with the dead

You can tell a lot about a city's living population from the way they treat their dead. Edinburgh has traditionally treated its own fairly well, as evidenced both by the grand monuments in its kirkyards and cemeteries, and by the kirkyards' often prominent locations: Greyfriars, the Canongate and St Cuthbert's are all in the city centre. Others, such as Warriston, stand in gentle decay; others still, such as Old Calton, could be missed by pedestrians walking a mere 15 feet above. The kirkyard of St Giles, the last resting place of hundreds of dead, has all but gone, built over as the city expanded.

Greyfriars (*see pp95-96*), perhaps the most famous of Edinburgh's kirkyards, houses some of the finest monuments in the UK. Among those buried here, memorialised with varying degrees of dignity and affection, are George Buchanan (died 1582), tutor to Mary, Queen of Scots and James VI; the poets Allan Ramsay (d.1758), Duncan Ban MacIntyre (d.1812) and William McGonagall (d.1902); James Craig (d.1795), designer of the New Town; and John Gray (d.1858), whose tomb was reputedly guarded by his dog Bobby until he too died (and got his own headstone). Also here are the remains of physician Archibald Pitcairn (d.1713), who ordered a quantity of wine to be interred with him. The wine, he stated, was to be consumed only when the Stuart dynasty was restored. Unfortunately for Pitcairn, his tomb was renovated in 1800, and the wine was apparently drunk.

But Greyfriars' macabre side is also in evidence. Alongside the impressive statuary, decked in carved Romanesque swags, reclining sleepers, attendant angels and upturned torches, stand the remains of mortsafes. The iron grilles were erected to protect corpses from body snatchers.

Sombre monuments bear testament to wrongs done to the living. Those who died in prison or were executed at the Grassmarket were buried in an area set aside for criminals. The Martyrs' Memorial honours the executed Covenanters, who were incarcerated for five cold winter months in the area now known as the Covenanters Prison. It's bitterly ironic that one of the finest mausoleums here is that of Sir George 'Bluidy' Mackenzie, relentless persecutor of the Covenanters. His tomb is elegantly classical, complete with Corinthian pillars and a Grecian urn.

Others fared less well than Mackenzie, and few met a more unfortunate earthly afterlife than poet Robert Fergusson (1750-1774). Plagued by 'the horrors', he died in a mental asylum and was interred in a pauper's grave in the **Canongate Kirkyard** (*see p91*). It remained unmarked until Robert Burns, who described Fergusson as 'my elder brother in misfortune, by far my elder brother in the Muse', funded the purchase of a headstone. Fergusson was finally honoured in 2004 with a statue outside the kirk, portraying the poet in exuberant mid-stride.

Fergusson lies in interesting company. Adam Smith (d.1790), author of the *Wealth of Nations*, was interred here in neo-classical splendour, while a fairly plain table stone gravemarker is commonly agreed to be the grave of David Rizzio (d.1766), the murdered secretary of Mary, Queen of Scots. Here, too, stands the grave of music publisher Thomas Este, notable for an inscription that uses both sides of the stone, and the remains of Mrs Agnes McLehose, Burns's beloved 'Clarinda'.

Neglect of the dead can take many forms. Walk down the **High Street** and you'll pass the site of St Giles' Kirkyard, long gone under the likes of the Signet Library. The location of John Knox's grave is marked in Parliament Square with a plaque in the car park. And while David Hume's Robert Adam-designed mausoleum in **Old Calton Hill Kirkyard** is imposing, many other tombs here are crumbling.

Elsewhere, author Thomas de Quincey and mathematician John Napier are buried at **St Cuthbert's Kirk** (*see p101*); the Great Lafayette, illusionist extraordinaire, rests at **Piershill**; James Young Simpson, pioneer of anaesthesia, lies in **Warriston**; and the remains of 'Colonel' Anne Mackintosh, who raised a battalion for Bonnie Prince Charlie in 1745, lie in **Old Leith Cemetery**. The modest stones at Old Leith, complete with gruesome skulls, trade carvings, winged angels and touching lists of children lost to families, are a sight. And then there's **Holyrood Abbey**, home to the remains of assorted Scottish royals and worthies (*see p94*).

Don't forget that the living who haunt kirkyards can be dangerous. Avoid walking alone, and take care not to step on discarded syringes. Choose your time of day carefully, or you may have a far more frightening experience than you bargained for.

Sightseeing

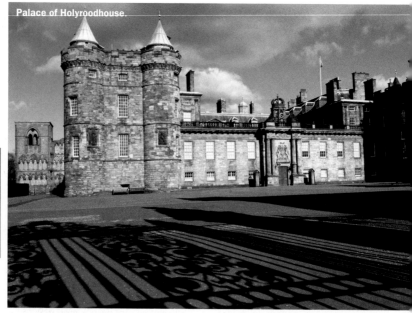
Palace of Holyroodhouse.

visitors back to the creation of the universe nearly 14 billion years ago, then bring them forward to the present day. Tilted primarily at school-age children, it's a science museum that combines natural history with simulated natural disasters, and attempts to make geology fun.

There's only one way through the exhibition, so it's worth taking your time. Staff play different roles as you're led through the ageing world, and interactive exhibits are used to great effect: experience an earthquake simulation on a shuddering platform, touch an iceberg, and take a dizzying virtual helicopter ride around some glaciers. The scientific explanations are simplistic without being patronising; as you near the end, there are philosophical musings from French anthropologist Claude Levi-Strauss, Polish scientist Jacob Bronowski and, er, Sting.

Additions in 2006 included the Earthscape Scotland gallery, which explores the country's geological history with (among other displays) million-year-old rocks and the chance to burrow to the centre of the earth. The FutureDome, meanwhile, offers a range of intriguing 'what if' scenarios, with simulated news updates that allow visitors to make decisions regarding climate change and then see how it all pans out. Once you return to the present day, there's also a café and gift shop. **Photo** *p91*.

Palace of Holyroodhouse

Holyrood Road (524 1120/www.royalresidences.com). Bus 35, 36. **Open** *Apr-Oct* 9.30am-6pm daily (last entry 5pm). *Nov-Mar* 9.30am-4.30pm daily (last entry 3.30pm). Closed 15 May-3 June, 27 June-8 July, 7 Nov & during royal visits. **Admission** £8.80; £4.80-£7.80 concessions; free under-5s; £22.50 family. **Credit** AmEx, MC, V. **Map** p79 H1, p327/p331 L6.

The Palace of Holyroodhouse has its origins in the Abbey of Holyrood (now picturesque ruins), established in 1128 by David I. When Edinburgh was confirmed as the nation's capital city, royal quarters were built adjacent to the abbey and have been gradually upgraded and renovated over the years. It's still used by the Queen as an official residence. When she's elsewhere, parts of the building are open to the public, as an audio tour details the history of a series of plush bedrooms, galleries and dining rooms.

The tour takes you back to 1566 when, six months pregnant, Mary, Queen of Scots watched as four Scottish noblemen murdered her secretary David Rizzio here with the consent of her husband, Lord Darnley. Some say Darnley wanted to kill the baby she was carrying (the future James VI), believing it not to be his. Darnley died soon after in deeply suspicious circumstances (*see p18*).

After Queen Victoria acquired the Balmoral estate, she began to use Holyroodhouse as a stop-off point on the long journey north. It was Victoria who extensively redecorated the building's then-drab walls with the paintings and tapestries that remain on view today, just a small part of the extensive Royal Collection housed here.

The intricate and ornate entrance to the Queen's Gallery leads most visitors to expect a grand, ornate and old-fashioned room; in fact, the interior is surprisingly contemporary. Made up of a series of flexible spaces, the gallery hosts a changing programme of exhibitions from the Royal Collection, with a focus on works from the Royal Library at Windsor Castle. There's also computer access to an e-Gallery, with interactive online exhibition catalogues and details of other works from the collection.

A café can be found on what was formerly the Palace Mews, while the gift shop sells a range of royal-related goods. There are facilities for disabled visitors and parents with small children, although wheelchair access to the State Apartments is currently limited due to fire safety concerns.

People's Story

Canongate Tolbooth, 163 Canongate (529 4057/ www.cac.org.uk). Bus 35, 36. **Open** *Aug* 10am-5pm Mon-Sat; noon-5pm Sun. *Sept-July* 10am-5pm Mon-Sat. **Admission** free. **Map** p79 F1, p327/p331 K6.

With Edinburgh's Tolbooth long since consigned to history, the Canongate Tolbooth is one of the most emotionally resonant buildings in the Old Town. It's where justice was meted out and prisoners awaited their fate, whether hanging, beheading, branding, burning, transportation or any of the other official punishments of the day. These days it houses the People's Story museum, but visitors are reminded of its history by the ground-floor tableau of three of the city's less illustrious citizens.

The museum itself is dedicated to the colourful story of the lives of Edinburgh's working classes over the last four centuries or so. The exploits of the feared Edinburgh mob are recorded, but most of the displays are concerned with more sedate day-to-day life, concentrating on the role of Edinburgh's guilds, unions and friendly societies. Various trades are represented: printers, ship-builders, fishwives and even the redoubtable tram clippies. The exhibits continue to the present day, including a section on Thatcher's Scotland (complete with an amusing mannequin punk) and testimonies from fans of the city's football teams. The museum also affords a glimpse into the grinding poverty that some of Edinburgh's citizens endured long into the 20th century, and continue to endure to this day in run-down estates. Take the time to read their testimonials, and a very different side to the city is revealed.

Scottish Parliament

Canongate (348 5200/www.scottish.parliament.uk). Bus 35, 36. **Open** *Apr-Oct* 10am-6pm Mon, Fri; 9am-7pm Tue-Thur; 10am-4pm Sat, Sun. *Nov-Mar* 10am-4pm Mon, Fri; 9am-7pm Tue-Thur; 10am-4pm Sat, Sun. **Admission** free (last admission 45mins before closing). **Map** p79 H2, p327/p331 L6.

The people of Edinburgh had a long wait to see the building that houses their new parliament. When the scaffolding and coverings were finally removed, a confident, dynamic and innovative complex was revealed, utterly different from any other parliamentary building in the UK. If you've time, take the 45-minute tour (£3.50/£1.75, not available Tue-Thur when Parliament is sitting), which explores areas that are not normally accessible to the casual visitor. If you just want to drop in, however, there's an exhibition about the building, plus a café, a shop and crèche facilities. On business days tickets are available for the public gallery in the debating chamber for those who book ahead: seating is limited.

Even if you don't have the time or inclination to venture inside, the building's exterior, along with the garden areas and water features, provides plenty of points of interest. The parliament's dedicated arts strategy is reflected by design components and art installations. Among them is the Canongate Wall, which is covered with quotations from centuries of Scottish writers engraved into blocks of different types of Scottish stone. At the end of the wall is a line drawing of the Old Town based on a sketch made by the building's architect Enric Miralles, who died before the project's completion.

Scottish Poetry Library

5 Crichton's Close, Canongate (557 2876/ www.spl. org.uk). Bus 35, 36. **Open** 11am-6pm Mon-Fri; 1-5pm Sat. **Admission** free; donations welcome. *Membership* £20; £10 concessions. **No credit cards. Map** p79 G1, p327/p331 L6.

Founded in 1984, the Scottish Poetry Library is housed in an impressive contemporary building, one of the unlikely architectural surprises concealed down Edinburgh's closes. Robert Burns, unquestionably Scotland's best-known bard, is well represented on the library's shelves, but so are scores of other poets, writing in Scots, English, Gaelic or perhaps a language of their own invention. The library also has a small selection of books for sale, including works by local poets. Staff are happy to help with recommendations and will even try to help you track down a poem, even if you can only remember a line or two.

The Cowgate & south

At the junction of the Cowgate and Holyrood Road, turn off and head south along the Pleasance. Halfway up is the 16th-century boundary of the Old Town, marked by a remaining corner of the **Flodden Wall**. Turning from here on to Drummond Street provides a neat shortcut to the **Museum of Scotland** and the **Royal Museum** on Chambers Street (*see p99*). Alternatively, turn northwards where the Cowgate and Holyrood Road meet, up shop-packed St Mary's Street towards the Netherbow. This crossroads was at one time an entrance to the Old Town, known as the Cowgate Port.

The Cowgate

The **Cowgate** was originally used by cows and their keepers passing to and from the fields. However, little of its history is tangible today: later developments have obscured its distant past, and the Old Town fire of 2002 managed to spirit away a block of the Cowgate adjacent to South Bridge. Legal and architectural wrangles have delayed rebuilding; there's been much debate in the local press about precisely what should be constructed on the site of the fire, with 2009 currently pinned as the completion date for a complex that should include private housing, an arts centre and a hotel.

Until the middle of the 20th century, the Cowgate was known as the 'Irish quarter', due to the thousands of Irish immigrants who arrived here following the Great Famine in 1846. Many chose to settle in the area because of the presence of **St Patrick's** on South Gray's Close, a Catholic church built in 1771. Its gardens, accessible from South Gray's Close, are a tranquil spot these days.

Nearby, on the corner of Blackfriars Street, is **St Cecilia's Hall**, which houses the Russell Collection of Early Keyboard Instruments. Owned by the University of Edinburgh, the hall also hosts musical performances and recitals (*see p227*). Infirmary Street, opposite, leads up to the Old High School (1777), the Old Surgeon's Hall (1697) and the Victorian premises that once housed the Royal Infirmary, where Joseph Lister discovered the benefits of antiseptic surgery. At the end of Infirmary Street, on Nicolson Street, is **New Surgeon's Hall**, built in 1832.

By the middle of the 19th century, the Cowgate had become one of the most densely populated areas of the city, crammed with impoverished inhabitants. Today it is an ever popular centre for alcoholic hedonism. Come the weekend, the huge **Three Sisters** pub (No.139, 622 6801) takes the lion's share of the street's punters, with the nearby **Subway** nightclub (*see p231*) providing cheap and cheerful competition to similar establishments on Lothian Road. In an attempt to reduce the number of drink-related accidents, the Cowgate is now closed to traffic at night.

Beyond the towering backs of the Sheriff's Court buildings, the Cowgate passes under George IV Bridge. Immediately on the left is the **Magdalen Chapel** (*see below*), dwarfed by surrounding tenements. In the bloody days of the late 17th century the chapel served as a mortuary for the executed Covenanters, whose bodies were to be buried around the corner in **Greyfriars Kirkyard** (*see right*).

Magdalen Chapel

41 Cowgate (220 1450). Bus 2, 23, 27, 41, 42, 45. **Open** *9.30am-4pm Mon-Fri.* **Admission** *free.* **Map** *p78 B2, p330 H8, p336 D4.*

Built between 1541 and 1547 (the steeple was added in 1626), Magdalen Chapel is the headquarters of the Scottish Reformation Society. The chapel held the first congregation of the Church of Scotland in December 1560, which included John Knox. Its walls are lined with 'brods' (receipts for gifts of money or goods donated to the Chapel) from the 16th to the 19th centuries, which wrap round the walls like a frieze. The chapel also contains the only surviving pre-Reformation stained-glass window in Scotland.

The Grassmarket

There has been a market in the **Grassmarket** since at least 1477; a 1977 plaque on a rock here commemorates the 500th anniversary of the date when the area first received its charter from James III. Along **King's Stables Road** at the north-west corner of the Grassmarket, gardens provided the raw material for a vegetable market from the 12th century; the Grassmarket itself held livestock sales. When England's Edward III occupied the castle in the 1330s, King's Stables Road held a medieval tournament ground, but it didn't last long: David II put a stop to it when Scotland regained the castle in the mid 14th century (*see p14*).

Later the Grassmarket developed a darker history as a regular venue for executions; for the gruesome details, *see p16*. These days it's dominated by a row of pubs and restaurants, among them the **White Hart Inn**. Robert Burns reputedly wrote 'Ae Fond Kiss' here; it's also where the protagonist in Iain Banks' novel *Complicity* gets some hints about the whereabouts of a dismembered body. The state-of-the-art **Dance Base** (*see p246*) is a more recent arrival.

At the west end of the row are Granny's Green Steps, which lead up to **Johnston Terrace** and, for the intrepid stroller, a possible walk around the base of **Castle Rock**. If you don't fancy it, head up the West Bow, which quickly turns into steep, bending **Victoria Street**. There's an eclectic range of shops here, selling everything from antique lace and hand-stitched leather bags to henna tattoos. Add some interesting bars and popular live music venue the **Liquid Room** (*see p231*), and it's one of Edinburgh's quirkiest streets.

Greyfriars & Chambers Street

Candlemaker Row, off the Cowgate, leads up to where **Greyfriars Kirk** overlooks George IV Bridge. At the top of Candlemaker Row stands one of Edinburgh's more curious attractions, a small statue of a dog named Greyfriars Bobby. When a man named John Gray was buried in the kirk's graveyard, so the story goes, his loyal Skye terrier Bobby kept constant watch over his grave for 14 years until his own death in 1872. It's not uncommon to see passers-by kiss the doggy statue.

However, Bobby's long vigil is far from the strangest occurrence reputed to have happened at Greyfriars Kirk, which is said to be one of the most haunted burying grounds in Britain (see p98). Sightings of ghosts and ghouls have been recorded at regular intervals down the years, and some night-time visitors have reported receiving scratches and bruises. The 'violence' is often attributed to the ghost of the 17th-century judge and Lord Advocate Sir George Mackenzie. Commonly known as Bluidy Mackenzie, he was the scourge of the Covenanters, many of whom were buried here after being executed. Perhaps it's the undulating ground, the result of centuries of burials, or maybe it's Mackenzie (or another of the kirkyard's incumbents), but even hardened sceptics admit to finding the place spooky.

Greyfriars Kirk and its kirkyard have played a pivotal role in the history of Scotland. The National Covenant was signed before the pulpit in 1638; later the survivors of the Battle of Bothwell Brig (1679) were kept in the south-west corner of the yard in the Covenanters' Prison for five months under desperate living conditions. Not all of them survived their incarceration; the **Martyrs' Monument**, with its chilling inscription, 'Halt passenger, take heed of what you do see, This tomb doth shew for what some men did die', is their memorial, and stands in the north-eastern part of the yard.

Opposite the entrance to Greyfriars, the bold, impressive lines of the **Museum of Scotland** (see p99) mask a warren of winding corridors that open up on to spectacular drops and huge spaces. The museum's roof and its **Tower** restaurant (see p147) boast fantastic views of Arthur's Seat and the castle. Next door, along Chambers Street, is the **Royal Museum** (see p99), designed by Captain Francis Fowke along conventional, Victorian lines and completed in 1888. Although they are separate institutions, the two museums are linked inside. Across from the imposing steps leading into the Royal Museum is the Matthew Architecture Gallery (closed to the public).

Old College, bordered on its northern edge by Chambers Street, is the oldest of the city's university buildings. Architect Robert Adam began work on the building in 1789, only to be interrupted by the Napoleonic Wars. William Playfair then finished it, and Rowand Anderson added the landmark dome in 1883. Entrance to the main courtyard is either through the small entrance of the **Talbot Rice Gallery**, up West College Street (see p99), or through the monumental arch on Nicolson Street.

Greyfriars Bobby. See p96.

Certain areas of Old College are open to the public. Most notable are the **Playfair Library**, with its superb classical interior (the University of Edinburgh runs the odd guided tour in the Easter and summer holidays; available by special arrangement) and the old Upper Museum, now part of the Talbot Rice Gallery. The museum features a table from Napoleon's lodgings on St Helena, complete with a cigar burn that was allegedly made by the little Corsican. For details of how to join the tours, contact the University of Edinburgh Centre on Nicolson Street (No.7, 650 2252).

Two of Edinburgh University's student unions are situated nearby, on either side of Bristo Square. **Teviot Row House** is the grander of the two – it's the oldest purpose-built student union in the world – while **Potterrow** is easily identifiable by its domed roof. The latter hasn't aged well in its short life, but is nonetheless being considered for listed status. Next to Teviot Row House is the **Reid Concert Hall** (see p228), which hosts classical concerts and houses the Edinburgh University Collection of Historic Musical Instruments.

George Heriot's School, off Lauriston Place, was used in its early days as a military hospital for Cromwell's troops. School prefects give historical tours of this fine 17th-century building, named for the goldsmith and jeweller to James VI of Scotland (James I of England).

Greyfriars Kirk

2 Greyfriars Place, Candlemaker Row (226 5429/www.greyfriarskirk.com). Bus 2, 23, 27, 41, 42, 45. **Open** *Apr-Oct* 10.30am-4.30pm Mon-Fri; 10.30am-2.30pm Sat. *Nov-Mar* 1.30-3.30pm Thur or by appointment. **Admission** free. **Map** p330 H8.

Formerly the site of a Franciscan friary, Greyfriars dates back to 1620. The west end of the church was reduced to ruins in 1718, however, after the local council's nearby gunpowder store exploded; 127 years later, much of the kirk was then gutted by a fire. After recent renovations, both the exterior and the interior are impressive once more, with some sympathetic, traditional harling on the outer walls and elegantly sparse spaces within.

Worshippers from the Highland Tolbooth St John's (now the Hub; see p83) joined the Greyfriars congregation in 1979. Known as the Highland Kirk, St John's held services in Gaelic; alongside its regular services in English, Greyfriars now does the same each Sunday. The small visitors' exhibition on the church's 400-year history contains a display about the National Covenant, but most people go to see the portrait of Greyfriars Bobby, painted by John MacLeod in 1887. Check online for details of the regular musical recitals held here.

Things that go bump in the night

Auld Reekie Tours

557 4700/www.auldreekietours.co.uk. **Tours** Ultimate Ghost & Torture hourly, 7-10pm daily. Underground City hourly, 12.30-3.30pm daily. **Meeting point** Tron Kirk, High Street, Old Town. **Tickets** Ultimate Ghost & Torture £6; £5 concessions. Underground City £5. **Credit** AmEx, MC, V.

Sacrificing some factual accuracy for engaging pantomime, tour guides lead you through the streets of Edinburgh to a section of the Underground Vaults, where you'll allegedly find a working pagan temple. The same company runs the Medieval Torture Exhibition (45 Niddry Street, Old Town, 10am-7pm daily, £2).

City of the Dead Tours

225 9044/www.blackhart.uk.com. **Tours** Nov-Easter 7.30pm, 8.30pm daily. Easter-Oct 8.30pm, 9.15pm, 10pm daily. **Meeting point** Mercat Cross, High Kirk of St Giles, High Street, Old Town. **Tickets** £8.50; £6.50 concessions. **No credit cards**.

The City of the Dead tours delve into Edinburgh's history, but the focus is all on the trip to Greyfriars' graveyard. Many a visitor, petrified after the guide's careful build-up, faints upon entering the secluded section of the cemetery where the MacKenzie poltergeist reportedly lingers.

Mercat Walking Tours

557 6464/www.mercattours.com. **Tours** Ghosthunter Trail Apr-Sept 9.30pm, 10.30pm daily. Oct-Mar 9.30pm daily. Ghosts & Ghouls Apr-Sept 7pm, 8pm, 9pm daily. Oct-Mar 7pm, 8pm daily. Haunted Underground Experience Apr-Sept 5pm, 6pm daily. Oct-Mar 6pm Mon-Thur, Sun; 5pm, 6pm Fri, Sat. Secrets of the Royal Mile 2.30pm daily. The Vaults May-Sept noon, 2pm, 3pm, 4pm daily. Oct-Mar 2pm, 4pm daily. **Meeting point** Mercat Cross, High Kirk of St Giles, High Street, Old Town. **Tickets** Ghosthunter Trail £7; £6.50 concessions. Ghosts & Ghouls, Secrets of the Royal Mile £7; £3.50-£6.50 concessions. Haunted Underground Experience, The Vaults £6; £2.50-£5.50 concessions. **Credit** AmEx, MC, V.

The longest established and most professional of all the companies prides itself on historical accuracy. Don't expect a lecture, though: the black-cloaked guides feed the customers a grisly portrait of Old Edinburgh. All Mercat's walks pass through the extensive Underground Vaults. The earlier tours are less sinister than those from 9.30pm onwards.

Real Mary King's Close

0870 243 0160/www.realmarykings close.com. **Tours** Apr-Oct every 20mins, 10am-9pm daily. Nov-Mar every 20mins, 10am-4pm Mon-Fri, Sun; every 20mins, 10am-9pm Sat. **Meeting point** Mary King's Close, via Warriston Close. **Admission** £8; £6-£7 concessions. **Credit** MC, V.

The remains of a street beneath the City Chambers have been turned into an historical attraction, overseen by a costumed guide. It's a fascinating look at life in Edinburgh over the centuries, but with only the barest whisper of supernatural possibilities: the focus here is on the historical rather than the paranormal. More supernaturally focused tours are usually scheduled to run around Hallowe'en; call for details.

Witchery Tours

225 6745/www.witcherytours.com. **Tours** Ghost & Gore May-Aug 7pm, 7.30pm daily. Murder & Mystery 9pm, 9.30pm daily. **Meeting point** outside Witchery restaurant, Castlehill, Old Town. **Tickets** £7.50; £5 concessions. **Credit** AmEx, MC, V.

Moving from the castle through the Cowgate, a character guide entertains in agreeably light-hearted fashion, with a costumed mad monk sidekick and other characters – including Burke and Hare the body snatchers – frequently popping up to startle the unwary tourist. It's an amusing evening out, though it's not the scariest of the tours on offer.

Museum of Scotland

Chambers Street (247 4422 /www.nms.ac.uk).
Bus 2, 23, 27, 41, 42, 45. **Open** 10am-5pm daily.
Admission free. **Credit** *Shop* MC, V. **Map** p330 H8.
Designed by architects Benson and Forsyth, the museum was judged to be the Scottish Building of the Year after its opening in 1998. The huge, airy complex is full of stairways and windows that lead to or look out on other levels, reminiscent of the city's architecture of centuries gone by. Thousands of artefacts are on display, from small everyday objects to a steam locomotive. Grim relics of the darker side of Edinburgh's past are also on show, among them the Maiden of Edinburgh guillotine and an iron gaud used to restrain prisoners on the old Tolbooth. If you enter via the (unaffiliated) Royal Museum, be sure to exit by the Museum of Scotland: the ramped entry has a lovely frieze by the late Ian Hamilton Finlay.

Royal Museum

Chambers Street (247 4422 /www.nms.ac.uk). Bus 2,
23, 27, 41, 42, 45. **Open** 10am-5pm daily.
Admission free. **Credit** *Shop* MC, V. **Map** p330 H8.
The Royal Museum is in the throes of a Herculean reinvention (due to finish in 2011), but the beautifully airy main hall, with its wrought-iron 'birdcage' construction, is sure to remain. Although many more exhibits will be on show by the time the work is complete, there are still thousands to enjoy in the meantime. The Millennium Clock certainly deserves more than a cursory glance: ask at the information desk for its display times before you start your visit. It's a phantasmagorical glory; although it may be relentlessly gruesome, kids seem to love it.

There are currently three floors of displays, and while some are rather dated – the stuffed tigers look particularly sad – they have a peculiar charm. The Connect Room is more up-to-date, housing a rocket, Dolly the sheep, interactive robots and energy transfer machines. It gets very busy, so be prepared to queue. There's a café in the main hall (*see p141*) and another to the back of the building, a pretty well-stocked shop catering to a range of budgets, facilities for disabled visitors, and parenting rooms.

Talbot Rice Gallery

Old College, South Bridge (650 2211/www. trg.ed.ac.
uk). Nicolson Street–North Bridge buses. **Open**
10am-5pm Tue-Sat. **Admission** free. **Map** p331 J8.
Opened in 1975 and situated off William Playfair's stately, grand Old Quad in Old College, the Talbot Rice Gallery is named after the Watson Gordon Professor of Fine Art, David Talbot Rice, famed for his writings on Islamic art. There are three main exhibition spaces: the White Gallery, which stages five temporary exhibitions per year on mid-career artists and emergent talents; the Georgian Gallery, a neo-classical room designed by Playfair that houses a permanent exhibition of pieces from the university's Torrie Collection of Dutch and Italian Old Masters; and the round room, home to small-scale exhibitions and experimental artwork.

Something old, something new at the **Museum of Scotland**.

The New Town

Well, we *say* new...

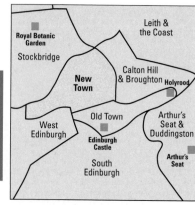

Although estate agents and property developers may tell you otherwise, Edinburgh's New Town has firm boundaries: the area comprises the regimented grid of streets and gardens that runs from **Princes Street** down to **Cumberland Street**. The result of two huge successive construction projects, it represents 18th-century Britain's biggest and best piece of town planning, and still holds some of the finest Georgian architecture in the country.

As the Old Town became more and more congested, the city fathers realised that they needed to take steps to provide alternative housing for the city's residents. However, this wasn't social housing as we understand the term today: the scheme was motivated not by concern for the general populace's health and welfare, but to allow the city's monied classes a means of escape from the tumbling tenements and questionable hygiene in what then constituted the city centre.

More salubrious districts had already been erected to the south of the Old Town's confines, most notably Brown Square in 1763 and George Square three years later, but more were needed. A competition was announced in April 1766, inviting architects to submit plans for an area north of the castle that was newly accessible following the draining of the Nor Loch and the ongoing construction of North Bridge. The contest was won by a then-unknown 22-year-old architect named James Craig, whose genteel, regimented vision remains in place today.

While the warren-like Old Town was Scottish through and through, from the architecture to the very street names, the New Town's identity centred around wider British influences. Although his designs were altered prior to construction, Craig's original plans echoed the lines of the Union Flag. Even the area's street names honoured the Hanoverian rulers (George Street, King Street), their families (Princes Street, Charlotte Square) and the Act of Union of 1707 (Rose Street and Thistle Street). Despite the obvious advantages of New Town life, the new *quartier* was initially shunned by Edinburghers, who considered it too exposed to the high winds blowing in from the Firth of Forth. But they soon saw the error of their ways, and abandoned the chaotic jumble of the Old Town for its refined streets and mansions.

The neighbourhood is dotted with impressive boutiques and intimate cafés (*see pp148-153*), as well as the usual gamut of high-street shopping emporia. However, it's still chiefly a residential area, especially in its northern extremities. Now, as then, the New Town is home to some of Edinburgh's richest residents, from arriviste traders and trust-fund students to distinguished members of the Scottish aristocracy. Indeed, those who believe Scotland is run by a small, conspiratorial elite look towards these streets for their evidence. The richest pitch in for imposing townhouses (around £1 million, on average), which often come with keys to the fabulous but exclusive communal gardens; those with lesser budgets inhabit the tenement blocks that dot the area.

However, the abundance of influential residents haven't had it all their own way. Locals have been locked in a long-running but prosaic battle over whether they should be forced to suffer the indignity of having wheelie-bins on their streets. While the rest of the city succumbed to the inevitable practicality and efficiency of communal waste disposal, New Town residents have fought fiercely for their right to deposit rubbish in bin bags by the side of the road, even enlisting UNESCO's help. Certain streets have thus far managed to evade the threat of giant communal bins, while others have been allotted smaller green wheelie bins, triggering fresh rows over collections and bin storage space issues. It looks like this one could run and run...

Princes Street

Although **Princes Street** represented the first phase of New Town construction, it's suffered more than any other thoroughfare here in the two-plus centuries since it was built. Today it's an unsympathetic jumble of Edwardian aesthetic delights, functional 1970s blocks and modern glass-fronted edifices, all of which 'seemed a good idea at the time'. But while it's easy to see why Scottish broadcaster Moray MacLaren pronounced it 'one of the most chaotically tasteless streets in the UK', its mix of high-street chain stores, cheap homewares retailers and insipid souvenir shops continues to attract sizeable crowds.

In the last few years, steps have been taken to improve the appearance of Princes Street, and some of its least appealing buildings have been and will be demolished. However, since the street is part of a World Heritage Site, any changes to the landscape are fraught with complications. The concept of a galleried mall gets mooted once every few years, but it seems unlikely to make any leeway until the existing buildings are further improved.

Although Edinburgh's citizens rejected the idea of congestion charging, a range of traffic control measures are in place in and around Princes Street, including one-way systems and areas where access is restricted to buses, taxis and emergency vehicles. The return of trams is also on the cards, hopefully by 2010, although the scheme has proven highly contentious.

The verdant **Princes Street Gardens** act as a buffer between the New Town and Old Town; protected by an Act of Parliament since 1816, they're the one part of the area that most people agree shouldn't be changed. Indeed, the first thing that strikes most visitors about Princes Street is how lopsided it appears, with solid rows of buildings on one side and green expanses on the other. Numerous statues are dotted around the gardens, and the far western end is home to two churches: the Episcopalian **St John's Church** (*see p102*) and, at the foot of Edinburgh Castle, the Presbyterian **St Cuthbert's Kirk** (*see below*). In summer, the gardens are packed with sunbathers listening to the music emanating from the **Ross Bandstand**; During winter, a Christmas market is set up behind the Scott Monument, and an ice-rink is installed (*see p209*).

St Cuthbert's Kirk

5 Lothian Road (229 1142/www.st-cuthberts.net). Princes Street buses. **Open** *Apr-Sept* 10am-4pm Mon-Sat. Closed Oct-mid Mar. **Admission** free. **Map** p330 E7, p336 A2.

Along with Duddingston Kirk and Kirkliston's parish church, St Cuthbert's has claim to being one of the oldest places of worship in the city. However, although its steeple dates back to 1789, the church's current incarnation was built as recently as 1894. Its kirkyard is the resting place of some notable names: artist Alexander Nasmyth, writer Thomas de Quincey, mathematician John Napier and the Reverend David Williamson, the church's covenanting, seven-times-married minister celebrated in song

The well-trodden path of **Princes Street**.

as 'Dainty Davie'. When Williamson was buried here in 1706, no stone was erected by his widow, presumably because she would have had to list on it the names of her six predecessors.

St John's Episcopal Church

3 Lothian Road (229 7565/www.stjohns-edinburgh. org.uk). Princes Street buses. **Open** 8am-4pm Mon-Fri; 8am-noon Sat. **Admission** free. **Map** p330 E7, p336 A2.

Designed in the perpendicular Gothic style by the Scottish architect William Burn, the man behind the Melville Monument in St Andrew's Square and the 19th-century additions to Lauriston Castle, St John's Episcopal Church began in 1816, just before the Act of Parliament that outlawed any further building on Princes Street Gardens; as such, the church's view of Edinburgh Castle is legally protected. The collection of stained glass is said to be the finest in Scotland, although the church's relentless 19th-century worthiness and sheer Victorian vulgarity can be overwhelming. Spare a moment to examine the intricate plaster ceiling vault. At the north-eastern end of the church the mural area often features thought-provoking, politicised images. The café below (*see p163*) is a pleasing oasis from the bustle outside.

East end of Princes Street

Opponents of the current redevelopment of Princes Street need look no further than the **St James Centre** to see what can happen if you leave town planning to fashionable architects. What may have seemed a good idea in 1964 now looks like a truly ghastly one. Thankfully, it's the worst offender for a while; heading west, Princes Street gets a lot prettier.

In front of the **General Register House** (*see right*), one of numerous buildings that are currently undergoing refurbishment, stands James Gowans' statue of the **Duke of Wellington** on his horse Copenhagen. It's dramatic stuff: most equestrian statues have four feet firmly on the ground, but Wellington's horse here rears up on its hind legs as his master points symbolically towards Waterloo Place. West Register Street leads past New Register House (housing the **General Register Office**; *see right*) through to St Andrew Square and George Street, passing the **Café Royal** en route (*see p173*). The interior of this 19th-century building is listed, its spectacular central bar offset by a succession of ceramic murals depicting famous inventors such as Michael Faraday and James Watt.

Across the road is the posh **Balmoral Hotel** (*see p57*). Its clock, facing the Old Town, famously runs three minutes fast in order to hurry passengers to the adjacent Waverley Station. Nearby is **Jenners** (*see p186*), the city's grande dame of retail therapy. Founded in 1838

by two Leith drapers, the shop was rebuilt in 1893 after a fire. An estimated 25,000 people gathered for the unveiling of its elaborately carved, statue-encrusted frontage, inspired by the façade of Oxford's Bodleian Library.

This stretch of Princes Street best exemplifies the city's 19th-century extravagance. And perhaps no one structure exemplifies it better than George Meikle Kemp's colossal **Scott Monument**, which points 200 feet (61 metres) into the Edinburgh clouds. It was originally meant to have been sited in residential Charlotte Square, but instead dominates the skyline on the corner of Waverley Bridge (named for Scott's *Waverley* novels) and rather overshadows the statue of Lanarkshire-born explorer David Livingstone. After a failed expedition to discover the source of the Nile, an emaciated Livingstone was found by journalist Henry Morton Stanley, who famously introduced himself with the words, 'Dr Livingstone, I presume'. Close by are statues of Adam Black, twice Lord Provost of Edinburgh and founder of the *Edinburgh Review*, and John Wilson, a professor of moral philosophy at the University of Edinburgh.

General Register House

2 Princes Street (535 1314/www.nas.gov.uk). Princes Street buses. **Open** 9am-4.30pm Mon-Fri. **Admission** free with reader's ticket. **Map** p326/p330 H6, p336 F2.

Designed by Robert Adam and planned while North Bridge was still being built, General Register House first opened in 1789, despite being only half complete. Under architect Robert Reid's supervision, it was finally completed in the 1820s; the Corinthian pillars, beautifully balanced front elevation and restrained friezework are magnificent. Home to the National Archives of Scotland, it's the oldest purpose-built archive repository still in use in Europe, holding public records of government, churches, the law and businesses. Archival access for historical research purposes is free. A series of construction projects is currently under way; until well into 2007 general access to the building is likely to be via side entrances.

General Register Office

New Register House, 3 West Register Street (334 0380/www.gro-scotland.gov.uk). Princes Street buses. **Open** 9.30am-4.30pm Mon-Fri. **Admission** £17 day pass; £10 part-day pass (after 1pm); £65 week pass. **Credit** MC, V. **Map** p326/p330 H6, p336 F1.

Scotland's purpose-built General Register Office, completed in 1863, contains records of all births, marriages and deaths in the country since 1855, census records up to 1901, and 3,500 old parish registers from between 1553 and 1854. Like the old General Post Office building across the road, it was the work of Robert Mathieson, who designed it to be in harmony with the General Register House next door. A pass is required to view the records; booking ahead is advisable.

Scott Monument

East Princes Street Gardens (529 4068/www.cac.org.uk). Princes Street buses. **Open** *Apr-Sept* 9am-6pm Mon-Sat; 10am-6pm Sun. *Oct-Mar* 9am-3pm Mon-Sat; 10am-3pm Sun. **Admission** £3. **No credit cards. Map** p326/p330 G6, p336 E2.

Travellers emerging from Edinburgh's Waverley Station expecting to see austere classical architecture will gawp in disbelief at the Victorian Gothic ostentation of the Scott Monument. Designed by the self-taught architect George Meikle Kemp, the monument houses a vast white marble statue of Sir Walter Scott (by Edinburgh sculptor John Steell) as well as 64 statuettes, mostly of Scott's characters but with a few notable figures from Scottish history thrown in for good measure. It was completed in 1846, 14 years after Scott's death, using funds raised from public donations, which shows how dearly Edinburghers held the famous author. The views from the top are quite superb, but the final flight of steps up to the pinnacle are a tight squeeze and can be rather claustrophobic.

The Mound

On the west side of the junction between the Mound and Princes Street stands a handsome 1903 statue of wigmaker-turned-poet Allan Ramsay. However, the area is dominated by the twin Doric temples of the **Royal Scottish Academy** (*see p104*) and the **National Gallery of Scotland** (*see right*), two 19th-century buildings designed by prolific architect William Playfair. The plainer and more refined National Gallery was built 20 years after the rather more florid Academy, topped by sphinxes and an incongruous statue of the young Queen Victoria. Completed by John Steell in 1844, the statue was originally displayed at street level, but it's said Victoria, displeased by her chubby appearance, demanded that it was elevated to a rooftop location in order that she should avoid close scrutiny by her subjects.

Extensive work has taken place in and around these galleries over the last few years. Both may appear stolidly traditional from the outside, but refurbishments mean that the gallery space within is state of the art, with temperature and humidity controls, air conditioning and specialised lighting. While the two buildings seem to stand in splendid isolation of each other, they're now connected by the **Weston Link**, an adventurous complex accessed from Princes Street Gardens. The project contains an IT gallery, an education centre (comprising a 200-seat lecture theatre and a cinema), a restaurant, a café and a shop.

On a lower-tech note, Edinburgh's national galleries are linked by a free bus service that picks up passengers at half-hour intervals from outside the National Gallery on the Mound and goes to the **National Portrait Gallery** (*see p105*), the **Dean Gallery** (*see p112*) and the **National Gallery of Modern Art** (*see p113*).

National Gallery of Scotland

The Mound (624 6200/www.nationalgalleries.org). Princes Street buses. **Open** 10am-5pm Mon-Wed, Fri-Sun; 10am-7pm Thur. **Admission** free; £1-£5 for special exhibitions. **Credit** *Shop* MC, V. **Map** p330 G7, p336 D3.

Edinburgh has a wealth of institutions serving the visual arts, but perhaps none is as grand as the National Gallery. Built by William Playfair in 1848, it opened 11 years later as the home to both the Royal Scottish Academy and the National Gallery, before becoming sole home to the latter in 1910.

The gallery boasts excellent collections of paintings and sculptures, but has been criticised for the way it displays them. Some have objected to the way it over-crowds its walls with works, while others have made pointed remarks about the gallery's apparent desire to try and cater for every artistic taste. However, the sheer wealth of great works is undeniable, from Byzantine-like Madonnas through the Northern Renaissance and High Renaissance (highlights include Raphael's *Bridgewater Madonna* and a handful of pieces by Titian) and right on to the early 20th century. Impressionist and post-Impressionist work includes Monet's *Haystack*, Gauguin's *Vision after the Sermon* and Cézanne's *Montagne Sainte-Victoire*. In January, the gallery displays the Turner watercolours that were bequeathed to it in 1900 by Henry Vaughan.

Scott Monument.

Sightseeing

As you might expect, one particular forte is the permanent collection of Scottish art, encompassing works by artists such as Ramsay, Wilkie and McTaggart. Among the favourites is Raeburn's *The Reverend Walker Skating on Duddingston Loch* (aka the 'Skating Minister'), despite the fact that the background landscape looks distinctly unlike any view possible at Duddingston. The management of the gallery's shop are clearly unconcerned by such trifling details, and sell the work in print, jigsaw, mug and even fridge-magnet form. Check online for details of the regular temporary exhibitions and related special events.

Royal Scottish Academy

The Mound (225 6671/www.royalscottish academy. org). Princes Street buses. **Open** 10am-5pm Mon-Wed, Sat, Sun; 10am-7pm Thur. **Admission** free; £2-£4 for special exhibitions. **Credit** MC, V. **Map** p326/p330 G6, p336 D2.

This grand structure on the Mound was completed in 1826 to the designs of William Playfair, but its exterior dates from eight years later, after Playfair was asked to remodel his work. The building's 16 columns give it a Grecian air that finds echoes in numerous other Playfair buildings around the city. It was originally built for the Royal Institution for the Encouragement of Fine Arts in Scotland, and dramatically renovated in the 1910s to accommodate the RSA. The beginning of the 21st century saw another overhaul of the building, including the addition of cruciform-shaped lower-level galleries.

The building is effectively a large-scale temporary exhibition space, supplementing big-ticket blockbusters on the likes of Monet and Titian with shows devoted to less well-known artists both ancient and modern. A number of annual events focus on Scottish art; chief among them is the RSA Annual Exhibition, an open show held each spring, though it's also worth looking for the Royal Scottish Society of Painters in Watercolour's semi-open exhibition, which runs for a month each summer. Special events sometimes accompany the shows; call for details.

St Andrew Square

Named after Scotland's patron saint, St Andrew Square sits at the eastern end of George Street, a relatively tranquil grassy haven adding punctuation to one of the city's more upmarket thoroughfares. For years the square was the heart of Edinburgh's financial industries, until regeneration programmes encouraged key institutions to expand into glass and brick new-builds in the western environs of the city. Right in the centre of the square stands the **Melville Monument**, a 135-foot (41-metre) Doric column – inspired by the Trajan Column in Rome – topped by a statue of Henry Dundas, first Earl of Melville, the right-hand man of prime minister William Pitt and an infamous 18th-century political wheeler-dealer.

The **Royal Bank of Scotland** has long since moved its headquarters out to Gogarburn, but its registered office remains a former mansion on the square. Set behind a private lawn, an extremely rare sight in the New Town, the Palladian-style edifice was built in 1772 for Sir Laurence Dundas on a site that, in James Craig's plan for the New Town, was reserved for St Andrew's Church. It's a mark of Sir Laurence's political muscle that he was able to overrule the council's planning orders. The building is still a working branch of the bank; the sumptuously decorated iron dome of the Telling Room (added by J Dick Peddie in 1857) is open during banking hours. Next door sits another working institution with a fine

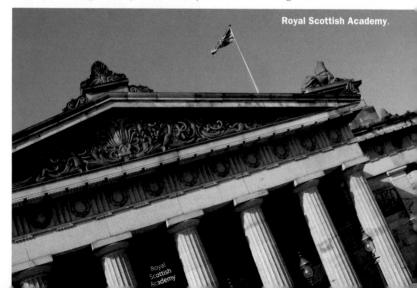
Royal Scottish Academy.

banking hall: **Bank of Scotland**, housed in an outlandishly loud 1851 pseudo-palazzo complete with rooftop statues.

The north-east corner of the square has been the subject of a multi-million-pound commercial redevelopment programme in recent years. First to be completed was Edinburgh's branch of **Harvey Nichols** (*see p186*), which provided a shot in the arm for the town's shopping scene when it opened in 2002. The town's new bus station opened next, albeit without attracting the same levels of media coverage as its neighbour. Between them sits **Multrees Walk**, a tidy pedestrianised road lined with smart designer boutiques (*see p185*); it's Edinburgh's own little Bond Street.

The **Scottish National Portrait Gallery** (*see below*) sits just north of the square, at the eastern end of Queen Street. Designed by Sir Robert Rowand Anderson with financial help from *Scotsman* owner JR Findlay and completed in the late 19th century, it's a confident building, its neo-Gothic style – dotted with pinnacles and sculptures of intellectual heroes from down the ages – representing a definite departure from the Georgian neo-classical constraint of much of the New Town. Its red sandstone façade is best seen in the late evening summer sun, but the huge foyer, decorated with an astrological ceiling and a processional frieze that recounts Scotland's history, is well worth a look at any time of day.

Scottish National Portrait Gallery

1 Queen Street (624 6200/www.nationalgalleries.org). Princes Street buses. **Open** 10am-5pm Mon-Sat; noon-5pm Sun. **Admission** free; £1-£5 for special exhibitions. **Credit** MC, V. **Map** p326 G5.
Sir Richard Rowand Anderson's impressive building originally housed the National Museum of Antiquities, but now contains busts and portraits of Scottish heroes, heroines and notable historical figures from the 16th century through to the present day. The foyer is decorated with stunning murals depicting key moments in Scottish history; further in, paintings of kings and queens – Mary, Queen of Scots and Bonnie Prince Charlie among them – offer a rich visual guide to the rise and fall of the Scottish monarchy. However, cultural figures are also represented throughout the collection, among them poet Robert Burns, philosopher David Hume, football manager Sir Alex Ferguson, actor Sir Sean Connery, and author Irvine Welsh. Temporary exhibitions provide added entertainment.

George Street

Named in honour of King George III, **George Street** was conceived as the New Town's main thoroughfare. It quickly became Edinburgh's financial district, but many of the banking institutions once resident here have been transformed to meet more modern needs. It's now a major shopping drag with more than its fair share of upmarket style bars, but the ambience is decidedly different from that of nearby Princes Street: the pace is more leisurely and the price tags are higher. One constant throughout its history has been the excellent views afforded from here of the steep descent down into Stockbridge and, on clear days, the hills of Fife, particularly down Dundas Street.

Through all the changes, the street has retained its dignity remarkably well, and remains the lynchpin in Edinburgh's claim to truly continental style. National fashion chains – and the ubiquitous Starbucks – have crept in behind the street's toned-down façades, but many of the city's traditional names remain; among them are **Gray's** (No.89, 225 7381), which has offered all kinds of household wares from this location for around a century, and the jewellers **Hamilton & Inches** (*see p195*). Other buildings lend a suitably stylish austerity to an array of new restaurants, bars and hotels.

The **Assembly Rooms**, built by public subscription, have been a feature of the street since 1787. The rooms became a favoured haunt of Edinburgh's Regency partying set: it was here, in 1827, that George Street resident Sir Walter Scott revealed that he was the author of the *Waverley* novels. Though it briefly served as a labour exchange and recruiting centre during World War I, it's remained a popular venue for concerts, plays and performances of all kinds, and is busy more or less all the time during August.

This stretch of George Street was once a popular quarter for Edinburgh's literary types. The poet Shelley and his first wife Harriet Westbrook honeymooned at 84 George Street, and Scott lived around the corner at 39 North Castle Street. No.45 George Street was the headquarters of the influential literary journal, *Blackwood's Magazine*, which counted Henry James and Oscar Wilde among its contributors.

St Andrew's & St George's Church, built in 1787, was originally intended for a plot of land on St Andrew Square. However, the site was appropriated by the entrepreneur and politician Sir Lawrence Dundas, and the New Town's first church was instead built on George Street. It was later the site of what became known as 'the Disruption' of the Church of Scotland: in 1843, 472 ministers marched from here to the Tanfield Hall at Canonmills and established the Free Church of Scotland. Opposite the church is the **Dome** bar and restaurant (*see p175*). Like many buildings on George Street, it was once a bank, and much of its interior decoration has been retained. Pop in for a coffee, if only to see its richly decorated, domed interior.

Charlotte Square

Designed by Kirkcaldy-born architect Robert Adam in 1791 (the year before his death), **Charlotte Square** is one of the most pleasant spaces to be found in the city centre. Initially named St George's Square, it was planned by New Town architect James Craig to mirror St Andrew Square to the east. But when George III's daughter Charlotte was born, it was renamed in her honour, helping to clear up confusion with the other George Square in the south of the city. Adam designed the palatial frontages, discreetly ornamented with sphinxes and pediments, but each house was then built separately by individual plot owners, creating an effect of harmony in diversity. Numerous illustrious types have lived here down the years; among them was Alexander Graham Bell, the inventor of the telephone, who was born at 16 South Charlotte Street in 1847.

The best preserved façades are on the north side of the square, an excellent example of Adam's famous 'palace-front' design. At No.7 is the **Georgian House** (*see right*), which offers visitors the chance to see how the interior of a domestic house might have looked when the square was built. Next door's **Bute House** is the official residence of Scotland's First Minister; as a result, the square can be awash with lobbyists and parliamentary hangers-on.

Two other buildings on the square merit particular mention. On the west side is **West Register Office** (535 1314; free entry), a stuffy edifice that contains the National Archive's collection of maps. And to the south is the head office of the **National Trust for Scotland** (*see right*), which owns and operates the aforementioned Georgian House as a visitor attraction. A monument to Prince Albert, husband of Queen Victoria, sits in the central grassy area overlooked by West Register House, a grandly domed and porticoed affair originally built as St George's Church. Each summer, this area plays host to the tented village of the **Edinburgh International Book Festival** (*see p46*).

Tucked away from the grander streets, **Young Street** was traditionally home to the New Town's less financially blessed residents. In latter years it's become a favoured haunt of one Inspector John Rebus, who drinks at the **Oxford Bar** (*see p177*) in Ian Rankin's best-selling detective novels. To the north of Young Street, and parallel to George Street, lie **Queen Street** and the **Queen Street Gardens**. Like many of the green spaces that punctuate the New Town, they were created as retreats for the residents of the grand squares and terraces to enjoy, and are still open only to residents.

Further along Queen Street, at No.8, is a townhouse built by Robert Adam; at No.9 stands Thomas Hamilton's neo-classical Royal College of Physicians.

Georgian House

7 Charlotte Square (226 3318/www.nts.org.uk). Princes Street buses. **Open** *Mar & Nov* 11am-3pm daily. *Apr-Jun, Sept, Oct* 10am-5pm daily. *July & Aug* 10am-7pm daily (last admission 30 mins before closing). Closed Dec-Feb. **Admission** £5; £4 concessions; £10-£14 family. **Credit** *Shop* MC, V. **Map** p325 D6, p336 A1.

When John Lamont, the 18th Chief of Clan Lamont, bought this house in 1796, it cost him the princely sum of £1,600 (around £200,000 in today's money). It's open to visitors these days and run by the National Trust for Scotland, its excellent reconstructions providing a window into how the upper classes lived during the 18th century. The rooms are packed with period furnishings and detail, right down to sugar cones, locked tea caddies, chamber pots and newspapers. The basement contains an informative video presentation; well-informed guides in each room are happy to answer questions.

National Trust for Scotland

26-31 Charlotte Square (243 9300/restaurant reservations 243 9339/www.nts.org.uk). Princes Street buses. **Open** *Gallery* 11am-3pm Mon-Fri. *Shop/coffeehouse/restaurant* 9.30am-5.30pm Mon-Sat. **Admission** free. **Credit** *Shop* MC, V. **Map** p326 E7, p336 A1.

The National Trust for Scotland has spent some £13.6 million restoring these four townhouses to their original state, and making them suitable for modern offices. The public rooms, which are entered at No.28, allow visitors to see many of the original features, including ornate plasterwork and wallpaper. The galleries upstairs give the NTS the opportunity to show off some of its art collection, including some fine pieces by Scottish Colourists. Pleasantly eclectic, other notable gallery inclusions are two cases of relief portraits and a fantastic Achille Castiglioni-designed music system. There's a pleasant café on the ground floor, with an outdoor courtyard for sunny days.

Dundas Street

One of six developments built in the early 19th century, as landowners cashed in on the city's need for upmarket dwellings, **Dundas Street** is the backbone of what was known as 'the Second New Town'. Scottish property laws allowed landowners to stipulate architectural style, so the New Town's cohesive classical formality is played out with little interruption.

Resolutely residential and exclusive, these new areas were designed to deter outsiders or Old Town riff-raff. Churches aside, there were originally no public buildings, squares or markets. Shops and restaurants have opened

In memoriam

As may be apparent by now, Edinburgh loves, revels in and depends upon its history. It follows, then, that the city contains an almost innumerable array of statues paying tribute to those residents who helped shape the city. The tallest is the **Scott Monument** (*see p103*); the most imposing may be the statue of **John Knox** outside the High Kirk of St Giles (*pictured*; *see p88*); and the best known is the tribute to **Greyfriars Bobby** (*see p96*) on the George IV Bridge. But there are myriad others throughout the town: some are grand and some are unassuming, but all have a measure of local resonance.

It should come as little surprise that royalty has been regularly honoured across the city. Perhaps most notable among them is James Smith's statue of **Charles II** in Parliament Square; erected in 1685, it's believed to be the oldest statue in the city. Elsewhere, James Hill's 1755 statue of **George II** stands in Lauriston Place, while John Rhind sculpted the statues of **Queen Victoria** (1907), at the northern end of Leith Walk, and **Edward VII**, unveiled in Victoria Park six years later. And then there's the Scott Monument, which finds room for tributes to **Charles I** (John Hutchison, 1882), **James VI** (DW Stevenson, 1874) and **Robert the Bruce** (George Lawson, 1874) among a 64-strong cast of other historic notables and characters of Scott's invention.

Sir Walter Scott isn't the only literary figure to have been memorialised in and around Edinburgh. An SNP campaign to replace the statue of the **Duke of Wellington** outside General Register House (*see p102*) with one of **Robert Burns** came to naught, but the poet is honoured with a rather pompous bronze at the corner of Constitution and Bernard Streets in Leith. Created by Ratho-born sculptor DW Stevenson, it was unveiled in 1898. At Picardy Place stands Gerald Laing's bronze of **Sherlock Holmes**

(1989), erected by the Conan Doyle Society near the author's birthplace. The pipe bears the words 'Ceci n'est pas une pipe' ('This is not a pipe'), in homage to the painting of the same name by surrealist René Magritte.

Another literary figure, publisher **Adam Black**, was memorialised in 1877 with a Hutchison statue in Princes Street Gardens. He has plenty of company: the green expanse also contains tributes to poet **Allan Ramsay** (John Steell, 1864), **Dr David Livingstone** (Amelia Hill, 1876), anaesthetist **James Young Simpson** (William Brodie, 1877) and minister **Thomas Guthrie** (FW Pomeroy, 1910).

Many local notables honoured by having streets or even institutions named after them are also recollected with statues in the city. Ukrainian sculptor Valentin Znoba's portrayal of mathematician **John Napier** (died 1617) surveys the Craighouse Road campus of Napier University. A rendering by John Steell of **Robert, Viscount Melville**, former First Lord of the Admiralty, stands tall in – where else? – Melville Crescent. And the two men who lend their names to Heriot-Watt University are commemorated in a pair of 19th-century sculptures by Peter Slater: goldsmith **George Heriot** perches on the Scott Monument, while industrial pioneer **James Watt** keeps guard at the Edinburgh Conference Centre.

Monuments in the care of Edinburgh City Council are deemed to be a 'collection' in the museum sense of the word. Under the council's Adopt-a-Monument scheme, groups and individuals maintain landmarks with which they have an association or feel a particular affinity. Francis Chantrey's Frederick Street statue of **William Pitt**, who introduced the income tax system, has been adopted by a tax consultancy firm, while the tribute to Greyfriars Bobby is tended by a breeder of Skye terriers.

But perhaps the most controversial statues in the city's history are the anonymous naked nymphs that adorn the **Ross Fountain**, erected in Princes Street Gardens in 1877. Its cast-iron figures, rendered in still-glorious gold by Jean-Baptiste Klagmann, weren't to everyone's taste: Dean Ramsay, minister of nearby St John's, decried it as 'grossly indecent and disgusting'.

Sightseeing

along the main roads in recent decades, and Dundas Street itself contains a number of art galleries (*see p220*), but it remains the residential heart of the New Town. The best way to explore this part of town is simply to follow your feet; it's almost impossible to get lost. A high-class, well-upholstered dignity still pervades, especially on its upper reaches, but the area is now home to a wider social mix than ever before.

Like much of Edinburgh, the area has a literary heritage. At 17 Heriot Row, look out for the stone-carved inscription commemorating the fact that author Robert Louis Stevenson once lived here. It's said that when Stevenson was a sickly child, the gardens here provided inspiration for his novel *Treasure Island*, and the gas light that once stood outside the house was the source for his poem *The Lamplighter*. Nearby, JM Barrie, author of *Peter Pan*, lodged at 3 Great King Street when he was a student. Just beyond lies Drummond Place, a crescent-shaped street once called home by *Whisky Galore* author Compton Mackenzie (at No. 31). And just over the intersection is Scotland Street, the setting for bestselling Edinburgh novelist Alexander McCall Smith's recent novel *44 Scotland Street*. Further west is the **Moray Estate**. Designed by James Gillespie Graham in 1822 at the behest of the Earl of Moray, it's one of the grandest of the New Town's residential quarters.

The Western New Town

The western end of the New Town is a quiet and pleasant place for a wander, but it's almost entirely bereft of activity. With most of the buildings now either high-rent offices, flats or hotels, it pales in comparison to the east side of the New Town. One notable exception is the **Hilton Caledonian Hotel** (*see p60*), a colossal red-brick edifice built in 1903, but even this was originally the subject of complaints: many locals believed such a vulgarian effort was better suited to Glasgow. More than a century of respectability has helped it blend in.

The only thoroughfare of any real distinction is **Melville Street**, which ends with the episcopal cathedral of **St Mary's** (enter from Palmerston Place; *see p229*). The foundation stone was laid in 1874, complete with what would now be called a time capsule, on land gifted for the purpose by two sisters, Barbara and Mary Walker. The main building completed and consecrated five years later, but the triple spires, which form an integral part of Edinburgh's skyline, were not finished until World War I. With its 270-foot (82-metre) central spire, the rose window of the south transept and the fossils in the granite steps of the High Altar, the cathedral is filled with artistic and ecclesiastical points of interest; Edinburgh has many beautiful churches, but perhaps none is more beautiful than this.

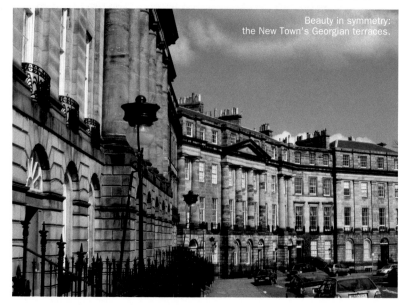

Beauty in symmetry: the New Town's Georgian terraces.

Stockbridge

Come and meet Edinburgh's village people.

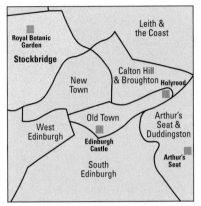

Village backwater, Georgian vision, Bohemian enclave, workers' utopia: Stockbridge has been many things to many people over the centuries. But while housing trends and shopping fashions continue to come and go, Stockbridge still feels like an urban neighbourhood and more like a village that just happens to have a city on its doorstep.

Independent businesses thrive here: cafés, pubs and small restaurants galore, and a handful of small local stores and well-stocked charity shops, including **Oxfam**'s specialist book and music stores (Nos.25 and 64 Raeburn Place, 332 9632/332 7593). The area is also a foodie's paradise: breathe in the ripe rinds at **IJ Mellis, Cheesemonger** (6 Bakers Place, 225 6566), raid the deli shelves at **Herbie of Edinburgh** (see p199), or enjoy the own-grown delights of the **Store** (13 Comely Bank Road, 315 0030). For more, see p200 **Walk**.

The architecture is as varied as the shopping opportunities, and several centuries' worth of building styles can be seen during the course of a gentle stroll around the area. But the sense of gentility often associated with Stockbridge is perhaps best reflected in the elegant curves of **Royal Circus**, designed by William Playfair. The prolific architect (for some of his other works, see p116) was also responsible for the baroque tower of **St Stephen's Church** at the foot of St Vincent Street, one of the first buildings you'll see as you walk down Howe Street from the city centre. The enormous

arched entrance was Playfair's answer to the awkward shape and sloping ground of the site. The church's clock pendulum, meanwhile, is reputed to be the longest in Europe.

From St Stephen Street to the Botanics

St Stephen Street came into its own in the '70s, known for its bric-a-brac shops and boho aura (former Velvet Underground chanteuse Nico lived there at the time). All that raffish ambience has more or less given way to the requirements of Edinburgh in the 21st-century: art galleries, beauty salons, bridal shops and clothes stores. However, a few less highfalutin spots remain, among them the **Blue Parrot Cantina** (No.49, 225 2941) and the reassuring presence of the **Antiquary** pub (No.72, 225 2858). Some glorious remnants of the old days also endure, with vintage clothing, clocks and other assorted bits of bric-a-brac still on sale here and there, but don't expect the shops to keep regular hours.

Trends for feng shui, herbal teas, tantric sex and the like may come and go, but two Stockbridge worthies have been helping to align Edinburghers' chi and provide an alternative to a diet of antibiotics for years. At the **Edinburgh Floatarium** (see p203), you can float in relaxing isolation, be indulged with a beauty regime or just browse through an array of crystals, candles, oils and unguents. And at the end of Hamilton Place sits **Napiers** (No.35, 315 2130, www.napiers.net): one of the city's long-established herbalists, it offers a wide variety of over-the-counter remedies, therapies and consultations.

Head on to India Place to see a cluster of old buildings that together make up **Duncan's Land**: look out for the higgledy-piggledy doors and windows, the crow-step gables, and the lovely lintel that reads 'Fear only God'. Built in the 1790s using stones recovered from buildings in the Lawnmarket that had been demolished as part of the construction of the Mound, Duncan's Land was the birthplace of artist David Roberts (1796-1864), who specialised in visions of souks, monuments of Egypt and the vistas of the Holy Land, and who was known for dressing in clothing as exotic as the sheiks who inhabit his landscapes. The more

Walk this way

At just over 28 miles, the **Water of Leith** is by no means the longest river around Edinburgh. But for its easy accessibility and richly colourful history, it takes some beating. Rising in the Pentland Hills, it takes a meandering path through the outlying villages of Balerno, Currie, Juniper Green and Colinton, then flows on through the heart of Edinburgh, past Murrayfield and Roseburn, by Dean Village, through Stockbridge, past Warriston and on out into the Firth of Forth at Leith.

Dean Village would probably never have existed were it not for the river, which provided the power for its mills. At one time there were 11 flour mills here, grinding meal for much of Edinburgh and its environs. This is the most dramatic stretch of the river, with rushing weirs, old mill buildings and, spanning the gorge, the huge Dean Bridge. Downriver in Stockbridge, the water is put to more holistic use: a mineral water spring is housed in St Bernard's Well, a gloriously over-the-top Doric temple designed by painter Alexander Nasmyth in 1788.

While it may look benign, the river has flooded periodically throughout the centuries. The most recent outpouring occurred in April 2000, when it burst its banks – and the walls – at the Stockbridge Colonies and

at Warriston, where it flooded residents' homes. One of the more aesthetic outcomes of the rebuilding and flood prevention programme will hopefully be a replacement bridge to span the river at Bell Place at the Colonies. The innovative design will incorporate a pulley system, enabling the bridge to be raised in times of flooding; work is expected to begin on site in 2007.

Around 12 miles of the river's course can now be navigated on foot (or by bike) along the **Water of Leith Walkway**. The river is easily accessible: you can join it at the Gallery of Modern Art and wander to Stockbridge, or pick it up in Stockbridge at Pizza Express and meander along its course to Canonmills without leaving the path. As well as mallards, there are a couple of herons that live along this stretch and can frequently be seen fishing in the river. During the annual **Stockbridge Festival**, which normally runs for nine days towards the end of June, the river plays host to an annual Duck Race, so don't be surprised if you see the odd stray bobbing along from Stockbridge to Canonmills one summer's day. The path makes for a cooling walk on hotter days, but parents should hold on tight to their kids' hands: there are a few stretches without barriers.

Sightseeing

utilitarian-looking blocks of flats opposite Duncan's Land replaced a series of slums that were demolished in the 1960s and 1970s.

Another memento of the area's past can be found in the form of the towering gateway that once led to Stockbridge's meat and vegetable market. It now stands in attractive isolation between St Stephen Street and Hamilton Place, but still announces the availability of 'Butcher Meat, Fruits, Fish and Poultry'. The market, built in 1826 after a public campaign, was a spit in the eye to the city officials of the day who had hoped that Stockbridge would leave behind such working class ideas and remain market-free like its neighbouring areas.

Join the riverside path from the stairs beside Pizza Express, and you can cut along to the **Stockbridge Colonies**, a series of 11 one-ended streets that follow the curve of the Water of Leith. Conceived and built by the Edinburgh Co-operative Building Company, they're named after its members and supporters. The design is interesting insofar as that while the buildings are two-storey houses, they're double-sided: the entrance to the upper dwelling is accessed from stairs on one street, with access to the ground floor from the street on the opposite side. It's obvious from the properties' narrow doorways, not to mention the thin cobbled roads that run between them, that they weren't originally built for the monied classes. These days, though, they're highly desirable residences.

From here, head up Arboretum Avenue to the delightful **Royal Botanic Garden**, with **Inverleith House** standing at its heart.

Inverleith House

Royal Botanic Garden, Inverleith Row (552 7171/ www.rbge.org.uk). Bus 8, 17, 23, 27. **Open** *Nov-Feb* 10am-3.30pm Tues-Sun. *Mar-Oct* 10am-5.30pm Tues-Sun. *During festival* 10am-5.30pm daily. **Admission** free. **Map** p325 D2.

Standing in the centre of the Botanics, this imposing, austere, late Georgian building was designed in 1774 by David Henderson for James Rocheid, whose family owned the Inverleith estate. Part of the estate was bought to provide a home for the Botanic Garden in 1820, but it wasn't until 1877 that the house was sold, at first becoming the home of the garden's Regius Keeper. It was transformed into an art gallery in the 20th century, housing the Scottish National Gallery of Modern Art from 1960 until 1984, but is now owned and run by the Royal Botanic Garden. Exhibitions taking place in the recently reburbished gallery space often make reference to the natural world, but it also houses temporary exhibitions by some big-hitters of modern art, including Edinburgh-born Callum Innes, Ulrich Rückriem, Agnes Martin, minimalist sculptor Carl Andre and Turner Prize nominee Jim Lambie, as well as shows by up-and-coming local talent.

Royal Botanic Garden

Inverleith Row (552 7171/www.rbge.org.uk). Bus 8, 17, 23, 27. **Open** *Nov-Feb* 10am-4pm daily. *Mar, Oct* 10am-6pm daily. *Apr-Sept* 10am-7pm daily. **Admission** *Garden* free. *Glasshouses* £3.50; £1-£3 concessions; £8 family. *Audiopass sound guide hire* 50p. **Credit** *Shop* V. **Map** p325 D2.

The Royal Botanic Garden has delighted both plant-lovers and those just out for a casual stroll for almost two centuries. (The city's original physic garden was the smaller-scale St Anne's Yard, part of the grounds of Holyrood. The site, now occupied by Waverley Station, is commemorated by a plaque on platform 11.) The Botanics is Edinburgh's most peaceful tourist attractions, but it's also a noted centre for botanical and horticultural research, and houses the oldest botanical library in Britain.

The glasshouses are divided into ten different themed zones. Among them are the Orchids and Cycads House, where some of the species are over 200 years old, and the Plants and People House, with a pond dominated in summer by gigantic water lilies. The gardens are constantly being remodelled and improved, and there's usually something new to see: the Rock Garden Stream is one notable recent addition. However, perhaps the main highlight in the gardens is the Chinese Hillside, which focuses on intrepid Scottish plant-hunters of the past such as George Forrest and Robert Fortune. Plant specimens in this area grow in drifts beside winding paths and carved bridges. There's also a T'ing, a traditional poolside pavilion.

In the summer, during the Fringe and the International Festival, outdoor art installations and exhibits are often set up around the site, making for an interesting series of diversions. Perhaps surprisingly, there's also plenty that appeals to children here. The pond, with its resident ducks and swans, and the waterfall in the rock garden area, where a heron sometimes fishes, are particularly popular. If your visit leaves you or them inspired, there's a small plant centre on site, accessed through the Botanics shop at the East Gate. The latter stocks an array of gifts, stationery and pocket-money toys, as well as a good range of publications about the gardens, plants native to Scotland and horticulture in general. The Terrace Café, adjacent to Inverleith House, serves hot and cold refreshments, snacks and meals (*see p155*). There's seating inside and out, although you may have to fend off pigeons and the occasional marauding squirrel if you choose the open air option.

The Raeburn Estate

Back in Stockbridge, at the top of Leslie Place, sits **St Bernard's Crescent**. It's all that remains of the **Raeburn Estate**, a property development financed by artist and Stockbridge native Sir Henry Raeburn. Although St Bernard's House, the central focus of the development, is long gone, the Georgian

The old market gate. *See p111.*

Named for the dean (deep valley) found at its heart – see for yourself at the vertiginous **Dean Bridge**, which crosses the Water of Leith between Stockbridge and the West End – the neighbouring territory of **Dean Village** has undergone plenty of changes down the years. The mills and tanneries that once stood here were replaced by breweries and distilleries in the 19th century, buildings that now form part of a very pleasant conservation area. But mementos of the flour milling trade that thrived here for around 700 years still remain.

At the top of Bell's Brae stands the quirky **Kirkbrae House**. Eagle-eyed visitors will spot a panel taken from the ruins of a granary named Jericho, which was built for the Incorporation of Baxters (bakers) in 1619 and once stood in the dean immediately below the house. The ornate panel depicts a cherubic head and scrolls, with an inscription reading 'In the sweat of thy face shalt thou eat bread, Gen.3 verse 19'. By **Bell's Brae Bridge** is another panel, dated 1643 and carved with two crossed bakers' peels (used for taking hot loaves out of ovens); beside it is a window lintel, inscribed 'Blesit be God for al his Giftis'. The building opposite carries another panel with crossed peels and the words, 'God's Providence is our Inheritans'; a door lintel bears the words 'God bless the Baxters of Edinbrugh who bult this Hous 1675'.

The history of nearby **Canonmills**, meanwhile, has almost vanished under successive waves of civic improvement. Over the years, it's lost its loch, its mills and even the historic Tanfield Hall, to which the ministers who broke away from the Church of Scotland to form the Free Church marched in 1843. However, it's still a very pleasant place, its array of good cafés supplemented by a number of second-hand and antiquarian bookshops.

Dean Gallery

Belford Road (624 6200/www.nationalgalleries.org). Bus 13 (or free shuttle bus from the Mound). **Open** 10am-5pm daily. **Admission** free; £1-£6 for special exhibitions. **Credit** MC, V. **Map** p329 A7.

Opened in 1999 and housed in an impressive 19th-century building, the Dean Gallery is conveniently situated directly across the road from the Scottish National Gallery of Modern Art (*see p113*); you can easily combine a visit to both in a day. The exhibitions it hosts are often enlightening, and the gallery currently holds one of Britain's largest collections of surrealist and Dadaist artworks, including pieces by Dalí, Giacometti, Miró and Picasso. However, its layout is rather sterile, and the curators dedicate what is arguably an excessive amount of space to work by Edinburgh-born artist Sir Eduardo Paolozzi: in

crescent remains a fine example of New Town elegance. Its western end is quite plain, but the central section, with reeded Doric columns, astragalled windows and fanlights, is very fine. It's become a popular filming location for period dramas; don't be too surprised if you see ladies in crinolines or gentlemen sporting greatcoats and top hats wandering around the neighbourhood.

Nearby **Ann Street**, thought to have been designed by James Milne and named after Raeburn's wife, is arguably the prettiest street in Edinburgh. It's notable particularly for the fact that each of the Georgian houses on it has its own front garden; properties on the grander crescents in the city have only shared occupancies of immaculately maintained communal gardens. Thomas de Quincy, the author of *Confessions of an English Opium Eater*, lived here for a time here, while a nearby street provided a home for a certain Mrs Dora Noyce. For 30-odd years, the entrepreneurial Noyce ran a 'house of leisure and pleasure' at No.17 Danube Street (adjacent to St Bernard's Crescent) in this heartland of gentility, serving liquid refreshments out of silver teapots as her clients selected and then retreated upstairs with one of her 15 live-in girls. Something of a local legend, Noyce was sent to jail in 1972, at the age of 71, but carried on working when she emerged four months later.

addition to a large array of his works, there's even a mock-up of his studio here. (For more on Paolozzi, *see p117* **Eduardo sculpturehands**.)

Scottish National Gallery of Modern Art

Belford Road (624 6200/www.nationalgalleries.org). Bus 13 (or free shuttle bus from the Mound). **Open** 10am-5pm daily **Admission** free; £1-£6 for special exhibitions. **Credit** MC, V. **Map** p329 A7. Since 1984 Scotland's national collection of modern art has been housed in this neo-classical structure, designed by William Burn in the 1820s as an institution for fatherless children. The permanent collection features numerous well-established artists, with a strong showing from the so-called 1980s Glasgow Boys: Peter Howson, Steven Campbell, Adrian Wiszniewski, Ken Currie and others. The ground level is usually devoted to special exhibitions, with the upper floor accommodating works by big international names such as Matisse, Picasso and Pollock. The entire supporting wall on the stairs linking the two floors has been given over to the artist Douglas Gordon, who has neatly printed the names of every person he has ever met and whose name he can remember.

The attractions continue outside. The gallery is impressively set in the middle of plush parkland, part of which was remodelled recently by American landscape architect Charles Jencks into a sculpture entitled *Landform*. Dotted with sculptures by the likes of Henry Moore, Sir Eduardo Paolozzi and Dan Graham, the grounds are a great picnic location.

Back to school

Perhaps Stockbridge's greatest asset is its architecture. Alternately crumbling and grand, austere and curious, its buildings reward closer attention from both expert eyes and design novices. And some of the finest buildings in Stockbridge are its schools, solid and imposing edifices that still stand as temples to the glories of learning.

The **Edinburgh Academy** on Henderson Row (*pictured*), designed by William Burn and opened in 1824, exudes neo-classical gravitas. The inscriptions on its portico remind passers-by that the academy's founders and directors, among them Henry Cockburn, John Russell and Sir Walter Scott, wanted their educators to place an emphasis on Greek: their aim was to improve on the standards of classical education at their own alma mater, the Royal High School, but also to create a school that would rival England's finest educational establishments. The adjacent building, formerly Donaldson's School for the Deaf, was acquired by the Academy in 1977; eight years previously it had provided a suitably austere location for the filming of Muriel Spark's *The Prime of Miss Jean Brodie*.

In contrast to such stolid neo-classicism, **Stewart's Melville College**, on Queensferry Road, could be mistaken for an Elizabethan mansion: check out the symmetrical scattering of square towers and elegantly leaded roofs. It's thought that David Rhind, the building's Edinburgh-born architect, simply reworked the designs he had earlier submitted for the Houses of Parliament in London.

But for sheer flights of architectural fancy, **Fettes** wins hands down. Architect David Bryce blended the Scottish Baronial style with influences from French chateaux, creating what has been termed – slightly clumsily, it should be said – Edinburgh Loire Gothic. With its gargoyles, turrets, intricate stonework and clock tower spire, it's easy to believe that there's some of Fettes in JK Rowling's vision of Hogwarts. Former pupils include Tilda Swinton, Tony Blair and James Bond.

Finally, don't miss the relatively unheralded **Stockbridge Primary School**, the Gothic design of which was considered radical when it was completed in 1877. Sir Robert Rowand Anderson's other Edinburgh buildings include the Scottish National Portrait Gallery and the McEwan Hall, but this is the last extant example of his educational architecture.

Sightseeing

Calton Hill & Broughton

Where the giraffes roam free…

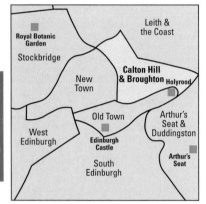

Royal Botanic
Garden

Stockbridge

New
Town

Leith &
the Coast

**Calton Hill
& Broughton** Holyrood

Old Town

West
Edinburgh

Edinburgh
Castle

South
Edinburgh

Arthur's
Seat &
Duddingston

Arthur's
Seat

Sightseeing

It was from the top of Calton Hill that Robert Louis Stevenson drew much of the inspiration that fuelled his writing on Edinburgh. Although *The Strange Case of Dr Jekyll and Mr Hyde* was set in London, its atmosphere of moral hypocrisy was charged with what Stevenson saw from the hill: it was a prime location for procuring the services of local prostitutes, and hence an ideal place to bear witness to the seamier side of the city. Calton Hill, according to Stevenson in his 1878 work *Edinburgh: Picturesque Notes*, is the best vantage point over Edinburgh, 'since you can see the Castle, which you lose from the Castle, and Arthur's Seat, which you cannot see from Arthur's Seat'.

Calton Hill remains an atmospheric spot. The smoking chimneys are long gone, but when a sunny summer afternoon turns chilly and a sea mist (known here as a 'haar') sweeps up from the Forth, the view of mist-torn chimneys and tenements creates an impression of what Edinburgh must have been like when it was nicknamed 'Auld Reekie'.

The hill is on the edge of old Edinburgh and is home to the **City Observatory**, from which 19th-century science regimented time. But it also lies in the heart of new Edinburgh, and is the site of the modern **Beltane** celebrations (see *p208*), commemorating the days when time's passage was marked by pagan rituals. In the run-up to Hogmanay, meanwhile, it's the destination for the annual torchlight procession, culminating in fireworks and boat-burning; it's

also a great place from which to view the spectacular fireworks that close the Edinburgh International Festival each year.

Waterloo Place

Most visitors approach Calton Hill from the west: along Princes Street or across North Bridge. Looking up, the succession of neo-classical monuments that crown the hill make it easy to understand why Edinburgh retains the accolade 'Athens of the North'. What's rather more strange is that the name came before the Grecian architecture was built, instead resulting from the city's inclusion in the itineraries of the grand tours of the late 18th century and its relationship with imperial Roman London. It was only later that the classical-styled architecture followed to justify and immortalise the phrase.

Turning the corner from North Bridge into **Waterloo Place** brings the visitor face to face with the full impact of Edinburgh's 19th-century neo-classical architecture. The austere grey buildings clash acutely with the intricately designed extravagances elsewhere in the city. It's buildings like these that fuel Edinburgh's reputation for dour rectitude, even if it's slightly less strong than in the past.

A few yards further along, Waterloo Place bisects the **Old Calton Burial Ground**. The steps to the right lead up to the largest part of the graveyard, the last resting place of many of the main figures of the Enlightenment. The two most imposing memorials are Robert Adam's tower for the philosopher and historian David Hume and the tall Cleopatra's Needle, an obelisk to the political reformers of 1793-4 who were transported for having had the audacity to demand the vote for Scots. The statue of Abraham Lincoln is part of a monument to the Scots who died during the American Civil War. Up against the burial ground's east wall, there stands what little remains of **Calton Gaol**; the turreted ruins are often mistaken for Edinburgh Castle by over-excited tourists disembarking at Waverley train station. The Burial Ground was divided into two in 1818, with the construction of Waterloo Place. Before then, access to Calton Hill had been via the steep road of the same name, which now runs from the end of Waterloo Place down to Leith Street.

Rock House, set back above the road on the north side, is one of the only houses in Edinburgh to have good views both north and south, and was home to a succession of photographers from the 1830s until 1945. Among them was David Octavius Hill, whose work, in collaboration with Robert Adamson, gave photography credibility as a modern art form. Around 5,000 of their calotypes form the basis of the extensive photographic collection at the **Museum of Scotland** (see p99).

The most direct route up Calton Hill from here is via the steps at the end of Waterloo Place. After the first flight, go straight ahead and meander up the side of the hill or, if you have more energy, take the steep steps to the right.

Regent Road

Originally the home of the Scottish Office and now the base of the Scottish Executive, **St Andrew's House** is the first point of interest on the right as Waterloo Place becomes **Regent Road**. The site was originally host to Calton Gaol, described by Robert Louis Stevenson as 'castellated to the point of folly'. The prison was demolished to make way for St Andrew's House, but one of its turreted walls remains in place and is visible from Waverley Station.

The old **Royal High School** building, where Sir Walter Scott was educated, is perhaps the finest example of neo-classical architecture in the city. Completed in 1829, it was designed by Glasgow-born architect Thomas Hamilton, an internationally renowned leader in the Greek

revivalist school. Modelled on the Temple of Theseus in Athens (since reassigned to the god of fire and called the Hephaisteion), the building consists of a massive Doric central block with pillared wings. Because of the structure's monumental size, it's difficult to get a proper perspective on it, even when walking past on the other side of Regent Road. It's best to focus on the detail here and then contemplate its grandeur from one of the closes at the lower end of the Royal Mile.

The school was the site of a five-year round-the-clock vigil in the 1990s, as protestors gathered to campaign for Scottish devolution. It seemed an auspicious location: having been converted into a debating chamber before the failed referendum for a Scottish Assembly in 1979, the school was fully expected to house the new Scottish Parliament. However, after the 'yes-yes' vote of autumn 1997, the government said 'no-no' to the site and chose Holyrood instead. Look carefully and you'll find a small plaque commemorating the 1,980-day vigil. Plans are now in place to transform the building into the **Scottish National Photography Centre** (www.snpc.org.uk).

Just across the road from the Royal High School is Hamilton's **Robert Burns Memorial**, a small circular Greek temple that seems completely out of sync with its purpose. The large collection of Burns memorabilia that was once displayed here can now be seen in the **Writers' Museum** (see p85). It's worth straying this far in order to take in the fantastic view up to the castle and down

Sightseeing

Hamilton's obelisk and the old Calton Gaol **Governor's House**. See p114.

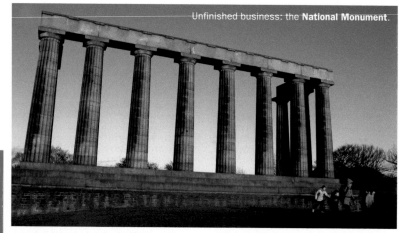
Unfinished business: the **National Monument**.

to the **Palace of Holyroodhouse**, the **Scottish Parliament**, the dome of **Our Dynamic Earth** and the **Canongate Kirkyard** (for all, *see pp91-95*). The paths on the right lead down to Calton Road, and provide a suitable shortcut to Holyrood if you're not going back up the hill. Alternatively, head along Regent Terrace (closed to through traffic to protect the American Embassy in the jumpy post-9/11 world) and on to Royal Terrace for a leafy stroll to the top of Leith Walk.

Calton Hill

Though the views from it are terrific, **Calton Hill** is most famous for its bizarre selection of architecture. And no single structure on it is more bizarre that the 12 Doric columns that form the **National Monument** to those who lost their lives in the Napoleonic Wars. The project was designed by William Playfair, the architect responsible for some of Edinburgh's finest neo-classical architecture, as a replica of the Parthenon in Athens. Sadly, the funds ran out before the building was completed and it remains unfinished. Known as 'Scotland's Disgrace', it's rivalled only by the new Scottish Parliament as Edinburgh's most famous monument to poor budgeting.

Playfair wasn't responsible for the **Nelson Monument** (*see below*), the telescopic tower on the top of the hill; it was designed by Robert Burn and completed in 1816. But Playfair did build the **Monument to Dugald Stewart**, a homage to the Lysicrates Monument on the Acropolis in Athens and a tribute to an early 19th-century professor of moral philosophy at the University of Edinburgh.

The **City Observatory** (1774), based on the Temple of the Winds in Athens, is another of Playfair's projects. Built as a commercial venture and consisting of three buildings (the Old, New and City observatories), it was granted Royal Observatory status in 1822 during the visit of George IV. However, as the city became increasingly polluted, views from Calton Hill diminished and the institution was moved to its current site at Blackford Hill in 1895. Attempts have been made to re-open the old buildings and grounds as a visitor attraction, but at present, the only way to visit is through the Astronomical Society of Edinburgh (556 4365).

Although most parts of Calton Hill are open to the public, the **Regent Gardens** to the east are private and belong to the residents of the Regent, Carlton and Royal Terraces. Also designed by Playfair, they follow the contours of the hill rather than a grid pattern and are regarded as further testament to his talent.

Nelson Monument

Calton Hill (556 2716/www.cac.org.uk). Playhouse buses. **Open** *Apr-Sept* 1-6pm Mon; 10am-6pm Tue-Sat. *Oct-Mar* 10am-3pm Mon-Sat. **Admission** £3. **No credit cards. Map** p327 K5.

If the views from Calton Hill aren't grand enough for your liking, you can get an even better vantage point from the top of the Nelson Monument, designed in the shape of Nelson's telescope. Be warned, though: despite its sturdy structure the viewing deck can feel very exposed on windy days, and the parapet isn't very high. In 1852, a time ball was erected at the top of the monument; nine years later, a steel wire more than 4,000ft (1,200m) long was attached between the monument and the Edinburgh Castle to facilitate the firing of the latter's 1pm gun, which still shocks the unwary today.

Broughton

Broughton has been home to Edinburgh's gay community for many years, and the area defined by Broughton Street, Picardy Place and the top of Leith Walk has been nicknamed 'the pink triangle' (*see p223*). However, there's far more to the neighbourhood, which has steadily become one of the most fashionable corners of the city. The atmosphere has always been cultured and unconventional; it was once a notorious centre for witchcraft in Edinburgh.

The tone of Broughton, once a village in its own right, has been somewhat lowered in recent years by the addition of the monstrous **Omni Centre**, towering over the area from the top of Leith Walk. The glass-fronted edifice is filled with chain eateries, a health centre, a comedy club (**Jongleurs**; *see p219*) and a cineplex (*see p219*), and is topped by the **Glasshouse** hotel (*see p65*), which boasts beautiful views over both Calton Hill and the city. Just down the road is the **Playhouse Theatre** (*see p244*).

Picardy Place, flanking the huge roundabout at the top of Leith Walk, was once home to a colony of Protestant French silk weavers who fled to Edinburgh from Picardy in 1685. Today, assuming you're not a member of swanky private members' club the Hallion

(No.12), the main reason to visit is for a peek at the statue of Sherlock Holmes; his creator, Sir Arthur Conan Doyle, was born at a now demolished property at No.11. Nearby, in front of **St Mary's Roman Catholic Cathedral** are a set of outsize sculptures by Sir Eduardo Paolozzi (*see p117*), but the two scrap metal giraffes by Helen Denerley that were erected outside the Omni Centre in 2005 are more likely to delay the camera-toting tourist.

Broughton Street itself is teeming with cafés and restaurants, not to mention a couple of excellent delicatessens (including Edinburgh's best butcher, **Crombie's**; *see p199*). At the bottom of the street, across the roundabout, is **Mansfield Church**, the walls of which are covered in murals by leading Arts and Crafts artist Phoebe Traquair. The church was bought by the Mansfield Traquair Trust; although the building now houses offices, the murals have been restored for public display.

Continuing down the hill, a look down Bellevue Crescent on the left reveals some of the most elegant New Town façades. Further north, on Warriston Road, is **Warriston Cemetery**. It was here that cremation first became available in Edinburgh in 1929. To the west of the cemetery lie the **Royal Botanic Garden** (*see p111*) and **Stockbridge** (*see p109*).

Eduardo sculpturehands

As you circle the roundabout at the top of Leith Walk, you'll spot two scrap metal giraffes in front of the Omni Centre and, across the road, a statue of Sherlock Holmes. Less immediately obvious, but more artistically significant, are four sculptures hidden behind the bushes in front of St Mary's Roman Catholic Cathedral: an open hand, a foot and an ankle, all strikingly larger than life, and an arrangement of stones taken from the old Leith train station. All are the work of Sir Eduardo Paolozzi, arguably the city's most famous artistic son.

Born near the station at the other end of Leith Walk in 1924 to a family of Scots-Italian ice-cream parlour owners, Paolozzi started out as a surrealist painter but went on to become one of the progenitors of pop art, acclaimed as a major figure by critics and peers. Although his work can be seen all over the UK (perhaps most famously in the form of the brilliant mosaics he created for London's Tottenham Court Road underground station), nowhere is he more celebrated than in his home city.

Two venues are of particular interest. The **Scottish National Gallery of Modern Art** (*see p113*) holds a sizeable body of his work, plenty of it donated by Paolozzi himself in 1994. The adjacent **Dean Gallery** (*p112*) stages periodic exhibitions of his formidable output (surrealist collages to sculptures, screenprints to tapestries), and also contains a mesmerising life-size reproduction of Paolozzi's studio in all its chaotic splendour. Other Paolozzi works are scattered around town, among them some ancient-looking bronze heads in the **Museum of Scotland** (*see p99*) the stained glass windows in **St Mary's Episcopal Cathedral** in Palmerston Place (*see p229*); two figures, Parthenope and Egeria, outside the Michael Swann Building at the University of Edinburgh's Kings Buildings campus; six woodcuts dedicated to Charles Rennie Mackintosh on the walls of the **Scottish Parliament** (*see p95*); and The Wealth of Nations, a bronze sculpture outside the South Gyle headquarters of the Royal Bank of Scotland.

Arthur's Seat & Duddingston

The hills are alive.

Arthur's Seat

The point is made often, but it's worth making again: no other city in Europe has an extinct volcano within its limits. From the south and east, the soft shoulders and rounded summit that form the silhouette of **Arthur's Seat**, the tallest of Edinburgh's seven hills, seem the result of simple erosion, its outline often compared with that of a recumbent lion. But from the west and north, the sheer cliffs known as Salisbury Crags reveal a violent past.

The 'Edinburgh volcano' last erupted some 350 million years ago, into a shallow and ancient sea; what now remains is a basalt lava plug that choked the volcano's neck. Movements in the Earth's crust resulted in the volcano being submerged underwater, under thousands of feet of sediment. It eventually moved to the surface again; erosion and glaciation wore away its slopes and revealed the ancient volcano once more, but it had been tilted by 25 degrees by the Earth's geological processes. More on how the landmark was formed can be found at the excellent **Our Dynamic Earth** (*see p92*).

Humans first inhabited the area around 10,000 years ago, and the remains of prehistoric settlements, farming and even fortifications are there for those who know how to look. There are cultivation terraces just below the east side of Arthur's Seat which may date to the Bronze Age. Two stone ramparts on the hill have been associated with a fort of possible Iron Age vintage.

While its name hints at myth and legend, there's no reason to suspect that Arthur's Seat has any connection with King Arthur. The most plausible explanation is that the hill is named after Arthur, Prince of Strathclyde in the sixth century, but a more romantic notion is that the name comes from a corruption of the Gaelic *Ard-na-Said*, meaning 'the height of arrows'. The explanation gains currency from the fact that during the 12th century, when the area was owned jointly by the Church and the Scottish royal family, it was used as a royal hunting ground.

According to legend, King David I (the de facto creator of Scotland as we now know it) was attacked by a stag as he hunted here in 1128. The stag wounded the king, but fled when he grasped a crucifix that had miraculously appeared between its antlers. In thanksgiving, David founded **Holyrood Abbey** (holyrood means 'holy cross'), and bequeathed it his lands on Arthur's Seat. It remained in the abbey's possession until the Reformation, when it came into the hands of the Crown once more.

Arthur's Seat stands 823 feet (251 metres) above sea level within the 650-acre **Holyrood Park**. The park is Edinburgh's playground, an opportunity to get a taste of the Scottish countryside without leaving the city. There are three main entrances to Holyrood Park: via Holyrood Park Road, by the University of Edinburgh's Pollock Halls of Residence; directly next to **Holyrood Palace** and the **Scottish Parliament**; and by the east gate, along Duke's Walk near **Meadowbank Stadium**.

Climbing the hill is a regular but rewarding challenge for many Edinburghers. Numerous families make the hike on weekends; the walk isn't a cinch, but it's certainly within the ability of any moderately fit adult and child. Some cross-country runners ascend the hill every day; conversely, drink-fortified teens have been

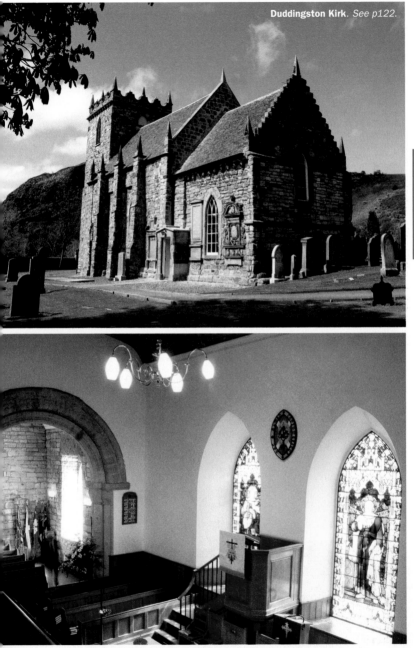

Duddingston Kirk. *See p122.*

Sightseeing

known to climb the peak after a night on the tiles. Every May Day hundreds of faithful souls take a pre-dawn jaunt to follow the pagan tradition of washing their faces in the dew at sunrise, said to bring clear skin and great beauty. The precise origins of the ritual are unknown; as, for that matter, is the identity of the person or persons who left 17 miniature coffins, each containing a tiny wooden doll, in a hillside cave during the 19th century. The eight surviving coffins can be seen to this day in the **Museum of Scotland** (*see p99*); the mystery of their origin has never been solved.

Several paths lead to the top of Arthur's Seat; all can be taken at an easy pace with plenty of pauses to enjoy the views and catch your breath. A word of warning, though: it might be in the centre of the city, but the park has seen its share of tragic accidents. If you plan to climb Arthur's Seat, wear strong shoes that will not slip on the grass or slopes, and take an extra layer of clothing: even on mild days there's no shelter from the often fearsome wind.

The most popular way to top is from the man-made **Dunsapie Loch** on the hill's west side. It's accessible from Queen's Drive, the road that circles Holyrood Park. Whether you walk around to it or bring the car (there's parking), it's a straight and easy pull from Dunsapie Loch up a grass slope to the summit.

However, more challenging hikes to the top can be enjoyed by ambling into the park through the Holyrood Park Road entrance. Once inside, go right at the second, upper roundabout and walk uphill on Queen's Drive. An obvious track soon cuts in to your left, between the south end of Salisbury Crags and the *massif* of Arthur's Seat itself. The track leads down into a small valley known as Hunter's Bog; at the lip of the valley, immediately up to the right, you'll see a zig-zagging and rough-cut stone pathway

leading directly up the bump known as Nether Hill. It's an arduous yomp at first, but the upper slopes are less punishing. Once you're up, it's an easy walk over to the summit.

One alternative route, from the same Holyrood Park Road entrance, is to bypass the track into Hunter's Bog and continue around Queen's Drive for another 50 yards, where there are wooden steps leading directly off the road. Again, it's a steep ascent and the steps only go so far; when they end, you'll have a little scramble to reach the upper slopes. This track joins up on Nether Hill with the one from the entrance to Hunter's Bog, effectively offering two routes around and through the crags that buttress Nether Hill to its south west.

You can also reach the summit by entering the park via the **Holyrood Park Education Centre** (No.1 Queen's Drive, 652 8150, www.historic-scotland.gov.uk), which holds plenty of information about the park and stages regular events. From the Education Centre, head along Queen's Drive in the direction of St Margaret's Loch. But before you get there, walk in behind the ruins of the 15th-century St Anthony's Chapel; here, an easy rising glen, the Dry Dam, leads uphill to the south. The path to the rocky outcrops at the top of Arthur's Seat is obvious.

St Margaret's Loch itself is a picturesque spot and good for those who can't manage a more strenuous hike. Not only does it boast those Gothic chapel ruins, but also a resident flock of mute swans, mallard ducks and other wildfowl. The loch was created in 1856 as part of an extensive series of works drawn up by Prince Albert (husband of Queen Victoria), intended to make the park more pleasant for recreation. Just before the loch is a grille set into the wall on the right. This is St Margaret's Well, which, during the plague years, was relied upon as a source of clean and safe drinking water.

Arthur's Seat affords the best views of Edinburgh itself, but the glorious 360-degree panorama from the top encompasses the Bass

Rock and the hills of North Berwick Law and Traprain Law to the east, the Lammermuir and Moorfoot hills to the south-east, the Pentland Hills to the south and the Firth of Forth and Fife to the north. On clear days, walkers are rewarded by views of up to 80 miles, all the way to the peaks of the southern Highlands. Once you're taken it all in, head back down the eastern side of Arthur's Seat back towards Dunsapie Loch. To the south of the loch, take the steps that lead down to Duddingston and the Sheep Heid Inn (see p122).

Another popular walk on Arthur's Seat is along the **Radical Road**, which skirts the foot of Salisbury Crags. Built in 1820 as a means of providing employment, at the suggestion of the novelist Sir Walter Scott, it is so called because of the radical political views held by the group of unemployed weavers who built it. Part of the rock face alongside the road here is known as Hutton's Section; in the late 18th century it was used by James Hutton, the 'father of modern geology', to demonstrate that Salisbury Crags were formed by molten lava. In the evening sun, the fiery ochre crags still seem to glow from within.

Despite the deep history, millennia of human occupation, and amazing views, Holyrood Park still has one more trick up its sleeve with various locations where it can offer respite from the city – countryside all around and hardly a glimpse of buildings in sight. In Hunter's Bog, for example, enclosed on one side by Arthur's Seat itself, on the other by the slope running up behind Salisbury Crags, it's hard to believe that Princes Street is only a mile away on the other side of the ridge.

Duddingston

You don't need to venture far from central Edinburgh to experience a Scottish village atmosphere. Designated an Outstanding Conservation Area in 1975, **Duddingston** is a peaceful haven, as tranquil as it is surprising.

Traditionally, the village was a busy hub for the weaving of a coarse linen cloth known as Duddingston hardings, but its parishioners also made use of the advantageous natural conditions. Farming was a common occupation, as the land surrounding Arthur's Seat is extremely fertile, and there was also a small salt industry here.

If you're walking around Queen's Drive, you can descend into Duddingston from the steps near Dunsapie Loch (see p120). Otherwise, the easiest stroll is from the park's Holyrood Park Road entrance, taking a right turn at the first roundabout and following the 'Low Road' that skirts under the cliffs of the Lion's Haunch, past Duddingston Loch and into the village. It's an easy walk, but it does miss the view of the loch and the adjacent 64-acre Bawsinch Nature Reserve afforded by the 'High Road' (another section of Queen's Drive directly above it). Bawsinch is now a site of Special Scientific Interest in the care of the Scottish Wildlife Trust, and is dotted with bird-watching hides. The road also overlooks **Prestonfield Golf Club** (see p240), one of the city's prettiest.

Duddingston Village itself is very small and made up of two parallel streets, Old Church Lane (a busy weekday rat run for commuter traffic) and the Causeway. The village's main feature is **Duddingston Loch**, a bird sanctuary since 1925 and home to a thriving colony of greylag geese, along with swans, ducks and other birdlife. Otters have returned for the first time in a century, probably attracted by a ready supply of trout and perch.

A cache of Bronze Age weapons and tools was dredged up from the bottom of the loch in 1778. They had been broken before being discarded, and it remains a mystery whether they were thrown in as offerings to the water spirits, or simply because they were scrap metal. Six years later the loch also provided the setting for Scotland's most famous painting:

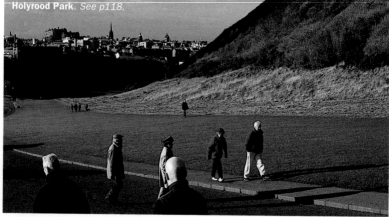
Holyrood Park. *See p118.*

Sir Henry Raeburn's *Reverend Robert Walker Skating on Duddingston Loch*, better known as 'The Skating Minister'. A much-replicated image on everything from mugs to mouse mats, you can see the original in the **National Gallery of Scotland** (*see p103*).

Dating from 1124, **Duddingston Kirk** is one of the oldest churches in Scotland still used for regular worship. Next to its gates is a two-storey tower, now called the Session House, once used as a graveyard lookout point. Such

Off the rails

Approaching Holyrood Park from its south side along Holyrood Park Road, take a left along East Parkside into a newish housing development; after about 50 yards, take a sharp right at the 'Resident Parking Only' sign. Here, you can enter an extraordinary, 350-yard Victorian tunnel, paved over for walkers and cyclists, through which ran Edinburgh's very first railway line. Planned by engineer Robert Stevenson, grandfather of Robert Louis Stevenson, the track that ran along here was dubbed the Innocent Railway, either because of its impeccable safety record (not a single fatality despite carrying up to 400,000 passengers a year) or because of the sedate pace of travel: the carriages were originally drawn by horses. When you emerge at the other end of the tunnel, you can keep going on the cycle path that eventually runs east out of the city, or turn right and follow the path back to the road leading to Duddingston.

features were common in Edinburgh kirkyards in the 19th century, with grave-robbers such as Burke and Hare on the prowl for fresh cadavers to sell to the medical schools. Look out also for the 'loupin'-on-stane' (jumping-on stone), used for mounting horses, and a punishment collar known as the Jougs.

The small, octagonal building found at the foot of the Duddingston Kirk manse (and the edge of the loch) is **Thomson's Tower**. The structure was named after the Reverend John Thomson (1778-1840), one of the parish's best-known ministers and also, in his spare time, a landscape painter. It was Thomson who coined the Scots phrase 'We're a' Jock Tamson's bairns', meaning that all men are equal in the eyes of God. Thomson's visitors included the artist JMW Turner and the writer Sir Walter Scott, who wrote part of his novel *The Heart of Midlothian* in the tower.

Most visitors to Duddingston end up in the **Sheep Heid Inn** (*see p179*) on the Causeway, a country pub that feels removed from urban life. The pub was a firm favourite with King James VI, who later united the thrones of Scotland and England, and has also hosted Mary, Queen of Scots, and Charles Edward ('Bonnie Prince Charlie') Stuart, who, on 19 September 1745, held his council of war here before a famous victory over the English at the Battle of Prestonpans a few miles away. Today the pub oozes atmosphere, with its dark wood circular bar, leaded glass partitions, knick-knack festooned walls and, taking pride of place, a large painting of the aforementioned battle. There's also a beer garden with overhanging trees, better than average pub food and even a skittle alley to help while away an hour or two.

South Edinburgh

Strippers, suburbs and pathological remains.

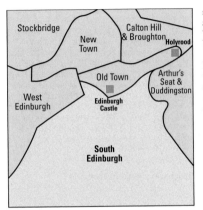

Starting at the new Quartermile residential development on Lauriston Place, South Edinburgh stretches off like a slice of cake, taking in everything from the green spaces of the Meadows and Blackford Hill to tenemented suburbs such as Marchmont and Bruntsfield. There are students galore here, thanks to the campus outposts of Edinburgh and Napier universities and the presence of Edinburgh College of Art; their influence ensures that the area boasts plenty of takeaways, pubs and second-hand bookshops. But what really defines much of South Edinburgh is the middle-class reserve apparent in any leafy backstreet in the Grange or Morningside, where the grandest houses sit discreetly behind the highest walls.

Lothian Road & Tollcross

Lothian Road is a living laboratory, almost custom-built to test the proposition that life really can come to imitate art. The thoroughfare has long had a reputation for carousing: when Robert Louis Stevenson was a young man, more than 130 years ago, it was here he came here with his friends for a beer. It was also in the kirkyard of **St Cuthbert's Kirk** (*see p101*) that Stevenson was said to have found a gravestone with the name Jekyll, which he later used in *The Strange Case of Dr Jekyll and Mr Hyde* (1886). The novel has long served as a peg for theories of human nature and even as a symbol of Edinburgh's Janus face, with the

stifling and respectable New Town on one side and the saltier closes and encounters of the Old Town on the other. But the same distinction can be drawn about 21st-century Lothian Road.

Over the years, a degree of respectability has crept in to the area. The construction of the **Royal Lyceum** theatre (*see p246*) in 1883 and the elegant **Usher Hall** (*see p228*) three decades later helped matters; while the later arrival of the **Filmhouse** (*see p218*) and the **Traverse Theatre** (*see p246*) created an artistic cluster that offers everything from cutting-edge drama to classical music. However, the seediness remains. Lothian Road, Tollcross and the nearby West Port, drily dubbed the Pubic Triangle by locals, are currently home to an assortment of lap-dancing joints and strip show bars. As darkness falls, the area's pubs and clubs are magnets for groups of young drinkers out on Friday- or Saturday-night benders. Within the space of about 100 yards here, you could watch traditional ballet or watch exotic dancing, get into a discussion about Orson Welles or get into a fight. Jekyll and Hyde indeed.

Barclay Church. See p124.

Sightseeing

Inhabitants of the **Surgeons Hall Museums**.

At the top of Lothian Road is **Tollcross**, a crossroads now dominated by the **Princes Exchange**. Built in 2001 to house financial-sector offices, it might be big but it's hardly beautiful. For a building with a little more soul, keep walking up Home Street and Leven Street until the **Barclay Church** (photo *p123*) looms out of nowhere. With one of the tallest spires in Edinburgh, this Franco-Venetian Gothic extravaganza was created by FT Pilkington in 1864. So much for progress.

Edinburgh College of Art

Lauriston Place (221 6000/www.eca.ac.uk). Bus 23, 27, 35, 45. **Open** hours vary. **Admission** free. **Map** p330 F9.

The ECA operates a year-round programme of exhibitions. For many, the highlight is the annual degree show in June, when the public can eye up (and, hope the artists, purchase) works of future art stars. However, the college puts on regular shows by artists from all over the world; check online for details. For the college's Wee Red Bar, *see p236*.

George & Nicolson Squares

George Square should cause the city fathers of yore to hang their heads in shame. The handsome central gardens, open 9am-4.30pm daily (until 7pm in summer), were once lined by elegant houses dating back to the 18th century; No.25 was home to a young Walter Scott. Some survive along the west side of the square, but many were levelled in the 1960s so that the **University of Edinburgh** could build modern facilities for its arts and social science faculties. The squat University Library (1967) on the south side was constructed to replace the much more elegant library in Old College (*see p97*), while the Appleton Tower (1963), set back from the east side, is widely regarded as one of the city's most objectionable buildings. A multi-million-pound refurbishment in 2006 hasn't improved it.

Facing on to the neighbouring **Bristo Square** is **Teviot Row House**; built in 1889, it's Britain's oldest purpose-built student union. The square itself has become a favourite spot among skaters, and is packed all year round with big-trousered youths and their entourages. They're overlooked by the **McEwan Hall**, designed by Sir Robert Rowand Anderson in decorative Renaissance style. The hall was paid for by Sir William McEwan, the Victorian brewing magnate, and constructed in 1897.

Over on Nicolson Street sits another building by celebrated architect Sir William Playfair. Completed in 1832, **Surgeons Hall** was where Burke and Hare brought their freshly deceased victims. It remains home to the Royal College of Surgeons of Edinburgh, a body that can trace its roots to 1505, and the celebrated **Surgeons Hall Museums**. If half a millennium of medical development gets too much, adjourn to **Pear Tree House** (*see p179*), which has a huge beer garden that's perfect for sunny days.

Surgeons Hall Museums

Royal College of Surgeons of Edinburgh, 18 Nicolson Street (527 1649/www.rcsed.ac.uk). Nicolson Street–North Bridge buses. **Open** *July-Sept* 10am-4pm daily. *Oct-June* noon-4pm Mon-Fri. **Admission** £5, £3 concessions. **Credit** MC, V. **Map** p331 J8.

This series of collections formerly felt like an adjunct to the workings of the Royal College, but a 2005 rethink turned the Surgeons Hall Museums into a much more coherent and user-friendly experience. Here you can trace the history of medicine in the city from 1505, when the Barber Surgeons of Edinburgh were incorporated as a craft guild, through to the development of modern surgical techniques. One of the real curios is a pocketbook covered with the tanned skin of William Burke who, with accomplice William Hare, killed at least 16 Edinburgh citizens in 1827-8 and sold their bodies for dissection. You'll either love or loathe the John Menzies Campbell dentistry section. But the main attraction is the celebrated pathology collection, the largest in the UK. The museum helpfully suggests that some people might find the pickled remains 'unsettling', and under-15s must be accompanied by an adult, but seeing the workings – and failures – of the human body is never less than fascinating.

The southern suburbs

The immediate centrepiece of South Edinburgh is the **Meadows**, stretching east to west from Newington to Tollcross and north to south from Quartermile (the site of the old Royal Infirmary) to Marchmont. Formerly the site of the Burgh Loch of Edinburgh, it was drained in the late 17th century, leaving the flat, grassy area that stands today. Tree-lined paths (complete with cycle lanes) cut across in every direction; it's a popular spot for joggers and amateur sports. A lack of lighting means caution should be taken at night, but it's generally a safe place. For one day every August, it's packed out for **Fringe Sunday** (*see p43* **Special events**).

The Meadows was the site of the ambitious International Exhibition of Industry in 1886, housed in a temporary structure at its western end. This left the city with several permanent souvenirs, including the whale jawbones at Jawbone Walk (a gift of improbable provenance that came from the Zetland and Fair Isle knitting stand) and the memorial pillars where Melville Drive joins Brougham Place.

South of the Meadows, **Marchmont** is composed almost entirely of baronial tenement buildings, built between 1876 and 1914. The cobbled sweep of Warrender Park Road gives a general flavour of the district, which now has the atmosphere of a genteel student ghetto in places thanks to its proximity to the University of Edinburgh. The nearby **Warrender Swim Centre** (55 Thirlestane Road, 447 0052), housed in a beautiful Victorian building, is worth a visit.

To the south-west, the Meadows opens out into old **Bruntsfield Links**, all that remains of the old Burgh Muir (or town heath) gifted to the city by David I in 1128. Once open ground extending towards the Pentlands, this is where medieval plague victims were banished to die. Much less traumatic is its golfing reputation: people have been playing here since the 17th century at least. There's still a modest pitch and putt course, free if you bring clubs and balls.

Bruntsfield itself is a thriving neighbourhood, with specialist independent shops selling everything from surfboards to designer cakes. Like Marchmont, it's almost wholly residential, but a clutch of classy bars and restaurants sets it apart. Further south is **Morningside**, once notoriously snooty and home to blue-rinsed ladies with strangulated accents. Visitors would be hard-pressed to find anyone like that in the area now, but with some property prices here – and in the nearby **Grange** – reaching seven figures, it's still an exclusive locale.

One characteristic that Morningside and the Grange share with Bruntsfield and Marchmont is that all were at least partly built over the Burgh Muir, which also served as a rallying point for Scottish armies (the last time this happened was before the disastrous defeat at Flodden in 1513). On these occasions the royal standard would be pitched in the **Bore Stone**, now displayed on a plinth on Morningside Road next to the old kirk at the corner of Newbattle Terrace. Close by, on Newbattle Terrace itself, is the art deco **Dominion Cinema** (*see p218*).

Beyond these suburbs is **Blackford Hill**; here stands the twin-teacake structure of the **Royal Observatory**, completed in 1896. The observatory does have a visitor's centre, but only offers Friday night openings for families in summer, and occasional one-off events (see www.roe.ac.uk). Further south still lie the **Braid Hills**; like the Blackford Hill, these offer amazing views back over the city.

Pedal power

Edinburgh, like Rome, is built on seven hills – so when it comes to gentle leisure cycling, it's not exactly in the class of Amsterdam and Copenhagen. Whether you're trying to get from the bottom of Leith Walk to the Royal Mile or from Stockbridge to Princes Street, you'll face some pretty relentless gradients.

But it would be wrong to rule out Edinburgh as a cycling city, at least according to the folks at Spokes (*see p239*). Provision is made for cyclists on its major roads, and it's also the perfect centre for trips as far afield as St Andrews and the Borders. But those seeking a gentler pace need not be discouraged. Many of the city's former train lines have been turned into cycle paths, forming one of the most extensive off-road networks in the country. Trains, like bikes, don't care for hills, which makes for easy and safe cycling over a surprisingly large area.

To the north of the city is the Water of Leith Walkway (*see p110* **Walk this way**), leading to the **Scottish National Gallery of Modern Art** (*see p113*) in one direction and the port of Leith in the other. From the same starting point, you can get as far as **Cramond** (*see p128*). On the other side of town, join the **Union Canal** towpath at Fountainbridge, then rejoin the walkway leading right out to Balerno. On the south side of Holyrood Park, the charmingly named **Innocent Railway Path** will set you en route for Musselburgh. However, make sure you wear a helmet where the paths cross the city's less reputable housing schemes. This affords at least some protection when local urchins engage in their popular 'throw a rock at a cyclist' game. The worst spots are on the cycle path running from Victoria Park to Crewe Toll, parallel with Ferry Road. For more on cycling, *see p239*.

West Edinburgh

And they said you should never mix business and pleasure...

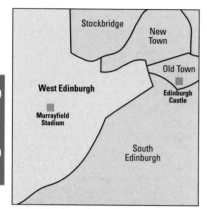

Stockbridge

New Town

Old Town

West Edinburgh

Edinburgh Castle

Murrayfield Stadium

South Edinburgh

Aside from a handful of iconic attractions – **Edinburgh Zoo**, **Murrayfield Rugby Stadium** – West Edinburgh is not an area that generally detains or diverts visitors to the city. But it's here that various layers of Edinburgh's economic history fit together like some topological puzzle, just as a few old buildings hidden away in residential warrens hint at a less urban past. The most surprising feature may well be the **Union Canal**, its terminus tucked discreetly away just off Lothian Road. Well, that and the penguins...

Fountainbridge

Sliced in two by the West Approach Road, **Fountainbridge** doesn't win many beauty contests. It's the only neighbourhood within two miles of the Castle to betray any hint of old industries, and while the arrival of the Fountain Park leisure centre in 1999 (bowling, bingo, and a 13-screen cinema) added amenities for the locals, it didn't improved things aesthetically.

Edinburgh was once a world centre for beer production, with more than 40 breweries located in the city. Even into the 21st century, the multinational Scottish & Newcastle retained an industrial-scale brewing plant at Fountainbridge, dating back to 1856, while out on Slateford Road, the small Caledonian firm produced award-winning beers such as Caledonian 80/- and Deuchars IPA at a brewery only 13 years younger.

But after Scottish & Newcastle closed its Fountainbridge plant in 2004, the company then bought the Caledonian brewery (but not the company itself) in order that it could continue brewing McEwan's 80/-, its signature Scottish ale, in Edinburgh. Caledonian still brews its own ales at Slateford Road, but no longer runs tours for the public. Just another tale of modern capitalism then, but one that holds particular resonance for West Edinburgh: this kind of economic shift has been played out in the area before, such as with the superhighway of the 1820s...

The Union Canal

Before railways made their impact on the city, the last word in 19th-century transport was the **Union Canal**. Built by Irish navvies and French stonemasons and completed in 1822, it ran all the way from Lothian Road (where the Odeon cinema currently stands) to Camelon, near Falkirk, linking with the **Forth & Clyde Canal** that ran on to Glasgow. Coal, building materials and passengers came in to Edinburgh; merchants' goods, horse manure and more passengers went out. However, the canal's heyday proved short-lived, and it was bought out by a competitor railway company in 1848. Traffic died out altogether after the 1860s; the Lothian Road terminus was built over in 1922, and the waterway was officially mothballed in the 1960s.

It took another few decades before the idea of the canal as civic amenity and potential green transport option gained critical mass. However, the notion of opening up the waterway all the way to the Clyde eventually found favour, and the £84.5 million **Millennium Link Project** (www.millenniumlink.org.uk) was born. The Forth & Clyde Canal was officially reopened in 2001 and the Union Canal in 2002, with the city centre terminus established at Lochrin Basin off Fountainbridge. A new housing development, offices, restaurants and cafés immediately arrived, lending it the air of a prosperous little yacht marina. Formally known as Edinburgh Quay, the area won an award for the best regeneration project in Scotland in 2005.

The canal towpath is popular with walkers, joggers and cyclists, and will take you from Lochrin Basin right through the city, out into

A new lease of life: the **Lochrin Basin** development. *See p126.*

West Lothian and beyond. Those who make it as far as the small village of **Ratho** (around eight miles away) can reward themselves with a decent pint at the **Bridge Inn**, which has outdoor seating that overlooks the canal (27 Baird Road, 333 1320, www.bridgeinn.com). Two miles further on, you can enjoy the view from the viaduct high above the River Almond.

The Exchange

Throughout the history of West Edinburgh, grand businesses, even those with massive infrastructures, have regularly flourished before fading. However, the financial services companies that are the real drivers of today's Edinburgh economy haven't been deterred by history. The Royal Bank of Scotland opened enormous new corporate headquarters out on the city's western edge in 2005, but many of the city's others big employers are clustered around Lothian Road and Morrison Street in an area known as the **Exchange**.

Perversely, the first big name to put down roots here, before a formal development strategy was hatched, was the **Sheraton Grand** hotel on Festival Square (*see p72*). Its brutalist façade has been a feature of the area since 1985, but it wasn't until three years later that the city council decided to promote the locale as a dedicated financial district. So began

a £350 million construction extravaganza, described at the time – with a complete lack of understatement – as the most important thing to happen in Edinburgh since the New Town.

At first, development centred around the **Edinburgh International Conference Centre**, which arrived on Morrison Street in 1995. Designed by Terry Farrell, this circular, flat-topped structure beats its own drum. A slew of new buildings followed. Designed by Michael Laird Architects and completed in 1997, the **Standard Life** head office on Lothian Road made an effort to incorporate creative elements into its design, with an entrance and gates by sculptor John Maine and lights and railings by artist Jane Kelly. The sweeping crescent roof of the **Scottish Widows** building landed on Semple Street the next year, courtesy of Glasgow's Building Design Partnership. Then, in 2001, the Sheraton redeemed itself (to an extent) with the addition of the Farrell-designed **One Spa** (*see p203*).

Walk around this area now, though, and every scrap of land seems to be taken up with identikit offices. The paucity of imagination that afflicts some of these brash upstarts is only too evident when they're compared with the nearby tenements at the corner of Grove Street. They're the work of maverick Victorian architect FT Pilkington, and the touch of his Gaudí-esque imagination is still unmistakable.

Gorgie & Dalry

West of the castle, Edinburgh was once a bucolic stretch of farms and small hamlets. From the 12th century on, possibly earlier, the area in immediate proximity to the castle was given over to market gardening. Such rural tranquillity hardly seems credible given the riot of tenements and modern developments that are crammed into the area today. But seek out some of the older buildings, and the picture of a time when the pace of life was much slower gradually emerges. Down Distillery Lane, for instance, off Dalry Road at Haymarket Station, sits a beautiful 18th-century mansion called **Easter Dalry House**. However, it's now occupied by offices and obscured by later developments, and it's hard to imagine it as the old Scots manor with extensive grounds that it once was.

Further along Dalry Road at Orwell Terrace is **Dalry House** (1661), originally the country seat of the Chiesly family. Entirely hemmed in by tenements these days, it was restored as an old folks' home in the 1960s, then transformed into private apartments in 2006. Way back in 1689, though, John Chiesley – son of the original owner – was found guilty of murder, had his hand hacked off before being hanged, and was allegedly buried in the back garden. The building is said to be haunted by 'Johnny One-Arm', Chiesley's ghost.

Keep going and you'll come to the **Gorgie** area, where **Heart of Midlothian** (or 'Hearts') play their football at **Tynecastle Stadium** (*see p238*). Opposite is the child-pleasing **Gorgie City Farm** (*see p212*), and at the junction of Gorgie Road and Balgreen Road is the hidden surprise of **Saughton Park**. Here you'll find beautifully kept winter gardens, centred around a public greenhouse, and a rose garden. It's also a good point to access the **Water of Leith Walkway**, which meanders through the city (*see p110* **Walk this way**).

Further west still, just off the western end of Gorgie Road, sits the architectural mishmash of **Saughton Prison**, Edinburgh's lock-up since 1919. Its ghoulish claim to fame is that, although only four men were dispatched at Saughton, it was the site of the city's most recent execution: after being found guilty of murder, George Alexander Robertson was hanged here in June 1954. His body, along with those of the other three men, lies buried inside the jail's precincts.

Close to Saughton, and even more anomalous than its fellow old country houses in West Edinburgh, is **Stenhouse Mansion**. This solid, three-storey 16th-century pile was built on a meander of the Water of Leith; out of sight and largely out of mind, it's now used by Historic Scotland as a conservation centre, and isn't open to visitors. The motto above the door reads 'Blisit be God for all his giftis', which, back in the day, would have included an uninterrupted view of the castle, two-and-a-half miles away, over open land.

Corstorphine & Cramond

Murrayfield Stadium (*see p239*) is the 67,500-capacity home of rugby union in Scotland, an extraordinary place during any Six Nations match. It's one of the UK's largest sporting arenas, but also hosts major gigs: the Red Hot Chili Peppers played in summer 2004, and Live8 took place here the following year. Further out still is **Edinburgh Zoo** (*see p129*).

Corstorphine Hill, just behind the zoo, offers tremendous views. Best accessed via the steep Kaimes Road, the wooded hill is a favourite with mountain bikers and dog walkers. The trees hide the best panoramas from Corstorphine Hill Tower on the peak, but there are good lookout points to the east of the higher reaches of the zoo. This is the point known as 'Rest-and-be-thankful', where travellers journeying in from the west could get their first real view of Edinburgh.

Back towards the Firth of Forth again, the road to Cramond village passes **Lauriston Castle**. Although hardly typical of other large houses nearby, it does exemplify a particular style of wealthy Edinburgh living: secluded and overlooking the Forth, but not too far from the city centre. The magnificent croquet lawns at the front of the house are home to the **Edinburgh Croquet Club** (661 9994).

Cramond, home to the fictional Mr Lowther to whom Muriel Spark's Miss Jean Brodie paid visits on Sunday afternoons, was actually the earliest known settlement in the Lothians. Waste has been found from the camps of Mesolithic people who inhabited the area in 8500 BC. The Romans arrived in about AD 140; remains were excavated behind the sea wall car park in the Manse gardens, where boards provide information about their second-century bathhouse. The finds, including a remarkable sandstone statue of a lioness that was discovered in the River Almond, are on display in the **Museum of Edinburgh** (*see p92*).

Cramond became both a commuter town and a summer retreat for Edinburgh residents during the 20th century , but it was a thriving port in previous years. During the 18th century the water power available from the Almond proved irresistible to industrialists, who built iron mills along its banks; the village became an exporter of nails around the world. The small **Cramond Heritage Trust** exhibition (www.cramondheritagetrust.org.uk) offers an intriguing slant on local history, and is open on the quayside during summer weekends.

Edinburgh Zoo

Corstorphine Road, Murrayfield (334 9171/www. edinburghzoo.org.uk). Bus 12, 26, 31. **Open** *Apr-Sept* 9am-6pm daily. *Oct, Mar* 9am-5pm daily. *Nov-Feb* 9am-4.30pm daily. **Admission** £10; £7-£7.50 concessions; free under-3s; family £32-£35.50. **Credit** MC, V.

Opened in 1913 on the side of Corstorphine Hill, Edinburgh Zoo is now home to over 1,000 different species of animal. While it's principally a family-orientated attraction (*see p212*), albeit one that puts an increasing emphasis on conservation, its penguin parade is one of the most bizarre and hilarious sights in the city whatever your age; check with zoo staff for times. Legend has it that the parade began in the 1950s, when a keeper accidentally left the door to the penguin enclosure open and they all followed him out. The zoo has maintained a self-sustaining colony for nearly a century; it's now the largest in Europe. Wow-factor mammals such as gorillas, lions, polar bears

and more are among the other inhabitants. There are several play areas for children, plus two cafeterias (one, the Oasis, is only open for meals during the school holidays) and a more formal restaurant.

Lauriston Castle

Cramond Road South, Davidsons Mains, Cramond (336 2060/www.cac.org.uk). Bus 1, 41, 42. **Open** *House Apr-Oct* 11am-5pm Mon-Thur, Sat, Sun. *Nov-Mar* 2-4pm Sat, Sun. *Grounds* 9am-dusk daily. **Admission** *House* (guided tour only) £4.50; £3 concessions. *Grounds* free. **No credit cards**.

Set in large, reasonably well-kept grounds on the way to Cramond, this 16th-century neo-Jacobean fortified property was built as a 1590s tower house for Sir Archibald Napier, extended during the 1820s and last used as a private residence from 1902 to 1926, when then-owner William Reid left it in trust to the nation. Reid and his wife were enthusiastic antiques collectors who furnished the entire house with their finds, and the property's Edwardian interiors have been carefully preserved. The house can only be viewed on a 50-minute tour, which starts at 20 minutes past the hour (during regular opening times).

Sightseeing

Poets' corner

Out in the south-west of the city, set against the backdrop of the two Craiglockhart Hills (Easter and Wester), lies Napier University's Craiglockhart campus. The great sense of space and panoramic views around Edinburgh mean it's almost impossible to link the setting with the slaughter of the Great War, but what went on here for a few months in 1917 did much to create the lines of poetry that were to shape later thinking about the conflict.

A swathe of land here was acquired in 1877 by the Craiglockhart Hydropathic Company, which built a grand Victorian pile that offered fashionable Turkish baths, vapour baths and other 'treatments' for the well-to-do. Some 39 years later the premises were requisitioned by the British Army for use as a hospital, specifically for officers suffering from 'neurasthenia', or shellshock.

Siegfried Sassoon had openly criticised the way the war was being conducted, but was lucky to be deemed 'ill' and sent to Craiglockhart to recuperate; the alternative would have been a guilty verdict at a court martial. Wilfred Owen, though, was suffering a far more obvious bout of shellshock, brought on by a German artillery bombardment. The two met here, and immediately hit it off. Sassoon encouraged Owen in his writing, and also contributed one of his own most celebrated poems, 'The Dreamers', to *Hydra*,

the hospital magazine that Owen edited. Owen, for his part, was inspired to write such pieces as 'Dulce et Decorum Est' and 'Anthem for Doomed Youth'. Their time at the hospital is explored in Pat Barker's critically-acclaimed novel *Regeneration*.

After their months at Craiglockhart, both men returned to active service. Sassoon headed to Palestine and then returned to the Western Front; he was wounded but survived and lived on until 1967. Owen wasn't so fortunate: after returning to the Front in September 1918, he was killed just a week before the armistice.

The building where Sassoon and Owen spent their time together now houses Napier University's Business School; within it, the Craiglockhart Campus Library is home to the **War Poets Collection**. The permanent exhibition, which opened in its current form in late 2005, contains material on the Great War, concentrating on the poets, patients and staff at Craiglockhart in those years. It's open to all, and admission is free.

War Poets Collection

Napier University: Craiglockhart Campus, 219 Colinton Road (455 6021/www.napier.ac.uk/ warpoets). Bus 4, 10, 27, 45. **Open** 8.45am-9pm Mon-Thur; 8.45am-8pm Fri; 10am-4pm Sat, Sun. **Admission** free.

NEW TIME OUT
SHORTLIST GUIDES 2007

Time Out SHORTLIST 'The slickest city guide publisher' The Times

Barcelona 2007
WHAT'S NEW | WHAT'S ON | WHAT'S NEXT

London 2007
WHAT'S NEW | WHAT'S ON | WHAT'S NEXT

New York 2007
WHAT'S NEW | WHAT'S ON | WHAT'S NEXT

Paris 2007
WHAT'S NEW | WHAT'S ON | WHAT'S NEXT

Prague 2007
WHAT'S NEW | WHAT'S ON | WHAT'S NEXT

Rome 2007
WHAT'S NEW | WHAT'S ON | WHAT'S NEXT

The MOST up-to-date guides to the world's greatest cities

UPDATED ANNUALLY

WRITTEN BY LOCAL EXPERTS

Available at all major bookshops at only
£6.99 and from timeout.com/shop

Time Out SHORTLIST

Leith & the Coast

These days, a stroll by the Shore no longer means a walk on the wild side.

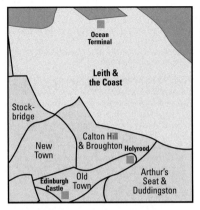

Ocean
Terminal

Leith &
the Coast

Stock-
bridge

Calton Hill
& Broughton Holyrood

New
Town

Edinburgh   Old
Castle   Town

Arthur's
Seat &
Duddingston

The history of Leith, a couple of miles north-east of the Old Town, is almost as chequered as that of its neighbour. At various points a medieval fishing settlement, a crucial port, a shipbuilding centre and a crime-riddled suburb, it's now on the up once more, and in quite spectacular fashion. Despite its proximity to central Edinburgh, it's very much a separate place, with an atmosphere and a history all of its own.

When David I founded Holyrood Abbey in 1128, he endowed it with various patches of land, among them a small area around the **Water of Leith** that included some fishermen's huts. David promptly built another fishing village of his own nearby, roughly based around the site of the modern cobbled street called **The Shore**. The settlement grew comfortably enough, and international trade began to be carried out through its port. But, in 1329, Robert the Bruce, in one of his very last acts as King of Scotland, granted Leith Harbour to the burgesses of Edinburgh, a move that was to have dramatic repercussions down the years.

Since Leith didn't have burgh status of its own, Edinburgh tried to keep it under its thumb over the next 500 years, despite the fact that for much of that time, it was Scotland's premier port. When cargoes were landed at Leith, for example, someone had to walk or ride the three miles to the Edinburgh Tolbooth to pay duty on them before they could be unloaded. The absurd situation sums up the relationship between the two towns, with Leith as the conduit to the sea and Edinburgh the commanding capital skimming a share of its trade. Leithers saw Edinburgh as interfering and incompetent when it came to running a port; Edinburgh saw Leithers as a troublesome breed. Mutual mistrust simmered down through the years, with Leith always maintaining a sense of distance and separation from the capital.

Leith was often caught in the middle of the ongoing conflicts between Scotland and England. Its strategic importance saw it burned by the English in 1544 as part of Henry VIII's 'Rough Wooing', a campaign designed to persuade the Scots to let their infant Mary (later Queen of Scots) marry Henry's son, Edward. The Scots turned down Henry, so the English came back and burned Leith again in 1547. Then, 13 years later, they besieged it.

Leithers appeared to view such destruction as a minor impediment to progress, and had set up strong trade links with the Low Countries, Scandinavia, the Baltic and other countries even further afield by the second half of the 18th century. The harbour had capacity for hundreds of ships; business was booming, with brandy, wine, and citrus arriving from France, Spain and Portugal, and rum, rice and timber from America and the West Indies.

Through all this, the tensions between Leith and Edinburgh never went away, and the pair were eventually destined for a formal divorce in 1833 over mismanagement of the docks, corruption and other financial issues. During its period as a separate burgh, the docks themselves saw massive growth. But then, in 1920, the irresistible expansion of modern Edinburgh saw it swallowed up once more, before the post-war economic doldrums saw it virtually crumble. There are few sights more down-at-heel than a fading port town, but Leith's troubles were compounded in the 1960s and '70s by ill-considered public housing, unemployment and prostitution; eventually, drugs appeared on the scene too. By the late 1970s, Leith was hardly a brand consultant's dream. So what happened?

In the 1980s, encouraged by cheap rents, a few intrepid restaurateurs and creative white-collar entrepreneurs decided to take the plunge and set up in Leith, leavening the social mix in the area while also encouraging others to follow. The area gradually began to improve, but things really started to take off when, in 1992, the docks were privatised, and new owners Forth Ports looked at alternative uses for the empty land. The massive **Scottish Executive** building was completed at Victoria Quay in 1995, followed in short order by the 1998 arrival of the **Royal Yacht Britannia** and the opening of the **Ocean Terminal** shopping mall in 2001.

However, the most dramatic changes in Leith have been residential. Numerous new apartment blocks have sprung up over the last decade, some affordable and some decidedly plush. And the docks are a key component in the grandiose plans for Edinburgh Forthside (www.edinburghforthside.co.uk), a long-term development that incorporates housing, schools, retail and leisure into what will eventually become virtually a whole new city by the sea.

The other most noticeable novelty in recent years has been the number of Polish voices on the streets. Following the 2004 expansion of the EU, thousands of young Poles headed for Scotland to find work, and many gravitated to Leith. With more shops, restaurants and bars opening to cater to incomers in the new seafront developments, the relationship between Poles and Leithers seems to be an economic symbiosis, the modern equivalent of the Baltic trade from centuries past. While the Leith of today is a very different proposition to the Leith of even 15 years ago, some things stay the same.

Leith Walk & the Kirkgate

Leith Walk, the most direct route to Leith from Edinburgh city centre, only came into its own after the construction of North Bridge in 1769. The thoroughfare was built on the line of an old earthwork running from Calton Hill to Leith, which had been thrown up as a defence against Cromwell's invading army in 1650. These days it's flanked by tenements, with shops, pubs and cafés running all the way from the **Playhouse Theatre** at the city end (see p244) down to the **New Kirkgate Shopping Centre** in Leith.

The **Kirkgate** itself was, for centuries, Leith's main street. However, it's now covered by 1960s public housing, and only two structures give any clue as to what the road was once like. The first is **Trinity House** (see below), fast approaching its 200th birthday; the other is **South Leith Parish Kirk**, a Victorian structure erected on the site of a 15th-century church that was damaged when the English besieged Leith in 1560. Both are still handsome buildings, but they're virtually overwhelmed by the crass modern architecture that surrounds them.

Trinity House
99 Kirkgate, Leith (554 3289/www.historic-scotland. gov.uk). Bus 1, 7, 10, 11, 12, 14, 16, 22, 25, 32, 34, 35, 36. **Open** by appointment only. **Admission** £3.50; £1.50-£2.50 concessions. **No credit cards.** **Map** p324 Y4.

The original Trinity House was built in 1555 as the Hospital for the Fraternity of Masters & Mariners of Leith. Completely rebuilt in classical Georgian style in 1816 by Thomas Brown, it has a fabulous interior, and still serves as a museum to Leith's seafaring history, with an outstanding collection of maritime artefacts. It operates by guided tour only; call ahead to book. **Photo** p134.

Leith Links

Before the development of Leith's docks and the addition of the various waves of urban housing in the 19th and 20th centuries, **Leith Links** was a flat, grassy stretch of land by the Firth of Forth. This was once the site of Edinburgh's first racecourse: there are records of silver cups being presented as prizes as far back as 1655, and an annual race week took place here every summer during the 18th century. Boggy ground and boisterous behaviour led to the course being moved east to Musselburgh in 1816. However, the racecourse isn't Leith Links' sole claim to sporting fame. The Honourable Company of Edinburgh Golfers, the oldest golf club in the world, first teed off here in 1744, and went on to draw up the rules that were adopted by the Royal & Ancient Club at St Andrews ten years later.

What's left of the old links, at the foot of Easter Road, is surrounded by houses and tenements sitting around a mile inland. These days, the land is generally used by amateur footballers, cricketers and others simply out to enjoy the summer sunshine. At night, though, it's a different story: despite crackdowns, there are still problems with street prostitution here, and single women should be particularly wary of the area (and nearby Seafield Road) after dark.

The Shore

Leith's Shore is, in a nutshell, where it all began, the site of the 12th-century fishing settlement that eventually grew into a major international port. **The Shore** itself is actually the name of the street running down the south bank of the Water of Leith, home to an assortment of bars and restaurants that face across to an assortment of new apartment blocks on the water's northern edge. A stroll along it reveals just how speedy and dramatic the area's recent regeneration has been. However, it's by no means the whole story.

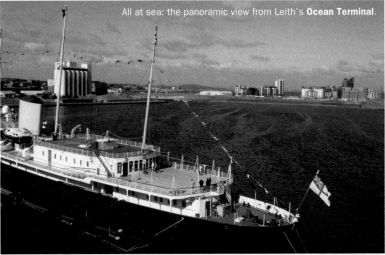
All at sea: the panoramic view from Leith's **Ocean Terminal**.

Just behind the Shore is a maze of narrow old streets that gives some indication of what the area was like before redevelopment. The oldest building here is **Andrew Lamb's House** on Burgess Street, a 16th-century warehouse with merchants' quarters; it's now a home for the elderly. A short walk away, at the corner of Giles Street, is the **Vaults**, a 1682 wine warehouse topped off with an upper storey tacked on in 1785. The ground floor is home to the **Vintners Rooms** restaurant (*see p168*), with the **Scotch Malt Whisky Society** based above (*see p183*).

Signs of Leith's early 19th-century prosperity are visible just a few minutes' walk from the Shore, with grand edifices such as the old, domed **Leith Bank** in Bernard Street (1804), the **Exchange Buildings** and **Assembly Rooms** in Constitution Street (1809), the **Custom House** at the east end of Commercial Street (1812), and the **Municipal Buildings** in Constitution Street (1827), now a police station. The buildings' exteriors give a sense of how the port squared up to the new century with confidence. Back on the quayside, opposite 30 The Shore, a plaque commemorates the arrival here in 1822 of George IV, the first British monarch to set foot in Scotland for nearly two centuries. 'Geo IV Rex O Felicem Diem', it reads, or 'George IV rules on this happy day'.

North Leith

Dividing Leith north and south, the **Water of Leith** is a tourist attraction in its own right. Once described by Robert Louis Stevenson as

'that dirty Water of Leith', it's not the most bucolic of waterways even today. However, it has been cleaned up in recent years, and the addition of a walkway has improved public access to it. Start at the northern end of the Sandport Place Bridge and follow the river back uptown; it's a great way to see behind the façade of the city.

North and South Leith are also connected by Junction Bridge at the corner of Ferry Road and North Junction Street, overlooked by a gable-end mural depicting the history of Leith as a jigsaw. The final piece of the puzzle is a picture of a Sikh man reaching to take the outstretched hand of the community. Many of Edinburgh's Sikhs live in Leith, and a Sikh temple now occupies a converted church, just back over the bridge and down Mill Lane towards the Shore. To the left of the mural are two imposing but unfussy buildings, **Leith Library** and the **Leith Theatre**. Both opened in 1932 and are curious examples of between-the-wars architectural design, with the theatre's portico following the curve of the library's semicircular reading room.

Along North Junction Street, the Leith School of Art inhabits the oldest Norwegian seamen's church outside Norway, a small Lutheran kirk dating from 1868. Walk on to the corner of North Junction Street and Prince Regent Street and you'll discover a dramatic contrast of the old and new. Facing the top of Prince Regent Street is the Doric portico and classical steeple of **North Leith Parish Kirk**, dating from 1813. Spin around and you'll be looking down

Trinity House. *See p132.*

Sightseeing

towards a phalanx of contemporary apartments on the dockside, built next to the Ocean Terminal shopping mall.

At **Ocean Terminal**, designed by Sir Terence Conran (and overlooking the now stationary **Royal Yacht** *Britannia*; *see below*), you get a sense of the sheer scale of the changes the area has undergone in the last few years. To the east of the big retail shed is **Commercial Quay**, a row of bonded warehouses that have been renovated into apartments, upmarket shops, restaurants and offices. Facing them across the quayside is an implacable chunk of modern architecture housing the **Scottish Executive** (*see p35*). The uncompromising design may not be to everyone's taste, but its brashness epitomises the new Leith.

Royal Yacht *Britannia*

Ocean Terminal, Ocean Drive (555 5566/www.royal yachtbritannia.co.uk). Bus 1, 11, 22, 34, 35, 36. **Open** *Apr-Oct* 9.30am-6pm daily (last admission 4.30pm). *Nov-Mar* 10am-5pm daily (last admission 3.30pm). **Admission** £9; £5-£7 concessions; free under-5s; £25 family. **Credit** AmEx, DC, MC, V. **Map** p324 X1.

Launched in 1953, the year of Queen Elizabeth II's coronation, the Royal Yacht *Britannia* was used by the Royal family for state visits, holidays and diplomatic functions for more than four decades. It was decommissioned at the end of 1997 and now resides permanently in Leith, where it has consistently drawn big crowds: in autumn 2005 the old girl clocked up her two millionth visitor since opening to the public in late 1998.

Although the ship's exterior has an art deco beauty, stepping on board – enter from the second floor of Ocean Terminal, via the Britannia Experience – is like regressing into a 1950s nightmare of suburban taste. The chintzy drawing room is perhaps the worst offender in this regard. However, visitors do get to see the state dining room, which has entertained everyone from Gandhi to Reagan, and the engine room, favoured more by grease monkeys. The price of admission includes an audio guide that's packed with anecdotes and points of reference.

Newhaven & Granton

Following the shoreline west along Lindsay Road, on past the gleaming white silos of Chancelot Mill, will lead you to the old fishing village of **Newhaven**. Up until the 20th century, this was an insular community whose residents are thought to have descended from the intermarriage of locals and the shipbuilding craftsmen brought over from France, Scandinavia, Spain, and Portugal by James II. Newhaven became famous for its sturdy and colourfully dressed fishwives,

who used to carry their creels full of fresh fish up to Edinburgh to sell every morning. Much of the original village has been pulled down, but there are still some fishermen's cottages in the streets near the shore. The small but history-packed **Newhaven Heritage Museum** (24 Pier Place, Newhaven Harbour, 551 4165) gives a flavour of what life here was once like.

Across the road from the museum sits the former St Andrew's Kirk, now used by **Alien Rock** (*see p241*) as an indoor climbing centre. However, the major recreational and fitness centre in Newhaven is the huge **Next Generation Club** at Newhaven Place (554 5000, www.nextgenerationclubs.co.uk). When the club first opened back in the 1990s, it was an anomaly on what was then a sparse stretch of waterfront. But now that the Western Harbour area has been designated a major part of the mammoth Edinburgh Forthside development, a huge residential commercial expansion project that also takes in a sizeable chunk of Leith docks, it has been joined by some decidedly chi-chi neighbours.

Further west, **Granton Harbour** first opened in 1838 and was built by the fifth Duke of Buccleuch as part of his estate. Engineering expertise for the project came courtesy of one of the lighthouse-building Stevenson family (relatives of Robert Louis Stevenson). Like Newhaven, Granton was once the base for a fishing fleet, although only small leisure craft are found there today. It also once boasted the world's first ferry train, offering the most direct route to Fife before the construction of the Forth Rail Bridge in 1890.

Portobello

The current focus of attention along Edinburgh's coastline is very much on Leith and all points west, but **Portobello** is still worth a peek. The town was founded in 1739 by George Hamilton, a retired sailor. Having fought in Panama against the Spanish, Hamilton was part of the successful capture of Puerto Bello; when he retired to the shore of Edinburgh, he named his house 'Portobello' in its honour. For a time, the town consisted more or less solely of Hamilton's home, but it soon became a staging post for passengers travelling on the stagecoach to Musselburgh and on towards London.

Once a proper Victorian holiday resort, Portobello was often referred to, seemingly without irony, as 'the Brighton of the North'. Like many other British seaside towns, its glamour has faded somewhat down the years. Nevertheless, on sunny days, its seafront and long stretch of sand can get packed with pale

Sightseeing

On the air tonight

Anything Edinburgh can do, Leith can do too.

Such was the rationale behind the launch of the **Leith Festival** (www.leithfestival.com), an annual community arts shindig that's begun to take off in recent years. However, although audience figures increased fourfold between 2002 and 2005, the festival is still a pretty modest affair; a typical year might take in a gala day on Leith Links, some folk gigs and a number of exhibitions by local artists and photographers.

In 2003 a handful of local enthusiasts began to wonder aloud that if Leith could have a community arts festival, why couldn't it also have a community radio station to broadcast during it? Astonishingly, they got their way, winning a restricted service licence for **Leith FM** (87.7 FM, www.leithfm.co.uk). The station settled into a steady rhythm of biannual broadcasts: a couple of weeks around the festival in June, then another few weeks during the Christmas holidays. As an open-access community broadcaster, it set up a schedule that was beyond eclectic: programmes on healthy living sat alongside classic rock and Arab-language talk shows. Emboldened by its success, the station's volunteers began asking themselves if they could possibly broadcast all the time. They're about to find out.

Leith FM won a five-year community radio licence for North Edinburgh and Leith in early 2006, and aims to be on air 24/7 by 2007. Issues about filling two fortnights a year with material have now been superseded by far more pressing matters: how do you run a real radio station with no money? Although it's easy enough to find wannabe DJs who don't require payment for the privilege of subjecting listeners to obscure techno at 3am, persuading people to work behind the scenes (accounts, administration, sweeping up, making the tea) is a different matter. But with all of North Edinburgh and Leith within range of its transmitter, an area that includes the swanky new developments between Leith docks and Granton, Leith FM does have a great opportunity to establish itself as the voice of the waterfront.

bodies catching some sun, visitors munching on ice-creams or fish and chips, kids playing on the slot machines, and locals indulging in the simple pleasure of a stroll along the beach. There's also a mood of determined enjoyment whatever the weather that is peculiarly British.

Unlikely as it may seem, Portobello does have something of a musical heritage. Wander over to 4 Bridge Street, and you'll see a plaque announcing it as the birthplace of Sir Harry Lauder (1870-1950). Known as the 'Laird of the Music Hall', he wrote many of the popular tunes of the day, including 'Roamin' in the Gloamin' and 'I Love a Lassie'. Nearly 30 years after Lauder's death, Edinburgh punk band the Valves mocked the traditional family resort and calm sea with their classic 'Ain't No Surf in Portobello'.

Portobello Swim Centre

57 Promenade, off Bellfield Street (669 6888). Bus 12, 15, 15A, 26, 32, 42, 49. **Open** *Pool* 7am-9pm Mon-Thur; 7am-7.40pm Fri; 9am-3.40pm Sat, Sun. *Turkish Baths* (women only) 3-9pm Mon; 9am-9pm Wed; (men only) 9am-9pm Tue, Thur; (mixed) 3-9pm Mon, 9am-9pm Thur, Fri; 9am-3.40pm Sat, Sun. **Admission** *Pool* £1.10-£3.10; free under-5s. *Baths* (over-16s only) £5-£7. **Credit** MC, V.

Housed in an elaborate building that dates back to 1901, the old Portobello Baths have had a couple of facelifts in their century-plus lifespan. A Lottery grant in 1998 turned the splendid old pile into the Portobello Swim Centre, adding new fitness facilities and a family-friendly café with views out to the beach. The famous Turkish baths are still there (with hot rooms, a steam room and a plunge pool); note that some days are designated as men- or women-only.

Eat, Drink, Shop

Plaisir du Chocolat. *See p201.*

Restaurants & Cafés

Where to find a bit of local flavour.

Blooming lovely: tea and cakes at **Always Sunday**. *See p141.*

At long last, there seems to be a sense around Edinburgh that the local restaurant scene has reached some kind of equilibrium. The gathering prosperity of the 1990s saw an explosion not just in restaurants but also in stylish, modern café-bars. The boom reached an apogee around the turn of the millennium with some major investments and big openings. The likes of **Oloroso** (*see p153*) and **Forth Floor** (*see p152*) managed to find a niche, but others proved short-lived; for them, the wave just broke too high.

On the face of it, the problem was one that the restaurateurs should have predicted: it's hard to run a truly top-class venue when you're only busy at weekends with people celebrating special occasions. A surer route to success is

to set up a more modest operation and focus on building a reputation in the immediate locale. And so it's proved. After Edinburghers' eyes had adjusted to the dazzle emanating from all the new arrivals, they found that a string of accomplished neighbourhood eateries had sneaked along and caught them unawares. Richard and Michelle Heller's **New Bell** (*see p163*), opened in 2000, was one of the first; three years later, the MacRae brothers opened the acclaimed **First Coast** (*see p164*); and more recently, chef Jason Gallagher has transformed the **Stockbridge Restaurant** (*see p155*).

At the more elevated end of the market, the most interesting developments have been low key. In 2005, rising-star chef Alex Thain made his entrance not at some freshly created style palace but at **Cosmo**, a real old stager (*see p151*). In the same year, the celebrated Gullane hotel **Greywalls** managed to tempt chef David Williams from the accomplished, critically lauded Chapter One in Kent to give its kitchen a new direction.

> ❶ Purple numbers given in this chapter correspond to the location of each restaurant and café on the street maps. *See pp324-336.*

Back in the city, Thai restaurants are still popping up at a positively alarming rate, testament to their enduring popularity. And thanks to a few adventurous, innovative establishments such as **Saffrani** (see p141) and **Roti** (see p148), Edinburgh has never been better off when it comes to Indian cuisine. Add in some memorable seafood spots and a couple of Michelin-starred eateries, and it's plain that the restaurant scene in Edinburgh is still punching well above its weight.

CAFE CULTURE
The irresistible rise of the café-bar as a venue that puts eating and drinking on a relatively equal footing has been a boon here, but such establishments don't suit every occasion. Sometimes you simply fancy a pot of tea and a slice of carrot cake, preferably unaccompanied by an over-zealous DJ playing his favourite tunes, or a noisy gaggle of office refugees on their third bottle of chenin blanc. You're in luck.

The city has been swamped by the well-known chains in recent years, but the more individual local cafés – traditional spots such as **Clarinda's** (see p141), contemporary venues such as **Glass & Thompson** (see p149) and one-offs like the **Chai Teahouse** (see p160) – have held firm. A certain schizophrenia has also proven a sound business move at operations such as the **Honey Pot** (see p143), **Maxi's** (see p155) and **Toast** (see p161), which operate as cafés during the day but which also serve more substantial meals in the evening.

The café-bar culture in Edinburgh is great for residents but a nightmare for guidebook editors, who have to decide whether a venue is best approached for its food or its drinks. Generally speaking, where a venue's dining operation is more noteworthy than its bar scene, we've included it in this chapter. However, it's also worth checking the **Pubs & Bars** section (see pp169-184) for other café-bar ventures that, while generally attracting more drinkers than diners, also serve food. Indeed, many operate more as cafés than bars during the day, with most visitors favouring coffee and a sandwich over beer and a bag of nuts.

PRACTICALITIES
Few restaurants have a strict dress code these days. As a general rule, the pricier the joint, the smarter the clientele; if you're unsure, it's wise to call ahead first.

It's standard practice to pay ten per cent on top of the bill for service. Some restaurants will add a service charge automatically, even while insisting that it's 'optional'; if service wasn't up to scratch, you should ask for this to be deducted. Be wary of places that include a service charge on the bill but still leave a space for a gratuity on your credit card slip.

Note that during August, when various festivals take over the city (see pp41-50), many restaurants and cafés remain open beyond their regular opening hours in order to meet demand. If in doubt, call ahead to check. Whenever you turn up, though, you'll need to stub out your cigarette before entering: smoking has been outlawed in all enclosed public spaces in Scotland since March 2006, and violation of the law could leave you with a £50 fine. If you want to light up, you'll have to go outside on the street.

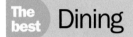

The best Dining

Top restaurants
Atrium: keeps on keeping on. See p161.

Cosmo: a new chef and a new style. See p151.

Number One: fine food with a touch of grand hotel class. See p153.

Restaurant Martin Wishart: the best stand-alone restaurant in the city. See p168.

Witchery: this good all-rounder has a brilliant atmosphere. See p148.

Good lookers
Dragon Way: miles over the top. See p157.

Forth Floor: Space: 1999 lands in the classical surrounds of St Andrew's Square. See p152.

La Garrigue: you'll either love or loathe the work of furniture man Tim Stead. See p144.

Rhubarb: a 17th-century mansion benefits from an opulent £2.5 million refurbishment. See p163.

Shapes: a perversely appealing riot of fixtures and fittings in a big shed on an industrial estate. See p164.

Neighbourhood eats
Le Bistrot des Arts: authentic French cuisine from Eric Ortiz. See p161.

First Coast: bistro brilliance from the brothers MacRae. See p164.

New Bell: a great family-run spot in an attractive old building. See p163.

Stockbridge Restaurant: ambitious cooking on St Stephen Street. See p155.

Sweet Melinda's: the name comes courtesy of Bob Dylan's 'Just Like Tom Thumb's Blues'. See p161.

Eat, Drink, Shop

Triple Award Winning
ROTI
is open for both
Lunch and Dinner

The ROTI concept of quality Indian cuisine
can now be experienced at lunchtimes with a

Fixed Price Lunch Menu
Choose from our normal menu
Enjoy a la carte choice
but at a Table d'Hote price

2 Courses £15.95
3 Courses £19.95

Off the beaten track but in the heart of the city centre
ROTI is ideally placed for that discreet business lunch
or a break from the George Street shops.

Come and see why ROTI has won 3 awards since the start of 2006
Best Newcomer in The List Magazine's Food and Drink Awards
Best Eating Experience in the Theme Bar & Restaurant Awards
Highly Commended (second place) in SLTN Catering Restaurant of the Year Awards

Book now to share the experience of.........

Indian food as it is meant to be

Fixed price lunch Tues ~ Fri, 12.00pm ~ 2.00pm
A la Carte dinner Tues ~ Sat, 6.00pm ~ 11.00pm

Telephone 0131 225 1233
email info@roti.uk.com
70 ROSE STREET NORTH LANE • EDINBURGH • EH2 3DX
(Between Castle St. and Frederick St.)

Old Town

Asian

Namaste
15 Bristo Place (225 2000). Bus 2, 41, 42.
Open 5-11pm Tue-Sun. **Main courses** £6-£12.
Credit MC, V. **Map** p330 H8 ❶
Billing its fare as 'Frontier Cuisine', this is an old
hippy dream of North India: candles, cushions,
and Love's *Forever Changes* playing in the background. The signature brass pots contain decep-
tively large quantities of food. A short menu keeps
the quality control high: there are familiar kormas
and rogan josh, but there's also a fine dhal makhni
(black lentils). The swordfish tikka starter is
brilliant, and even the nan breads display a pleasing lightness of touch.

Saffrani
11 S College Street (667 1597). Bus 35/Nicolson
Street–North Bridge buses. **Open** noon-2pm, 5.30-
11pm Mon-Fri; 5.30-11pm Sat, Sun. **Main courses**
£5-£13. **Credit** MC, V. **Map** p331 J8 ❷
Tucked away up a street to the side of the university's classical Old College, this site has played host
to a number of restaurants over the last decade.
Saffrani has been in situ since 2004, and looks
like it should be around for a while. It looks like a
fairly unassuming Indian restaurant from the outside, but owner Khalil Mansoori displays a welcome
sense of adventure in the kitchen: try halibut with
spinach and fenugreek leaves, a signature dish.
Far superior to the average curry house.

Cafés

Always Sunday
170 High Street (622 0667/www.alwayssunday.
co.uk). Bus 35/Nicolson Street–North Bridge
buses. **Open** 8am-6pm Mon-Fri; 9am-6pm Sat,
Sun. **Main courses** £4-£8. **Credit** MC, V.
Map p330 H7, p336 F4 ❸
Thanks to its prime site, bang on the Royal Mile, this
contemporary café can get terribly crowded in
August. But it's well worth trying for a table:
the quality of food on offer (soups, salads, decent
bread and daily specials) means it's simply a great
place to have lunch, an afternoon snack or even a
leisurely Sunday breakfast. No frills, but quite a
gem. **Photo** *p138.*

Beanscene
67 Holyrood Road (557 6549/www.beanscene.co.uk).
Bus 35, 36. **Open** 8am-10pm Mon-Sat; 10am-10pm
Sun. **Main courses** £3-£9. **Credit** MC, V.
Map p331 L7 ❹

▶ For pubs and bars serving food in the
Old Town, see pp170-173.

There are other outlets in Ayr, Glasgow, St Andrews
and Stirling along with four here in Edinburgh (this
one is the most convivial), but Beanscene is very
much a homegrown Scottish affair rather than a
pan-global retail assault. It's hardly elaborate, but
simple pleasures such as the toasted cinnamon and
raisin bagel with cream cheese are not to be scorned.
The chain hosts regular in-store gigs and even has
its own record label, Luna; check online for more.
Other locations: 2 Grosvenor Street, New Town
(346 8043); 99 Nicolson Street, South Edinburgh
(667 8159); 1 Edinburgh Quay, Fountainbridge,
West Edinburgh (656 0520).

Café DeLos
Royal Museum of Scotland, Chambers Street (274
4114/www.nms.ac.uk/royal). Bus 23, 27, 42, 45.
Open 10am-4.30pm daily. **Main courses** £4-£7.
Credit MC, V. **Map** p330 H8 ❺
Completed in 1888 and built by Captain Francis
Fowke, also responsible for the Royal Albert Hall in
London, the Royal Museum is a Victorian marvel,
and its spectacular, soaring atrium is one of the most
impressive places in Edinburgh to sit and have a cup
of coffee and a slice of cake. The more peckish may
prefer one of the stromboli, or a choice of sandwiches, soups and other platters.

Caffè Lucano
37-39 George IV Bridge (225 6690/www.caffelucano.
co.uk). Bus 23, 27, 42, 45. **Open** 10am-10pm
Mon-Sat; 10am-8pm Sun. **Main courses** £3-£15.
Credit MC, V. **Map** p330 H8 ❻
A simple Italian establishment with a relaxed and
friendly atmosphere, Caffè Lucano offers breakfast
(scrambled egg and smoked salmon on toast), filled
ciabatta and focacce, cakes, coffees and even full-on
plates of fettucini, steak or chicken washed down
with a glass or two of house wine. The good-natured
staff and sheer lack of whimsy or pretension make
it a welcome find.

Clarinda's
69 Canongate (557 1888). Bus 35, 36. **Open** 9am-
4.30pm Mon-Sat; 10am-4.30pm Sun. **Main courses**
£2-£5. **No credit cards**. **Map** p331 L6 ❼
Hanging baskets of flowers outside, politesse inside:
nothing changes at Clarinda's, a traditional tea room
par excellence. Along with your pot of tea, sample a
chocolate crispy, sherry trifle or melting moment.
It's all very Scottish and home-made, with cakes and
biscuits your grandmother might have baked, but it
also runs to breakfasts, sandwiches and lunches.

Elephant House
21 George IV Bridge (220 5355/www.elephant-
house.co.uk). Bus 23, 27, 42, 45. **Open** 8am-10pm
daily. **Main courses** £3-£6. **Credit** MC, V.
Map p330 H8 ❽
This popular café draws everyone from juice-sipping
students to grannies out with the grandkids. Some
of the teas and coffees are first-rate (and organic), but
there's also a short and affordable wine list. The food
menu runs to salads, baguettes and savouries, and

Eat, Drink, Shop

the main room at the back has fantastic views out over the Old Town. For Elephants & Bagels, their sister operation on Marshall Street, *see p160*.

Fruitmarket Gallery
45 Market Street (226 1843/www.fruitmarket.co.uk). Bus 36/Nicolson Street–North Bridge buses. **Open** 11am-5.30pm Mon-Sat; noon-4.30pm Sun. **Main courses** £2-£7. **Credit** MC, V. **Map** p330 H7, p336 F3 **9**
This modern art gallery (*see p221*) challenges the viewer to ponder what they've just seen long after they've left the gallery itself. Just as well, then, that this light, airy café is on the premises, providing some space to think along with some excellent salads, light meals and cakes.

Honey Pot
46 George IV Bridge (226 3269/www.honeypot experience.co.uk). Bus 23, 27, 42, 45. **Open** 9.30am-10.30pm daily. **Main courses** £3-£9. **Credit** MC, V. **Map** p330 H8 **10**
Although the dining space here is below street level, it feels fairly light and spacious during the day. The menu kicks off with breakfast (porage, poached eggs on toast), moves on to wraps, sandwiches and light meals, and then gets more serious in the evenings with heartier dishes such as stroganoff, lasagne and paella. Free Wi-Fi access is an added bonus.

Lot
4 Grassmarket (225 9924/www.the-lot.co.uk). Bus 2, 23, 27, 41, 42. **Open** 11am-9.30pm Mon-Sat; noon-6pm Sun. **Main courses** £4-£9. **Credit** MC, V. **Map** p330 G8, p336 C4 **11**
Hidden away in a converted church, the Lot is a not-for-profit bistro and arts venue run by An Airde, a charity that promotes Christian musicians. There are gigs upstairs, while downstairs is a neat dining room. Pop in for a coffee or enjoy a full evening meal from the short but eclectic menu: small haggis, neeps and tatties to start, say, followed by Thai green curry.

Plaisir du Chocolat
251-253 Canongate (556 9524/www.plais chocolat.com). Bus 35, 36. **Open** 10am-6pm daily. **Main courses** £2-£20. **Credit** MC, V. **Map** p331 K7 **12**
This spot has much to offer the visitor: fin-de-siècle decor, gourmet teas and light bistro meals (moules, savoury tarts, even fondue in winter). But its name gives away its main attraction, which comes as cakes, gateaux, truffles and more. Whatever you do, order a steaming cup of hot chocolate, served with a dash of cinnamon, nutmeg or even chilli.

Spoon
15 Blackfriars Street (556 6922). Bus 35/Nicolson Street–North Bridge buses. **Open** 9am-5pm Mon-Fri; 10am-5pm Sat. **Main courses** £2-£6. **Credit** MC, V. **Map** p331 J7 **13**
This fresh, modern café has a reputation for decent food and great smoothies. The clientele is more varied than you might expect given its proximity to the Royal Mile; indeed, the café can be a great escape from the tourist madness a few yards away. The menu features light breakfasts, panini, soups and ever-changing specials. It's also licensed, so you can have a glass of wine to go with that focaccia.

Fish & seafood

Creelers
3 Hunter Square (220 4447/www.creelers.co.uk). Bus 35/Nicolson Street–North Bridge buses. **Open** *June-Sept* noon-2.30pm, 5.30-10.30pm Mon-Thur, Sun; noon-2.30pm, 5.30-11pm Fri, Sat. *Oct-May* 11.30am-2.30pm, 5.30-10pm Mon-Thur; 11.30am-2.30pm, 5.30-11pm Fri, Sat; noon-3pm, 6-10pm Sun. **Main courses** £9-£30. **Credit** MC, V. **Map** p330 H7, p336 F4 **14**
Owners Tim and Fran James opened this smart seafood restaurant, a sister establishment to the Arran original, in 1994. The formula is simple: good

Spoon.

produce sourced from Scotland's crinkly west coast. Food may arrive unadorned (a signature seafood platter) or with more elaborate preparation (king scallops with sweetcorn risotto). The menu always includes one or two meat and vegetarian options for those not fishily inclined.

Mediterranean

Barioja
19 Jeffrey Street (557 3622). Bus 35/Nicolson Street–North Bridge buses. **Open** 11am-late Mon-Sat. **Main courses** *Tapas £2-£7.* **Credit** AmEx, DC, MC, V. **Map** p331 J7 ⑮
Sister venture to Igg's next door (*see below*), Barioja is a smart, modern tapas bar. All of the old favourites are here (tortilla, gambas a la plancha, manchego); the lunchtime special offers four tapas for a set price. You could just come here to sit and drink wine, but you'll crack and order some food eventually.

Igg's
15 Jeffrey Street (557 8184). Bus 35/Nicolson Street–North Bridge buses. **Open** noon-2.30pm, 6-10.30pm Mon-Sat. **Main courses** £16-£22. **Credit** AmEx, MC, V. **Map** p331 J7 ⑯
Aside from a recent move towards a more seafood-slanted menu, not much has changed at Iggy Campos's upmarket Iberian restaurant since it first opened in 1989: the table linens are still white, the glassware still shines, and the food still relies on good ingredients presented with Spanish flair. The two-course set lunch (£12.50) is excellent value. For the more informal Barioja, *see above*.

La Garrigue
31 Jeffrey Street (557 3032/www.lagarrigue.co.uk). Bus 35/Nicolson Street–North Bridge buses. **Open** noon-2.30pm, 6-9.30pm Mon-Sat. **Main courses** £9-£20. **Credit** AmEx, MC, V. **Map** p331 J7 ⑰
The quality-rustic decor of Edinburgh's specialist Languedoc restaurant – tables and chairs are by the late, great furniture-maker Tim Stead – are in keeping with chef Jean Michel Gauffre's food philosophy. Highlights include 'three meat cassoulet' with pork, lamb and duck (plus Toulouse sausage, of course), but there are also meat-free options for vegetarians.

Maison Bleue
36-38 Victoria Street (226 1900). Bus 2, 23, 27, 41, 42. **Open** noon-3pm, 5-11pm Mon-Sat; noon-3pm, 5-10pm Sun. **Main courses** £7-£23. **Credit** MC, V. **Map** p330 G7, p336 D4 ⑱
The menu at atmospheric Maison Bleue is split into bouchées (one equates to a starter, two or three to a main), bouchées doubles (more substantial) and brochettes (chargrilled skewers). Set menus are good value, especially early evening. With Marrakech-influenced decor, the second branch opened in 2006. **Other locations**: Maison Bleue & Boudoir Bar, 3-5 Infirmary Street, Old Town (557 9997).

Modern European

Café Hub
Castlehill (473 2067/www.eif.co.uk/thehub). Bus 2, 23, 27, 41, 42. **Open** 9.30am-6pm Mon, Sun; 9.30am-10pm Tue-Sat. **Main courses** £5-£15. **Credit** AmEx, MC, V. **Map** p330 G7, p336 D4 ⑲

Scottish cuisine

Scotland has a tremendous natural larder. Venison, wildfowl, salmon and shellfish have been used ever since the country was settled after the last Ice Age. The Vikings probably introduced sea fishing, while barley and beef cattle have long been mainstays of Scottish farming. Diplomatic ties with France – before the Scottish and English crowns merged in 1603 – brought rich sauces, cakes, pastries and desserts, largely for the aristocracy. The more prosaic potatoes, oats and mutton came along later.

This wealth of raw materials sits rather at odds with current folk memories. Since the Industrial Revolution, most Scots have lived in cities and traditionally opted for cheap and wholesome staples: porridge, Scotch broth, stovies, or mince and tatties. These dishes are still thought of as Scottish cooking, but in the last generation or two have been brushed aside by takeaways, ready-meals and the like.

As such, a restaurant aiming to create something 'typically Scottish' has a problem. In cafés and bars, homely and cheap Scotch broth or stovies may go down well, but not in more aspirational establishments. That said, some traditional fare does stand being posed up: Cullen skink (creamy smoked haddock soup), for example, or cranachan (cream, oatmeal, whisky and raspberries).

The general compromise taken by many restaurateurs has been to take the raw materials of Scottish cuisine and deal with them in a classic French style. Both **Off the Wall** (*see p147*) and **Haldanes** (*see p152*) are good examples of this Franco-Scots approach, although no Edinburgh granny ever made seared venison loin with *port jus*. But at more typically Scottish restaurants such as **Dubh Prais** (*see p148*) and **Stac Polly** (*see p153*), it just comes down to atmosphere, attitude and invention.

Shaws Bistro & International Tapas Bar. *See p147.*

The catering wing of the Edinburgh International Festival HQ, Café Hub sits in a building dating to 1845, originally an assembly hall and offices for the Church of Scotland. The daytime menu is flexible, with more ambitious food (halibut, maize-fed chicken) served in the evenings, but it's also a great place to have an alfresco beer on a sunny day. It gets stupidly busy in August, of course, both on the inside (with soaring ceilings) and out on the terrace.

Grain Store

30 Victoria Street (225 7635/www.grainstore-restaurant.co.uk). Bus 2, 23, 27, 41, 42.
Open noon-2pm, 6-10pm Mon-Thur; noon-2pm, 6-11pm Fri; noon-3pm, 6-11pm Sat; noon-3pm, 6-10pm Sun. **Main courses** £9-£30. **Credit** MC, V. **Map** p330 G7, p336 D4 ⑳
Looking out from first-floor level down a curving, cobbled brae, the Grain Store is a comforting presence. Stone-walled, wooden-floored and candlelit, it's been a city favourite for years. The menu is generally Franco-Scots with the odd Euro foray, but there are few better places to neck half a dozen Loch Fyne oysters, followed by venison, lamb or fresh fish. It's also an ideal location for lingering lunches (£10 for two courses, £13.50 for three) over a bottle of wine.

North Bridge Brasserie

Scotsman Hotel, 20 North Bridge (556 5565/www.thescotsmanhotel.com). Nicolson Street–North Bridge buses. **Open** noon-2.30pm, 6-10pm daily. **Main courses** £9-£18. **Credit** AmEx, DC, MC, V. **Map** p330 H7, p336 F3 ㉑
Housed in the former offices of the *Scotsman* newspaper, this upmarket hotel (*see p53*) gave the local scene a real boost when it opened in 2001. Since then, its brasserie has settled down into an established hangout for lunch, dinner or drinks. It looks suitably sleek and imposing, with the requisite modern fittings and huge displays of flowers at the door. Food ranges from shepherd's pies to charcuterie platters.

Off the Wall

105 High Street (558 1497/www.off-the-wall.co.uk). Bus 35/Nicolson Street–North Bridge buses.
Open noon-2pm, 6-10pm Mon-Sat. **Main courses** £10-£21. **Credit** AmEx, MC, V. **Map** p331 J7 ㉒
Located up a flight of stairs off the city's main tourist drag, this is an ideal retreat, at the pricier but more accomplished end of the city's eating out continuum. Chef David Anderson has built a solid reputation for himself: all his meat, game and seafood comes from Scottish sources, but his cooking nods to France with mains such as supreme of Barbary duck and saddle of venison.

Outsider

15-16 George IV Bridge (226 3131). Bus 23, 27, 42, 45. **Open** noon-11pm daily. **Main courses** £7-£15. **Credit** MC, V. **Map** p330 H8, p336 D4 ㉓
A bigger and altogether more urbane sister to the Apartment (*see p161*), the Outsider has been a hit since it opened in 2002. The food is similar to the Apartment, but the Outsider scores extra points for

its views over the Castle and the Old Town from the rear of the building. With a sometimes overweening attitude towards fashion, however, it's possibly not the best choice for grumpy old men (or women).

Shaws Bistro & International Tapas Bar

21 Old Fishmarket Close (226 1300/www.shaws restaurant.com). Nicolson Street–North Bridge buses. **Open** noon-11pm daily. **Main courses** *Tapas* £4-£8. **Credit** AmEx, MC, V. **Map** p330 H7, p336 E4 ㉔
This two-level bar-bistro sits at the foot of a steep cobbled brae, in an award-winning building (*see p34* **Small is beautiful**). These are 'international-style' rather than Spanish tapas; the choice includes sardines, ostrich steak, crab claws, kangaroo and much more. Your best bet is to grab one of the bar's black leather sofas, have a few drinks, and order a tapas dish or two as the mood takes you. **Photo** *p145*.

Tower

Royal Museum of Scotland, Chambers Street (225 3003/www.tower-restaurant.com). Bus 23, 27, 42, 45. **Open** noon-4.30pm, 5-11pm daily. **Main courses** £12-£28. **Credit** AmEx, DC, MC, V. **Map** p330 H8 ㉕
A 1998 offering from star restaurateur James Thomson, this is definitely one for the beautiful people. Perched atop the Museum of Scotland, Tower offers self-conscious chic, good views and a terrace (weather permitting). The menu is flexible – combine a salad and a side if you like – with an emphasis on fresh seafood and well-hung meat. The menu

Indian food with flair at **Roti**. See *p148*.

also boasts some serious wines, with 180 bins or thereabouts. Most are affordable, but there's always the 1982 Margaux for moments of madness.

Vermilion

Scotsman Hotel, 20 North Bridge (556 5565/www. thescotsmanhotel.com). Nicolson Street–North Bridge buses. **Open** 6-9.30pm Wed-Sun. **Main courses** £16-£25. **Credit** AmEx, DC, MC, V. **Map** p330 H7, p336 F3 ㉖

Located at the bottom of an ostentatious marble staircase, subterranean Vermilion is the manor of chef Beth McTaggart. Low lighting and a crepuscular colour scheme make you feel as if you're in a grotto, far removed from the city outside. The menu might include pigeon breast to start, with monkfish fillet to follow, cooked with some neat creative flourishes.

Witchery & Secret Garden

352 Castlehill (225 5613/www.thewitchery.com). Bus 2, 23, 27, 41, 42. **Open** noon-4pm, 5.30-11.30pm daily. **Main courses** £15-£50. **Credit** AmEx, DC, MC, V. **Map** p330 G7, p336 D4 ㉗

One 16th-century venue, two dining rooms and tons of ambience. James Thomson opened the Witchery back in 1979, its wood panelling, red leather and candlelit interior immediately lending it a reputation for destination dining. The possibly even more romantic Secret Garden then followed in 1989. Neither are cheap, and some critics grumble that the cooking (whole grilled Dover sole and roast loin of Scottish deer are typical mains) isn't consistently top class, but it's still of a high standard, served with a legendarily good wine list. Try the post-theatre supper to experience the Witchery without breaking the bank.

Scottish

Dubh Prais

123b High Street (557 5732/www.dubhprais restaurant.co.uk). Bus 35/Nicolson Street–North Bridge buses. **Open** noon-2pm, 6.30-10.30pm Tue-Fri; 6.30-10.30pm Tue-Sat. **Main courses** £12-£19. **Credit** AmEx, DC, MC, V. **Map** p331 J7 ㉘

This small, discreet cellar doesn't exactly trumpet its presence among the tourist delights of the Royal Mile. Scottish ingredients served with little fuss define the menu: Aberdeen Angus steak on Arran mustard sauce, chicken breast stuffed with ham from Argyll and cheese from Mull. It's tiny, so book ahead.

Vegetarian

David Bann

56-58 St Mary's Street (556 5888/www.davidbann. com). Bus 35/Nicolson Street–North Bridge buses. **Open** 11am-10pm daily. **Main courses** £9-£12. **Credit** AmEx, MC, V. **Map** p331 J7 ㉙

There are Indian vegetarian venues in Edinburgh, and Michelin-starred establishments with meat-free menus. But when it comes to modern, European-style and completely vegetarian eateries, David Bann is the market leader. The approach is flexible:

it's fine for a quick coffee and a light snack, but also for a full lunch or dinner: try parmesan and basil polenta to start, followed by spinach and smoked cheese strudel. The wine list is short and affordable.

New Town & West End

Asian

Dusit

49a Thistle Street (220 6846/www.dusit.co.uk). Princes Street buses. **Open** noon-2.30pm, 6-10.45pm Mon-Sat; noon-10pm Sun. **Main courses** £9-£18. **Credit** AmEx, MC, V. **Map** p326/p330 F6, p336 C1 ㉚

Edinburgh hasn't so much experienced a wave of new Thai restaurants in the last few years as a continuous spring tide of green curry and tom yum soup. Although it is comparatively pricey, Dusit is among the most accomplished and interesting. For the most part traditional, it does make a few departures (a dash of whisky here and there, for example).

Kweilin

19-21 Dundas Street (557 1875/www.kweilin.co.uk). Bus 13, 23, 27. **Open** noon-2pm, 5-11pm Tue-Sat; 5-11pm Sun. **Main courses** £10-£36. **Credit** MC, V. **Map** p326 F5 ㉛

Kweilin's longevity (it's been open since 1984) bodes well for the quality of its Cantonese food, and the kitchen delivers. The simple, calming decor and somewhat aspirational atmosphere mean that it's perhaps not the best place to familiarise the kids with dim sum, but grown-ups will enjoy wrestling with crab claws to start, before tackling some roast duck or properly handled sea bass as a main.

Roti

70 Rose Street North Lane (225 1233/www.roti.uk. com). Princes Street buses. **Open** noon-2pm, 6-11pm Tue-Fri; 6pm-midnight Sat. **Main courses** £12-£15. **Credit** AmEx, MC, V. **Map** p326/p330 F6, p336 C1 ㉜

The much-loved Martin's closed its doors in 2005, but within weeks Tony Singh of Oloroso (*see p153*) had moved in and reopened as Roti. It's a modern take on the Indian restaurant that works brilliantly: in place of korma or bhuna you'll find Goan fish, Kashmiri lamb and seared halibut in coconut and vegetable stew. Desserts are an aesthetic treat. **Photo** *p147.*

Cafés

Queen Street Café

Scottish National Portrait Gallery, 1 Queen Street (557 2844/www.natgalscot.ac.uk). Bus 4, 8, 10, 11, 12, 15, 15A, 16, 17, 26, 44, 45. **Open** 10am-4.30pm Mon-Sat; 2-4.30pm Sun. **Main courses** £2-£5. **No credit cards. Map** p326 G5 ㉝

▶ For pubs and bars serving food in the **New Town**, *see pp173-177.*

The very fabric of this fantastic Victorian-Gothic building has a reassuring air of tradition. The café is good for gossip and a scone, or light meals such as soups, pasta, salads or focacce after a look round the gallery (*see p105*). Although the food won't come with any fashionista flourishes, the standard is high.

Glass & Thompson
2 Dundas Street (557 0909). Bus 13, 23, 27.
Open 8am-6pm Mon-Fri; 10.30am-4pm Sun. **Main courses** £3-£7. **Credit** MC, V. **Map** p326 F5 ㉞
For more than a decade, G&T has been on every list of Edinburgh's best cafés. Given the New Town location and premium prices, it's not the most populist of places, but the food is excellent: the cakes are sublime, while the assorted tarts and platters would put some local restaurants to shame. The decor is modern, with a couple of outside tables for sunny days.

Palm Court
Balmoral Hotel, 1 Princes Street (556 2414/ www.thebalmoralhotel.com). Princes Street buses.
Open 9am-1am daily. **Main courses** £10-£25. *Afternoon tea* £15-£20. **Credit** AmEx, DC, MC, V. **Map** p326/p330 H6, p336 F2 ㉟
Now renamed 'the Bollinger Bar at Palm Court', this is an imposing spot for afternoon tea. Choose between the Balmoral, Tartan and Chocolate teas (2-6pm daily) and book ahead, then kick back and feel like a mon-eyed aristocrat of the old school for an hour or two.

Fish & seafood

Fishers in the City
58 Thistle Street (225 5109/www.fishersbistros. co.uk). Princes Street buses. **Open** noon-10.30pm. **Main courses** £10-£22. **Credit** AmEx, MC, V. **Map** p326/p330 F6, p336 C1 ㊱

The owners of Fishers in Leith (*see p165*) ventured into the city centre in 2001 with this smart, modern seafood eatery. Hardy perennials include the excellent creamy fish soup, oysters and a seafood platter; alternative mains might include west coast scallops with smoked haddock Welsh rarebit.

Mediterranean

Café Marlayne
76 Thistle Street (226 2230). Princes Street buses. **Open** noon-2pm, 6-10pm Tue-Sat. **Main courses** £11-£15. **Credit** MC, V. **Map** p326/p330 F6, p336 C1 ㊲
Wicker chairs and wooden tables create a relaxed environment at this café, where you can count on finding solid French cuisine based around such raw materials as pigeon breast, crab, lamb and beef fillet. Puddings are delicious too: the pear and frangipane tart is a triumph.
Other locations: 7 Old Fishmarket Close, Old Town (225 3838).

Centotre
103 George Street (225 1550/www.centotre.com). Princes Street buses. **Open** *Italian Bar* 8am-11pm Mon-Thur; 8am-midnight Fri, Sat; 11am-6pm Sun. *Café* 9am-10pm Mon-Thur; 9am-10.30pm Fri, Sat; 11am-5pm Sun. **Main courses** £4-£16. **Credit** MC, V. **Map** p326/p330 F6, p336 B1 ㊳
Victor and Carina Contini are part of the family behind the celebrated Valvona & Crolla (*see p199*). However, in 2004, the duo decided to set up on their own in this former bank, still grandiose but done out with modern fixtures and fittings. The culinary aim is simple: to produce high-quality Italian food. At the front, the Italian Bar caters to coffee fiends, wine-sippers and snackers. **Photo** *p151*.

Glass & Thompson.

Duck's at Le Marche Noir
2-4 Eyre Place (558 1608/www.ducks.co.uk).
Bus 8, 17, 23, 36. **Open** noon-2.30pm, 6-10pm
Tue-Thur; 6.30-10pm Fri-Sun. **Main courses** £13-
£24. **Credit** AmEx, DC, MC, V. **Map** p326 F3 **39**
At this intimate and polished space (owned, if you
were wondering, by Malcolm Duck), food comes with
a French accent: goat's cheese tartlet to start, perhaps, followed by a pork fillet casserole. The award-
winning wine list incorporates everything from
easy-drinking lunchtime plonk at under £15 to serious (and seriously expensive) vintage French reds.

Valvona & Crolla Vin Caffè
Multrees Walk, St Andrew's Square (557 0088/
www.valvonacrolla.com). Princes Street buses.
Open 10am-9.30pm Mon-Wed; 10am-10.30pm Thur,
Fri; 9am-10.30pm Sat. **Main courses** £10-£20.
Credit AmEx, MC, V. **Map** p326 H5, p336 F1 **40**
Valvona & Crolla (*see p199*) launched the ambitious
Vin Caffè, a modern space with a café on the ground
floor and restaurant upstairs, in 1999. The latter offers
dark wood, leather banquettes and acclaimed (if not
inexpensive) food. Dishes include great pizzas, grid-
dled venison and pasta dishes as simple as taglierini
with cream, butter and parmesan.

Middle Eastern

Nargile
73 Hanover Street (225 5755/www.nargile.co.uk).
Princes Street buses. **Open** noon-2pm, 5.30-10pm
Mon-Thur; noon-2pm, 5.30-11pm Fri, Sat.
Main courses £7-£22. **Credit** AmEx, MC, V.
Map p326/p330 G6, p336 D1 **41**

Decor-wise, this city centre Turkish eaterie is bright,
modern and cliché-free. Meze features prominently
on the extensive menu, but kebabs, couscous, veggie options, seafood and specials such as chicken
tossed in mustard and honey are also on offer, as are
Turkish wines. Sit-down cuisine from this corner of
the globe is still pretty rare in Scotland, so praise is
due to manager and co-owner Seyhan Azak for carv-
ing out this unique and enduring fixture.

Modern European

Bonham
35 Drumsheugh Gardens (623 9319/www.the
bonham.com). Bus 13, 19, 37, 41, 47. **Open**
7am-10pm Mon-Sat; 12.30-3pm, 6.30-10pm Sun.
Main courses £12-£25. **Credit** AmEx, DC, MC, V.
Map p329 C7 **42**
Although it is just a few minutes' walk from the
bustling west end of Princes Street, the Bonham
hotel (*see p59*) feels delightfully secluded. The menu
served in its light and spacious dining room reflects
head chef Michel Bouyer's French origins, but offers
a decidedly modern take on his native cuisine. Set
lunches (£13.50 for two courses, £16 for three) are
good value. On one day a week, dubbed Fishy
Friday, the focus at this fine, contemporary restaurant is on seafood.

Cosmo
58a N Castle Street (226 6743/www.cosmo-
restaurant.co.uk). Princes Street buses. **Open**
12.30-2.15pm, 7-10.30pm Mon-Fri; 7-10.30pm Sat.
Main courses £13-£22. **Credit** AmEx, MC, V.
Map p326/p330 E6 **43**

Eat, Drink, Shop

Resistance is futile at **Centotre**. *See p149.*

Poles apart

Since the expansion of the EU in 2004, a large number of young Polish people have come to seek work in the UK. Around 20,000 Poles had registered as residents in Scotland by spring 2006; however, the actual number may be much higher. Many of these new arrivals have headed for the economic buoyancy of Edinburgh; within the city, a large proportion have settled in Leith.

As the Polish community expanded, a tranche of bars and eateries opened to cater to them. The most ambitious is **Cenzor** (*see p173*), where you sense that the street-smart bar staff are getting a little tired of monoglot drinkers asking how to pronounce words such as Zywiec (a brand of lager). Polish cooking may not have the immediate appeal of other national cuisines, but the bar food here offers taste of home for ex-pats: potato pancakes, *pierogi* (stuffed dumplings) and *bigos* (the national dish, a meat and cabbage stew).

The latter platter clearly inspired **Bigos** (277 Leith Walk, Leith, no phone), a small and simple café-bistro that serves a few varieties of *bigos* and *pierogi* alongside pork and chicken dishes and even burgers. Nearby are a couple of Polish shops. **Polski Smak** (25 Albert Place, Leith Walk, mobile 07796 094738, www.polski-smak.co.uk) is a fairly modest affair selling Polish branded food in tins and jars, plus breads, sausages and Polish-language magazines. **Deli Polonia** (237 Leith Walk, Leith, 555 1281) is a labour of love for owner Lucyna Ellis: a proper delicatessen with a meat counter, a good selection of foodstuffs, a takeaway service and even a few tables at which to sup coffee and munch snacks. But it's not all confined to Leith – South Edinburgh also has its own neighbourhood Polish store, **Bona Deli** (86 South Clerk Street, South Edinburgh, mobile 07724 388413).

Established in 1969 as an old-fashioned and upmarket Italian, Cosmo was fully refurbished in 2005 and set off in a new direction under chef Alex Thain. The chandeliers and deep red colour scheme mean that its classic look lives on, but Thain has drawn on his experiences with Gordon Ramsay to introduce a modern Franco-Scottish menu. With an eminently capable sommelier and an excellent kitchen crew, this is one of the very best restaurants in the city.

Dining Room

Scotch Malt Whisky Society, 28 Queen Street (220 2044/www.smws.com). Bus 4, 8, 10, 11, 12, 15, 15A, 16, 17, 26, 44, 45. **Open** *Non-members, pre-theatre menu* 5-6.30pm Mon-Sat. *A la carte* 7-9pm Wed-Sat. **Main courses** £13-£20. **Credit** AmEx, DC, MC, V. **Map** p326 F5 ㊵
Complementing the Leith original (*see p183*), the Scotch Malt Whisky Society opened a second venue in a restored Georgian townhouse with some modern interior design touches. The ground floor holds a rather splendid Dining Room. Non-members are currently restricted to the pre-theatre menu (reasonably priced at £12.50 for two courses, £15 for three), but members can invite as many people as they like for a full meal.

Forth Floor

Harvey Nichols, 30-34 St Andrew's Square (524 8350/www.harveynichols.com). Princes Street buses. **Open** *Brasserie* 10am-5.30pm Mon-Sat; noon-4pm Sun. *Restaurant* noon-3pm Mon; noon-3pm, 6-10pm Tue-Fri; noon-3.30pm, 6-10pm Sat; noon-3.30pm Sun. **Main courses** *Brasserie* £7-£11. *Restaurant* £12-£18. **Credit** AmEx, DC, MC, V. **Map** p326 H5 ㊸

Even the anti-fashion brigade has had to admit that Harvey Nicks' fourth-floor restaurant and brasserie are pretty good. The views over the Forth are tremendous, the decor is funky, and the kitchen operates at an elevated standard. During the day it caters for footsore shoppers, but at night there's a real buzz. The restaurant has a slightly more elaborate menu than the brasserie, but it's all effectively one space with a discreet partition. There's jazz on Sunday afternoons.

Haldanes

13b Dundas Street (556 8407/www.haldanes restaurant.com). Bus 13, 23, 27. **Open** noon-1.45pm, 5.45-9.30 Mon-Thur; noon-1.45pm, 5.45-10pm Fri; 5.45-10pm Sat; 5.45-9.30pm Sun. **Main courses** £17-£26. **Credit** AmEx, DC, MC, V. **Map** p326 F5 ㊹
Chef and proprietor George Kelso built Haldanes' reputation as one of the city's most accomplished Franco-Scottish restaurants. In early 2006, it moved from Albany Street to these New Town premises, which incorporate a louche lounge bar that offers decent daytime ciabatte, and a warren of adjoined lower basement dining spaces with stone walls and the odd Jack Vettriano print. Kelso has stuck to his tried and tested style (tian of crab, panache of monkfish).

Iglu

2b Jamaica Street (476 5333/www.theiglu.com). Bus 24, 29, 36, 42. **Open** *Bar* 4pm-1am Mon-Thur; noon-1am Fri-Sun. *Restaurant* 6-10pm Tue-Thur, Sun; noon-2pm, 6-10pm Fri; noon-10pm Sat, Sun. **Main courses** £9-£15. **Credit** AmEx, MC, V. **Map** p326 F5 ㊼
The ground floor bar is pleasingly modern (with free Wi-Fi access); upstairs is a small organic restaurant, added in 2005 by energetic proprietor Charlie

Cornelius (he also runs the Wild in Scotland tour business). Dishes include wood pigeon, venison, salmon and vegetarian options, all from carefully sourced ingredients. Not 'haute', but worthwhile and fun.

Number One

Balmoral Hotel, 1 Princes Street (557 6727/www.the balmoralhotel.com). Princes Street buses. **Open** 6.30-10pm Mon, Tues, Sat, Sun; noon-2pm, 6.30-10pm Wed-Fri. **Main courses** £25-£28. **Credit** AmEx, DC, MC, V. **Map** p326/p330 H6, p336 F2 ❹❽

An enviable address, a keen reputation and a very talented chef (Jeff Bland) all conspire to make this a first-class dining experience, one of only two venues in Edinburgh with a Michelin star. The spacious dining room pulls off the trick of being contemporary and classic at once, as the menu brings you into the heady territory of foie gras roulade with pineapple chutney, followed by poached beef sirloin with horseradish gratin.

Oloroso

33 Castle Street (226 7614/www.oloroso.co.uk). Princes Street buses. **Open** noon-2pm, 7-10.15pm daily. **Main courses** £15-£50. **Credit** AmEx, MC, V. **Map** p326/p330 F6, p336 B1 ❹❾

Since opening in 2001, this destination bar-restaurant has, under Tony Singh's watchful eye, consolidated its reputation for quality cooking. The restaurant leads on its beef, veal and seafood grills and modish à la carte menu, and there's a roof terrace from which to enjoy the ephemeral Scottish summer. That said, the bar is usually buzzing, and many people come simply to drink or snack.

Pompadour

Caledonian Hilton Hotel, Princes Street (222 8888/ www.hilton.com). Princes Street buses. **Open** 12.30-10pm Tue-Fri; 7-10pm Sat. **Main courses** £19-£26. **Credit** AmEx, DC, MC, V. **Map** p330 E7, p336 A2 ❺⓪

While faddish eateries come and go, the Pompadour endures. The dining room is effortlessly traditional in a dainty rococo manner, with the odd concession to modernity. With a classic French repertoire and a great sense of history, it's popular with tourists and couples on romantic breaks. With luck, newish head chef Kenny Coltman will lead Pompadour away from its 'Edinburgh institution' reputation and towards greater things once more.

Urban Angel

121 Hanover Street (225 6215/www.urban-angel. co.uk). Princes Street buses. **Open** 10am-10pm Mon-Thur; 10am-11pm Fri, Sat; 10am-6pm Sun. **Main courses** £3-£10 **Credit** MC, V. **Map** p326 G5 ❺❶

Urban Angel has a smart country-city crossover look, with wooden floors and white walls. It maintains high ethical standards, using organic, free range and Fair Trade ingredients. In the daytime, it's a café and takeaway serving up brunches, sandwiches and salads, but it comes into its own in the evening as a relaxed and popular restaurant. Try the fantastic tapas to start, followed by a bowl of crayfish risotto. There are also top-notch veggie options.

Scottish

Stac Polly

29-33 Dublin Street (556 2231/www.stacpolly.co.uk). Bus 10, 11, 12, 23, 27. **Open** noon-2pm, 6-9.30pm Mon-Fri; 6-9.30pm Sat, every other Sun. **Main courses** £18-£21. **Credit** AmEx, DC, MC, V. **Map** p326 G5 ❺❷

Like many restaurants trying to collar Scottishness as a unique selling point, the clubbish if rustic Stac Polly does offer haggis (in filo pastry with plum and red wine sauce). However, it also serves dishes such as duck with pineapple relish, and its Caledonian credentials are more in its general approach than in the way it draws on the homelier elements of the traditional Scots kitchen. The prix fixe lunch is terrific value at £10 for three courses; set lunches are £15.95 (two courses) and £18.95 (three)

Other locations: 8-10 Grindlay Street, South Edinburgh (229 5405).

Vegetarian

Henderson's Bistro

25 Thistle Street (225 2605/www.hendersonsof edinburgh.co.uk). Princes Street buses. **Open** noon-10pm Tue, Wed, Sun; noon-10.30pm Thur-Sat. **Main courses** £5-£6. **Credit** MC, V. **Map** p326/ p330 G6, p336 D1 ❺❸

The Henderson's that so many people know and love (the Salad Table, established in 1963) is just around the corner, but is effectively a basement canteen. You queue, you choose and you pay. Another glass of wine? Repeat the process. Thankfully, the Bistro is just a few yards away: it serves up the same kind of food (including soups, salads, chunky stews and pasta), but it's brought to you by waiting staff. It comes with less hassle involved, but it is admittedly a less atmospheric room.

Other locations: Henderson's Salad Table, 94 Hanover Street, New Town (225 2131).

Stockbridge

American

Bell's Diner

7 St Stephen Street (225 8116). Bus 24, 29, 36, 42. **Open** 6-10.30pm Mon-Fri, Sun; noon-10.30pm Sat. **Main courses** £7-£12. **Credit** MC, V. **Map** p326 E4 ❺❹

It's said that modern sharks evolved something like 144 to 208 million years ago, and have been such a great success in terms of natural selection that they haven't changed much since. And so to Bell's Diner, a burger joint par excellence since 1972; in terms of Edinburgh restaurant turnover, this actually makes

▶ For pubs and bars serving food in **Stockbridge**, *see pp177-178*.

FORTH FLOOR

RESTAURANT BAR & BRASSERIE

"...EVERYTHING ABOUT THIS RESTAURANT
IS A CLASS ACT..." HERALD

"...ONE OF THE CITY'S
PREMIUM RESTAURANTS...BASED ON
SOURCING AND SEASONALITY" THE LIST

HARVEY NICHOLS

it fitter than your average great white. It's small and simple, cooking up fabulous burgers (including vegetarian options), good steaks and hearty desserts to delight your inner child.

Cafés

Gallery Café
Scottish National Gallery of Modern Art, 75 Belford Road (332 8600/www.natgalscot.ac.uk). Bus 13. **Open** 10am-4.30pm daily. **Main courses** £4-£6. **Credit** MC, V. **Map** p329 A7 ⑤⑤
A perennially popular eaterie, and not just with the city's art hounds. The light basement space always has a selection of soups, salads and a couple of hot dishes, as well as a decent cheese selection, but its real value becomes apparent in the summer, when diners can sit on the terrace next to the garden outside the classical 19th-century building.

Café Newton
Dean Gallery, 72 Belford Road (623 7132/www.natgalscot.ac.uk). Bus 13. **Open** 10am-4.30pm daily. **Main courses** £4-£7. **Credit** MC, V. **Map** p329 A7 ⑤⑥
With more than a nod to the grandeur of the Viennese coffee houses (and a rather spectacular Victoria Arduino coffee machine), Café Newton is worth a visit just to look. But the lemon polenta cake is rather wonderful, and the rest of the offerings are good (soup, platters, specials and more). The only downside is that while it may look big, the floorspace isn't extensive and it can get crowded.

Circle
1 Brandon Terrace, Canonmills (624 4666). Bus 8, 17, 23, 27, 36. **Open** 8.30am-5pm Mon-Sat; 9am-4.30pm Sun. **Main courses** £3-£7. **Credit** MC, V. **Map** p326 F3 ⑤⑦
Walk past the counter at the entrance and you'll discover a long, thin, stone-walled café offering decent breakfasts, lunches and afternoon teas. Whether you're after scrambled eggs with sausage or smoked bacon, a chocolate brownie and an espresso, or even a glass of merlot accompanied by brie and oatcakes, Circle can deliver. Lunches include chorizo and bean salad.

Maxi's
33 Raeburn Place (343 3007/www.eveningatmaxis.com). Bus 24, 29, 42. **Open** 8.30am-6pm Mon-Wed; 8.30am-10.30pm Thur-Sat; 10am-5pm Sun. **Main courses** £3-£7. **Credit** MC, V. **Map** p325 D4 ⑤⑧
A friendly and popular café with a few deli bits and bobs for sale, Maxi's is approaching its tenth anniversary. A light and airy space with blond wood tables, it's modern but still accessible. Stop for breakfast or a quick coffee, or dawdle over a bottle of red with a panino and salad. At night (Thur-Sat), another pair of hands takes over to offer a bistro dinner menu, with a focus on local ingredients; mains might include pot roast shoulder of pork, or beef and cider pie. A decent neighbourhood eaterie.

Terrace Café
Royal Botanic Gardens, Inverleith Row (552 0616/www.rbge.org.uk). Bus 8, 17, 23, 27. **Open** May-Sept 9.30am-6pm daily. Oct-Apr closes earlier; phone for details. **Main courses** £2-£7. **Credit** MC, V. **Map** p325 D2 ⑤⑨
The Botanics are a popular spot for an afternoon wander, and the café next to Inverleith House (*see p111*) is a handy pit-stop. There are seats inside and out, light lunches of the quiche-and-salad or baked potato variety, plus sandwiches and cakes. If you sit outside on a fine day, the views of the central Edinburgh skyline are unparalleled.

Modern European

Channings
12-15 S Learmonth Gardens (315 2225/www.channings.co.uk). Bus 19, 37, 41, 47. **Open** noon-2.30pm, 6-10pm Mon-Fri; 12.30-3pm, 6-10pm Sun. **Main courses** £12-£18. **Credit** AmEx, DC, MC, V. **Map** p325 B4 ⑥⓿
One of a small chain of boutique hotels in the city, Channings (*see p64*) has two eateries: a wine bar with a good choice of light meals and snacks and – more importantly – a fine dining room under the supervision of Hubert Lamort, serving some of the best modern Franco-Caledonian cuisine in the city (pan-fried scallops to start; roast squab with couscous, dried fruits, harissa and sweet jus as a main, perhaps). Located just up the hill from the main Stockbridge 'village', it feels very discreet.

Circus Café
15 North West Circus Place (220 0333/www.circuscafe.co.uk). Bus 24, 29, 36, 42. **Open** 10am-9.30pm Mon-Sat; 10am-5pm Sun. **Main courses** £8-£15. **Credit** MC, V. **Map** p326 E5 ⑥①
The Circus Café is a combination of café-restaurant, bar (open until 11pm Mon-Sat), bakery, deli, takeaway and wine store, occupying the ground floor and basement of a former bank. The environment is suitably grand but the fixtures and fittings much more contemporary – art deco even. Breakfast starts at 10am, lunch lasts all afternoon (saffron linguini or a neat take on fish 'n' chips), then the slightly more extensive dinner menu kicks in after 5pm. The perfect hideaway for a lazy and leisurely afternoon.

Stockbridge Restaurant
54 St Stephen Street (226 6766/www.thestockbridgerestaurant.com). Bus 24, 29, 36, 42. **Open** 7-9.30pm Tue-Fri; 7-10pm Sat; 12.30-2pm Sun. **Main courses** £15-£24. **Credit** AmEx, MC, V. **Map** p326 E4 ⑥②
If the Edinburgh restaurant market is maturing, then the growing profile of this small, smart, basement eaterie, run by chef Jason Gallagher since 2004, is part of the trend. The dishes betray no lack of ambition: grilled halibut fillet with a crab crust, for instance. But it's no city centre hangout: it's a neighbourhood establishment, albeit in a fairly swish locality, providing great food without hubris. Local foie gras for local people? Drop by anyway.

Simple pleasures at **Embo**.

Calton Hill & Broughton

Asian

Thai Me Up
4 Picardy Place (558 9234/www.tmeup.com).
Playhouse buses. **Open** 5-10.30pm Mon, Sun;
noon-2.30pm Wed-Sat. **Main courses** £10-£14.
Credit AmEx, MC, V. **Map** p327 J5 ⑬
The small, informal Thai Me Up has got a lot more
going for it than its punning name would suggest.
There's no pretension here (the truncated wine list
has just two choices by the glass): diners really do
come for the food. Simple dishes such as spring rolls
and tom yum soup are competently cooked, as are
various familiar stir-fries and curries. However, the
kitchen also stretches to more elaborate dishes such
as marinated cod with king prawn. A good pre-
theatre option if you're off to the Playhouse.

Cafés

Blue Moon Café
36 Broughton Street (556 2788). Bus 8, 13, 17/
Playhouse buses. **Open** 11am-midnight Mon-Fri;
10am-midnight Sat, Sun. **Main courses** £5.95-
£7.95. **Credit** MC, V. **Map** p326 H4 ⑭

▶ For pubs and bars serving food in **Calton
Hill & Broughton**, *see pp178-179.*

Gay-run but straight-friendly, the Blue Moon is a
popular meet-and-eat place during the week, but the
atmosphere steps up a notch to accommodate the
pre-club crowd. The food tends to be simple and filling (burgers, nachos, macaroni cheese) while there
are some good bottled lagers and economy wines.
If you want to know anything about the city's gay
scene, just ask the friendly staff.

Embo
29 Haddington Place, Leith Walk (652 3880/
www.embodeli.com). Bus 7, 10, 12, 14, 16, 22,
25, 49. **Open** 7.30am-4.30pm Mon-Fri; 9am-4.30pm
Sat. **Main courses** £3-£5. **No credit cards**.
Map p327 K4 ⑮
Up a short flight of steps from the pavement on one
of Leith Walk's terraces, Embo is a small but well-
run establishment. If you're in the area and fancy a
high-quality focaccia, salad or wrap, then head here.
The food on offer is very good, whether you decide
to eat in or have a takeaway. The decor is simple but
attractive, and the staff are a matey lot.

Manna House
22-24 Easter Road (652 2349/www.manna-house-
edinburgh.co.uk). Bus 1, 35. **Open** 9am-8pm
Mon; 8am-8pm Tue-Thur; 8am-6pm Fri, Sat.
Main courses £2-£5. **No credit cards**.
Map p327 M4 ⑯
Manna House bears testament to the changes that
property-price inflation has wrought in Edinburgh.
Easter Road has always been a solid, working-class
street, but the sheer cost of flats these days has
brought in a wave of new residents. Businesses have

moved in to cater for the new arrivals; among them is this brilliant patisserie, where shoppers can stop for coffee, cake, elaborate tarts or savouries.

Renroc

91 Montgomery Street (556 0432/www.renroc.co.uk). Bus 1, 7, 10, 12, 14, 16, 22, 25, 35, 49. **Open** 7.30am-6pm Mon-Wed; 7am-7.30pm Thur, Fri; 9.30am-7.30pm Sat; 10.30am-6pm Sun. **Main courses** £2-£5. **Credit** MC, V. **Map** p327 K4 ⑤

If Manna House (*see p156*) demonstrates the gentrification of the upper end of Easter Road, nearby Renroc goes one better, offering not only an extensive café menu but also a complementary health studio in its basement. Sample soups, sandwiches, panino and specials – ideally at one of the tables outside, which are something of a suntrap on the right day.

Valvona & Crolla Caffè Bar

19 Elm Row, Leith Walk (556 6066/www.valvona crolla.com). Bus 7, 10, 12, 14, 16, 22, 25, 49. **Open** 8am-6pm Mon-Sat; 10.30am-4.30pm Sun. **Main courses** £8-£15. **Credit** AmEx, MC, V. **Map** p327 J4 ⑥⑧

The most celebrated delicatessen in Scotland (*see p199*) includes this simple and tasteful space at the rear of the shop (a converted stables) with white walls and wooden beams. The food (breakfast, panatella sandwiches and more substantial dishes) draws on the quality of raw materials, shipped in from Italian markets. Pick any bottle from the deli to drink in the Caffè Bar for a corkage fee of £5.

Mediterranean

Tapas Tree

1 Forth Street (556 7118/www.tapastree.co.uk). Playhouse buses. **Open** 11am-11pm daily. **Main courses** *Tapas* £2-£8. **Credit** AmEx, DC, MC, V. **Map** p326 H4 ⑥⑨

This old Spanish dependable throws out classic tapas (Serrano ham, tortilla Española and so on), but doesn't rest on its laurels: there's a good-value lunch menu, a Spanish guitar night on Wednesdays and flamenco on Thursdays. The emphasis is on fun, free-flowing conversation and sharing; no wonder locals are grateful that the Tapas Tree keeps on going.

Modern European

No.3 Royal Terrace

3 Royal Terrace (477 4747/www.no3royalterrace. com). Bus 1, 4, 5, 15, 15A, 19, 26, 34, 44, 45. **Open** noon-2pm, 5.30-11pm daily. **Main courses** £9-£23. **Credit** AmEx, DC, MC, V. **Map** p327 K5 ⑦⓪

Occupying two floors of a Georgian townhouse, No.3 possesses a certain grandeur. Most diners are seated on the ground floor, complete with ornate bar and chandeliers; upstairs is generally reserved for busier evenings or private functions. The signature dish is charcoal-grilled steak, but there's a fair choice à la carte, too, plus a handy pre-theatre menu and a nice garden at the back.

South Edinburgh

Asian

Ann Purna

45 St Patrick Square (662 1807). Nicolson Street–North Bridge buses. **Open** noon-2pm, 5.30-11pm Mon-Fri; 5.30-11pm Sat. **Main courses** £6-£13. **Credit** MC, V. **Map** p331 J9 ⑦①

The family-run Ann Purna has a wholly vegetarian, South Indian-style menu and a relaxed and homely feel. It's very close to the George Square and Buccleuch Place buildings of Edinburgh University, and is extremely popular with staff and students alike: the bargain business lunch is extraordinarily good value. An unprepossessing wee gem.

Bonsai

46 W Richmond Street (668 3847/www.bonsaibar bistro.co.uk). Nicolson Street–North Bridge buses. **Open** noon-late daily. **Main courses** £2-£7. **Credit** MC, V. **Map** p331 K8 ⑦②

The Japanese team in this small, uncluttered establishment produces a range of dishes, many of which won't spook the Scots palate too much. There's assorted tempura, user-friendly *makizushi* (rice rolled in seaweed), and bowls of noodles, for example, so raw fish isn't compulsory. But if you want a more adventurous culinary experience, you'll find tuna or salmon sashimi and squid *nigirizushi* on the menu.

Dragon Way

74-78 S Clerk Street (668 1328). Nicolson Street–North Bridge buses. **Open** noon-2pm, 5-11.30pm Mon-Sat; 4-11.30pm Sun. **Main courses** £5-£18. **Credit** MC, V. **Map** p331 K10 ⑦③

Most diners are too gobsmacked by the gilded birds and dragons on the walls, the small waterfall and various other decorative extravagances to notice the menu, but once you add in the food, you have a truly memorable restaurant. Dishes are generally Cantonese, but with Peking and Sichuan influences. The kitchen also fits in specials, which often depend on the seafood catch of the day. **Photo** *p159*.

Jasmine

32 Grindlay Street (229 5757). Bus 1, 2, 10, 11, 15, 15A, 16, 17, 23, 24, 27, 34, 35, 45. **Open** noon-2pm, 5-11.30pm Mon-Thur; 1-2pm, 5pm-12.30am Fri; 1pm-12.30am Sat; 1-11.30pm Sun. **Main courses** £5-£18. **Credit** MC, V. **Map** p330 E8, p336 A4 ⑦④

Jasmine has been around for years, but the premises have been spruced up and refurbished along the way, and currently feature lemon walls, dark wood flooring and banquette seating. Local workers are lured in with a bargain lunch menu; regulars rave about the almond chicken with orange sauce. The seafood specials here can also be great.

▶ For pubs and bars serving food in **South Edinburgh**, see pp179-181.

Kalpna

2-3 St Patrick Square (667 9890). Nicolson Street–North Bridge buses. **Open** noon-2.30pm, 5.30-10pm Mon-Sat. **Main courses** £6-£16. **Credit** MC, V. **Map** p331 K9 🄎

Restaurant trends have come and gone over the last few decades, but nothing much has changed at Kalpna. The sign above the door still reads 'You do not have to eat meat to be strong and wise', and the Gujarati vegetarian fare remains successful; try a thali if you're having trouble deciding. The interior is far from contemporary, but the food is a welcome departure from Indian cliché: freshly made, delicately spiced and often enjoyably inventive.

Kwok

44 Ratcliffe Terrace (668 1818). Bus 3, 3A, 7, 8, 29, 31, 37, 49. **Open** noon-2.30pm, 5-11pm Tue-Fri; 5pm-1am Fri, Sat; 5-11.30pm Sun. **Main courses** £6-£16. **Credit** MC, V.

This great little Chinese eaterie gets less recognition than it should because of its location half a mile south of the Meadows, in lands where visitors generally fail to tread. Dark red decor and a backdrop of jazz and lounge music set the scene, and the brasserie-like atmosphere is quite unlike that of any other Chinese establishment in the city. The food is of an impressive quality and freshness.

Suruchi

14a Nicolson Street (556 6583). Nicolson Street–North Bridge buses. **Open** noon-2pm, 5-11.30pm Mon-Sat; 5-11.30pm Sun. **Main courses** £8-£14. **Credit** MC, V. **Map** p331 J8 🄎

Under the direction of Herman Rodrigues, Suruchi has consolidated its position as one of Edinburgh's best Indian restaurants. Here you'll find jazz gigs, food festivals, cultural displays and, alongside old favourites such as prawn masala, some innovative dishes that nod to the Scottish larder (salmon tikka, for instance, or the unlikely but decent haggis pakora). Vegetarians do well too, though, and even simple sundries such as coconut rice can be sublime. **Other locations**: Suruchi Too, 121 Constitution Street, Leith (554 3268).

Thai Lemongrass

40-41 Bruntsfield Place (229 2225). Bus 11, 15, 15A, 16, 17, 23, 45. **Open** noon-2.30pm, 5-11.30pm Mon-Thur; noon-11.30pm Fri, Sat; 1-11.30pm Sun. **Main courses** £7-£15. **Credit** MC, V. **Map** p330 E10 🄎

When it first opened in 2002, this was acclaimed as one of the best Thai eateries in the city. So why change a winning formula? Staff in traditional costume serve fresh dishes (from an extensive menu) that command attention with their punchy flavours, such as stir-fried roast duck with basil leaves. There are also some good seafood specials, and a short vegetarian menu. Try the coconut ice-cream to finish.

Thaisanuk

21 Argyle Place (228 8855/www.thaisanuk.com). Bus 24, 41. **Open** 6-11pm daily. **Main courses** £9-£15. **No credit cards. Map** p330 H11 🄎

Thaisanuk started life with a slightly hand-knitted feel, as an appealing but tiny room where the tom yum soup had the zing of authenticity and the noodles came in generous portions. After opening a

Eat, Drink, Shop

Forget calm, understated decor: it just isn't the **Dragon Way**. *See p157.*

Candlelit cool at **Atrium**. See p161.

sister establishment out east and a takeaway in the west, the owners extended the original in spring 2006. Happily, it's still as laid-back and likeable as ever. **Other locations**: 27 Jock's Lodge, East Edinburgh (661 0202); *takeaway only* 112a Gorgie Road, West Edinburgh (346 8755).

Cafés

Chai Teahouse

9 W Richmond Street (662 0990/www.chaitea house.co.uk). Nicolson Street–North Bridge buses. **Open** 10am-6pm Mon-Wed, Fri, Sat; 10am-7pm Thur; noon-4pm Sun. **Main courses** £1-£3. **Credit** MC, V. **Map** p331 J8 ⑳
Small but perfectly formed, the Chai Teahouse arrived in 2005. While it's more of a specialist tea shop than a café, there are a few seats where aficionados can order anything from a China black to beautiful 'display teas' such as jasmine strawberry with lotus, which often contain flowers that unfurl when the water is added. Aside from cashew nuts, Indian sweets and a few other nibbles, no food is served.

Elephants & Bagels

37 Marshall Street, Nicolson Square (668 4404/ www.elephant-house.co.uk). Nicolson Street–North Bridge buses. **Open** 8.30am-5pm Mon-Fri; 9.30am-5.30pm Sat, Sun. **Main courses** £3-£6. **Credit** MC, V (over £5). **Map** p331 J8 ⑳
The baby sister of the Elephant House (*see p141*) doesn't sell many elephants, but is big on the bagel side of things. It's particularly popular with students

from the university, who take away the sweet and savoury goodies for impromptu picnics in nearby George Square during the summer.

Engine Shed

19 St Leonard's Lane (662 0040/www.engineshed. org.uk). Nicolson Street–North Bridge buses. **Open** 10.30am-3pm Mon-Thur; 10.30am-2.30pm Fri. **Main courses** £2-£6. **No credit cards. Map** p331 L9 ⑪
Based in a former train maintenance depot, this vegetarian/vegan wholefood café is a good pit-stop if you've been hiking around Arthur's Seat. Mains such as cashew nut pie and spinach bake are wholesome and hearty, and the bread is excellent, but what really sets this venture apart is its training role for adults with learning difficulties, who work on the other side of the counter. Worth supporting.

Made in France

5 Lochrin Place (221 1184/www.madeinfrance.co.uk). Bus 11, 15, 15A, 16, 17, 23, 45. **Open** 9.30am-5pm Mon-Fri; 10am-4pm Sat. **Main courses** £2-£5. **Credit** MC, V. **Map** p330 E10 ⑫
Made in France only arrived on the Tollcross scene at the end of 2004, but quickly established itself as a local favourite thanks to the Francophile enthusiasms of owners Craig and Amanda Nash. French cheeses, *saucisson*, nice terrines, authentic baguettes and *tartiflettes* are among the well-sourced temptations on offer. It's great for a croissant and coffee, or for a more substantial lunch.

Metropole

33 Newington Road (668 4999). Nicolson Street–North Bridge buses. **Open** 9am-10pm daily. **Main courses** £2-£7. **Credit** MC, V. **Map** p331 K11 ⑬
Deep in the heart of studentland, this café is lent an air of faded grandeur by its setting in a converted bank. You could pop in for a coffee and cake during the daytime or lunch on a baked potato or plate of lasagne, but it's also a good place to come for straightforward eats in the evening.

Ndebele

57 Home Street (221 1141/www.ndebele.co.uk). Bus 11, 15, 15A, 16, 17, 23, 45. **Open** 8.30am-6pm Mon-Sat; noon-5pm Sun. **Main courses** £2-£6. **Credit** MC, V. **Map** p330 F10 ⑭
The city's only African café-deli, Ndebele has foods on offer that you'd be hard-pressed to find anywhere else in Scotland. It's a pleasantly scruffy, student-style hangout in Tollcross, with staff who seem to be on a mission to bring African cuisine such as *boerewors* and biltong shavings to a new audience. There are daily hot dishes and soups (largely vegetarian), but sandwiches are the mainstay.

S Luca

16 Morningside Road (446 0233/www.s-luca.co.uk). Bus 11, 15, 15A, 16, 17, 41. **Open** 9am-10pm daily. **Main courses** £3-£7. **Credit** MC, V.
S Luca is famed for the ice-cream served at its legendary Musselburgh café, while this branch – located near Holy Corner, so called because it has

more churches per square foot than Vatican City – offers a range of sandwiches and panini melts as well as pizza. Still, who needs them when there are nut sundaes and Caribbean longboats to be scoffed? **Other locations**: 28-32 High Street, Musselburgh (665 2237).

Toast

146 Marchmont Road (446 9873). Bus 5, 24, 41. **Open** 10am-5pm Mon; 10am-10pm Tue-Sun. **Main courses** £3-£9. **Credit** MC, V.

Formerly Kaffe Politik, Toast looks very smart and contemporary, with understated art on the walls and lots of blond wood. The menu changes as the day progresses, kicking off with really good breakfast choices, moving through to sandwiches, salads and light meals, then becoming somewhat bistro-like in the evenings. It's an ideal place to relax and cast an eye over the Sunday papers.

Two Thin Laddies

103 High Riggs (229 0653). Bus 11, 15, 15A, 16, 17, 23, 45. **Open** 8am-6pm Mon-Fri; 8am-5pm Sat, Sun. **Main courses** £2-£5. **No credit cards.** **Map** p330 F9 ➏➎

This friendly café in the heart of Tollcross opens early for those seeking breakfast en route to work, unlike those café-bars that don't emerge blinking into the daylight until 11am or noon. It's bright and wholesome, with a menu featuring bakes, salads, and more, plus the enduring legend that is the Two Thin Laddies' macaroni cheese.

Fish & seafood

Sweet Melinda's

11 Roseneath Street (229 7953). Bus 24, 41. **Open** 7-10pm Mon; noon-2pm, 7-10pm Tue-Sat. **Main courses** £12-£15. **Credit** MC, V. **Map** p330 H11 ➏➏

The bright, compact Sweet Melinda's is an oasis in the culinary desert of Marchmont. It's not billed as a seafood restaurant, but there are some good fishy choices supplied by the acclaimed fishmonger a few doors down: scallops with chilli sauce, halibut and crab risotto, fabulous Thai-style fishcakes. The kind of neighbourhood restaurant where diners walk in with limited expectations and walk out with a smile.

Mediterranean

Le Bistrot des Arts

19 Colinton Road (452 8453/www.lebistrotdesarts. com). Bus 11, 15, 15A, 16, 17, 23, 45. **Open** noon-2pm, 6.30-10pm Mon-Sat. **Main courses** £15-£22. **Credit** MC, V.

Chef-patron Eric Ortiz has an impressive CV, having earned a Michelin star on a couple of occasions back in France. His Edinburgh establishment has restrained and simple decor, leaving the (very) French cuisine to take centre stage: *tarte flamiche, raviolis d'escargots, coquilles St Jacque.* There are also plenty of nice French wines.

Modern European

Apartment

7-13 Barclay Place (228 6456). Bus 11, 15, 15A, 16, 17, 23, 45. **Open** 6-11pm Mon-Fri; noon-3pm, 6-11pm Sat, Sun. **Main courses** £6-£10. **Credit** MC, V. **Map** p330 E10 ➏➐

Apartment's success obviously depends on the food, but its status as an informal designer eaterie for middle-class Edinburgh hipsters also owes much to its location: Bruntsfield, Marchmont and Merchiston are right on the doorstep. Key dishes include the chunky, healthy lines or CHLs (chargrilled chunks on a skewer); the rest of the menu has a modern, fusion feel. A spring 2006 makeover showed that the management isn't resting on its laurels. For the Outsider, its Old Town sister, *see p147.*

Atrium

10 Cambridge Street (228 8882/www.atrium restaurant.co.uk). Bus 1, 2, 10, 11, 15, 15A, 16, 17, 23, 24, 34, 35, 45. **Open** noon-2pm, 6-10pm Mon-Fri; 6-10pm Sat. **Main courses** £16-£22. **Credit** AmEx, MC, V. **Map** p330 E8, p336 A3 ➏➒

Sharing a building with the Traverse Theatre, Andrew Radford's flagship restaurant changed the rules of Edinburgh fine dining when it opened back in 1993. These days its design still looks contemporary, with low-key lighting, dark wood and clean lines all adding to a sense of occasion and otherness. Destination dining that's stood the test of time, this is still well worth a visit. **Photo** *p160.*

Blonde

75 St Leonard's Street (668 2917/www.blonde restaurant.com). Nicolson Street–North Bridge buses. **Open** 6-10pm Mon; noon-2.30pm, 6-10pm Tue-Sun. **Main courses** £8-£11. **Credit** MC, V. **Map** p331 K9 ➏➒

This modern neighbourhood restaurant, named for its blond-wood interior, has been a real asset to the area since opening in 2000. The menu takes an eclectic approach: dishes such as mussels in coconut milk, lime and basil to start, then beer-braised venison as a main course. The wine list is brief and affordable, and the waitresses are as sharp as tacks.

Blue Bar-Café

10 Cambridge Street (221 1222/www.bluebarcafe. com). Bus 1, 2, 10, 11, 15, 15A, 16, 17, 23, 24, 27, 34, 35, 45. **Open** noon-2.30pm, 5.30-10.30pm Mon-Thur; noon-2.30pm, 5.30-11pm Fri, Sat. **Main courses** £5-£12. **Credit** AmEx, MC, V. **Map** p330 E8, p336 A3 ➒➊

Upstairs from the Atrium restaurant (*see above*) and also run by Andrew Radford, Blue was a real smash when it opened in 1997. It's moved in and out of vogue over the years, but is still hugely popular. On a good day, Blue produces the best café-bar food in town, and can whip you up a pretty good salmon and smoked haddock fishcake with salsa rossa. There's a large, open dining space at the front and a bar area to the rear of the premises, open all day.

CAFE HUB

CAPPUCCINO

SALADS

CIABATTA

SMOKED SALMON

MERLOT

PASTA

INSPIRED CUISINE

CAFE HUB - OPEN DAY AND NIGHT
For coffee + cakes, relaxed lunches and informal evening dining

EDINBURGH'S FESTIVAL CENTRE

The Hub, Castlehill, Edinburgh EH1 2NE
Tel: 0131 473 2067
www.thehub-edinburgh.com
cafehub@eif.co.uk

Borough

72-80 Causewayside (668 2255/www.boroughhotel. com). Bus 41, 42. **Open** *Bar* 11am-1am Mon-Sat; 12.30pm-midnight Sun. *Restaurant* noon-5pm daily. **Credit** MC, V. **Map** p331 K11 **㉚**

The most obvious feature of this boutique hotel (*see p68*) is the spacious lounge area with newspapers to browse and leather sofas on which to slump. You can drink here, but you'd also do well to eat. There's generally a good standard of Modern European cooking (also available in the adjacent restaurant space, dotted with discreet booths), and the brunch menu is probably the best in the city. It's calming when quiet, but DJs play on busier nights. The kitchen closes around 10pm.

Howies

208 Bruntsfield Place (221 1777/www.howies.uk. com). Bus 11, 15, 15A, 16, 17, 23, 45. **Open** noon-2.30pm, 6-10pm Mon-Fri; noon-3.30pm, 6-10pm Sat, Sun. **Main courses** *Lunch* £6. *Set dinner* £12.95-£16.50/2 courses; £18.95/3 courses. **Credit** AmEx, DC, MC, V.

With four venues in Edinburgh, Howies adeptly fills a niche as the kind of accessible bistro that young couples might choose for an economical night out, but also the sort of spot to which mums and dads can take their student kids for a relaxed Sunday lunch (lamb and rosemary burger and venison casserole are typical mains). This branch is a converted bank, with big wooden tables and the odd piece of art on the walls. While it follows a formula, the feel is more artisan than mass-market. **Other locations**: 10-14 Victoria Street, Old Town (225 1721); 29 Waterloo Place, Calton Hill (556 5766); 1a Alva Street, New Town (225 5553).

Marque Centrale

30b Grindlay Street (229 9859/www.marquecentrale. co.uk). Bus 1, 2, 10, 11, 15, 15A, 16, 17, 23, 24, 27, 34, 35, 45. **Open** noon-2pm, 5.30-10pm Tue-Thur; noon-2pm, 5.30-11pm Fri, Sat. **Main courses** £10-£17. **Credit** AmEx, MC, V. **Map** p330 E8, p336 A4 **㉜**

Located next door to the Royal Lyceum Theatre (and hence a good bet for its pre- and post-theatre menus), Marque Centrale probably doesn't get the recognition it deserves. That might be because the decor is polite and inoffensive, and the clientele (thankfully) aren't garbed in uniform designer black. But the kitchen operates to a commendable standard, and the food is easily as good as you might find in more heavily-hyped restaurants.

New Bell

233 Causewayside (668 2868/www.thenewbell.com). Bus 42. **Open** 5.30-9pm Mon-Sat; noon-2pm, 5.30-9pm Sun. **Main courses** £9-£15. **Credit** MC, V.

Few visitors have reason to head into this slightly suburban part of town, but the award-winning New Bell is certainly worth the trip. Opened back in 2000 by Richard and Michelle Heller, the eaterie occupies the first floor of a 17th-century building, above a pub called (you guessed it) the Old Bell. The menu offers acclaimed bistro-style food.

Rhubarb

Prestonfield, Priestfield Road (225 7800/www. rhubarb-restaurant.com). Bus 2, 14, 30. **Open** noon-3pm, 6-11pm daily. **Main courses** £17-£30. **Credit** AmEx, DC, MC, V.

James Thomson, the brains behind the Witchery (*see p148*) and the Tower (*see p147*), took over the old Prestonfield House Hotel, gave it a major makeover and reopened it as Prestonfield in 2003 (*see p68*). Rhubarb, its restaurant, aims for the same standards as Thomson's other establishments (pan-seared scallops to start; sea bass fillet as a main; *assiette* of rhubarb desserts to finish, perhaps). But the opulent decor means you come here not just for the food but for the whole experience.

West Edinburgh

Asian

Chop Chop

248 Morrison Street (221 1155). Bus 2, 22, 30. **Open** 11.30am-2.30pm, 5.30-10.30pm Tue-Fri, Sun; 5-10.30pm Sat. **Main courses** £3-£8. **Credit** MC, V. **Map** p329 C8 **㉝**

This sparse room certainly isn't a romantic venue – or, indeed, an eaterie where you might linger at all – but it has a secret weapon in the form of the excellent boiled or fried dumplings. It's a rewarding pitstop on anyone's night out and perfect for larger groups, who can share a selection.

Rainbow Arch

8-16a Morrison Street (221 1288). Bus 2, 22, 30. **Open** noon-11.30pm daily. **Main courses** £5-£12. **Credit** AmEx, MC, V. **Map** p330 E8 **㉞**

Rainbow Arch has the look and atmosphere of a plush, traditional Chinese restaurant (as invented for westerners), and a menu so wide in scope it's almost intimidating. There are authentic Cantonese dishes, though, and the Chinese clientele bodes well for the quality of the food. The waitresses are friendly, the dim sum is great, and on most nights it stays open long past its advertised closing time, making it *the* place to go for a late prawn dumpling or two.

Cafés

Cornerstone Café

St John's Church, Princes Street & Lothian Road (229 0212/www.stjohns-edinburgh.org.uk). Princes Street buses. **Open** 9.30am-4pm Mon-Sat. **Main courses** £3-£6. **No credit cards. Map** p330 E7, p336 A2 **㉟**

A popular lunch haunt for weary shoppers and office staff, the Cornerstone can be found in the basement of St John's Episcopalian Church (1818), bang on the

▶ For pubs and bars serving food in
West Edinburgh, *see pp181-182.*

Eat, Drink, Shop

corner of Princes Street and Lothian Road. It serves robust canteen-style meals such as baked potatoes, tortilla and pasta. In summer, you can sit outside on the terrace and contemplate the adjacent cemetery.

Mediterranean

La Bruschetta
13 Clifton Terrace (467 7464/www.labruschetta. co.uk). Bus 2, 3, 3A, 4, 12, 25, 26, 31, 33, 38, 44, 44A. **Open** noon-10.30pm Tue-Sat. **Main courses** £7-£13. **Credit** MC, V. **Map** p329 C8 ❾❻
There's nothing elaborate about La Bruschetta: it's just a fabulous little Italian restaurant. The interior is neat and modern, but the focus is very much on owner Giovanni Cariello's food, familiar Italian dishes such as insalata caprese, spaghetti carbonara and risotto ai frutti di mare. No surprises, then, but it is a joy to see this kind of thing done with such skill.

La Partenope
96 Dalry Road (347 8880). Bus 2, 3, 3A, 4, 25, 33, 44, 44A. **Open** 5-10.45pm Mon, Sun; noon-2pm, 5-10.45pm Tue-Fri; noon-10.45pm Sat. **Main courses** £7-£16. **Credit** MC, V. **Map** p329 B9 ❾❼
Unlike some Italian spots in town, Rosario Sartore's traditional Neopolitan restaurant has great specials, with seafood very much at the forefront of the menu. There are some interesting wines from southern Italy, waiters are upbeat and chatty, and decor-wise it looks just like an Italian restaurant should. The name relates to one of the sirens who killed herself after failing to cop off with Ulysses; Naples was built on the spot where her body washed up.

Santini & Santini Bis
Sheraton Grand, 8 Conference Square, Western Approach Road (221 7788). Bus 2, 3, 3A, 4, 25, 33, 44, 44A. **Open** noon-2.30pm, 6.30-10.30pm Mon-Fri; 6.30-10.30pm Sat. **Main courses** £7-£17. **Credit** AmEx, DC, MC, V. **Map** p329 D8 ❾❽
This twin operation occupies the ground floor of the One Spa building, attached to the Sheraton Grand (*see p72*). Santini is the more formal restaurant; Santini Bis the adjacent bistro, serving up great pizza and pasta. Both arrived in 2001 and were immediately acclaimed as among the very best Italians in the city. Contemporary, sharp and not for scruffs. There are branches in London and Milan.

Modern European

First Coast
99-101 Dalry Road (313 4404/www.first-coast.co.uk). Bus 2, 3, 3A, 4, 25, 33, 44, 44A. **Open** noon-2pm, 5-10.30pm Mon-Sat. **Main courses** £7-£14. **Credit** MC, V. **Map** p329 B9 ❾❾
The MacRae brothers, who hail from the Isle of Skye, opened this Dalry Road bistro in 2003. Decor-wise, it's all done out in white and light blue, with touches of bare stone and dark wood. The food, like the general atmosphere, is very approachable

(haricot bean stew with chorizo, black pudding and pork belly, for example, and truly excellent mash). Affordable wines add to the appeal.

Shapes
Bankhead Avenue, Sighthill (453 3222/www.shapes restaurant.co.uk). Bus 3, 3A, 20, 25, 32, 34, 35. **Open** 9am-6pm Mon-Thur; 9am-midnight Fri, Sat. **Main courses** £9-£20. **Credit** MC, V.
As part of an auction house and upmarket furniture business, Shapes has the most unlikely restaurant address in the city, on an unlovely and far-flung industrial estate. It looks like a big green shed from the outside, but the decor is an eclectic riot of expensive fixtures and fittings, stopping just short of overkill. The food is excellent, the wine list is decent and service is right on the button. Anyone can come for lunch, but you have to be a member for dinner on Friday or Saturday. Worth the schlep. **Photo** *p165*.

Leith & the Coast

Asian

Britannia Spice
150 Commercial Street (555 2255/www.britannia spice.co.uk). Bus 1, 10, 16, 22, 35, 36. **Open** noon-2pm, 5-11.45pm Mon-Sat; 5-11.45pm Sun. **Main courses** £6-£11. **Credit** AmEx, DC, MC, V. **Map** p324 W2 ❿⓿⓿
This nautical-themed venue tries to cover the whole subcontinent rather than just India, with some Thai dishes thrown in for good measure. The menu covers all the usual suspects, but plenty more besides: you can have Himalayan trout or chicken jalfrezi, lamb biryani or Bangladeshi baked fish. A popular, populist and award-winning feature of the new Leith.

Joanna's
42 Dalmeny Street (554 5833). Bus 1, 7, 10, 12, 14, 16, 22, 25, 35, 49. **Open** 5.30-10.30pm Tue, Wed, Sun; 5.30-11.30pm Thur-Sat. **Main courses** £8-£11. **Credit** MC, V. **Map** p327 L2 ❿⓿❶
The last thing you expect to find in the tenement hinterlands between Leith Walk and Easter Road is a tiny Chinese restaurant specialising in dishes from Beijing. But Joanna Wong's eaterie has been a city secret for many years, and has a loyal band of devotees who are happy to make the trek (despite an interior that won't win any design awards). The premises are small, and booking is advisable.

Cafés

Café Truva
77 The Shore (554 5502). Bus 1, 10, 16, 22, 35, 36. **Open** 9am-6.30pm daily. **Main courses** £4-£12. **Credit** MC, V. **Map** p324 Y3 ❿⓿❷

▶ For pubs and bars serving food in **Leith & the Coast**, *see pp182-184*.

Less isn't more at **Shapes**. See p164.

This wee Turkish delight of a café, located right down by the Water of Leith, serves the kind of light meals and sweets that may remind you of holiday excursions to that end of the Mediterranean: not only moussaka and meze, but also breakfasts, filo pastry savouries and teeth-melting baklava. Try to nab one of the outside seats on a sunny day.

Cairn Café at Tiso Edinburgh Outdoor Experience

41 Commercial Street (555 2211/www.thecairncafe. co.uk). Bus 1, 10, 16, 22, 35, 36. **Open** 9am-5.15pm daily. **Main courses** £3-£5. **Credit** MC, V. **Map** p324 X2 **103**

Tiso (*see p206*) is Scotland's premier outdoors activity store: come for the gear that could get you up Ben Nevis or even more challenging mountains. This handy addition at the back offers breakfast rolls, some serious panini, quiches, soups and salads, plus pies and baked potatoes. There's nothing complicated or surprising; this is just a dependable café serving decent food in bright, breezy surroundings.

Fish & seafood

Fishers

1 The Shore (554 5666/www.fishersbistros.co.uk). Bus 1, 10, 16, 22, 35, 36. **Open** noon-10.30pm daily. **Main courses** £10-£25. **Credit** AmEx, MC, V. **Map** p324 Y2 **104**

The nautical theme in Fishers' decor and fittings is pretty much justified by the fact that the docks are on the doorstep, and you can see working ships as

you're walking down the Shore. Eat in the bar or the small adjacent raised area, where a starter such as crab stuffed with mozzarella and artichoke is almost a meal in itself. This has been one of the city's leading seafood restaurants since 1991, and you'll leave replete and happy. It now has a sister establishment in the New Town (*see p149*). **Photo** *p168*.

Skippers

1a Dock Place (554 1018/www.skippers.co.uk). Bus 1, 10, 16, 22, 35, 36. **Open** 12.30-2pm, 7-10pm Mon-Fri, Sun; 12.30-2pm, 6.30-10pm Sat. **Main courses** £8-£24. **Credit** AmEx, MC, V. **Map** p324 Y2 **105**

Skippers has been around for over 25 years, and was a real pioneer in the pre-refurbished docklands. It has an excellent reputation for its bistro-style seafood cookery; dishes such as Cullen skink or fishcakes are fixtures on the menu, but the catch of the day will influence the specials on offer. The owners also run the Waterfront over the street (*see below*).

Waterfront

1c Dock Place (554 7427/www.waterfrontwinebar. co.uk). Bus 1, 10, 16, 22, 35, 36. **Open** noon-3pm, 6-9.30pm daily. **Main courses** £7-£19. **Credit** AmEx, MC, V. **Map** p324 Y2 **106**

This informal venue caters for all-comers, with a conservatory restaurant and a floating barge out back for alfresco moments *sur mer* (even if you just want a glass of wine and a bowl of olives; the bar is open all day). Owned by the folks behind Skippers (*see above*), it's been a mainstay of the Leith scene ever since the docks started to come up in the world more than 20 years ago.

Mediterranean

Daniel's

88 Commercial Street (553 5933/www.daniels-bistro.co.uk). Bus 1, 10, 16, 22, 35, 36. **Open** 10am-10pm daily. **Main courses** £8-£15. **Credit** AmEx, MC, V. **Map** p324 X2

A long stretch of Leith's Commercial Street is occupied by refurbished warehousing. It's unremarkable enough facing the street, but the north side holds a terrace of offices and restaurants that face over to the huge Scottish Executive. Plenty bars and restaurants have been established here since the mid 1990s, and the casualty list is frightening. The survivor par excellence is Daniel Vencker, whose Alsatian-influenced modern French bistro still packs 'em in after all these years with dishes such as pork knuckle on the bone.

Domenico's

30 Sandport Street (467 7266). Bus 1, 10, 16, 22, 35, 36. **Open** noon-3pm, 5-10.30pm Mon-Fri; noon-10.30pm Sat, Sun. **Main courses** £5-£16. **Credit** MC, V. **Map** p324 Y3

This tiny, informal Italian sits just around the corner from Commercial Street, and isn't immediately apparent to passers-by. The food combines

My Edinburgh Martin Wishart

herbs from Skye and the Lothians. So coming back to Edinburgh was an easy choice for me: I always felt there was an opportunity to open a restaurant here that suited my style, with prime, seasonal ingredients. The lifestyle is also great here. It's a large part of the reason why I came back.

'Restaurants in Edinburgh have evolved dramatically over the past five years or so. There's a lot more diverse cooking, with more personalised dining. Food-lovers visiting the city have also got a great choice of shops where they can buy good produce. **Valvona & Crolla** on Elm Row (*see p199*) and **Iain Mellis, Cheesemonger** (*see p201*) are absolute musts. The **Valvona & Crolla Vin Caffè** on Multrees Walk (*see p151*) is also a great place to stop for something to eat; I often take my own family there.

'My wife is from Mexico, so we have a lot of visitors from out of town. We try to take them to some of the bars around the Old Town like the **Canny Man's** (*see p179*) in Morningside; it's one of the oldest bars in Edinburgh and has a great selection of whiskies. There's also **Kay's Bar** on Jamaica Street (*see p175*). They're both privately owned, so they have a more personalised atmosphere. The **Port o' Leith** on Constitution Street (*see p183*) is also fantastic, with a real mix of characters.

'**Arthur's Seat** (*see p118*) and the **Royal Botanic Garden** (*see p111*) are always nice places to spend an afternoon, and I'd also recommend taking a day trip to **East Lothian** (*see pp284-286*), where there are some fantastic walks and beaches. **Yellowcraigs** is lovely, with **North Berwick** in walking distance. And **Gullane**, in the opposite direction, has some of the best golf courses around Scotland.'

Edinburgh-born chef Martin Wishart left school at 15 to pursue his career, travelling the globe to work with such luminaries as Albert Roux, Michel Roux Jr and Marco Pierre White. He returned to Edinburgh in 1999 to open his eponymous restaurant (Restaurant Martin Wishart; see p168); granted a coveted Michelin star in 2001, it won the Good Food Guide*'s Scottish Restaurant of the Year award in 2005.*

'I've been fortunate to travel around the world, but, in many places I worked, a lot of the best ingredients came from Scotland. Game is particularly good here, especially winged game, not to mention the wild mushrooms, shellfish and seafood, beautiful

Eat, Drink, Shop

heartiness with joie de vivre, and it makes up in personality what it lacks in finesse. Once you've struggled through the generous antipasti (assorted charcuterie, cheeses and roast vegetables), the impending plate of spaghetti alla vongole might just finish you off. Book ahead and bring an appetite.

La Favorita

325-331 Leith Walk (554 2430/www.la-favorita.com). Bus 7, 10, 12, 14, 16, 21, 22, 25, 49. **Open** noon-11pm daily. **Main courses** £7-£16. **Credit** MC, V. **Map** p327 L2 **109**

A locally owned attempt at Pizza Express-style dining: modern decor, a wood-fired pizza oven and better-than-average pasta plates. The formula works nicely, and it's enormously popular with a cross section of Leithers, from families to young couples. As a result, it can be seriously busy at weekends, but it's still ideal for a pizza fiorentina and a cold Peroni.

Modern European

Restaurant Martin Wishart

54 The Shore (553 3557/www.martin-wishart.co.uk). Bus 1, 10, 16, 22, 35, 36. **Open** noon-2pm, 6.45-9.30pm Tue-Fri; 6.45-9.30pm Sat. **Main courses** £21-£60. **Credit** AmEx, MC, V. **Map** p324 Y3 **110**

Located in the historical heart of Leith, Wishart's establishment has retained a Michelin star since 2001, and the food is sublime. Subtle frothy pumpkin purée with vegetable shavings, served in a small glass vase as an *amuse-bouche*. Intense Jerusalem artichoke soup as a starter, with a dainty bouillaisse to follow. Then, for dessert, achingly good almond and pear tart with Armagnac ice-cream. The sommelier is brilliant, the

front of house staff are approachable and efficient, and the kitchen crew are the best in the city. Marks out of ten? Eleven. *See also p167* **My Edinburgh**.

Smoke Stack

19 Shore Place (476 6776/www.smokestack.org.uk). Bus 1, 10, 16, 22, 35, 36. **Open** noon-2.30pm, 6-10.30pm Mon-Fri; noon-10.30pm Sat; 5-10.30pm Sun. **Main courses** £7-£22. **Credit** MC.V. **Map** p324 Y3 **111**

This 18th-century warehouse, one street back from the Water of Leith, has hosted some pretty upmarket restaurants in its time, and the interior is still fairly swish. Smoke Stack took over the premises in 2003, offering more of an informal chargrill menu: some ribs to start with, then a burger or a steak as a main. Vegetarians need not be deterred, though: fajitas, pasta and crêpes are also available. The other (original) Smoke Stack has been around since 1996. **Other locations**: 53-55 Broughton Street, Broughton (556 6032).

Vintners Rooms

Vaults, 87 Giles Street (554 6767/www.thevintners rooms.com). Bus 1, 10, 16, 22, 35, 36. **Open** noon-2pm, 7-10pm Tue-Sat. **Main courses** £18-£25. **Credit** AmEx, MC, V. **Map** p324 Y3 **112**

At the corner of a Leith backstreet sits a former wine warehouse with a history dating back to the late 16th century. Its first floor is home to the Scotch Malt Whisky Society (*see p183*), while the ground floor hosts the Vintners Rooms, a classy French-style fixture since 1985. Diners have the choice of tables in the homelier bar area or in a small adjacent room with elaborate plasterwork. The latter tends to be a little stark during the day, but is better at night.

Fishers: nautical but nice. *See p165.*

Pubs & Bars

Here comes that drinking feeling...

As with so many aspects of life here, Edinburgh's drinking culture is defined by its history, and specifically by its historic pubs and bars. The **Café Royal** (*see p173*) dates from 1862, while the **Guildford** next door (*see p175*) was built even earlier (but only became a bar in the 1890s). Up at Tollcross sits **Bennet's**, another Victorian survivor (*see p179*), but the history of the **King's Wark** in Leith (*see p182*) takes the cake. After the 15th-century building that once occupied the site was destroyed in the Hertford invasion in 1544, it was rebuilt in the time of James VI of Scotland (also James I of England, *see p18*) and still stands today.

Although pubs such as these have appealed for years, the Edinburgh drinking scene of two decades ago also had a lot of dross. But as the city grew more prosperous, things improved, with the arrival on the scene of new style bars and the ceaseless growth of the café-bar (*see below*). After a fashion for dazzlingly designed venues (such as **Halo**, *see p175*), recent years have seen the informal and homely likes of **Boda** (*see p182*) take an anti-style approach to decor. However, changes in the local bar scene tend to be evolutionary rather than revolutionary, and local drinkers will just have to wait and see.

CAFE-BARS

In the beginning, it was all very simple. Restaurants were for food, pubs were for drink, and cafés were either egg-and-chips affairs or rooms in which old ladies could sip tea and eat scones. The idea of a single venue that served food, alcohol and coffee throughout the day was simply anathema for years, but how things have changed. Perhaps the growth in foreign travel helped turn things around (the concept is certainly more continental than British), or maybe an entrepreneur simply spotted a gap in the market. Either way, the rise and rise of the café-bar has been an enduring trend in Edinburgh for more than 20 years.

The pioneer was **Negociants** (*see p173*), which opted for a vaguely French decor that's remained essentially unchanged since the '80s.

> ❶ Pink numbers given in this chapter correspond to the location of each pub and bar on the street maps. *See pp324-336.*

Another early pace-setter was **City Café** (*see p171*), whose retro-Americana fittings took a completely different decorative tack. After all, what was a café-bar *supposed* to look like? However, it was the self-conscious commitment to design and chunky metal flourishes at the **Basement** (*see p179*), which opened in 1994, that really set the template for café-bars here. Look at venues such as **Baroque** (*see p179*) or **Bar Sirius** (*see p184*) and you can still see its influence, even through layers of refurbishment.

A decade or so later, design trends have moved on a little, with dark wood, low tables and sharp lines all the rage these days. At the

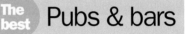

The best Pubs & bars

For beer-hounds
Cask & Barrel: football and ale both on tap. *See p178.*

Cumberland: a true New Town boozehouse. *See p173.*

Guildford: sup awat in Victorian splendour. *See p175.*

For cocktail hour
Amicus Apple: new in the New Town for 2006. *See p173.*

Dragonfly: girl, I wanna take you to a fey bar. *See p179.*

Halo: louche and casual in Edinburgh's West End. *See p175.*

For al fresco drinking
Assembly and **Negociants**: neighbours by the university. *See p171 & p173.*

Cargo: a new look for the old canal. *See p182.*

Ocean Bar: terrace views high above the Western Harbour. *See p182.*

For breakfast or brunch
City Café: robust and filling, before or after a big night out. *See p171.*

King's Wark: Sunday brunch, best washed down with a pint. *See p182.*

Rick's: eggs benedict served with additional hotel swank. *See p177.*

Eat, Drink, Shop

Plenty of spirit: the **Bow Bar**.

populist end of the market, both **Assembly** (*see p171*) and the **Human Be-In** (*see p181*) have elements of this approach, but in design terms, the look works far better at **Borough** (*see p163*), **Rick's** (*see p177*) and especially **Opal Lounge** (*see p177*). However, while decorative fashions come and go, the general concept behind café-bars remains the same: to be all things to all people. Stop by for a latte, a lager or a lunch, but do stop by.

Old Town

Bars & pubs

Bar Kohl

54-55 George IV Bridge (225 6936). Bus 23, 27, 42, 45. **Open** 4pm-1am daily. **Credit** MC, V. **Map** p330 H8, p336 E4 ❶
Bar Kohl has provided Edinburgh's vodka connoisseurs with a second home since its launch in 1993. There are innumerable imported varieties of vodka, including many flavoured versions; staff can even knock up a vodka milkshake. The room itself has a contemporary look (bare stone walls, stone floor), and gets louder and livelier as the night wears on.

Black Bo's

57-61 Blackfriars Street (557 6136). Nicolson Street–North Bridge buses. **Open** 4pm-1am daily. *Food served* 6-10.30pm daily. **Credit** MC, V. **Map** p331 J7 ❷
This relaxed and bohemian little howf, with no style bar flourishes in sight, is a two-part operation. The pub is a winning little spot that even boasts a basement pool room (albeit one without much elbow

room); next door is an often adventurous vegetarian restaurant. Both pub and eaterie are handy places if you want to escape the overkill of the Royal Mile.

Bow Bar

80 West Bow (226 7667). Bus 2, 23, 27, 41, 42. **Open** noon-11.30pm Mon-Sat; 12.30-11pm Sun. *Food served* noon-2.30pm Mon-Sat. **Credit** MC, V. **Map** p330 G8, p336 D4 ❸
This small and simple one-room pub has one of the largest and most interesting ranges of single malt scotch in the city. The Port Ellen distillery on Islay, for instance, was mothballed in 1983, but the Bow may still have three different bottlings on offer. There's also a good choice of ales, along with some interesting Nicaraguan rums.

Canons' Gait

232 Canongate (556 4481). Bus 35, 36. **Open** noon-midnight daily. *Food served* noon-3pm Mon-Sat. **Credit** AmEx, MC, V. **Map** p331 K7 ❹
Roomy and comfortable, with a pub-grub lunch menu and music on some evenings, the Canons Gait offers a modern take on what a Royal Mile bar should be. Despite its location in the middle of tourist country, the place still attracts its share of locals. After all, any pub with a wall-mounted display about the cost overruns on the nearby Scottish Parliament has to be worth a look.

Medina

45-47 Lothian Street (225 6313). Nicolson Street– North Bridge buses. **Open** 10pm-3am daily. **Credit** MC, V. **Map** p330 H8 ❺
The sister venue to Negociants (*see p173*), Medina is a late and often lively basement with a North African theme. Although it's a kind of club-bar crossover,

with DJs, drinks promos and a young profile, you can just lie on the cushions, relax and listen to music (Latin night on Mondays, for example). There's usually a cover charge, but it's no bank-breaker.

Royal Oak

1 Infirmary Street (557 2976/www.royal-oak-folk. com). Nicolson Street–North Bridge buses. **Open** 1pm-2am Mon-Sat; 2pm-2am Sun. **No credit cards.** **Map** p331 J8 ⑥
Fall through the doors of this tiny, two-floor pub and you're virtually guaranteed to be regaled with a flurry of fiddles, squeezeboxes and guitars. There are nightly folk sessions here, with the Wee Folk Club taking over the Lounge Bar on Sundays for an organised programme of guest artists. No frills: just beer and tunes.

Sandy Bell's

25 Forrest Road (225 2751). Bus 35/Nicolson Street–North Bridge buses. **Open** noon-1am Mon-Sat; 12.30-11pm Sun. **No credit cards.** **Map** p330 H8 ⑦
Like the Royal Oak, this is a folkies' hangout: there's an open session every night from around 9pm. You can get the gist of the place from the bust of poet Hamish Henderson above the bar, author of 'Freedom Come All Ye', a tune that can still get the hairs standing up on the backs of some Scots' necks.

Whistlebinkies

6 Niddry Street (557 5114/www.whistlebinkies.com). Nicolson Street–North Bridge buses. **Open** 5pm-3am Mon-Thur; 1pm-3am Fri-Sun. **Credit** MC, V. **Map** p331 J7, p336 F4 ⑧
Edinburgh's primary live music pub, Whistlebinkies takes in rock and pop acts along with resident

singer-songwriters. Monday is open-mic night and Tuesdays are for up-and-coming bands; the rest of the week, you could find anything from earnest troubadours to indie wannabes.

Café-bars

Assembly

41 Lothian Street (220 4288/www.assemblybar.co.uk). Nicolson Street–North Bridge buses. **Open** 9am-1am daily. *Food served* noon-8pm Mon-Fri; 10am-8pm Sat, Sun. **Credit** MC, V. **Map** p330 H8 ⑨
If you're in an upbeat mood, with company, and looking for nachos and lager or wine, Assembly is a good option. Hit it on the wrong day or come on your own, though, and the uninterested (or should that be overstretched?) service can grate nearly as much as the student-heavy clientele. There are outdoor tables, and Sunday barbecues in summer.

City Café

19 Blair Street (220 0125). Nicolson Street–North Bridge buses. **Open** 11am-1am daily. *Food served* 11am-11pm Mon-Thur; 11am-10pm Fri-Sun. **Credit** MC, V. **Map** p330 H7, p336 F4 ⑩
The City Café was one of the first modern café-bars on the scene; these days it feels as much a part of Edinburgh as the castle. The ground floor features a pool table and fill-you-up meals, to be devoured in the booths at the back or the more open seating upfront. Downstairs is more club-like, with DJs spinning. It's packed with pre-clubbers at weekends; the late mornings bring a clientele in search of a serious breakfast (carnivore or veggie versions). And still the famous spelling error behind the bar endures.

Wine! Here! **Ecco Vino**. *See p172.*

Eat, Drink, Shop

A beginner's guide to whisky

Walk into any Edinburgh bar, and the cheapest and biggest-selling whisky on the optic will be a blended scotch, made up of around one-third malt whisky (from assorted distilleries) and two-thirds bulk grain whisky. Blends have been the dominant style in the industry since it first really got going in the 1820s. The Famous Grouse is Scotland's top-seller, although it is fairly sweet; J&B Rare is cleaner. Any blend labelled as 'deluxe' will have more mature single malts in its make-up, and will tend to be more complex: Johnny Walker Black Label, for instance, with its medicinal edge.

It wasn't until the 1960s, when Glenfiddich began to market its single malt scotch in its distinctive triangular green bottle, that the industry cottoned on to the possibility that whisky could be sold as a luxury item. Whisky of a certain age from a single distillery had cachet, rather like French wine and its *terroir*, but no one had yet exploited it. These days malt whisky is a huge industry in Scotland, but also a confusing one for the novice. Where to start?

The character of individual malt whiskies is to an extent defined by the area of the country in which they're made. From Islay come single malts with a maritime, smoky, peaty character: Ardbeg, Laphroaig and Lagavulin, for example. The archetypal Speyside single malt is the Macallan, aged in casks formerly used for sherry. Then there is the subtlety of Cragganmore (Speyside again), the toffee tones of a good old Springbank (Campbeltown) and the sheer all-round class of Orkney's Highland Park. It really does come down to a matter of taste. Whichever flavour you favour, you should add a little water to cask-strength whiskies (and, if you like, when supping on regular-strength whiskies). The only other failsafe rule is that

asking for an 18-year-old Talisker *and Coke* will get you laughed not just out of the premises but out of the country.

But where to drink them? One good spot to start is **Bennet's** (*see p179*), which has more than 100 whiskies sitting on its gorgeous Victorian gantry; try sampling a few on a quiet afternoon. The **Canny Man's** (*see p179*), a much more upmarket venue in Morningside, also has a tremendous choice, with some rare bottlings. The selection at **Kay's** (*see p175*) is more limited, but its cosiness gels nicely with whisky drinking. For rare single cask bottlings, you'll have to join the **Scotch Malt Whisky Society** (*see p183*). But if you just want to walk in off the street to a simple Old Town pub and be blown away by some of the more premium whiskies, the **Bow Bar** is top of the list (*see p170*).

Ecco Vino

19 Cockburn Street (225 1441). Bus 35/Nicolson Street–North Bridge buses. **Open** noon-midnight Mon-Thur; noon-1am Fri, Sat; 12.30pm-midnight Sun. *Food served* noon-9.45pm Mon-Sat; 12.30-9.45pm Sun. **Credit** AmEx, MC, V. **Map** p330 H7, p336 E3 ⑪
The formula at this perennial Old Town favourite has a simplicity bordering on genius. Create a basic Italian menu (antipasti, risotto, focacce, pasta) and throw in the odd special. Devise an Italian-slanted wine list. Store the bottles of wine along one wall as a design feature, run the bar along the other

side of the room, light some candles and abracadabra: watch as eager drinkers and diners flock in. A good spot for a relaxed tête-à-tête. **Photo** *p171*.

Favorit

19-20 Teviot Place (220 6880). Bus 2, 41, 42. **Open** 8am-3am Mon-Fri; 10am-3am Sat, Sun. *Food served* bar hours. **Credit** AmEx, MC, V. **Map** p330 H8 ⑫
As its opening hours suggest (note that the kitchen may close early on slow nights), Favorit provides everything from breakfast for office workers in a hurry to nightcaps for clapped-out clubbers in a room

that comes with the flavour of an American diner. It's popular for quick lunches (a glass of wine to wash down a selection of small dishes), but it's also a fine place to while away a lazy afternoon or long evening.

Negociants
45 Lothian Street (225 6313). Nicolson Street–North Bridge buses. **Open** 11am-1am Mon-Thur, Sun; 11am-3am Fri, Sat. *Food served* noon-midnight daily. **Credit** MC, V. **Map** p330 H8 ⑬
Negociants feels as if it's been here forever. The fixtures and fittings are French-ish, but the band posters – it's a students' favourite – are more Britpop than brasserie. It's pleasantly spacious and light, with plenty of mirrors and big windows. There has been a marked improvement in the evening menu of late: you can now chow down on risotto, coq au vin or a salad niçoise. Equally laid-back sister operation Medina (*see p170*) is downstairs.

New Town & West End

Bars & pubs

Abbotsford
3 Rose Street (225 5276). Princes Street buses. **Open** 11am-11pm Mon-Sat; 12.30-11pm Sun. *Food served* noon-3pm Mon-Sat; 12.30-3pm Sun. **Credit** MC, V. **Map** p326/p330 G6, p336 E1 ⑭
The Abbotsford may count Sainsbury's and Fopp (*see p205*) among its neighbours these days, but it's been a no-nonsense drinking den since 1901: dark wood, bench tables, a fine central island bar, a decorative ceiling, four real ales and virtually no concessions to modernity. The food here is better than you might imagine.

Amicus Apple
17 Frederick Street (226 6055/www.amicusapple.com). Princes Street buses. **Open** 10am-1am Mon-Sat; 11am-1am Sun. **Credit** MC, V. **Map** p329 D7 ⑮
When it opened in summer 2006, this central cocktail bar introduced a new aesthetic to Edinburgh (designer stools, white leather banquettes, a pop-erotic mural) and brought a dedicated attitude to a menu of good drinks, fine bar snacks (and even a small restaurant space). Cool but not pretentious, and only seconds from Princes Street.

Café Royal Circle Bar
19 West Register Street (556 1884). Princes Street buses. **Open** 11am-11pm Mon-Wed; 11am-midnight Thur; 11am-1am Fri, Sat; 12.30-11pm Sun. *Food served* 11am-10pm Mon-Sat; 12.30-10pm Sun. **Credit** MC, V. **Map** p326/p330 H6, p336 F2 ⑯
An island bar dominates this attractive and elegant Victorian pub, where the walls are decorated with Royal Doulton tiles of famous inventors. It gets very busy after work, and is positively packed if Scotland are playing a home rugby international. The bar food is of a very high standard, but for more formal eats, try the beautiful Café Royal Oyster Bar next door (17A West Register Street, 556 4124).

Cenzor
1-3 York Place (07971 230574/www.szkocja.net/cenzor). Playhouse or Princes Street buses. **Open** 5pm-1am Mon-Fri; 2pm-1am Sat, Sun. *Food served* pub hours. **Credit** MC, V. **Map** p326 H5 ⑰
Catering to the recent wave of young Polish incomers to the city, the labyrinthine Cenzor has annexed much of what was once an Indian restaurant called 9 Cellars. There's now a chilled cabinet full of bottled Polish beer, and *bigos* and *pierogi* on the menu. A little piece of Poznań in York Place. *See p152* **Poles apart**.

Clark's Bar
142 Dundas Street (556 1067). Bus 13, 23, 27. **Open** 11am-11pm Mon-Wed; 11am-11.30pm Thur-Sat; 12.30-11pm Sun. *Food served* pub hours. **No credit cards. Map** p326 F4 ⑱
Sparse and traditional, this old howf opened in 1899 and hasn't changed in years: the decor still features red leather seats, shiny brass table tops and a dark red ceiling. You'll find a reasonable malt whisky selection, a few cask ales, and basic bar food such as toasties and baguettes. Definitely somewhere to sit and talk.

Cumberland
1-3 Cumberland Street (558 3134/www.cumberlandbar.co.uk). Bus 13, 23, 27. **Open** 11am-1am Mon-Sat; 12.30-1am Sun. *Food served* noon-3pm daily. **Credit** MC, V. **Map** p326 G4 ⑲

Cumberland.

The Cumberland is perhaps the most user-friendly of the city's acclaimed cask ale bars. It feels light and spacious during the day, and the leafy beer garden is an absolute joy in the summer. There's a fair choice of wine and bar food, in addition to the nine or so ales on tap. All in all, it's the opposite of a misogynist drinking den.

Guildford

1-5 West Register Street (556 4312). Princes Street buses. **Open** 11am-11pm Mon-Thur; 11am-midnight Fri, Sat; 12.30-11pm Sun. *Food served* noon-2.30pm, 6-9.30pm Mon-Fri; noon-10pm Sat; 12.30-3pm, 6-9.30pm Sun. **Credit** MC, V. **Map** p326/p330 H6, p336 F2 ㉑
Established in 1898 (the building dates back a further 60 years), the Guildford is one of Edinburgh's most accessible Victorian pubs, just a hop, skip and jump away from Waverley Station. The rotating selection of cask ales is excellent, the whisky choice is decent and the bar food is better than average: try to eat in the small gallery overlooking the main bar.

Halo

3 Melville Place (539 8500/www.halobar.co.uk). Bus 13, 19, 36, 37, 41, 47. **Open** 4pm-1am daily. *Food served* pub hours. **Credit** MC, V. **Map** p329 D7 ㉑
Along with Dragonfly (*see p179*), Halo is currently the high water mark of design on Edinburgh's drinking scene. Its features include a riveted, leather-clad bar, leather panelling, contemporary chandeliers, and faux classical mirrors by the door, but the punters are really here for the cocktails more than anything (though snacks are also served). A style bar that actually manages to be stylish.

Kay's

39 Jamaica Street (225 1858). Bus 24, 29, 36, 42. **Open** 11am-midnight Mon-Thur; 11am-1am Fri, Sat; 12.30-11pm Sun. *Food served* noon-2.30pm daily. **Credit** MC, V. **Map** p326 E5 ㉒
Drink has been a mainstay here for nearly two centuries: before morphing into a pub in 1976, these premises housed a wine merchant for more than 150 years. Now, along with a reputation as a patrician New Town howf, this palpably historic spot offers an excellent choice of single malt whiskies and a perfect environment in which to sample them.

Living Room

113-115 George Street (0870 442 2718/www.the livingroom.co.uk). Princes Street buses. **Open** 11am-1am Mon-Sat; 11am-12.30am Sun. *Food served* noon-10pm Mon, Tue, Sun; noon-11pm Wed; noon-11.30pm Thur; noon-midnight Fri, Sat. **Credit** AmEx, MC, V. **Map** p326/p330 E6, p336 B1 ㉓
The Living Room, part of a UK-wide chain, arrived in 2003 and quickly built a reputation as a somewhat more mature venue (pianist, sober dark wood fittings) in a part of the city where office nights out are common. While there is a restaurant, the clubbish bar area is the main feature. There are plans to start serving breakfast in late 2006; call to check.

Eat, Drink, Shop

Roll out the barrel: beer drinkers at **Kay's**.

The spirit of *Cocktail* lives on at the **Opal Lounge**. *See p177.*

Oxford

8 Young Street (539 7119/www.oxfordbar.com).
Princes Street buses. **Open** 11am-1am Mon-Sat;
12.30pm-midnight Sun. **No credit cards.**
Map p326/p330 E6, p336 B1 ㉔
Cramped, dowdy and clannish, the Oxford's bar area
offers no space at all, and while the adjacent room has
been given a lick of paint lately, it's still pretty basic.
Sometimes it feels as if you have to be a member to
drink here. So why come? Because it ploughs its own
furrow, and doesn't give a toss about the white noise
of contemporary style. It enjoys minor celebrity status as a favoured haunt of Ian Rankin's Inspector
Rebus (and, for that matter, Rankin himself).

Café-bars

Dome

14 George Street (624 8624/www.thedomeedinburgh.
com). Princes Street buses. **Open** 10am-
late daily. *Frazer's bar* 10am-late Thur-Sat. *Food*
served noon-10pm Mon-Wed, Sun; noon-11pm
Thur-Sat. **Credit** AmEx, MC, V. **Map** p326/p330 G6,
p336 E1 ㉕
In the 1840s, the Commercial Bank of Scotland built
this grand old pile as its head office; it remained a
bank almost until the Dome took it over in 1996.
There's a striking classical frontage, and the central
hall is a soaring, decadent space with a marble
mosaic floor. The whole thing is crowned by the
eponymous dome, housing a bar and restaurant (the
Grill Room); the building also has a separate 1930s-
style cocktail bar.

Indigo Yard

7 Charlotte Lane (220 5603/www.indigoyard
edinburgh.co.uk). Princes Street buses. **Open**
8.30am-1am Mon-Fri; 9am-1am Sat, Sun. *Food*
served 8.30am-10pm Mon-Fri; 9am-10pm Sat, Sun.
Credit AmEx, MC, V. **Map** p329 D7 ㉖
Has it really been a decade or so since Indigo Yard
made such a splash in the West End? It's showing a
little wear and tear these days, but it still endures,
popular both with post-work drinkers during the
week and a more mixed clientele during the day and
at weekends. Available to tables on the ground floor
or the mezzanine, the menu offers pretty good breakfasts, fusion-style mains and some pure comfort food
(sausages from Crombie's, for example).

Opal Lounge

51a George Street (226 2275/www.opallounge.co.uk).
Princes Street buses. **Open** 5pm-3am Sun-Fri; noon-
3am Sat. *Food served* 5-10pm Sun-Fri; noon-10pm Sat.
Credit AmEx, MC, V. **Map** p326/p330, p336 C1 F6 ㉗
Opal Lounge has been going great guns since its
arrival in 2002. The food is predominantly eastern:
sushi, bento boxes, noodle bowls and little 'bites' of
tempura or Thai fishcakes. A good choice for lunch,
the contemporary, minimal and relaxed basement
space becomes much buzzier in the evenings, thanks
to a roster of DJs (including a Vegas-themed night
on Fridays) and a fine cocktail list. **Photo** *p176*.

Rick's

55a Frederick Street (622 7800/www.ricksedinburgh.
co.uk). Princes Street buses. **Open** 7am-1am daily.
Food served 7am-10pm Mon-Sat; 7am-11pm
Thur-Sat. **Credit** AmEx, MC, V. **Map** p326/p330 F6,
p336 C1 ㉘
On busier evenings, the café-bar at Rick's hotel (*see*
p63) tends to attract girls with a certain look (*that*
blonde hair, *that* black top) and guys with a certain
demeanour (*that* aspirational wristwatch), but it's still
a lively spot. You can grab a very decent breakfast
(kippers with poached egg); later in the day, the menu
offers the likes of oysters, venison and duck breast.

Tonic

34a N Castle Street (225 6431/www.devilskitchen.
co.uk). Princes Street buses. **Open** noon-1am daily.
Food served noon-4pm daily. **Credit** MC, V.
Map p326/p330 E6, p336 B1 ㉙
Tonic's identikit style bar look and 13-page cocktail
list (combined with a meagre choice of wines) may
spark doubts about its approach. However, the
kitchen may well surprise you: since going into partnership with a catering firm, it's offered a nice line in
one-dish lunchtime meals (focacce, salads, chargrilled
burgers and a few more elaborate efforts). Menus are
put away as the convivial evening clientele appears.

Whigham's Wine Cellars

13 Hope Street, Charlotte Square (225 8674/
www.whighams.co.uk). Princes Street buses.
Open noon-midnight Mon-Thur; noon-1am Fri, Sat.
Food served noon-10pm daily. **Credit** AmEx, MC, V.
Map p330 E7, p336 A2 ㉚
The old alcoves, candles and low ceilings give this
well-established basement wine bar a cosy, intimate
feel, but it's not completely subterranean: a 2004
expansion into next door's basement created a
brighter, more open space. The menu tends towards
good bistro fare (including a signature seafood platter); the wine list is a decent international mix.

Stockbridge

Bars & pubs

Avoca

4-6 Dean Street (315 3311). Bus 24, 29, 42.
Open 11am-midnight Mon-Thur, Sun; 11am-1am
Fri, Sat. *Food served* noon-7.30pm daily. **Credit**
MC, V. **Map** p325 D4 ㉛
Despite bearing the name of a village in County
Wicklow, this is no Oirish theme bar. Instead, it's a
compact, modern pub in one of the city's most bour-
geois *quartiers*, with wooden fittings, friendly staff
and decent bar food (including late breakfasts).

Bailie

2 St Stephen Street (225 4673). Bus 24, 29, 42.
Open 11am-midnight Mon-Thur; 11am-1am Fri,
Sat; 12.30-11pm Sun. *Food served* 11am-9pm
Mon-Thur, Sat, Sun; 11am-5pm Fri. **Credit** MC, V.
Map p326 E5 ㉜

Eat, Drink, Shop

Totally unwired

As recently as 2004, the options for a laptop-toting web surfer in Edinburgh were fairly limited. You could go to a chain coffee bar and pay through the nose, or you could fork out the fee at one of BT's Wi-Fi hotspot kiosks around the city centre. And that, more or less, was that. Happily, however, the proprietors of some of the city's cafés and pubs have realised that free Wi-Fi access is a big pull these days, and options are increasing.

The benefits for the café or bar appear small at first: two or three itinerant surfers popping in for a couple of coffees while sorting through their inbox won't send profits soaring into the stratosphere. However, as word spreads, business picks up, and a few of the coffee-suppers stick around for a bite to eat. All the surfer has to worry about is spilling a milky latte or a pint of Guinness over their brand-new MacBook Pro. It's a win-win situation.

Edinburgh was named as one of BT's 12 Wireless Cities in 2006, which means that there'll be even more Wi-Fi hotspots in the city before long. However, since access is expected to cost money, going to a café or bar would still seem to be the more amenable option. **Baroque** (*see p179*), the **Honey Pot** (*see p143*), the **Traverse Theatre Bar** (*see p181*) and **Iglu**, a restaurant upstairs but a bar on the ground floor (*see p152*), all now offer free Wi-Fi access for customers; more are sure to follow their lead.

This old-style basement pub – all striking blacks and reds, focused on a central island bar – somehow manages to combine New Town money with Stockbridge bohemia. Food is typical pub grub (fish and chips, steak pie) with a few more ambitious dishes. The only change of late is that the old regulars look testier than ever, presumably because they have to go outside to smoke.

Café-bars

Hector's
47-49 Deanhaugh Street (343 1735). Bus 24, 29, 42. **Open** noon-midnight Mon-Wed, Sun; noon-1am Thur-Sat. *Food served* noon-3pm, 6-10pm Mon-Fri; noon-4pm Sat, Sun. **Credit** AmEx, MC, V. **Map** p325 D4 ⓸
Formerly a pioneering designer restaurant, this establishment is now a less ostentatious style bar, good for cosy chats by candlelight or nestling by the

---

fire. The menu features the usual suspects (nachos, burgers, salads). A handy stop if you've been wandering around the nearby Royal Botanic Garden.

Watershed
44 St Stephen Street (220 6189). Bus 24, 29, 42. **Open** 4pm-midnight Mon-Wed; noon-1am Thur-Sat; 12.30pm-1am Sun. *Food served* 4-8pm Mon-Fri; noon-8pm Sat; 12.30-8pm Sun. **Credit** MC, V. **Map** p326 E4 ⓸
The Watershed's recent facelift has cheered up its fading style bar image with a blast of design eclecticism that the new management say 'just seemed like a good idea at the time': a celebration of Koh Samui beach bar chic in an Edinburgh basement. It has a reasonable bar food menu at lunchtime and in the afternoon; as with many other venues of this ilk, it gets buzzier and pubbier in the evening.

Calton Hill & Broughton

Bars & pubs

Barony
81-83 Broughton Street (557 0546). Bus 8, 13, 17/Playhouse buses. **Open** 11am-1am Mon-Sat; 12.30-11pm Sun. *Food served* 11am-10pm Mon-Sat; 12.30-10pm Sun. **Credit** MC, V. **Map** p326 H4 ⓹
The Barony is a very traditional-looking pub, but by no means without character or charisma. The clientele is pretty mixed, and wouldn't seem entirely out of place in one of the more contemporary café-bars nearby. There's pub grub, various cask ales (with regular guest offerings), plus occasional live music.

Cask & Barrel
115 Broughton Street (556 3132). Playhouse buses. **Open** 11am-1am daily. *Food served* noon-2pm daily. **Credit** MC, V. **Map** p326 H4 ⓺
Beer heaven: this old-fashioned pub offers local brews, obscure artisan cask ales from around the UK, and bottled beers from Germany and the Low Countries. Wherever you choose to sit or stand, you'll be able to watch the football on one of the screens.

Pivo
2-6 Calton Road (557 2925). Nicolson Street–North Bridge buses. **Open** 4pm-3am daily. **Credit** AmEx, MC, V. **Map** p327/p331 J6 ⓻
It's not so much a Czech bar as a Czech-themed bar, but Pivo has the look (and the lager) all the same. Two minutes from the east end of Princes Street, it's a popular late-night DJ bar for a cheery, up-for-it crowd; if you want to savour that Staropramen in relative peace and quiet, best go early in the evening.

Café-bars

Baroque
39-41 Broughton Street (557 0627). Bus 8, 13, 17. **Open** 11am-1am Mon-Sat; noon-1am Sun. *Food served* 11am-10pm Mon-Fri; 11am-8pm Sat; noon-8pm Sun. **Credit** MC, V. **Map** p327 J5 ⓼

You can trace the last ten years of Edinburgh's café-bar trends through this one venue. Baroque was a complete design riot when it first opened, but trimmed back the excess a few years later and then added free Wi-Fi access in 2005. Open to the street in summer, the bar has all the usual booze choices alongside a basic menu. It's more of a pre-club venue at night, so don't go expecting peace and quiet.

Basement

10a-12a Broughton Street (557 0097/www.the basement.org.uk). Bus 8, 13, 17/Playhouse buses. **Open** noon-1am daily. *Food served* noon-10.30pm daily. **Credit** AmEx, MC, V. **Map** p326 H5 ㉝

Broughton Street's original style bar still feels much the same as it did back when it opened in 1994, albeit with the odd improvement decor-wise. Incorporating a dim-lit, split-level room and a separate dining space, it can get pretty buzzy in the evenings, when the music is even louder than the staff's Hawaiian shirts. The menu changes through the week, but avocado salad or steak pie for lunch are good benchmarks.

Outhouse

12a Broughton Street Lane (557 6668). Bus 8, 13, 17/Playhouse buses. **Open** noon-1am daily. *Food served* noon-10pm Mon-Fri; noon-7pm Sat, Sun. **Credit** MC, V. **Map** p327 J5 ㊵

Down an unlovely lane off Broughton Street, the Outhouse could easily be just another style bar. However, it works hard at attracting a lively clientele with regular DJs, and scores with the urban beer garden out back. There's not much of a view, but it is away from all the traffic pollution. Of course, all the smokers congregate out there these days…

Arthur's Seat & Duddingston

Bars & pubs

Sheep Heid Inn

43-45 The Causeway (656 6951). Bus 4, 44, 44A, 45. **Open** 11am-11pm Mon-Thur; 11am-midnight Fri, Sat; 12.30-11pm Sun. *Food served* noon-8pm Mon-Sat; 12.30-8pm Sun.

Legend has it that the Sheep Heid Inn got its name from the motif on a snuff box presented by King James VI before he legged it to London to become James I of Britain (yes, the same James as the King's Wark, for which *see p182*). For many, the enticing bar menu and selection of guest beers is a reward for tramping over Arthur's Seat. As close as you'll get to an historic country pub in Edinburgh.

South Edinburgh

Bars & pubs

Bennet's

8 Leven Street (229 5143). Bus 11, 15, 15A, 16, 17, 23, 45. **Open** 11am-1am daily. *Food served* noon-2pm, 5-8.30pm daily. **Credit** MC, V. **Map** p330 F10 ㊶

A marvel of Victorian design. A long wooden bar occupies one side of the room (with alcoves along the top of the gantry accommodating a huge selection of single malts), while the opposite wall has fitted red leather seats and more wooden fittings. Enjoy the cask ales, hearty pub grub and stained glass, but don't bother with the overspill room out back.

Blue Blazer

2 Spittal Street (229 5030). Bus 1, 2, 10, 11, 15, 15A, 16, 17, 23, 24, 27, 34, 35, 45. **Open** 11am-1am Mon-Sat; 12.30pm-1am Sun. **Credit** MC, V. **Map** p330 F8, p336 B4 ㊷

Sandwiched between the lads-night-out chaos of Lothian Road and the lap-dancing bars at the top of the West Port, the Blue Blazer is no more or less than a cosy place to hide away and chat with a decent pint, especially in the wee room through the back.

Canny Man's

237 Morningside Road (447 1484). Bus 11, 15, 15A, 16, 17, 41. **Open** noon-11pm Mon-Wed; noon-midnight Thur, Sat; noon-1am Fri; 12.30-11pm Sun. *Food served* noon-3pm, 6.30-9pm Mon-Sat; 12.30-3pm Sun. **No credit cards.**

It's been around since 1871. It looks as if it was decorated by a mad maiden aunt from the Victorian era. It has a good wine list, an excellent bar menu (the open sandwiches are legendary), and a truly exceptional selection of single malt whiskies. The catch? The sign by the door says 'Dress smart but casual', and it means it. Also known as the Volunteer Arms.

Cloisters

26 Brougham Street (221 9997). Bus 11, 15, 15A, 16, 17, 23, 45. **Open** noon-midnight Mon-Thur, Sun; noon-1am Fri, Sat. *Food served* noon-8pm Mon-Thur; noon-5pm Fri, Sat. **Credit** MC, V. **Map** p330 F9 ㊸

The decor at Cloisters, housed in a former manse, is simple, but it's the rare cask ale that's the selling point. It puts on a good showing on the whisky front too, with around 40 varieties on the shelf.

Dragonfly

52 West Port (228 4543/www.dragonflycocktailbar. com). Bus 2, 35. **Open** 5pm-1am Mon-Thur, Sat, Sun; 4pm-1am Fri. *Food served* pub hours. **Credit** AmEx, MC, V. **Map** p330 F8 ㊹

This address has hosted many a venue over the years, but perhaps plush cocktail bar Dragonfly will stick. Some might see hints of a Graham Norton stage set in the decor, but there are absolutely no quibbles with the quality of the drinks. A hit with the beautiful people, it's definitely not to be confused with the strip joints nearby. *See p183* **My Edinburgh.**

Pear Tree House

36 West Nicolson Street (667 7533). Nicolson Street– North Bridge buses. **Open** 11am-midnight Mon-Thur; 11am-1am Fri, Sat; 12.30pm-midnight Sun. **Credit** MC, V. **Map** p331 J9 ㊺

Literally over the road from Edinburgh University's George Square campus, the Pear Tree's cobbled beer garden has played host to generations of thirsty

Eat, Drink, Shop

students in its time. Inside, the decor is classic trad Scots pub, but with a big screen for the football. Outside termtime, it's fairly placid.

Café-bars

Filmhouse Café Bar

88 Lothian Road (229 5932/www.filmhousecinema. com). Bus 1, 2, 10, 11, 15, 15A, 16, 17, 23, 24, 27, 34, 35, 45. **Open** 10am-11.30pm Mon-Thur, Sun; 10am-12.30am Fri, Sat. *Food served* 10am-10pm daily. **Credit** MC, V. **Map** p330 E6, p336 A4 ⓯

The city's independent arthouse cinema (*see p218*) has been around since the 1980s, but a 2002 refurbishment means the bar doesn't look dated. With coffee, snacks, light meals and a couple of good beers on tap, it's the perfect place to meet friends before or after a movie. If you're brave enough to take on the city's cinema buffs, there's a film quiz on the second Sunday of every month.

Human Be-In

2-8 West Crosscauseway (662 8860/www.human be-in.co.uk). Nicolson Street–North Bridge buses. **Open** 10am-1am daily. *Food served* noon-9pm daily. **Credit** AmEx, MC, V. **Map** p331 J9 ⓱

The interior of this polished style bar is all about the dark woods and clean lines. There are cosy booths to the rear, as well as low, comfortable seats in front of the big windows that look out over the street, and outside tables in the summer. Food includes some fairly ambitious dishes (baked sea bream with clams, duck salad). However, many people come here just for a drink – especially on weekend evenings, when DJs play.

Montpeliers

159-161 Bruntsfield Place (229 3115/www. montpeliersedinburgh.co.uk). Bus 11, 15, 15A, 16, 17, 23, 45. **Open** 9am-1am daily. *Food served* 9am-10pm daily. **Credit** AmEx, MC, V.

Although it has been around since 1992, the odd refurb has ensured that Montpeliers hasn't become dated or dowdy. The decor is currently clean cut, with sofas by the window and dark woods galore. The bar is to one side with the dining space partitioned off to the other; here, you can sample salads, steaks, burgers or comfort food (Irish stew, perhaps). The breakfast menu is also justly celebrated at what remains Bruntsfield's café-bar of choice.

Traverse Theatre Bar

10 Cambridge Street (228 5383/www.traverse.co.uk). Bus 1, 2, 10, 11, 15, 15A, 16, 17, 23, 24, 27, 34, 35, 45. **Open** 10.30am-midnight Mon-Wed, Sun; 10.30am-1am Thur-Sat. *Food served* 10.30am-midnight Mon-Wed, Sun; 10.30am-1am Thur-Sat. **Credit** MC, V. **Map** p330 E8, p336 A3 ⓭

The bar at the Trav (*see p246*) gets very busy pre- and post-performance, especially during the Fringe. The modern, roomy establishment is generally open-plan, but offers a more closed-off dining space in one corner. It attracts a typical café-bar crowd: you can

pick up anything from a veggie sausage sandwich or a haggis baguette for breakfast through to nachos, Thai fish cakes or a stilton and walnut salad at night. Another bonus is the free wireless internet access, allowing you to check your emails over a smoothie or a glass of wine.

West Edinburgh

Bars & pubs

Athletic Arms

1-3 Angle Park Terrace (337 3822). Bus 2, 3, 3A, 4, 25, 33, 44, 44A. **Open** noon-midnight Mon-Thur; 11am-midnight Fri, Sat; 12.30-11pm Sun. *Food served* pub hours. **Credit** MC, V. **Map** p329 A11 ⓭

Before the growth in style bars, Edinburgh had a few 'classic' pubs. Some were Victorian and ornate, while others traded on a different reputation: the Athletic Arms was famous for serving the best pint of McEwan's 80/- in town. Some things remain unchanged: the beer here is still decent, and most locals still call the place the Diggers, after the gravediggers from the nearby cemetery who used to drink here.

Caledonian Ale House

1-3 Haymarket Terrace (337 1006). Bus 2, 3, 3A, 4, 12, 25, 26, 31, 33, 38, 44, 44A. **Open** 11am-12.30am Mon-Sat; 12.30pm-11.30am Sun. *Food served* noon-9pm Mon-Thur; noon-9.30pm Fri, Sat; 12.30-5pm Sun. **Credit** MC, V. **Map** p329 B9 ⓾

A haven for travellers killing time before catching a train from Haymarket station next door. With a bistro upstairs, the bar food is a cut above the usual standard; the ground floor bar has cask ales and a fair selection of whiskies. Gender-wise, the clientele here is more mixed than in some of the more robust drinking dens in these parts. Get in quick, though: in years to come, it may be demolished to make way for Edinburgh's planned tram scheme.

Caley Sample Room

58 Angle Park Terrace (337 7204). Bus 2, 3, 3A, 4, 25, 33, 44, 44A. **Open** noon-midnight daily. *Food served* 6-9pm daily. **Credit** MC, V. **Map** p329 A11 ⓾

The Caley is red brick on the outside and roomy on the inside, with wooden benches and simple, functional decor. With good cask ales on offer, it invariably gets packed out before Hearts games at nearby Tynecastle (*see p238*).

Golden Rule

28-30 Yeaman Place (622 7112). Bus 22, 30. **Open** noon-nidnight Mon-Sat; noon-11pm Sun. *Food served* pub hours. **Credit** MC, V. **Map** p329 B11 ⓾

The Golden Rule is a fine old-fashioned pub with a selection of cask ales, plus a more contemporary lounge bar downstairs that has a glowing reputation for its excellent jukebox. The western tenemental suburbs of the city tend to be a bit of a desert when it comes to decent pubs, so this one stands out all the more.

Eat, Drink, Shop

Café-bars

Cargo
Edinburgh Quay, 129 Fountainbridge (659 7880/ www.cargobar.co.uk). Bus 1, 34, 35. **Open** 11am-1am daily. *Food served* noon-10pm daily. **Credit** AmEx, MC, V. **Map** p330 A9 ⓺⓷

Cargo could be viewed as a cavernous 'retail leisure experience', catering to the outspill from the financial services sector offices nearby. But since opening in 2004, it's offered reasonable food and the chance to sit outside by the terminus of the Union Canal, all as part of an award-winning urban regeneration scheme. Busy, but nicely placed.

Leith & the Coast

Bars & pubs

Boda
229 Leith Walk (553 5900). Bus 7, 10, 12, 14, 16, 22, 25, 49. **Open** 2pm-1am Mon-Fri; noon-1am Sat; 1pm-midnight Sun. *Food served* bar hours. **Credit** MC, V. **Map** p327 L2 ⓹⓸

Boda arrived in 2004 and is run by a Swedish couple with a friendly and laid-back style. It feels like a café-bar but operates like a pub, albeit one with cheese platters and moose sausages on the menu. Nearby sister pub Sofi's runs on the same lines but might also host such unlikely events as knitting evenings. **Other locations:** Sofi's, 63 Henderson Street, Leith (555 7019).

Cramond Inn
30 Cramond Glebe Road, Cramond (336 2035). Bus 24, 41. **Open** 11am-11pm Mon-Thur; 11am-midnight Fri, Sat; 12.30-11pm Sun. *Food served* 12.30-3pm, 6-9pm Mon-Fri; noon-9pm Sat; 12.30-7pm Sun. **Credit** MC, V.

On the coast stretching west of Leith, tucked away in a conservation village on the banks of the River Almond, this cosy, family-friendly venue is full of welcoming nooks and crannies. In the summer it's particularly busy on Sundays, when Edinburgh folk come up to these parts for a walk. Dating from the 17th century, the inn is now owned by Yorkshire brewery Samuel Smith's.

Dalriada
77 The Promenade, Portobello (454 4500/www. dalriada-restaurant.co.uk). Bus 12, 15, 15A, 32, 42, 49. **Open** 11am-11pm Mon-Thur, Sun; 11am-midnight Fri, Sat. *Food served* noon-3pm, 5-9pm Mon-Sat; noon-7pm Sun. **Credit** MC, V.

At this pub down at Portobello beach, about three miles east of Leith, you can get a decent pint of cask ale and sit in the front garden overlooking the sands, head for the enclosed beer garden at the back, or just hang out in the spacious interior. With a bar menu that runs to club sandwiches, burgers, steak, fish and chips and the like, this former hotel is an ideal stop if you've been walking along the Prom.

King's Wark
36 The Shore (554 9260). Bus 1, 10, 16, 22, 35, 36. **Open** noon-11pm Mon-Thur; noon-midnight Fri, Sat; 11am-11pm Sun. *Food served* noon-3pm, 6-10pm Mon-Sat; 11am-3pm, 6-10pm Sun. **Credit** MC, V. **Map** p324 Y3 ⓹⓹

Built on the site of an original 15th-century building, the current King's Wark was part of an early 17th-century royal complex used by King James VI of Scotland (who became King James I of England). The main room is simply a well-worn, welcoming pub, but there's a smaller space to one side for slightly more formal dining. The beer-battered fish and chips is always a winner, and Sunday brunch is terrific.

Noble's
44a Constitution Street (554 2024). Bus 1, 10, 16, 22, 35, 36. **Open** 11am-midnight Mon-Wed, Sun; 11am-1am Thur-Sat. *Food served* noon-3pm Mon-Fri. **Credit** MC, V. **Map** p324 Z4 ⓹⓺

This old Victorian bar has gone through many changes in its long lifetime, the latest being a serious refurbishment in 2006 that brought an added sense of gravitas to the already ornate interior (which boasts stained glass and a maritime frieze). There's now plush leather seating, and a more upmarket style in both food and general tenor.

Ocean Bar
Ocean Terminal, Ocean Drive (553 8073). Bus 1, 10, 16, 22, 35, 36. **Open** noon-midnight Mon-Thur, Sun; noon-1am Fri, Sat. *Food served* noon-10pm daily. **Credit** AmEx, MC, V. **Map** p324 X1 ⓹⓻

On the first floor of Ocean Terminal mall (see *p187*), the Ocean Bar has great views out over the Western Harbour (home of the Royal Yacht *Britannia*, see *p135*). Good for cocktails, it's best when you can go outside to the balcony and look out over the water. Shoppers seem wary of even the slightest breeze, so it's often fairly quiet out there. One of the more unusual places to drink in the city.

Old Chain Pier
32 Trinity Crescent (552 1233). Bus 10, 11, 16, 32. **Open** noon-11pm Mon-Wed; noon-midnight Thur-Sat; 10am-11pm Sun. *Food served* noon-9pm Mon-Sat; 10am-8pm Sun. **Credit** MC, V.

Refurbished after a fire in 2004, this bar sits on the coast between the small harbours at Newhaven and Granton. It was built on the site of (yes) an old chain pier, constructed in 1821 and swept away in a storm in 1898. Now it functions as a friendly neighbourhood pub, with a conservatory for more formal dining (steak, lamb stew, chowder). However, it's still best for a pint and a bar meal while gazing out over the Forth. Free Wi-Fi access is a nice touch.

Pond
2 Bath Road (467 3825). Bus 1, 10, 16, 22, 35, 36. **Open** 4pm-1am Mon-Thur; 2pm-1am Fri, Sat; 1pm-1am Sun. **No credit cards.**

The encroachment of new apartment blocks has put paid to the Pond's former reputation as 'the pub at the end of the universe', but it's still in a fairly

Eat, Drink, Shop

My Edinburgh Kyles Dignall

*A Godzilla among local lounge lizards,
Edinburgh-born Kyles Dignall opened his
first bar, the **Villager** (49-50 George IV Bridge,
Old Town, 226 2781), in 2003 with partners
Anthony Boyle, Brendan Denahy and Annalese
McDermott. It was an instant hit; Dignall
followed by launching **Dragonfly** (see p179)
in 2004 and starting Stolen, a modelling
agency, the following year.*

'I've lived in Edinburgh my entire 32 years.
Apart from a year's IT work in Milton Keynes,
that is, which particularly outlined what a
cultural pleasure Edinburgh is.

'Edinburgh's bar culture is unique in that
the city centre buzz goes on within such
a small geographic area. The top ten bars
in the city are all within a 20-minute-walk
radius. Given the huge influx of tourists
and business travellers
from out of town,
the locals still retain
enormous influence on
the city's character.

'Our best bars are
among the finest in the
UK in terms of aesthetic,
service, drinks and
bartenders (who smile!).
Coupled with that are the
relaxed licensing laws,
which give an amazing,
cosmopolitan air to
the city and a prime
opportunity for late-night
fun. The recent smoking
ban is one of Scotland's
best moves of all time,
right up there with Archie
Gemmill in 1978.

'Apart from our own multi-award-winning
bars, the best cocktails are to be found at
Tonic on Castle Street (see p177) and **Rick's**
on Frederick Street (see p177). For all-round
good stuff, try **Sygn** in the West End (15
Charlotte Lane, 225 6060, www.sygn.co.uk).
When the sun's out (and I can't make the
journey to Leith's **Shore**; see p184), I head to
the **Human Be-In** (see p181). I'm also excited
about two new openings: **Amicus Apple** on
Frederick Street (see p173) and **Tigerlily** on
George Street (see p61).

'Villager and Dragonfly are definitely unique.
Our high standards and attention to detail are
combined with a genuine, relaxed and local
vibe. But the best kept secret in Edinburgh is
an amazing old school bar in the Old Town.
I'm not telling which one, unless you buy me
a champagne Mojito at Villager or Dragonfly...'

unlovely street between Leith Links and the docks
(albeit less than half a mile away from the Shore and
the heart of Leith). It has the look of a hand-knitted
university common room, but with a decent pint and
some bombay mix in your hand, and a seat on one
of the sofas, it can seem like a home from home.

Port O' Leith
*58 Constitution Street (554 3568). Bus 1, 10, 16,
22, 35, 36.* **Open** *9am-1am Mon-Sat; 12.30pm-1am
Sun.* **No credit cards. Map** *p324 Z3* ⑬
Both this pub and its proprietor, Mary Moriarty, are
legends on the Edinburgh pub scene. It's a small,
neatly kept pub, patronised by everyone from merchant mariners to locals and students. You could sit

for hours looking at the details: ships' flags, lifebelts,
snuff for sale and so on. With bucketloads of character, it captures the true essence of Leith.

Scotch Malt Whisky Society Members' Room
*The Vaults, 87 Giles Street (555 2266/www.smws.
com). Bus 1, 10, 16, 22, 35, 36.* **Open** *10am-5pm
Mon, Tue; 10am-11pm Wed-Sat; 11am-10pm Sun.
Food served noon-5pm Mon, Tue; noon-9pm
Wed-Sat; 12.30-3pm Sun.* **Credit** *AmEx, MC, V.*
Map *p324 Y3* ⑬
The SMWS was set up in 1983 to buy individual
casks of whisky from distilleries, bottle them and sell
them to members. The idea proved a hit, but the

changes in the industry (and an investment in a second room in the New Town) stretched the society; it was bought by Glenmorangie in 2004, which itself was then snapped up by luxury brand conglomerate LVMH. It remains largely unchanged: the atmosphere is still tranquil, the food is still good and the range of rare whiskies is the city's best. It's open to members only; membership starts at £75 a year.

Other locations: 28 Queen Street, New Town (220 2044).

Shore

3-4 The Shore (553 5080/www.theshore.biz). Bus 1, 10, 16, 22, 35, 36. **Open** 11am-midnight Mon-Sat; noon-11pm Sun. *Food served* noon-2.30pm, 6.30-10pm Mon-Fri; noon-3pm, 6.30-10pm Sun. **Credit** MC, V. **Map** p324 Y2 ⑳

The Shore has a small, bustling bar and tables outside on the pavement – on finer days, you can even take your drink across the street to the quayside and sit watching the Water of Leith flow into the docks. It's essentially a gastropub: the bar menu is fabulous, and a small adjoining room operates as a restaurant, serving some excellent fresh fish and seafood dishes. There is often live music in the bar.

Starbank Inn

64 Laverockbank Road (552 4141/www.starbank inn.co.uk). Bus 10, 11, 16, 32. **Open** 11am-11pm Mon-Wed; 11am-midnight Fri, Sat; 12.30-11pm Sun. *Food served* noon-2.30pm, 6-9pm Mon-Fri; noon-9pm Sat; 12.30-9pm Sun. **Credit** MC, V.

Set back and slightly raised on the other side of the street from the sea wall, the Starbank arguably has better views of the Forth than the nearby Old Chain

Pier (*see p182*). Like its neighbour, it offers good cask ales, as well as a rotating selection of guest ales, but is the more patrician of the two establishments. The menu offers solid, traditional fare; roast lamb and mint sauce, poached salmon or a ploughman's lunch.

Café-bars

Bar Sirius

7-10 Dock Place (555 3344). Bus 1, 10, 16, 22, 35, 36. **Open** noon-11.30pm Mon-Thur; noon-1am Fri-Sun. *Food served* noon-8pm daily. **Credit** MC, V. **Map** p324 Y2 ㉛

When Sirius arrived in Leith a decade ago, its like had never been seen before. But the original ostentation of its design was calmed down a little, and in spring 2006 a refurb freshened the whole place up once more. It's still very popular, both as a venue for a good night out and for café-bar eats.

Malmaison Bar

1 Tower Place (468 5000/www.malmaison.com). Bus 1, 10, 16, 22, 35, 36. **Open** 9am-1am daily. **Credit** AmEx, DC, MC, V. **Map** p324 Y2 ㉜

The name is now well known thanks to a string of boutique hotels across the UK, but this was the very first of their number (*see p72*). The ground floor has a fine contemporary bar space, with outdoor seating on the terrace that overlooks the water. The food is good, but the Malmaison Brasserie next door has a more extensive menu, serving up dishes such as chargrilled burgers, monkfish, great salads and a fabulous Sunday brunch.

Home comforts at the **Scotch Malt Whisky Society** in Leith. *See p183.*

Shops & Services

Off the tourist trail, there's a lot more to Edinburgh than twee souvenirs.

Savvy shopper's paradise or tourist trap? There are two distinct sides to Edinburgh's retail experience. On the one hand, you'll see whisky, kilts and shortbread in every other store. However, perhaps in a bid to prove to the outside world that the city's shopping circuit isn't simply about tradition, an increasing number of independent fashion boutiques, music stores and design shops offer locals and visitors rather more appealing wares.

The city's best-known shopping drag is **Princes Street**. Retail outlets line the north side of the road, while on the south side, in the shadow of the castle, lie expansive and immaculately maintained gardens. However, the street sports the same shops that you'll find in any other British high street. Marks & Spencer, Boots, Gap… you'll find everything you need here, but nothing that really inspires.

Thankfully, things improve just a few yards away. In recent years, the grand old banks and offices of parallel **George Street** have been converted into boutiques, bars and restaurants. The result is an upmarket alternative to Princes Street, with fashion brands such as Whistles, Coast and Hobbs sitting alongside renowned jewellers Hamilton & Inches and diamond specialists Lime Blue. The arrival of Harvey Nichols on **St Andrew's Square**, at the street's eastern end, was another boost; next door, **Multrees Walk** has become the city's version of London's Bond Street, home to Emporio Armani, Louis Vuitton and Mulberry stores.

Edinburgh's most interesting shops are a little off the beaten track. In the West End, **William Street** is home to a range of inspiring boutiques, from Helen Bateman's exclusive shoes to Arkangel's show-stopping jewellery. Head to the buzzing **Grassmarket** for a less well-heeled but livelier shopping experience. Vintage clothes emporium Armstrong's and a good selection of antique shops create a raffish vibe; nearby sit Odd One Out on Victoria Street and Godiva on West Port, both offering fashionable new kit.

On **Cockburn Street**, three independent music shops – Avalanche, Underground Solu'shn and the increasingly ubiquitous Fopp – offer an alternative to the high street megastores. The twisting street leads up to the **Royal Mile**, which caters to your every Scottish-themed need (and then some). Treat yourself to a sugary box of Edinburgh rock and a tartan scarf by all means, but don't miss out on the fine Scottish malts at Royal Mile Whiskies, Ness Scotland's vibrant knitwear and quirky accessories and the 21st-century kilts on sale at Geoffrey (Tailor).

One often unheralded feature of Edinburgh's shopping landscape is its preponderance of great food shops. Valvona & Crolla is the most famous of several delis around the city, but there are also a number of terrific speciality shops. Try Plaisir du Chocolat for melt-in-the-mouth chocolates, Crombie's on Broughton Street for top quality sausages, or Iain Mellis's famous cheese shop on Victoria Street – you'll smell it before you see it.

The best Shops

For Italian food
Marcella Italian Bakery. See p199.

For German homewares
Designshop UK. See p204.

For English records
Underground Solu'shn. See p205.

For American beauty products
Space NK. See p202.

For Scottish souvenirs
Royal Mile Whiskies. See p198.

OPENING HOURS

Usual shop opening hours are from 9am or 10am to 6pm from Monday to Saturday, but lots of shops do stay open late on Thursdays. Many stores now also open on Sundays, but the majority operate shorter hours than normal. Shops often extend their hours during the festivals and in the run-up to Christmas.

General

Department stores

With the conspicuous exception of Selfridges, all of the UK's top department store chains can be found in Edinburgh, dotted on and around

Cockburn Street.
See p185.

Located at the west end of Princes Street, Fraser's offers a reasonable selection of cosmetics, contemporary and classic fashions, homewares and gifts.

Harvey Nichols

30-34 St Andrew Square, New Town (524 8388/ www.harveynichols.com). Princes Street buses. **Open** 10am-6pm Mon-Wed; 10am-8pm Thur; 10am-7pm Fri, Sat; 11am-6pm Sun. **Credit** AmEx, DC, MC, V. **Map** p326 H5, p336 E1.

When Harvey Nichols opened in Edinburgh in 2003, it heralded a shift in the city's shopping landscape. Designer togs have always been available here, but no one presents them quite so glossily as Harvey Nicks. As well as fashions, you'll find exclusive cosmetics brands and a top-floor food hall, bar and restaurant, Forth Floor, with truly breathtaking views (*see p152*).

Jenners

48 Princes Street, New Town (0870 607 2841/ www.jenners.com). Princes Street buses. **Open** 9am-6pm Mon-Wed, Fri, Sat; 9am-8pm Thur; 11am-5pm Sun. **Credit** AmEx, DC, MC, V. **Map** p326/p330 G6, p336 E2.

You could easily fill a couple of hours exploring this vast shop, its 100 departments laid out rather eccentrically over six floors. The store includes fashions, cosmetics, homewares, food, gifts, an interior design studio, stationery and toys. However, tears were shed when the shop, founded in 1838 and Scotland's oldest independent department store, was bought by House of Fraser in 2005; under its new owners, the range doesn't seem as extensive as it once was.

John Lewis

69 St James Centre, Leith Street, New Town (556 9121/www.johnlewis.com). Playhouse or Princes Street buses. **Open** 9am-6pm Mon-Wed; 9.30am-8pm Thur; 9am-8pm Fri; 9am-6.30pm Sat; 11am-5pm Sun. **Credit** MC, V. **Map** p326 H5.

John Lewis's Edinburgh store has undergone an estimated £25 million refurbishment in recent years, and it shows: it's now a shop very much fit for the 21st century. The stock, while expanded, nonetheless takes the same tack as ever: from haberdashery to hats, furniture to fashion, it's all very sensible – albeit with the store's famed 'never knowingly undersold' pledge guaranteeing value for money.

Marks & Spencer

54 & 91 Princes Street, New Town (225 2301/ www.marksandspencer.com). Princes Street buses. **Open** 9am-7pm Mon-Wed, Fri; 9am-8pm Thur; 8.30am-7pm Sat; 11am-6pm Sun. **Credit** AmEx, DC, MC, V. **Map** p326/p330 G6 & p330 F7, p336 D2 & C2.

The Edinburgh outpost of M&S, on the up again after a spell in the doldrums, is a tale of two stores. The 54 Princes Street operation is home to menswear, childrenswear, homewares and the above-average food hall, while a full selection of casual and smart womenswear is a short walk away at No.91.

Other locations: 21 Gyle Avenue, West Edinburgh (317 1333).

Princes Street. **Jenners**, over a century old, is the grande dame, with **Harvey Nichols** the new kid on the block; pitched in between the pair is the recently refurbished **John Lewis**.

Bhs

64 Princes Street, New Town (226 2621/www.bhs. co.uk). Princes Street buses. **Open** 9am-6pm Mon-Wed, Fri, Sat; 9am-8pm Thur; 11am-5pm Sun. **Credit** AmEx, DC, MC, V. **Map** p326/p330 G6, p336 D2.

Affordable mainstream fashions, homeware and a surprisingly decent selection of confectionery gifts at reasonable prices.

Debenhams

109-112 Princes Street, New Town (225 1320/ www.debenhams.com). Princes Street buses. **Open** 9.30am-6pm Mon-Wed, Fri; 9.30am-8pm Thur; 9am-6pm Sat; 11am-6pm Sun. **Credit** AmEx, DC, MC, V **Map** p330 F7, p336 B2.

Negotiating your way around this ageing building can be tricky. Still, once you've got your bearings, you'll find the fashions above average (the Designers at Debenhams range features outfits by Ben de Lisi, John Rocha and other well-known names), and decent ranges of homewares, accessories and cosmetics.

Fraser's

145 Princes Street, New Town (0870 160 7239/ www.houseoffraser.co.uk). Princes Street buses. **Open** 9.30am-6pm Mon-Wed, Fri; 9.30am-7.30pm Thur; 9am-6pm Sat; 11am-5pm Sun. **Credit** AmEx, DC, MC, V. **Map** p330 E7, p336 A2.

Eat, Drink, Shop

Malls

Most of the shopping malls in the Edinburgh area contain the same retailers you'll find on the high street. However, a few also house cinemas, all feature eating options and most will keep you dry when it's raining outside.

Cameron Toll

6 Lady Road, South Edinburgh (666 2777/ www.camerontoll.co.uk). Bus 24, 32, 33, 38, 49. **Open** 10am-6pm Mon-Wed, Sat; 10am-7pm Thur, Fri; 11am-5pm Sun.

Located a ten-minute bus ride south of the city centre, Cameron Toll houses around 50 stores. Among them are Bhs, Boots, Ottakar's, Virgin and a sizeable branch of the Sainsbury's supermarket chain.

Fort Kinnaird

Newcraighall Road, South Edinburgh (www.fort kinnaird.com). Bus 30. **Open** 9am-8pm Mon-Fri; 9am-6pm Sat, Sun.

This popular out-of-town shopping destination, accessible via a 20-minute bus journey from the city centre or a ten-minute train ride to Newcraighall, is home to branches of Borders, H&M and Gap, among others. There's also an Odeon multiplex (*see p218*).

Gyle Centre

South Gyle Broadway, West Edinburgh (539 8828/ www.gyleshopping.co.uk). Bus 12, 21/Edinburgh Park rail. **Open** 9.30am-8pm Mon-Wed, Fri; 9.30am-9pm Thur; 9am-6pm Sat; 10am-6pm Sun.

A 20-minute drive west of the city, the Gyle is home to Sainsbury's, Marks & Spencer, Next and other well-known high street names.

Ocean Terminal

Ocean Drive, Leith (555 8888/www.oceanterminal. com). Bus 1, 11, 22, 34, 35, 36. **Open** 10am-8pm Mon-Fri; 10am-7pm Sat; 11am-6pm Sun. **Map** p324 X1.

After a slow start, this Conran-designed building is now attracting decent numbers of retailers and customers, helping to regenerate the Leith waterfront. Shops include French Connection and Debenhams, and there's a Vue cinema on the second floor (*see p219*). The food isn't anything special, but the views over the Forth from the eating area can't be beaten.

Princes Mall

Princes Street (east end), New Town (557 3759/www. princesmall-edinburgh.co.uk). Princes Street buses. **Open** 8.30am-6pm Mon-Wed, Fri, Sat; 8.30am-7pm Thur; 11am-5pm Sun. **Map** p326/p330 H6, p336 E2.

Right next door to Waverley train station, Princes Mall also incorporates the city's tourism office. High street names such as Warehouse, Oasis and Kookai rub shoulders with Scottish-themed gift shops.

St James Centre

Leith Street, New Town (557 0050/www.thestjames. com). Playhouse or Princes Street buses. **Open** 9am-6pm Mon-Sat; 11am-5pm Sun. **Map** p326 H5.

The bleak concrete exterior of the St James Centre is often criticised, but its interior has been immeasurably improved with the refurbishment of the flagship John Lewis store. Among the other attractions are familiar names such as HMV, Next and Topshop, plus a post office.

Markets

A combination of new building developments and trading standards clampdowns have put paid to some of the city's longest-running markets and car boot sales. However, the weekly farmer's market continues to do a brisk trade, and temporary specialist markets are often set up in the city centre during August to coincide with the festivals, or as part of the Christmas festivities in December.

Farmers' Market

Castle Terrace, South Edinburgh (557 9201/ www.edinburghcc.com/ECC/farm_market.htm). **Open** 9am-2pm Sat. **Map** p330 F8, p336 B4.

Held weekly at the foot of Edinburgh Castle, this market caters to hungry foodies desperate for local produce. More than 50 specialist stalls sell meat, fish, free-range eggs, cheeses, fruit and veg and all manner of homemade chutneys, breads and chocolates.

Specialist

Books & magazines

In addition to the independent stores detailed below, there are branches of the **Waterstone's** and **Blackwells** general book chains around town. The former are at 13 and 128 Princes Street (www.waterstones.co.uk); the latter at 53-62 South Bridge (www.blackwells.co.uk).

Analogue

102 West Bow, Old Town (220 0601/www.analogue books.co.uk). Bus 2, 23, 27, 41, 42. **Open** 10am-5.30pm Mon-Sat. **Credit** MC, V. **Map** p330 G8, p336 D4.

Analogue deals in books on design and contemporary culture. As well as glossy tomes on fashion, illustration, graffiti and graphic design, there's a gallery space (*see p221*) and interesting ranges of T-shirts, magazines and prints.

Armchair Books

72-74 West Port, South Edinburgh (229 5927/ www.mochaholic.org/acb). Bus 2, 35. **Open** 10am-8pm Mon-Sat; 11am-5pm Sun. **Credit** MC, V. **Map** p330 F8.

An archetypal second-hand bookshop, with thousands of old volumes stacked precariously on shelves in every available space. Specialising in Victorian, illustrated and antiquarian books, it's a browser's paradise.

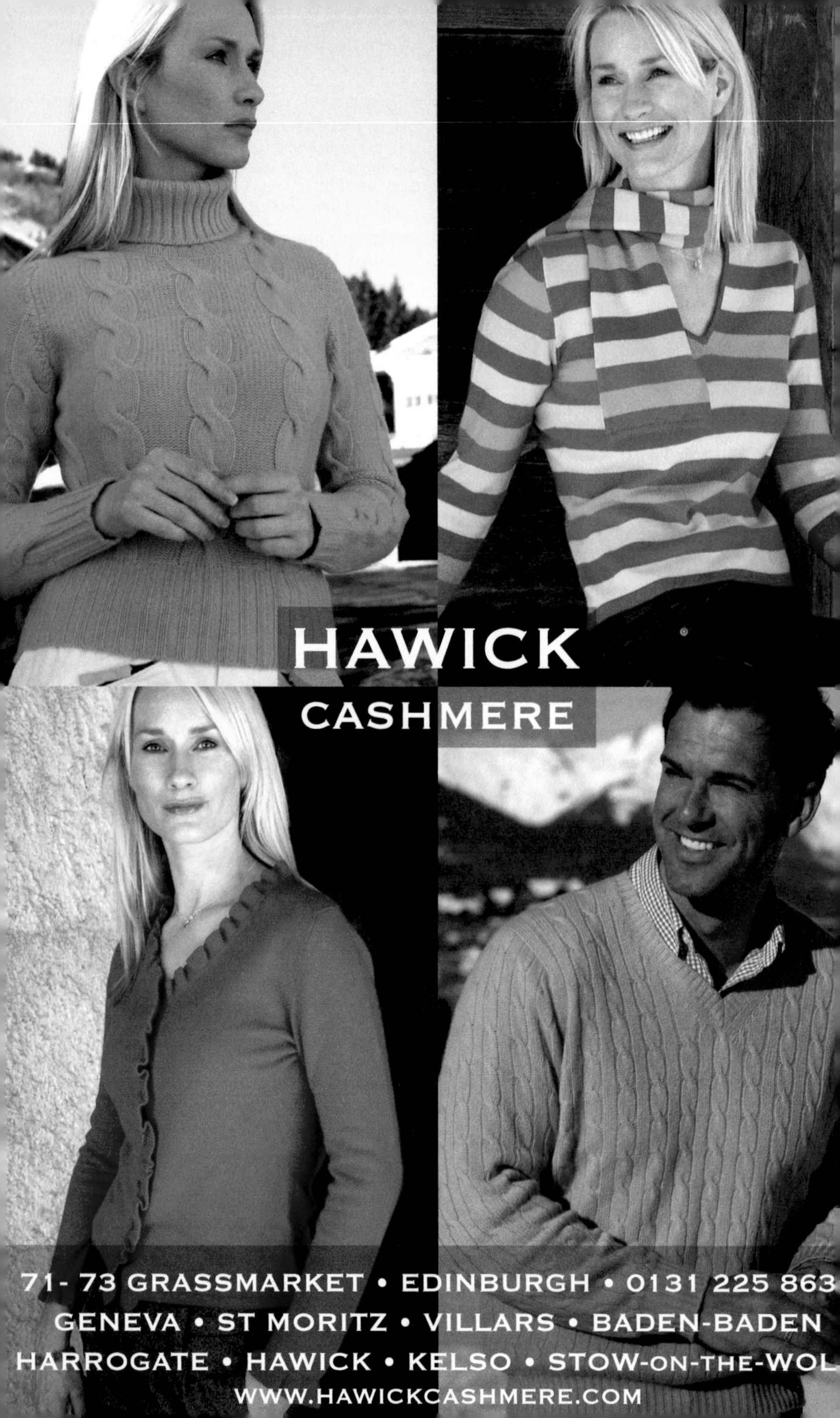
HAWICK
CASHMERE
71- 73 GRASSMARKET • EDINBURGH • 0131 225 863
GENEVA • ST MORITZ • VILLARS • BADEN-BADEN
HARROGATE • HAWICK • KELSO • STOW-ON-THE-WOL
WWW.HAWICKCASHMERE.COM

Beyond Words

42-44 Cockburn Street, Old Town (226 6636/www. beyondwords.co.uk). Bus 35/Nicolson Street–North Bridge buses. **Open** 10am-6pm Mon-Sat; 1-6pm Sun. **Credit** MC, V. **Map** p330 H7, p336 F3.

Scotland's only photographic bookshop stocks coffee table-friendly tomes featuring everything from landscapes to celebrity portraits.

Other locations: 45 Broughton Street, Broughton (556 3377).

Deadhead Comics

27 Candlemaker Row, Old Town (226 2774/ www.deadheadcomics.com). Bus 2, 23, 27, 41, 42. **Open** 10am-6pm Mon-Sat; 12.30-5.30pm Sun. **Credit** MC, V. **Map** p330 H8.

Behind the gloomy exterior lies a fine selection of American superhero titles, as well as lesser-known indie works and second-hand comics.

Forbidden Planet

40-41 South Bridge, Old Town (558 8226/ www.forbiddenplanet.co.uk). Nicolson Street–North Bridge buses. **Open** 10am-5.30pm Mon-Wed, Fri, Sat; 10am-6pm Thur; 11am-5pm Sun. **Credit** MC, V. **Map** p331 J7, p336 F4.

Action figures, science-fiction and fantasy novels, comics, DVDs and toys compete for shelf space here.

International Newsagents

351 High Street, Old Town (225 4827). Bus 35/ Nicolson Street–North Bridge buses. **Open** 6am-6pm Mon-Fri; 7am-7pm Sat; 7.30am-5.30pm Sun. **Credit** MC, V **Map** p330 H7, p336 E4.

This truly global outlet on the Royal Mile stocks everything from *Le Monde* to *USA Today*.

Old Town Bookshop

8 Victoria Street, Old Town (225 9237/ www.oldtownbookshop.com). Bus 2, 23, 27, 41, 42. **Open** 10.30am-6pm Mon-Sat. **Credit** MC, V. **Map** p330 H7, p336 D4.

Antiquarian maps and prints sit alongside a wide collection of historical, children's and general used titles at this Victoria Street shop.

West Port Books

145 West Port, South Edinburgh (229 4431). Bus 2, 35. **Open** 10.30am-6pm Mon, Tue, Fri; 12.30pm-6pm Wed, Thur, Sat. **Credit** MC, V **Map** p330 F8.

While away a happy afternoon in this sizeable second-hand book shop, which houses over 25,000 volumes, not to mention a large selection of sheet music.

Word Power

43 West Nicolson Street, South Edinburgh (662 9112/www.word-power.co.uk). Nicolson Street–North Bridge buses. **Open** 10am-6pm Mon-Fri; 10.30am-6pm Sat; noon-5pm Sun. **Credit** AmEx, MC, V. **Map** p331 J9.

This radical bookstore sells titles from new writers and small presses alongside copies of *Stupid White Men* and *The God of Small Things*. Warmly supported by local and international writers, the shop hosts an annual Radical Book Fair in October.

Computing & electronics

Basic electronics and computing needs can be taken care of on Princes Street or at one of the out-of-town retail parks, most of which are home to a branch of all-rounders Comet or Currys. There's an **Apple Centre** at 95-97 Nicolson Street, South Edinburgh (0845 606 2641), and a branch of gamers' haven **Game** at 127 Princes Street (225 3453, www.game.net).

Blacks & Lizars

6 Shandwick Place, New Town (225 2195/www. blacksandlizars.com). Bus 3, 3A, 4, 12, 25, 26, 31, 33, 44. **Open** 9am-5.30pm Mon-Wed, Fri, Sat; 9am-7pm Thur, Sun. **Credit** AmEx, MC, V. **Map** p329 D7.

Blacks & Lizars are best known as optometrists, but this store specialises in photographic equipment: digital, compact and SLR cameras, plus camcorders, lenses and accessories.

Edinburgh Cameras

219 Bruntsfield Place, South Edinburgh (447 9977/ www.edinburghcameras.co.uk). Bus 11, 15, 15A, 16, 17, 23, 45. **Open** 9am-5.30pm Mon-Sat. **Credit** MC, V. **Map** p330 E11.

This independent retailer, in the trade for over 50 years, stocks a wide variety of camera equipment and binoculars, and also offers a repair service.

Ideal Computing

78 Bruntsfield Place, South Edinburgh (0871 700 0156/www.idealcomputing.co.uk). Bus 11, 15, 15A, 16, 17, 23, 45. **Open** 10am-6pm Mon-Sat. **Credit** MC, V. **Map** p330 E11.

If you're overwhelmed by the PC superstores, this small outlet, which custom-builds and sells its own systems, is a good alternative.

Fashion

Children

Blessings & Blossoms

132 St John's Road, West Edinburgh (334 8322/ www.blessingsandblossoms.co.uk). Bus 12, 26, 31, 38. **Open** 9.30am-5pm Mon-Sat. **Credit** MC, V.

Smart togs for babies and children, with outfits for christenings, weddings or other special occasions.

Ideal Cottons

72a Madeira Street, Leith (553 4191/www.ideal cottons.com). Bus 1, 10, 32, 34. **Open** by appointment only. **Credit** MC, V. **Map** p324 W3.

All of the clothing here is made from 100 per cent cotton, created by designer Tania Chamberlain.

JnR Station

Princes Mall, Princes Street (east end), New Town (557 5858/www.jnrstation-online.co.uk). Nicolson Street–North Bridge or Princes Street buses. **Open** 9am-6pm Mon-Wed, Fri, Sat; 9am-7pm Thur; 11am-5pm Sun. **Credit** MC, V. **Map** p326/p330 H6, p336 E2.

Eat, Drink, Shop

My Edinburgh Joey D

After moving to Edinburgh from Leicester on the advice of a medium, Joey D's fortunes certainly took an upward turn. From staging fashion shows in New York to kitting out KT Tunstall and Elton John, the boy's done good since opening his eponymous Broughton Street shop (see p191), now a much-loved Edinburgh institution, back in 1998.

'I just fell in love with the city, really; it's beautiful. I love the buzz of the people here, the excitement of the place and the fact that there's always something to do.

'I tend to be too busy these days to spend as much time in the clubs and bars as I'd like. These days, you're just as likely to find me having a coffee in **Sala** on Broughton Street (*see p223*), which is nice and chilled, but I still try and go to the **City Café** on Blair Street (*see p171*) as much as I can. Everyone who visits Edinburgh will go through that place at some point – and so they should. It's got such a beautiful vibe. I love the Cuban Brothers, too. If they're playing anywhere in town, they're well worth checking out: they're often at the Snatch Social at the **Liquid Room** (*see p231*), which is where it all started for them.

'Scottish people generally, and Edinburghers in particular, are always willing to try something different and assert their own identity. This is what really defines the Edinburgh style for me. It's unlike any other city. My own designs and store (**Joey D**; *see p191*) are influenced more by my customers and their feedback than anything else. I love that they can come in to the shop and chill out and chat anytime. Outside of my own place, visitors to the city really should check out **Armstrongs** in the Grassmarket (*see p193*). If you want to find something extreme, that's the place to go. It's all second-hand, but definitely worth a gander.

'Perfect day out? Probably a visit to my shop, then some of the art galleries on Dundas Street, rounding off with a show of some sort. Possibly a live sex show. Failing that, a trip to the sea is always nice, isn't it?'

Start the kids on those designer brands nice and early, with gear from the likes of Diesel and Levi's.

Nippers for Kids
131 Bruntsfield Place, South Edinburgh (228 5086/ www.nippersforkids.com). Bus 11, 15, 15A, 16, 17, 23, 45. **Open** 9.30am-5.30pm Mon-Sat. **Credit** MC, V. **Map** p330 E11.
Almost 20 years ago, Karen Mackay spotted a gap in the children's clothing market. Today, her company produces its own affordable designs, and also stocks brands such as Uttam and Confetti.

Designer

A few major designer stores have branches in Edinburgh, among them **Emporio Armani** (23 Multrees Walk, St Andrew Square, 523 1580, www.emporioarmani.com) and **Louis Vuitton** (1-2 Multrees Walk, St Andrew

Square, 652 5900). There's also an outpost of luxury leather goods label Mulberry at No.6 (Multrees Walk, St Andrew Square, 557 5439).

Corniche
2-4 Jeffrey Street, Old Town (556 3707/www. corniche.org.uk). Bus 35/Nicolson Street–North Bridge buses. **Open** 10.30am-5.30pm Mon-Sat. **Credit** AmEx, MC, V. **Map** p327/p331 J6.
Corniche has been introducing new labels to the city for years. Designers such as Westwood and Gaultier are represented, with menswear and womenswear pieces, alongside local girl Holly Campbell Mitchell.

Cruise Woman
31 N Castle Street, New Town (220 4441/ www.cruiseclothing.co.uk). Princes Street buses. **Open** 9.30am-6pm Mon-Wed, Fri, Sat; 10am-8pm Thur; 11am-5pm Sun. **Credit** AmEx, MC, V. **Map** p326/p330 E6, p336 B1.

Voted the Most Stylish Retailer 2005 at the Scottish Style Awards, Cruise has been catering to fashion-conscious Scots for 20 years. Brands stocked include Prada, Gucci, Dolce & Gabbana and Galliano.
Other locations: Cruise Man, 94 George Street, New Town (226 3524); Cruise Jeans, 80 George Street, New Town (226 0840).

Jane Davidson
52 Thistle Street, New Town (225 3280/ www.janedavidson.co.uk). Princes Street buses. **Open** 9.30am-6pm Mon-Wed, Fri, Sat; 9am-7pm Thur. **Credit** MC, V. **Map** p326 G5.
This chic boutique has been attracting in-the-know locals since 1969, with designs by Christian Lacroix, Diane von Furstenberg, Missoni and more.

Sam Thomas
18 Stafford Street, New Town (226 1126). Bus 3, 3A, 4, 12, 25, 26, 31, 33, 44. **Open** 9.30am-6pm Mon-Wed, Fri, Sat; 9.30am-6.30pm Thur; 12.30-5pm Sun. **Credit** MC, V. **Map** p329 D7.
The price tags in this friendly boutique are, pleasingly, a little lower than you might expect. Clothes, including hard-to-find labels such as Great Plains and Avoca, are laid out on colour-co-ordinated rails.

Discount

Edinburgh isn't great for discount shopping, but there is a branch of bargainous chain **TK Maxx** at Meadowbank Retail Park (London Road, Calton Hill, 661 6611, www.tkmaxx.co.uk)

General

Princes Street is home to **Gap** (No.131, 220 3303), **Next** (No.107, 0870 386 5103), **Top Shop** (No.30, 556 0151) and all the usual high street fashion retailers, while George Street is home to more upmarket chains such as **Karen Millen** (No.53, 220 1589), **Whistles** (No.97, 226 4398) and **Hobbs** (No.47, 220 5386). However, venture beyond the high street and you'll find an inspiring range of boutiques, stocking everything from urban labels to local designers.

Big Ideas
96 West Bow, Old Town (226 2532/www.bigideasfor ladies.co.uk). Bus 2, 23, 27, 41, 42. **Open** 10am-5.30pm Mon-Sat. **Credit** AmEx, MC, V. **Map** p330 G8, p336 D4.
This friendly shop stocks a good range of well-designed smart and casual clothes in plus sizes.
Other locations: 116 West Bow, Old Town (226 2532).

Concrete Wardrobe
317-319 Cowgate, Old Town (558 7130). Nicolson Street–North Bridge buses. **Open** noon-6pm Tue-Fri; noon-5pm Sat. **Credit** MC, V. **Map** p331 J7.
There aren't many shops where the designer might be on hand to give you advice on which of their outfits would work best for you, but this shop is staffed

by the artists whose work it stocks. Labels include Roobedo, Mal & Leith and PickOne. *See also p204* **Concrete Butterfly**. Photo *p192*.

Cookie
29a-31 Cockburn Street, Old Town (622 7260). Bus 35/Nicolson Street–North Bridge buses. **Open** 9.30am-6pm Mon-Wed, Fri, Sat; 9.30am-7pm Thur; noon-5pm Sun. **Credit** AmEx, MC, V. **Map** p330 H7, p336 F3.
Its arrays of colourful dresses, tops and skirts lend Cookie the feel of a vintage shop. However, the stock here is all new, and features plenty of unusual labels.

Cult Clothing
7-9 North Bridge, Old Town (556 5003/www. cult.co.uk). Nicolson Street–North Bridge buses. **Open** 9.30am-6pm Mon-Wed, Fri, Sat; 10am-7pm Thur; noon-5pm Sun. **Credit** AmEx, MC, V. **Map** p326/p330 H6, p336 F3.
An essential pitstop for students during freshers' week, Cult caters to casual twentysomethings with brands such as Bench, GV and Road.

Godiva
9 West Port, South Edinburgh (221 9212/www. godivaboutique.co.uk). Bus 2, 35. **Open** 10am-6pm Mon-Fri; 10.30am-6pm Sat; 10.30am-5pm Sun. **Credit** MC, V. **Map** p330 G8.
Vintage and custom-made clothing for men and women, all fashioned by local designers, ranging from funky retro kit to unique cashmere pieces.

Impractical Clothes
5 East Fountainbridge, South Edinburgh (221 1722/ www.impracticalclothes.com). Bus 1, 2, 10, 11, 15, 15A, 16, 17, 23, 24, 27, 34, 35, 45. **Open** noon-6pm Mon-Sat. **Credit** MC, V. **Map** p330 E9.
This corner of town is better known for its strip bars, but concentrate instead on Irene Wadsworth's inspired little boutique. Many of her outfits are limited editions or one-offs; bustiers are a speciality.

Joey D
54 Broughton Street, Broughton (557 6672/www. joey-d.co.uk). Bus 8, 13, 17. **Open** 10.30am-6pm Mon-Sun. **Credit** MC, V. **Map** p326 H4.
The cutting-edge garments here are best described as reconstructed. Tweed, boiler suits, jeans and other items are ripped up and put back together to create something more interesting. **Photo** *p193*.

Odd One Out
16 Victoria Street, Old Town (220 6400/www.odd oneout.com). Bus 2, 23, 27, 41, 42. **Open** 10am-6pm Mon-Sat; noon-5pm Sun. **Credit** MC, V. **Map** p330 H7, p336 D4.
Odd One Out has been supplying a mixture of cult, underground and street brands (including Ladysoul and Silas) to style-savvy shoppers for the last ten years. Look out for Oddities, the in-house range.

Psycho-Moda
22 St Mary's Street, Old Town (557 6777). Bus 35/ Nicolson Street–North Bridge buses. **Open** 11am-6pm Mon-Sat. **Credit** MC, V. **Map** p331 J7.

Eat, Drink, Shop

Just off the Royal Mile, this small boutique deals in own-label clothing for women, including dresses in luxurious fabrics.

Slater Menswear

100 George Street, New Town (220 4343/ www.slatermenswear.com). Princes Street buses. **Open** 8.30am-5.30pm Mon-Wed, Fri, Sat; 8.30am-7.30pm Thur; 11.30am-4.30pm Sun. **Credit** AmEx, MC, V. **Map** p326/p330 F6, p336 B1.
This independent operator will have you measured up and kitted out in a new suit in minutes. The flagship Glasgow store is in the *Guinness Book of World Records* as the world's largest menswear store; while it's not on the same scale, the Edinburgh operation should have something that fits the bill.

Swish

22-24 Victoria Street, Old Town (220 0615). Bus 2, 23, 27, 41, 42. **Open** 10am-6pm Mon-Sat; noon-5pm Sun. **Credit** AmEx, MC, V. **Map** p330 J7, p336 D4.
Cool urban styles for men and women by Bench, Free Soul and the like, plus funky T-shirts for kids.

Xile

Princes Mall, Princes Street (east end), New Town (556 6508/www.xileclothing.com). Nicolson Street– North Bridge or Princes Street buses. **Open** 9.30am-6pm Mon-Sat; 11am-5pm Sun. **Credit** MC, V. **Map** p326/p330 H6, p336 E2.

One of the city's leading independent purveyors of branded goods, Xile is now spread over three units in the Princes Mall. Expect to find labels like Replay, Diesel, Fornarina and True Religion on the shelves.

Traditional

Finding traditional clothing in Edinburgh isn't hard: just wander down the Royal Mile and you'll find yourself surrounded by Highland outfitters and woollen mills. Amid the mass-produced gear, a number of independent operators offer high-quality, original items. For **Belinda Robertson Cashmere** and **Ragamuffin**, *see p194* **Made in Scotland**.

Geoffrey (Tailor) Kiltmakers & Weavers

57-61 High Street, Old Town (557 0256/www. geoffreykilts.co.uk). Bus 35/Nicolson Street–North Bridge buses. **Open** 9am-5.30pm Mon-Wed, Fri, Sat; 9am-7pm Thur; 10am-5pm Sun. **Credit** AmEx, MC, V. **Map** p331 J7.
One of the city's best Highland outfitters is also home to 21st Century Kilts. Launched in 1996, this innovative range is made from materials such as denim and leather and is favoured by Robbie Williams and Vin Diesel.

God is in the details at **Concrete Wardrobe** & **Concrete Butterfly**. *See p191 & p204.*

Rip it up and start again: fashion gets reconstructed at **Joey D**. *See p191.*

Kinloch Anderson

*4 Dock Street, Leith (555 1390/www.kinlochanderson.
com). Bus 1, 11, 22, 34, 35, 36.* **Open** 9am-5.30pm
Mon-Sat. **Credit** AmEx, DC, MC, V. **Map** p324 X2.
Kinlock Anderson may be the city's most renowned
kiltmaker, although it's far from the cheapest. The
shop includes a small tartan museum.

Hawick Cashmere

*71-81 Grassmarket, Old Town (225 8634/
www.hawickcashmere.com). Bus 2, 23, 27, 28, 42,
45.* **Open** 10am-6pm Mon-Sat; noon-4pm Sun.
Credit AmEx, MC, V. **Map** p330 G8, p336 D4.
Hawick has been trading since 1874, but the shop is
contemporary rather than twee, with colourful racks
loaded with everything from socks to sweaters.

Ness Scotland

*336 Lawnmarket, Old Town (225 8815/www.nessby
post.com). Bus 2, 23, 27, 41, 42.* **Open** 10am-6pm
daily. **Credit** AmEx, MC, V. **Map** p330 G7, p336 D4.
Compared to some of the dreary Royal Mile stores,
Ness feels reassuringly modern. Knitwear and accessories are available in vibrant colours at reasonable
prices; highlights include Harris tweed corsages.
Other locations: 367 High Street, Old Town
(226 5227).

Romanes & Pattersons

*62 Princes Street, New Town (225 4966).
Princes Street buses.* **Open** 9am-8pm Mon-Sat;
10am-8pm Sun. **Credit** AmEx, MC, V. **Map**
p326/p330 G6, p336 D2.
Now part of the Edinburgh Woollen Mill group of
shops, Romanes & Pattersons have been trading on
Princes Street since 1808. Prices are fair.

Scottish Designer Knitwear

*42 Candlemaker Row, Old Town (220 4112/
www.joyce.forsyth.btinternet.co.uk). Bus 2, 23, 27,
41, 42.* **Open** 10am-5.30pm Tue-Sat. **Credit** MC, V.
Map p330 H8.
Vibrant, colourful creations from Scottish knitwear
designer Joyce Forsyth, such as dramatic flared jackets and matching hats.

Vintage

Armstrongs

*83 Grassmarket, Old Town (220 5557). Bus 2, 23,
27, 41, 42.* **Open** 10am-6pm Mon-Sat; noon-6pm
Sun. **Credit** MC, V. **Map** p330 G8, p336 D4.
Everyone from the Kaiser Chiefs to Kylie have
stopped to browse at this massively popular
Edinburgh institution. Clothing here spans the last
100 years, with everything from ballgowns to kaf-
tans. Kilts are cheap here too.
Other locations: 64-66 Clerk Street, South
Edinburgh (667 3056).

15 The Grassmarket

*15 Grassmarket, Old Town (226 3087).
Bus 2, 23, 27, 41, 42.* **Open** noon-6pm Mon-Sat.
No credit cards. Map p330 G8, p336 C4.
This treasure trove of a shop has an impressive
array of Victoriana, from curtains to coats, with a
particularly noteworthy selection of trilbies and vintage suits for gents.

Herman Brown

*151 West Port, South Edinburgh (228 2589).
Bus 2, 35.* **Open** 12.30-6pm Mon-Sat. **Credit** MC, V.
Map p330 F8.

Made in Scotland

Marketing coup or marketing curse? To some, the 'Made in Scotland' label smacks of tradition and tradition alone: kilts, shortbread and big woolly sweaters. Those who don't see Scotland as a romantic, misty *Brigadoon* would prefer that the tag sent out a more cutting edge, contemporary message. But why take sides? Both camps are well represented in Edinburgh, and in some cases the boundaries have blurred.

Take **Belinda Robertson Cashmere** (13A Dundas Street, New Town, 557 8118, www.belindarobertson.com), for example. The Glasgow-born designer uses yarns that are spun and dyed in the Scottish Borders using centuries-old techniques, but employs them in the creation of modern clothing; she's probably best known for her cheeky cashmere knickers. It's a similar story at **Ragamuffin** (278 Canongate, Old Town, 557 6007, www.ragamuffinonline.co.uk): the firm may have originated on the Isle of Skye, but

its woollies prove Scottish knitwear doesn't have to be dowdy. The Angels Don't Trudge label features jackets and accessories made from pure wool tweed and decorated with buttons and trims from around the world.

Further proof that the old and the new can co-exist harmoniously is found at **Geoffrey (Tailor) Kiltmakers & Weavers** (*pictured; see p192*). The family business is well known as a traditional Highland outfitters, but prodigal son Howie Nicolsby has established a distinctly modern line for it: 21st Century Kilts features kilts made from leather, denim or even PVC. Further forward-thinking design can be found at **Godiva** (*see p191*), a funky boutique that draws on the talents of fashion students and graduates of Edinburgh College of Art; **Joey D** (*see p191*), whose designs are the perfect antidote to high street uniformity; and **Concrete Wardrobe** (*see p191*), staffed by the designers whose clothes it sells. Tartan: who needs it?

The vintage clothing and accessories sold at this family-run shop have been carefully selected before being put on sale. There are plenty of classy finds at good prices, plus a glamorous jewellery selection.

Rusty Zip
14 Teviot Place, Old Town (226 4634). Bus 2, 41, 42. **Open** 10am-5.30pm Mon-Thur; 10am-6pm Fri, Sat; noon-6pm Sun. **Credit** MC, V. **Map** p330 H8.
Whether you're looking for an antique wedding dress or psychedelic swirls to wear to a '70s retro night, there's plenty to tempt. Prom dresses, waistcoats and second-hand kilts are among the specialities.

Fashion accessories

Hats

Fab Hatrix
13 Cowgatehead, Old Town (225 9222/www.fab hatrix.com). Nicolson Street–North Bridge buses. **Open** 10.30am-6pm Mon-Sat. **Credit** AmEx, MC, V. **Map** p330 G8, p336 D4.
Top hats, cloches, trilbies, bowlers, berets, straw hats and just about every other kind of smart headgear is stocked in this bright, inspiring store, along with wraps, scarves and accessories.

Yvette Jelfs
656 6500/www.yvettejelfs.com. **Open** by appointment only. **Credit** MC, V.
Renowned milliner-to-the-stars Yvette Jelfs recently closed her William Street shop and now sells direct from her workshop. If you'd prefer to wear a creation of your own, sign up for one of the day-long millinery courses run on the premises.

Jewellery

Your first stop should be **Rose Street**: there are about a dozen jewellers here, selling contemporary, antique and Celtic designs.

Alistair Wood Tait
116a Rose Street, New Town (225 4105). Princes Street buses. **Open** 10am-6pm Mon-Fri; 9.30am-5.30pm Sat. **Credit** AmEx, MC, V. **Map** p326/p330 F6, p336 C1.
Tait sells its own collections, featuring Scottish gemstones mounted in platinum, silver and gold. Look out, too, for antique pieces, including traditional Scottish pebble brooches.

Argento
18a Frederick Street, New Town (226 1704/ www.argentosilver.com). Princes Street buses. **Open** 9.30am-6pm Mon-Wed, Fri, Sat; 9.30am-7.30pm Thur; noon-5pm Sun. **Credit** MC, V. **Map** p326/p330 F6, p336 C1.
If you're looking to step up from Accessorize without blowing the budget, head to Argento. The shop stocks a wide range of colourful fashion pieces, as well as Celtic and Macintosh designs.

Arkangel
4 William Street, New Town (226 4466/www. arkangelfashion.co.uk). Bus 3, 3A, 4, 12, 25, 26, 31, 33, 44. **Open** 10am-5.30pm Mon-Wed, Fri, Sat; 10am-6.30pm Thur. **Credit** MC, V. **Map** p329 D7.
This boutique feels like a giant dresing-up box, with unusual clothes as well as a fabulous range of jewellery. Designs come from big names such as Butler & Wilson, Ruyi and Les Nereides.

Gallerie Mirages
46a Raeburn Place, Stockbridge (315 2603). Bus 24, 29, 42. **Open** 10am-5.30pm Mon-Sat; noon-4.30pm Sun. **Credit** MC, V. **Map** p325 C4.
Sheila Dhariwal travels the globe in search of interesting jewellery to stock in her gallery, but also makes her own designs using antique beads. A good selection of silver pieces is also on offer.

Hamilton & Inches
87 George Street, New Town (225 4898/www. hamiltonandinches.com). Princes Street buses. **Open** 9.30am-5.30pm Mon-Fri; 9am-5pm Sat. **Credit** AmEx, MC, V. **Map** p326/p330 F6, p336 C1.
Scotland's best-known jewellers, Hamilton & Inches have a royal warrant as silversmiths to the Queen. The wares are every bit as grand as the Georgian shop: watches, silverware and a stylish (if pricey) selection of contemporary and classic jewellery.

Joseph Bonnar
72 Thistle Street, New Town (226 2811/www.joseph bonnar.com). Princes Street buses. **Open** 10.30am-5pm Mon-Sat. **Credit** AmEx, MC, V. **Map** p326 G5.
Antique and period jewellery for occasions when you really want to splash out.

Lime Blue
107 George Street, New Town (220 2164/www. lime-blue.co.uk). Princes Street buses. **Open** 10am-6pm Mon-Wed, Fri, Sat; 10am-7pm Thur; 1-5pm Sun. **Credit** MC, V. **Map** p326/p330 E6, p336 B1.
Diamonds are the name of the game at Lime Blue, with two large showrooms devoted to rocks of all shapes and sizes. Giftware includes hip flasks and jewellery boxes.

Laundry & repairs

City Alterations
123 Hanover Street, New Town (220 6004/www. cityalterations.co.uk). Princes Street buses. **Open** 8.30am-7.30pm Mon-Fri; 8.30am-6.30pm Sat; 11am-5pm Sun. **No credit cards.** **Map** p326/p330 G6.
Stop by for dry cleaning, alterations and repairs, including a one-hour alterations service.

Kleen Cleaners
10 St Mary's Street, Old Town (556 4337). Bus 35/ Nicolson Street–North Bridge buses. **Open** 9am-5pm Mon-Fri; 10am-4pm Sat. **Credit** MC, V. **Map** p331 J7.
Instantly recognisable by the display of wedding dresses in the window, this store offers dry cleaning as well as alterations and repairs.

Eat, Drink, Shop

For fresh, colourful, inspired interiors

The ultimate collection
of contemporary designer
furnishings & accessories

Leather goods & luggage

Fling
18 William Street, New Town (226 4115/www.
fling-scotland.com). Bus 3, 3A, 4, 12, 25, 26, 31, 33,
44. **Open** 9.30am-6pm Mon-Fri; 9.30am-5.30pm Sat.
Credit MC, V. **Map** p329 D7.
There's more to Fling than leather, but it's a good
place to start. All products are produced in Scotland;
highlights include leather-bound notebooks, travel
bags and a dinky – if rather unnecessary – wallet
for holding a pack of gum.

Mackenzie Bags
34 Victoria Street, Old Town (220 0089/www.
mackenziebags.co.uk). Bus 2, 23, 27, 41, 42.
Open 10am-5.30pm Mon-Fri; 10am-5pm Sat.
Credit AmEx, MC, V. **Map** p330 J7, p336 D4.
Mackenzie has been making leather bags and cases
in Scotland for a quarter of a century. The hand-fin-
ished bags come with a lifetime guarantee.

Lingerie

There's a branch of **Calvin Klein Underwear**
at 6 Multrees Walk, by St Andrew Square (557
6971, www.cku.com).

Boudiche
15 Frederick Street, New Town (226 5255/www.
boudiche.co.uk). Princes Street buses. **Open** 10am-
6pm Mon-Wed, Fri, Sat; 10am-7pm Thur; noon-4pm
Sun. **Credit** MC, V. **Map** p326/p330 F6, p336 C2.
From its crystal chandeliers to the luxury lingerie
on sale, the vibe at Boudiche is deeply decadent.
Brands include La Perla Black Label, Damaris,
Spoylt and Elle Macpherson Intimates. **Photo** *p198.*

La Jolie Madame
22 Morningside Road, South Edinburgh (447 6715/
www.lajoliemadame.com). Bus 11, 15, 15A, 16, 17,
41. **Open** 9.30am-5.30pm Mon-Sat. **Credit** MC, V.
The city's largest independent retailer of lingerie,
stocking nightwear, swimwear and bridal undies for
all shapes and sizes.

Shoes

Clarks (No.79, 220 1261) and **Nine West**
(No.99, 220 1444) are among the familiar chain
shoe shops on Princes Street, while there's a
branch of **Dolcis** in the St James Centre (*see*
p187; 556 1940) and other high street names
scattered elsewhere.

Bagatt
22 Multrees Walk, St Andrew Square, New
Town (558 1600/www.bagatt.it). Princes Street
buses. **Open** 10am-6pm Mon-Wed, Fri, Sat;
10am-7pm Thur; noon-5pm Sun. **Credit** MC, V.
Map p326 H5, p336 F1.
The only UK outlet for the famed Italian brand,
selling footwear, clothing and accessories.

Helen Bateman
16 William Street, New Town (220 4495/www.helen
bateman.com). Bus 3, 3A, 4, 12, 25, 26, 31, 33,
44. **Open** 9.30am-6pm Mon-Sat. **Credit** MC, V.
Map p329 D7.
This Scottish independent brand features seasonal
collections in limited runs, as well as plenty of classic footwear and accessories.

Pam Jenkins
41 Thistle Street, New Town (225 3242/www.pam
jenkins.co.uk). Princes Street buses. **Open** 10am-
5.30pm Mon-Sat. **Credit** AmEx, MC, V. **Map** p326 G5.
A dangerously tempting array of designer shoes and
accessories from well-known names such as Jimmy
Choo, Nicole Farhi, Christian Louboutin and Kate
Spade. Shoe-lovers, enter at your peril.

Rogerson Fine Footwear
126-128 Rose Street (220 1775). Princes Street
buses. **Open** 9.30am-6pm Mon-Wed, Fri, Sat;
9.30-7pm Thur; noon-5pm Sun. **Credit** MC, V.
Map p326/p330 F6, p336 C1.
High quality European footwear, including shoes
from Ecco, Hispanitas, Think and Mephisto.

Schuh
6-6a Frederick Street, New Town (220 0290/www.
schuh.co.uk). Princes Street buses. **Open** 9am-6pm
Mon-Wed, Fri; 9am-8pm Thur; 11am-6pm Sun.
Credit AmEx, MC, V. **Map** p326/p330 F6, p336 C2.
Rocket Dog and Red or Dead are just two of the
brands on offer at Schuh, which also stocks the highest, weirdest stilettos you're ever likely to see.
Other locations: 32 North Bridge, Old Town (225
6552); Ocean Terminal, Leith (555 3766).

Food & drink

In search of basic groceries in the centre of
Edinburgh? On Princes Street, try **Marks
& Spencer** (No.54, 225 2301) or **Boots**
(Nos.101-103, 225 6397), or **Sainsbury's**
on St Andrew Square (225 8400).

Alcohol

For details of the **Scotch Malt Whisky
Society**, *see p183.*

Cadenhead's Whisky Shop
172 Canongate, Old Town (556 5864/www.edinburgh.
wmcadenhead.com). Bus 35, 36. **Open** 10.30am-
5.30pm Mon-Sat; 12.30-5.30pm Sun. **Credit** MC, V.
Map p331 K7.
Scotland's oldest independent bottler, established in
1842, has a fine selection of whiskies, encompassing
both rare brands and more recognisable names. The
company is also known for its Old Raj gin.

Cornelius
18-20 Easter Road, Calton Hill & Broughton
(652 2405). Bus 1, 35. **Open** noon-9pm Mon-Sat.
Credit AmEx, MC, V. **Map** p327 M4.

Eat, Drink, Shop

Knickers and knick-knacks at **Boudiche**. *See p197.*

Another example of gentrification in a far from tra-ditionally middle-class area (the southern end of Easter Road), Cornelius is a decent wine merchant in a neighbourhood that's previously been served only by cheap supermarkets and chains. There's an excellent choice of bottled beers.

Demijohn
32 Victoria Street, Old Town (225 3265/ www.demijohn.co.uk). Bus 2, 23, 27, 41, 42. **Open** 10am-6pm Mon-Sat; 12.30-5pm Sun. **Credit** MC, V. **Map** p330 J7, p336 D4.
Dubbed 'the liquid deli', this unusual Victoria Street shop lets you try before you buy. Liqueurs, wines and spirits from around the world are joined by olive oils and vinegars; you can even choose your own bottle. Hampers packed with goodies are a new addi-tion to its wares.

Noble Grape
21-27 Brandon Terrace, Stockbridge (556 3133/ www.thenoble-grape.co.uk). Bus 8, 17, 23, 27, 36. **Open** 9.30am-5.30pm Mon, Tue, Thur-Sat; 9.30am-1pm Wed. **Credit** AmEx, MC, V. **Map** p326 F3.
Fine wines from around the world, including bottles that are imported by the owners direct from chateaux in France and Spain.

Peter Green
37a-b Warrender Park Road, South Edinburgh (229 5925). Bus 5, 24, 41. **Open** 10am-6.30pm Tue-Thur, Sat; 10am-7.30pm Fri. **Credit** MC, V. **Map** p330 G11.

This independent wine merchant in Marchmont also stocks large selections of spirits and beers alongside cases of reds, whites and rosés.

Royal Mile Whiskies
379 High Street, Old Town (225 3383/www.royal milewhiskies.com). Bus 35/Nicolson Street–North Bridge buses. **Open** 11am-7pm Mon-Sat; noon-5pm Sun. **Credit** MC, V. **Map** p330 H7, p336 E4.
Staff at this award-winning malt whisky shop are likely to encourage you to sample a few of the 300-plus varieties on offer before you buy.

Scottish Whisky Heritage Centre
354 Castlehill, Old Town (220 0441/www. whisky-heritage.co.uk). Bus 2, 23, 27, 41, 42. **Open** *May-Sept* 9.30am-6.30pm daily (last tour 5.30pm). *Oct-April* 10am-6pm daily (last tour 5pm). **Credit** AmEx, MC, V. **Map** p330 G7, p336 D4.
Located by Edinburgh Castle at the top of the Royal Mile, this is a whisky shop and theme park all in one. Still, you don't have to take the Whisky Heritage Tour or do the barrel ride to enjoy the shop, home to around 270 different malt and blended whiskies.

Villeneuve Wines
49a Broughton Street, Broughton (558 8441/www. villeneuvewines.com). Bus 8, 13, 17. **Open** 10am-10pm Mon-Thur; 9am-10pm Fri, Sat; 1-8pm Sun. **Credit** AmEx, MC, V. **Map** p326 H4.
A well-stocked and reasonably priced fine wine and whisky shop.

Delicatessens & bakeries

Herbie of Edinburgh

66 Raeburn Place, Stockbridge (332 9888). Bus 24, 29, 42. **Open** 9.30am-7pm Mon-Fri; 9am-6pm Sat. **Credit** MC, V. **Map** p325 C4.

This friendly neighbourhood deli has plenty of fresh-baked breads and an extensive range of cheeses that you can try before you buy.

Lupe Pinto's Deli

24 Leven Street, South Edinburgh (228 6241/ www.lupepintos.com). Bus 11, 15, 15A, 16, 17, 23, 45. **Open** 10am-6pm Mon-Wed, Sat; 10am-7pm Thur, Fri; 12.30pm-5.30pm Sun. **Credit** MC, V. **Map** p330 F10.

Tequila, chillies and just about every other ingredient you might need to create a Mexican feast, along with Caribbean, Spanish and Asian produce.

Marcella Italian Bakery

20a Brougham Place, South Edinburgh (622 5781). Bus 11, 15, 15A, 16, 17, 23, 45. **Open** noon-10pm Mon-Sat; 5-10pm Sun. **No credit cards.** **Map** p330 F9.

It's worth making the trip to Tollcross for Marcella's delicious Italian breads, continental produce and lasagnes, which can be eaten in or taken away.

Margiotta's

31 Dundas Street, New Town (476 7070). Bus 13, 23, 27. **Open** 7.30am-10pm Mon-Sat; 8am-10pm Sun. **Credit** MC, V. **Map** p326 F5.

This popular deli has branches around the city, selling standard groceries along with good selections of wines, cheeses, olives and gourmet snacks. **Other locations**: throughout the city.

Peckham's

155-159 Bruntsfield Place, South Edinburgh (229 7054/www.peckhams.co.uk). Bus 11, 15, 15A, 16, 17, 23, 45. **Open** 8am-midnight Mon-Sat; 9am-11pm Sun. **Credit** MC, V. **Map** p330 E11.

Fresh fruit, breads, luxury chocolates, vegetarian haggis and a great wine selection. **Other locations**: 48 Raeburn Place, Stockbridge (332 8844).; 49 S Clerk Street, South Edinburgh (667 0077).

Valvona & Crolla

19 Elm Row, Leith Walk, Broughton (556 6066/ www.valvonacrolla.com). Bus 7, 10, 12, 14, 16, 22, 25, 49. **Open** 8am-6pm Mon-Sat; 10.30am-5pm Sun. **Credit** AmEx, MC, V. **Map** p327 G4.

Edinburgh's best-known destination for gourmet treats, this family-run Italian deli has been operating since the 1930s. Shelves are stacked from floor to ceiling with a delicious range of products, and there's a small café at the back of the shop serving moreish breakfasts and lunches.

Victor Hugo

29 Melville Terrace, South Edinburgh (776 1827). Bus 24, 41. **Open** 8am-6pm Mon-Fri; 9am-6pm Sat. **Credit** MC, V. **Map** p331 J10.

A great place to get picnic provisions, this deli stocks produce from around the world: Polish fudge, Scots cheeses and Russian rye bread, for example.

Fruit & vegetables

Certain parts of town – usually those without a nearby supermarket giant – seem to attract fruit and veg shops by the dozen. The best choices are on Argyle Place, Marchmont, Leith Walk and Clerk Street.

Health food

Henderson's

94 Hanover Street, New Town (225 6694/www. hendersonsofedinburgh.co.uk). Princes Street buses. **Open** 8am-7pm Mon-Fri; 9am-6pm Sat. **Credit** MC, V. **Map** p326/p330 G6, p336 D1.

Henderson's has been promoting natural food in Scotland for over 40 years through its shop and restaurant. You'll find a good supply of breads, cheeses and healthy snacks; in particular, look out for the vegetarian haggis roll.

Real Foods

37 Broughton Street, Broughton (557 1911/www. realfoods.co.uk). Bus 8, 13, 17. **Open** 9am-7pm Mon-Wed, Fri; 9am-8pm Thur; 9am-6.30pm Sat; 10am-6pm Sun. **Credit** MC, V. **Map** p326 H4.

Opened in 1975, the well-stocked Real Foods shop is still the place to go if you're looking for organic, vegetarian and wheat-free products. **Other locations**: 8 Brougham Place, South Edinburgh (228 1201).

Specialists

Coco

174 Bruntsfield Place, South Edinburgh (228 4526/ www.cocochocolate.co.uk). Bus 11, 15, 15A, 16, 17, 23, 45. **Open** 10am-6pm Mon-Sat. **Credit** MC, V. **Map** p330 E11.

All of the chocolates produced and sold here are organic and ethically traded, and staff can describe the process from bean to bar. Check online for details of the ever-popular tasting evenings.

Crombie's of Edinburgh

97-101 Broughton Street, Broughton (557 0111/ www.sausages.co.uk). Bus 8, 13, 17. **Open** 8am-5.30pm Mon-Fri; 8am-5pm Sat. **Credit** MC, V. **Map** p326 H4.

This high-quality butcher is best known for its extensive array of sausages: boar, port and stilton, and pork, mango and apple are stocked alongside more traditional bangers.

Fudge House

197 Canongate, Old Town (556 4172/www.fudge house.co.uk). Bus 35, 36. **Open** 10am-5.30pm Mon-Sat; 11am-5.30pm Sun. **Credit** MC, V. **Map** p331 K7.

Eat, Drink, Shop

Walk Pick up a picnic

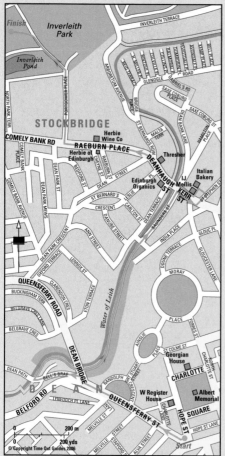

Brae; take a left, then take an immediate right on to Miller Row. At the bottom of Miller Row, you'll connect with the Water of Leith. Follow the path north-east along the stream; it really is a beautiful stroll.

Exit at Saunders Street; this leads up towards Raeburn Place, the 'high street' of Stockbridge. Make a right at the first junction (Deanhaugh Street looking left, Kerr Street looking right) and you'll soon find **IJ Mellis, Cheesemonger** (6 Baker's Place; *see p201*), nothing short of Nirvana for any friend of fromage. Be daring with your choices: you can try before you buy if you're feeling a wee bit mousey, and it's not every day you'll see an array like this. After making your selection, pop into the **Italian Bakery** (7 Baker's Place, 225 2685) next door for your bread.

Double back and walk up towards Raeburn Place, perhaps stopping off at one of the many grocery stores for some fresh fruit and veg: try **Edinburgh Organics** (10 Deanhaugh Street, 315 2580, www.edinburghorganics.co.uk). You're spoiled for choice for booze around here, from established chains such as **Oddbins** (30 North West Circus Place, 220 1555, www.oddbins.co.uk) and **Thresher** (35 Deanhaugh Street, 332 2223, www.victoriawine.co.uk) to the more select list of truly terrific wines available from **Herbie Wine Co** (66 Raeburn Place, 332 9858), sister to the **Herbie of Edinburgh** deli across the street (*see p199*). Cold meats and condiments, olives, snacks, breads, cheeses...

The enduring mystery of how they manage to fit so much magic into such a small space has been solved only by Intel engineers and Tardis mechanics.

Now you have your picnic, you can pick your spot. Just around the corner, leading off Portgower Place to the right, is **Inverleith Park** (*see p111*). Settle down on the banked hill on the other side of the swans' reservoir and enjoy your goodies with perhaps the finest view of the city's unique skyline.

The one essential ingredient in any good picnic is spontaneity, and this is especially true in Edinburgh. The weather can change so suddenly here that you really need to seize the moment if you don't want to end up sucking your rain-sodden sandwiches through a straw. Forget packing hampers: simply stock up en route. And there's no finer route to take than through Stockbridge.

Start at the west end of Princes Street. Head down Queensferry Street as far as Bells

Huge blocks of fudge in every imaginable flavour, all made on site – heaven for sweet-toothed shoppers. There's also a coffee shop on site.

IJ Mellis, Cheesemonger

30a Victoria Street, Old Town (226 6215/www.ij mellischeesemonger.com). Bus 2, 23, 27, 41, 42. **Open** 10am-6pm Mon-Sat; noon-5pm Sun. **Credit** MC, V. **Map** p330 J7, p336 D4.

Wandering past this shop will either make you wince or grin, so pungent is the smell of the cheeses within. Delicious farmhouse cheeses from all over Europe sit alongside Scottish favourites.
Other locations: 6 Bakers Place, Stockbridge (225 6566); 205 Bruntsfield Place, South Edinburgh (447 8889).

Macsween of Edinburgh

Dryden Road, Loanhead (440 2555/www.macsween. co.uk). Bus 37. **Open** 9am-5pm Mon-Fri. **Credit** MC, V.

One of Scotland's best-known haggis manufacturers. Their wares, which include a delicious vegetarian haggis, are also stocked in Peckham's and other delis around the city.

Pat's Chung Ying Chinese Supermarket

199-201 Leith Walk, Broughton (554 0358). Bus 7, 10, 12, 14, 16, 22, 25, 49. **Open** 10am-6pm Mon-Sun. **Credit** MC, V. **Map** p327 K3.

Edinburghers come here to pick up spices, noodles, seafood, oriental wines and beers, and other Chinese, Japanese and Korean ingredients, with fresh produce imported weekly.

Plaisir du Chocolat

251-253 Canongate, Old Town (556 9524/www. plaisirduchocolat.com). Bus 35, 36. **Open** 10am-6pm daily. **Credit** MC, V. **Map** p331 J7.

If you buy something from this store's huge range of luxurious chocolates and truffles as a gift, don't be too surprised if you end up eating it yourself. Try the ever-popular truffles, or buy a steaming mug of rich hot chocolate in the Salon de Thé. Also available at Harvey Nichols (*see p186*). **Photo** *p202*.

Gifts & souvenirs

There's plenty of cheap tartan tat on sale, both on and near the Royal Mile, but there are more inventive alternatives to be found.

Crystal Clear

52 Cockburn Street, Old Town (226 7888). Bus 35/Nicolson Street–North Bridge buses. **Open** 10am-6pm Mon-Sat; noon-5pm Sun. **Credit** MC, V. **Map** p330 H7, p336 F3.

CDs, books and assorted other ephemera offering some measure of spiritual guidance. Golden, Thom McCarthy's other shop, is a larger space with a wider selection of stock.
Other locations: Golden, 109 High Street, Old Town (624 3777).

Flux

55 Bernard Street, Leith (554 4075/www.get2flux. co.uk). Bus 12, 16, 35. **Open** 11am-6pm Mon-Sat; noon-5pm Sun. **Credit** MC, V. **Map** p324 Y3.

Quirky, British-made crafts are a speciality, with an ever-changing range of gifts, jewellery and art.

Just Scottish

4-6 North Bank Street, Old Town (226 4806). Bus 2, 23, 27, 41, 42. **Open** 10am-6pm Mon-Fri; 9.30am-5.30pm Sat; noon-4pm Sun. **Credit** AmEx, MC, V. **Map** p330 G7, p336 D3.

Among the tasteful, Scottish-themed gifts on sale here are Shirley Pinder's beautiful, eclectic scarves.

One World Shop

St John's Church, Princes Street (229 4541/ www.oneworldshop.co.uk). Princes Street buses. **Open** 10am-5pm Mon-Wed, Fri, Sat; 10am-7pm Thur. **Credit** AmEx, MC,V. **Map** p330 E7, p336 A2.

Offerings at Edinburgh's Fair Trade shop include crafts, textiles, toys, clothing and foods.

Paper Tiger

53 Lothian Road, West Edinburgh (228 2790/www. papertiger.ltd.uk). Bus 1, 2, 10, 11, 15, 15A, 16, 17, 23, 24, 27, 34, 35, 45. **Open** 9.30am-6pm Mon-Wed, Fri, Sat; 9.30am-7pm Thur; 11am-5pm Sun. **Credit** MC,V. **Map** p330 E8, p336 A3.

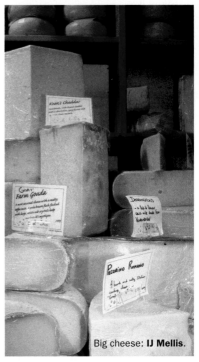

Big cheese: **IJ Mellis.**

Eat, Drink, Shop

A good source of innovative stationary, greetings cards and wrapping paper, among other goodies. **Other locations**: 16 Stafford Street, New Town (226 2390).

Russian Shop
18 St Mary's Street, Old Town (556 0181). Bus 35/ Nicolson Street–North Bridge buses. **Open** 10am-5pm Mon-Sat. **Credit** AmEx, MC, V. **Map** p331 J7.
Russian dolls and all sorts of decorative items line the shelves of this cosy shop.

Scotland Shop
18-20 High Street, Old Town (557 2030/www. scotlandshopdirect.com). Bus 35/Nicolson Street– North Bridge buses. **Open** *Summer* 9am-8pm daily. *Winter* 10am-6pm Mon-Sat; 11am-6pm Sun. **Credit** AmEx, MC, V. **Map** p331 J7.
Head here to pick up some Celtic jewellery, a *Braveheart*-style sword, a kiddy's kilt and virtually anything else in tartan.

Studio One
10-16 Stafford Street, New Town (226 5812). Bus 3, 3A, 4, 12, 25, 26, 31, 33, 44. **Open** 9.30am-6pm Mon-Wed, Fri, Sat; Thur 9.30am-6pm; noon-5pm Sun. **Credit** MC, V. **Map** p329 D7.
A wealth of interesting household items and quality gifts line the shelves here, from scented candles and soaps to paper lanterns and colourful rugs. **Other locations**: Studio One Cookshop, 71 Morningside Road, South Edinburgh (447 0452).

Follow the pleasure principle at **Plaisir du Chocolat**. See p201.

Whigmaleeries Ltd
334 Lawnmarket, Old Town (225 4152). Bus 2, 23, 27, 41, 42. **Open** 9am-7.30pm daily. **Credit** AmEx, MC,V. **Map** p330 G7, p336 D4.
The lethal-looking window displays contain all the reproduction weapons you'll ever need, while a not-very-Scottish replica gladiator's helmet will set you back £150.

Health & beauty

Alternative medicine

Glover's Intergrated Healthcare
10 William Street, New Town (225 3161/www. glovers-health.co.uk). Bus 3, 3A, 4, 12, 25, 26, 31, 33, 44. **Open** 9.30am-5pm Mon-Fri. Appointments outside these hours by request. **Credit** MC, V. **Map** p329 D7.
Christine Glover, a former president of the Royal Pharmaceutical Society, sells a wide range of alternative health products at this shop. The clinic offers homeopathy, reflexology and other therapies.

Napiers Dispensary
18 Bristo Place, Old Town (225 5542/www.napiers. net). Bus 2, 41, 42. **Open** 10am-6pm Mon; 9am-6pm Tue-Fri; 9am-5.30pm Sat; 12.30-4.30pm Sun. **Credit** MC, V. **Map** p330 H8.
Napiers, which dates back to 1860, offers treatments from herbalists, acupuncturists and other practioners. The shop is well stocked with homeopathic and herbal medicines, as well as natural cosmetics.

Cosmetics

Jo Malone
93 George Street, New Town (478 8555/ www.jomalone.co.uk). Princes Street buses. **Open** 10am-6pm Mon-Wed; 10am-7pm Thur; 9.30am-6pm Fri, Sat; noon-5pm Sun. **Credit** AmEx, MC, V. **Map** p326/p330 F6, p336 B1.
The Jo Malone collection of fragrances and toiletries comes at a price, but has quite a following nonetheless. Popular scents include Red Roses & Nutmeg and Lime, Basil & Mandarin.

Lush
44 Princes Street, New Town (557 3177/www.lush. co.uk). Princes Street buses. **Open** 9.30am-6.30pm Mon-Wed, Fri, Sat; 9.30am-7pm Thur; 11.30am-5.30pm Sun. **Credit** AmEx, MC, V. **Map** p326/p330 G6, p336 E2.
Huge, colourful cakes of soap greet you as you walk through the door of this chain store. Beyond sits a host of fragrant lotions, potions and bath bombs.

Space NK
97-103 George Street, New Town (225 6371/ www.spacenk.co.uk). Princes Street buses. **Open** 10am-6pm Mon-Wed, Fri; 10am-7.30pm Thur; 9am-6pm Sat; noon-5pm Sun. **Credit** AmEx, MC, V. **Map** p326/p330 F6, p336 B1.

This chic store hawks the wares of cult beauty brands from around the world, including Kiehl's, Ren, Eve Lom, Caudalie and Chantecaille.

Hairdressers

The city has plenty of old-school barbers; just look for the red and white poles.

Charlie Miller

13 Stafford Street, New Town (226 5550/www. charliemiller.com). Bus 3, 3A, 4, 12, 25, 26, 31, 33, 44. **Open** 9am-5.30pm Mon-Wed, Fri; 9am-6.30pm Thur; 8.30am-5pm Sat. **Credit** AmEx, MC, V. **Map** p329 D7.
Established in 1966, this popular local hairdressing name now has a number of salons throughout the city. Prices are staggered to reflect the experience of the stylist.
Other locations: throughout the city.

Cheynes

46 George Street, New Town (220 0777/ www.cheyneshairdressing.com). Princes Street buses. **Open** 9am-6pm Mon-Wed, Fri; 9am-7.30pm Thur; 9am-5pm Sat. **Credit** MC, V. **Map** p326/ p330 F6, p336 D1.
Another well-known Edinburgh hairdressing chain, with several branches.
Other locations: throughout the city.

Medusa

6-7 Teviot Place, Old Town (225 6627/www.medusa hair.co.uk). Bus 2, 41, 42. **Open** 9am-6pm Mon-Wed, Fri; 9am-8.30pm Thur; 9am-4.30pm Sat. **Credit** MC, V. **Map** p330 H8.
This reasonably priced unisex hairdresser always seems to be busy, with customers young and old. Staff throw in a free drink to keep 'em happy. There's also an entire whole floor devoted to colour.
Other locations: 26 Bread Street, South Edinburgh (622 7277).

Paterson SA

129 Lothian Road, West Edinburgh (228 5252/ www.psahair.com). Bus 1, 2, 10, 11, 15, 15A, 16, 17, 23, 24, 27, 34, 35, 45. **Open** 9am-6pm Mon-Wed, Fri; 9am-7.30pm Thur; 9am-4pm Sat. **Credit** MC, V. **Map** p330 E8, p336 A4.
Award-winning hairstylists, operating in a laid-back and stylish setting.
Other locations: 60 George Street, New Town (228 5252).

Opticians

The **Dollond & Aitchison** (558 1149, www. danda.co.uk) and **Vision Express** (556 5656, www.visionexpress.co.uk) chains have stores at the St James Centre on Leith Street (*see p187*).

Eyes Optometrist

63 Thistle Street, New Town (225 4004). Princes Street buses. **Open** 9.30am-5.30pm Mon-Fri; 9.30am-4pm Sat. **Credit** MC, V. **Map** p326 G5.

An independent operation specialising in handmade spectacle frames, though designer names such as Philippe Starck and Eye DC are also represented.

Pharmacies

Edinburgh doesn't have a 24-hour pharmacy, but some of the pharmacies attached to larger supermarkets remain open into the evening.

Boots

101-103 Princes Street, New Town (225 8331/www. boots.co.uk). Princes Street buses. **Open** 8am-6.30pm Mon-Wed, Fri, Sat; 8am-8pm Thur; 10am-6pm Sun. **Credit** AmEx, MC, V. **Map** p326/p330 F6, p336 C2.
The largest of several Boots stores scattered around Edinburgh has huge ranges of toiletries and cosmetics, as well as a pharmacy and an optician.
Other locations: throughout the city.

Spas

Cowshed Relax Spa

Scotsman Hotel, 20 North Bridge, Old Town (622 3800/www.thescotsmanhotel.co.uk). Nicolson Street–North Bridge buses. **Open** 9am-8pm Mon-Wed, Fri; 9am-6pm Thur; 10am-6pm Sat, Sun. **Credit** AmEx, MC, V. **Map** p326/p330 H6, p336 F3.
The prices here are a little high, but how can you resist any posh spa that offers a massage called 'pampered cow', or an exfoliation treatment by the name of 'rawhide'?

One Spa

Sheraton Grand, 8 Conference Square, Western Approach Road (221 7777/www.one-spa.net). Bus 2, 3, 3A, 4, 25, 33, 44, 44A. **Open** 6.30am-10pm Mon-Fri; 7am-9pm Sat, Sun. **Credit** AmEx, MC, V. **Map** p329 D8.
From the rooftop whirlpool to the heat and steam experiences, One Spa offers the ultimate in luxurious urban relaxation. Take a high-priced treatment, opt for a manicure or check in for an entire day of utterly blissful pampering.

Zen Lifestyle

9 Bruntsfield Place, South Edinburgh (477 3535/ www.zen-lifestyle.com). Bus 11, 15, 15A, 16, 17, 23, 45. **Open** 8am-10pm Mon-Fri; 9am-5.30pm Sat; 10am-5.30pm Sun. **Credit** MC, V. **Map** p330 E10.
With a whole host of awards to its name, this soothing urban retreat offers a comprehensive range of health and beauty treatments.
Other locations: 2-3 Teviot Place, Old Town (226 6777).

Treatments & therapies

Edinburgh Floatarium

29 North West Circus Place, Stockbridge (225 3350/ www.edinburghfloatarium.co.uk). Bus 24, 29, 36, 42. **Open** 9am-8pm Mon-Fri; 9am-6pm Sat; 9.30am-4pm Sun. **Credit** MC, V. **Map** p326 E5.

Eat, Drink, Shop

As well as the floatation tank, relaxing experiences on offer here include aromatherapy massage, chiropody, reiki and shiatsu.

Neal's Yard Remedies
102 Hanover Street, New Town (226 3223/www. nealsyardremedies.com). Princes Street buses. **Open** 10am-6pm Mon-Wed, Fri, Sat; 10am-7pm Thur; 1-5pm Sun. **Credit** MC, V. **Map** p326/p330 G6.
Lovely soaps, moisturisers and bath oils are among the body and beauty essentials on sale, made using essential oils and other natural ingredients. (The ultra-rich Frankincense Nourishing Cream is highly recommended.) The treatment rooms here also offer a host of options.

Whole Works
Jackson's Close, 209 High Street, Old Town (www.the wholeworks.co.uk). Bus 35/Nicolson Street–North Bridge buses. **Open** 9.30am-7.30pm Mon-Fri; 9.30am-4.30pm Sat. **No credit cards. Map** p330 H7, p336 F4.
In addition to offering a wide range of treatments, from homeopathy to massage, this complementary health centre runs evening and weekend courses.

Homewares

Antique & vintage
The Grassmarket has plenty of places selling jewellery, ceramics and other small items, as well as furniture.

Organised chaos at **Backbeat**. *See p205.*

Edinburgh Architectural Salvage Yard
31 West Bowling Green Street, Leith (554 7077/ www.easy-arch-salv.co.uk). Bus 7, 11, 14, 21. **Open** 9am-5pm Mon-Fri; noon-5pm Sat. **Credit** MC, V. **Map** p324 W4.
EASY has been supplying Edinburgh's citizens with period pieces for more than 20 years. Georgian, Victorian, art nouveau and art deco styles are all represented, in the form of everything from door handles to bath tubs.

Georgian Antiques
10 Pattison Street, Leith (553 7286/www.georgian antiques.net). Bus 21. **Open** 8.30am-5.30pm Mon-Fri; 10am-2pm Sat. **Credit** MC, V. **Map** p324 Z3.
Spread over 50,000sq ft of floor space in a converted whisky bond, this is the largest collection of quality antiques and collectibles in town.

New

Anta
91-93 West Bow, Old Town (225 4616/www.anta. co.uk). Bus 2, 23, 27, 41, 42. **Open** 10am-6pm Mon-Sat; 11am-5pm Sun. **Credit** AmEx, MC, V. **Map** p330 G8, p336 D4.
A family-run Scottish design company, Anta sells a selection of hand-painted stoneware and textiles, plus quirky accessories.

Concrete Butterfly
317-319 Cowgate, Old Town (558 7130). Nicolson Street–North Bridge buses. **Open** noon-6pm Mon-Fri; noon-5pm Sat. **Credit** MC, V. **Map** p331 J7.
If you're into interiors you'll love Concrete Butterfly, staffed by some of the designers whose innovative products are on show. Look out for Tessuti's printed textiles (the ironing board cover is a real treat) and Meg Hamilton's metalwork items. *See also p191* **Concrete Wardrobe. Photo** *p192.*

Designshop UK
116-120 Causewayside, South Edinburgh (667 7078/ www.designshopuk.com). Bus 2, 3, 3A, 5, 7, 8, 14, 29, 30, 31, 33, 37, 47, 49. **Open** 10am-6pm Tue-Sat. **Credit** MC, V. **Map** p331 K11.
Stocking covetable contemporary furniture and accessories from world-famous names such as Vitra and Panton, this is the ideal place to come if you're in your early thirties and looking to furnish a loft apartment in a putatively fashionable part of town. Just remember, design classics don't come cheap.

Halibut & Herring
89 West Bow, Old Town (226 7472). Bus 2, 23, 27, 41, 42. **Open** 9.30am-5.30pm Mon-Sat; 11am-5pm Sun. **Credit** MC, V. **Map** p330 G8, p336 D4.
There's a pretty big selection of gifts at this shop, with a particular focus on bathroom accessories: colourful shower curtains, locally made ceramics and bath toys abound.
Other locations: 108 Bruntsfield Place, South Edinburgh (229 2669).

Inhouse
*28 Howe Street, New Town (225 2888/www.
inhouse-uk.com). Bus 24, 29, 42.* **Open** 9.30am-6pm
Mon-Wed, Fri; 10am-7pm Thur; 9.30am-5.30pm Sat.
Credit MC, V. **Map** p326 F5.
A large selection of contemporary minimalist furniture is stocked here, alongside a stylish (and less
expensive) selection of Alessi kitchenware.

Lakeland
*26 George Street, New Town (220 3947/
www.lakelandlimited.co.uk). Princes Street buses.*
Open 9am-5.30pm Mon-Sat. **Credit** MC, V.
Map p326/p330 G6, p336 D1.
Gadgets you never knew you needed, along with all
the essentials for your kitchen.

Tangram Furnishers
*33-37 Jeffrey Street, Old Town (556 6551/www.
tangramfurnishers.co.uk). Bus 35/Nicolson Street–
North Bridge buses.* **Open** 10am-5.30pm Tue-Fri;
10am-5pm Sat. **Credit** MC, V. **Map** p331 J7.
Tangram deals in super-stylish furniture, lighting
and rugs from leading European manufacturers.

Music

CDs & vinyl

Avalanche
*17 West Nicolson Street, South Edinburgh (668
2374/www.avalancherecords.co.uk). Nicolson Street–
North Bridge buses.* **Open** 9.30am-6pm Mon-Sat.
Credit MC, V. **Map** p331 J9.
Opened by Kevin Buckle more than 20 years ago,
Avalanche is the best small music shop in town.
Alongside the new CDs (dominated by Indie artists),
there's a decent selection of cut-price DVDs and a
mixed bag of second-hand discs.
Other location: 63 Cockburn Street, Old Town
(225 3939).

Backbeat
*31 East Crosscauseway, South Edinburgh (668 2666).
Bus 35/Nicolson Street–North Bridge buses.* **Open**
10am-5.30pm Mon-Sat. **Credit** MC, V. **Map** p331 K9.
Although the proprietor assures us he knows where
everything is, Backbeat always looks like chaos. CDs
and old vinyl are piled high in boxes all over the
place; bring a shopping list to save time. **Photo** *p204*.

Coda Music
*12 Bank Street, Old Town (622 7246). Bus 2, 23,
27, 41, 42.* **Open** 9.30am-5.30pm Mon-Sat; 11am-
4.30pm Sun. **Credit** MC, V. **Map** p330 H7, p336 E3.
Scottish folk music dominates this friendly store on
the Mound, though there's also plenty of traditional music from elsewhere in the world.

Fopp
*55 Cockburn Street, Old Town (220 0133/www.fopp.
co.uk). Bus 35/Nicolson Street–North Bridge buses.*
Open 10am-6.30pm Mon-Sat; 11am-6pm Sun.
Credit AmEx, MC, V. **Map** p330 H7, p336 F3.

Wind Things: the sky's the limit. *See p206.*

Scotland's largest independent music retailer always
has great deals on new releases, plus back-catalogue
bargains galore and a wide array of books and DVDs.
Other location: 7 Rose Street, New Town (220 0310).

McAlister Matheson Music
*1 Grindlay Street, South Edinburgh (228 3827/www.
mmmusic.co.uk). Bus 1, 2, 10, 11, 15, 15A, 16, 17,
23, 24, 27, 34, 35, 45.* **Open** 9.30am-6.30pm Mon-Fri;
9am-5.30pm Sat. **Credit** AmEx, MC, V. **Map** p330 E8.
Classical music and opera are the focus, and the shop
stays open later when there's a concert at Usher Hall.

Ripping Music & Tickets
*91 South Bridge, Old Town (226 7010/www.ripping
records.com). Bus 35/Nicolson Street–North Bridge
buses.* **Open** 9.30am-6pm Mon-Sat; noon-5.30pm
Sun. **Credit** MC, V. **Map** p331 J8.
Ripping stocks a good selection of rock, pop, dance
and indie CDs, but the main attraction is the gig tickets. From local nights to stadium shows, everything
that's available is pinned up in the window display.

Underground Solu'shn
*9 Cockburn Street, Old Town (226 2242/www.
undergroundsolushn.com). Bus 35/Nicolson Street–
North Bridge buses.* **Open** 10am-6pm Wed, Fri,
Sat; 10am-7pm Thur; noon-5pm Sun. **Credit** AmEx,
MC, V. **Map** p330 H7, p336 E3.
Unbeatable for vinyl dance imports, with a huge
choice of house, garage, techno and jungle sounds.
The vibe is friendly rather than intimidating and the
shop also sells tickets for forthcoming club nights.

Instruments

Bagpipes Galore
82 Canongate, Old Town (556 4073/www.bagpipe. co.uk). Bus 35, 36. **Open** 9.30am-5pm Mon-Sat. **Credit** AmEx, MC, V. **Map** p327/p331 L6.
A huge range of new and second-hand pipes, plus a beginner's tutoring kit for under £30. Probably best ask the neighbours first.

Sound Control
1 Grassmarket (229 8211/www.soundcontrol.co.uk). Bus 2, 23, 27, 41, 42. **Open** 9am-6pm Mon-Fri; 9am-5.30pm Sat. **Credit** AmEx, MC, V. **Map** p330 G8, p336 C4.
The east coast's biggest selections of guitars, keyboards, amps and everything else you might need to start a band. The store is also home to Scotland's first rock academy.

Sports & fitness

Boardwise
4 Lady Lawson Street, South Edinburgh (229 5887/ www.boardwise.com). Bus 2, 35. **Open** 10am-6pm Mon-Sat. **Credit** AmEx, MC, V. **Map** p330 F8.
Whether your board of choice rides on snow, surf or wheels, you'll find what you need here, alongside skater and surfing clothing labels.

Edinburgh Bike Co-op
8 Alvanley Terrace, South Edinburgh (228 3565/ www.edinburghbicycle.com). Bus 11, 15, 15A, 16, 17, 23, 45. **Open** Apr-Sept 10am-7pm Mon-Fri; 10am-6pm Sat, Sun. Oct-Mar 10am-6pm Mon-Wed, Fri-Sun; 10am-7pm Thur. **Credit** MC, V. **Map** p330 F11.
Scotland's first co-operatively run bike shop, open for almost 30 years, has an extensive selection of bikes, panniers, protective gear and other accessories. The friendly staff are happy to give advice on good local cycling routes.

Freeze
116 Bruntsfield Place, South Edinburgh (228 2355/ www.freeze-scotland.com). Bus 11, 15, 15A, 16, 17, 23, 45. **Open** 10am-7pm Mon-Fri; 10am-5.30pm Sat. Oct-Apr also noon-5pm Sun. **Credit** AmEx, MC, V. **Map** p330 E11.
An extensive range of ski and snowboard gear.

Run & Become
33 Dalry Road, West Edinburgh (313 5300/www. runandbecome.com). Bus 2, 3, 3A, 4, 25, 33, 44, 44A. **Open** 9.30am-6pm Mon-Sat. **Credit** MC, V. **Map** p329 B9.
This dedicated running shop has an impressive array of specialist shoes and clothing.

Tiso
123-125 Rose Street, New Town (225 9486, www. tiso.com). Princes Street buses. **Open** 9.30am-5.30pm Mon, Tue, Fri, Sat; 10am-7.30pm Thur; 11am-5pm Sun. **Credit** MC, V. **Map** p326/p330 F6, p336 B2.

Effectively Scotland's outdoors superstore, Tiso stocks a massive variety of clothing, equipment, books and maps. The Leith store has a mini climbing wall and a Gore-Tex waterproof test shower. **Other locations**: 41 Commercial Street, Leith (554 0804).

Wind Things
11 Cowgatehead, Old Town (662 7032/www.wind things.co.uk). Nicolson Street–North Bridge buses. **Open** 10am-5.30pm Mon-Sat; noon-5pm Sun. **Credit** MC, V. **Map** p330 G8, p336 D4.
If you've seen folk flying in kites in Holyrood Park and have the urge to join in, this is the place to visit. More adventurous souls can investigate the kitesurfing equipment. **Photo** *p205.*

Toys & games

Aha Ha Ha
99 West Bow, Old Town (220 5252). Bus 2, 23, 27, 41, 42. **Open** 10am-6pm Mon-Sat. **Credit** MC, V. **Map** p330 G8, p336 D4.
Probably the city's best-known joke shop. You can't miss it: just look for the oversized Groucho moustache and glasses above the front door. It also sells magic tricks and costumes.

Harburn Hobbies
67 Elm Row, Leith Walk, Broughton (556 3233/ www.harburnhobbies.com). Bus 7, 10, 12, 14, 16, 22, 25, 49. **Open** 9.30am-6pm Mon-Sat. **Credit** MC, V. **Map** p327 J4.
This family-run business has been selling models from the likes of Hornby and Corgi since the 1930s. Stock includes specially commissioned Scottish-themed railway models.

Owl & the Pussycat
166 Bruntsfield Place, South Edinburgh (228 4441). Bus 11, 15, 15A, 16, 17, 23, 45. **Open** 9.30am-5.30pm Mon-Sat. **Credit** MC, V. **Map** p330 E11.
Selling sturdy painted wooden toys that are very much built to last, this shop is sheer heaven for plastic-hating parents.

Toys Galore
193 Morningside Road, South Edinburgh (447 1006/ www.toys-galore.co.uk). Bus 11, 15, 15A, 16, 17, 41. **Open** 9.30am-5.30pm Mon-Sat. **Credit** MC, V.
All of the leading brands (Playmobil, Brio et al) are sold here, as well as specialist lines from the likes of Steiff Bears and Alberon Dolls.

Wonderland
97 Lothian Road, West Edinburgh (229 6428/www. wonderlandmodels.com). Bus 1, 2, 10, 11, 15, 15A, 16, 17, 23, 24, 27, 34, 35, 45. **Open** 9.30am-6pm Mon-Fri; 9am-6pm Sat. Oct-Dec also noon-5pm Sun. **Credit** MC, V. **Map** p330 E8, p336 A4.
Boasting a massive selection of model cars, trains and planes, dinosaurs, monsters and skeletons, plus doll's houses, Scalextric sets and kites, Wonderland should keep the children amused.

Arts & Entertainment

Cabaret Voltaire. *See p227.*

Festivals & Events

An 11-month calendar of the year.

The array of cultural events held in Edinburgh during August captures the headlines (and get their own chapter in this guide; see pp41-50), but there are plenty of other festivals that enliven the calendar all year round. With the darkness of winter comes the light and festivity of the Christmas and Hogmanay celebrations, while spring and autumn throw up everything from pagan fire rituals to left-slanted literary get-togethers. Where possible, we've included precise dates for the events listed in this section; for confirmation, check online nearer the time.

Spring

Ceilidh Culture Festival
Various venues (228 1155/www.ceilidhculture.co.uk). **Dates** 24 Mar-17 Apr 2007; 2008 dates tbc.
Gaelic singing, traditional dancing, bagpipe blowing… it's all here in this month-long celebration of Celtic culture. Prices vary by event.

Edinburgh International Science Festival
Various venues (558 7776/www.sciencefestival.co.uk). **Dates** 2-15 Apr 2007; 2008 dates tbc.
This hugely enjoyably festival gives an accessible slant on scientific subjects without dumbing down. The UK's largest science festival, it stages around 200 events, from free talks to hands-on workshops.

Beltane Fire Festival
Calton Hill (228 5353/www.beltane.org). **Date** 30 Apr.
This druidic tradition, marking the transition from winter to spring, was revived in 1988 after two millennia in hiatus. It's grown into a mass of fire, drumming and exhibitionists, watched by roughly 10,000 people. Tickets cost around £3 in advance (from the Hub) or £5 on the night. **Photo** *p209.*

The best Festivals

For a cultural feast
August's festivals. *See pp41-50.*

For a haggis feast
Burns Night. *See p209.*

For an alcoholic feast
Hogmanay. *See p209.*

Summer

Royal Highland Show
Royal Highland Centre, Ingliston (335 6200/www.royalhighlandshow.org.uk). **Dates** 21-24 June 2007; 19-22 June 2008.
If sheep shearing is your thing, head to the Highland Show, which celebrates Scottish rural life with everything from organic food to fancy tractors. A day ticket is around £20; under-16s get in free.

Autumn

Doors Open Day
Various venues (557 8686/www.cockburnassociation. org.uk). **Date** 1 day, Sept.
The Cockburn Association persuades the owners of many of Edinburgh's finest private buildings, from sewage plants to stately homes, to open their doors to the public for one day a year. Admission is free.

Edinburgh Independent Radical Book Fair
Call for venue details (662 9112/www.word-power. co.uk). **Dates** 4-5 days, Oct.
Readings, launches and discussions focusing on small, independent and radical publishing houses. The event moved from the Assembly Rooms to the Out of the Blue Drill Hall (*see p245*) in 2006, which also saw it shift to later in the calendar year.

Hallowe'en: Samhuinn
High Street, Old Town (228 5353/www.beltane.org). **Date** 31 Oct.
Samhuinn marks the end of the Celtic summer, six months after Beltane. The Beltane Fire Society takes to the streets once again, from Castle Esplanade, down the Royal Mile to Parliament Square, where the summer court, led by the Green Man, is banished to the magical realm for winter.

Bonfire Night
Various venues. **Date** 5 Nov.
The fact that Guy Fawkes' gunpowder plot of 1605 was against Scotland's James VI is masked by the fact that it was also meant to destroy the hated English Parliament. The biggest fireworks display in the city is held at Meadowbank Stadium.

St Andrew's Day
Date 30 Nov.
… As if you needed an excuse to come to Edinburgh and go for a drink. St Andrew's Day is nowhere near as debauched as St Patrick's Day is for the Irish, but it's still a pretty decent reason to go and raise a glass.

Beltane Fire Festival.
See p208.

Winter

Capital Christmas

Various venues (www.edinburghschristmas.com).
Date Dec.
What started out as a few casual events to brighten up December has grown into a large and very popular festival. The event usually includes a Winter Wonderland in Princes Street Gardens, complete with fairground rides, a mini-market and the largest outdoor skating rink in Britain, and the Edinburgh Wheel, a large temporary Ferris wheel adjacent to the Scott Monument.

Edinburgh's Hogmanay

Throughout the city (www.edinburghshogmanay.org).
Date 29 Dec-1 Jan.
Scotland is the home of Hogmanay, and Edinburgh is the best place to celebrate it. Tradition demands that on New Year's Eve, the people of Scotland take to the streets, kiss everyone in sight as the bells ring out midnight, and afterwards go 'first footing' with a lump of coal, a bun and a bottle of spirits.

Edinburgh's official Hogmanay celebration is now a four-day extravaganza, featuring a torchlight procession, bands and singers in Princes Street Gardens, street performers, marching bands, fireworks, and even a mini-triathlon on New Year's Day for those with the hardiest of constitutions. However, the street party on the evening of 31 December is the highlight: a vast whirl of activity, it sees the city centre cordoned off for safety reasons, and the police place strict limits on numbers. It's a truly massive event, and brings thousands of visitors (and many more thousands of pounds) into the city each year.

In previous years, passes for the street party were allocated via a ballot, but in 2005, they were sold from the Hub (*see p83*) and online for £2.50 per person. Those buying tickets for one of the major concerts are also eligible. Passes usually go on sale in October, when most of the event details are finalised. But don't worry if you can't get hold of one: there's plenty of fun to be had on the streets outside the cordon, and you can see the extravagant and beautiful Seven Hills fireworks display from vantage points such as the Meadows, North Bridge and, for the intrepid, Salisbury Crags. Check online for full details.

Burns Night

Throughout the city (www.rabbie-burns.com).
Date 25 Jan.
Robert 'Rabbie' Burns, Scotland's unofficial poet laureate, was born on 25 January 1759, and it's long been the custom of Scots to gather on the anniversary to consume haggis, sup whisky and recite the virtually sacred texts. Around Edinburgh, theatres and bookshops play host to readings of Burns's work. Some of the poems are very bawdy, although 'Tam o' Shanter' is a great story and the 'Address to a Haggis' is a true celebration of the working man.

▶ For all of **August's cultural festivals**, see pp41-50.
▶ For the **Scottish Storytelling Festival**, see p90.
▶ For **children's festivals**, *see p214*.
▶ For **Pride Scotia**, *see p243*.
▶ For **music festivals in Edinburgh**, see p229.

Arts & Entertainment

Children

The kids are alright in the Scottish capital.

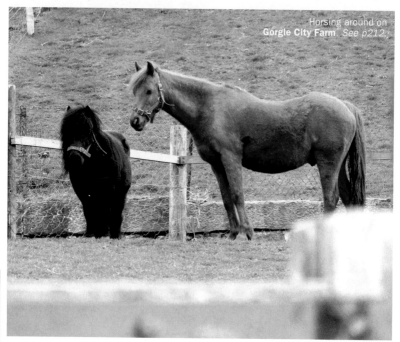

Horsing around on **Gorgle City Farm**. See p212.

Boredom isn't the problem when you visit Edinburgh with kids: the real difficulty is deciding what to skip. There are dedicated play venues, of course, but there are also plenty of child-friendly galleries, kid-orientated theatres, and fantastic museums with loads of hands-on exhibits, not forgetting an extinct volcano, a castle, a palace fit for a fairytale, and acres of green spaces where they can run and run.

Despite being built on a series of hills, Edinburgh is compact, meaning that you don't have to walk very far to reach any of the key points of interest. If little legs do stage a walk-no-more mutiny, the city's bus system is pretty good. Under-fives travel free, while five- to 15-year-olds ride for a 60p flat fare. If you're planning to hop on and off, day tickets are available, priced at £2 for five- to 15-year-olds and £2.30 for adults. For more on the city's public transportation system, see pp296-297. Alternatively, buy a ticket on one of the open-top tour buses, some of which have audio guides aimed at children. It's a more expensive option, but it means you can incorporate a bus tour with a ride to the venue of your choice, and is a good way to get your bearings. Taxis are even more expensive, but black cabs do seat five and you won't need to fold your pushchair.

If you're visiting the city with very young children, it's worth remembering that it's a criminal offence in Scotland to harass or otherwise prevent a mother from breastfeeding a child under two years old; the law also includes other carers feeding such children milk. This applies to public places or licensed premises where children are welcome, such as family-friendly pubs. Parents travelling to Edinburgh with younger kids will also find *Edinburgh for Under Fives* (£6.95) an invaluable guidebook. Edition 10 also includes information regarding access to attractions for disabled children.

Sightseeing

Old Town, Arthur's Seat & further south

Edinburgh Castle (*see p81*) possesses most children's prerequisites for a 'good' castle: dark spaces, cannons, courtyards and mysterious stairways. Get there in good time for the gun salute, fired at 1pm daily (except Sundays) with a satisfyingly big bang and a puff of smoke. Just down from the castle, the **Camera Obscura** (*see p80*) may or may not be of interest to kids (it really depends on their age), but the holographic exhibits usually are.

The **Royal Museum** and the **Museum of Scotland** (*see p99*) are fabulous, especially if the weather lets you down. Don't leave without admiring the phantasmagorical Millennium Clock (ask at the information desk for its current chiming hours) or the Connect exhibit, where you can control various robots, indulge in virtual Formula 1 driving, or create your own electricity. The museum buildings also have well-appointed nappy changing and feeding rooms.

If you're after room for the kids to stretch their legs (and yours), head south to the **Meadows** (*see p124*). As well as open parkland, there are three playgrounds; the one next to the tennis courts is specifically for toddlers. Alternatively, head to **Holyrood Park** and **Arthur's Seat** (*see p118*). The Park Rangers (140 Holyrood Road, open 10am-4pm Mon-Fri) will give you maps and suggest suitable walks. It can get very blustery up there, so keep hold of small hands. Best to take a picnic, or make a pit-stop at the café at **Our Dynamic Earth** (*see p92*) at the bottom of the hill; you don't need a ticket to get into it.

New Town, Calton Hill, Stockbridge & further west

Princes Street Gardens (*see p101*) are an ideal place in which to recover from any time spent shopping. Divided by the Mound and further bisected by the railway, the gardens feature grass banks, winding paths up to the castle, the odd ruin, loads of statues, a floral clock (in summer) and a Winter Wonderland (at Christmas; www.edinburghschristmas.com). Tiny trainspotters should go to the bridge behind the **Ross Bandstand**: wave like crazy and passing train drivers will usually toot their whistle in return. In the westernmost corner of the gardens are a snack bar, toilets and often a delightful Edwardian merry-go-round. Alternatively, enter the **Weston Link** building

at the Mound (which connects the National Gallery of Scotland and the Royal Scottish Academy), and enjoy the café and facilities there. **Calton Hill** (*see pp114-116*), to the east of Princes Street, offers great views of the city and more space to run around and explore: a flight of steps from Waterloo Place will get you to the top in no time.

In Stockbridge, **Inverleith Park** (*see p111*) has acres of space and lots to see, including a refurbished play park, a boating lake (go on Sunday mornings to see the model boats) and a pétanque club that plays on Sundays. Just across Arboretum Place is the **Royal Botanic Garden** (*see p111*): not only does it have endless greenery and absolutely no dog mess, but there are also friendly squirrels and ducks to feed, glasshouses, a pricey café with high chairs, an outdoor eating area, and nappy-changing facilities. However, no ball games, picnics or bikes are permitted within its bounds, as it's not a park.

North-west of Stockbridge, the **Scottish National Gallery of Modern Art** (*see p113*) and the **Dean Gallery** (*see p112*) conveniently sit across the road from each other. The art in the latter will probably appeal more to youngsters: it includes Paolozzi's two-room high metal giant, *Vulcan*, and a replica of his chaotic studio. However, the grounds of both galleries offer interesting examples of sculpture and art set into the environment, which kids love to touch and explore.

A steep path from the rear of the Gallery of Modern Art takes you to the **Water of Leith Walkway** (*see p110* **Walk this way**), a series of riverside pathways that meander north-east through the city back towards the docks in Leith. Open to walkers and cyclists alike, the walkway offers the chance to spot a rich array of wildlife and plants. For information, visit the Water of Leith Visitors' Centre, which also holds interactive exhibits allowing children to examine the river and its plant and animal life in detail. Leith itself boasts the **Royal Yacht** *Britannia* (*see p135*).

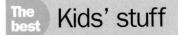

The best Kids' stuff

For raindrops on roses
Princes Street Gardens. *See left.*

For cream-coloured ponies
Gorgie City Farm. *See p212.*

For silver-white winters
Winter Wonderland. *See left.*

Edinburgh Zoo

*Corstorphine Road, Murrayfield (334 9171/www.
edinburghzoo.org.uk). Bus 12, 26, 31.* **Open**
Apr-Sept 9am-6pm daily. *Oct, Mar* 9am-5pm daily.
Nov-Feb 9am-4.30pm daily. **Admission** £10;
£7-£7.50 concessions; free under-3s; family
£32-£35.50. **Credit** MC, V.

While Edinburgh Zoo has many species of animal
and birds on show, its principal claim to fame is its
army of penguins, the largest number assembled in
captivity anywhere. The zoo's very own march of
the penguins, held at 2.15pm every day between
April and August (as long as the birds are in the
mood), is one of the city's most bizarre sights. Also
check the daily schedule of talks on the zoo's various
inhabitants, from rhinos to red pandas.

Gorgie City Farm

*Gorgie Road, West Edinburgh (337 4202). Bus 1, 2,
3, 21, 25, 33, 34, 38.* **Open** *Mar-Oct* 9.30am-4.30pm
daily. *Nov-Feb* 9.30am-4pm daily. **Admission** free;
donations welcome.

This lovely, informal spot has the usual farmyard
favourites, plus a pet lodge (housing guinea pigs,
rabbits, fish, tortoises and the like), a playground
and a good café with high chairs. **Photo** *p210.*

Out of town

Almond Valley Heritage Centre and **East
Link Farm Park**, to the west and east of
Edinburgh respectively, offer train rides, farm
animals, play zones and soft play areas, as well
as cafés. The seabirds and ancient monastic
ruins of **Inchcolm Island** and **Inchcolm
Abbey**, together with the ferry boat trip to get
there, are a sure-fire hit. **Linlithgow Palace** is
well worth a visit, as is **Tantallon Castle**, but
both have vertigo-inducing drops, so watch
the children: and your own step. Good beaches
include **Gullane** (which has a paying car
park, with a playpark and toilets nearby),
Yellowcraig (again, a paying car park, plus
a recently-renovated playpark with a toddler
area), and the beaches at **North Berwick**.
For details on all these venues, *see pp285-294.*

Butterfly & Insect World

*Dobbies Garden World, Lasswade, Midlothian (663
4932/www.edinburgh-butterfly-world.co.uk). Bus 3,
3A, 29.* **Open** *Summer* 9.30am-5.30pm daily.
Winter 10am-5pm daily (last admission 4.30pm).
Admission £4.90; £3.75 concessions; free under-3s;
family from £16. **Credit** MC, V.

Butterflies of every size flutter free in this enclosed,
tropically humid greenhouse. Safely behind glass,
however, are the lizards, bats, glow-in-the-dark scorpions
and numerous other creepy-crawlies. For the
more adventurous of your offspring, the jovial keepers
lead handling sessions, involving snakes, tarantulas
and very brave children, at noon and 3pm
daily. On Fridays, after the 3pm session, you can
cure more phobias at the snake-pit feeding session.
A useful option if the weather turns.

Free and easy

Sightseeing with the family in tow can be a
costly business. Take out a second mortgage
to fund a visit to some must-see attraction,
and it's even money that the kids'll want to
leave after five minutes. Happily, Edinburgh
has plenty of attractions that won't dent your
wallet too much – and if you're prepared to
take a couple of fairly pleasant strolls, you can
spend an entire day enjoying the city for free.

Edinburgh Castle (*see p81*) is a good
starting point, its esplanade holding enough
of interest for younger children without you
having to fork out the entrance fee to go
inside. The hall of mirrors mounted on the
exterior of the **Camera Obscura** (*see p80*)
is equally appealing. From Castlehill, you're
spoilt for choice: entrance to the museums
on Chambers Street (*see p99*) is free, and
there are frequent free children's art events.
Heading down the High Street and through
the Canongate takes you to the **Museum of
Childhood** (*see p90*) and the **People's Story**
(*see p95*), both worth a look.

August offers a good deal of entertainment
for youngsters, with a few special events
really jumping out of the calendar. **Fringe
Sunday**, held at the Meadows during the
Edinburgh Fringe (*see p43* **Special events**),
offers an exuberant snapshot of what's on
offer that year at the Fringe. For parents with
young children, there's usually a feeding and
changing tent courtesy of the NCT. And the
fireworks extravaganza that marks the end
of the **Edinburgh International Festival** (*see
pp41-50*) can be viewed for free from Princes
Street or somewhere less crowded like
Inverleith Park: take a radio and tune in
to the programme covering the event to hear
the music while you view the spectacle.

To the west of the city, **Lauriston Castle**
(*see p128*) hosts events throughout the
year. Some are free of charge, although they
may require pre-booking. And, of course,
Christmas is great for kids, with Santa
himself making a special appearance to
turn on the lights on Princes Street.

Leith Waterworld.

Deep Sea World

North Queensferry, Fife (01383 411 880/www.deep seaworld.com). North Queensferry rail, then 10min walk (down steep hill). Free bus in summer 01383 621249 for details. **Open** 10am-5pm Mon-Fri; 10am-6pm Sat, Sun. **Admission** £8.55; £6.30-£6.75 concessions; free under-3s; family £29.50. **Credit** MC, V.

Aquariums, a moving walkway and a feely fish pool, plus films, educational lectures and a café are on offer here. You can even learn to dive to PADI-accepted standards among the sharks and stingrays.

Scottish Seabird Centre

The Harbour, North Berwick (01620 890202/www. seabird.org). North Berwick rail, then 10min walk. **Open** *Apr-Oct* 10am-6pm daily. *Nov-Jan* 10am-4pm Mon-Fri; 10am-5.30pm Sat, Sun. *Feb-Mar* 10am-5pm Mon-Fri; 10am-5.30pm Sat, Sun. **Admission** £6.95; £4.50 concessions, 5-15s; under-4s free; family £13.95-£21.95. **Credit** MC, V.

Perched on the shore, this excellent attraction lets you zoom in on nesting birds with live-action video cameras or watch them through telescopes; alternatively, head indoors to watch some short films. There are good nappy-changing facilities, and a nice café.

Activities

Adventurous kids will love the **Ratho Adventure Centre** (*see p241*), though under-16s must be accompanied by an adult and must to be at least 4ft 7in to have a go.

Laserquest

56b Dalry Road, West Edinburgh (346 1919/www. laserquest.co.uk). Bus 2, 3, 3A, 4, 25, 33, 44, 44A. **Open** 11am-11pm Mon-Sat; 11am-8pm Sun. **Admission** £4.50 per game. **No credit cards.** **Map** p329 B9.

You can zap them with laser fire and they can zap you back (as long as they're 3ft 6in or taller, that is), and you all go home in one piece afterwards.

Leith Waterworld

377 Easter Road, Leith (555 6000). Bus 1, 12, 21, 25, 32, 34, 35, 49. **Open** 10.30am-4.45pm Fri; 10am-4.45pm Sat, Sun. **Admission** £3.20; £2.65 concessions; free under-5s. **No credit cards.**

Edinburgh's most kid-friendly pool includes a gently sloping beach for toddlers, plus water cannons, a wave machine, flumes, river rapids and bubble beds. The pool also has a soft play and a multi-sensory area. There are strict parent:child ratios in place for children under nine years old. Note the limited opening hours.

Indoor play centres

Molly's Playcentre

Top Floor, Ocean Terminal, Leith (0845 123 5593). Bus 1, 11, 22, 34, 35, 36. **Open** 10am-6pm Mon-Thur, Sat; 10am-7pm Fri; 11am-6pm Sun. **Admission** *1hr session* free under-18mths; £2.50 18mths-3yrs; £3 3-12s. **Map** p324 X1.

This great, compact soft play centre has equipment suitable for both able-bodied and disabled children, and huge windows that let in plenty of natural light. Staff police the play structure, which includes cargo nets, tunnels, rollers and a large slide; parents or carers do have to stay within the centre, though. There are plenty of sofas and benches on which adults can relax, plus a range of snacks and drinks on sale.

Clambers

Royal Commonwealth Pool, 21 Dalkeith Road, South Edinburgh (667 7211). Bus 2, 14, 30, 33. **Open** 10am-6pm Mon-Fri; 9am-7pm Sat, Sun. **Admission** *1hr session* £2.50. **No credit cards.** **Map** p331 M11.

After a 2006 facelift, Clambers emerged as one of the largest facilities of its kind in the Edinburgh area. The new format includes dedicated areas for babies and toddlers, as well as a new double level for slightly older children, and an enclosed space for ballgames.

Eating & drinking

Restaurants & cafés

Just a hop, skip and jump away from the Chambers Street museums, **Monster Mash** (4a Forrest Road, 225 7069) is a retro café dishing up old-time faves such as bangers and mash. The special children's menu is complemented by high chairs and nappy-changing surfaces. Pachyderm fans will love the **Elephant House** (see p141), a busy, informal café with elephants everywhere you look. For child-friendly Italian eats, take a trip to the **Valvona & Crolla Vin Caffè** (see p151). **Spoon** (see p143), just off the Royal Mile, also has a child-friendly policy.

If pizza's the thing, you could head for North Bridge, where you'll find **Pizza Express** (No.23, 557 6411), or Elm Row on Leith Walk, where sits the **Jolly Pizzeria** (No.9, 556 1588). However, kids can make their own pizzas at **Est Est Est** (135a George Street, New Town, 225 2555), **Ti Amo** (16 Nicolson Street, South Edinburgh, 556 5678), **Giuliano's on the Shore** in Leith (1 Commercial Street, 554 5272). Many cafés and restaurants around town offer drawing materials to make everyone's visit a little easier. If you don't have your own, it's always worth asking.

Outside the centre of Edinburgh, **Circle** (see p155) is a good stop-off point before going on to the Royal Botanic Garden. Offering seasonally changing menus, it's very accomodating to kids: there are a couple of high chairs, and staff are happy to supply half-portions on request. In Leith, the **Waterfront** wine bar and grill (see p165) welcomes families and has a dedicated children's menu, while the **Engine Shed** (see p160), a community-run enterprise, has a bakery and a cheerful vegetarian café.

Pubs

Pubs that serve full meals are, at the bar staff's discretion, allowed to admit children until 8pm. Try the **Cramond Inn** (Glebe Road, Cramond Village, 336 2035) or the **Botanic Park Hotel** (27 Inverleith Row, Inverleith, 552 2563) – especially on a nice day, when your offspring can enjoy the beer gardens. The **Standing Order** (62-66 George Street, 225 4460), part of the ubiquitous JD Wetherspoon's chain, has a family dining room.

Arts & entertainment

Many of Edinburgh's special events (see pp208-209) include a kid-friendly element, but there are also several events designed purely for younger audiences. Chief among them is the **Scottish International Children's Theatre Festival** in May (www.imaginate. org.uk), aimed at three- to 14-year-olds, held in various child-friendly venues and with a free crèche for under-fives. October's **Scottish International Storytelling Festival**, at the lively **Scottish Storytelling Centre** (www.scottishstorytellingcentre.co.uk, see p90), has plenty to entertain the youngsters, as does Easter's **Puppet Animation Festival** (www.puppetanimation.org).

Many theatres in the city stage a children's show at Christmas. The **Royal Lyceum** (see p245) always has an excellent reinterpretation of a classic fairy story for five- to ten-year-olds, while the **Theatre Workshop** (see p246) produces a small-scale contemporary alternative for over-fives. For a traditional pantomime (*Mother Goose, Cinderella* and the like), head to the **King's Theatre** (see p245). Other events occur on a much more regular basis. The **City Art Centre** (see p221) excels in large-scale exhibitions that are frequently of interest to parents and children. Once a week, the **Cameo** and the **Filmhouse** for both, (see p218) both hold morning film screenings for parents and carers with babies, entitled 'The Big Scream', and 'For Crying Out Loud!' respectively. The **North Edinburgh Arts Centre** (see p246), meanwhile, offers a full programme of theatre and dance, as well as various children's summer schools and holiday arts activities, ranging from creative writing and drama to 'aerial dance'.

Practicalities

Babysitting/childminding

Butterfly Personnel
7 Earlston Place, London Road, Calton Hill (659 5065). No credit cards.

Family Circle Recruitment
22 Tower Street (554 9500). Credit MC, V.

Accidents & emergencies

Royal Hospital for Sick Children
23 Sciennes Road, South Edinburgh; direct A&E access can be made from Sylvan Place (536 0000). Map p330 H11.
This hospital is orientated to the needs of babies and children aged up to 13 years old.

Comedy

Something funny going on?

The **Stand** delivers. *See p216.*

Edinburgh is the feast or famine capital of comedy. During August's Fringe, stand-up fans get to gorge themselves, but for the other 11 months of year, the lack of consistent top-notch comedy is no laughing matter. Comedy nights launched by local promoters and frustrated comedians come and go with alarming regularity, making it virtually impossible to predict which will still be running in a few months' time. The only guarantee is that **Jongleurs** and the **Stand** are here to stay.

So how do you like your laughter: poured from a can or served fresh using hand-picked local ingredients? This, in essence, is the choice that's available. At Jongleurs, you always know exactly what you're going to get, which is the multinational chain's greatest strength and biggest weakness. At the Stand, which operates seven days a week, the superior environment makes up for the occasional blips in line-ups that mix home-grown talent with luminaries from the international circuit.

In addition to this indigenous activity, the big UK comedy guns periodically pass through, playing the **Queen's Hall** (*see p228*), the **Traverse** (*see p246*) or the **Festival Theatre** (*see p246*). But if you like your entertainment raw and edgy and prefer to support upcoming local talent, check out the more sporadic pub gigs – see local listings for details.

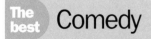

Comedy

For traditional stand-up
Stand. *See p216.*

For adventurous cabaret
Snatch Social. *See p216.*

For better, for verse
Big Word Performance Poetry. *See right.*

Big Word Performance Poetry

Tron, 9 Hunter Square, Old Town (226 0931/ www.bigword.co.uk). North Bridge–Nicolson Street buses. **Shows** fortnightly Thur. **Admission** £3; £2 concessions. **No credit cards. Map** p331 J7, p336 F4.

It's not strictly comedy, but laughter is high on the agenda at these fortnightly performances. Expertly hosted by Jenny Lindsay, Big Word features a mix of serious poets and well-versed stand-ups. The Poetry Slam, held regularly at the Bongo Club (*see p235*), is in a similar vein.

Jongleurs

Unit 6/7, Omni Centre, Greenside Place, Calton Hill (08707 870707/www.jongleurs.com). Bus 8, 12, 16, 17, 25. **Shows** 8.30pm Fri, Sat. **Tickets** £10-£12. **Credit** AmEx, MC, V. **Map** p327 J5.

On the plus side, you're likely to find some of the biggest names in the business taking the mic at Jongleurs. But this is also, unashamedly, comedy for the masses, so even comedians known for dark, edgy material may jettison their riskier gags in favour of the crowd-pleasers; not for nothing has the club's empire spread from humble London beginnings to an astonishing 17 branches around the UK. The ticket price includes entrance to the post-gig club; no wonder it's popular with large parties.

Snatch Social

Liquid Room, 9c Victoria Street, Old Town (07795 255400/www.snatchsocial.com). Bus 2, 23, 27, 41, 42. **Shows** 10.30pm Thur. **Admission** £5. **No credit cards. Map** p330 H7, p336 D4.

Harry Ainsworth and Tony Carter (aka Garth Cruikshank and Will Andrews, respectively past winners of the Perrier Best Newcomer and Tap Water Awards) continue to ply offbeat absurdity at the weekly club night that helped launch media darlings the Cuban Brothers on to an unsuspecting world. The antithesis of straight stand-up.

Stand

5 York Place, New Town (558 7272/ www.thestand.co.uk). Playhouse or Princes Street buses. **Shows** 8.30pm (doors 7.30pm) Mon-Wed; 9pm (doors 7.30pm) Thur-Sat; 1pm (doors 12.30pm), 8.30pm (doors 7.30pm) Sun. **Tickets** free-£10. **No credit cards. Map** p326 H5.

The Stand's big weekend shows see its 160-capacity basement space at its uproarious best; arrive early for a good seat. However, weekday shows can offer some surprises. Established performers such as Miles Jupp and Craig Hill cut their teeth at Monday's popular Red Raw newcomers' night (£1); Wednesdays are generally devoted to more diverse forms of comedy, including sketch shows and satire. Increasingly, though, the Thursday shows are the ones to catch, with Frankie Boyle often taking on compère duties. Sunday afternoons have a more laid-back vibe, with battered sofas, a simple menu and free improv. **Photo** *215*.

You're having a laugh

When, in 2006, Perrier let lapse its sponsorship of the Fringe's comedy awards, online bank Intelligent Finance stepped into the breach. As part of the deal, the company managed to shoehorn its URL into the cringeworthy new moniker: the if.comeddie awards (immediately nicknamed the Eddies). But has it missed its moment?

Comedy on the Fringe began not with stand-up but with revue shows; most famously, 1960's *Beyond the Fringe*, starring Jonathan Miller, Peter Cook, Dudley Moore and Alan Bennett. Youthful Pythons such as Michael Palin, Eric Idle and Terry Jones cut their teeth here later in the '60s; the following decade saw such notables as Rowan Atkinson and Billy Connolly appear on the Fringe. But then, in 1981, along came Perrier, followed swiftly by alternative comedy and Channel 4.

The British comedy landscape changed beyond recognition during the early and mid 1980s. *The Young Ones* and *The Comic Strip Presents...* appeared on television, and alternative comedy clubs sprang up around the country. Venue managers on the Fringe realised stand-up was both fashionably anti-establishment and, compared with amateur theatre productions, easy to stage: the turnaround time between shows could be virtually eliminated if all the acts needed was a microphone and a mic-stand. Economically,

it was a no-brainer, and stand-up began to take over from theatre as the Fringe's main draw. A boom followed: the city was swamped with stand-ups every August during the 1990s, chasing their fortune while simultaneously losing one playing to empty rooms.

Some critics grumble that comedy here is now less about entertainment, more about career-building. Newcomers are desperate to get noticed by the award judges (unsurprising, given the boost it's given to past winners such as Frank Skinner, Lee Evans and Dylan Moran), while talent-spotters up from London are desperate to find the next big thing, a process that can be about as amusing as a job interview. Many established comics now either avoid the event or jet in for lucrative three- or four-night theatre engagements.

There's also a sense of anxiety about the current career opportunities for young comics. Commissioning editors are now favouring sketch-based acts over stand-ups, and the national club circuit seems reliant on a number of trusted faces. The unjustly maligned Perrier judges generally did a great job of finding the gifted unknowns amid the star names and hopeless hopefuls. But even so, the production-line programming at some slicker Fringe venues means the next Rich Hall or Dylan Moran may appear from the blind side. Let's hope someone's paying attention.

Film

Hooray for Holyrood…

Lights, **Cameo**, action. *See p218.*

For a small city, Edinburgh packs a cinematic punch. Sean Connery, the city's most famous son, *is* James Bond; without JK Rowling's scribblings in local cafés, there'd be no record-setting Harry Potter movie franchise. And with the filming in the city of countless Dickens tales, *The Da Vinci Code* (at nearby Rosslyn Chapel), *The Prime of Miss Jean Brodie* and *Trainspotting*, Edinburgh has long been favoured by film-makers looking to adapt great literary classics. (And Dan Brown novels.)

For all that, there are scant rewards for those who want to go location-spotting in the city. A small plaque marks Connery's former home in Fountainbridge; Calton Road and the Mound are recognisable from *Trainspotting*'s opening shots (the rest was shot in Glasgow); and, if you're really desperate, you can head to the parts of West Lothian that Adrien Brody and Keira Knightley were contractually obliged to visit while shooting *The Jacket*. But that's about it.

As in most big cities, filmgoers in Edinburgh depend on a number of multiplexes, many close to the city centre, and a handful of independent,

cinephile-friendly operations. Housed in a B-listed building, the **Dominion** (*see p218*) harks back to the days before popcorn and Coke: you may be greeted at the door by the tuxedo-clad owner, before being ushered to your 'Gold Class' armchair seats or two-seater leather sofa. There's similar luxury at the Sundays-only **Scotsman Screening Room** (*see p218*). Lovers of art-house and foreign films are well served by the **Filmhouse** (*see p218*) and the

The best Cinemas

For a big-screen blockbuster
Vue Omni Centre. *See p219.*

For a small-screen treat
Scotsman Screening Room. *See p218.*

For the visiting cineaste
Filmhouse. *See p218.*

Cameo (see p218), both of which supplement their screenings with talks and Q&As. However, as of mid 2006, the latter was in danger of closure and conversion into a bar, a restaurant or even a lap-dancing club; check listings before pitching up to avoid a nasty surprise.

Established in 1947, the **Edinburgh International Film Festival** (see p43 and p50) is the second longest-running such event in the world. However, plenty of other series festivals run throughout the year; check listings for details. Documentary screenings are staged by Docspace (www.docspace.org.uk) and the Scottish Documentary Institute (www.scottish docinstitute.com). Scottish short films are screened on the first Monday of the month at the Filmhouse's Shoot First night; shorts from around the world are shown monthly at the **Left Bank** (37 Guthrie Street, 225 9744) as part of Future Shorts (www.futureshorts.com).

PRACTICAL INFORMATION

Cinema programmes change on Fridays; listings appear in *Metro*, the *Edinburgh Evening News*, the *Scotsman*, the *Herald*, *The List* and online. Films are classified as follows: (U) – universal viewing; (PG) – parental guidance advised for young children; (12a) – under-12s must be accompanied by an adult; (15), (18) – no entry for those under-15 and under-18s respectively. Most but not all of the city's cinemas are fully disabled-accessible; call ahead to check.

Cinemas

Necessity may well have spawned Edinburgh's healthy crop of cinemas: on days when the rain hits you horizontally, seeing a film becomes a most attractive option.

Cameo

38 Home Street, South Edinburgh (information 228 2800/bookings 228 4141/www.cameocinema.co.uk). Bus 11, 15, 15A, 16, 17, 23, 45. Tickets Mon £4; Tue-Sun £4.90-£5.90; £4 concessions. Credit MC, V. Map p330 E9.
Nestled in Tollcross, this indie cinema is a real treat, picking four films a week from the edges of the mainstream. Chat up the friendly staff at the bar, totally refurbished in 2005, then take your pint through when the film begins. Sunday's weekly double-bill of classic cinema is just £5. Photo p217.

Cineworld Fountain Park

Fountain Park, 130-133 Dundee Street, West Edinburgh (0871 200 2000/www.cineworld.co.uk). Bus 2, 3, 3A, 4, 25, 33, 44, 44A. Tickets £3.70-£6; £3-£4 concessions. Credit AmEx, MC, V. Map p329 C10.
Located in Sean Connery's old stomping ground of Fountainbridge, Cineworld is a sprawling, comprehensive 13-screener. Unusually for a multiplex

cinema, standard Hollywood fare is often supplemented with more risky film choices, particularly on Monday evenings and other off-peak times.

Dominion

18 Newbattle Terrace, Morningside, South Edinburgh (information 447 2660/bookings 447 4771/www.dominioncinemas.net). Bus 11, 15, 15A, 16, 17, 41. Tickets £4.90-£12.50; £4.90 Mon-Fri before 6pm. Credit MC, V.
A beautiful reminder of what cinemas used to be like in the days before the multiplex, the Dominion's art deco interior dates from 1938. A full hot menu is available before 6pm in the basement café/bar, with toasted baguettes on offer until 9pm. The more expensive tickets are for impossibly comfortable reclining armchairs and Pullman seats.

Filmhouse

88 Lothian Road, South Edinburgh (information 228 2689/bookings 228 2688/www.filmhousecinema.com). Bus 1, 2, 10, 11, 15, 15A, 16, 17, 23, 24, 27, 34, 35, 45. Tickets £4.20-£5.90 (Mon-Thur, Sat, Sun); £3.20-£5.90 (Fri); £1.80-£4.30 concessions. Credit MC, V. Map p330 E8, p336 A4.
A mix of arty new films and classics is screened at the Filmhouse, which supplements its day-to-day programming with a variety of festivals (the annual Dead by Dawn is a gory treat) and screenings on Sundays and Wednesdays organised by the long-running Edinburgh Film Guild (www.edinburgh filmguild.com). On the second Sunday of the month, you can go head-to-head with Edinburgh's cinema-going cognoscenti at the notoriously competitive quiz night. The café/bar serves drinks and home-cooked food, if you don't mind the slow service.

Odeon Lothian Road

118 Lothian Road, South Edinburgh (information 221 1477/bookings 0871 224 4007/www.odeon.co.uk). Bus 1, 2, 10, 11, 15, 15A, 16, 17, 23, 24, 27, 34, 35, 45. Tickets £5.50-£6.50; £3.50-£4.20 concessions. Credit MC, V. Map p330 E8.
Filling both a geographical and cultural gap between its independent neighbours, the Cameo and the Filmhouse, the Odeon supplies the city centre with mainstream and family films. The city's other two Odeon multiplexes boast 20 screens between them. **Other locations: Odeon Fort Kinnaird** Kinnaird Park, Newcraighall Road, East Edinburgh (669 0777); **Odeon Wester Hailes** Westside Plaza, 120 Wester Hailes Road, West Edinburgh (453 1569). **Both** bookings 0871 224 4007/www.odeon.co.uk.

Scotsman Screening Room

Scotsman Hotel, 20 North Bridge, Old Town (www.scotsmanscreenings.com). Nicolson Street–North Bridge buses. Tickets Movie £8.50. Movie & meal £39. Credit MC, V. Map p330 H7, p336 F3.
The 46 leather armchairs lend this intimate and luxurious cinema the feel of a private viewing room; unsurprising, since that's what it is during the week. The Sunday-night public programme concentrates

My Edinburgh Richard Baker

Having worked for five years as Marketing Manager for the Edinburgh International Film Festival (EIFF), Richard Baker was headhunted by Miramax founder Harvey Weinstein and moved to New York to take up the post of Vice President of International Marketing at the newly formed Weinstein Company. However, he's still a frequent visitor to the city, as he explains...

'Edinburgh feels European, and more connected to the rest of "the continent" than anywhere in England. It's got a vibe that's comparable to somewhere like Prague; a sophisticated, modern city, but bijou enough

that you can stand in the city centre, walk for an hour and enjoy the peace of a national park.

'The **Cameo** (*see p218*) houses my favourite screen, but otherwise it's not a scratch on the **Filmhouse** (*see p218*), which is, hands down, the best cinema in Edinburgh, Scotland and maybe even the UK. I love that rather than simply serving those in the know, it chooses to share its passion for cinema with everybody. Everyone who works for the cinema is unselfconsciously evangelical about great movies, and it's infectious.

'Scotland has the highest number of film attendances outside London. There's a big bunch of cine-literate people residing in Edinburgh, usually found in the café-bars of the Filmhouse and the Cameo, arguing into the early hours about the final shot of *Caché*, or if it really is his cock in *Brown Bunny*.

'On my last day in Edinburgh, I took a final walk around, bought some sausages from **Crombie's** on Broughton Street (*see p199*) – the best sausages I have ever eaten; seriously! – and some whisky from the **Scotch Malt Whisky Society** (*see p183*). I took myself to the top of **Arthur's Seat** (*see p118*) and drank tea from a flask. After a pint in **Bennet's** bar (*see p179*) with my pal, I had a fish supper on the way home. I miss Bennet's terribly.

'Edinburgh's not done with me yet. My heart's there and I can see myself moving back at some point. The quality of life is too good to be away from for too long. It would be a brilliant place to have kids, I think. Maybe I'll work on the girlfriend thing first.'

on classic films that rarely get an outing on the big screen (or, for that matter, the small one). Tickets are a tad pricey but probably worth it, especially when combined with dinner in the hotel's critically acclaimed Vermilion restaurant (*see p148*). It's definitely an impressive place to take a date.

Vue Omni Centre
Omni Centre, Greenside Place, New Town (information 0870 240 6020/bookings 0871 224 0240/www.myvue.com). Playhouse or Princes Street buses. **Tickets** £5.25-£6.30; £4-£4.30 concessions. **Credit** MC, V. **Map** p327 J5.

The giant glass cheesecake at the top of Leith Walk houses the closest cinema to Princes Street, a perfectly comfortable multiplex set-up. Expect big releases rather than art-house flicks, as the regular programme here rarely strays from the blockbuster path. It's a similar story over at Leith's ultra-modern Ocean Terminal. Nonetheless, with 12 screens at each Vue, you should be able to find something you want to see.
Other locations: Vue Ocean Terminal Ocean Drive, Leith (information 553 0700/bookings 0871 224 0240/www.myvue.com).

Galleries

The art of Midlothian.

doggerfisher. *See p221.*

Edinburgh residents are notoriously bad at leaving the house; anything located more than 15 minutes' walk away tends to fall off the radar. The city's contemporary art galleries are clearly wise to this state of affairs: many are clumped around Waverley Station, while **doggerfisher** and **Edinburgh Printmakers** are near the top of Leith Walk. It helps make a contemporary arts tour less of a pilgrimage and more of an easy perambulation.

In the shape of the **Royal Scottish Academy** (*see p104*) and the **National Galleries** (*see p103, p105 and pp112-113*), Edinburgh's artistic old guard still stands firm.

The best Galleries

For international names
Fruitmarket. See p221.

For national up-and-comers
doggerfisher. See p221.

For a snapper's delights
Stills. See p222.

Although both have done much to boost interest in modern art, the city's visual arts scene has been under-funded for years. This, combined with the country-wide economic recession of the 1980s and early '90s, spurred many local artists to leave, dissatisfied with an unadventurous buying climate that still preferred its art historical rather than contemporary (something that is still reflected, to a point, in the somewhat parochial galleries on Dundas Street).

Others, though, reacted to the situation by setting up their own art spaces. One inspired example of this trend is the **Collective**, which ambles along on a shoestring budget but still hosts successful, offbeat shows year-round. And then there's the **Embassy**: run by a committee of young artists, who submit to a tri-annual turnover in order to keep things fresh, it resolutely snubs Edinburgh's established institutions with its series of in-house exhibitions and off-site happenings.

Although Edinburgh's art scene hasn't mushroomed as greatly as that of Glasgow, things have moved away from a conservative modus operandi towards a youthful miscellany of artist-led initiatives. Siphoning off ambitious Edinburgh College of Art (ECA) graduates, the city has benefited from an enthusiastic,

Arts & Entertainment

irreveverent DIY attitude towards exhibitions. Keeping a eye on noticeboards at the **Forest Café** (3 Bristo Place, Old Town, 220 4538, www.theforest.org.uk), Totalkunst and the ECA, or on flyers stacked in more established galleries, the eager art tourist can track down one-off shows squatting in temporary shop lets, private flats or other off-site areas around town.

INFORMATION

The *Edinburgh Gallery Guide* is an essential companion; usually found nestling in flyer-stands and at the entrances of museums and galleries (but also online at www.edinburgh-galleries.co.uk), the free magazine contains full listings for all major shows. For more detailed information, pick up *The List* (*see p303*).

Galleries

Analogue

102 West Bow, Old Town (220 0601/www.analogue books.co.uk). Bus 2, 23, 27, 41, 42. **Open** 10am-5.30pm Mon-Sat. **Admission** free. **Credit** MC, V. **Map** p330 G8, p336 D4.

Stowed away behind Edinburgh's finest graphic arts shop (*see p187*), this intimate space packs in works from Britain's hippest illustrators and design-ers. The gallery functions as an extension to the shop floor, with shows rotating on a monthly basis; works can also be viewed and purchased online.

City Art Centre

2 Market Street, Old Town (529 3993/www.cac. org.uk). Princes Street buses. **Open** 10am-5pm Mon-Sat; noon-5pm Sun. **Credit** MC, V. **Map** p330 H7, p336 F3.

Treading the thin line between public edutainment and contemporary art, this six-floor gallery positive-ly dwarfs the Fruitmarket opposite (*see below*), but tends to have problems grappling with its own size. The CAC hosts civic shows alongside large touring exhibitions (for which there's sometimes an admis-sion charge); there's also a spacious café and shop.

Collective

22-28 Cockburn Street, Old Town (220 1260/www. collectivegallery.net). Bus 35/Nicolson Street–North Bridge buses. **Open** noon-5pm Tue-Sat. **Admission** free. **Credit** MC, V. **Map** p330 H7, p336 E3.

Located a stone's throw from Stills (*see p222*), this artist-led gallery has provided a small but influen-tial platform for diverse up-and-coming local talents, as well as internationally established artists, since opening in 1984. The recent addition of the Black Cube space has allowed for regular exhibitions of video art and film from around the world.

doggerfisher

11 Gayfield Square, Broughton (558 7110/ www.doggerfisher.com). Playhouse buses. **Open** 11am-6pm Wed-Fri; noon-5pm Sat; also by appointment. **Credit** AmEx, MC, V. **Map** p327 J4.

Housed in a converted tyre garage, doggerfisher has racked up an impressive roster of mainly Scottish artists since its 2001 inception – among them Moyna Flannigan, Nathan Coley and Rosalind Nashashibi – and is an increasingly conspicuous player at art fairs around the world. Prices can be high, but the gallery's penchant for delicate materials and fine crafts means it's always worth a visit. **Photo** *p220*.

Edinburgh Printmakers

23 Union Street, Broughton (557 2479/www. edinburgh-printmakers.co.uk). Playhouse buses. **Open** 10am-6pm Tue-Sat. **Credit** MC, V. **Map** p327 J4.

This pioneering open-access printmaking workshop often shows prints by its in-house artists alongside works by more notorious names, including Tracey Emin, Gillian Wearing and Jake and Dinos Chapman. Much of the work is archived, but staff can help you to sift through prints. Hands-on types can enrol on print-making courses or one-day taster workshops.

Embassy

76 East Crosscauseway, South Edinburgh (667 2808/ www.embassygallery.co.uk). Bus 35/Nicolson Street– North Bridge buses. **Open** noon-6pm Thur-Sun. **No credit cards. Map** p331 K9.

Although sometimes criticised as a cliquey second home for art school grads, this committee-run space nonetheless sticks a forever-young V-sign to the Edinburgh bourgeoisie while playing host to emerg-ing European artists. An endearingly shambolic approach means that the gallery's posters around the ECA and its own website are the best ways to keep up with forthcoming events.

Fruitmarket Gallery

45 Market Street, Old Town (225 2383/ www.fruitmarket.co.uk). Princes Street buses. **Open** 11am-6pm Mon-Sat; noon-5pm Sun. **Credit** MC, V. **Map** p330 H7, p336 F3.

Expect thoroughbred shows by the likes of Louise Bourgeois, Jeff Koons and Fred Sandback at the Fruitmarket, Edinburgh's leading venue for con-temporary art. The pint-sized bookshop sells a wide range of art book ephemera, while the café (*see p143*) will revive even the weariest gallery-goer.

Ingleby Gallery

6 Carlton Terrace, Calton Hill (556 4441/www.ingleby gallery.com). Bus 35. **Open** 10am-5pm Wed-Sat; also by appointment. **Credit** AmEx, MC, V. **Map** p327 L5.

Set up in 1998 and largely devoted to abstract art, this Georgian townhouse doubles up as the home of Richard and Florence Ingleby, who reside on the upper floors. The tranquil, exquisite gallery holds an impressive clutch of prints and paintings, pre-dominantly by Scottish artists such as Ian Hamilton Finlay, Andy Goldsworthy and Alison Watt.

Inverleith House

Royal Botanic Garden, 20A Inverleith Row, Stockbridge (248 2931/www.rbge.org.uk). Bus 23, 27. **Open** *Sep-July* 10am-5.30pm Tue-Sun. *Aug* 10am-5.30pm daily. **No credit cards. Map** p325 D2.

Arts & Entertainment

This beautiful house-cum-gallery is an unexpected find in the middle of Edinburgh's Royal Botanic Garden (*see p111*). Built in in 1774, it was home to the Scottish National Gallery of Modern Art from the 1960s to the mid '80s. Since a 2004 refurbishment, it has hosted a wide-ranging programme of temporary exhibitions featuring the work of both new and established artists (Roni Horn, Barbara Hepworth and the like).

Merz

Mobile 07876 373247/www.merzart.com.
Currently without a permanent space, the eclectic Merz stages regular exhibitions of affordably priced works from around the world in various spaces around the city, ranging from bars and restaurants to the Holmes Place health club on Greenside Place.

Red Door

42 Victoria Street, Old Town (477 3255/ www.edinburghart.com). Bus 2, 23, 27, 41, 42. **Open** 11am-5.30pm Mon-Sat; noon-5pm Sun. **Credit** MC, V. **Map** p330 G7, p336 D4.
Sandwiched into a narrow space on Victoria Street, this mini-gallery touts a selection of works by local designers, graphic artists, Lomographers and contemporary jewellers. Prices are generally reasonable.

Scottish Gallery

16 Dundas Street, New Town (558 1200/www. scottish-gallery.co.uk). Bus 13, 23, 27. **Open** 10am-6pm Mon-Fri; 10am-4pm Sat. **Credit** MC, V. **Map** p326 F5.

The gallery's rather drab name belies the merit of the work it houses. The lower floor is one of the best spots in town for contemporary ceramics; upstairs, modern paintings rub shoulders with works by recent graduates and emerging Scottish artists. 'Traditional' is not a dirty word here: open since 1842, the gallery is currently headed up by Guy Peploe, the grandson of Scottish colourist SJ Peploe.

Sleeper

6 Darnaway Street, New Town (225 8444/ www.sleeper1.com). Princes Street buses. **Open** 2-5pm Mon-Fri. **No credit cards. Map** p326 E5.
Running chiefly on word-of-mouth publicity, Sleeper is a wilfully under-promoted white cube found under the offices of Reiach & Hall Architects. After explaining your mission to the firm's receptionist, walk along the plushly-carpeted corridor and down the stairs to find the gallery. Past exhibitors include Bruce Nauman and Douglas Gordon.

Stills

23 Cockburn Street, Old Town (622 6203/ www.stills.org). Bus 35/Nicolson Street–North Bridge. **Open** 11am-6pm daily. **Credit** MC, V. **Map** p330 H7, p336 E3.
After languishing in obscurity for a few years, Stills is beginning to recoup its reputation as the city's leading photography venue. Alongside year-round shows, it's hosted the annual Jerwood Photography Awards exhibition. On-site resources include darkrooms, editing suites and digital labs; photography and design-based courses are open to the public.

Top drawer

Sublime and surreal, the craft of **Malcy Duff** is a grubby tirade against all things pleasant. Since entering the mini-press scene in 1997, Duff has become something of a local hero through humble ramblings such as *I Can't Draw: Part 2*, gathering a cult following among UK collectors of indie comics and zines.

Although often likened to the crude musings of David Shrigley, Duff's work revels in an even more grotesque menagerie of characters than that of his Glaswegian counterpart, and

adopts a comic book layout. Works such as *Rainbows Don't Have Black* are indicative of Duff's spirited tone; wry visual gags and puerile reveries unite under his prolific pen. Displaying a distinctly local humour, Duff draws many of his comics at his day job, sitting behind the box office desk or in the kiosk at the **Cameo** cinema in Tollcross (while it's still open; *see p218*).

Duff prefers the lavish tactility of the limited-edition signed comic print to shows at white-cube spaces, issuing his work through Monkey Loft Comics and the Giant Tank label. The latter also provides an outlet for Duff's free-noise band Usurper, orchestrated with fellow remedialist Alasdair Robertson. The duo often gig around the country, hawking Duff's work on their merchandise tables; check www.gianttank.com for updates. If there aren't any events scheduled when you're in town, Edinburgh outlets such as **Analogue** (*see p187*) and **Avalanche Records** (*see p205*) stock Duff's works.

Gay & Lesbian

The scene gets heard.

The preponderance of students and young professionals in Edinburgh means that the pace of its gay scene is fast. Yet there's refreshingly little attitude on show: if you try talking to someone you don't know, you can expect a demure and even shy friendliness that's typical of the capital as a whole. Many young gay men and lesbians here favour bleached hair and tight clothes, but not fitting into this stereotype is unlikely to raise an immaculately plucked eyebrow or cause bouncers to question your sexuality. Come one, come all.

Centred on an area known as the **Pink Triangle**, bounded on two sides by Broughton Street and Leith Walk, Edinburgh's gay scene thrives on drinking and late-night hedonism. There's only one permanent gay club (*see p225*), but a diverse variety of gay nights at otherwise straight venues around the city provide plenty of entertainment. The quality and quantity of LGBT bars has also increased substantially, leaving the scene in healthy shape.

The influx of thespian tourists and drama queens visiting during August (*see pp41-50*) doubles the city's population and galvanises the queer scene, filling the pubs all day long and allowing some clubs to extend their hours until 5am. The other big event in the gay calendar is June's **Pride Scotia**, a huge annual festival held alternately in Edinburgh (2007, 2009 and so on) and Glasgow (2008, 2010 etc). Each spring and autumn, the **Lothian Gay & Lesbian Switchboard** (*see p300*) organises a ceilidh, where you can reel past midnight in homo-friendly surroundings. And look out for the London Lesbian & Gay Film Festival on Tour, which brings the best in gay cinema to the **Filmhouse** (*see p218*) each July.

The best | Gay stuff

For a bite
Blue Moon Café. *See p223.*

For a brew
Street. *See p224.*

For a ball
Vibe. *See p226.*

HELP & INFORMATION

The most comprehensive coverage on the local scene is in *Scotsgay,* which can be found in bars or online at www.scotsgay.co.uk. The gay section of *The List* has previews and listings, as does free listings newspaper the *Skinny* (www.skinnymag.co.uk). For Edinburgh's **LGBT Centre**, and other local organisations offering advice and information, *see p300.*

Restaurants & cafés

Blue Moon Café

1 Barony Street, New Town (556 2788/www. broughtonstreet.co.uk/theblue.htm). Bus 8, 13, 17. **Open** 11am-midnight Mon-Fri; 9am-12.30am Sat, Sun. **Main courses** £3-£10. **Credit** MC, V. **Map** p326 H4.

Right at the heart of Edinburgh's gay scene, the welcoming, laid-back Blue Moon offers good food and drink. The staff are cute and sassy: ask here if you have any questions or need any information about what's on in the local clubs. There's a heartening open fire in winter.

Sala

60 Broughton Street, Broughton (478 7069). Bus 8, 13, 17. **Open** 4pm-midnight Tue-Thur; 12.30pm-1am Fri; 11am-12.30am Sat; 11am-11pm Sun. **Main courses** £5-£10. **No credit cards.** **Map** p326 H4.

One of queer Edinburgh's more genteel hostelries, café-bar Sala has become a favourite with girls who like girls. Still, all are welcome, whether for a drink on one of the highly prized sofas at the front or for a selection of tapas from the diminutive kitchen. **Photo** *p225.*

Bars

Many of Edinburgh's gay bars have been spruced up of late, making them look much more appealing and attractive both to the LGBT community and to straight folk. The division between women and men has also become less polarised recently. Outside of the scene, a variety of other bars draw a good proportion of gay drinkers, among them **Black Bo's** (*see p170*), the **Outhouse** (*see p179*), the **Basement** (*see p179*) and the bars at the **Filmhouse** (*see p181*) and the **Traverse Theatre** (*see p181*). Many venues listed below will extend their hours during August's festival. Call for details.

Claremont

133-135 East Claremont Street, Broughton
(556 5662/www.claremontbar.co.uk). Bus 8, 13,
17, 23, 27. **Open** 11am-midnight Mon-Thur;
11am-1am Fri, Sat; 12.30am-11pm Sun. *Food served*
11.30am-2.30pm, 6-10pm Mon-Sat; 12.30-6pm Sun.
Credit MC, V. **Map** p326 H2.

A mecca for those with a fetish: various Saturdays
throughout the month here are turned over to bears,
kilt-wearers, transvestites and glamorous goth
types. During the rest of the week, the Claremont
attracts a friendly, cruisy, male-dominated crowd
sporting denim or leather. On the food front, the
inexpensive bar menu is great and chef Jean-
Philippe makes exceedingly good cakes.

Frenchies

89 Rose Street North Lane, New Town (225 7651).
Princes Street buses. **Open** 1pm-1am Mon-Sat;
2pm-1am Sun. **No credit cards. Map** p326/p330
F6, p336 B1.

Coming across more like a local pub in a Highland
village than a bar in the Scottish capital, Frenchies
is the oldest gay hangout in Edinburgh. Despite its
central location the bar is quite difficult to spot, as
the entrance is just a small doorway in between
boarded-up windows. It's a charm, however. Happy
hour runs from 6-8pm daily.

Habana

22 Greenside Place, Leith Walk, Calton Hill (558
1270/www.gayscotland.com/habana). Playhouse
buses. **Open** noon-1am Mon-Sat; 12.30pm-1am
Sun. **No credit cards. Map** p327 J5.

The distinguishing feature of this Calton Hill
favourite is the balcony that overlooks the hubbub
of the colourful, energetic and sociable bar. Look

down on proceedings, and it's likely you'll find the
gay community, perhaps joined by the odd hen
party, having an outrageously fabulous time.

Planet Out

6 Baxter's Place, Leith Walk, Calton Hill (556 5551).
Playhouse buses. **Open** 4pm-1am Mon-Fri; 2pm-1am
Sat, Sun. **Credit** MC, V. **Map** p327 J4.

Planet Out is settling nicely into its role as a staple
of the Edinburgh scene. It's particularly popular
with students (there are cheap drinks on Mondays),
and the vibe is very relaxed. However, the clientele
has been more mixed of late, so prepare to have your
hopes dashed with the dreaded, 'Sorry, I'm not gay'.

Regent

2 Montrose Terrace, Calton Hill (661 8198).
Bus 1, 4, 5, 15, 15A, 19, 26, 34, 35, 44, 44A,
45. **Open** 11am-1am Mon-Sat; 12.30pm-1am Sun.
Credit MC, V. **Map** p327 M5.

Proud of its credentials as a real ale pub, this boozer
eschews the jukebox in favour of encouraging conversation. The atmosphere is in keeping with the
pub's traditional decor, and staff are friendly. A fine
alternative to the city's more frenetic bars and clubs,
if a little bit out of the way. There's free Wi-Fi access
for those toting a laptop.

Street

2 Picardy Place, Calton Hill (556 4272). Playhouse
buses. **Open** noon-1am Mon-Sat; 12.30am-1am Sun.
Credit MC, V. **Map** p327 J5.

Located on the corner of Broughton Street, this is a
jewel in the crown of the local gay and lesbian communities; some diehard regulars even rate it as one
of the best bars in the city. Sit upstairs on chrome
and cream leather barstools and gaze at the fishtank,

Claremont.

Sala. *See p223.*

or descend to the intimate bar below. Run by Trendy Wendy, the scene's most famous face, and Louise, ex-manager of Planet Out, it's not to be missed.

Twist

26b Dublin Street, New Town (538 7775/www.bar-twist.co.uk). Bus 4, 8, 10, 11, 12, 15, 15A, 16, 26, 44, 45. **Open** *noon-1am Mon-Thur; noon-2am Fri, Sat; 12.30pm-1am Sun. Food served noon-7pm Mon-Fri; noon-4pm Sat, Sun.* **Credit** MC, V. **Map** p326 G4.
Twist was formerly a real men's den, but a major refurbishment in a style bar vein has made it a far more welcoming prospect. It's mellow during the day, as the kitchen serves snacks to laptop-carrying customers (there's free Wi-Fi access). The basement club has a female DJ on Fridays and Saturdays.

Shops & services

Q Store

5 Barony Street, New Town (477 4756). Bus 8, 13, 17. **Open** *11am-7pm Mon-Fri; 11am-6pm Sat; 1-5pm Sun.* **Credit** MC, V. **Map** p326 H4.
Just off Broughton Street, this queer shop is pleasingly clean and airy. Head here to buy mucky DVDs and magazines, as well as skimpy underwear and a full range of sex contraptions and accoutrements. It's the only licensed gay store north of the border.

Nightclubs

Although **Ego** (*see p236*) is no slouch, with an increasing range of gay club nights on its calendar, **CC Blooms** is still Edinburgh's only permanent gay club.

CC Blooms

23-24 Greenside Place, Calton Hill (556 9331). Playhouse buses. **Open** *6pm-3am Mon, Fri, Sat; 8pm-3am Tue-Thur, Sun.* **Admission** free. **Credit** MC, V. **Map** p327 J5.
Ah, CC's, where great romances start and end, often in the same evening. The capital's only full-time gay venue may be offensive to both eye and ear (bad pop galore!), but its cheeky charm attracts girls and boys alike. The weekend queues to get downstairs provide the perfect opportunity to make your move. After all, as soon as you get down there, the pair of you will both be itching to leave.

Club nights

Below are a list of Edinburgh's regular gay and lesbian nights, generally staged either weekly or monthly. In the local bars, look out for flyers granting money off the entrance fee, and don't worry too much about any dress code they might claim to enforce: none of the clubs are particularly strict.

Blaze

Ego, 14 Picardy Place, New Town (478 7434/ www.jameslongworth.com). Playhouse buses. **Open** *11pm-3am 1st & 3rd Fri of mth.* **Admission** £5. **No credit cards. Map** p327 J5.
Following the resounding success of Tuesday's Vibe (*see p226*), also held at Ego, DJ James Longworth adds another string to his bow with Blaze. Essentially, it serves up more of the same: lashings of commercial tunes, funky house and chart music, with a camp cherry on top.

Arts & Entertainment

Booty

Medina, 45-47 Lothian Street, Old Town (667 5193/ www.bootylushous.com). North Bridge–Nicolson Street buses. **Open** 10pm-3am Sun. **Admission** £2-£4. **No credit cards. Map** p330 H8.

Now firmly established in the intimate, Moroccan-themed Medina, Booty grooves on with funk, disco, soul and R&B for an open-minded audience. Cheap drink deals are an added bonus, and clubbers are keen to strut their stuff on the dance floor.

Burly Too

Mariners, 39-40 Commercial Street, Leith (07930 357401/www.dv8scots.co.uk). Bus 1, 10, 11, 16, 22, 34, 35, 36. **Open** 10pm-2am last Sat of mth. **Admission** £6-£7. **No credit cards. Map** p324 X2.

The brother of Glasgow's award-winning Burly, this Leith night welcomes *real* men: over 25, and into denim, sportswear, industrial wear, uniforms, rubber, kilts and leather. Confounding expectations, it's a relaxed affair, with plenty of familiar faces trying out their fantasies while the music pumps, or simply gossiping in the bar area.

Disko Bloodbath

Ego, 14 Picardy Place, New Town (478 7434/ www.clubego.co.uk). Playhouse buses. **Open** 11pm-3am 1st Wed of mth. **Admission** £3. **No credit cards. Map** p327 J5.

Those whose tastes run to tough electro or edgy rock will enjoy this small club, which attracts youngsters who are into glamming it up in a deliberately trashy kind of way.

Fever

Ego, 14 Picardy Place, New Town (478 7434/ www.taste-clubs.com). Playhouse buses. **Open** 11pm-3am last Sat of mth. **Admission** £8-£10. **No credit cards. Map** p327 J5.

The guys behind Taste (*see below*) decamp to Ego once a month to spin quality house to a similarly mixed/gay audience. The main room has a harder edge than downstairs, where what pops out of the record bag is anybody's guess.

Fur Burger

Ego, 14 Picardy Place, New Town (478 7434/ www.clubego.co.uk). Playhouse buses. **Open** 11pm-3am 2nd Thur of mth. **Admission** £3. **No credit cards. Map** p327 J5.

This delightfully named ladies' night takes place in the smaller Cocteau Lounge area of Ego. The organisers demand that clubgoers wear good shoes and bring beautiful people. Chaps wishing to attend must be accompanied by a lady.

Luvely

Liquid Room, 9c Victoria Street, Old Town (225 2564/www.luvely.com). Bus 2, 23, 27, 41, 42. **Open** 10.30pm-3am first Sat of mth. **Admission** £8-£12. **No credit cards. Map** p330 H7, p336 D4.

Luvely is where serious clubbers go to have fun, drawn by the mix of funky house and harder-edged tunes from the US. Every month the party has a dif-

ferent dress theme, such as doctors and nurses, tartan, cops and robbers or cowboys and Indians: arrive suitably attired and you'll receive a discount on the admission price.

Tackno

Ego, 14 Picardy Place, New Town (478 7434/ www.clubego.co.uk). Playhouse buses. **Open** 11pm-3am last Sun of mth. **Admission** £5-£7. **No credit cards. Map** p327 J5.

Cross a school disco with a village fête and add a dose of hedonism, and you'll get some idea of the atmosphere at Tackno. Cheesy, one-hit wonders jostle for attention with daft competitions and giveaways, all under the beady eye of Trendy Wendy. There's a fresh theme each month.

Taste

Liquid Room, 9c Victoria Street, Old Town (225 2564/www.taste-clubs.com). Bus 2, 23, 27, 41, 42. **Open** 11pm-3am Sun. **Admission** £5-£8. **No credit cards. Map** p330 H7, p336 D4.

Taste is gay-friendly rather than exclusively gay, which makes for a better night out all round. Whether you like your house music deep, American or just plain ready-salted, resident DJs Fisher and Price and Martin Valentine (plus assorted guest players) will sort you out.

Upstairs Downstairs

Ego, 14 Picardy Place, New Town (478 7434/ www.clubego.co.uk). Playhouse buses. **Open** 11pm-3am 3rd Sat of mth. **Admission** £6. **No credit cards. Map** p327 J5.

The closure of the Venue has left Joy and Mingin', Alan and Maggie Joy's longstanding nights, with an uncertain future. In the meantime they're joining forces with Habana's Graeme F and Chris Paton for a night that offers fun party tunes in the main arena, and trancey house in the Cocteau Lounge beneath.

Velvet

Mariners, 39-40 Commercial Street, Leith (555 4242). Bus 1, 10, 16, 22, 35, 36. **Open** 10pm-2am 1st Sat of mth. **Admission** £4-£6. **No credit cards. Map** p324 X2.

The longer-running of the city's two girl-oriented nights, Velvet has recently been voted the best women's club night in Scotland. The eclectic, genre-spanning music policy includes a 'foreplay lounge set' in the first hour. Good boys are allowed in as guests of their gal pals.

Vibe

Ego, 14 Picardy Place, New Town (478 7434/ www.jameslongworth.com). Playhouse buses. **Open** 11pm-3am Tue. **Admission** £4. **No credit cards. Map** p327 J5.

The ever-popular Vibe is Scotland's most successful gay club night. It entertains a young, trendy audience – spiky-haired and chain-store clad – with pop tunes and cuts from the better end of the commercial dance spectrum. The atmosphere says 'get on your feet'; few try to resist.

Music

Beyond the bagpipes…

Charlie Winston, at **Cabaret Voltaire**.
See p230.

Classical & opera

Classical music in Edinburgh really began to
take off in the 18th century, after the Edinburgh
Musical Society moved into St Cecilia's Hall
on the Cowgate. Named for the patron saint
of music and musicians and completed in 1763,
it was the first purpose-built concert hall in
Scotland. Despite outbreaks of fire, plague and
urban regeneration, **St Cecilia's** still stands
and hosts concerts to this day (Niddry Street,

The best **Music**

For something old
Usher Hall. See p228.

For something new
Cabaret Voltaire. See p230.

For something borrowed
Royal Oak. See p171.

For something blue
Jazz Centre at the Lot. See p232.

Cowgate, Old Town, 650 2805). Fast-forward
to the present and classical music still thrives
in Edinburgh, although audiences have not
necessarily swelled enough to guarantee
packed houses for every event.

The two most notable ensembles playing
regularly in the city are the **Royal Scottish
National Orchestra** (www.rsno.org.uk)
and the **Scottish Chamber Orchestra**
(www.sco.org.uk). The RSNO performs a
lively programme of concerts, highlighted by
a Proms season in June, at both the Usher Hall
and Glasgow's Royal Concert Hall. The SCO,
meanwhile, mainly divides its time between
the Usher Hall and the Queens Hall, both
in Edinburgh, and the Glasgow City Halls.

A few other native groups play frequently in
the city, led by the **BBC Scottish Symphony
Orchestra** (www.bbc.co.uk/scotland/bbcsso).
The **Scottish Ensemble** (www.scottish
ensemble.co.uk) and the **Paragon Ensemble**
(www.paragon-ensemble.com) specialise in
less celebrated works that may not otherwise
see the light of day. And keep a close eye
out for performances from **Mr McFall's
Chamber** (www.mcfalls.co.uk), an ingenious
experimental project that unites SCO players

Arts & Entertainment

And wave 'em like you just don't care...
the **Liquid Room**. *See p231*.

and other talented, broadminded musicians who are equally at home tackling Frank Zappa as they are Franz Liszt.

Edinburgh has no dedicated opera house, which may be a good thing given the financial and artistic troubles that have beset the **Scottish Opera** (www.scottishopera.org.uk) in recent years. After running into financial trouble, the company was forced to cancel all major productions for a year, but returned in 2006. The group is currently staging four productions a year at the glass-fronted **Edinburgh Festival Theatre** (*see p246*) and the **Theatre Royal** in Glasgow (*see p281*).

Major venues

Queens Hall

Clerk Street, South Edinburgh (box office 668 2019/ administration 668 3456/www.queenshalledinburgh. co.uk). Nicolson Street–North Bridge buses. **Box office** *In person* 10am-5.30pm Mon-Sat (or until 15mins after showtime). *By phone* 10am-5pm Mon-Sat. **Tickets** £9-£25. **Credit** AmEx, MC, V. **Map** p331 K10.

Self-consciously squeezed in among a row of shops, this former church retains a distinctly spiritual vibe, right down to the pews arranged on the ground floor. The venue attracts performers from all genres, and plays host to as many jazz, folk and rock gigs (*see pp229-232*) as it has classical recitals. The programmes staged by the Scottish Ensemble and the Paragon Ensemble are always worth a look.

Reid Concert Hall

Bristo Square, Old Town (650 2423/www.music.ed. ac.uk). Bus 2, 41, 42. **Concerts** *Lunchtime*: Oct-May 1.10pm Tue, Fri. **Tickets** free-£7. **Map** p330 H8.

On selected days during termtime, wander in and enjoy a free lunchtime concert from students at the University of Edinburgh's music faculty, or established performers such as the Edinburgh Quartet. The hall also hosts a roots music series in August.

Usher Hall

Lothian Road, South Edinburgh (box office 228 1155/administration 228 8616/www.usherhall.co.uk). Bus 1, 2, 10, 11, 15, 15A, 16, 17, 23, 24, 27, 34, 35, 45. **Box office** 10am-8pm Mon-Fri; 10am-5.30pm (or until 15mins after showtime) Sat. **Tickets** £8-£27. **Credit** AmEx, MC, V. **Map** p330 E8, p336 A4.

A great deal of time and money have been spent returning the Usher Hall to its former glory; from the cosmetic refurbishments to the restoration of the colossal pipe organ, it's paid off nicely. Impressive acoustics mean that the venue, which first opened in 1914, is in constant demand by everyone from the RSNO to rock acts such as Mogwai and jazz artists of the calibre of John Scofield. Most of the major music events at August's Festival take place here.

Churches

Some of Edinburgh's wonderful old churches are used as concert venues, particularly during the Fringe. **Canongate Kirk** (153 Canongate, Old Town, 668 2019, www.canongatekirk.com), the Queen's preferred place of worship when she's in residence at Holyroodhouse, stages shows by small choral groups and chamber orchestras. As well as holding free concerts at 6pm most Sundays, the **High Kirk of St Giles** (*see p88*) also plays host to travelling choirs. Regular concerts are also held at the central **Greyfriars Kirk** (*see p97*).

Edinburgh has exploited its relatively civilised licensing hours to blend clubbing with live music in a way that Glasgow, hampered by relatively draconian alcohol laws, has been unable to do. Many venues in the city start out the evening as live music spots before morphing, in some cases seamlessly, into a nightclub around 10.30pm or 11pm. For details on the town's nightclubs scene, *see pp233-236.*

A handful of festivals enliven the calendar. **Triptych** (www.triptychfestival.com) stages a jumble of alternative-slanted acts in the run-up to the May Day bank holiday at many venues around Edinburgh and Glasgow. And then, in July, it's **T in the Park** (www.tinthepark.com), a weekend-long indie-fest up in Perthshire.

INFORMATION & TICKETS

For details on what's on, check *The List* (*see p304*). Online, Jockrock (www.jockrock.org) provides a scurrilous look at all things indie, while bi-monthly mag *Is This Music?* picks up on new local acts. Less comprehensive listings can be found in freesheets such as the *Fly* and the *Skinny*.

The main ticket outlets in Edinburgh are **Ripping Music** (*see p205*) and **Tickets Scotland** (127 Rose Street, New Town, 220 3234), but **Ticketmaster** (0870 534 4444, www.ticketmaster.co.uk) may also be of help.

St Mary's Episcopal Cathedral

Palmerston Place, New Town (225 6293/www. cathedral.net). Bus 12, 13, 26, 31, 38. **Open** *Evensong* 5.30pm Mon-Fri; 3.30pm Sun. *Sung Eucharist* 10.30am Sun. **Tickets** *concerts only* prices vary. **No credit cards. Map** p329 C8.
St Mary's is unique in Scotland in maintaining daily sung services. Organ recitals at 4.30pm on Sundays during the Festival are another musical highlight.

Rock, pop & dance

Edinburgh's contribution to rock 'n' roll history has been patchy. A few local acolytes have hit the headlines down the years, from tartan-clad popsters the Bay City Rollers to Garbage singer Shirley Manson. However, compared with Glasgow, the city hasn't produced its fair share of million-sellers. The musical relationship between the two cities was summed up in 2004, when Glasgow's world-conquering Franz Ferdinand asked Edinburgh's largely forgotten Fire Engines, whom they cite as a big influence, to reform in order to support them at the SECC. Around 7,000 Franz fans sat through their set with a mix of bemusement and disinterest, but the clamour for their rare-as-hen's-teeth records became nothing short of ridiculous.

Thanks to Edinburgh's modest size and the fluid nature of its young populace (tourists, travellers and students abound), new bands and music scenes can find it harder to anchor themselves here. Watching the progress of local outfits such as punky rock duo the Very, the country-tinged Sundowns and eccentric electronica boffins Mammal over the next couple of years will be a good benchmark for the city's musical potential.

Venues

In addition to venues detailed below, a couple of the city's concert halls also stage regular rock and pop shows: the **Queens Hall** (*see p228*) hosts gigs from cultured acts such as Richard Thompson and Eddi Reader, while the **Usher Hall** (*see p228*) has staged everyone from Ladysmith Black Mambazo to the Flaming Lips. **Whistlebinkies** (*see p171*) is home to live music nightly (singer-songwriters and bands); the **Bongo Club** (*see p235*) sometimes features live acts, as does the **Wee Red Bar** (*see p236*), which runs a showcase every Friday at 6pm during termtime. Even the **Edinburgh Playhouse** (*see p244*) squeezes the odd gig into its programme of theatrical blockbusters.

Bannermans

212 Cowgate, Old Town (556 3254/www. bannermansgigs.co.uk). Nicolson Street–North Bridge buses. **Admission** £3-£7. **No credit cards. Map** p331 K7, p336 F4.
The cavernous network of wee rooms that make up this well-worn boozer have hosted all manner of musicians over the years. Formerly a folkie favourite, it's now a bolt-hole for the indie fraternity, small enough to feel busy when you're starting off and positively riotous when a band can draw a crowd. There's something going on most nights of the week.

My Edinburgh Riley Briggs

Following the success of Young Forever, *their acclaimed 2004 debut, Edinburgh-based band Aberfeldy released* Whatever Turns You On *in 2006. Riley Briggs (centre), the band's singer and songwriter, has been playing around Edinburgh since the age of 15 in a variety of bands spanning every musical style, from Stones and Vapors covers to garage, punk, synth-garage-prog, cajun-zydeco and just plain acoustic music. He's even played guitar for the Jewish Elvis Presley.*

'I love the open-mindedness of Edinburgh, the beautiful architecture and wide-open spaces like **Calton Hill** (*see p114*) and **Arthur's Seat** (*see p118*); so rare in a major city. And the **Fringe** (*see pp41-50*) is great – the first sighting of Greg Proops being the traditional signal that summer is here. Visitors to the city should really get off the High Street and explore hidden gems like **Leith**, where there are great pubs such as the **Pond** – it's got

fishtanks, basket chairs, Space Invaders, good beer and sounds (*see p182*) – and the **Port o' Leith** (*see p183*). The **Cameo Bar** (23 Commercial Street, 554 9999) and the **Shore** (*see p184*) are both great for food.

'Edinburgh punches above its weight musically. It's most visible in the traditional scene. On any given night it's possible to hear some of the world's best musicians playing informally in pubs such as **Sandy Bell's** (*see p171*), the **Royal Oak** (*see p171*) and the Shore in Leith. Sessions are usually open, which is great for travelling musicians. The city also has some great jazz musicians: the **Jazz Bar** (*see p232*) is your best bet.

'For rock and pop, there's never really been a cohesive scene here, but exciting new bands are formed (and split up) every day: there seems to be something in the air. I think that the **Subway** (*see p231*) could become Edinburgh's CBGB – it's got the right atmosphere – while the **Bongo Club** (*see p235*) has a reliably eclectic calendar and is always worth a gamble, as is the arts lab-esque **Forest Café** (3 Bristo Place, Old Town, 220 4538, www.theforest.org.uk). My favourite local bands are the Thanes (a 1960s-style beat group), the arty Dominic Waxing Lyrical, über-rockers Moniack, the frightwig cabaret of Alleschwindel and the anarcho fury that is Oi Polloi. Then there are Preston Pfanz & the Seaton Sands, the Very, the Gussets... the list goes on.'

Cabaret Voltaire

36 Blair Street, Old Town (220 4638/www.the cabaretvoltaire.com). Nicolson Street–North Bridge buses. **Admission** *free-£15.* **No credit cards.** **Map** *p331 J7, p336 F4.*

This brick-lined basement space makes the most of the enthusiastic local support for innovative new music, providing the shot in the arm that the city's music circuit has needed for a while. Touring indie acts such as ¡Forward Russia!, the Research and Union of Knives have all been given the chance to shine in this fairly sophisticated room, which hosts around 30 gigs a month. There are also myriad club nights held here after the bands have finished for the night; *see p235.* **Photo** *p227.*

Caledonian Backpackers

3 Queensferry Street, New Town (476 7224/ www.caledonianbackpackers.com). Princes Street buses. **Admission** *£4-£5 Fri, Sat.* **No credit cards.** **Map** *p329 D7.*

It may be the rough and ready bar of a New Town backpackers' hostel, but thanks to canny local promoters such as Baby Tiger (www.baby-tiger.net), the eclectic bills of indie, rock, folk, pop and experimental electronica it stages are often worth a look.

Corn Exchange

11 New Market Road, South Edinburgh (477 3500/box office 443 0404/www.ece.uk.com). Bus 4, 20, 34, 35, 44, 44A. **Admission** *£14-£28.* **Credit** *AmEx, MC, V.*

Basement Jaxx, Starsailor and Futureheads have all raised the roof in this converted slaughterhouse, but the 2,500-capacity venue's finest moment remains the N.E.R.D MTV Awards aftershow party back in 2003, where Justin Timberlake was guest of honour.

Exchange
55 Grove Street, West Edinburgh (228 2141/ www.livemusicx.com). Bus 1, 34, 35. **Admission** *£6-£18.* **Credit** *AmEx, MC, V.* **Map** *p329 D9.*
Owned by the same company as the Corn Exchange (*see above*), this 460-capacity space plays host to sporadic shows from acts of the calibre of the Arctic Monkeys and the Dresden Dolls. However, its mainstays here are local showcases, tribute acts and the occasional gang of old rocker lags such as Nazareth.

Forest
3 Bristo Place, Old Town (220 4538/www.theforest. org.uk). Bus 2, 41, 42. **Admission** *free.* **No credit cards.** **Map** *p330 H8.*
The Forest provides an antidote to the creeping commercialism of other venues. Housed in a converted church, it contains an art gallery, a non-profit café and a club-cum-music venue at which all-comers are encouraged to get organised and get up on the stage. It hardly needs adding that the quality control can be a little unreliable, but all events are free.

Henry's Cellar Bar
8-16 Morrison Street, West Edinburgh (221 1288). Bus 1, 2, 10, 11, 15, 15A, 16, 17, 23, 24, 27, 34, 35, 45. **Admission** *£4-£8.* **No credit cards.** **Map** *p330 E8.*
Assembly Direct, the city's foremost jazz promoters, have decamped to the altogether more dapper Lot (*see p232*), leaving Henry's to become the unofficial heart of Edinburgh's experimental music scene. In addition to the odd touring act, Axis (www.sublive.co.uk) and MRW44 records stage an array of accomplished local noisemongers. Weird and exciting.

Jam House
5 Queen Street, New Town (226 4380/bookings 226 5875/www.thejamhouse.com). Princes Street buses. **Admission** *free-£10.* **Credit** *MC, V.* **Map** *p326 G5.*
Housed in the beautiful former BBC Broadcasting House, this music-and-dining venue is a real looker, a grand and expansive space with tables on the main floor and seating upstairs. The problems are with the anodyne programming, cover bands mixing with turns from the likes of Hue & Cry. **Photo** *p232.*

Liquid Room
9c Victoria Street, Old Town (225 2564/www.liquid room.com). Bus 2, 23, 27, 41, 42. **Admission** *£5-£15.* **No credit cards.** **Map** *p330 H7, p336 D4.*
On a busy night, the Liquid Room is as claustrophobic as a riot in a prison cell. Happily, the lack of cat-swinging capacity doesn't prevent it from being a great gig venue: everyone from Bloc Party to De La Soul have received a rapturous reception here. The club nights are generally just as popular; for details, *see p235.* **Photo** *p228.*

Studio 24
24-26 Calton Road, Calton Hill (558 3758/www. studio24edinburgh.co.uk). Nicolson Street–North Bridge buses. **Admission** *£5-£10.* **No credit cards.** **Map** *p327/p331 J6.*
Studio 24 boasts a long and storied musical history (Mudhoney, Fugazi and Teenage Fanclub all made their Edinburgh debuts here). These days the flourishing underground goth and metal scene predominates, especially at Saturday's Mission night and its under-18s sister club Junior Mission. Despite continued resilience on the part of the McArthur family, who own it, Studio 24 has been threatened with closure as developers continue to 'gentrify' the Old Town. Check online before setting out.

Subway
69 Cowgate, Old Town (225 6766/www.subway clubs.co.uk). Nicolson Street–North Bridge buses. **Admission** *£2-£5.* **No credit cards.** **Map** *p331 J7.*
Despite its location on the main Edinburgh drag for boozy, low-rent entertainment, this peculiar L-shaped room rattles to the sounds of everything from experimental noise to alt-country. For the latter, local promoters Lonesome Highway (www. lonesomehighway.co.uk) are the best in town.

Folk & roots

In the years since poet Hamish Henderson (composer of 'Freedom Come All Ye', which many believe should be the Scots national anthem) spearheaded the 1960s Scottish folk revival by founding the Edinburgh Folk Club, a younger generation of artists has picked up on other world traditions and influences to create a mongrel hybrid of ethnocentric sounds. Acts such as Croft No.5, Shooglenifty and the mighty Salsa Celtica lead the vanguard these days, but Fife's Fence Collective continues to thrive, regularly bringing members of their lo-fi folk clan from the Kingdom to charm the capital.

The best way to discover the Edinburgh's folk scene is to head to one of the various pub sessions. Arguably the best are held at the **Sandy Bell's** and the **Royal Oak** (for both, *see p171*), the latter also home to Sunday's Wee Folk Club, but they're the tip of the iceberg. The music at the **Hebrides** (17 Market Street, Old Town, 220 4213) is usually interesting, but a walk down the High Street will bring you within earshot of several similar pub sessions.

Venues

Edinburgh Folk Club
Pleasance, 60 Pleasance, South Edinburgh (556 6550/www.edinburghfolkclub.org.uk). Nicolson Street–North Bridge buses. **Gigs** *Edinburgh Folk Club* 8pm Wed. **Admission** *£6; £5 concessions.* **No credit cards.** **Map** *p331 K8.*

The Pleasance's Cabaret Bar hosts the Edinburgh Folk Club's weekly sessions for 11 months in every 12; the exception is August, when the venue becomes subsumed by the Fringe.

Folk 'n' Friends

Waverley, 3-5 St Mary's Street, Old Town (556 8855). Nicolson Street–North Bridge buses.
Gigs *Folk 'n' Friends* 9pm-midnight Thur.
Admission free. **No credit cards. Map** p331 J7.
This quiet upstairs room in an even quieter bar was a major venue during the 1960s folk revival. These days, it hosts Folk 'n' Friends (www.singing session.com), a loose-knit session of songs from around the globe.

Out of the Bedroom

Canon's Gait, 232 Canongate, Old Town (556 4481). Nicolson Street–North Bridge buses.
Gigs *Out of the Bedroom* 8pm Thur. **Admission** free. **No credit cards. Map** p331 K7.
This nifty little basement space is now the home of Out of the Bedroom (www.outofthebedroom.co.uk), a regular weekly event bringing together aspiring local singer/songwriters.

Jazz

While its rock scene sometimes underwhelms, Edinburgh's jazz circuit is often impressive. The **Lot** has been a very welcome replacement for the fabled sessions at Henry's Cellar Bar (now hosting experimental music; *see 231*), and the reborn **Jazz Bar** (*see below*) has gone from strength to strength under the watchful eye of

Jam House.
See p231.

renowned drummer Bill Kyle. Both the **Usher Hall** (*see p228*) and the **Queens Hall** (*see p228*) also stage regular concerts from some of the music's bigger names, many of them visitors from the US. Look out for other big names at the Starbucks-sponsored **Edinburgh Jazz & Blues Festival** (*see p47 and p50*), held in late July and early August.

Wester Hailes-born saxophonist Tommy Smith remains the figurehead of the local scene, his involvement with the **Scottish National Youth Jazz Orchestra** (www.nyos.co.uk) nurturing countless new players. The **Scottish National Jazz Orchestra** (www.snjo.co.uk), which plays several times a year at the Queens Hall, is worth a peek. But there's plenty of note on a grassroots level, from bands such as **Trio AAB**, **Salsa Celtica** and **Trianglehead** and from roving musicians like saxophonist **Konrad Wiszniewski**, trumpeter **Colin Steele** and guitarist **Haftor Medbøe**.

Venues

Eighty Queen Street

80 Queen Street, New Town (226 5097/www.eighty-queen-street.com). Princes Street buses. **Gigs** 9pm Wed; 2pm, 9pm Sat; 2pm Sun. **Admission** free. **Credit** MC, V. **Map** p326/p330 E6.
This spacious cellar bar offers regular sets of unobtrusive modern jazz, with guest artistes often featuring on Saturdays and mellow, acoustic sounds on Sunday afternoons. It's worth dropping by on Wednesdays for the well-established open sessions.

Jazz Bar

1a Chambers Street, Old Town (220 4298/www.the jazzbar.co.uk). Nicolson Street–North Bridge buses. **Gigs** from 9pm Mon-Wed, Fri; from 10.30pm Thur; from 3.30pm, 9pm Sat, Sun. **Admission** free-£5. **Credit** MC, V. **Map** p331 J8.
One of the vicitims of the massive Old Town fire of 2002 was the Bridge Jazz Bar on Cowgate. Proprietor Bill Kyle turned to the local jazz scene and asked for their help backing a new venture to replace the much-loved old place; aficionados dug deep, and the Jazz Bar duly arrived on Chambers Street. There's jazz here seven nights a week, Kyle bringing in players from near and far to provide the entertainment.

Jazz Centre at the Lot

4-6 Grassmarket, Old Town (467 5200/www.jazz centre.co.uk). Bus 2, 23, 27, 28, 42, 45. **Gigs** 8.30pm Wed, Thur; from 7.30pm Fri, Sat. **Admission** £7-£12. **Credit** MC, V. **Map** p330 G8, p336 C4.
Assembly Direct (www.jazzmusic.co.uk), the pro-moters behind the Edinburgh International Jazz Festival, left their previous haunt at Henry's Cellar Bar to set up an altogether classier jazz venue at this converted church. Better-known faces from the Scottish jazz scene mix with more exotic imports from Europe and the US.

Nightclubs

The late late show.

Espionage. *See p236.*

Fevered obituaries were penned for Edinburgh's club scene after the 2006 closure of the city's minimally named Venue. Far more than just another after-hours haunt, the Calton Hill hangout played host to innumerable influential club nights during its near two-decade history, and gave bands such as the Stone Roses, Radiohead and Coldplay their Scottish debuts. The recent closure of the Honeycomb and the continued question marks surrounding the future of **Studio 24** have provided further ammunition for those who favour Glasgow's rightly celebrated nightlife. Many have recently been quick to decry Edinburgh as a social wilderness. But while the city's reputation might suffer in comparison with that of its West Coast neighbour, locals know how to find the best of a vibrant scene in flux.

INFORMATION AND PRICES
The most comprehensive source of information on the local scene is *The List* (*see p304*). Both the *Skinny*, a free newspaper available in cafés, shops and club venues, and the *Edinburgh Evening News* feature club listings; national papers such as the *Daily Record*, Thursday's *Metro* and the *Herald* (in their Thursday 'Going Out' supplement) offer similar information.

Information on venue websites isn't always up to date, so word of mouth is the best bet when identifying the buzz nights of the week. Ask in record shops such as **Underground Solu'shn** and **Fopp** (for both, *see p205*) or any of the bars detailed below; most will also have an array of flyers.

The admission prices listed in this section should be taken as guidelines rather than gospel: when new nights launch, prices often change. Rates often rise substantially on weekends. Note, too, that opening hours for many of these venues will be extended during August's festival spell.

The best Clubs

For a pre-club drink
Dragonfly. *See p179.*

For all manner of music
Ego. *See p236.*

For a post-club feed
City Café. *See p171.*

Pre-club bars

Almost every corner of the compact and easily traversed centre of Edinburgh seems to hold a style bar or a traditional pub. Among those that make a perfect base from which to embark on an evening's clubbing are the **City Café** (*see p171*), a faux-American diner with food, pool tables and DJs, and **Dragonfly** (*see p179*), recently voted the most stylish bar in Scotland. **Assembly** (*see p171*) and **Human Be-In** (*see p181*) are equally refined venues, with a DJ-focused appeal that's designed to appeal to the dedicated clubber. **Wash** (11-13 North Bank Street, Old Town, 225 6193) has overcome tacky origins and reinvented itself as a credible retro-styled bar, while the **Street** (*see p224*) has added a touch of colour to the east end since its takeover by Trendy Wendy. The beer garden at the **Outhouse** (*see p179*) finds itself well used by smokers during the summer.

A number of bars are allowed to open beyond the usual curfew of 1am until the club curfew of 3am (or from 3am to 5am during the Festival and the week leading up to Hogmanay). Most offer free admission; those that don't will levy only a minimal door charge. **Pivo** (*see p178*) is the most renowned of these late-openers, its loose Czech theme adding little to what is an already bustling bar. House and techno DJs play seven nights a week. **Opium** (71 Cowgate, 225 8382) offers a similar vibe but with a larger two-level floorspace and rock DJs, while basement lounge **Medina** (*see p170*) is enlivened by a dynamic mix of house and funk. And don't miss the **Opal Lounge** (*see p177*), where the weekly programme of events is highlighted by Tuesday's Motherfunk.

Clubs

In addition to the venues listed in full below, a handful of hangouts operate dual existences as venues for both live music and club nights. Chief among them is **Cabaret Voltaire** (*see p230*), a compact but vibrant space that was recently taken over by the former management of the Liquid Room. Its expanding range of club nights includes **Ultragroove** (house; fortnightly on Saturdays), the **Sugarbeat Club** (electro and bastard house, run by Utah Saints; monthly on Fridays), **Trouble** (nu-jazz and funk; monthly on Fridays), **We Are Electric** (techno and electro; Wednesdays) and band-orientated indie nights **Spies in**

▶ For **gay and lesbian club nights**, see pp225-226.

the **Wires** (monthly on Thursdays) and **I Fly Spitfires** (monthly on Sundays).

The **Liquid Room** itself (*see p231*) continues to thrive on a repertoire of long-running and well-established nights. Chief among them are indie and alternative shindig **Evol** (Fridays), pumping monthly house night **Progression** (Saturdays) and the utterly unique blend of comedy, cheese and cheap drinks that makes up Thursday's **Snatch Social**, hosted by Harry Ainsworth (aka Garth Cruickshank, winner of the Perrier Best Newcomer award in 2001).

The newly refurbished **Henry's Cellar Bar** (*see p231*) has ditched the jazz and broadened its musical remit in recent times. The live music here tends to be more experimental these days, and the club nights are often just as interesting. Goths and metalheads would do well to investigate the nights at **Studio 24** (*see p231*), though it's presently under threat of closure due to complaints from neighbours. The **Subway** (*see p231*) is used by a number of enterprising promoters. And keep your eyes peeled for a trio of nights that, in mid 2006, were all looking for new homes following the closure of the Venue: '60s-themed gig **Mondo A-Go-Go**, drum 'n' bass club **Xplicit** and house shindig **Tokyoblu**. Check local listings for details.

Bongo Club

37 Holyrood Road, Old Town (558 7604/www.the bongoclub.co.uk). Nicolson Street–North Bridge buses. **Open** times vary. **Admission** £3-£9. **No credit cards. Map** p331 K7.

A convergence point for the city's aspirant music, art and club scenes, the Bohemian Bongo moved to the former Edinburgh University students' union building in 2003. More or less anything goes at this café-venue: the calendar usually features a mix of eclectic club nights (reggae at Messenger Sound System, hip-hop at Headspin, punky noise at Fast) the occasional gig (look out for Scottish Hobo Society nights, which draw the cream of local performers) and all manner of other odds and sods. The venue is used for comedy during the Fringe.

Caves

12 Niddry Street South, Old Town (557 9933/ www.undergroundedinburgh.com). Bus 35/Nicolson Street–North Bridge buses. **Open** times vary. **Admission** prices vary. **No credit cards. Map** p331 J7

Though it's mostly used for corporate parties, one-off themed nights and, in August, Fringe shows, this atmospheric, vaulted venue under the Old Town's South Bridge is occasionally hired out by club promoters, most notably for monthly funk, Latin and afrobeat fiesta Departure Lounge (www.departure lounge.me.uk). Once seen, the place is certainly not forgotten: the interior is spectacular.

Arts & Entertainment

Citrus Club

40-42 Grindlay Street, South Edinburgh (622 7086/
www.citrus-club.co.uk). Bus 1, 2, 10, 11, 15, 15A,
16, 17, 23, 24, 27, 34, 35, 45. **Open** 11pm-3am
Wed, Thur, Sat; 10.30pm-3am Fri. **Admission**
free-£5. **No credit cards. Map** p330 E8, p336 A4.
At this cheap and cheerful mainstay of the
Edinburgh nightlife scene, located just off Lothian
Road, regular nights Tease Age (indie), Planet Earth
(1980s) and Genetic (alt-rock) have been providing
bargain-minded clubbers with predictable thrills for
some years now.

Ego

14 Picardy Place, Broughton (478 7434/www.
clubego.co.uk). Playhouse buses. **Open** *Club*
nights vary. **Admission** £2-£10. **No credit cards.**
Map p327 J5.
The ground floor of this elegantly appointed ex-
casino and dancehall plays host to a number of fine
nights, including numerous gay nights (*see p226*).
More alternative adventures can be found in the
downstairs Cocteau Lounge, with 1960s-slanted
night Modern Lovers and the tremendously rowdy,
band-focused Goulag Beat. The main room is in the
venue's former ballroom, while the courtyard out
back is one of Edinburgh's plushest smoking zones.

Espionage

4 India Buildings, Victoria Street, Old Town
(477 7007/www.espionage007.co.uk). Bus 2, 23,
27, 41, 42. **Open** 7pm-3am daily. **Admission** free.
No credit cards. Map p330 G8, p336 D4.

This nightclub-and-bars complex on Victoria Street
extends over five levels. The upper stories house the
Lizard Lounge bar, the middle level contains the
Moroccan-themed Kasbar, while the lower floors are
rather clubbier. Drinks promos and long hours draw
a student-heavy, up-for-it crowd. **Photo** *p233.*

Massa

36-39 Market Street, Old Town (226 4224).
Bus 36/Nicolson Street–North Bridge buses.
Open 10.30pm-3am Mon, Wed, Sun; 8pm-3am
Thur; 10pm-3am Fri, Sat. **Admission** free-£5.
No credit cards. Map p330 H7, p336 E3.
It may have lost out on the hugely enjoyable Tackno
night to rival Ego (*see above*), but Massa is still one
of the more popular watering holes for weekenders
who don't pick their clubs by genres. Admission is
normally cheap, and drinks won't break the bank.

Wee Red Bar

Edinburgh College of Art, Lauriston Place, South
Edinburgh (office 229 1442/bar 229 1003/www.wee
redbar.co.uk). Bus 2, 23, 27. **Open** *Club nights*
10.30pm-3am Fri; 11pm-3am Sat. **Admission** £3-£5.
No credit cards. Map p330 F9.
The bijou, scarlet-painted students' union at the
Edinburgh College of Art has played host to indie
and '60s club nights so busy you could believe you're
frugging your way into a triptastic movie. The Egg,
held every Saturday, is possibly the city's finest
indie disco. Every Friday at 6pm during term-time,
there's a free get-ready-for-the-weekend showcase
of local alternative talent.

Massa.

Sport & Fitness

Welcome to the unlikely home of floodlit horse racing and one-day cricket.

It's not easy being green: fans of **Hibernian FC**. *See p238.*

Is Edinburgh's sport circuit any good? Ask a jogger who's just turned in a personal best at one of the mass participation races, or a bike rider fresh from completing the annual charity cycle ride to St Andrews in Fife, and the reply is likely to be in the affirmative. But ask a fan of the **Edinburgh Gunners** rugby team, lost in the immensity of Murrayfield Stadium, or a **Hibernian** supporter grumbling into his pint about the talent that's left the club in recent years, and things might not be so clear-cut. Even followers of **Heart of Midlothian** football club are in two minds: glad that their club is in the

running for the big prizes after some fallow years, but concerned about its massive debt, held at their owner's bank in Lithuania.

In football terms, Edinburgh isn't London or Barcelona. In club rugby terms, it's not even Leicester or Bath, and Scotland aren't going to beat Australia or England at cricket any time soon. But the city does offer some lively football spectacles, whether local derbies or visits from Celtic and Rangers. International rugby matches at Murrayfield are stirring events; and the national cricket team is improving.

There's just as much for the participant as for the spectator, thanks to the accessibility of green spaces and the profusion of gyms and fitness centres. Down the coast at Pease Bay, past Dunbar, daring souls even go surfing. **SportScotland** (www.sportscotland.org.uk), has more information about local events, clubs and governing bodies, while extreme sports are covered at www.godoscotland.com.

The best Sports

For adrenalin
The skyride at the **Ratho Adventure Centre**. *See p241.*

For appearance
The stainless-steel pool at the Scotsman Hotel's **Escape Club**. *see p53.*

For atmosphere
Hearts v Hibs. *See p238.*

Spectator sports

Cricket

Cricket has taken giant strides since Scotland joined the International Cricket Council (ICC) in 1994. The national team played in the English county set-up for three seasons from 2003, and wins in the ICC Intercontinental Cup (2004) and the ICC Trophy (2005) saw them rise high enough in the global rankings to achieve one-day international status and a guaranteed berth in the 2007 World Cup. Most matches are played at the small but civilised **Grange** (Portgower Place, 332 2148, www.cricketscotland.com); the season runs from April to August.

Football

Edinburgh's two football teams, **Heart of Midlothian** (Hearts) and **Hibernian** (Hibs), hail from opposite ends of the city: respectively, Gorgie in the west and Leith in the north-east. While the derbies are always passionate affairs, there's less of the bigotry that has plagued football in Glasgow. Hearts have been the stronger side of late, finishing second in the Scottish Premier League in 2005/6 and collecting the Scottish Cup for only the third time since World War II. Hibs, meanwhile, lack the financial backing that new owner

Vladimir Romanov has brought to Hearts (*see below*), and have struggled to keep pace with their rivals. The football season runs from August to May.

Heart of Midlothian FC

Tynecastle Stadium, McLeod Street, West Edinburgh (0870 787 1874/www.heartsfc.co.uk). Bus 1, 2, 3, 3A, 4, 22, 25, 30, 33, 44, 44A. **Open** *Shop* 9.30am-5.30pm Mon-Fri; 9.30am-3pm match days. *Ticket office* 10am-5pm Mon-Fri; 10am-2pm Sat; 10am-KO match days. **Tickets** £6-£35. **Credit** AmEx, MC, V. Hearts have been operating at close to capacity since their upturn in fortune in 2005, so getting tickets on matchdays might prove tricky. Book ahead, particularly for matches against Celtic, Rangers and Hibs. European ties are played at Murrayfield (*see p239*).

Hibernian FC

Easter Road Stadium, 12 Albion Place, Leith (661 2159/tickets 661 1875/www.hibernianfc.co.uk). Bus 1, 34, 35, 39. **Open** *Shop* 9am-5pm Mon-Sat. *Ticket office* 9am-5pm Mon,Tue, Thur, Fri; 10am-5pm Wed; 9am-3pm Sat; 9am-KO match days. **Tickets** £10-£25. **Credit** AmEx, MC, V.

The Romanov dynasty

Heart of Midlothian FC was in deep trouble in 2005. Years of overspending had resulted in huge debts, and the board was thinking of selling the team's Tynecastle ground. Although the team finished in the top half of the Scottish Premier League that season, the mood was grim. Then along came a Baltic businessman called Vladimir Romanov, and things started to happen.

Born in Russia but brought up in Lithuania, Romanov built a business empire that encompassed banking, textiles and metals just as the USSR fell apart, making him a multi-millionaire. He's also a keen football fan, and Hearts were only too pleased to find a backer who could help dig them out of their financial hole.

Romanov's first radical move was to replace manager John Robertson, former striker and club hero, with George Burley, who had experience of managing in England. New signings from the Baltic and Eastern Europe joined a decent core of Scottish internationals, and the team got off to a flier at the start of the 2005/6 season: in late October they stood at the top of the league, undefeated in the campaign.

But when Romanov finally assumed total control of the club, things quickly grew sour. Burley left due to 'irreconcilable differences', followed soon after by the club's chairman

and chief executive. Burley's replacement, former Arsenal and England player Graham Rix, lasted only four months before being peremptorily sacked with Hearts struggling to maintain their form. Rumours flew about Romanov's interference in team affairs, and they hardly abated when he hired Valdas Ivanauskas to be his fourth manager in the space of a year; Ivanauskas was formerly the coach at Lithuania's FBK Kaunas, another club in which Romanov has an interest. But despite all the turmoil, the team still managed to finish second in the league, nabbing a Champions League qualifying-round spot in the process, and lifted the Scottish Cup.

There's no doubt that Romanov is in total control. His Lithuanian bank, Ukios Bankas, holds the club's considerable debt, and his son Roman has been installed as Hearts' chairman. The nagging question, though, is why? Competing against Rangers and Celtic will always be difficult; Champions League football is not guaranteed; Scottish football has limited television revenues; and paying top wages with average crowds of just under 17,000 doesn't add up. Many Hearts fans are resigned to enjoying the ride, while some opposing teams' supporters have been quick to conclude that Romanov will get bored soon enough and the club will be doomed. For the time being, though, the saga continues...

Hibs may not have the spending power of their city rivals, but the side has played some thrilling football of late, and is well established in the top half of the Scottish Premier League. Stadium capacity is only around 17,500 and season ticket sales have been buoyant lately; buy tickets in advance, especially for games against Hearts, Celtic and Rangers.

Golf

Golf was born in Scotland, and the historic courses here regularly host major tournaments. **Muirfield** (www.muirfield.org.uk) in East Lothian is home to the Honourable Company of Edinburgh Golfers, which can trace its roots back to 1744. The 2007 Open will be held at **Carnoustie**, near Dundee (www.carnoustie golflinks.co.uk); two years later it'll be at **Turnberry** in Ayrshire (www.turnberry.co. uk). For more on playing golf, *see p240*.

Horse racing

These are exciting times for the city's racing aficionados. Just outside the city's eastern boundary, **Musselburgh** (665 2859, www. musselburgh-racecourse.co.uk) is currently constructing a £9-million floodlit, all-weather track. Protests slowed the project, but it should be up and running in 2007. Elsewhere, there are courses at **Ayr** (01292 264179, www.ayr-racecourse.co.uk), **Hamilton Park** (01698 283806, www.hamilton-park.co.uk), **Kelso** (01668 280800, www.kelso-races.co.uk), and **Perth** (01738 551597, www.perth-races.co.uk). See www.scottishracing.co.uk for more.

Ice hockey

The **Edinburgh Capitals** finished bottom of the Elite League in season 2005/6, prompting the damning chant: 'You're even worse than Basingstoke'. However, some interesting player signings and a league expansion mean things may get better soon. The team play at the 3,800-capacity Murrayfield Ice Rink (Riversdale Crescent, 313 2977, www.edinburgh-capitals. com); the season runs from September to April.

Rugby union

Scottish rugby is currently facing two very different problems. In international terms, a shrinking pool of potential players has meant Scotland has lagged behind England and France: the national side has won the Five (now Six) Nations tournament, held from February to April, just once since 1990. Despite this, though, support is still as strong as ever. International matches at 67,500-capacity **Murrayfield Stadium** (West Edinburgh,

346 5100, www.scottishrugby.org) still draw sell-out crowds; try and buy tickets well ahead. Assuming there's no big match that day, stadium tours (£5) are offered at 2.30pm from Monday to Friday; call 7346 5044 to book.

Scottish club rugby has been looking for a way forward since the game went professional in the mid 1990s. Traditionally, clubs were based either in small communities (in the Borders, say, where rugby is the leading sport) or tied to fee-paying schools, but the system has struggled to retain its relevance of late. The relatively recent creation of a few professional 'super clubs' may have made organisational sense, but they haven't attracted much interest.

Along with the Border Reivers and Glasgow Warriors, the **Edinburgh Gunners** (346 5252, www.scottishrugby.org/pro-rugby/edinburgh-gunners) take on teams from Ireland and Wales in the Celtic League from September to May. They play at Murrayfield but draw small crowds; advance ticket purchase isn't necessary.

Active sports

Curling

Curling has a dedicated (if small) following, and interest has grown since Britain's success in the 2002 Olympics. Whether you're an experienced player or a novice looking for an introduction, the **Royal Caledonian Curling Club** is the best starting point (333 3003, www. royalcaledoniancurlingclub.org).

Cycling

The velodrome at Meadowbank Sports Centre (*see p241*) is home to the **Scottish Cyclists' Union** (652 0187, www.scuonline.org), which has details of clubs and races all over the country. The city has an annual bike week each June (www.bikeweekedinburgh.info); in the same month there's a sponsored bike ride to St Andrews in aid of the leprosy charity Lepra (www.lepra.org.uk). **Spokes**, the Lothian Cycle Campaign (313 2114, www.spokes.org.uk) and the **Edinburgh Bicycle Cooperative** (331 5010, 228 3565, www.edinburghbicycle.com) both offer information on cycling in Edinburgh and the surrounding area. For details of bike routes on old train lines, *see p125* **Pedal power**; for more on cycling in general, go to www.sustrans.org. Both **Biketrax** (7-11 Lochrin Place, South Edinburgh, 228 6633, www.biketrax.co.uk) and **Cycle Scotland** (29 Blackfriars Street, Old Town, 556 5560, www.cyclescotland.co.uk) offer bike rentals; depending on the bike, expect to pay around £10-£20 a day or £50-£90 a week.

Arts & Entertainment

Golf

Scotland is the home of golf, something readily apparent from a glance at a map of Edinburgh: there are more than 30 courses near the city centre and dozens more within easy driving distance. The more prestigious courses are very popular with American golfing tourists and well-heeled day-trippers from London. While there are a few snooty establishments, the majority welcome visitors with open arms.

Wherever you play, don't expect just to turn up and get a tee time: always book in advance. Prices listed in this section are for peak season, but discounted green fees may be available in winter. If you're hoping to hire clubs, be sure to bring a credit card to act as a deposit. Casual golfers may enjoy **Bruntsfield Links**, a fun pitch-and-putt course adjacent to the Meadows.

Braid Hills

22 Braid Hills Approach, South Edinburgh (447 6666/www.edinburghleisure.co.uk). Bus 11, 15, 15A. **Open** dawn-dusk daily. **Green fee** £18 Mon-Fri; £22 Sat, Sun. **Club hire** £16. **Credit** MC, V.
This pair of tricky municipal courses represent one of the city's best golfing bargains. Situated against the backdrop of the Pentland Hills to the south and the Firth of Forth to the north, Braids One provides perhaps the most stunning views in Edinburgh. Book at least a week in advance.

Duddingston

Duddingston Road West, Arthur's Seat (661 7688/www.duddingston-golf.com). Bus 4, 42, 44, 44A, 45. **Open** dawn-dusk daily. **Green fee** £38. **Club hire** £15. **Credit** MC, V.
A demanding, tree-lined course set in undulating parkland south-east of Arthur's Seat. The Braid Burn (stream) winds throughout the course, and is in play on a disturbing number of holes.

Lothianburn

106a Biggar Road, Hillend, South Edinburgh (445 2206/www.lothianburngc.co.uk). Bus 4, 15, 15A. **Open** dawn-dusk daily. **Green fee** £19.50 Mon-Fri; £25 Sat, Sun. **Club hire** £12.50. **Credit** MC, V.
A swooping, testing hillside course perched around 900ft (270m) above sea level, again affording great views of the city. One of the cheaper private courses in or near the city.

Muirfield

Duncur Road, Muirfield, Gullane (01620 842123/www.muirfield.org.uk). **Open** dawn-dusk Tue, Thur. **Green fee** £145-£180. **Club hire** call for details. **Credit** MC, V.
It's possible to follow in the footsteps of Tiger by playing one of the world's finest links courses. But visitors are only allowed two days a week, which limits the opportunities for bookings, and a single round is very expensive indeed.

Murrayfield

43 Murrayfield Road, West Edinburgh (337 3479/www.murrayfieldgolfclub.co.uk). Bus 12, 13, 26, 31. **Open** 8am-4.30pm Mon-Fri. **Green fee** £35. **Club hire** £15. **Credit** AmEx, MC, V.
Murrayfield's handsome 18-hole course is set around Corstorphine Hill to the west of the city. Visitors must book in advance.

Musselburgh Links Old Golf Club

Balcarres Road, Musselburgh (665 5438/www.musselburgholdlinks.co.uk). Bus 30. **Open** dawn-dusk daily. **Green fee** £9/9 holes; £18/18 holes. **Club hire** £15-£25. **Credit** MC, V.
It's worth a visit here simply to pay homage to the world's oldest active golf course. You can even hire a set of hickory clubs and guttie balls for a taste of the 19th-century game.

Prestonfield

6 Priestfield Road North, Prestonfield (667 8597/www.prestonfieldgolf.com). Bus 2, 14, 30, 33. **Open** dawn-dusk daily. **Green fee** £29 Mon-Fri; £35 Sat, Sun; £39 day ticket. **Club hire** £10. **Credit** MC, V.
A not too taxing scenic parkland course within easy reach of the city centre.

St Andrews

West Sands Road, St Andrews, Fife (01334 466666/www.standrews.org.uk). **Open** dawn-dusk daily. **Green fee** varies according to course & time of year. **Club hire** £20-£30. **Credit** AmEx, MC, V.
The world's most famous golf complex is only a 50-mile drive from Edinburgh. There are six courses here (a seventh should open in 2007), as well as non-members' clubhouses and a driving range. For the Old Course, the minimum handicap is 24 (men) and 36 (women); the course is booked up months in advance, though some slots are available daily via a lottery system. The other four 18-hole courses can all be booked online (reserve at least one month ahead except for Saturday play, which can only be booked 24 hours ahead); reservations aren't accepted on the nine-hole Balgove course.

Gyms & fitness centres

In addition to the gyms detailed in full below, there are also extensive fitness facilities at the **Craiglockhart Tennis & Sports Centre** (*see p242*). The über-stylish **One Spa** (*see p64*) also has a pool and workout facilities.

Holmes Place

Omni Centre, Greenside Place, Calton Hill (550 1650/www.holmesplace.com). Playhouse buses. **Open** 6.30am-10.30pm Mon-Fri; 8am-8pm Sat, Sun. **Rates** members only; phone for details. **Credit** AmEx, MC, V. **Map** p327 J5.
This stylish members-only complex offers separate male and female sauna and steam rooms, spa baths, a health and beauty clinic, and a restaurant. The centrepiece is the 25m stainless steel swimming pool.

Braid Hills One. *See p240.*

LivingWell

89 Newcraighall Road, East Edinburgh (657 6800/ www.livingwell.com). Bus 30. **Open** 6am-10pm Mon-Fri; 8.30am-8pm Sat, Sun. **Rates** members only; phone for details. **Credit** AmEx, MC, V.

This club has a serious pool and well-equipped gym, plus saunas and steam rooms. A smaller LivingWell is attached to the Hilton Caledonian (*see p60*).

Meadowbank Sports Centre

139 London Road, Abbeyhill, Leith (661 5351/ www.edinburghleisure.co.uk). Bus 4, 5, 15, 15A, 19, 26, 34, 44, 44A, 45. **Open** 7.30am-10pm daily. **Rates** vary. **Credit** MC, V.

Meadowbank has facilities for athletics, badminton, squash, basketball and football, as well as a velodrome. There are classes for children, adults and the over-50s, in everything from archery to martial arts.

Pleasance Sports Centre

46 Pleasance, South Edinburgh (650 2585/www. sport.ed.ac.uk/facilities/pleasance). Nicolson Street–North Bridge buses. **Open** 7.30am-9.30pm Mon-Fri; 8.50am-5.30pm Sat; 9.50am-5.30pm Sun. **Rates** *Non-members* £4/session; £2 concessions. *Membership* call for details. **Credit** MC, V. **Map** p331 K8.

The University of Edinburgh's sports centre has an impressive gym and sports injury centre, plus badminton, squash, basketball facilities and more. Non-students can pay a day fee or take out membership.

Ice-skating

Murrayfield Ice Rink

Riversdale Crescent, West Edinburgh (337 6933/ www.murrayfieldicerink.co.uk). Bus 12, 26, 31. **Open** 2.30-4.30pm, 7-9pm Mon, Tue, Thur; 2.30-4.30pm, 7.30-10pm Wed; 2.30-4.30pm, 7.30-10.30pm Fri; 10am-noon, 2.30-4.30pm, 7.30-10.30pm Sat; 2.30-4.30pm Sun. **Admission** (includes skate hire) £4-£6. **No credit cards.**

Home to the Edinburgh Capitals ice hockey team (*see p239*), this large rink is also used for public skating sessions and curling. Disco skating sessions on Friday and Saturday nights attract a young crowd; family sessions take place on Thursday evenings and Saturday mornings; and Sundays from noon to 1.45pm are set aside for learn-to-skate sessions.

Rock climbing

Meadowbank Sports Centre (*see above*) has an old-fashioned, mainly brick climbing wall.

Alien Rock

8 Pier Place, Leith (552 7211/www.alienrock.co.uk). Bus 10, 11, 16, 32. **Open** *Summer* noon-10pm Mon-Fri; 10am-7pm Sat, Sun. *Winter* noon-11pm Mon-Thur; noon-10pm Fri; 10am-9pm Sat, Sun. **Admission** £5.50-£6.50; £4-£6 concessions. **Credit** MC, V. **Map** p324 U1.

Located in a former church, Alien Rock offers a 30ft (10m) surface, 40 top-ropes and 12 lead lines, with ten different walls and ever-changing routes. All equipment can be hired, including footwear, though novices will need to take an introductory course. The Alien 2 centre offers freestyle climbing ('bouldering') over 300sq m of wall space.

Other locations: Alien 2, 23-53 West Bowling Green Street, Leith (552 7211).

Ratho Adventure Centre

South Platt Hill, Ratho, Newbridge (333 6333). Bus X48, then 10min along canal. **Open** *Arena* 2-10pm Mon-Fri; 10am-6.30pm Sat, Sun. **Admission** *Arena* £8-£11; concessions £6.50. *Skyride* £8; concessions £6. **Credit** MC, V.

This multi-million-pound climbing arena ran into financial problems just five months after it launched in late 2003, but by summer 2006 was in the final stages of being taken over by Edinburgh Leisure.

A temporary closure was planned for autumn 2006, before a relaunch later in the year. Based in an old quarry in West Lothian, it's a hugely ambitious facility, with indoor and outdoor surfaces, freestanding boulders, a suspended assault course and more. If you're not up for scaling the walls, there's the Skyride, an aerial ropes adventure challenge.

Skiing

Midlothian Snowsports Centre

*Biggar Road, Hillend (445 4433/http://ski.
midlothian.gov.uk). Bus 4, 15, 15A.* **Open** *May-Aug*
9.30am-9pm Mon-Fri; 9.30am-7pm Sat, Sun. *Sept-Apr*
9.30am-9pm Mon-Sat; 9.30am-7pm Sun. **Rates** *Main
slope/nursery slopes* £8 first hr, £3.30 per extra hr;
£5.40 concessions, £2.30 per extra hr. *Lessons* £11.60/
£7.60 1hr; £23.20/£15.20 2hr. *Snowboarding 2hr open
class* £24.70/£16.70. **Credit** MC, V.
Situated just south of Edinburgh, the Midlothian Centre is in proud possession of the longest artificial ski slope in Europe, measuring 1,150ft (400m), as well as a jump slope and learning slopes. Prices include the hire of boots, skis and poles. There's a club for 7-12s, Sno'Cats, on Saturdays.

Swimming

Aside from those in gyms and fitness centres (*see p240*), public pools are run by Edinburgh Leisure (www.edinburghleisure.co.uk). The website details prices and opening times for 11 pools, from the serious, competition-sized **Royal Commonwealth** (21 Dalkeith Road, South Edinburgh, 667 7211) to the fun-oriented **Leith Waterworld** (377 Easter Road, Leith, 555 6000) and the Victorian **Glenogle Swim Centre** (Glenogle Road, Stockbridge, 343 6376).

Tennis

Craiglockhart Tennis & Sports Centre

*177 Colinton Road, Craiglockhart (443 0101/
www.edinburghleisure.co.uk). Bus 4, 10, 27, 45.*
Open 7am-11pm Mon-Fri; 9am-10pm Sat, Sun.
Rates phone for details. **Credit** MC, V.
Scotland's most comprehensive tennis centre has six indoor and eight outdoor courts, and provides coaching to all standards. The sports centre has a fitness room, badminton and squash courts, and a crèche. It also runs step and aerobics classes.

Meadows Tennis Courts

*East Meadows, Melville Drive, South Edinburgh
(444 1969). Bus 41, 42.* **Open** phone for details.
Rates £4-£7/hr. **No credit cards. Map** p331 J10.
Open each year from April to September, the facility at the Meadows has 16 tar courts.

Track & field

Most formal athletic activities are organised around the **Meadowbank Sports Centre** (*see p241*). **Edinburgh Leisure** (650 1001, www.edinburghleisure.co.uk) has details of other activities and venues, while **SportScotland** (317 7200, www.sportscotland.org.uk) holds a database of Scottish sports bodies. The city has plenty of green spaces for joggers, including the **Meadows** (*see p125*) and **Holyrood Park** (*see p118*). Mass-participation runs include the **BUPA Great Edinburgh Run** each May (www.greatrun.org), and the **Race for Life** (www.raceforlife.org) and **Seven Hills of Edinburgh** in June (www.seven-hills.org.uk).

Midlothian Snowsports Centre.

Theatre & Dance

August's drama glut gives the city a year-round taste for the theatrical.

Theatre

Edinburgh provides endless opportunities to stumble across theatre, or something like it, whenever you least expect. Whether it's exotic outdoor performances on George Street at **Hogmanay** (*see p209*), educational shows in the Royal Botanic Garden during the **Science Festival** (*see p208*) or the explosion of buskers on the High Street during the **Fringe** (*see pp41-50*), there's always some curious event or other on the horizon. And then, of course, there are the more straightforward indoor performances staged on the **Edinburgh International Festival** (*see pp41-50*) in August, not to mention the high-quality junior entertainment provided by the **Bank of Scotland International Children's Theatre Festival** in May and the **Puppet Animation Festival** in April (for both, *see p214*).

The vast majority of temporary venues that spring up during August revert to other functions for the remainder of the year, but a handful of theatres and arts centres keep things ticking over. The city's two main producing houses, the **Traverse** (for the new and untried) and the **Royal Lyceum** (for the more established), sit back-to-back near the Usher Hall (*see p228*) in the self-styled arts quarter by Lothian Road. If you're looking for large-scale mainstream entertainment, it's most likely you'll end up at the **King's**, the **Playhouse** or the **Edinburgh Festival Theatre**. The city lacks a dedicated permanent space for up-and-coming performers. However, many innovative companies are based here (*see p244* **Coming up**) and often stage shows in

less conventional theatres. Among those worth tracking are **Grid Iron** (www.gridiron.org.uk) and **Highway Diner** (www.highwaydiner.org).

The Traverse, once housed in a down-at-heel corner of the Grassmarket, but now found beneath a swanky Cambridge Street office block, is starting to form tighter bonds with a new generation of theatre-makers by offering £5,000 bursaries to emerging companies (in addition to its support of new playwrights). It'll be fascinating to see who emerges from this process to join the ranks of established local companies such as **Boilerhouse** (www.boilerhouse.org.uk), with its enterprising large-scale street-theatre ethic, and **Stellar Quines** (www.stellarquines.com), with its high-quality pro-female drama programme.

You may well get the chance to see stars treading the Edinburgh boards, but the theatre scene here is not driven by celebrity or glamour. Audiences are just as likely to be attracted to the standard of the ensemble in question, or the promise of a new work by one of Scotland's many celebrated playwrights (among them David Greig, Liz Lochhead, David Harrower, John Clifford, Henry Adam, Douglas Maxwell and Gregory Burke). In this regard, theatre is keenly attuned to the broader cultural life of Scotland and, at its best, can provide an illuminating snapshot of a nation.

INFORMATION & TICKETS

The List remains the best source for theatre listings in Edinburgh, but it's also worth taking a look at www.scottishtheatres.com, run by the Federation of Scottish Theatres, and the student-run site at www.scottishtheatre.co.uk. Tickets for many major venues can be booked through **Ticketline** (0870 444 5556, www.ticketline.co.uk) or **Ticketmaster** (0870 534 4444, www.ticketmaster.co.uk).

The best Theatre

For high drama and low farce
Royal Lyceum Theatre. *See p246*.

For a play for today
Traverse. *See p246*.

For tales tall and short
Scottish Storytelling Centre. *See p246*.

Venues

For the **Edinburgh Festival Theatre**, which stages some theatrical events, *see p246*.

Bedlam Theatre

11b Bristo Place, Old Town (information 225 9873/ box office 225 9893/www.bedlamtheatre.co.uk). Bus 2, 41, 42. **Box office** from 45mins before performance. **Tickets** £3-£7.50. **Credit** *Festival only* MC, V. **Map** p330 H8.

Coming up

Scots have been talking about its creation since 1819, so it's understandable that the launch of the **National Theatre of Scotland** (www.nationaltheatrescotland.com; *pictured*) in 2006 prompted a collective sigh of relief. The rest of the world took note, too, because this national theatre is unique. It has no building and no permanent company, just a core administrative team that spends its £7.5m budget on celebrating Scottish theatre at large. This it achieves by creating shows in conjunction with other companies, some as co-productions and others as special commissions. The resultant output

encompasses everything from site-specific experiments to mainstage classics and musicals for children.

Freed from the constraints of running a building, the NTS has diversity at its heart. The productions seen in Edinburgh are a case in point, among them a revival of *Elizabeth Gordon Quinn*, Chris Hannan's powerful rent-strike drama; *Roam*, a thrilling show that took place beyond the check-in desks of Edinburgh International Airport; and Gregory Burke's *Blackwatch*, a timely piece of documentary theatre about the old Scottish Regiment.

Still, even before the NTS, Edinburgh was blessed when it came to theatre-makers. Although it is eclipsed by Glasgow in the quantity of activity, it is home to several key playwrights – among them Chris Hannan, David Greig, Zinnie Harris and John Clifford – and many independent companies. Leading the field is **Grid Iron** (*see p243*), which has staged a string of hit performances in places as unlikely as the supposedly haunted Mary King's Close in the Old Town, and a department store. **Highway Diner** (*see p243*) has a similar taste for the unconventional, and once performed to an unsuspecting audience at a Franz Ferdinand gig.

For a more traditional experience, look out for classic drama from **Prime Productions** (www.primeproductions.co.uk), new writing from **Nutshell** (552 7364) and women-centred plays from **Stellar Quines** (*see p243*). Children are also well served, thanks to the brilliant **Licketyspit** (www.licketyspit.com), **Catherine Wheels** (www.catherinewheels.co.uk), and **Wee Stories** (www.weestoriestheatre.org).

The Bedlam Theatre is home to the Edinburgh University Theatre Company, which produces a rolling programme of student drama that can total as many as 40 shows a year. EUTC alumni include Ian Charleson, star of *Chariots of Fire*, actress and TV presenter Daisy Donovan, and Greg Wise, otherwise known as Mr Emma Thompson.

Brunton Theatre

Bridge Street, Musselburgh (665 2240/www.brunton theatre.co.uk). Bus 15, 15A, 26, 30, 44, 44A. **Box office** 10am-7.30pm Mon-Sat (closed 12.30-1pm Sat). **Tickets** £6.50-£12.50. **Credit** MC, V.
A 20-minute bus ride out of town, this comfortable, 300-seat civic theatre produces its own pantomime at Christmas. For the rest of the year, it hosts adult and children's companies on the touring circuit, plus the occasional community show.

Edinburgh Playhouse

18-22 Greenside Place, Calton Hill (0870 606 3424/ www.ticketmaster.co.uk). Playhouse buses. **Box office** *In person* 10am-8pm Mon-Sat (closes 6pm on non-performance days). *By phone* 24hrs daily. **Tickets** £10-£36.50. **Credit** AmEx, MC, V. **Map** p327 J5.
Run by global entertainment conglomerate Clear Channel, the 3,000-seat Playhouse is the regular home for touring West End musicals such as *Mamma Mia!* and *Chitty Chitty Bang Bang*. The Edinburgh International Festival regularly uses the auditorium, the largest of its kind in the UK, for bigger dance and opera productions, while grown-up rock stars and big-name comedians treat the Playhouse as a stopping-off point: Nick Cave, Katie Melua and Ross Noble have all visited recently, and it's apparently Lou Reed's all-time favourite venue.

King's Theatre

2 Leven Street, Tollcross, South Edinburgh (529 6000/www.eft.co.uk). Bus 11, 15, 15A, 16, 17, 23, 45. **Box office** *In person* from 1hr before performance. *By phone* 11am-8pm Mon-Sat (closes 6pm on non-performance days). **Tickets** £7-£21. **Credit** AmEx, DC, MC, V. **Map** p330 F10.

Built in 1905, this elegant old-time institution is managed, along with the Edinburgh Festival Theatre, by the Festival City Theatres Trust. The programme mixes musicals with star-studded serious drama, usually on pre- or post-West End tours. Highlights of recent seasons have included Simon Callow in *Present Laughter* and David Soul starring in *Mack and Mabel*. In 2005, David Harrower's acclaimed play *Blackbird* had its première here, later transferring to London's West End.

North Edinburgh Arts Centre

15a Pennywell Court, Muirhouse (315 2151/ www.northedinburgharts.co.uk). Bus 17, 27, 32, 37, 42. **Box office** 8am-4pm Mon-Fri; 10am-3pm Sat. **Tickets** £3-£8. **No credit cards.**

Tucked away behind one of the least inviting – if not downright scary – shopping arcades in the city, this community centre has a busy programme of small-scale touring productions for children and adults.

Out of the Blue Drill Hall

36 Dalmeny Street, Leith (555 7101/www.outofthe blue.org.uk). Bus 7, 10, 12, 14, 16, 22, 25, 49. **Box office** call for details. **Tickets** call for details. **No credit cards. Map** p327 L2.

Primarily a studio space for scores of artists, Out of the Blue has undergone a £500,000 redevelopment in recent times in order to make it suitable for performances, rehearsals and screenings. It was used in 2005 by the International Festival for the flamboyant Spanish spectacular *Nuts CocoNuts*.

Royal Lyceum

Grindlay Street, South Edinburgh (information 248 4800/box office 248 4848/www.lyceum.org.uk). Bus 1, 2, 10, 11, 15, 15A, 16, 17, 23, 24, 27, 34, 35, 45. **Box office** 10am-7.45pm Mon-Sat (closes 6pm on non-performance days). **Tickets** £1-£21. **Credit** AmEx, MC, V. **Map** p330 E8, p336 A4.

At its peak in the 1970s, the Lyceum was at the vanguard of a renaissance of local theatrical culture, and a breeding ground for leading directors such as Bill Bryden and Richard Eyre. The intervening decades were less radical but audiences remained loyal; since 2003, artistic director David Mark Thomson has built the company into one of the most popular in Scotland. Notable moments include John Clifford's bold translation of Goethe's *Faust* and a pre-*Doctor Who* David Tennant starring in *Look Back in Anger*.

Scottish Storytelling Centre

43-45 High Street, Old Town (0131 557 5724/ www.scottishstorytellingcentre.com). Bus 35/Nicolson Street–North Bridge buses. **Box office** 10am-6pm Mon-Sat; later on performance days. **Tickets** £2-£9. **Credit** MC, V. **Map** P331 J7.

The newly refurbished former Netherbow Arts Centre, located on the Royal Mile, now serves as a home for storytelling, arguably Scotland's most indigenous art form. The venue presents regular storytelling events pitched at all ages, with opportunities both to hear stories and to tell them.

Theatre Workshop

34 Hamilton Place, Stockbridge (226 5425/ www.theatre-workshop.com). Bus 23, 27, 36. **Box office** *Show runs only* 9.30am-5.30pm Mon-Fri. **Tickets** £10; £6 concessions. **Credit** MC, V. **Map** P326 E4.

Those who recall this small, boho establishment as an epicentre of Stockbridge life will be saddened to see how underused it is these days. Once a thriving receiving house of radical touring theatre, the building's focus is now on its own professional company, the first professional mixed physical ability ensemble in Europe. Its shows tackle single-issue politics head-on, from anti-globalisation marches to disabled activism. Aesthetic sensibilities, alas, are often buried in the desire to get the message across.

Traverse Theatre

10 Cambridge Street, South Edinburgh (228 1404/ www.traverse.co.uk). Bus 1, 2, 10, 11, 15, 15A, 16, 17, 23, 24, 27, 34, 35, 45. **Box office** 10am-8pm Mon-Sat (closes 6pm on non-performance days); from 2hrs before performance Sun. **Tickets** £4-£12. **Credit** MC, V. **Map** p330 E8, p336 A3.

Born in the 1960s, the Traverse was first housed in a former brothel on the High Street; a legend was born on its second night when actor Colette O'Neill was accidentally stabbed during a production of Sartre's *Huis Clos*. By the time it moved to its second

home in the Grassmarket, the emphasis on European experimentalism was shifting towards homegrown fare from writers such as John Byrne and Tom McGrath. In 1992, the Traverse moved to its current home, a purpose-built subterranean expanse beneath an office complex. Two performance spaces showcase a lively array of new plays from writers developed by the company – among them David Greig, David Harrower and Douglas Maxwell – as well as a rolling programme of touring shows. In August, it's always one of the hottest spots on the Fringe.

Dance

The fan base for ballet and dance in Edinburgh is a devoted one, but also adventurous enough to appreciate regular visits from the likes of Mark Morris, Nederlands Dans Theater and Michael Clark, as well as Ashley Page's rejuvenated Scottish Ballet. Smaller companies regularly tour to the **Traverse** (*see above*) and the **Brunton** (*see p244*).

Venues

Dance Base

14-16 Grassmarket, Old Town (225 5525/www. dancebase.co.uk). Bus 2, 23, 27, 41, 42. **Box office** 10am-5pm Mon-Fri; 10am-1pm Sat. **Tickets** prices vary. **Credit** MC, V. **Map** p330 G8, p336 C4.

This beautifully airy, purpose-built state-of-the-art venue in the shadow of Edinburgh Castle has become the focal point for the capital's thriving dance community. With four studios housing an extensive programme of classes and workshops, all levels and areas of interest are accommodated. Ever wanted to learn Highland or gumboot dancing? Feldenkrais and Alexander technique? This is the place. Regular performances have yet to happen here, though it's full of life nonetheless.

Edinburgh Festival Theatre

13-29 Nicolson Street, South Edinburgh (529 6000/ www.eft.co.uk). Nicolson Street–North Bridge buses. **Box office** *In person* 10am-8pm Mon-Sat (closes 6pm on non-performance days); 4pm-start of performance Sun. *By phone* 11am-8pm Mon-Sat (closes 6pm on non-performance days); 4pm-start of performance Sun. **Tickets** £4-£55. **Credit** AmEx, DC, MC, V. **Map** p331 J8.

The EFT began life as the Empire Palace Theatre, playing host to the biggest old-time variety stars during its early years. By the mid-1980s, it was another story: then the run-down Empire bingo hall, it suffered the indignity of staging shows by the likes of trash-sleaze merchants the Cramps. However, in 1994 major restoration turned the EFT into the most opulent of commercial receiving houses, with one of the biggest dance stages in the UK. Its programme is a mix of dance, opera and large-scale musical productions, and it's always a major venue for opera and dance during the Edinburgh International Festival.

Trips Out of Town

Falkirk Wheel. *See pp288-289*.

Getting Started

A Scottish sampler.

Edinburgh's relatively compact size gives the tourist two great advantages. The first is that the city is easy to explore; the second is that it's easy to escape. In less than an hour, you can find yourself in the countryside of East Lothian, the fishing villages of Fife or the cosmopolitan bustle of Glasgow; with a little more time, you can reach corners of Scotland that are the closest Britain comes to genuine wilderness.

In the following pages, we concentrate on **Glasgow**, which has a long-standing and healthy cultural rivalry with Edinburgh. Scotland's biggest city, it's a vibrant place, in the midst of a cultural renaissance that's been building for nigh on 15 years. On a less frenetic note, we highlight the attractions of the **Lothians**, **Stirling**, **Fife** and the **Borders**, and offer hints about how to get further afield.

Most of this section is pitched at the independent traveller. Intrepid visitors will be particularly attracted to the Highlands, ideal terrain for a number of adventure and winter sports. However, if you don't want to strike out alone, there are plenty of organised outings to destinations all around Scotland (*see p291*).

PLANNING A TRIP
The **Edinburgh & Lothians Tourist Board** on Princes Street (*see p298*) can provide information on travel, sightseeing and accommodation throughout Scotland. If you're planning on heading into the wilds, it's worth investing in good maps from **Ordnance Survey** (OS), which has the whole of Great Britain mapped in intimate detail. The two series likely to prove of greatest use are the Landranger (scale 1:50,000) and the Explorer (scale 1:25,000); buy them at **TSO Scotland** (71 Lothian Road, South Edinburgh, 659 7036, www.tso.co.uk) and most major bookshops.

GETTING AROUND
Many of Scotland's more rural regions are ill-served by public transport. Driving is often the best option and sometimes the only option. For details of car hire firms, *see p298*.

That said, the rail system is fairly efficient and provides a network of trains to most of the larger towns. **First Scotrail** (*see p297*) sells a variety of flexible travel passes that allow you to roam by train, bus and ferry, chief among them the **Freedom of Scotland Travelpass** (£96 for four days' travel over an

eight-day period, or £130 for eight days' travel over 15 consecutive days). The **Central Scotland Rover** (£31 for three days' travel over a seven-day period) covers a more limited area. If you're heading to the Highlands, invest in an eight-day **Highland Rover** pass (£62.50 for four days' travel, including ferries to, and bus travel on, Mull and Skye) and discover parts of Scotland that aren't accessible by car.

Bus travel is another possibility, although bear in mind that services in more remote areas may be as infrequent as twice a week. Buses from Edinburgh usually depart from **St Andrew Square Bus Station** (*see p296*).

PRECAUTIONS
Scotland's mountain scenery is one of the country's greatest assets, but is also potentially dangerous for hillwalkers and climbers who do not observe these basic safety precautions.

● Don't overestimate your ability and fitness.
● Always tell someone where you're going and what time you plan to get back.
● Take a map, a compass and a torch.
● Wear suitable footwear and carry waterproof clothing.
● Carry a water bottle and emergency rations.
● Pay close attention to the weather, which can change very quickly; if it looks like turning bad, get off the mountain.

If you're travelling to the Highlands, prepare for midges, tiny flying insects with a voracious appetite for human blood. Midges breed on boggy ground and prefer still days, and are at their worst between late May and early August. No one has yet found a repellent for them that works; however, they are deterred by citronella and herb oils such as thyme or bog myrtle.

The best Trips

For rest
A lazy summer in **East Neuk**. See p290.

For recuperation
Hiking in the **Pentland Hills**. See p287.

For recreation
A few days in **Glasgow**. See pp249-283.

Glasgow

It's certainly bigger than Edinburgh… but is it better?

Gallery of Modern Art.
See p251.

The rain falls on Glasgow two days out of three, the clouds rolling in from the low-pressure systems of the North Atlantic to hang over the Clyde valley. But Glasgow remains undaunted. The town – or 'toon', as the locals have it – has absorbed every shock and adapted to every change without breaking stride. If plagues, fires, cholera epidemics, the boom and bust of colonial trade and the collapse of local industry haven't spoiled the general mood, then a few drops of water will never bring it down.

Glasgow seems to convert adversity and rivalry into energy, continually redefining itself in proud, progressive opposition not only to Edinburgh, its smaller, prettier, bureaucratic senior, but also to London. Once the second city of the British Empire, Glasgow has become an enclave for the cultured and creative, offering its own range of urban diversions and possibilities. Between 1990, when it was nominated European City of Culture, and 1999, when it was appointed UK City of Architecture and Design, Glasgow spent serious time and money on remodelling, redirection and rebranding. A dark period of post-war and post-industrial decline – with poverty and unemployment giving rise to drug addiction, razor gangs and grim council tower blocks – was painstakingly shifted into a brighter future

of high-tech business, service-based commerce and hyperactivity in the arts and media. If anything, the rate of change is accelerating.

These days, the whole town is image-conscious to the point of vanity. At the upper end of the market, there's an infatuation with designer clothing, while at the lower end lies an obsession with curing the natural pallor: the city has more tanning salons per head than anywhere else in the world. Appropriately, then, many of the changes through which the city has gone of late are cosmetic. Older problems haven't been solved: they've just been pushed to outer estates and overspill towns as the centre becomes busily middle-class. Conditions in certain peripheral areas of south and east Glasgow are still defined by abysmal poverty.

Glasgow's history of sectarianism, a lingering product of antagonism between Irish Catholic and Scottish Protestant workers and unions, still finds ugly expression in the ugly 'Old Firm' football clashes (*see p276* **Which side are you on?**). But any fears that the city might be forgetting its long traditions of industriousness, socialism, free-thinking and fun-loving have so far proved unfounded. Glasgow is once again adapting to the times, but its physical character remains essentially unchanged, a central, compact grid of grand, bold architecture exemplified by the magnificent work of Charles Rennie Mackintosh and Alexander 'Greek' Thomson.

Glasgow's personality remains progressive, curious, innovative and wildly sociable. Entertainment is prized and thrillingly indulged every night of the week, without any of the self-consciousness that can often make fashionable city-dwellers reluctant to be seen to have a good time. A Wednesday night in the **Ben Nevis** bar (*see p268*), listening to awesomely talented folk musicians, is just as worthwhile an experience as a Saturday at the **Soundhaus** (*see p279*), tuned to awesomely talented DJs.

While Glasgow's reputation for toughness and drunkenness isn't unjustified, neither are reports of its good humour and friendliness, and the frank, realist brand of *joie de vivre* that permeates the character of the city's residents is infectious. Outsiders often imagine a huge rivalry between Edinburgh and Glasgow, but, in truth, both cities are happy to get on with their own lives in their very different ways. Taken together, they make a scintillating pair.

Sightseeing

The City Centre

The wealth generated by Glasgow's once-dominant place in the world of trade and commerce transformed the semi-rural medieval city into one of the most elegant urban centres in Scotland. It's a small but perfectly formed arrangement of decorative stone canyons: laid out in an easily negotiable grid akin to that found in a modern American city, but definitively Victorian.

The heart of Glasgow is **George Square**, a former swamp first laid out in the late 18th century; it's benefited handsomely from a recent renovation and is now back to something like its best. The square's centrepiece is a soaring statue of Sir Walter Scott, not as grand as the tribute paid to him in Edinburgh's Princes Street Gardens but impressive all the same. Robert Burns, William Gladstone and Queen Victoria are commemorated in other statues around the square. The most notable building is the magnificent **City Chambers** to the east: opened by Queen Victoria in 1888, it's a potent reminder of Glasgow's former importance in the British Empire. The square hosts a year-round programme of public events, including the city's wildly rowdy Hogmanay celebrations (*see p275* **Festivals and events**).

Queen Street station sits at the north-west side of George Square, with Buchanan Street underground immediately adjacent. The main shopping thoroughfare is **Buchanan Street**, home to several major malls and numerous stand-alone stores. The pedestrianised road pulses with activity on weekends.

Following Buchanan Street north past the vast **Buchanan Galleries** mall (*see p271*) and the **Royal Concert Hall** (*see p274*), you'll connect with busy **Sauchiehall Street**, a fairly boring commercial thoroughfare at its eastern extremity but increasingly interesting the further west you walk along it. As you do so, stop in for a snack at the **Willow Tea Rooms** (No.217, 0141 332 0521, www.willowtearooms.co.uk): commissioned by the formidable Kate Cranston, a pioneer of the art tearoom society prevalent in 19th-century Glasgow, it was designed by Charles Rennie Mackintosh and remains a beautiful spot. Close by, the **Centre for Contemporary Arts** (CCA, *see p251*) is housed in a building by Alexander 'Greek' Thomson, Glasgow's other visionary architect, and is now one of the UK's most stylish venues for visual and performance art. This section of Sauchiehall Street is also home to a number of very worthwhile bars and music venues, among them the newly revitalised **ABC** (*see p276*) and **Nice 'n' Sleazy** (*see p267*).

A sharp incline to the north leads up **Garnethill**, a mainly residential area that's the centre of Glasgow's small Chinese community. The **Glasgow School of Art** (*see p252*), Mackintosh's masterpiece, balances on this perilously steep hill; the view south from here takes in the exotic spire of the **St Vincent Street Free Church**, another Thomson construction. Even today, these two great architects still battle for mastery of Glasgow's skyline. Further west are two other notable sights: **Garnethill Synagogue** (127 Hill Street), the oldest Jewish place of worship in the city, and interesting **Tenement House** (*see p252*).

Returning to Buchanan Street, a stroll southwards along it afford access to two of the city's more engaging cultural institutions. To the east, dominating handsome **Royal Exchange Square**, is the **Gallery of Modern Art** (GOMA; *see p251*). And just off to the west on Mitchell Lane – lit by blue streetlamps after dark – is the first public building designed by Charles Rennie Mackintosh, constructed in 1895 to house the offices of the Glasgow *Herald*. An ultramodern makeover has transformed it into the **Lighthouse**, an architecture and design centre (*see p252*).

The Mack daddy

Glasgow's architecture is largely defined by the sudden influx of capital in the Victorian period. Wherever you go in the city, you'll find Grecian fixtures, Renaissance parodies and Baroque stonework. They may seem impressive now, but to critics such as Ruskin and Pugin, they represented the height of arriviste vulgarity. Worse still, the pagan associations were seen as frivolous, effete and out of keeping with mainstream Victorian values. Ruskin encouraged a homegrown architecture that was integrated with nature, and it was his influence that laid the ground for the arrival of **Charles Rennie Mackintosh**.

Mackintosh, born in 1868, was a sickly child who drew thistles and flowers in the countryside while other boys played sports. With the MacDonald sisters and Herbert MacNair, he formed 'the Four', a group of artists influenced by the delicate beauty and exotic minimalism of the Japanoiserie that had begun to circulate in Britain. Mackintosh joined the firm of Honeyman and Keppie as a draughtsman in 1889, where he refined his unique combination of natural light and minimalistic ornamentation on such projects as the Martyrs' School and the Herald Building (now the Lighthouse), becoming a partner in 1901.

Architect, graphic designer, interior decorator, and creator of radical furniture, Mackintosh's singular vision demanded an extraordinary level of integration. He was a pure design auteur, who brought something distinctively his own to everything from spoons to staircases: the first thing that strikes you about his designs is that they are like no one else's. The lightshades in the Glasgow School of Art library are strange cuboid things, while his chairs look distorted enough to have sprung to life from a surrealist painting. The rooms recreated in the Hunterian Museum (see p261) are profoundly interesting due to the tension between minimalism and ornamentation.

Thanks to the ubiquitous Mockintosh lettering, the gift shops selling tourist knick-knacks, and four (at least partly devoted) museums, Mackintosh is everywhere in Glasgow. But despite his ubiquity, it's hard to find many Glaswegians whose interest in his works goes beyond the financial. His dandyish moustache, billowing silk bow tie and general aestheticism don't sit well with their chippy common sense. Indeed, although he was briefly fashionable in his native city, his career ended in disappointment: after the commissions dried up, he turned to the bottle. A Mackintosh festival during 2006 helped raise his profile, as part of the latest push towards achieving World Heritage City status off the back of his work.

Centre for Contemporary Arts (CCA)

350 Sauchiehall Street (0141 352 4900/ www.cca-glasgow.com). Cowcaddens underground. **Open** *Centre* 11am-11pm Tue-Thur; 11am-midnight Fri, Sat; 11am-6pm Sun. *Gallery* 11am-6pm Tue, Wed, Fri-Sun; 11am-8pm Thur. **Admission** *Centre* free. *Gallery* prices vary. **Credit** MC, V. **Map** p332 D2.

Threatened with closure after recent financial problems, a chastened Centre for Contemporary Arts is quietly regaining its strength under its new administrators, the Scottish Arts Council. Part of the CCA's problem – and, simultaneously, the reason it's so essential – is that it's always spurned the populism of GOMA for more challenging work, in terms both of its exhibition programme and its choice of films. The imposing courtyard café, though known locally as 'the prison', is actually a quietly convivial spot, even on a Saturday night; a raucous upstairs bar hosts DJs throughout the week (*see p267*).

Gallery of Modern Art (GOMA)

Queen Street (0141 229 1996/www.glasgow museums.com). Buchanan Street underground/ Queen Street rail. **Open** 10am-5pm Mon-Wed; 10am-8pm Thur; 11am-5pm Fri, Sun; 10am-5pm Sat. **Admission** free. **Map** p333 E4.

The traffic cone now almost permanently attached to the equestrian statue of the Duke of Wellington gives a neat Glaswegian touch to the classical grandeur of GOMA. Since it was built in 1778, the Cunningham Mansion has been used a town house for a tobacco baron and as offices for the Royal Bank of Scotland. Today, it's the second most visited contemporary art gallery in the UK outside London. The permanent collection contains significant works by Euan Uglow, Grayson Perry and Douglas Gordon; it's supplemented by a programme of first-class touring shows. Photo *p249*.

Glasgow School of Art

167 Renfrew Street (0141 353 4500/www.gsa.ac.uk). Cowcaddens underground/Charing Cross rail. **Tours** *April-Sept* 10.30am, 11am, 11.30am, 1.30pm, 2pm, 2.30pm daily. *Oct-Mar* 11am, 2pm Mon-Sat. *Shop open* 10am-5pm Mon-Fri; 10am-1pm Sat. **Admission** £6.50; £4.80 concessions; free under-10s. **Credit** AmEx, MC, V. **Map** p332 D2.
An icon of 20th-century design and arguably the world's first modernist building, Mackintosh's masterpiece is full of surprising details. The best angles are around the façades of the north and west wings. The interior is open only for guided tours, for which reservations are required, but it's well worth booking for a stroll that takes in the extraordinary library and its wonderful lights and desks.

Lighthouse

11 Mitchell Lane (0141 221 6362/www.thelight house.co.uk). Buchanan Street or St Enoch underground/Central Station rail. **Open** 10.30am-5pm Mon, Wed-Sat; 11am-5pm Tue; noon-5pm Sun. **Admission** £3; £1.50 concessions. **Credit** MC, V. **Map** p333 E4.
Tucked away down an alleyway off Buchanan Street, Mackintosh's Glasgow Herald building is now the hypermodern Centre for Architecture, Design & the City, and was central to Glasgow becoming UK City of Architecture and Design in 1999. Several years on, its evolving programme of exhibitions and events continues to make it an exciting part of Glasgow's cultural scene. The well-contextualised Mackintosh Interpretation Centre leads to a daunting helical staircase that offers those fit enough to climb it stunning views over the whole city.

Tenement House

145 Buccleuch Street (0141 333 0183/www.nts. org.uk). Cowcaddens underground/Charing Cross rail. **Open** *Mar-Oct* 1-5pm daily. **Admission** *Tours* £5; £4 concessions; free under-5s. **Credit** AmEx, MC, V. **Map** p332 C2.
The former home of Miss Agnes Toward, an ordinary Glaswegian shorthand typist, offers a remarkable glimpse into Victorian home life, with its bed recesses in the kitchen and lounge and perfectly preserved knick-knacks. An exhibition on the ground floor about tenement life, the clearance of the slums and the city's continuing gentrification gives a real insight into Glasgow's journey.

The Merchant City & around

Spreading away from the south-east of George Square, the **Merchant City** was developed in the 18th century by the city's sugar and tobacco traders, who conducted their business on the nearby River Clyde and built mansions here in order to make their daily commute that much easier. In the 19th century, a number of markets sprung up in the area, before it steadily declined. However, the boom years of the 1990s spurred a renaissance in the area, which is still spawning new bars, cafés, boutiques, arts venues and suitably expensive apartment conversions.

Running east from Royal Exchange Square, **Ingram Street** connects the Merchant City to the centre proper. The street, and those immediately surrounding it, is dotted with high-fashion boutiques such as Ralph Lauren and Cruise (*see p272*); while neighbouring Buchanan Street is dominated by fairly familiar chains, the Merchant City offers more exclusive – and, it follows, expensive – shopping opportunities. A few streets east is **Candleriggs**, home to a number of restaurants and bars. And just past it, sandwiched between Candleriggs and Albion Street south of Ingram Street, is the old **Glasgow City Halls** complex, now enjoying a new lease of life as a concert venue (*see p276*). One of its halls was originally built as a market in the 19th century; its name, the **Old Fruitmarket**, pays homage to its history.

To the south, more or less parallel to Ingram Street, lies the slightly ragged but still imposing **Trongate**. The 16th-century clocktower belongs to vital local playhouse the **Tron Theatre** (*see p280*), originally built as a church. Wandering westwards, Trongate becomes **Argyle Street**, the third and shabbiest of Glasgow's major shopping streets. The **Argyle Arcade**, an airy Victorian glass-roofed passageway lined with jewellers' shops, hooks off Argyle Street to the north and connects with Buchanan Street.

However, there's more of interest to the south: gentrification has been slower to arrive in the roads and alleys below Argyle Street and the Trongate, and Old Glasgow remains appealingly tangible. Nowhere is this more the case than in the three pubs that make up the **Stockwell Triangle** on **Stockwell Street**, chief among them the 250-year-old Scotia Bar (*see p268*). Together, this trio gives off a more palpable, atmospheric sense of Glasgow's history than any of the city's museums. Onwards past the dusty, half-forgotten **Old Wynd** and **New Wynd**, **Chisholm Street** and **Parnie Street** are composed of an eye-catching fusion of red and yellow sandstone tenements and dotted with an unlikely mix of shops: if you want to get a tattoo, browse some rare comics or buy a tropical fish, you're in luck.

Nearby **King Street** is a mini art-district, home to the **Transmission Gallery** (No.45, 0141 552 7141, www.transmissiongallery.org), the **Glasgow Print Studio** (No.22, 0141 552 0704, www.gpsart.co.uk) and the **Street Level Gallery** (No.48, 0141 552 2151, www.street levelphotoworks.org); **Art Exposure** is back along nearby Parnie Street (No.19, 0141 552 7779, www.artexposuregallery.co.uk). Above many of the galleries sit artists' studios. King Street culminates in King's Court and **Mono**, a combination vegan café, microbrewery and record shop. **Paddy's Market**, a rundown palace of junk, lies just over the road.

At the eastern end of the Trongate, at its intersection with High Street, Gallowgate, London Road and Saltmarket, is **Glasgow Cross**. The junction is marked by the seven-storey **Tolbooth Steeple**, formerly part of the city's long-vanished Tolbooth. It's the point at which the City Centre becomes the East End.

The East End

Although Glasgow has redefined itself many times over the centuries, it has tended to do so while moving westwards, leaving a rich vein of history in its wake. From the construction of Glasgow Cathedral in 1136 through to the wealth-driven expansions of the 19th century, the East End essentially *was* Glasgow. And it

is in the East End, with all its adversity and good humour, that the Glaswegian spirit persists most strongly.

Glasgow's origin myth says it was founded at the point where the Molendinar Burn flowed into the Clyde, now the site of the High Court. Opposite the court stands the **McLennan Arch**, which originally formed part of Robert Adam's Assembly Rooms. When the rooms were demolished, local MP James McLennan funded their reconstruction in the Barras. The arch was eventually moved to its present location in 1922, and now marks the entrance to **Glasgow Green**.

Dating back to the 15th century, when King James II designated the land as common grazing ground, Glasgow Green is Europe's oldest public park. It once doubled as fairground and hanging place, although these days, the public events it hosts – such as the **Glasgow Show** and **Proms in the Park** – tend to be rather more sedate. The **People's Palace** and the **Winter Gardens** (*see p254*) are the main permanent attractions on the Green, but don't miss – not that you can, really – the extraordinary **Templeton Carpet Factory**, a colourful Glaswegian version of Venice's Doge's Palace that now houses the **West Brewing Company** (*see p268*).

Just off the Green, where it borders on Greendyke Street, is the **Homes for the Future** development. A cornerstone project of Glasgow's year as the UK City of Architecture and Design, replaced some of the wasted urban

People's Palace. *See p254.*

Trips Out of Town

spaces north of the Green with attractive, imaginative housing. Close by is **St Andrew's in the Square** (559 5902, www.standrewsin thesquare.com), a former church that now hosts a variety of concerts. There's a café here, too.

Edging still further north, the twin thoroughfares of Gallowgate and London Road form part of the boundary of the **Barras**, Glasgow's monumental weekend market (*see p271*). Next door is the legendary **Barrowland** ballroom (*see p277*). The gigantic trademark neon sign outside the venue was temporarily removed during World War II, when it was realised that German bombers were using it as a guiding light. And up the High Street, north of Gallowgate, sit **Glasgow Cathedral** (*see below*), **Provand's Lordship** (*see below*), the **Necropolis** (*see p255* **Death on the rock**) and the **St Mungo Museum of Religious Life & Art** (*see below*). This little corner is all that really remains of medieval Glasgow, and seems increasingly strange and wonderful amid the 21st-century metropolis that surrounds it.

Glasgow Cathedral

Castle Street (0141 552 6891/www.glasgow cathedral.org.uk). High Street rail. **Open** *Apr-Sept* 9.30am-6pm Mon-Sat; 1-5pm Sun. *Oct-Mar* 9.30am-4pm Mon-Sat; 1-4pm Sun. **Admission** free. **Map** p333 H3.
Until the rise of the British Empire, Glasgow was chiefly known as an ecclesiastical town: pilgrims came here regularly to visit the tomb of St Mungo, who founded Glasgow Cathedral during the sixth century. The earliest parts of the cathedral date back more than 700 years, though the building was regularly amended and extended through to the 19th century. The exterior is begrimed with soot from the industrial age, but it's still an impressive example of Gothic architecture and the only medieval Scottish cathedral to have survived the Reformation unscathed.

Martyrs' School

Parson Street (0141 552 2356/www.glasgow museums.com). High Street rail. **Open** by appointment only. **Admission** free. **Map** p333 H2.
Mackintosh's first school project, commissioned in 1895 and completed two years later, shows many of his characteristic design details in an embryonic form that would later flourish at Scotland Street. Closed as a school in 1974, it was saved from destruction by the Mackintosh Society.

Necropolis

Glasgow Necropolis Cemetery, 50 Cathedral Square (0141 552 3145). High Street rail. **Open** 24hrs daily. **Admission** free.
The first interdenominational 'hygienic' graveyard in Scotland was inspired by the famed Père Lachaise cemetery in Paris. Almost 180 years after it was established, it's now a curiously haunting place. For more, *see p255* **Death on the rock**.

People's Palace/Winter Gardens

Glasgow Green (0141 271 9262/www.glasgow museums.com). Bridgeton rail. **Open** 10am-5pm Mon-Thur, Sat; 11am-5pm Fri, Sun. **Admission** free. **Map** p333 G6.
Built in 1898, the red sandstone People's Palace originally served as a municipal and cultural centre for the city's working classes. It now houses a much-cherished exhibition that covers all aspects of Glaswegian life, but pays particular attention to the city's social and industrial history. The adjoining Winter Gardens is one of the most elegant Victorian glasshouses in Scotland, a very pleasant spot in summer or winter. Just outside the People's Palace is the Doulton Fountain: built to celebrate Queen Victoria's rule over the Commonwealth, it's the largest terracotta fountain in the world. **Photo** *p253*.

Provand's Lordship

3 Castle Street (0141 552 8819/www.glasgow museums.com). High Street rail. **Open** 10am-5pm Mon-Thur, Sat; 11am-5pm Fri, Sun. **Admission** free. **Map** p333 H3.
Glasgow's oldest house, built in 1471, is a delightful refuge on wet and windy afternoons. A well-worn staircase leads to a homely recreation of the former Bishop's bedroom; a new physic garden provides some meditative calm away from the din of cars heading to or from the motorway. **Photo** *p256*.

St Mungo Museum of Religious Life & Art

2 Castle Street (0141 553 2557/www.glasgow museums.com). High Street rail. **Open** 10am-5pm Mon-Thur, Sat; 11am-5pm Fri, Sun. **Admission** free. **Map** p333 H3.
Glasgow's ugly sectarianism is quickly forgotten in this wide ranging museum that investigates how different cultures have dealt with life's most fundamental concerns. Temporary photographic exhibitions provide further food for thought, engaging with modern problems from other cultures. You can contemplate it all in the café, which looks out on to a Zen garden.

The Waterfront

Essentially where Glasgow began, when St Mungo settled here in the sixth century, the **River Clyde** is where the city is most visibly regenerating itself with a series of huge new development schemes. A stroll along its banks offers some instructive insights into how today's city fathers would like to see their town continue to develop.

Along the north bank, the **Clyde Walkway** runs underneath the numerous city-centre bridges. Beginning at the west end of Glasgow Green, head westwards along Clyde Street, then the Broomielaw and Anderston and Lancefield Quays, and you'll arrive at one of the city's new sci-fi riverside landmarks, Foster and Partners'

Death on the rock

Scotland's religious Reformation. Towering 70 feet into the air, the Knox Monument is notable for its size, but also for the fact that, unlike the monuments and mausoleums that eventually came to be scattered beneath, its subject had nothing to do with its construction.

Six years after the Knox Monument arose, John Strang, the chamberlain of the Merchants' House, pushed forward the idea of establishing a cemetery around it, 'dedicated to the genius of

In her 1943 novel Anger in the Sky, English writer Susan Ertz mused on how 'Millions long for immortality [yet] don't know what to do with themselves on a rainy Sunday afternoon.' Today, Glaswegians spend their rainy afternoons ambling around the tombs of those citizens who, just over a century ago, longed so dearly for immortality. Perched conspicuously atop a hill just east of the city's cathedral, the Necropolis is one of Glasgow's most involving tourist attractions, because its existence, its design and its current state of repair unwittingly tell tourists a great deal about the ambitions of those who helped build the city they've come to see.

The hill on which the Necropolis stands was developed as parkland in the 17th and 18th centuries. Fir Park, it was called, a reference to the trees planted on it after it was acquired in 1650 by the Merchants' House, a guild of local businessmen and craftsmen. With money comes influence, and so it followed that as the local merchants grew more affluent, their power over the city expanded. By the 18th century, Glasgow was thriving, as trade conducted on the River Clyde brought with it mountains of cash. Commerce was king, and the Merchants' House became, in many regards, the de facto town council, setting business rates, overseeing local construction and even, to an extent, controlling the city's purse-strings.

It was the Merchants' House that first proposed converting Fir Park into a cemetery, modelled to a degree on Père Lachaise in Paris. However, the cemetery's most dramatic monument predates its establishment by several years: Thomas Hamilton's 1825 tribute to John Knox, the progenitor of

memory and calculated for the extension of religious and moral feeling'. Progress was speedy; the first interment was made in 1832. During the next half-century, Glasgow's great and good were laid to rest in its windswept grounds, beneath monuments and mausoleums of increasingly deliberate grandeur. Theatrical impresario John Alexander lies beneath an elaborate circular tomb decorated with theatrical avatars; John Dick, a religious figure of no little repute, is honoured with a simple, almost gracious memorial; Reverend William Brash has a vast monument that tallies with his surname. Not everyone was so lucky: amid such daunting, haughty magnificence lie tens of thousands of ordinary citizens who weren't deemed of sufficient social importance to merit so much as a simple plaque marking their remains. With money comes influence, and they had neither.

A century or so after its establishment, its grounds full to bursting, the Necropolis had already begun to fall into disrepair. Glasgow had expanded further westwards, and the men – and men they mostly were – who had laid the groundwork for the city's growth were left to rot atop the hill. Today, the Necropolis remains in a state of listless decay, battered by the weather and rendered drowsy by the fumes blown across from the nearby Tennent's brewery. Beer cans and scotch bottles litter the ground, left by lads destined to end up in tombs less memorable but perhaps more dignified than those they regularly deface. 'Do not try to live forever,' counselled George Bernard Shaw (who chose not burial but cremation). 'You will not succeed.'

Provand's Lordship. *See p254.*

Clyde Auditorium (*see p277*). The Armadillo, as it's inevitably been nicknamed, is certainly an impressive building, but its hard, funky glisten has been eclipsed by the spectacular shine of the new **Glasgow Science Centre** (*see below*), across the Clyde at Pacific Quay.

Directly adjacent to the Science Centre stands the 127-metre (417-foot) **Glasgow Tower**, the tallest free-standing structure in the city. As you'd expect, it affords unsurpassed views; or, at least, it has done during the brief periods it's been open to the public. As of 2006, it remained closed due to technical problems, which is Glasgow all over: progressive, but prone to glitches. Still, the Science Centre's glass frontage offers a good view of the **Tall Ship at Glasgow Harbour** (*see below*), the *SV Glenlee*, one of the few Clyde-built sailing ships still in existence. In summer, look out for the **Waverley** (*see below*): the world's only sea-going paddle steamer, it cruises to the Isle of Bute and other west coast locations. The **Clyde Waterbus** (*see p283*) is a little less handsome, but does at least operate all year round, ferrying passengers to the Braehead Shopping Centre and the nearby **Clydebuilt Maritime Museum** (*see below*).

Clydebuilt Maritime Museum
King's Inch Road, Braehead (0141 886 1013/ www.scottishmaritimemuseum.org). Bus 23, 101. **Open** 10am-5.30pm Mon-Sat; 11am-5pm Sun. **Admission** £4.25; £2.50-£3 concessions; family £10. **No credit cards.**
One of the Scottish Maritime Museum's three sites (the others are at Dumbarton and Irvine), Clydebuilt tells the worthwhile, intertwined story of Glasgow and the Clyde, from trading to shipbuilding. Double the fun by taking the Clyde Waterbus from the city centre (*see p283*).

Glasgow Science Centre
Pacific Quay (0141 420 5000/www.glasgowscience centre.org). Exhibition Centre rail. **Open** *Science Mall* 10am-6pm daily. *IMAX* film times vary. **Admission** *Single attraction (Science Mall, IMAX or Glasgow Tower)* £6.95; £4.95 concesssions. *Two attractions* £9.95; £7.95 concessions. *Scottish Power Planetarium* add £2 to Science Mall ticket. **Credit** MC, V.
This futuristic titanium and glass structure boasts three riotously stimulating floors of hands-on science and technology exhibits as part of the Science Mall. Since opening in 2001, it's become deservedly popular with kids and armchair scientists for its well-run displays and planetarium. The centre also houses an IMAX cinema. The Glasgow Tower, which rotates 360 degress to reduce wind resistance, would give spectacular views over the city if it ever worked properly.

Tall Ship at Glasgow Harbour
Stobcross Road (0141 222 2513/www.thetallship. com). Exhibition Centre rail. **Open** *Nov-Feb* 11am-4pm daily. *Mar-Oct* 10am-5pm daily. **Admission** £4.95; £3.75 concessions. **Credit** MC, V. **Map** p332 A4.
The tall ship *SV Glenlee* is one of only five Clydebuilt sailing ships that remain afloat. Launched in 1896, she stands as an impressive reminder of the Clyde's shipbuilding legacy. The accompanying exhibitions explore what life was like on the open seas, encompassing everything from pirates to mermaids.

Waverley Paddle Steamer
Waverley Excursions, Waverley Terminal (0845 130 4647/www.waverleyexcursions.co.uk). Anderston rail. **Sailings** call or check online for details **Admission** varies. **Credit** MC, V.
Built in 1947, the Waverley paddle steamer is a unique summer attraction. The breezy, Huckleberry charm of a quiet churn down the water has been known to cure hangovers and shopping exhaustion.

The South Side

The West End may be the city's bohemian quarter, but Glasgow's **South Side** is much more cosmopolitan: diverse, fascinating and under-visited by tourists. Most of it is residential, from distant and affluent districts such as Newton Mearns to less monied housing estates like Castlemilk. (Previously one of the most moribund areas of the city, the Gorbals is fast becoming a respectable address, thanks to the effects of a wide-ranging regeneration programme.) The area also boasts several notable cultural institutions, chief among them the egalitarian **Citizens' Theatre** and the consistently challenging **Tramway** in Pollokshields. For both, *see p280*.

Some of the best examples of Alexander 'Greek' Thomson's architecture stand on the South Side, among them the Acropolis-inspired **Caledonia Road Church** (1856) on Cathcart Road. A fire in 1965 destroyed the painted interior, leaving only the portico and tower intact, but it's still worth the diversion. The Thomson-designed terraces of **Regent Park**, in the Strathbungo district, have fared better, and have been a designated conservation area since the 1970s. Both Thomson and Mackintosh lived here.

The South Side opens out into several large parks; indeed, the city as a whole boasts more parks per head than any other in Europe. Among them is **Bellahouston**, which holds the **House for an Art Lover** (*see below*), a modern construction based on plans submitted by Mackintosh in 1901. In **Pollok Park**, Glasgow's largest, you'll find the main South Side attractions: **Pollok House** (*see below*) and the wonderful phantasmagorical **Burrell Collection** (*see below*). But most visitors to the South Side are heading to **Hampden Park**, home to Scotland's national football team. The stadium contains a museum (*see p258*) with permanent displays and temporary exhibitions on Scottish football's finest moments. Most of them, alas, happened quite a long time ago.

Burrell Collection

Pollok Park, 2060 Pollokshaws Road (0141 287 2550/www.glasgowmuseums.com). Pollokshaws West rail, then 10min walk. **Open** 10am-5pm Mon-Thur, Sat; 11am-5pm Fri, Sun. **Admission** free.
When Sir William Burrell gave his prodigious collection of art and artefacts to the city of Glasgow in 1944, he stipulated that it must be kept at least 16 miles from the city centre to avoid it being covered in soot. Thankfully, Glasgow's air has improved since he died, and his estate agreed to it being exhibited fairly nearby in Pollok Park. The collection encompasses treasures from ancient Egypt, Greece and Rome, ceramics from various Chinese dynasties, and an assortment of European decorative arts, including rare tapestries and stained glass. It also boasts one of the finest collections of Impressionist and post-Impressionist paintings and drawings in the world. Try to come on a sunny day, when the reflected light in the interior glass-roofed courtyard is breathtaking. **Photo** *p258*.

Glasgow Museums Resource Centre

200 Woodhead Road, Nitsill (0141 276 9300/www.glasgowmuseums.com). Nitsill rail. **Open** *Tours* 2.30pm daily. **Admission** free.
Space constraints mean that only five per cent of Glasgow Museums' works are able to be displayed at any one time. Much of the remainder are stored in this modern day Aladdin's cave, open to the public through daily tours.

Holmwood House

61-63 Netherlee Road, Cathcart (0141 637 2129/www.nts.org.uk). Cathcart rail. **Open** *Apr-Oct* 1-5pm Mon, Thur-Sun; access may be restricted at peak times. **Admission** £5; £4 concessions; £14 family. **No credit cards**.
Thomson was given carte blanche by paper mill owner James Couper when designing Holmwood in the middle of the 19th century; the freedom he was granted inspired his most elaborate villa. The richly ornamental classical interior is a testament to Thomson's lovable eccentricities.

House for an Art Lover

Bellahouston Park, 10 Dumbreck Road (0141 353 4770/www.houseforanartlover.co.uk). Dumbreck rail. **Open** *Apr-Sept* 10am-4pm Mon-Wed; 10am-1pm Thur-Sun. *Oct-Mar* 10am-1pm Sat, Sun. Times may vary; phone to check. **Admission** £3.50; £2.50 concessions. **Credit** MC, V.
Built according to plans Mackintosh submitted to a German architecture competition in 1901, the House for an Art Lover was completed in 1996 to mixed reactions. Externally it has stark Modernist curves, but inside, the grids and flowers seem more Mockintosh than Mackintosh.

Pollok House

Pollok Park, 2060 Pollokshaws Road (0141 616 6410/www.nts.org.uk). Pollokshaws West rail, then 10min walk. **Open** 10am-5pm daily. **Admission** £8; £5 concessions. **Credit** MC, V.
This magnificent 18th-century mansion displays the Stirling Maxwell collection of Spanish and European paintings, including beautiful works by Goya, El Greco and Murillo. The highlight, though, is William Blake's exquisite tempera painting of Chaucer's Canterbury pilgrims.

Scotland Street School Museum

225 Scotland Street (0141 287 0500/www.glasgow museums.com). Shields Road underground. **Open** 10am-5pm Mon-Thur, Sat; 11am-5pm Fri, Sun. **Admission** free. **Map** p332 B6.
A real Mackintosh treat, this majestic school building is now a newly refurbished museum offering an insight into Glaswegian schooling in the first half of the 20th century. It also presents a detailed look at the architectural plans of Mackintosh's final commission in Glasgow, showing how he added numerous ornamental details once the drafts had been approved (much to the understandable annoyance of the School Board).

Trips Out of Town

Scottish Football Museum

National Stadium, Hampden Park (0141 616 6139/
www.scottishfootballmuseum.org.uk). King Park
or Mount Florida rail. **Open** 10am-5pm Mon-Sat;
11am-5pm Sun. **Admission** *Museum* £5.50; £2.75
concessions; free under-5s. *Stadium tour* £6; £3
concessions; free under-5s. **Credit** MC, V.
This display of Scottish football history is comprehensive to the point of obsession, documenting all
the players, kits and trophies since 1867. Pride of
place is given to a life-size model of Archie Gemmill
scoring his famous goal against Holland in the 1978
World Cup. While the Scottish national side hasn't
troubled Brazil, England or even Belgium for a while,
names like Dalglish, Law, Shankly and Stein still
inspire a nostalgic pride.

The West End

Beginning at the huge dome and imposing
façade of the **Mitchell Library** just beyond
the M8 motorway, the West End has a character
all of its own: it's Glasgow all right, but the
neighbourhood doesn't really seem to fit with
the rest of the city. Leafy, hilly, prettier and
lazier than the city's other quarters, the West
End remains a middle-class enclave, populated
mainly by students, rich folks and creative
types. A high-quality range of bars, coffee
shops, delis and record stores cater for most
of their tastes.

The main artery through the West End is
the long, straight **Great Western Road**, built
in 1836 so Glasgow's bourgeoisie could get out
of the crowded, soot-blackened city centre in a
hurry. Nowadays, it's often a choked snarl of
traffic, heading out past the **Botanic Gardens**
(*see p259*) and towards Loch Lomond. South
of the road sit an array of domestic terraced
buildings; dating from the 19th century,
they remain among the city's most beautiful.
Flanking Great Western Road, **Great
Western Terrace** is perhaps the finest
example of such architecture in the city:
designed by Alexander 'Greek' Thomson in
1867, it's now home to **Timorous Beasties**
(384 Great Western Road, 0141 337 2622,
www.timorousbeasties.co.uk), a small
wallpaper and fabrics shop that was nominated
for the Design Museum's Designer of the
Year award in 2005. Just up from here is
Devonshire Gardens, where you'll find
the city's most impressive hotel (*see p282*).

Arguably Glasgow's two greatest museums: the **Burrell Collection** (*see p257*)...

Further south, a few blocks away from the Great Western Road, sit two more fine residential streets, **Park Circus** (1857-63) and **Park Terrace** (1855), which sit mere steps away from **Kelvingrove Park**. First laid out as pleasure grounds in the 1850s, the park becomes packed on sunny days with dogs, bongo players and cheerful displays of public drunkenness: indeed, the open stretch of grass is known locally as the 'Green Beach'. The **Kelvingrove Art Gallery & Museum**, a striking red Victorian palace, reopened in 2006 after a three-year refurbishment, and dominates the end of the park. On those rare evenings when the sunset hits it, Glasgow takes on an exotic, storybook magic.

Just beyond the park is the **University of Glasgow**, whose dark fairytale neo-Gothic tower dominates the whole West End. The bizarre concrete façade of the Mackintosh House at the **Hunterian Art Gallery** next door (*see p261*) helps shape a strange and beautiful skyline. And just beyond all this is **Byres Road**, the heart of the West End. An assortment of charming little streets – among them **Dowanside Lane** and

Cresswell Lane – edge off this main thoroughfare, and are distinguished by a variety of stores selling vintage clothes and unusual gifts. The busiest and most beautiful is **Ashton Lane**, home to the **Grosvenor** cinema and bar complex (*see p274*) and the **Ubiquitous Chip** restaurant (*see p266*).

Botanic Gardens & Kibble Palace

730 Great Western Road (0141 334 2422/www. glasgow.gov.uk). Hillhead underground. **Open** *Palace Apr-Oct* 10am-4.45pm daily. *Nov-Mar* 10am-4.15pm daily. *Gardens* 7am-dusk daily. **Admission** free.
Glasgow's Botanic Gardens are dominated by the huge dome of Kibble Palace, a marvel of Victorian engineering that is currently being restored to its original glory. Look out, too, for the abandoned railway station, the extensive herb garden and, in summer, open-air Shakespeare performances (*see p279*).

Fossil Grove

Victoria Park (0141 950 1448/www.glasgow museums.com). Jordanhill rail/44 bus. **Open** *Apr-Sept* 10am-5pm Mon-Thur, Sat; 11am-5pm Fri, Sun. **Admission** free.
The petrified remains of a 300-million-year-old carboniferous forest at Fossil Grove give visitors pause to reflect on the transience of life, especially when

... and the newly reopened **Kelvingrove Art Gallery & Museum** (*see p261*).

they learn that, back then, Glasgow was equatorial. Discovered when Victoria Park was created on the site of a disused quarry, the fossils are housed in an Victorian ironwork warehouse, something of an antique in its own right.

Hunterian Museum & Art Gallery

University of Glasgow, Hillhead Street (museum 0141 330 4221/gallery 0141 330 5431/www. hunterian.gla.ac.uk). Hillhead underground. **Open** *Museum & Art Gallery* 9.30am-5pm Mon-Sat. *Mackintosh House* 9.30am-12.30pm, 1.30-5pm Mon-Sat. **Admission** free. *Mackintosh House* £2.50.
The Hunterian is divided into two distinct but equally fascinating parts. The museum, found amid the Gothic grandeur of the Gilbert Scott building, features dinosaurs, archaeological finds and an engaging hands-on display of Glasgow scientist Lord Kelvin's inventions and experiments. The art gallery across the road houses Scotland's largest print collection and a fine collection of paintings, including a room devoted to Whistler. The gallery leads on to the Mackintosh House; it recreates the architect's home in Southpark Avenue, where he lived from 1906 to 1914.

Kelvingrove Art Gallery & Museum

Argyle Street (0141 287 2699/www.glasgow museums.com). Kelvinhall underground/Partick rail. **Open** 10am-5pm Mon-Sat; 11am-5pm Sun. **Admission** free.
Reopened in July 2006 after a massive refurbishment, the Kelvingrove is now Glasgow's must-see museum. Cleaned of a century of grime, the impressive atrium sparkles in the light that floods in through the windows. The ground-floor exhibitions cover every subject under the sun, from architecture to war; on the first floor, masterpieces by Dali, Rembrandt, Van Gogh and Botticelli add up to an embarrassment of riches. **Photo** *p259.*

Mitchell Library

North Street (0141 287 2999/www.mitchelllibrary. org). Charing Cross rail. **Open** 9am-8pm Mon-Thur; 9am-5pm Fri, Sat. **Map** p332 C2.
Despite its imposing appearance, the Mitchell is a welcoming place for quiet study and genealogical research. Containing over one million books and documents, the library also has a huge collection of photographic prints and lithographs that vividly illustrate Glasgow's past.

Museum of Transport

1 Bunhouse Road, Kelvinhall (0141 287 2720/www. glasgowmuseums.com). Kelvinhall underground/Partick rail. **Open** 10am-5pm Mon-Thur, Sat; 11am-5pm Fri, Sun. **Admission** free.
The Clyde Room, where Glasgow's shipbuilding industry is celebrated and mourned, helps to make this one of Britain's more engaging transport museums. Every conceivable mode of transport is represented, but the highlight is the recreation of a fictional 1930s shopping street, complete with underground station and operational cinema.

Eat, Drink, Shop

Restaurants & cafés

The City Centre

Arisaig

140 St Vincent Street (0141 204 5399/www.arisaig restaurant.co.uk). St Enoch underground/Argyle Street rail. **Open** noon-midnight Mon-Sat; 5pm-midnight Sun. **Main courses** £11-£23. **Credit** AmEx, MC, V. **Map** p333 E3 ➊
Named after the little coastal chunk of the country south of Mallaig, this is Glasgow's most accessible Scottish bistro. Initially launched at another site in the Merchant City, it shifted to this spacious and contemporary room in 2005. The menu concentrates on traditional local ingredients, making this a great place to eat Scottish and drink scotch.

Brian Maule at the Chardon d'Or

176 West Regent Street (0141 248 3801/www.brian maule.com). Cowcaddens underground/Charing Cross rail. **Open** noon-2pm, 6-9.30pm Mon-Fri; noon-2pm, 6pm-10pm Sat, Sun. **Main courses** £16-£23. **Credit** AmEx, MC, V. **Map** p332 D3 ➋
The back story: Ayrshire lad trains in France, becomes head chef at Le Gavroche in London, and returns to Scotland to open his own place in 2002. Since its launch, Maule's restaurant has been rated as one of the best in the city. The interior is modern, if polite, and the classic cuisine remains confident and unfussy. Try a light bar lunch if the evening menu is beyond the reach of your credit card.

Café Hula

321 Hope Street (0141 353 1660/www.cafehula.co. uk). Buchanan Street or Cowcaddens underground/Queen Street rail. **Open** 8am-8pm Mon-Thur; 8am-midnight Fri, Sat. **Main courses** £4.50-£9.95. **Credit** AmEx, MC, V. **Map** p333 E2 ➌
This wannabe-bohemian enclave is a decidedly un-Glaswegian eaterie, eschewing cutting-edge style in favour of scatter-cushion hippy chic. The food may include the likes of chickpea and chorizo stew, Moroccan lamb casserole and something happily, comfortably vegetarian. Sandwiches are available for takeaway; there's also a short, cheerful wine list.

Dragon-i

311-313 Hope Street (0141 332 7728/www.dragon-i. co.uk). Buchanan Street or Cowcaddens underground/Charing Cross rail. **Open** noon-2pm, 5-11pm Mon-Fri; 5-11pm Sat; 5-10pm Sun. **Main courses** £10-£17. **Credit** MC, V. **Map** p333 E2 ➍
This modern eaterie arrived in 2003. Foodwise, it's more Asian-eclectic than straightforward Chinese, but there are no *Madame Butterfly* design clichés here: the dining room is characterised by rich reds and blues, and dark wood fittings. The wine list shows some thought, and the desserts aren't half bad either.

Trips Out of Town

étain

Princes Square, Buchanan Street (0141 225 5630/
www.conran-restaurants.co.uk). Buchanan Street
or St Enoch underground/Argyle Street or Queen
Street rail. **Open** noon-2pm, 7-11pm Mon-Fri;
7-11pm Sat; noon-3pm Sun. **Main courses**
£24-£59 set menus. **Credit** AmEx, M,V.
Map p333 E4 ❺
Tucked away on the top floor of the upmarket
Princes Square shopping mall, this chic establishment is one of Terence Conran's elite fine-dining
restaurants. The food is modern and French;
following the departure in 2006 of chef Geoffrey
Smeddle, who left to take charge of the Peat Inn
in Fife (*see p290*), it's now overseen by Neil Clark.
The restaurant is accessible through the mall, but
also has its own entrance (via a lift) at Springfield
Court, to the rear of the building. **Photo** *p263*.

Fratelli Sarti

133 Wellington Street (0141 248 2228/
www.sarti.co.uk). Buchanan Street underground/
Queen Street rail. **Open** 8am-10.30pm Mon-Sat.
Main courses £7-£21. **Credit** AmEx, MC, V.
Map p332 D3 ❻
A Glasgow institution, no less. Fratelli Sarti now has
several branches in the city, but the deli-and-trat in
Wellington Street still retains its popular appeal, as
a welcoming and unpretentious place to stop for a
plate of pasta and a glass of wine. Basic Italian fare
made with fresh, flavoursome ingredients.
Other locations: 121 Bath Street, City Centre
(0141 204 0440); 42 Renfield Street, City Centre
(0141 572 7000).

Gamba

225a West George Street (0141 572 0899/www.
gamba.co.uk). Buchanan Street underground/Queen
Street rail. **Main courses** £10-£23. **Credit** AmEx, MC, V.
Map p332 D3 ❼
For some years now, this unassuming basement
joint has been the city's favourite upmarket seafood
restaurant. The approach is simple enough: source
good raw materials and let their quality shine
through. The menu is Asian-influenced, but also
includes more traditional fare. It's far from cheap,
but the pre-theatre menu is decent value.

Ichiban

50 Queen Street (0141 204 4200/www.ichiban.
co.uk). St Enoch underground/Argyle Street rail.
Open noon-10pm Mon-Wed; noon-11pm Thur-Sat;
1-10pm Sun. **Main courses** £7-£10. **Credit** AmEx,
MC, V. **Map** p333 F4 ❽
We have Wagamama to thank for the formula:
noodles, served in a sparse, modern first-floor room,
eaten by diners perched on benches and sharing
their table with others. However, Ichiban deserves
credit for being the first restaurant to bring the dining style to Scotland at the end of the 1990s. Bento
boxes and sushi appease the carbohydrate-averse.
Other locations: 184 Dumbarton Road, West End
(0141 334 9222).

MC @ ABode

ABode Hotel, 129 Bath Street (0141 221 6789/
www.abodehotels.co.uk). Buchanan Street or
Cowcaddens underground/Queen Street rail.
Open noon-2.30pm, 7-10pm Mon-Thur; noon-2.30pm,
6.30-10pm Fri, Sat. **Main courses** £17-£22.95.
Credit AmEx, MC, V. **Map** p332 D3 ❾
A contender for the accolade of Glasgow's best
restaurant, MC is the brainchild of Michelin-starred
chef Michael Caines, and opened in 2005 in the old
Arthouse Hotel. There are now several ABodes in
the UK, and Mr Caines can't be everywhere; fortu-
nately, local boy Martin Donnelly is a more than
capable head chef. If the carte is beyond your means,
the set lunches are more affordable at £12.50 for two
courses and £17 for three.

Paperino's

283 Sauchiehall Street (0141 332 3800/www.
paperinos.co.uk). Buchanan Street or Cowcaddens
underground/Queen Street rail. **Open** noon-3pm, 5-
10.50pm Mon-Thur; noon-3pm, 5-11.30pm Fri; noon-
11.30pm Sat; noon-10.50pm Sun. **Main courses**
£6.35-£15.95. **Credit** AmEx, MC,V. **Map** p332 D2 ❿
To visitors, Paperino's may seem like little more
than a basic pizza-pasta joint. However, 15 years on
Sauchiehall Street has granted it a place in the hearts
of Glaswegians who first came here as kids or for an
affordable first date. Sit in a booth, order some pap-
pardelle Monteprandone and a glass of house red,
and make up your own mind. From the same stable
as La Parmigiana (*see p266*), the restaurant opened
a bigger, brighter West End sibling in 2005.
Other locations: 227 Byres Road, West End (0141
334 3811).

Red Onion

247 West Campbell Street (0141 221 6000/www.
red-onion.co.uk). Buchanan Street or Cowcaddens
underground/Queen Street rail. **Open** 11am-10pm
Mon-Fri; noon-10.30pm Sat, Sun. **Main courses**
£6.95-£16.50. **Credit** AmEx, MC, V. **Map** p332 D3 ⓫
After travelling the world working as the private
chef to a slew of notable rock stars, John Quigley
returned home to open an upmarket restaurant
under his own name, before turning his hand to
Red Onion in 2004. A flexible place, it offers salads,
sandwiches and an eclectic main menu (sea bass
with Thai noodles, say, or chicken tagine). Critics
generally felt Quigley was overstretched in the
early months, but the venue has since settled into a
comfortable niche.

Rogano

11 Exchange Place (0141 248 4055/www.rogano.
co.uk). Buchanan Street or St Enoch underground/
Argyle Street or Queen Street rail. **Open** noon-11pm
Mon-Thur; noon-midnight Fri, Sat. **Main courses**
£8-£35. **Credit** AmEx, MC, V. **Map** p333 E4 ⓬
This Glasgow classic, boasting a beautiful 1930s
art deco interior (contemporary with the Clyde-built
Queen Mary steamship), contains a restaurant, an
oyster bar and a downstairs café. Snacks are served
at the bar, with a fuller menu offered elsewhere and

Shop until you drop in at Terence Conran's **étain**. *See p262.*

a very useful late menu after 10pm for the post-theatre crowd. Seafood is a speciality. At its best, it can be incomparably atmospheric.

TaPaell'Ya

Radisson SAS Hotel, 301 Argyle Street (0141 204 3333/www.radissonsas.com). St Enoch underground/ Argyle Street rail. **Open** 8am-10.30pm Mon-Fri; 6-10.30pm Sat. **Main courses** £8.50-£18.95. *Tapas* £2.50-£7.95. **Credit** AmEx, MC, V. **Map** p332 D4 ⑬
Don't let its laboured name deter you: this Spanish eaterie is a fine option. Lingering over a lunch of boquerones or calamares is a blessed relief from the retail-a-go-go outside; if you're after something more substantial in the evening, three-course meals are also available. The hotel (*see p281*) also houses Collage, which takes a more upmarket, Mediterranean approach.

Two Fat Ladies

118a Blythswood Street (0141 847 0088). Buchanan Street or St Enoch underground/Central Station rail. **Open** noon-3pm, 5-10.30pm Mon-Sat. **Main courses** £11-£17. **Credit** AmEx, MC, V. **Map** p332 D3 ⑭
Following its success in the West End, Two Fat Ladies – nothing to do with the TV series of the same name – ventured into the centre of town to open this larger, smarter second branch in 2005. It's a modish, contemporary space, buzzing more often than not. As at the West End operation, the kitchen specialises in seafood. **Photo** *p264*.
Other locations: 88 Dumbarton Road, West End (0141 339 1944).

The Merchant City & the East End

Café Gandolfi & Bar Gandolfi

64 Albion Street (0141 552 6813/www.cafegandolfi. co.uk). St Enoch underground/Argyle Street or High Street rail. **Open** 9am-11.30pm Mon-Sat; noon-11.30pm Sun. **Main courses** £5-£12. **Credit** AmEx, MC, V. **Map** p333 G4 ⑮
Established way back in 1979, this stalwart is as popular as it's ever been. The distinctive L-shaped room is decorated with attractive, tactile wooden furniture by the late, great Tim Stead; the kitchen offers keenly-priced, Scottish-slanted food such as Arbroath smokies. Pop in for a sandwich and a glass of wine, or tuck into three full-on courses of good, solid cooking. Bar Gandolfi opened in the attic in 2002. **Photo** *p265*.

City Merchant

97-99 Candleriggs (0141 553 1577/www.city merchant.co.uk). Buchanan Street or St Enoch underground/Argyle Street or High Street rail. **Open** noon-10.30pm Mon-Sat. **Main courses** £9.75-£27.50. **Credit** AmEx, MC, V. **Map** p333 F4 ⑯
The City Merchant was one of the first restaurants to venture into the Merchant City almost 20 years ago; still run by the same family, it's endured while the area has gentrified around it. You can order a decent rib-eye steak, but the spectacular Scottish seafood platter is rather more in keeping with the eaterie's ethos.

Two Fat Ladies. See p263.

Dakhin

*89 Candleriggs (0141 553 2585/www.dakhin.com).
Buchanan Street or St Enoch underground/Argyle
Street or High Street rail.* **Open** noon-2pm, 5-10.30pm
Mon-Fri; 1-10.30pm Sat, Sun. **Main courses** £8-£17.
Credit AmEx, MC, V. **Map** p333 G4 ⑰

Glasgow has traditionally loved its robust Indian
food, invariably and inevitably washed down with
gallons of lager. In recent years, though, some more
mature Indian restaurants have sprung up around
the city, and none have impressed as much as
Dakhin. Housed in an open, first-floor room since
2004, the restaurant specialises in south Indian
cuisine, a lighter alternative to trenchant vindaloo.
Nearby Dhabba is the restaurant's north Indian
sister business.

Other locations: Dhabba, 44 Candleriggs (0141
553 1249/www.thedhabba.com).

Rab Ha's

*83 Hutcheson Street (0141 572 0400/www.rabhas.
com). Buchanan Street or St Enoch underground/
Argyle Street or High Street rail.* **Open** 5.30-10pm
daily. **Main courses** £9.95-£15.95. **Credit** AmEx,
MC, V. **Map** p333 F4 ⑱

Rab Ha's doubles as a small hotel and bar, but it's
best known for its restaurant (Perthshire lamb with
puy lentils, poussin, sirloin steaks) and the deriva-
tion of its name: the original Rab Ha', Robert Hall,
was a legendary 19th-century Glasgow trencherman
whose appetite even inspired children's songs. The
eaterie has been a mainstay of the Merchant City
scene for years; new owners took over in 2006 but
didn't change much, at least in the early going.

Smiths of Glasgow

*109 Candleriggs (0141 552 6539/www.smiths
restaurants.co.uk). Buchanan Street or St Enoch
underground/Argyle Street or High Street rail.*
Open noon-9.30pm Mon-Thur, Sun; noon-10.30pm
Fri, Sat. **Main courses** £9-£17. **Credit** AmEx, MC,
V. **Map** p333 G4 ⑲

This jolly joint has been serving decent French-style
food – cooked with Scottish influences – to a loyal
clientele since 1999. It's a good place to dawdle over
lunch on a Saturday afternoon, in the company of a
couple of bottles of wine.

The West End

Ashoka

*108 Elderslie Street (0141 221 1761/www.thebest
ashoka.com. Charing Cross or Exhibition Centre rail.*
Open noon-midnight daily. **Main courses** £6.95-
£14.95. **Credit** AmEx, MC, V. **Map** p332 B2 ⑳

Nothing to do with the chain of the same name,
Ashoka is located just west of the M8. The basement
dining space is decorated in rich red hues, almost
catering to a fantasy of how an old-fashioned curry
house should be decorated. Persian-influenced food
complements the traditional Caledonian-friendly
Indian dishes. If you're looking for a quiet night, it's
best to avoid the famous karaoke evenings.

Bothy

*11 Ruthven Lane (0141 334 4040/www.bothy
restaurant.co.uk). Hillhead underground.*
Open noon-10pm daily. **Main courses** £8.95-
£22.50. **Credit** MC, V.

The name (which means a small cottage or hut, generally in the Highlands), the decor (robust and rustic) and the food (haggis, smoked salmon and the like) all combine to create an avowedly Scottish restaurant. Some diners may find it all slightly contrived, but macaroni cheese, beef olives, and fish and chips are at least close to authentic local cuisine.

Buttery

652 Argyle Street (0141 221 8188/www.eatbuttery. com). Anderston or Argyle Street rail. **Open** noon-2pm, 6.30-9.30pm Tue-Fri; 6.30-9.30pm Sat. **Set meals** *Lunch* £12/1 course; £16/2 courses; £22/3 courses. *Dinner* £32/2 courses; £38/3 courses. **Credit** AmEx, MC, V. **Map** p332 B3 ㉑

One of Glasgow's best restaurants is also, perhaps, its most anomalous. It's housed on the ground floor of a 150-year-old tenement, its decor dark and distinguished. However, the ancient building is now ringed by swathes of modern development, and its immediate neighbours are ugly apartment blocks and the M8 flyover. The trip to these netherlands is well worth it, however, for the likes of chestnut-encrusted Perthshire lamb or grilled turbot.

Firebird

1321 Argyle Street (0141 334 0594/www.firebird glasgow.com). Kelvinhall underground. **Open** 11.30am-midnight Mon-Thur; 11.30am-1am Fri, Sat; 12.30pm-midnight Sun. **Main courses** £7-£18. **Credit** MC, V.

Not far from Kelvingrove Park, this bright, open plan café-bar has funky paintings on its walls and simple but well-executed dishes on its menu. The pizzas are among the best in the city, but there are also pasta dishes, salads, and specials, all made to order. Children are made very welcome.

Grassroots

97 St George's Road (0141 333 0534/www.grass rootsorganic.com). St George's Cross underground. **Open** 10am-10pm daily. **Main courses** £3-£8. **Credit** MC, V. **Map** p332 C2 ㉒

Glasgow's finest vegetarian café has sat just beside the M8 since 1999. Homely, wholesome and hand-knitted, it offers a few organic wines to go with your tofu noodles or veggie burger. There's also a shop and deli just round the corner (20 Woodlands Road, 0141 353 3278).

Mother India

28 Westminster Terrace (0141 221 1663/ www.motherindia.co.uk). Exhibition Centre rail. **Open** 5-10.30pm Mon-Thur; 5-11pm Fri; 1-11pm Sat; 1-10.30pm Sun. **Main courses** £7-£13. **Credit** AmEx, MC, V. **Map** p332 A2 ㉓

Often acclaimed as Glasgow's best Indian restaurant, Mother India is a cut above the average curry house. After 11 successful years, it expanded at the original premises by opening up its basement to create an additional and contemporary dining space in summer 2006, dubbed the Cellar. Its other branch, Mother India's Café, sits opposite the Kelvingrove Art Gallery & Museum; unusually for an Indian restaurant, the menu comes tapas-style, designed for sharing.

Other locations: Mother India's Café, 1355 Argyle Street, West End (0141 339 9145).

No.16

16 Byres Road (0141 339 2544/www.number16. co.uk). Kelvinhall underground. **Open** noon-2.30pm, 5.30-10pm Mon-Sat; 12.30-3.30pm, 5.30-9.30pm Sun. **Main courses** £13-£17. **Set menu** £11.50/2 courses; £13.50-£16/3 courses. **Credit** MC, V.

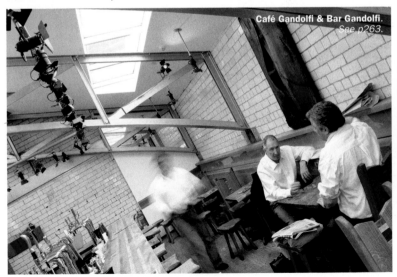

Café Gandolfi & Bar Gandolfi. See p263.

Nothing more or less than a very fine little restaurant, No.16 regularly pops up on 'best of' surveys, satisfying even the most recalcitrant of critics. The menu is French-influenced with international leanings, a testament to the creativity of head chef Grant Neil. Space is limited, so be sure to book ahead.

La Parmigiana

447 Great Western Road (0141 334 0686/www.la parmigiana.co.uk). Kelvinbridge underground. **Open** noon-2.30pm, 6-11pm Mon-Sat. **Main courses** £10-£17. **Credit** AmEx, MC, V.
The Giovanazzi family has been serving yer classic Italian posh nosh since 1978; the only thing to have changed substantially in those three decades is the decor (a rich, dignified 'art gallery' red). Come here for grilled langoustines followed by chunky seafood risotto, or perhaps some duck breast. Further tribute to the restaurant's authenticity is paid by the city's Italian residents, some of whom seem to use it as an unofficial community centre.

Shish Mahal

*66-68 Park Road (0141 334 7899/www.shishmahal. co.uk). Kelvinbridge underground.***Open** noon-2pm, 5-11pm Mon-Thur; noon-11pm Fri, Sat; 5-11pm Sun. **Main courses** £5-£10. **Credit** MC, V.
Since 1964, this curry house has shaped the tastebuds of generations of Glaswegians. The extensive menu contains all the usual, familiar dishes. The place has a familiarity to it that Johnny-come-lately competitors can't hope to match. However, despite its antiquity, it now looks fairly modern following a major refurbishment.

The Sisters, Kelvingrove

36 Kelvingrove Street (0141 564 1157/www. thesisters.co.uk). Kelvinhall underground. **Open** noon-2.30pm, 5.30-9pm Mon-Thur; noon-2.30pm, 5.30-9.30pm Fri, Sat; noon-7pm Sun. **Main courses** £9-£16. **Credit** MC, V. **Map** p332 A2 ㉔
The second establishment run by the two O'Donnell sisters (the other is in suburban Jordanhill) opened in 2005, and immediately set about winning over the West End girls and boys. The room is contemporary and smart but by no means stuffy; the food is modern, Scottish and generally excellent.
Other locations: 1a Ashwood Gardens, Jordanhill (0141 434 1179).

Stravaigin

28-30 Gibson Street (0141 334 2665/www.stravaigin. com). Kelvinbridge underground. **Open** 5-11pm Tue-Thur; noon-2.30pm, 5-11pm Fri-Sun. **Main courses** £12-£23. **Credit** AmEx, MC, V.
The 'think global, eat local' approach to cooking at this basement restaurant and ground-floor café-bar has made it one of Glasgow's leading eateries. The menu is as appealing as it is eclectic: a typically adventurous main dish could be Scottish pork loin marinated in maple, lemon and thyme, served with garlicky crushed sweet potato and black kale.
Other locations: Stravaigin 2, 8 Ruthven Lane, West End (0141 334 7165).

Ubiquitous Chip

12 Ashton Lane (0141 334 5007/www.ubiquitous chip.co.uk). Hillhead underground. **Open** noon-2.30pm, 5.30-11pm Mon-Sat; 12.30-5pm, 6-11pm Sun. **Main courses** £5-£19. **Credit** AmEx, MC, V.
The setting is impressive enough: either indoors, where there are murals by artist and author Alasdair Gray, or on an enclosed cobbled courtyard, surrounded by greenery and water features. But the food is the real draw at this impressive Scots restaurant, where you can feast on the likes of Perthshire wood pigeon and organic Orkney salmon. There's also a fine wee bar called, uh, the Wee Bar.

Pubs & bars

The City Centre

Arches

253 Argyle Street (0141 565 1035/www.thearches. co.uk). St Enoch underground/Argyle Street rail. **Open** 11am-midnight Mon-Sat; noon-late Sun. *Food served* noon-9pm daily. **Credit** MC, V. **Map** p332 D4 ❶
Housed under Glasgow Central Station, the cavernous Arches is all things to all people: a cultural centre known above all else for its theatre productions (*see p279*), a music venue, a gallery space, an integral part of the city's club scene (*see p279*) and an above-average café-bar. Both the lunchtime and evening menus are extensive, but it's also a good spot for a simple drink or two. DJs play from Friday to Sunday.

Bar 10

10 Mitchell Lane (0141 572 1448/www.bar10.info). St Enoch underground/Argyle Street rail. **Open** 11am-midnight daily. *Food served* noon-4.30pm daily. **Credit** MC, V. **Map** p333 E4 ❷
One of Glasgow's original style bars, Bar 10 has the unmistakable mishmash appearance of once having been something else entirely. Relaxed and perhaps even a little down-at-heel, it's still loveable, if not quite 'the greatest bar in the world' (as its website advertises, hopefully with its tongue in its virtual cheek). It serves a fullish menu during the day, but offers only snacks in the evenings.

Bunker

193-199 Bath Street (0141 229 1427/www.the bunkerbar.com). Buchanan Street or Cowcaddens underground/Charing Cross rail. **Open** noon-midnight Mon-Sat; 11.30am-midnight Sun. *Food served* noon-9pm Mon-Sat; 11.30am-9pm Sun. **Credit** MC, V. **Map** p332 D3 ❸
Glasgow loves its style bars: it seems as though barely a month passes before someone attempts another variation on the theme. The Bunker is one of the better-appointed hangouts, with an extensive food menu and some very affordable drinks. As the evening progresses, it morphs from café-bar into pre-club hangout, with DJs from Tuesday to Saturday and live bands on Sundays.

Butterfly and the Pig

153 Bath Street, City Centre (0141 221 7711/
www.thebutterflyandthepig.com). Cowcaddens
underground/Charing Cross rail. **Open** noon-
midnight Mon-Thur, Sun; noon-2am Fri, Sat.
No credit cards. Map p332 D3 **4**
This hybrid of style bar and convivial local pub is a
charming place, if perhaps a little chaotic at times.
DJs and bands provide entertainment; the bar is tied
to the Buff Club (*see p279*). The deliberately verbose
and misspelled menu seems designed to irritate, but
the food is decent.

Centre for Contemporary Arts (CCA)

350 Sauchiehall Street, City Centre (0141 352 4900/
www.cca-glasgow.com). Cowcaddens underground/
Charing Cross rail. **Open** *Café-Bar* 10.30am-10pm
Tue, Wed, Thur; noon-midnight Fri, Sat. *Bar* noon-
11pm Tue, Wed; noon-midnight Thur; noon-1am Fri,
Sat. **No credit cards. Map** p332 D2 **5**
Just one component of a warren of galleries and
workshops, the glass-roofed café-bar at the CCA (*see*
p251) is an extremely handsome spot. Stop for a
drink or tuck into the full menu. The bar itself (enter
on Scott Street) is packed at the weekend, a relaxed
and central meet-up point for scenesters.

Griffin

266 Bath Street (0141 331 5171). Cowcaddens
underground. **Open** 11am-midnight daily. *Food*
served noon-6.45pm daily. **Credit** MC, V. **Map**
p332 C2 **6**
Directly opposite the King's Theatre (*see p280*), this
Edwardian-era survivor is made up of an attractive
old bar and a couple of adjoining spaces for pub
grub (the Griffinette and the Griffiny). People spill
out of the popular performances at the theatre and
come here for a drink; it's also popular with staff
from nearby offices after work.

Horseshoe

17-19 Drury Street (229 5711). St Enoch
underground/Argyle Street rail. **Open** 11am-
midnight Mon-Sat; 12.30pm-midnight Sun.
Credit MC, V. **Map** p333 E4 **7**
Very near to Central Station (Drury Street runs
between Renfield Street and West Nile Street),
the Horseshoe is a classic old-school Glasgow bar.
There are few concessions to the 20th century here,
let alone the 21st: customers come for beer and ludi-
crously cheap pub grub. There's a basic restaurant
space upstairs, serving more substantial meals.

Nice 'n' Sleazy

421 Sauchiehall Street, City Centre (0141 333 0900/
www.nicensleazy.com). Cowcaddens underground.
Open 11.30am-11.45pm Mon-Sat; 12.30-11.45pm Sun.
No credit cards. Map p332 C2 **8**
Anyone who's anyone on the Glasgow music scene
will show their bearded face and skinny frame in
here at regular intervals, probably enjoying the
same combination of wicked cocktails, good food
and cheap bands downstairs as the rest of us. Not
nice, exactly, but not especially sleazy, either.

Variety Bar

401 Sauchiehall Street, City Centre (0141 332 4449).
Cowcaddens underground. **Open** 11am-midnight
Mon-Sat; 11.30am-midnight Sun. **No credit cards.**
Map p332 C2 **9**
Looking as though it once imagined itself as a
retro American diner but at some point during the
redecorations thought better of it, this dim-lit,
charismatic and extremely welcoming Sauchiehall
Street spot attracts a good pre- and post-gig crowd
from the nearby ABC (*see p276*) and Garage (490
Sauchiehall Street, 0141 332 1120). The daytime
atmosphere is less bustling but no less friendly.

The Merchant City & the East End

Babbity Bowster

16-18 Blackfriars Street (0141 552 5055). Buchanan
Street underground/Argyle Street or High Street rail.
Open 11am-midnight Mon-Sat; 12.30pm-midnight
Sun. *Food served* noon-10pm Mon-Sat; 12.30pm-10pm
Sun. **Credit** MC, V. **Map** p333 G4 **10**
You don't get many opportunities to bask in
the Glaswegian sunshine with a pint, but – weather
permitting – the tables outside Babbity Bowster's
offer precisely such a privilege. Drinks include cask
ales and the menu takes in Scottish dishes and
the occasional French favourite. The venue also has
hotel rooms and a first floor restaurant (Schtische),
but the lively beer garden is the finest feature.
Photo *p268*.

Horseshoe.

Trips Out of Town

Babbity Bowster. See p267.

Although parts of this building date back to the 16th century, it's only been in use as a theatre since 1980. Take your pick between the attractive Victorian restaurant, with its wooden-vaulted ceiling, or the light and bright modern conservatory bar to the side of the building. Either is well worth a visit, whether or not you're planning on seeing a play here.

West Brewing Company

Binnie Place, off Glasgow Green (0141 550 0135/ www.westbeer.com). St Enoch underground/High Street rail. Open 10am-11pm Mon-Thur; 10am-midnight Fri, Sat; 11am-11pm Sun. Food served 10am-9pm Mon-Sat; 11am-9pm Sun. Credit MC, V. Map p333 H6

One of Glasgow's most notable newcomers, the West Brewing Company launched in 2006 in a landmark East End building, the former Templeton Carpet Factory. The beer, brewed on site, aims for a German authenticity, and the pub has a Bavarian theme. The food is similarly Teutonic, but with a few Scottish dishes thrown in for good measure.

The West End

Ben Nevis

1197 Argyle Street (0141 576 5204). Exhibition Centre rail. Open noon-11pm Mon-Thur, Sun; noon-11.30pm Fri, Sat. Food served noon-6pm daily. No credit cards. Map p332 A2

There's no way Ben Nevis could be described as a designer bar, although it was clearly assembled with a kind of Neolithic chic in mind: dark wood and stone abound. With a wide whisky selection, decent beer, music sessions and good pub grub, it's a nice surprise at the Kelvingrove end of Argyle Street.

Bon Accord

153 North Street (0141 248 4427). Charing Cross rail. Open 11am-midnight Mon-Sat; 12.30-11pm Sun. Food served noon-7.45pm Mon-Sat; 12.30-7.45pm Sun. Credit MC, V. Map p332 C3

Often acclaimed as the best real ale pub in the city, Bon Accord usually has eight offerings on tap. Other attractions include fine music sessions, decent bar meals, and whisky served in proper tumblers. The only downside is the location, above the M8 motorway and opposite Glasgow's high-rise blocks.

Chinaski's

239 North Street (0141 221 0061/www.chinaskis. com). Charing Cross rail. Open noon-midnight daily. Food served noon-9pm daily. Credit MC, V. Map p332 C2

Close to the Bon Accord, Chinaski's is something of a departure for Glasgow: a style bar that's actually quite stylish, rather than just a glitzy excuse to raise the price of the house lager. The menu is good, there's free Wi-Fi access, and there's even a pleasant 'bourbon and cigar garden' (bourbon and cigars not mandatory). Heaven knows what Charles Bukowski, from whose writings the bar takes its name, would have made of it.

Corinthian

191 Ingram Street (0141 552 1101/www.corinthian. uk.com). Buchanan Street or St Enoch underground/ High Street rail. Open Lite Bar 11am-late daily. Piano Bar 9pm-3am daily. Slouch Bar 6pm-late daily. Food served: Lite Bar noon-5pm. Credit AmEx, MC, V. Map p333 F4

This entertainment complex is a beautifully extravagant spot. Housed in an ornate Victorian bank (later used as the High Court), it now contains several bars, a club and a restaurant. If you don't have the time to eat here, at least have a drink in the enormous Lite Bar, resplendent with gold leaf, cornicing and, directly overhead, an enormous glass dome.

Scotia

112 Stockwell Street (0141 552 8681). St Enoch underground/Argyle Street rail. Open 11am-midnight daily. Food served noon-3pm Mon-Fri; 12.30-4pm Sat, Sun. Credit MC, V. Map p333 F5

Just behind Argyle Street, new Glasgow falls apart, and you get a sense of what the city was like a few decades ago. Enter the Scotia, and you're transported back much further. The wood-panelled walls and old pictures just about convince you that this is the city's oldest bar, a prime place for music, beer and whisky. Along with the Victoria Bar (159 Bridgegate, 0141 552 6040) and the Clutha Vaults (167 Stockwell Street, 0141 552 7520), it's part of the so-called Stockwell Triangle, a trio of old-school folky bars.

Tron Theatre Bar

63 Trongate (0141 552 8587/www.tron.co.uk). St Enoch underground/Argyle Street rail. Open 10am-midnight Mon-Sat; 11am-midnight Sun. Food served 10am-5pm Mon, Sun; 10am-9pm Tue-Thur; 10am-10pm Fri, Sat. Credit MC, V. Map p333 F5

Trips Out of Town

Goat

*1287 Argyle Street (0141 357 7373/www.thegoat.
co.uk). Bus 9, 62/Kelvinhall underground.* **Open**
noon-midnight daily. *Food served* noon-3pm, 5-9pm
Mon-Thur; noon-9pm Fri-Sun. **Credit** Am Ex, MC, V.
The Goat has established itself as a city favourite in
recent years. It's essentially a gastropub: drinkers
tend to congregate downstairs, leaving the mezzanine area for diners munching on the decent food
(including a good bar bites menu). Other selling
points include occasional bands and DJs, free Wi-Fi
access, and leather sofas on which to lounge and
watch the football. An excellent all-rounder.

Halt

*160 Woodlands Road (0141 352 9996).
Kelvinbridge or St George's Cross underground.*
Open noon-midnight daily. *Food served* noon-8pm
daily. **Credit** MC, V. **Map** p332 B1 ⑲
The Halt has open-mic sessions and occasional gigs,
and serves a decent range of pub grub. But it's also
been a fine place for drink and conversation since
Edward VII was on the throne. Just a nice, simple,
pleasant pub.

Lansdowne Bar

*7A Lansdowne Crescent (0141 334 4653/
www.lansdownebar.co.uk). Bus 59/Kelvinbridge
underground.* **Open** noon-midnight Mon-Sat;
12.30pm-midnight Sun. *Food served* noon-9.45pm
Mon-Sat; 12.30-9.45pm Sun. **Credit** MC, V.
Located just off the Great Western Road, the
Lansdowne is a basement bar with a modern feel,
its decor characterised by clean lines and wooden
fittings. The superior pub grub (steaks, pastas, pizzas, fish and chips) is best washed down with decent
pint of Deuchars IPA. Other attractions include occasional DJs and, out back, a conservatory.

Liquid Ship

*171 Great Western Road (0141 331 1901/www.
stravaigin.com/liquid.htm). St George's Cross
underground.* **Open** 10am-midnight daily. *Food
served* 10am-8pm Mon-Thur, Sun; 10am-9pm Fri, Sat.
Credit MC, V.
Liquid Ship comes from the same stable of businesses as Stravaigin (*see p266*), which makes the
emphasis it places on food no surprise. The menu is
more about salads, snacks and platters than proper
sit-down dinners, but is done well all the same. The
Ship has also built up a strong reputation as a reliable venue for acoustic music.

Lismore

*206 Dumbarton Road (0141 576 0102).
Bus 8, 16, 20, 62, 64, 89/Kelvinhall underground.*
Open 11am-midnight Mon-Sat; 12.30pm-midnight
Sun. **No credit cards**.
Taking its name from a small Inner Hebridean
island, the Lismore is a straightforward, unpreten-
tious and traditional folk music pub with one of the
best selections of single malt whiskies in Glasgow.
The pub's decorative features include stained-glass
and references to the Highland Clearances.

Lock 27

*1100 Crow Road, Anniesland (0141 958 0853/
www.lock27.com). Anniesland rail.* **Open** noon-11pm
Mon-Thur; noon-midnight Fri; noon-11.45 Sat;
12.30-11pm Sun. *Food served* noon-9pm Mon-Sat;
12.30-9pm Sun. **Credit** MC, V.
Glasgow has few places to drink al fresco and
even fewer by the waterside. Lock 27, then, occupies
a fairly privileged niche, sitting on the Forth
and Clyde Canal just beyond the West End. It has a
fairly extensive menu and bargain wines, but really comes into its own on sunny days.

Òran Mór

*Top of Byres Road (0141 357 6200/www.oran-mor.
co.uk). Hillhead underground.* **Open** 9am-2am
Mon-Sat; 11.30am-2am Sun. *Food served* 9am-9pm
daily. **Credit** MC, V.
The cavernous bar at this converted church at the
corner of Byres Road and the Great Western Road
is supplemented by some lively arts programming
and a worthwhile restaurant. The ceiling mural in
the main auditorium was painted by Alasdair Gray,
and is one of Glasgow's most extensive pieces of
public art.

Sail aboard the **Liquid Ship**.

Trips Out of Town

Shops & services

Second only to London among all UK cities, Glasgow loves to shop. Virtually every one of the country's favourite high-street chain shops and big department stores are represented in the city, but there are also plenty of independent retailers scattered around town, hawking all manner of specialist goods to the hordes of local shopaholics.

In the **City Centre**, three streets dominate the shopping landscape: **Argyle Street**, which crosses the bottom of **Buchanan Street**, which in turn connects with **Sauchiehall Street**. All three are pedestrianised for much of their extents; a good job, given the massive volume of foot traffic that descends upon them at weekends. The busiest of the trio is Buchanan Street, home to malls, mainstream stores, and a handful of rarer chains such as Diesel and Jones the Bootmaker.

Just east of here, the **Merchant City** is home to the majority of Glasgow's smarter and more expensive clothing boutiques. Some are operated by individual designers: Armani and Ralph Lauren both have shops in the area. But others, such as Cruise, stock a wide and almost indiscriminate range of catwalk names. After innumerable false starts over the last few years, it's widely rumoured that Selfridges will open a shop in the area during 2007. Tucked away around the back of these highfalutin fashion-packed streets, in the alleys and alcoves behind the **Trongate**, are a cluster of delightfully tatty stores selling used this and second-hand that.

Standing apart from the heady consumerist familiarity of the City Centre, Glasgow's **West End** has its own commercial buzz, dotted with lively fashion boutiques and unusual gift shops. The main shopping streets are **Byres Road** and the **Great Western Road**, home to a jumble of music shops, clothing stores, grocers' shops and cafés, but don't miss cobbled Cresswell Lane and its **De Courcy's Arcade**, an enticing selection of one-off stores selling predominantly second-hand and vintage goods.

One-stop shopping

Glasgow's department stores generally think big, and none think bigger than **House of Fraser** (45 Buchanan Street, 0870 160 7243, www.houseoffraser.co.uk). The huge Victorian building is home to everything from Cath Kidston homewares to MAC cosmetics and designer togs. The shoe department is a highlight, with footwear to suit all budgets.

While Frasers represents historical Glasgow, **John Lewis** (Buchanan Galleries, 0141 353 6677, www.johnlewis.com) is the new kid on the block. As well as a wide selection of clothes, you'll find toys, homewares and haberdashery here, all at the store's famously keen prices. **Debenhams** (97 Argyle Street, 08445 616161, www.debenhams.com) has most basics that you could need for your home or wardrobe, while **Marks & Spencer** (2-12 Argyle Street, 0141 552 4546; 172 Sauchiehall Street, 0141 332 6097, www.marksandspencer.com) is as popular for its above-average food hall as for its inexpensive undies.

Several large malls dot the centre of town, each holding a large number of names familiar to British shoppers from high streets across the UK. The most popular of the malls – and, not coincidentally, the most mainstream – is the shiny **Buchanan Galleries** (220 Buchanan Street, 0141 333 9898, www.buchanangalleries.co.uk), home to the likes of Mango, H&M and Quiksilver. The **St Enoch Centre** (55 St Enoch Square, 0141 204 3900, www.stenoch.com), Europe's largest glass structure, is similarly stocked with stores such as HMV, JD Sports and the seemingly obligatory Gap.

Some variation on the mall theme is provided by **Princes Square** (48 Buchanan Street, 0141 221 0324, www.princessquare.co.uk). You'll find Monsoon and Accessorize here, but you'll also find the less ubiquitous likes of Whistles and Ted Baker, along with funky interiors store Bo Concept and fragrance boutique Jo Malone. But by far the town's most interesting mall isn't really a mall at all: the chain-free **De Courcy's Arcade** (5-21 Cresswell Lane, 0141 334 6673), home to a smile-inducing mix of cafes, vintage record shops and antique stores.

Two regular markets merit mention. Every weekend, **The Barras** (244 Gallowgate, 0141 552 4601, www.glasgow-barrowland.com). comes alive with 1,000 traders and shopkeepers offering you – yes, YOU! – the bargain of a lifetime. Sports socks, tea towels, clothes, CDs, DVDs and just about everything else you can think of is on offer, although you might wonder where some of it came from. Even if you have no use for 200 Benson & Hedges or a polyester bra, it's worth the journey simply to hear the local dialect in full flow. For a less full-on experience, head to the **Crafts & Designers Market** (Merchant Square, 71-73 Albion Street, 0141 552 5908, www.merchantsquare glasgow.com), held every Saturday.

Books

Perhaps surprisingly for a city of its size and stature, Glasgow isn't especially well served by bookshops. The City Centre contains branches of **Borders** (98 Buchanan Street, 0141 222 7700, www.borders.com) and **Waterstone's**

Trips Out of Town

Shopping on and around **Buchanan Street**.

(153-157 Sauchiehall Street, 0141 332 9105, www.waterstones.co.uk), both of which should cover most mainstream book needs. The two leading second-hand bookstores in the city are the relatively organised **Caledonia Books** (483 Great Western Road, 0141 334 9663, www.caledoniabooks.co.uk) and the decidedly cluttered **Voltaire & Rousseau** (18 Otago Lane, 0141 339 1811). And in De Courcy's Arcade (see p271), you'll find **Arthur's Books** (0141 334 6959), specialising in old magazines, comics and other illustrated tomes.

Fashion

Edinburgh might have Harvey Nichols and Multrees Walk these days, but shoppers in search of designer labels will find a wider range in Glasgow. For starters, head to **Cruise** (180 Ingram Street, 0141 572 3232; also **Cruise Jeans**, 223 Ingram Street, 0141 229 0000): one of the city's favourite independent retailers, it offers everything from carefully sharp suits to deliberately ragged jeans from labels including Dolce & Gabbana, Prada and Burberry. Other options include the **Italian Centre** (John Street, 0141 552 6368), which supplements branches of **Armani** and **Versace** with cafés and restaurants. **Ralph Lauren** (208 Ingram Street, 0141 204 6000) is just down the road.

If all you really want is a good quality suit, head straight for **Slaters** (165 Howard Street, 0141 552 7171, www.slatermenswear.com), listed in the *Guinness Book of Records* as the single largest menswear store in the world. And while Glasgow is better known for

fashion-forward clothing than traditional clobber, you can get kitted out in full Highland regalia. Try **Geoffrey (Tailor) Kiltmakers & Weavers** (309 Sauchiehall Street, 0141 331 2388, www.geoffreykilts.co.uk; see p192) or **Hector Russell, RG Lawrie Kiltmakers** (110 Buchanan Street, 0141 221 0217, www. hector-russell.com), which hawks everything from cashmere to shortbread.

The city is dotted with independent boutiques. On the top floor of Princes Square and run by two cousins, **Fifi & Ally** (Princes Square, 0141 229 0386, www.fifi-and-ally.co.uk) is the hippest, specialising in casually bohemian clothes, jewellery and lingerie. Stop for a quick break and a fantastic organic cake at the patisserie and café. Other city centre treats include **All Saints** (GPO Building, Ingram Street, 0141 248 6437), a cutting-edge fashion label where old meets new (think skinny jeans combined with Victoriana). The West End is also home to a pleasing array of one-off shops. Perhaps chief among them is **Felix & Oscar** (459 Great Western Road, 0141 339 8585, www.felixandoscar.co.uk), great for funky clothing and accessories. With its striking selection of clothes from names such as Zandra Rhodes, Betty Jackson and Diane von Furstenberg, **Moon** (10 Ruthven Lane, 0141 339 2315) also has a loyal clientele.

In addition to its new-clothing boutiques, the West End is also good for vintage gear. In particular, try **Starry Starry Night** (19 Downside Lane, 0141 337 1837) for everything from Victoriana to 1980s trends. If you're in the City Centre, visit **Mr Ben** (Kings Court, 99

King Street, 0141 553 1936), where the focus is on 1970s and '80s clothing. Going back in time, the **Victorian Village** (93 West Regent Street, 0141 332 0808) contains various antique and jewellery shops, as well as **Saratoga Trunk**, a vintage clothing emporium. It's just the tip of the iceberg, though: to visit the company's warehouse, the source for outfits worn in films such as *Star Wars: The Phantom Menace* and *Evita*, you'll need to make an appointment.

If the clothing you're after is contemporary, try **Dr Jives** (111-113 Candleriggs, 0141 552 5451, www.oddoneout.com), which stocks labels such as Silas and Stüssy for the gents and Eley Kishimoto for the ladies. **Aspecto** (18-20 West Nile Street, 0141 221 6321, www.aspecto.co.uk) has more of bent towards sportswear, stocking Duffer, G-Star and Adidas. **Cult Clothing** (63 Queen Street, 0141 226 6822) also takes care of Glaswegian's urban style needs, with labels such as Bench and Golddigga.

If you're looking for jewellery with which to accessorise your outfit, the easiest port of call is the **Argyll Arcade** (30 Buchanan Street, 0141 248 5257, www.argyll-arcade.com). Built in 1827, this ornate arcade features 32 jewellery shops, selling antique and cutting-edge pieces. Other good options include **Brazen Studios** (58 Albion Street, 0141 552 4551, www.brazen studios.co.uk), which showcases jewellery by some of Britain's best new designers, and **Orro Contemporary Jewellery** (12 Wilson Street, 0141 552 7888, www.orro.co.uk), where the innovative designs might be made of anything from platinum to plastic.

Health & beauty

The city's department stores (*see p271*) have a wide selection of cosmetics and fragrances by all the well-known brands. The larger branches of **Boots**, in the St Enoch Centre and Buchanan Galleries, also have good ranges, as well as health and grooming essentials. For a designer fix from Eve Lom, Stila or REN, go directly to **Space NK** (Princes Square, 0141 248 7931, www.spacenk.co.uk).

For a luxurious selection of bubble baths and body lotions, try **Molton Brown Cosmetics** (14 Royal Exchange Square, 0141 248 8090); visit **L'Occitane en Provence** (46 Buchanan Street, 0141 248 7940) for skincare and fragrances made using traditional French methods. **Lush** (111 Buchanan Street, 0141 243 2522; 136 Sauchiehall Street, 0141 333 9912; www.lush.co.uk) sells fresh and almost off-puttingly colourful soaps and bath products, while **Neal's Yard Remedies** (11 Royal Exchange Square, 0141 248 4230, www.neals yardremedies.com) has lots of sweet-smelling

jars of potions made with essential oils and herbal extracts. If you prefer the natural approach, **Napiers** (13 Bothwell Street, 0141 248 5407; 61-63 Cresswell Street, 0141 339 5859; www.napiers.net) is well stocked with herbal and homeopathic remedies, and also has practitioners offering holistic therapies.

Those in need of a little pampering are directed to the **Beauty Store** (1 Royal Exchange Court, 0141 204 2244, www.the beautystore.biz), described by *Tatler* as 'the best nail spa outside London'. As well as a full range of beauty treatments, it also offers an extensive selection of luxury cosmetics and skincare. Another soothing option is the **Oshi Spa** at Langs Hotel (*see p281*), where you can enjoy a massage or pedicure before relaxing in the aromatherapy steam room.

Complete your grooming with a haircut. **Taylor Ferguson** (106 Bath Street, 0141 331 1728, www.taylorferguson.com) is world-renowned for its award-winning stylists, while **Rainbow Room International** (125 Buchanan Street, 0141 248 5300, www.rainbow roominternational.com) has equally high standards. Gents can get the works at the **City Barbers** (99 West Nile Street, 0141 332 7114).

Music

Britain's major music department stores are both represented in Glasgow. There are two branches of **HMV** (154-160 Sauchiehall Street, 0141 332 6631; Lewis Building, Argyle Street, 0141 204 4787; www.hmv.co.uk), as well as a pair of run-of-the-mill **Virgin Megastores** (235 Buchanan Street, 0141 353 2993; 83 Argyle Street, 0141 221 2606; www.virgin.com). Given its alarmingly quick rate of expansion across the UK, Scots chain **Fopp** may soon cease to be seen as an alternative to these mainstream players. No matter: though the breadth of its stock sometimes leaves a little to be desired, there are always bargains at its two Glasgow branches (19 Union Street, 0141 222 2128; 358 Byres Road, 0141 357 0774; www.fopp.co.uk).

A few smaller independent shops battle to be heard. **Avalanche** (34 Dundas Street, 0141 332 2099, www.avalancherecords.co.uk) stocks music from across the board, but is perhaps best approached for its indie discs. **Monorail**, a bijou little shop located inside a vegan café named Mono (12 Kings Court, King Street, 0141 552 9458, www.monorailmusic.com), contains a hand-picked selection of alternative music in all manner of genres. **23rd Precinct** (23 Bath Street, 0141 332 4806, www.23rdprecinct.co.uk) specialises in dance, electronica and hip hop; **Classics in the City** (54 Dundas Street, 0141 353 6915, www.classicsinthecity.co.uk) should cover all your classical and opera needs; and **Folk Revolution** (22 Clarendon Place, 0141 353 1285, www.folkrevolution.co.uk) is a one-stop shop for CDs, instruments and books. For second-hand bargains, try Avalanche (*see p273*), **Lost in Music** (DeCourcy's Arcade, Cresswell Lane, 0141 339 8155) or **Missing Records** (48 Oswald Street, 0141 248 1661).

Arts & Entertainment

Comedy

Year-round, the local comedy scene is well served by the Glasgow outpost of the **Stand** (333 Woodlands Road, West End, 0870 600 6055, www.thestand.co.uk; *see p216* for the Edinburgh branch), which stages events nightly. It's also one of the main venues for March's two-week **Glasgow International Comedy Festival** (0141 552 2070, www.glasgowcomedyfestival.com), a mix of big names and circuit regulars. The city is also home to a branch of unavoidable national chain **Jongleurs**, in the same development as the Cineworld movie house (7 Renfrew Street, City Centre, 08707 870707, www.jongleurs.com).

Film

Glasgow is dotted with first-run cinemas, among them the centrally located **Cineworld** on the corner of Renfrew Street and West Nile Street (0870 200 2000, www.cineworld.co.uk) and the West End's **Grosvenor Cinema** (Ashton Lane, 0141 339 8444, www.grosvenorcinema.co.uk). Lovers of independent cinema are directed to the **Glasgow Film Theatre** (12 Rose Street, 0141 332 8128, www.gft.org.uk), which supplements arthouse flicks with older movies and occasional special events.

Galleries

In addition to major spaces such as the **Burrell Collection**, the **Gallery of Modern Art**, the **Lighthouse**, the **CCA**, the **Glasgow School of Art** and the **Kelvingrove Art Gallery & Museum** (for all, *see pp251-261*), Glasgow boasts a number of small, independent galleries. Aside from those on King Street (*see p253*), it's

▶ For details on **what's on in Glasgow** during your visit, pick up *The List* or the *Skinny* (*see p303*).

worth checking to see what's on at **Sorcha Dallas** (5 St Margaret's Place, www.sorchadallas.com). In addition, the gallery spaces at the **Arches** (*see p266*) and the **Tramway** (*see p280*) both stage engaging shows.

The **Glasgow School of Art Degree Show**, a free exhibition of student work held for a week or so each June at the Renfrew Street college (*see p252*), is one of the local arts community's social events of the year, with fine art from tomorrow's Turner Prize-winners and a suitably wild street party. The work is often superb, but the event is also a great opportunity to explore the Mackintosh Building. And look out for the **Glasgow International Festival of Contemporary Art** (www.glasgowinternational.org), an arts biennial that's growing in confidence and size. It's next due to be staged in April or May 2008.

Gay & lesbian

Aside from the **Polo Lounge** (*see p279*), which can draw a slightly mixed crowd on weekends, the city's other main gay venue is **Bennets** (80 Glassford Street, Merchant City, 0141 552 5761, www.bennets.co.uk), a cheery nightclub still going strong after 25 years. A little competition comes from the newly opened **CoCo** (18 Jamaica Street, 0141 847 0820).

The annual **Pride Scotia** festival is held alternately in Edinburgh and Glasgow; it'll be at the latter in 2008 and 2010. By way of compensation, the city holds its own citywide celebration of queer culture each year: **Glasgay!** (0141 552 7575, www.glasgay.co.uk), whose month-long programme takes in film screenings, theatrical performances and art exhibitions. It's held over a month or so each October/November.

Music

Classical & opera

Scottish Opera's Glasgow home is the **Theatre Royal** (*see p280*).

Glasgow Royal Concert Hall

2 Sauchiehall Street, City Centre (0141 353 8000/ www.grch.com). Buchanan Street underground/ Queen Street rail. **Box office** *In person & by phone* 10am-5pm Mon-Sat; until 9pm on concert days. **Tickets** £5-£30. **Credit** MC, V. **Map** p333 E3.
The construction of the the Royal Concert Hall was dogged with controversy. However, more than 15 years after it finally opened, it's regarded as one of the leading venues of its type in the UK. The classical programming is led by the Royal Scottish National Orchestra (*see p227*); other events range from Raymond Gubbay-promoted pop classics shows to the Celtic Connections festival in January.

Festivals and events

Undaunted by the shadow cast by Edinburgh's festivals, Glasgow's social calendar is crammed with events to cater for all tastes. In recent years, an explosion of festivals has brought many unexpected pleasures to the city's cultural life, with each quarter revelling in its own style of entertainment. Check the *Skinny* or *The List* for a rundown of what's on when you arrive. Discipline-specific events (music festivals, art biennales and the like) are detailed in their individual sections; *see pp274-280.* Unless stated, events are free.

Maydaze

Glasgow Green (0871 200 3940/www.may daze.org). Bridgeton rail. **Date** 1st Sun in May. Glasgow Green has been the site of popular rebellions since 1745, when Bonnie Prince Charlie camped there on his way to England, so it's proper that the city's May Day celebrations take place there after a union rally in George Square. Those not convinced by the politics can content themselves with free concerts, children's entertainments, outdoor sports and other attractions.

West End Festival

Various venues (0141 341 0844/www. westendfestival.co.uk). Hillhead underground. **Tickets** prices vary. **Dates** 2wks in June. A classy mix of music, theatre and gin-tasting. The undoubted highlight is the Mardi Gras and street party on Byres Road which, in 2006, linked up with Mela, Glasgow's vibrant multicultural festival on Kelvingrove Park.

Glasgow Show

Glasgow Green, G4 (0871 200 3940/www. glasgow.gov.uk). Bridgeton rail. **Admission** £3; £2 concessions. **Dates** wknd in early July. A rollicking day in the sun (weather permitting) which, in 2005, featured skydiving, stunt car racing and a concert from Peat Loaf (sic). Very much a people's festival, it's a perfect opportunity to experience the affection Glaswegians feel for their city.

Glasgow's River Festival

River Clyde (www.glasgowriverfestival.co.uk). Exhibition Centre rail. **Dates** wknd in July. Launched in 2003, the River Festival celebrates the Clyde's glorious past and its exciting future with a number of historical exhibits, some speedboat displays and a variety of musical entertainment.

World Pipe Band Championships

Glasgow Green (0141 564 4242/ www.secxtra.com). Bridgeton rail. **Tickets** £4-£19. **Date** 1 day in mid Aug. The truly international dimension of bagpiping becomes clear at this event: almost every continent is represented. The event reaches a crescendo of sound and colour as thousands of pipers and drummers participate in a mass march past the assembled crowds. As much of a spectacle as the Edinburgh Tattoo.

Whisky Live

George Square (www.whiskylive.com). Buchanan Street underground/Queen Street rail. **Tickets** £29.50 (includes 15 whisky vouchers). **Dates** wknd in early Sept. Whisky Live attempts to provide the participants with the ultimate whisky experience, with tastings, masterclasses, live music and regular nose-off competitions. A fun day out, if expensive.

Doors Open Day

Various venues (0141 221 1466/ www.doorsopendays.org.uk). **Dates** wknd in Sept. The magnificent City Chambers and the ornate Garnethill Synagogue are just two of the hidden gems opened to the public during this weekend.

Merchant City Festival

Various venues (www.merchantcityfestival. com). **Tickets** prices vary. **Dates** 1wk in Sept. An eclectic showcase of theatre, comedy, visual arts, street theatre, live music, food and fashion in the Merchant City quarter. Supported by Scottish Opera and Scottish Ballet, both of which performed for free during 2005, this is superior cultural entertainment.

Glasgow's Hogmanay

George Square (www.glasgowshogmanay. org.uk). Buchanan Street underground/ Queen Street rail. **Tickets** £5. **Date** 31 Dec. With more than 25,000 revellers (and almost as many police) in George Square for the city's Hogmanay celebrations, the countdown to midnight is a noisy, debauched yet controlled affair with bands, DJs and fireworks. 2005 was waved away with some polite MOR in the form of sets from Athlete, Hue & Cry and Deacon Blue.

Trips Out of Town

Glasgow City Halls & Old Fruitmarket

Candleriggs, Merchant City (0141 353 8000/www. glasgowcityhalls.com). Buchanan Street underground/ Queen Street rail. **Box office** *In person & by phone* 10am-5pm Mon-Sat; until 9pm on concert days. **Tickets** £5-£30. **Credit** MC, V. **Map** p333 G4.

Built in the 19th century, this complex of venues reopened in 2006 after extensive refurbishments, and is once again in terrific shape. The roster of concerts in the impressive, 1,000-capacity main hall is highlighted by regular shows from the BBC Scottish Symphony Orchestra. The Old Fruitmarket specialises in jazz and folk events, while the Recital Hall hosts small-scale concerts.

Royal Scottish Academy of Music & Drama

100 Renfrew Street, City Centre (information 0141 332 4101/box office 0141 332 5057/www.rsamd. ac.uk). Cowcaddens underground. **Box office** *By phone* 9am-5pm Sat; hours extended on concert days. **Tickets** £4-£10. **Credit** MC, V. **Map** p332 D2.

The concert hall of the Royal Scottish Academy of Music & Drama stages a regular array of recitals and masterclasses.

Rock, pop & dance

In addition to the venues featured below, **Nice 'n' Sleazy** (*see p267*) stages regular live music in its basement space, and there are frequent gigs at the **Woodside Social Club** (*see p279*) and the **Tron Theatre** (*see p280*). Big acts such as Corinne Bailey Rae play the **Glasgow Royal Concert Hall** (*see p274*). **Mono** (*see p273; www.monorailmusic.com*) also hosts singers and bands from time to time. **Stereo** closed in mid 2006, but a reopening is planned for the future (in a new building).

A number of music festivals appear on the city's cultural calendar throughout the year. The city's roots are celebrated at the **Celtic Connections** folk festival (353 8000, www. celticconnections.com), which runs for a fortnight each January. Previous years have seen picture-postcard Scottish group the Battlefield Band rub shoulders with Dhais, their Galician equivalent. Most big concerts during the event are held at the Royal Concert Hall (*see p274*).

Held over an early-September weekend in Victoria Park, **Indian Summer** (www.indian summerglasgow.com) gives Glasgow's thriving indie scene a chance to see what the current crop of *NME*-approved bands are up to. The event was headlined in 2006 by the Yeah Yeah Yeahs and Antony & the Johnsons. Either side of it, two niche events add a measure of exoticism: **Big Big Country Festival** (rockabilly, bluegrass, folk and all stripes of Americana; ten days in May) and **Big Big World** (world music; two weeks in October). Both are held in a variety of venues around the city; see www.soundsfine.co.uk.

ABC

300 Sauchiehall Street, City Centre (0141 332 2232/ www.abcglasgow.com). Cowcaddens underground/ Charing Cross rail. **Admission** £4-£15. **No credit cards. Map** p333 D2.

Which side are you on?

Forget Arsenal's hatred of Spurs, and the enmity that separates Manchester City and United: comfortably the fiercest rivalry in British sport is between Celtic and Rangers (aka the Old Firm), Glasgow's two football teams. The animus is partly sporting: the two teams have traditionally been the strongest in Scotland. But it also goes deeper. Plenty of the hostility is born from the religious bigotry of a considerable minority of fans: Celtic are held up as an icon of the Catholic community, while Rangers affect the role of Protestant defenders, a boorish and unpleasant borrowing from history that's turned violent on innumerable occasions.

The teams meet four times a year in the Scottish Premier League (SPL), and may also clash against each other in the Scottish knockout competitions. Tickets for these derby games are nigh-on impossible to come by, but it's usually rather easier to get into both teams' games against lesser opposition.

Celtic play at Celtic Park in the east of the city (95 Kerrydale Street, 0871 226 1888, www.celticfc.net, tickets £23-£31), while **Rangers** play to the south-west at Ibrox (Edmiston Drive, 0870 600 1993, www. rangers.co.uk, tickets £23-£24). If you can't make a game, both teams offer tours of their stadia. Celtic Park tours begin at 11am, noon, 1.45pm and 2.30pm daily (£8.50, £5.50 concessions), bookable on 0141 551 4308. Tours of Ibrox, meanwhile, run at 11am, 12.30pm and 2.30pm on Thursdays and Fridays and every 45 minutes between 10.30am and 4.30pm on Sundays (£7, £5 concessions); call 0870 600 1972 to reserve your place. There are no tours on matchdays.

Citizens' Theatre. *See p280.*

The regeneration of this old cinema has been extremely welcome in a city where most of the leading music venues are showing their age a little. The two halls between them stage a variety of events, with a concentration on mainstream music in all its myriad forms. Once the bands have finished, DJs take over, spinning music of a primarily indie bent.

Barfly
260 Clyde Street, City Centre (0870 907 0999/ www.barflyclub.com). St Enoch underground/Central Station rail. **Admission** £5-£10. **Credit** MC, V. **Map** p333 E5.
Bands not quite at the stage where they can fill King Tut's usually end up at this corner of the far-reaching, ever-growing Barfly enterprise.

Barrowland
244 Gallowgate, East End (0141 552 4601/ www.glasgow-barrowland.com). Argyle Street rail/ High Street rail. **Admission** £8-£25. **No credit cards. Map** p333 H5.
For years one of the greatest live music venues in the UK, the Barrowland is still going strong. Apart from the garish, gigantic neon sign, it's not much to look at, but the crowd regard it as their historical duty to go electrifyingly wild. There are actually two spaces here: the 1,900-capacity main room, and the considerably smaller Barrowland 2.

Carling Academy Glasgow
121 Eglinton Street, South Side (0141 418 3000/ www.glasgow-academy.co.uk). West Street underground. **Admission** £10-£25. **Credit** AmEx, MC, V. **Map** p332 D6.
First an art deco cinema, then a bingo hall, and now Glasgow's newest mid-sized live music venue, the Carling Academy is a pleasantly grubby space. Public Enemy, New Order, the Flaming Lips and Motörhead have all played of late.

Grand Ole Opry
2-4 Govan Road, South Side (0141 429 5396). Shields Road underground. **Open** 7pm-1am Fri, Sat. **Admission** £4-£12. **No credit cards.**
The Opry is a South Side institution for Glasgow's legions of country-music fans, who gather every weekend in this tacky hall, decorated in Confederate memorabilia, to imbibe cheap liquor, line-dance, witness the fake shoot-out and – yee-haw! – play bingo. Like nowhere else in Britain.

King Tut's Wah Wah Hut
272A St Vincent Street, City Centre (0141 221 5279/ www.kingtuts.co.uk). Central Station rail. **Admission** £5-£15. **No credit cards. Map** p332 D3.
Founded in 1990, this storied space in the middle of town is still the venue of choice for touring acts on their way up – or down – the *NME* ladder. Everyone from James Morrison to Sparklehorse has played here in recent years.

Scottish Exhibition & Conference Centre/Clyde Auditorium
Exhibition Way, City Centre (0141 248 3000/ box office 08700 404000/www.secctickets.com). Exhibition Centre rail. **Admission** £10-£65. **Credit** MC, V. **Map** p332 A3.
The SECC is a vast aircraft hangar of an arena, the main venue for big touring acts as they pass through Scotland. The smaller Clyde Auditorium (aka the 'Armadillo') provides the sit-down atmosphere sought by more mature performers (and audiences).

Jazz

While Glasgow's rock circuit is considerably livelier than Edinburgh's, the capital does trump its West Coast rival on the jazz front. Big names do trot through town as part of British or European tours, particularly during the two-week **Glasgow International Jazz Festival** held around June/July (0141 353 8000, www.jazzfest.co.uk), but the scene is otherwise quite small. The **Old Fruitmarket** (*see p276*) hosts many of the touring acts; for details of smaller venues, see the excellent **GlasJazz** website at www.glasjazz.co.uk.

Nightclubs

In clubbing terms, Edinburgh has a head start on its West Coast rival simply by dint of the fact that its city fathers have made it far easier for bar- and club-owners to obtain a late alcohol licence. However, while the club scene in Edinburgh is more or less dominated by cheesy indie nights and cornball retro-disco piss-ups, Glasgow's nightlife circuit retains a real edge.

In addition to the clubs below, a handful of music venues also stage club nights once the bands have finished. Among them are the **ABC** (*see p276*) and **Nice 'n' Sleazy** (*see p267*).

Where staying in is the new going out

Luxury accommodation

Irresistible cuisine

Fancy a night out? Then why not stay in with a sumptuous meal featuring the best local ingredients in our Michael Caines Restaurant, followed by an overnight stay in one of our Comfortable, Desirable, Enviable or Fabulous rooms? Rooms from £89 per room per night.

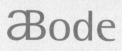

Arches

30 Midland Street, City Centre (0870 240 7528/
www.thearches.co.uk). St Enoch underground/Central
Station rail. **Open** hrs vary. **Admission** £4-£20.
Credit MC, V. **Map** p333 E4.
Reclaimed from the huge network of tunnels
beneath Central Station, this multi-purpose venue
hosts theatre performances (*see below*), exhibits
works by local artists and serves an above-average
menu in its café-bar (*see p266*). It's also, though, a
consistently terrific club venue: regular nights
include gay-oriented Burly (1st Fri of month), elec-
tro-rock favourite Blitzkrieg Bop (2nd Fri of month)
and the house- and trance-heavy Inside Out (last Sat
of month).

Buff Club

142 Bath Lane, City Centre (0141 248 1777/
www.thebuffclub.com). Cowcaddens underground/
Charing Cross rail. **Open** 11pm-3am Mon-Fri;
10.30pm-late Sat, Sun. **Admission** £3-£6.
No credit cards. Map p332 D3.
The Buff Club's primary focus is soul and funk, but
it also offers indie, electro and disco through its
seven-night opening schedule. The venue is tied to
the Butterfly & the Pig (*see p267*).

Glasgow School of Art

168 Renfrew Street, City Centre (0141 353 4531/
www.theartschool.co.uk). Cowcaddens underground/
Charing Cross rail. **Open** 11pm-3am Thur-Sat.
Admission free-£6. **No credit cards. Map** p332 D2.
The bar and club nights at Glasgow's Art School are
greatly venerated among the city's sizeable indie
cognoscenti. Regular nights include hip hop-heavy
Freak Menoovers (Thursdays) and northern soul-
tinged Divine (Saturdays); check the website for
other one-off events. Drinks, needless to say, are
pretty cheap.

Polo Lounge

84 Wilson Street, Merchant City (0141 553 1221).
Buchanan Street underground/Queen Street rail.
Open 5pm-1am Mon-Thur; 5pm-3am Fri-Sun.
Admission free-£5. **Credit** MC, V. **Map** p333 F4.
One of Glasgow's leading gay clubs (for others, *see*
p274), the Polo Lounge opens its doors every night
of the week. The DJs generally don't challenge
the punters too much, but the queues here on weekends are testament to the fact that the punters don't
really mind.

Soundhaus

47 Hydepark Street, Anderston (0141 221 4659/
www.soundhaus.co.uk). Anderston rail. **Open**
hrs vary. **Admission** £4-£8. **No credit cards.**
Map p332 B4.
It's located on an industrial estate a short distance
out from the city centre, but Soundhaus is worth the
walk. At nights such as Monox and Off the Record,
hard-edged techno styles come together in an agreeably underground atmosphere. The club is members
only: call for membership details or simply get someone else to sign you in.

Sub Club

22 Jamaica Street, City Centre (0141 248 4600/
www.subclub.co.uk). St Enoch underground/Central
Station rail. **Open** 11pm-3am Fri-Sun. **Admission**
£2-£12. **No credit cards. Map** p333 E4.
Favouring experimentalism over commercialism,
up-and-comers over veterans, this small but perfectly formed enterprise encapsulates all that can be
great about Glasgow clubbing. Subculture, held
every Saturday and featuring regular guest DJs, is
a brilliant house night, while Sunday's anything-
goes Optimo is commonly regarded as Scotland's
finest regular club night.

Woodside Social Club

329 North Woodside Road, Kelvinbridge (0141 337
1643). Kelvinbridge underground. **Open** hrs vary.
Admission £2-£5. **No credit cards**.
This old-school neighbourhood social club has been
shunted into the present day in recent years, thanks
to the efforts of a wily bunch of promoters keen to
stage events in memorably offbeat venues. National
Pop League, an indie night, has flourished here for
years; indie-friendly Pinup Nights, held on the first
Friday of the month, also does keen business.

Theatre & dance

Two very different events enliven the city's
theatrical calendar. Over a month or so
each February/March, **New Territories**
(www.newmoves.co.uk) brings an array of
contemporary dance and performance art
to the Tramway (*see p280*). The 2006 event
featured the convention-upending work of La
Ribot and the extreme body art of Ron Athey.
And then, in June/July, it's time for Scotland's
only outdoor Shakespeare festival: **Bard in**
the Botanics (www.glasgowrep.org), staged
in the fragrant surroundings of the Botanic
Gardens. Picnicking is encouraged.

Arches Theatre

253 Argyle Street, City Centre (0870 240 7528/
www.thearches.co.uk). St Enoch underground/
Central Station rail. **Box office** 9am-8pm Mon-Sat;
12-6pm Sun. **Tickets** £5-£15. **Credit** MC, V.
Map p333 E4.
The most atmospheric theatre in Scotland, this
subterranean warren has built itself into a vital
creative hub over the past 15 years. The hugely popular nightclub (*see above*) and renowned café-bar
(*see p266*) keep the money flowing in, allowing
young theatre-makers to take their first experimental steps and the resident company to stage adventurous productions of 20th-century classics. The
best shows use the myriad rooms for spooky promenade performances, as disorientating as they are
dramatic. Andy Arnold's company is a keen supporter of up-and-coming talent, through forums such
as the Arches Theatre Festival in the spring and
autumn's Arches Live.

Trips Out of Town

Citizens' Theatre

119 Gorbals Street, South Side (administration 0141 429 5561/box office 0141 429 0022/www.citz.co.uk). Bridge Street underground. **Box office** 10am-6pm Mon-Sat (until 9pm on performance days). **Tickets** £2-£20. **Credit** MC, V. **Map** p333 E6.

For 30-odd years, under the directorial triumvirate of Giles Havergal, Robert David MacDonald and Philip Prowse, the Citz was one of Europe's great theatrical powerhouses, famed for its blend of high camp, high risk and high intelligence. Since Jeremy Raison took over in 2003, the company has been going through the slow process of redefining itself for a new era without losing its old identity. As well as the attractive horseshoe auditorium, two studios are often used for touring productions. **Photo** *p277*.

King's Theatre

297 Bath Street, City Centre (0141 240 1111/ www.theambassadors.com/kings). Charing Cross rail. **Box office** *In person & by phone* 10am-8pm Mon-Sat. **Tickets** £10-£35. **Credit** AmEx, MC, V. **Map** p332 C2.

Under joint management with the Theatre Royal, the King's has a true place in the city's heart, not least for its earthy annual pantomime. Outside the Christmas season, the traditional theatre, built in 1904, hosts large-scale touring productions on post-West End runs, as well as some amateur musicals.

Pavilion Theatre

121 Renfield Street (0141 332 1846/www.pavilion theatre.co.uk). Cowcaddens underground/Queen Street rail. **Box office** 10am-8pm daily. **Tickets** £8-£19. **Credit** MC, V. **Map** p333 E2.

The Pavilion is that rare thing: a large, traditional theatre run without subsidy by an independent management. Unashamedly populist, it offers broad comedies, often with a Glasgow setting, as well as bands, comedians and risqué hypnotists. The raucous Christmas pantomime is a hoot.

Theatre Royal

282 Hope Street, City Centre (0141 332 9000/www. theatreroyalglasgow.com). Cowcaddens underground. **Box office** 10am-6pm Mon-Sat (until 8pm on performance days). **Tickets** £5-£30 (more for Scottish Opera productions). **Credit** AmEx, MC, V. **Map** p333 E2.

To ease its perennial financial woes, Scottish Opera handed over the operation of the Theatre Royal to the Ambassador Theatre Group in 2005, which means this grandest of Glasgow theatres shares its management with the King's Theatre. The association with Scottish Opera and Scottish Ballet endures, sustaining the Victorian theatre's reputation for the high arts; you're likely to come across serious drama and large-scale Shakespeare productions.

Tramway

25 Albert Drive, Pollokshields (0141 422 2023/ www.tramway.org). Pollokshields East rail. **Box office** *In person & by phone* 10am-8pm Tue-Sat; noon-6pm Sun. **Tickets** £5-£15. **Credit** MC, V.

Cutting edge art, theatre and performance, plus a year-round garden of tranquillity. The big warehouse-style space has struggled to maintain the momentum of its glory days following 1990, when Glasgow was European City of Culture and visitors included Peter Brook, Robert Lepage and the Wooster Group, but it's still a hive of activity and innovation, with performers from home and abroad.

Tron Theatre

63 Trongate, City Centre (0141 552 4267/www.tron. co.uk). St Enoch underground. **Box office** 10am-6pm Mon-Sat (hours extended on performance days). **Tickets** £5-£15. **Credit** MC, V. **Map** p333 F5.

This lively theatre puts on a variety of smaller touring productions to complement its own shows, which are usually of a high standard. Its collaborations with the Edinburgh International Festival, including David Greig's *San Diego* and Anthony Neilson's *The Wonderful World of Dissocia*, have been the highlights of recent seasons. The restaurant and bar are also highly recommended, humming with discussions between local dramatists.

Where to Stay

The City Centre

ABode

129 Bath Street, G2 2SZ (0141 572 6000/ www.abodehotels.co.uk/glasgow). Cowcaddens underground/Charing Cross rail. **Rates** £125-£225 double. **Credit** AmEx, DC, MC, V. **Map** p332 D3 ❶

This City Centre hotel found a measure of success under its former name, Arthouse. However, since a rebranding as part of the ABode mini-chain in late 2005, it's picked up even more plaudits. Part of this is down to the involvement of chef Michael Caines, who lends his name to the kitchen at MC @ Abode (*see p262*). However, the high-tech rooms are also impressive in a modish, undemonstrative way. **Photo** *p281*.

Bewleys

110 Bath Street, G2 2EN (0141 353 0800/fax 0141 353 0900/www.bewleyshotels.com). Cowcaddens underground/Charing Cross rail. **Rates** £69 double. **Credit** MC, V. **Map** p333 D4 ❷

The stepped, overhanging storeys, protuberant roof and glass frontage of Bewleys make it virtually impossible to miss. Part of a small chain, the Glasgow incarnation opened in 2000. It's essentially a budget hotel (the £69 room rate is valid every day), but comes with a reasonably stylish design that sets it apart from most cheapo bedboxes. Free Wi-Fi access is a bonus, and the location is perfect.

City Inn Glasgow

Finnieston Quay, G3 8HN (0141 240 1002/fax 0141 248 2754/www.cityinn.com/glasgow). Exhibition Centre rail. **Rates** £99 double. **Credit** AmEx, DC, MC, V. **Map** p332 A4 ❸

This modern hotel, part of an expanding UK chain, isn't bang in the City Centre, but does count among its neighbours such attractions as the Finnieston Crane and the Science Centre (*see p256*). Its restaurant (the City Café) is decent enough and the hotel offers free broadband internet access. However, the real selling point is the views afforded by the river-facing rooms. Be sure to specify when you book.

Ibis Glasgow

220 West Regent Street, G2 4DQ (0141 225 6000/ fax 0141 225 6010/www.ibishotel.com). Buchanan Street underground/Charing Cross or Queen Street rail. **Rates** £47-£52 double. **Credit** AmEx, DC, MC, V. **Map** p332 D3 ➍

There are around 50 Ibis hotels scattered around the UK. While we haven't been to them all, it's a fair bet that they all look something like this: clean, plain and completely forgettable. However, at these prices and this location, it's hard to argue with the formula.

Langs

2 Port Dundas Place, G2 3LD (0141 333 1500/fax 0141 333 5700/www.langshotels.co.uk). Buchanan Street underground/Queen Street rail. **Rates** £115 double. **Credit** AmEx, DC, V. **Map** p333 E2 ➎

Located up near the Royal Concert Hall, Langs has given the Malmaison a little competition since opening in 2000. Certainly, both hotels are aimed at a similar clientele: youngish, affluent urbanites here on either business or pleasure. It's a stylish place, the rooms crisp, clean and furnished with flat-screen TVs and Playstations. There are two bars and restaurants here, and Wi-Fi access throughout the building. However, the major selling point is the Oshi Spa, one of the best urban spas in Scotland.

Malmaison

278 West George Street, G2 4LL (0141 572 1000/ fax 0141 572 1002/www.malmaison-glasgow.com). Charing Cross rail. **Rates** £135-£155 double. **Credit** AmEx, DC, MC, V. **Map** p332 D3 ➏

The second hotel in the chain to open (Edinburgh was first, a month earlier), this Malmaison is housed for the most part in a 19th-century Greek Orthodox church. It's an impressive setting: check out the handsome, below-stairs restaurant, complete with stunning vaulted ceilings. The handsome, comfortable rooms are individually decorated; none are more individual than the tartan-heavy Big Yin Suite named in tribute to Billy Connolly. Other amenities include high-speed internet access.

Radisson SAS

301 Argyle Street, G2 8DL (0141 204 3333/fax 0141 204 3344/http://glasgow.radissonsas.com). St Enoch underground/Central Station rail. **Rates** £195 double. **Credit** AmEx, DC, MC, V. **Map** p332 D4 ➐

Just as the Malmaison makes a virtue of its historic building, so the Radisson isn't afraid to advertise its modernity. Confounding expectations that this might be just another chain hotel, it opened in 2004 in a strikingly modern, purpose-built structure that's impossible to miss. The interior isn't as memorable, but the guestrooms are nonetheless crisp, comfortable and welcoming. For TaPaell'Ya, the hotel's most accessible restaurant, *see p263*.

St Jude's

190 Bath Street, G2 4HG (0141 352 8800/fax 0141 352 8801/www.saintjudes.com). Charing Cross rail. **Rates** £95 double. **Credit** MC, V. **Map** p332 C2 ➑

ABode. See p280.

Hotel du Vin at One Devonshire Gardens.

Glasgow's original boutique hotel forms part of a terrace of Victorian townhouses in one of the more attractive pockets of the City Centre. The accommodation – just six rooms, so be sure to book well in advance – aims for a cool and stylish modernism, and the basement effectively serves as another Bath Street style bar; the ground-floor restaurant underwent a major refurbishment in spring and summer 2006.

The Merchant City & the East End

Brunswick

104-108 Brunswick Street, G1 1TF (0141 552 0001/fax 0141 552 1551/www.brunswickhotel. co.uk). Buchanan Street underground/Queen Street rail. **Rates** £65-£95 double. **Credit** MC, V. **Map** p333 F4 ⑨
'Contemporary, minimalist accommodation,' advertises the Brunswick's website, which just about covers it. No two of the 18 rooms are quite alike, but all are plain, stylish and devoid of clutter. Whoever named the hotel's carefully chic café-bar Brutti Ma Buoni ('ugly but good') clearly had a sense of humour. The location is handy, and prices are keen.

Cathedral House

28-32 Cathedral Square, G4 0XA (0141 552 3519/fax 0141 552 2444/www.cathedralhouse.com). High Street rail. **Rates** £65-£85 double. **Credit** MC, V. **Map** p333 H3 ⑩
The Cathedral House hotel started life in 1877 as a halfway house for a local prison, before being transformed into the diocesan headquarters of the Catholic Church. Today's operation attempts to balance this history with modern conveniences, and does so quite nicely. There aren't too many frills in the eight guestrooms, but the prices make them quite hard to resist.

The West End

Hotel du Vin at One Devonshire Gardens

1 Devonshire Gardens, G12 0UX (0141 339 2001/fax 0141 337 1663/www.hotelduvin.com). **Rates** £155-£295 double. **Credit** AmEx, DC, MC, V.
The city's smartest hotel sits in a leafy row of Victorian terraces. It's a handsome place, elegant and luxurious but never flashy. The guestrooms are supplemented by an array of appetising services and amenities, among them an air-conditioned gym, Wi-Fi access and 24-hour room service. Taken over in summer 2006 by the Malmaison group, the hotel was scheduled for refurbishments prior to a relaunch and rebranding under the Hotel du Vin umbrella. Hopefully it'll retain the same (very) high standards.

Directory

Arriving & leaving

By air

Glasgow Airport (0870 040 0008, www. glasgowairport.com) is eight miles south-west of the city, at Junction 28 of the M8. Buses 905 and 950 leave the airport for the city roughly every ten minutes during the day (every 15 minutes on weekends) and every half-hour from 8pm until midnight. The 25-minute journey costs £3.30 for a single and £5 return. Alternatively, a taxi will take about 20 minutes and cost about £16-£20.

Cheap flights operated by Ryanair arrive at **Glasgow Prestwick Airport** (0871 223 0700, www.gpia.co.uk), 32 miles south-west of the city. There's a regular train service between the airport and Glasgow's Central Station; journey time is 45 minutes. Upon presentation of the relevant plane ticket or boarding pass, all aeroplane passengers receive 50% off the fare.

By bus or coach

Long-distance buses arrive at and depart from **Buchanan Street Bus Station** (0141 333 3780) at Killermont Street. Citylink runs a service to and from Edinburgh roughly every 15 minutes (slightly more frequently during rush hour); journey time is around 80 minutes and the fare is around £5.

By car

Despite its all-ensnaring motorway system, Glasgow is actually easy to access by car. The M8 from Edinburgh delivers you into the heart of the city. Take junction 15 for the East End and Old Town, junction 16 for Garnethill, junction 18 for the West End, junction 19 for the City Centre and junction 20 for the South Side.

By train

Glasgow has two main-line train stations. **Queen Street Station** (West George Street) serves Edinburgh (trains every 15 minutes) and the north of Scotland, while **Central Station** (Gordon Street) serves the West Coast and south to England. The stations are centrally located and are within walking distance of each other. For further information on rail travel in Scotland, *see p297*.

Getting around

Central Glasgow is easy to negotiate on foot, but you'll need to use public transport or hire a car if you're going further afield. Nearly all the listings in this chapter refer only to the underground or train network for reasons of space. However, the frequent bus service that runs throughout the city is well signposted at the regular bus stops. Glasgow is also served by a fleet of capacious black taxis. They're cheap, but elusive in the early hours.

As for trains, besides the inter-city services, there's a good network of low-level trains serving Glasgow's suburbs, which is run by Scotrail. The slightly ramshackle underground system, affectionately known as the Clockwork Orange, is a single, circular line that loops between the centre and the West End. To enjoy another view of Glasgow, or to travel to Braehead shopping centre or the **Scottish Maritime Museum** (*see p256*), hop on the waterbus at Central Station bridge.

Clyde Waterbus

07711 250969/www.clydewaterbusservices.co.uk. **Ferry services** *From Glasgow* every 90mins, 10.45am-6.15pm Mon-Fri; 11.15am-5.15pm Sat; 11.45am-5.45pm Sun. *Departing Braehead* every 90mins, 10am-5.45pm Mon-Fri; 10.30am-4.30pm Sat; 11am-5pm Sun. **Tickets** *Single* £4.25; £3.25 concessions; £13 family. *Return* £7.50; £5.50 concessions; £22 family. **No credit cards.**

Traveline Scotland

0870 608 2608/www.travelinescotland.com. **Open** 8am-8pm daily.

Resources

Health

Glasgow Dental NHS Trust

378 Sauchiehall Street, City Centre, G2 (0141 232 6323). Cowcaddens underground. **Open** *Emergency clinic* 9-noon, 1.30-3.30pm Mon-Fri by appointment only. **Map** p332 D2.

Glasgow Royal Infirmary NHS Trust

84 Castle Street, East End (0141 211 4000). High Street rail. **Open** *Accident & emergency* 24hrs daily. **Map** p333 H2.

Western Infirmary NHS Trust

Dumbarton Road, Partick (0141 211 2000). Kelvinhall underground/Partick rail. **Open** *Accident & emergency* 24hrs daily.

Postal services

There are post offices throughout the city, the majority open during usual post office hours (*see p304*). To get information about your nearest, call 08457 223344 or see www.royalmail.com. There's a late-opening post office at 1606 Great Western Road, G13 (0141 954 8661).

Telephones

The area code for Glasgow and its environs is 0141.

Tourist information

Greater Glasgow & Clyde Valley Tourist Information Centre

11 George Square, City Centre (0141 204 4400/ fax 0141 221 3524/www.seeglasgow.com). Buchanan Street underground. **Open** *Oct-Apr* 9am-6pm Mon-Sat. *May* 9am-6pm Mon-Sat; 10am-6pm Sun. *June, Sept* 9am-7pm Mon-Sat; 10am-6pm Sun. *July, Aug* 9am-8pm Mon-Sat; 10am-6pm Sun. **Credit** MC, V. **Map** p333 F3.
The Tourist Information Centre will take credit card bookings for accommodation throughout the city (with a small booking fee), and can also answer general enquiries about sightseeing and local events.

Trips Out of Town

Around Edinburgh

Bring both golf clubs and walking boots.

East Lothian

The coastal town of **Musselburgh** is barely five miles from the bustle of the Royal Mile, but feels much further apart. It was settled by the Romans, who established a port at the mouth of the river Esk, as far back as AD 80, and remains proud of its history. Since the early 14th century, it's been known as the 'honest toun', a sobriquet gained when the locals refused to claim a reward offered to them after they cared for Randolph, Earl of Moray, through a long illness. This historic virtue is commemorated each year with the appointment of an Honest Lad and Honest Lass in the town.

Post-war development hasn't been especially kind to the town's outer reaches, but its centre remains a handsome place. The chief attractions are owned by the National Trust. Towards Edinburgh sits **Newhailes** (*see p285*), a 250-year-old house with rococo interiors and an 18th-century garden. And don't miss **Inveresk Lodge** (*see p285*): the building itself is private but the gardens are sublime, sloping down to the River Esk's peaceful banks. However, most visitors tend to head here for sporting reasons, whether to play the famous **Musselburgh Old Links** (*see p240*) or for a meeting at **Musselburgh Racecourse** (*see p239*).

After the racecourse, take the B1348 to head along the coast road, through small towns such as **Prestonpans**. Beyond the village of **Longniddry**, the full picturesque roll of the East Lothian coast takes hold. Nature thrives here: the **Aberlady Wildlife Sanctuary**, reached by crossing the footbridge from the car park just east of the village of Aberlady, is open all year, its sandy mudflats attracting bird-watchers in autumn. The waders are forced to jostle for position with the golfers who flood here to take advantage of some rugged links courses: **Craigielaw Golf Club** in Aberlady (01875 870800, www.craigielawgolfclub.com), the three courses that comprise **Gullane Golf Club** 01620 842255, www.gullanegolfclub.com), and the legendary **Muirfield** (*see p240*).

Five miles on, at the heart of the pretty village of **Dirleton**, are what remains of 13th-century **Dirleton Castle** (*see p285*). The castle sits atop a hill surrounded by hugely handsome gardens, its herbaceous border recognised by the *Guinness Book of World Records* as the

world's longest. The village itself is a gem, constructed around a green slightly unusual for this part of the world. Slightly further east sits the busier town of **North Berwick**, a quaintly traditional seaside settlement. Edinburghers head here during the summer to take advantage of its clean, sandy beaches, both of which have splendid rock pools that flank the old harbour.

However, the real draw in North Berwick is the **Scottish Seabird Centre** (*see p285*), an ingenious twist on the standard nature reserve. Much of the local wildlife – puffins, gannets, the occasional dolphin – sits on islands off the coast, on which the centre has placed cameras that visitors can remotely control. Boats leave North Berwick harbour (01620 892838, book ahead) during summer for trips to the gannet-smothered **Bass Rock**, a vast offshore lump of volcanic basalt that has been a prison, a fortress and a monastic retreat. The coast beyond North Berwick is dominated by **Tantallon Castle** (*see p285*), a formidable cliff-edge fortification largely built in the 14th century.

Past Tantallon, continue south along the A198 until you reach the A1. Immediately east is the **John Muir Country Park**, which covers more than 1,800 acres of country and coast and provides various habitats for local wildlife. Muir lived in Dunbar until he was 11, when his family emigrated; he was later instrumental in founding the US National Parks system. West along the A1, meanwhile, are the crumbling and slightly isolated remains of 13th-century **Hailes Castle** (*see p285*). And just a short drive north, in an old World War II airfield, sits the popular **National Museum of Flight** (*see p285*), a slightly grand name for a pleasingly low-key institution. Boys of all ages love the collection of old aircraft, including war bombers, passenger planes and even Concorde.

Ten minutes further along the A1 lies the royal burgh of **Haddington**, a well-heeled market town. The main attractions are historic buildings such as **St Mary's Collegiate Church** (aka the Lamp of the Lothians), handsome, undemonstrative and keenly preserved by locals quietly anxious that their town shouldn't embrace the 21st century with too much enthusiasm. However, an even more delightful settlement sits a few miles south along the B6369: built by the Marquis of Tweeddale in the 18th century for his estate workers, **Gifford** is almost too charming for

Dirleton Castle.

words. Continuing south to **Longyester** affords access to the **Lammermuir Hills**, popular with walkers.

Dirleton Castle & Gardens *Dirleton (01620 850330/www.historic-scotland.gov.uk).* **Open** *Apr-Sept* 9.30am-6.30pm daily. *Oct-Mar* 9.30am-4.30pm daily. **Admission** £4; £1.60-£3 concessions. **Credit** AmEx, MC, V.

Hailes Castle *1.5 miles south-west of East Linton (Historic Scotland 668 8600/www.historic-scotland.gov.uk).* **Open** all year, daily. **Admission** free.

Inveresk Lodge Garden *24 Inveresk Village, Musselburgh, East Lothian (01721 722502/www.nts.org.uk).* **Bus** 26, 30, 44, 44A. **Open** 10am-6pm (or dusk) daily. **Admission** £3; £2 concessions; free under-5s; £6-£8 family. **No credit cards**.

National Museum of Flight *East Fortune Airfield, East Fortune (01620 897240/www.nms.ac.uk/flight).* **Open** *Apr-June, Sept, Oct* 10am-5pm daily. *July, Aug* 10am-6pm daily. *Nov-Mar* 10am-4pm Sat, Sun. **Admission** £5; £4 concessions; free under-12s. **Credit** MC, V.

Newhailes *Newhailes Road, Musselburgh, East Lothian (653 5599/www.nts.org.uk).* **Bus** 30. **Open** *Easter wknd* noon-5pm daily. *May-Sept* noon-5pm Mon, Thur-Sun. **Admission** £10; £7 concessions; free under-5s; £20-£25 family. **Credit** MC, V.

Scottish Seabird Centre *Harbour, North Berwick (01620 890202/www.seabird.org).* **Open** *Apr-Oct* 10am-6pm daily. *Nov-Jan* 10am-4pm Mon-Fri; 10am-5.30pm Sat, Sun. *Feb, Mar* 10am-5pm Mon-Fri; 10am-5.30pm Sat, Sun. **Admission** £6.95; £4.50 concessions; £13.95-£21.95 family. **Credit** AmEx, MC, V.

Tantallon Castle *off A198, 2 miles east of North Berwick (01620 892727/www.historic-scotland.gov.uk).* **Open** *Apr-Sept* 9.30am-6.30pm daily. *Oct-Mar* 9.30am-4.30pm Mon-Wed, Sat, Sun. **Admission** £4; £1.60-£3 concessions. **Credit** AmEx, MC, V.

Where to eat & drink

Run by chef David Williams, the dining room at **Greywalls** (*see below*) is the best option, though with a nicely crafted three-course dinner costing £45, it's not the cheapest. Also in Gullane is **La Potinière** (01620 843214, www.la-potiniere.co.uk, £36.50/4 courses), which serves very agreeable French-slanted food. The **Waterside** in Haddington offers decent bistro fare (01620 825674, mains £9-£15), while **Bonars** is a more polite local choice (01620 822100, www.bonars.co.uk, mains £10-£17). On a more affordable note, **Luca's** in Musselburgh (Nos.32-38 High Street, 665 2237) sells the best ice-cream on the east coast. There are several decent little pubs around here, but the nicest is the old-fashioned **Drovers Inn** in East Linton (01620 860298).

Where to stay

The most impressive hotel east of Edinburgh is **Greywalls** in Gullane (01620 842144, www.greywalls.co.uk, double £240-£285), built by

Trips Out of Town

Unearthly garden of delights

Although it's relatively accessible from Edinburgh, the southwestern end of the Pentland Hills can seem harsh. This area is neither picturesque nor punctuated by volcanic outcrops and castles; it's really just a lonely upland. The highest point immediately to the north is named Bleak Law, which seems all too appropriate. Undeterred, it was this part of the world to which poet and artist Ian Hamilton Finlay relocated in 1966 with his wife Sue MacDonald-Lockhart, first moving into a semi-derelict farmhouse and then developing a garden on land surrounding it. Over the following four decades, **Little Sparta** grew into the most celebrated 20th-century garden in Scotland.

Finlay worked with the environment to create a harmonious meeting of horticulture and sculpture. Around the garden's natural features, he inscribed slogans in stone, wood and metal, on themes from philosophy and human rights to war and man's relationship with the sea. It all works on a pleasingly human scale. The tops of classical columns stand at eye level, while apparently natural rocks and simple span bridges carry inscribed definitions that give pause for thought. Little Sparta's trustees are quite right to describe it as a place for 'contemplation, intellectual receptiveness and enjoyment'.

The subtle surprises that Finlay's work can spring on the visitor are perhaps the chief pleasure of a visit here. But there is also a dramatic history to the garden – with its allusions to classical militarism, Little Sparta was the site of a much mythologised 'battle' in 1983, when the local authority claimed that Finlay had turned the locale into an art gallery and so should pay higher rates. He claimed it was a temple and therefore he should not. When sheriff officers appeared to seize artworks in lieu of payment, they were faced by Finlay, his friends, and television news cameras, so backed off. (Although, it should be added, they did come back later.)

In a survey of art experts conducted by *Scotland on Sunday* in 2004, Little Sparta was named the finest Scottish work of art of all time, a gem in a cussed environment. Finlay lived to witness this accolade, but finally passed away aged 80 in March 2006. He was survived by his wife, their two children, and – of course – by the garden, which remains open to visitors for a couple of days a week each summer.

Little Sparta

Just west of Dunsyre (01899 810252/www. littlesparta.co.uk). **Open** *June-Sept* 2.30-5pm Fri, Sun. **Admission** £10. **No credit cards**.

Edwin Lutyens in 1901 as a country retreat. Alternatives include **Browns** in Haddington (1 West Road, 01620 822254, www.browns-hotel. com, double £90-£105) and the **Eaglescairnie Mains** in Gifford (01620 810491, www.eagles cairnie.com, double £35-£70), a lovely old farmhouse B&B. North Berwick boasts a major outpost of the Macdonald chain, the **Marine Hotel & Spa** (Cromwell Road, 0870 400 8129, www.macdonaldhotels.co.uk, double £200-£270), while 17th-century **Kilspindie House** at Aberlady (Main Street, 01875 870504, www. kilspindie.co.uk, double £70-£100) is now run by noted Edinburgh restaurateur Malcolm Duck. However, it's worth noting that even as far out as North Berwick, you're only a 25-mile, 50-minute drive from the centre of Edinburgh.

Getting there

By bus

East Lothian is served by buses from St Andrew Square Bus Station. For further information, consult Lothian Buses or First Group (*see p297*).

By car

Take the A1 out of Edinburgh towards Haddington. The coastal trail is signposted.

By train

A branch line runs services from Edinburgh's Haymarket station through Waverley and on to Musselburgh, Prestonpans, Longniddry, Drem and North Berwick.

Tourist information

Dunbar *143a High Street (01368 863353).* **Open** *Apr, May, Oct* 9am-5pm Mon-Sat. *June, Sept* 9am-6pm Mon-Sat; 11am-4pm Sun. *July, Aug* 9am-7pm Mon-Sat; 11am-6pm Sun.

Musselburgh *Old Craighall, Granada Service Station, off A1 (653 6172).* **Open** *Apr, May, Oct* 9am-5pm Mon-Sat. *June-Sept* 9am-5pm Mon-Sat, 10am-5pm Sun.

North Berwick *1 Quality Street (01620 892197).* **Open** *Apr, May* 9am-6pm Mon-Sat. *June, Sept* 9am-6pm Mon-Sat; 11am-4pm Sun. *July* 9am-7pm Mon-Sat; 11am-6pm Sun. *Aug* 9am-8pm Mon-Sat; 11am-6pm Sun. *Oct-Mar* 9am-5pm Mon-Sat.

Midlothian

The graciously curving Pentland Hills cover 22,000 acres just south of the city on the A702, forming the **Pentland Hills Regional Park**. From here, you can travel further along the A702 to reach the Iron-Age fort of **Castle Law Hill** and explore even more genuine Scottish unadulterated ruralness.

Many head to the Pentlands to do some serious hill-walking, but those who don't fancy putting in much effort should make their way to the **Glencorse Reservoir**. A five-minute stroll up the gentle incline from the reservoir car park plunges you straight into the heather covered hills that form the image of classic Scottish countryside worldwide. Ready and waiting for you on the return trip is the inviting **Flotterstone Inn** (*see below*).

Rosslyn Chapel (*see below*) sits six miles south of Edinburgh at Roslin. The chapel was founded in 1446 by Sir William St Clair, Prince of Orkney, and remains an intensely and ornately carved demonstration of medieval religious syncretism. However, it's most famous for its starring role in both the book and the movie adaptation of Dan Brown's monstrously popular novel *The Da Vinci Code*. The ruins of Rosslyn Castle lie in the nearby woodlands of **Roslin Glen Country Park**, accessed from the B7003 Roslin–Rosewell road. The country park hugs the steep-sided valley of the river Esk, where there are many cliffs and caves. One of them is reputed to be the site of Robert the Bruce's famous encounter with a spider.

Rosslyn Chapel *Roslin (www.rosslynchapel.org.uk).* **Open** *Apr-Sept* 9.30am-6pm daily. *Oct-Mar* 9.30am-5pm Mon-Sat; noon-4.45pm Sun. **Admission** £7; £6 concessions. **No credit cards**.

Where to eat & drink

Eating and drinking options are relatively thin on the ground, but the **Old Bakehouse** in West Linton (01968 660830, mains £8-£18) is worth a look. The **Allan Ramsey Hotel** in Carlops (01968 660258, www.allanramsay hotel.com, mains £7-£13) is an old pub that also serves bar food upstairs. And if you're in the Pentland Hills, don't miss the food – or, for that matter, the beer – at the **Flotterstone Inn** (01968 673717, mains £6-£15) on the A702 at Milton Bridge.

Where to stay

There are a few hotels and B&Bs around these parts, but you're best off staying in Edinburgh, where there's greater quality and quantity.

Getting there

By bus

Buses leave from the St Andrew Square Bus Station for the Pentland Hills and Roslin. For Glencourse and Flotterstone Inn, ask for buses to Milton Bridge.

By car

Take the A701 to Roslin or the A702 from Edinburgh to the Pentland Hills.

Tourist information

There are no tourist information centres in this part of the world.

West Lothian

Just south of the airport lies the village of Ratho, a fairly unassuming little place that's the home of the **Ratho Adventure Centre** (*see p241*). The best parts of West Lothian, however, are closer to the Forth. Along the A90, and just off the B924 towards South Queensferry, is the village of **Dalmeny**, where you'll find **St Cuthbert's**, one of the finest Norman churches in Scotland. Overlooking the Forth is **Dalmeny House** (*see p289*), a Gothic revival mansion designed by William Wilkins in 1814 and home of the Earls of Rosebery. The property boasts the obligatory grand interior and, incongruously, an extensive collection of Napoleonic memorabilia.

Falkirk Wheel. *See p289.*

Just beyond the house is **South Queensferry**, the best place from which to view the imposing pair of Forth bridges. The newer of the two is the **Forth Road Bridge**, a vast suspension bridge completed in 1964 and a continuing source of controversy. But the more impressive, in terms of both construction and appearance, is the **Forth Rail Bridge**, an extraordinary 1.5-mile span completed in 1890. The other main reason to visit South Queensferry is to catch the Maid of the Forth ferry, which sails from South Queensferry to **Inchcolm Abbey** (*see p289*) on Inchcolm Island in the Firth of Forth. Founded in 1123, the abbey comprises a clutch of wonderfully preserved monastic buildings. Seal sightings are common during the boat trip.

West of South Queensferry stands the self-consciously grandiose **Hopetoun House** (*see p289*), designed by William Bruce in 1699 and enlarged by William Adam in 1721. The elegant simplicity of the building belies the opulence within: it really is quite extraordinary inside. Further west is **Blackness Castle** (*see p289*), used by Zefferelli in his film version of *Hamlet*. Its walls have crumbled since they were built in the 1440s, but the view across the Forth from the castle promontory remains spectacular.

Four miles south, just off the M9, is the attractive royal burgh of **Linlithgow**. The town is most famous for the beautiful, ruined **Linlithgow Palace** (*see p289*), where Mary, Queen of Scots was born in 1542. A walk around the bird-filled loch that the palace overlooks takes about an hour, and offers a real sense of the countryside that lies all around.

Behind the station in Linlithgow lies the **Canal Basin**; here you'll find the **Linlithgow Canal Centre** (*see p289*), which includes a museum and a tearoom. There's more for lovers of arcane transportation to the north in the once-thriving, now-ragged town of **Bo'ness**: the steam-powered trains of the **Bo'ness & Kinneil Railway** (*see p289*) regularly chug along the Firth of Forth to the **Birkhill Claymines**, where visitors can take a tour.

West of Bo'ness sits **Falkirk**, an entirely undistinguished town but for the presence of one of the most extraordinary attractions in Scotland. The **Falkirk Wheel** (*see p289*) acts as a link between the Forth & Clyde Canal and the Union Canal, thus connecting the waterways between Glasgow and Edinburgh. From that description, it doesn't sound overly exciting, but it needs to be stressed that one waterway is around 30 metres (95 feet) above

Abbotsford. *See p292.*

the other. Boats are scooped up from the Forth & Clyde Canal and gracefully airlifted up to the Union Canal above; the public can watch this process, or take a ride on a boat and experience the amazing machine in action.

Blackness Castle *Blackness, 4 miles north of Linlithgow on the A904 (01506 834807/ www.historic-scotland.gov.uk). Apr-Sept* 9.30am-6.30pm daily. **Open** *Oct-Mar* 9.30am-4.30pm Mon-Wed, Sat, Sun. Last admission 30min before closing. **Admission** £3.50; £1.50-£2.50 concessions. **No credit cards.**

Bo'ness & Kinneil Railway *Bo'ness (01506 822298/www.srps.org.uk/railway).* **Open** *Apr, May, Sept, Oct* Sat, Sun. *June* Tue, Thur, Sat, Sun. *July, Aug* Tue-Sun. Phone for train times. **Tickets** £5; £2.50-£4 concessions; £13 family. **Credit** AmEx, MC, V.

Dalmeny House *South Queensferry (331 1888/ www.dalmeny.co.uk).* **Open** *July, Aug* 2-5.30pm Mon, Tue, Sun. **Admission** £5; £3-£4 concessions; free under-10s. **No credit cards.**

Falkirk Wheel *Lime Road, Tamfourhill, 1.5 miles from centre of Falkirk (0870 050 0208/ www.falkirk-wheel.com).* **Tickets** *Boat trip* £8; £4.25-£6.50 concessions; £21.50 family. **Credit** MC, V. Photo *p287.*

Hopetoun House *South Queensferry (331 2451/ www.hopetounhouse.com).* **Open** *Mid Apr-Sept* 11am-5.30pm daily (last admission 4.30pm). **Admission** *House & grounds* £8; £4.25-£7 concessions; free under-5s; £22 family. *Grounds only* £3.70; £2.20-£3.20 concessions; free under-5s; £10 family. **Credit** MC, V.

Inchcolm Abbey *Inchcolm Island, Firth of Forth (01383 823332/www.historic-scotland.gov.uk).* **Open** *Apr-Oct* See sailing times for Maid of the Forth below. **Admission** £4; £1.60-£3 concessions. **Credit** AmEx, MC, V.

Linlithgow Canal Centre *Canal Basin, Manse Road, Linlithgow (01506 671215/www.lucs.org.uk).* **Open** *Easter-June, Sept, Oct* 2-5pm Sat, Sun. *July, Aug* 2-5pm daily. **Admission** *Museum* free. *St Magdalene cruise* £6; £3 concessions; £15 family. *Victoria cruise* £2.50; £1.50 concessions. **Credit** MC, V.

Linlithgow Palace *Kirkgate, Linlithgow (01506 842896/www.historic-scotland.gov.uk).* **Open** *Apr-Sept* 9.30am-6.30pm daily. *Oct-Mar* 9.30am-4.30pm Mon-Sat; 2-4.30pm Sun. **Admission** £3; £1-£2.30 concessions. **Credit** AmEx, MC, V.

Maid of the Forth *Ferry leaves from: Hawes Pier, South Queensferry (331 5000/www.maidof theforth.co.uk).* **Open** *Apr-Oct* phone for details. **Admission** *Ferry & abbey* £13; £4.70-£11 concessions; £32 family. *Cruise only* £9; £3-£8 concessions; £21 family. **Credit** AmEx, MC, V.

Where to eat & drink

The restaurant at **Orocco Pier** (*see below*; mains £10-£25) offers decent bistro cooking, with a lively update on Scottish cuisine. Also in South Queensferry, the **Hawes Inn**

(6 Newhalls Road, 331 1990, mains £6-£14) was immortalised by Robert Louis Stevenson in *Kidnapped* as the site of the abduction of David Balfour. The **Stables Tearoom** at Hopetoun House (331 3661, closed Oct-Mar) is very well regarded by cake aficionados. The **Bridge Inn** at Ratho (333 1320, www.bridgeinn.com, mains £9-£18), recently spruced up by a renovation, has two canal boat dining rooms (for parties only) and a restaurant on land.

There are a number of pubs and restaurants serving decent food along the High Street in Linlithgow. Among them is **Livingston's** (No.52, 01506 846565, www.livingstons-restaurant.co.uk, set dinner £33.50/3 courses), which is very popular for deliciously cooked Scottish beef and fish dishes. Good quality alternatives include the **Star & Garter Hotel** (No.1, 01506 846362, mains £5-£15) and the modern **Marynka** (No.57, 01506 840123, mains £10-£17. The best pint in the area can be enjoyed at the **Four Marys** just down the road (No.111, 01506 842171).

Arguably the best restaurant for miles is the **Champany Inn**, just outside Linlithgow via the northbound A803 (01506 834532, www.champany.com, mains £20-£40). Its reputation is based on steaks and lobster, so vegetarians should definitely call ahead.

Where to stay

Undoubtedly the most interesting and characterful place to stay in the immediate vicinity, the **Orocco Pier** in South Queensferry (17 High Street, 331 1298, www.oroccopier. co.uk, £100-£150 double) occupies an old coaching inn right between the Forth rail and road bridges. It's a sharp place, perhaps not quite as stylish as it thinks it is but still an excellent option. The **Macdonald Houstoun House** in Uphall (01506 853831, www.macdonaldhotels.co.uk/houstounhouse, £110-£130 double) is a more straightforward operation, while the **Thornton B&B** (Edinburgh Road, Linlithgow, 01506 844693, www.thornton-scotland.co.uk, £60 double) is a cheaper choice.

Getting there

By bus
A regular bus service departs from the St Andrew Square Bus Station.

By car
Take the A902 west of Edinburgh, then pick up the B974 for South Queensferry. Take the M9 for Linlithgow and Falkirk.

Trips Out of Town

By train

Trains depart regularly from Waverley and Haymarket stations in Edinburgh for South Queensferry, Bo'ness, Linlithgow and Falkirk. Linlithgow is on the main Glasgow–Edinburgh line, with four trains an hour from Edinburgh.

Tourist information

Bo'ness *Union Street (01506 826626).*
Open *Apr-June* 10am-5pm Sat, Sun. *July, Aug* 10am-5pm daily. *Sept, Oct* noon-5pm daily.
Falkirk *2-4 Glebe Street (01324 620244).* **Open** *Apr, May, Sept* 10am-5pm Mon-Sat. *June, July* 10am-5pm Mon-Sat; noon-4pm Sun. *Aug* 9.30am-5pm Mon-Sat, noon-4pm Sun. *Oct-Mar* 10am-4pm Mon-Sat.
Linlithgow *Burgh Halls, The Cross (01506 844600).* **Open** *Apr-Oct* 9am-5pm Mon-Sat; 10am-5pm Sun.

Fife

Fife stands on the far shore of the Firth of Forth, visible from Leith on all but the foggiest days. After North Queensferry and **Deep Sea World**, where a huge aquarium full of rays and sharks stretches over your head, the coast comes into its own around Largo Bay. This stretch, up to and around St Andrews, is known as **East Neuk**, but is also known as 'fringe of gold' for its sandy beaches. Its fishing villages, such as **Elie**, **St Monans**, **Pittenweem**, **Anstruther** and **Crail**, are delightful, tiny colourful houses huddled round harbours holding an array of too-perfect rustic boats.

According to legend, the university town of **St Andrews** is home to the bones of the apostle Andrew, the brother of St Peter. These days, though, it sells itself as a golfing destination, and with good reason. The **St Andrews Links** are the venue of golf, the venue at which the Royal & Ancient Golf Club has determined the rules of the game for more than 250 years. For details on playing the various courses here, *see p240*.

Deep Sea World *Battery Quarry, Fife (01383 411880/www.deepseaworld.com).* **Open** *July, Aug* 10am-6pm daily. *Sept-June* 10am-5pm Mon-Fri; 10am-6pm Sat, Sun. **Admission** £8.55; £6.30-£6.75 concessions; £28.70 family. **Credit** MC, V.

Where to eat

If you're looking for a treat, the restaurant at the **Inn at Lathones** (*see below*; mains £17-£30) uses local produce where possible. If you're looking for a cheap snack, the **Anstruther Fish Bar** (42/44 Shore Street, 01333 310518) is held by many to be the best chippie in Scotland. Also in Anstruther, the **Cellar** (24 East Green, 01333 310378, £35/3 courses) is a great seafood bistro.

In St Andrews, your best bet is the **Seafood Restaurant** (Below the Scores, 01334 479475, www.theseafoodrestaurant.com, £45/3 courses), the name of which rather gives its game away. Its sister restaurant, with the same name and pricing, is in the nearby village of St Monans nearby (16 West End, 01333 730327). Tucked away several miles inland is the **Peat Inn** (nr Cupar, 01334 840206, www.thepeatinn.co.uk), a pioneering gastropub-inn that changed hands in 2006 but will hopefully remain among the best eating options in the region under the auspices of Geoffrey Smeddle, formerly of étain in Glasgow. Anyone passing through Cupar should try the modern Scottish cuisine at **Ostlers Close** (25 Bonnygate, 01334 655574, www.ostlersclose.co.uk, mains £14-£20).

Where to stay

In Dunfermline, try the **Davaar House Hotel** (126 Grieve Street, 01383 721886, www.davaar-house-hotel.com, £85-£90 double). The **Inn at Lathones** (Lathones, by Largoward, 01334 840494, www.theinn.co.uk, £110-£220 double) is a 400-year-old former coaching inn. In Falkland, try the historic **Covenanter** (The Square, 01337 857224, www.covenanterhotel.co.uk, £62 double), another comfortable former coaching inn; if you'd like to stay in St Andrews, you could do worse than the cultured, traditional **Rufflets** Country House (01334 472594, www.rufflets.co.uk, £210-£250 double).

Getting there

By bus

Buses depart from Edinburgh's St Andrew Square Bus Station for Dunfermline and St Andrews. Many buses in the area are run by **Stagecoach Fife** (01383 621249, www.stagecoachbus.com/fife).

By car

Take the A90, then the M90. Turn onto the A823 for Dunfermline, or the A921 for the coastal route. For St Andrews, take the A91 off the M90.

By train

Trains depart Edinburgh's Waverley Station for Dunfermline, Kirkcaldy and Leuchars.

Tourist information

Dunfermline *1 High Street (01383 720999).*
Open *Apr-Sept* 9.30am-5.30pm Mon-Sat; 11am-4pm Sun. *Oct-Mar* 9.30am-5pm Mon-Sat.
St Andrews *70 Market Street (01334 472021).*
Open *Easter-June* 9.30am-5.30pm Mon-Sat; 11am-4pm Sun. *July, Aug* 9.30am-7pm Mon-Sat; 11am-5pm Sun. *Sept, Oct* 9.30am-6pm Mon-Fri, 11am-4pm Sun. *Nov-Easter* 9.30am-5pm Mon-Sat.

Trips and tours

Sightseeing tours

Celtic Trails
448 2869/www.celtictrails.co.uk.
Ancient sites near Edinburgh, with a particular
emphasis on the mythical and medieval.
The Rosslyn Chapel Trail lasts half a day
and costs £31 (£17 children).

Rabbie's Trail Burners
226 3133/www.rabbies.com.
Mini-coach tours of between one and
five days. A trip from Edinburgh to Skye
for three days costs £109 (peak season).
Accommodation costs extra.

Timberbush Tours
226 6066/www.timberbush-tours.co.uk.
Off-the-peg or tailor-made coach tours for
groups of up to 39 people, with your driver
doubling as your guide.

Touring Scotland
07815 886014/www.touringscotland.co.uk.
Personalised tours of Scotland for groups,
lasting half a day, a full day or perhaps
longer. Call for prices.

Backpacking tours

Celtic Connections
225 3330/www.thecelticconnection.co.uk.
Backpacking tours for smaller groups
(up to a maximum of 22 people, and generally
15 or fewer), covering Scotland and Ireland.
The nine-day tour of both countries costs
£225, setting off from Edinburgh.

Haggis Adventures
557 9393/www.haggisadventures.com.
Haggis will take you from Edinburgh to
destinations in the Highlands, on the West
Coast and across the sea to the Isle of Skye.

MacBacpackers
558 9900/www.macbackpackers.com.
A variety of Highland tours. The seven-day
Grand Tour, leaving from Edinburgh and
taking in Inverness, Fort William, Oban and
the Isle of Skye, costs £175; a three-day trip
to Inverness and Oban costs £75.

Wild in Scotland
478 6500/www.wild-in-scotland.com.
Wild in Scotland's tours include a seven-day
trip to Skye and the Hebrides for around
£310; a shorter three-day jaunt to Skye
and the Highlands costs around £120.

Hill-walking

See www.walkingwild.com.

Make Tracks Walking Holidays
229 6844/www.maketracks.net.
Guided walks along hill-walking trails, including
the Southern Upland Way, St Cuthbert's Way
and the Great Glen. The company arranges
accommodation and transports your luggage.
Prices start from £145 for three nights.

Walkabout Scotland
*0845 686 1344/www.walkabout
scotland.com.*
Guided hill-walking tours from Edinburgh to
the Highlands. There are day tours, weekend
breaks and longer walking holidays, and you
don't have to be an experienced hill-walker
to join. Day tours cost from £50.

Wild About Scotland
478 0435/www.wildaboutscotland.co.uk.
Tailored, eco-friendly minibus tours to
Sandwood Bay on the far north-west
coast, offering a taste of the wilderness.
Available in the summer months, a four-day
trip costs £240.

The Borders

A number of picturesque towns and villages
dot the Borders, but it's really what lies
between them that makes the area worth
visiting. Take **Peebles**, for example: while
a perfectly handsome town in its own right,
it's somewhat overshadowed by the rich,
unspoiled countryside that surrounds it.
Heading west will lead you to a couple
of castles: **Neidpath Castle** (*see p293*),
a moderately impressive 14th-century
construction converted into a private residence
during the 1800s, and the barely extant
remains of **Drumelzier Castle**, visible
from the B712. Carry on for a few more miles,
weaving along some handsome back roads,
and you'll get to the pleasant market town of
Biggar. If you've got kids in tow, try to time
your visit to coincide with a performance at
the **Biggar Puppet Theatre** (01899 220631,
www.purvespuppets.com).

Trips Out of Town

East of Peebles, meanwhile, lie a couple of popular attractions. Tucked away off the B7062, **Kailzie Gardens** (*see below*) is an delightful walled garden surrounded by handsome woodlands. And just outside the tidy village of **Innerleithen** is the 1,000-year-old **Traquair House** (*see p293*). Acclaimed as the oldest inhabited house in Scotland, it's served as a court for William the Lion, a hunting lodge for Scottish royalty, a refuge for Catholic priests and a stronghold of Jacobite sentiment.

Further east lie are ruins of **Melrose Abbey** (*see p293*), founded by St Aidan in about 660AD and the reputed resting place of Robert the Bruce's heart. Restored in 1822 by Sir Walter Scott, it's one of the most evocative sites in all the Borders. Perhaps inspired by this history, Scott moved out to this part of the world, building himself an appropriately romantic baronial pile on the banks of the Tweed. The writer died in 1832, only eight years after **Abbotsford** (*see below*) was completed; it's been open to the public since the following year. Two further attractions lie east of Melrose along the B6356: **Scott's View**, a panoramic vista across to the Eildon Hills, and the gargantuan **Wallace Statue**, in the grounds of nearby Bemersyde House.

Abbotsford *Melrose (01896 752043/www.scotts abbotsford.co.uk).* **Open** *Late Mar-Oct* 9.30am-5pm Mon-Sat; 2-5pm Sun. **Admission** £5; £2.50 concessions. **No credit cards. Photo** *p292.*

Dawyck Botanic Garden *Stobo, on B712 (01721 760254/www.rbge.org. uk).* **Open** *Feb, Nov* 10am-4pm daily. *Mar, Oct* 10am-5pm daily. *Apr-Sept* 10am-6pm. **Admission** £3.50; £1-£3 concessions; £8 family. **Credit** MC, V.

Kailzie Gardens *Kailzie (01721 720007/www. kailziegardens.com).* **Open** *Apr-Oct* 11am-5.30pm daily. *Nov-Mar* 11am-dusk daily. **Admission** £3; £1 concessions. **No credit cards.**

The High country

The Lowlands of Scotland are picturesque and rich in history, but it's the **Highlands** where the drama really begins. With awesome peaks of sandstone and granite reaching to 4,406 feet (1,343 metres), the region takes up half of the country's land mass. There are 790 islands, 130 of which are inhabited. If you have an opportunity to travel further afield and discover more of Scotland's staggering scenery, you should grab it. Here are some pointers to help plan trips to three of the most popular destinations. For details of organised tours, *see p291* **Trips and tours**. For further information, see www.visitscotland.com.

The Trossachs

The Highlands converge with the Lowlands at the Trossachs, an area of lochs, rivers and hills. It takes about 90 minutes to reach the region from Edinburgh, and you'll need a car to explore it thoroughly. Loch Lomond, to the west of the Trossachs, is Scotland's largest, and jostles with Ness for the title of most famous loch. For more on the area, check www.lochlomond-trossachs.org, the official site of the Loch Lomond & Trossachs National Park. There are tourist information centres in **Callander** (Ancaster Square, 01877 330342) and **Aberfoyle** (01877 382352).

The Highlands & Isle of Skye

Fort William is a good point from which to explore the Highlands, as many of the major mountains and glens are within striking distance: Glen Coe, Ben Nevis, Glen Nevis, the West Highland Way and Loch Ness. The Road to the Isles (more prosaically known as the A830) takes you from Fort William on a dramatic 46-mile journey through lochs, forests and mountains to Mallaig, where you can board a boat for Skye. Check www.gael-net.co.uk, www. ecossenet.com, www.visit-fortwilliam.co.uk and www.skye.co.uk for further information on the area. There are tourist information centres at Fort William (Cameron Square, 01397 703781) and on Skye (2 Lochside, Dunvegan, 01470 521581).

Isle of Mull

Mull is the most accessible of the major islands because its mainland ferry port, Oban, is only three hours' drive or four and a half hours on the train from Edinburgh. Mull has it all: castles, heathery hills, glistening sandy beaches, miniature train trips and boat excursions to Staffa and Fingal's Cave, and its own unique cheese and whisky. The main town, Tobermory, has recently been used as the set for popular children's TV series *Balamory*; a huge surge in family tourism followed. The comprehensive website at www.isle. of.mull.com lists all kinds of accommodation, and there's also a tourist information office on the island (Main Street, Tobermory, 01688 302610), as well as one in Oban (Albany Street, 01631 563122).

National Wallace Monument. *See p294.*

Melrose Abbey *Abbey Street, Melrose (01896 822562/www.historic-scotland.gov.uk).* **Open** *Apr-Sept* 9.30am-6.30pm daily. *Oct-Mar* 9.30am-4.30pm daily. Last entry 30mins before closing. **Admission** £4.50; £2-£3.50 concessions. **Credit** AmEx, MC, V.
Neidpath Castle *Peebles (01721 720333).* **Open** *May-Sept* 10.50am-5pm Wed-Sat; 12.30-5pm Sun. **Admission** £1.50-£3. **No credit cards**.
Traquair House *Innerleithen (01896 830323/www. traquair.co.uk).* **Open** *Apr, May, Sept* noon-5pm daily. *June-Aug* 10.30am-5pm daily. *Oct* 11am-4pm. *Nov* noon-4pm Sat, Sun. **Admission** *House & grounds* £6.20; £3.30-£5.60 concessions; £17.50 family. *Grounds* £3.50; £2 concessions. **Credit** DC, MC, V.

Where to eat & drink

A picturesque choice is the **Tibbie Shiels Inn** (St Mary's Loch, 01750 42231, www.tibbieshiels inn.com, mains £5-£10), which overlooks the water. **Kailzie Gardens** (*see p292*), has a tea shop that serves good home baking. At **Burts Hotel** (*see below*), you can eat in the convivial bar (mains £8-£15) or choose from a more sophisticated menu in the restaurant. The best bet in Peebles is the **Halcyon** (39 Eastgate, 01721 725100, www.halcyonrestaurant.com, mains £11-£20); **Marmions Brasserie** is the pick in Melrose (Buccleuch Street, 01896 822245, www.marmionsbrasserie.co.uk, mains £8-£15).

Where to stay

In Peebles, the **Peebles Hydro Hotel** (01721 720602, www.peebleshotelhydro.co.uk, £214-£296 double) has great views of the town and good facilities. Other options in Melrose include the **George & Abbotsford Hotel** (01896 822308, www.georgeandabbotsford.co.uk, £62.50-£90 double) and **Burts Hotel** (01896 822285, www.burtshotel.co.uk), which has doubles from around £100. For a country house experience, try the **Roxburghe** outside Kelso (01573 450331, www.roxburghe.net, £170-£280

double). The **Philipburn** in Selkirk (01750 720747, www.philipburnhousehotel.co.uk, doubles £120-£165) has a hearty bistro and an outdoor pool.

Getting there

By bus
Buses depart from St Andrew Square Bus Station.

By car
Take the A701, followed by the A703 to Peebles.

By train
It's almost impossible to reach the Borders by train. The nearest station is in Berwick-upon-Tweed, from where there are connecting buses to Galashiels and other destinations.

Tourist information

Jedburgh *Murray's Green (0870 608 0404).* **Open** *Apr, May* 9.15am-5pm Mon-Fri; 10am-5pm Sun. *June, Sept* 9am-6pm Mon-Fri; 10am-5pm Sun. *July, Aug* 9am-7pm Mon-Sat, 10am-6pm Sun. *Oct* 9.15am-5pm Mon-Sat; 10am-5pm Sun. *Nov-Mar* 9.15am-4.45pm Mon-Sat.
Kelso *Town House, the Square (0870 608 0404).* **Open** *Apr, May, Sept* 9.30am-5pm Mon-Sat; 10am-2pm Sun. *June* 10am-5.30pm Mon-Fri; 10am-2pm Sun. *July, Aug* 9.30am-5.30pm Mon-Sat; 10am-2pm Sun. *Oct* 10am-4pm Mon-Sat, 10am-1pm Sun. *Nov-Mar* 10am-2pm Mon-Sat.
Melrose *Melrose Abbey House, Abbey Street (0870 608 0404).* **Open** *Apr, May, Sept* 9.30am-5pm Mon-Sat; 10am-2pm Sun. *June* 10am-5.30pm Mon-Fri; 10am-2pm Sun. *July, Aug* 9.30am-5.30pm Mon-Sat; 10am-4pm Sun. *Oct* 10am-4pm Mon-Sat; 10am-1pm Sun. *Nov-Mar* 10am-2pm Mon-Sat.
Peebles *23 High Street (0870 608 0404).* **Open** *Apr, May* 9am-5pm Mon-Sat; 11am-4pm Sun. *June* 9am-5pm Mon-Sat; 10am-4pm Sun. *July, Aug* 9am-6pm Mon-Sat; 10am-4pm Sun. *Sept* 9am-5.30pm Mon-Sat; 10am-4pm Sun. *Oct* 9.30am-5pm Mon-Sat; 11am-4pm Sun. *Nov, Dec* 9.30am-5pm Mon-Sat; 11am-3pm Sun. *Jan-Mar* 9.30am-4pm Mon-Sat.

Stirling

Stirling's position just above the River Forth, at the meeting of Scotland's Highlands and Lowlands, made it into a key strategic stronghold for centuries. Two of the most significant battles against English rule took place nearby: William Wallace, subject of the film *Braveheart*, defeated the English at the Battle of Stirling Bridge in 1297, and then Robert the Bruce conquered Edward II's forces at **Bannockburn** 17 years later.

Both events are commemorated in the town. Wallace's achievement is celebrated by the **National Wallace Monument** (*see below*) just beyond Stirling Old Bridge, about a mile north-east of the town. An oddly shaped tower, it dominates the skyline; among the Wallace memorabilia stored with it is the great man's double-edged sword. The story of the Bannockburn battle, meanwhile, is told at the **Bannockburn Heritage Centre** (*see below*).

Castle Rock was probably first occupied in the 600s, yet today's **Stirling Castle** (*see below*) dates mainly from the 15th and 16th centuries. It's a magnificent sight, one of the finest castles in Scotland. Displays inside detail the history of the building: Alexander I died here in 1124, James II was born within its walls, Mary, Queen of Scots was crowned here and her son James VI (later James I of England) was christened in the chapel. The restoration of the wonderful Great Hall is impressive. But the castle's exterior is its greatest asset, a dramatic and daunting structure that retains every bit of the grandeur it's surely boasted for centuries. It's particularly haunting at night.

Below it, on Castle Wynd, is **Argyll's Lodging** (*see below*), one of Scotland's most storied townhouses. It's named in honour of the ninth Earl of Argyll, responsible for a sizeable renovation of the property in the late 17th century. Over the way is **Mar's Wark**, the impressive stone remains of what was once a grand Renaissance-style house built by the Earl of Mar; next door is the **Church of the Holy Rude**, which has one of the few surviving medieval timber roofs in Scotland, the intended rebuild having been halted by the Reformation. But while Stirling is dominated by its history, the town thrives today. Much of its atmosphere emanates from the university, its students enlivening the local pubs during termtime.

Argyll's Lodging *Castle Wynd (01786 431319/ www.historic-scotland.gov.uk)*. **Open** *Summer* 9.30am-6pm daily. *Winter* 9.30am-5pm daily. Last entry 30mins before closing. **Admission** *Stirling Castle & Argyll's Lodging* £8.50; £3.50-£6.50 concessions. *Argyll's Lodging* £4; £1.60-£3 concessions. **Credit** AmEx, DC, MC, V.

Bannockburn Heritage Centre *Glasgow Road, Stirling (01786 812664/www.nts.org.uk)*. **Open** *Feb, Mar, Nov-late Dec* 10.30am-4pm daily. *Apr-Oct* 10am-5.30pm daily. **Admission** £5; £4 concessions; free under-5s; £10-£14 family. **Credit** MC, V.
National Wallace Monument *Abbey Craig (01786 472140/www.nationalwallacemonument. com)*. **Open** *Jan, Feb, Nov, Dec* 10.30am-4pm daily. *Mar-May, Oct* 10am-5pm daily. *June* 10am-6pm daily. *July, Aug* 9.30am-6pm daily. *Sept* 9.30am-5pm daily. **Admission** £6.50; £4-£4.90 concessions; £17 family. **Credit** MC, V. **Photo** *p293*.
Stirling Castle *Castle Esplanade, Stirling (01786 450000/www.historic-scotland.gov.uk)*. **Open** *Apr-Sept* 9.30am-6pm daily. *Oct-Mar* 9.30am-5pm daily. Last entry 45mins before closing. **Admission** *Stirling Castle & Argyll's Lodging* £8.50; £3.50-£6.50 concessions. **Credit** AmEx, MC, V.

Where to eat & drink

Eating options include the fairly basic **Barnton Café** (3 Barnton Street, 01786 461698, mains £5-£7); **Hermann's** (Broad Street, 01786 450632, main courses £14-£19), which serves an unlikely fusion of Austrian and Scottish cuisine; and the **Tolbooth Café-Bar** (The Tolbooth, Jail Wynd, 01786 274010, www.stirling.gov.uk/ tolbooth), part of the city's arts centre. For a pint, try the **Portcullis** pub (Castle Wynd, 01786 472290, www.theportcullishotel.com).

Where to stay

Lodgings range from the grand-ish **Paramount Stirling** (Spittal Street, 01768 272727, www. paramount-hotels.co.uk, £75-£225 double), in an old 18th-century school, to the homelier **Golden Lion Flagship Hotel** (8 King Street; 01786 475351, www.thegoldenlionstirling.com, £99 double). There are also rooms above the **Portcullis** pub (£82-£87 double).

Getting there

By bus
The express bus run by Citylink leaves hourly from St Andrew Square Bus Station. Slower buses are run by First Bus.

By car
Stirling is 40 miles north of Edinburgh on the A91.

By train
There are hourly trains from Edinburgh's Waverley Station. The journey takes about 55mins.

Tourist information

Stirling *41 Dumbarton Road (01786 475019/ www.stirling.co.uk)*. **Open** *May, June, Sept, Oct* 9am-5pm daily. *July, Aug* 9am-7pm daily. *Nov-Apr* 10am-5pm daily.

Directory

Features

Directory

Getting Around

Arriving & leaving

By air

Edinburgh Airport

0870 040 0007/www.edinburgh airport.com.
Edinburgh Airport is about ten miles west of the city centre, and around 25 minutes' drive from Princes Street. The airport is served by all major UK airlines, among them **British Airways** and **BA Connect** (0870 850 9580, www.ba.com), **BMI** (0870 607 0555, www.flybmi.com) and **BMI Baby** (0871 224 0224, www.bmi baby.com), **ScotAirways** (0870 606 070, www.scotairways.co.uk), **Air Scotland** (0870 850 0958, www.air-scotland.com), **Easyjet** (0905 821 0905 (65p/min), www.easyjet.com) and **Ryanair** (0871 246 0000, www. ryanair.com). The only direct flights to and from the US are run by **Continental** (UK: 0845 607 6760, US: 1-800 231 0856, www.continental. com), to and from New York Newark. The airport's website contains a full list of airlines and destinations.

The best way to and from the airport is via the **Airlink 100 bus** service (555 6363, www.lothianbuses. co.uk), which stops at Maybury, Drum Brae, Edinburgh Zoo, Murrayfield, the Haymarket, the West End and Waverley Bridge. Buses leave the airport every 20mins from 4.50am to 6.50am (every 30mins between 5am and 8am on Sun), then every 10mins until 9.40pm, then every 15mins until 1.45am, with an hourly service all night. To the airport, buses leave Waverley Bridge every 20mins from 4am until 6.20am, then every 10mins until 9pm, then every 15mins until around 11.45pm, with an hourly service through the night. The journey takes around 25mins and costs £3 for a single or £5 return. **Taxis** run from a rank outside the UK Arrivals hall. The journey to central Edinburgh usually takes around 20-25 minutes (more during peak times) and costs around £20.

By bus/coach

St Andrew Square Bus Station

Elder Street, New Town. Princes Street buses. **Open** 6am-midnight daily. **Map** p326 H5, p336 F1.

National Express (0870 580 8080, www.nationalexpress.com) operates coach services between Edinburgh and destinations in England and Wales. Buses run by **Scottish Citylink** (0870 550 5050, www.city link.co.uk) serve a variety of towns around Scotland, while **Megabus** (www.megabus.com) runs budget bus services from Edinburgh to half a dozen Scottish destinations (including Glasgow) and a few in England. All buses and coaches arrive and depart from St Andrew Square Bus Station.

By train

Waverley Station

Waverley Bridge, New Town (0845 748 4950/www.nationalrail.co.uk). Princes Street buses. **Map** p326/ p330 H6, p336 F2.
Edinburgh's central station serves the East Coast main line to London and Aberdeen. GNER and Virgin run cross-border services, while First Scotrail run trains to destinations around Scotland, including a shuttle service (every 15mins) to Glasgow (which also stops at Haymarket Station). Local services go to East and West Lothian and into Fife.

Getting around

To fully appreciate the beauty, elegance, charm and contrasts of its city centre and its environs, Edinburgh is best explored on foot. Although the usual caution should be exercised at night, especially around those areas of the city with abundant and rowdy nightlife (Lothian Road and the Cowgate, to name but two), walking around the city is safe and rewarding.

Bus travel around the centre of Edinburgh is, on the whole, reasonably fast and reliable, and is certainly a better option than driving. Taxis are numerous, if rather pricey. Cycling is a fast and efficient way of getting around, as long as you don't mind a few cobbled streets and the odd hill.

For information on getting around **Glasgow**, *see p283*. Travel information for other destinations is given in the **Around Edinburgh** chapter on *pp284-294*.

Public transport

Buses

The city and its surrounding suburbs are very well served by a comprehensive bus network. **Lothian Buses** (555 6363, www.lothianbuses.co.uk) runs the majority of bus services throughout Edinburgh and into Mid and East Lothian; it's these services that we've listed throughout the guide.

Several parts of town are served by a great number of buses. In these cases, rather than list each individual bus numbers on every occasion, we've instead broken them into groupings. Below are the groupings used throughout the guide, together with a list of bus routes that serve the respective streets or areas.

Nicolson Street–North Bridge buses 3, 3A, 5, 7, 8, 14, 29, 30, 31, 33, 37, 47, 49.
Playhouse buses 1, 4, 5, 7, 8, 10, 11, 12, 14, 15, 15A, 16, 17, 19, 22, 25, 26, 34, 44, 45, 49.
Princes Street buses 1, 3, 3A, 4, 10, 11, 12, 15, 15A, 16, 17, 19, 22, 24, 25, 26, 29, 31, 33, 34, 36, 37, 44, 47.

Night buses, operated by Lothian Buses, run seven days a week on 11 different routes around the city and out into the suburbs. The services operate hourly starting from around midnight. For full information on routes and timetables, see www.night buses.com or visit any of the Lothian Buses Travelshops (*see p297*).

Single journeys within Edinburgh cost £1 for adults and 60p for children aged 5-16, regardless of the distance travelled. Under-5s travel free, up to a maximum of two kids per adult passenger. A single journey on the city's Night Bus network costs £2 (or £1 with a Ridacard; *see below*). Exact change is required for all single fares.

If you're planning on making several journeys during one day, it may be worth purchasing a **Daysaver** ticket, which allows for unlimited travel on the Lothian Buses network (excluding the Airlink 100 bus, special tour services and Night Buses). Daysavers cost £2.30 (£2 for children aged 5-15), and are available when you board your first bus of the day. Again, exact change is required.

The **Ridacard** affords the holder unlimited travel on the network (excluding tour services and Night Buses) for longer periods. The card costs £13 for one week (£11 for students aged 16-25, £9 for 5-15s) or £36 for one month (£30 for students aged 16-25, £24 for 5-15s). You can buy a Ridacard from Lothian Buses Travelshops (*see below*).

Lothian Buses Travelshops

27 Hanover Street *New Town. Princes Street buses.* **Open** 8.15am-6pm Mon-Sat. **Map** p326/p330 G6, p336 E2.
7 Shandwick Place *New Town. Princes Street buses.* **Open** 8.15am-6pm Mon-Sat. **Map** p329 D7.
Waverley Bridge *New Town. Princes Street buses.* **Open** 8.30am-6pm Mon-Sat; 9.30am-5pm Sun. **Map** p326/p330 H6, p336E2.

The region's other main bus services are run by the **First Group** (08708 727271, www.firstgroup.co.uk). Its services in East Lothian include a number of routes that run into Edinburgh's city centre. Unfortunately, day tickets are not transferable between First Group and Lothian Buses.

Trains

The majority of rail services in Scotland are run by **First Scotrail**. Details of the firm's various services and fares are available from National Rail Enquiries by calling 08457 484950 (lines are open 24 hours daily) or checking www. nationalrail.co.uk. Specific information on First Scotrail can be also be found at www.firstgroup.com/scotrail. The information desk at Waverley station (*see p296*) has timetables and details of discount travel, season tickets and international travel.

As well as Waverley and Haymarket stations, the city has several suburban stations including South Gyle, Slateford and Edinburgh Park. For full information on their locations, check National Rail Enquiries.

Taxis

Black cabs

Most of Edinburgh's taxis are black cabs, which take up to five passengers and have facilities for travellers with disabilities. When a taxi's yellow 'For Hire' light is on, you can hail it in the street. The basic fare, for the pick-up and the first 450 metres, costs £1.45 or £2.20 after 6pm; each subsequent 225 metres travelled costs 23p (or 24p at night). There's a 20p charge for every additional passenger over two.

Phoning for a taxi is particularly advisable at night or if you're based out of the city centre. To book, contact **Central Taxis** (229 2468, www.taxis-edinburgh.co.uk), **City Cabs** (228 1211, www. citycabs.co.uk) or **Computer Cabs** (272 8000, www.comcab-edinburgh.co.uk). While some taxi firms take credit cards, many others accept only cash: check when you book or get into the cab.

Private hire cars

Minicabs (saloon cars) are generally cheaper than black cabs and may be able to carry more passengers: some firms have people-carriers at their disposal, which can accommodate up to eight passengers (always specify when booking). Cars cannot be hailed on the street, and must be booked in advance. Reputable firms include **Bluebird** (621 6666) and **Persevere** (555 3377). It's a good idea to call around first to get the best price.

Complaints

Complaints or compliments about a taxicab or private hire company journey should be made to the Licensing Board, 343 High Street, Edinburgh EH1 1PW (529 4260). Be sure to make a note of the date and time of the journey and the licence number of the vehicle.

Cycling

Thanks to some successful lobbying by the local cycle campaign **Spokes** (*see p239*), Edinburgh is a pretty decent place for cyclists. The city council has invested in some off-road cycle paths and road-edge cycle lanes; although it's not compulsory for motorists to observe the latter, the lanes ease the flow of cyclists during rush hours and make some roads safer. Cyclists can travel freely along bus lanes.

Be sensible when tethering a bike in the street: bikes left on the Grassmarket and Rose Street are prone to vandalism and theft. Otherwise, the only real worries for cyclists are the steep and cobbled streets around the Old Town.

Spokes produces four cycle maps that show the cycle routes in Edinburgh and the Lothians. All cost £4.95 and are available from the

Directory

Spokes website. For more on cycling, including details of bike rentals, *see p239*.

Driving

If you're planning on staying within Edinburgh during the course of your visit, driving isn't recommended. For one thing, the town is reasonably small and thus very accessible either on foot or via the public transport system (*see p296*). And in addition, the city centre is awash with one-way streets and pedestrian-only areas, which can make driving a frustrating experience. Princes Street, in particular, has limited access for private vehicles and is best avoided. Plans to introduce a London-style congestion charge in the city were rejected in 2004.

A knock-on effect of this road-planning strategy is that the surrounding thoroughfares have become increasingly busy: slow-moving traffic is the norm, especially during rush hours (7.30-9.30am, 4.30-7pm Mon-Fri). There are also stringent parking restrictions throughout the city. And during August, the influx of visitors for the various festivals makes things even worse: the High Street is pedestrianised, while car parking on Chambers Street and elsewhere is requisitioned for use as coach parking for the Tattoo.

Breakdown services

If you're a member of a motoring organisation in your home country, check to see if it has a reciprocal agreement with a British organisation.

AA (Automobile Association) *Enquiries 0870 600 0371/ emergency breakdown 0800 887766 (08457 887766 from mobile)/ www.theaa.com.*
ETA (Environmental Transport Association) *Enquiries 0800 212810/emergency breakdown 0845 389 1010/www.eta.co.uk.*

RAC (Royal Automobile Club) *Enquiries 08705 722722/ emergency breakdown 0800 828282/ www.rac.co.uk.*

Car hire

Most car rental firms insist that drivers are over 21 (at the very least), with at least one year's driving experience and a current full driving licence with no serious endorsements. All the firms detailed below have branches at Edinburgh Airport (though Arnold Clark's is some way from the terminal building); several also have offices in the city centre. Prices vary: be sure to shop around for the best rate, and always check the level of insurance included in the price.

Alamo *UK: 0870 400 4562/www. alamo.co.uk. US: 1-800 522 9696/ www.alamo.com.*
Arnold Clark *UK & US: 0845 607 4500/www.arnoldclarkrental. co.uk.*
Avis *UK: 0844 581 0147/www. avis.co.uk. US: 1-800 331 1212/ www.avis.com.*
Budget *UK: 0844 581 2231/www. budget.co.uk. US: 1-800 472 3325/ www.budget.com.*
Enterprise *UK: 0870 350 3000/ www.enterprise.co.uk. US: 1-800 261 7331/www.enterprise.com.*
Europcar *UK: 0845 758 5375/ www.europcar.co.uk. US: 1-877 940 6900/www.europcar.com.*
Hertz *UK: 0870 844 8844/www. hertz.co.uk. US: 1-800 654 3001/ www.hertz.com.*
National *UK: 0870 400 4552/ www.nationalcar.co.uk. US: 1-800 227 3876/www.nationalcar.com.*

Car parks

All the car parks detailed below are open 24 hours a day. Rates vary; call for details. There's a full list of city centre car parks, complete with a map, online at www.edinburgh.gov.uk.

Castle Terrace *Old Town (229 2870/www.ncp.co.uk).* Map p326 E8, p336 A3.
Chalmers Street *South Edinburgh (229 2870/www.ncp.co.uk).* Map p330 G9.
Greenside Place *Calton Hill & Broughton (558 3518/www.ncp. co.uk).* Map p331 J5.

St James Centre *Leith Street, Broughton (556 5066/www. ncp.co.uk).* Map p331 J5.
St John's Hill *Old Town (229 2870/www.ncp.co.uk).* Map p331 K7.
St Leonard's Street *South Edinburgh (667 5601).* Map p331 K9.

Parking fines & vehicle removal

Edinburgh Council employs a notoriously efficient private company to keep the streets clear of illegally parked cars. If you park illegally, expect to receive a parking ticket.

Always carefully check street signs to find out the local parking regulations. For the purposes of on-street car parking, the city is divided up into central and peripheral zones. In the central zone, you must pay for parking between 8.30am and 6pm from Monday to Saturday; in the peripheral zone, payment must be made between 8.30am and 5pm. Parking payment should be made either at parking meters or on-street pay-and-display ticket vending machines.

The fine for parking illegally is £60, reduced to £30 if it is paid within 14 days. The clamping of vehicles is forbidden in Scotland, but don't let that lull you into a false sense of security: if you're parked illegally, your car can be towed away and impounded. If this occurs, a fee of £105 is levied for removal, plus a £12 storage fee for every day the vehicle remains uncollected. These fees are in addition to the cost of the parking ticket. Impounded cars are taken to the Edinburgh Car Compound, which keeps a log of all cars. If your car has been stolen, you should immediately report the theft to the police (*see p304*).

Edinburgh Car Compound *57 Tower Street, Leith (555 1742).* Bus 12, 16, 35. **Open** 7am-9pm Mon-Sat; 8.45am-11.30am Sun. **Credit** MC, V. Map p324 Z2.

Resources A-Z

Age restrictions

You have to be 18 to drink in Scotland, though some bars and clubs admit only over-21s. The legal age for driving is 17, though most car rental firms won't hire cars to under-21s. The legal age of consent is 16.

Attitude & etiquette

Edinburgh is, on the whole, an informal city. A handful of high-end restaurants may insist on jacket or jacket and tie (call to check).

Business

Conferences & conventions

Edinburgh Convention Bureau
29 Drumsheugh Gardens, EH3 7RN (473 3666/fax 473 3636/www. conventionedinburgh.com).
Assistance on arranging a conference.

Edinburgh International Conference Centre
The Exchange, 150 Morrison Street, West Edinburgh, EH3 8EE (300 3000/fax 300 3030/www.eicc.co.uk). Bus 2, 3, 3A, 4, 25, 33, 44, 44A. **Map** p329 D8.

In the modern surroundings of the city's new financial centre, the EICC's main space can accommodate up to 1,200 delegates.

Couriers & shippers

Call the numbers below to arrange an item pick-up.

DHL *0870 240 0555/www.dhl.co.uk.*
FedEx *0800 123800/08456 070809/www.fedex.com/gb.*
UPS *08457 877877/www.ups.com/gb.*

Office hire & business centres

Edinburgh Office Business Centre & Conference Venue
16-26 Forth Street, Broughton, EH1 3LH (550 3700/fax 550 3701/www. edinburghoffice.co.uk). Bus 8, 17. **Map** p331 J4.
A variety of office spaces, scattered over four locations around the city.

Regus
Conference House, The Exchange, 152 Morrison Street, West Edinburgh, EH3 8EB (200 6000/fax 200 6200/ www.regus.com). Bus 2, 3, 3A, 4, 25, 33, 44, 44A. **Map** p329 D8.
Office and conference spaces, conveniently close to the EICC.

Secretarial services

Office Angels *95 George Street, New Town, EH2 3ES (226 6112/fax 220 6850/www.office-angels.com).*

Translators & interpreters

Berlitz *26 Frederick Street, New Town, EH2 2JR (226 7198/www. languagecentres.com).*
Integrated Language Services *School of Languages, Heriot-Watt University, Riccarton, EH14 4AS (451 3159/www.hw.ac.uk/ils).*

Reed Employment Solutions
13 Frederick Street, New Town, EH2 2BY (226 3687/fax 247 5900/ www.reed.co.uk).

Useful organisations

Edinburgh Chamber of Commerce & Enterprise
Capital House, 2 Festival Square, West Edinburgh, EH3 9SU (221 2999/fax 221 2998/www.ecce.org). Bus 10, 11, 15, 15A, 16, 17, 22, 24, 30. **Open** 8.30am-5.30pm Mon-Fri. **Map** p326 E8, p336 A4.
Advice and support for businesses.

Scottish Enterprise Edinburgh & Lothian
Apex House, 99 Haymarket Terrace, West Edinburgh, EH12 5HD (313 4000/fax 313 4231/www.scottish-enterprise.com/edinburghandlothian). Bus 12, 26, 31. **Open** 9am-5pm Mon-Fri. **Map** p329 B8.
A government-funded economic development agency.

Scottish Executive
St Andrew's House, Regent Road, Calton Hill, EH1 3DG (556 8400/ www.scotland.gov.uk). Bus 3, 7, 8, 14, 19, 19A. **Open** 8.30am-5pm Mon-Fri. **Map** p327/p331 J6.
Access government departments here.

Consumer

If you pay with a credit card, you can cancel payment or get reimbursed if there is a problem. The **Citizens Advice Bureau** and the local trading standards office at the **Advice Shop** (for both, *see p301*) can help.

Customs

Citizens entering the UK from outside the EU must adhere to duty-free import limits:

Travel advice

For current information on travel to a specific country – including the latest news on health issues, safety and security, local laws and customs – contact your home country's government department of foreign affairs. Most have websites with useful advice for would-be travellers.

Australia
www.smartraveller.gov.au

Canada
www.voyage.gc.ca

New Zealand
www.safetravel.govt.nz

Republic of Ireland
http://foreignaffairs.gov.ie

UK
www.fco.gov.uk/travel

USA
http://travel.state.gov

Directory

- 200 cigarettes or 100 cigarillos or 50 cigars or 250g of tobacco.
- 2 litres still table wine plus either 1 litre spirits or strong liqueurs (over 22% abv) or 2 litres fortified wine (under 22% abv), sparkling wine or other liqueurs.
- 60cc/ml perfume.
- 250cc/ml toilet water.
- Other goods to the value of no more than £145.

The import of meat, poultry, fruit, plants, flowers and protected animals is restricted or forbidden; there are no restrictions on the import or export of currency. People over the age of 17 arriving from an EU country have been able to import unlimited goods for their own personal use, if bought tax-paid (ie not duty-free). For more details, see www.hmce.gov.uk.

Disabled

Listed buildings aren't allowed to widen their entrances or add ramps, and parts of the Old Town have wheelchair-unfriendly narrow pavements. However, equal opportunity legislation requires new buildings to be fully accessible. **Lothian Buses'** new fleet of vehicles are accessible to passengers in wheelchairs. Some routes still rely on older buses, but more than half the buses are now accessible. Call 555 6363 for details. Newer **black taxis** (*see p297*) are wheelchair-accessible; specify when booking. **Edinburgh City Council** publishes *Transport in Edinburgh: A Guide for Disabled People*. For a free copy, call 469 3891.

Most theatres and cinemas are fitted with induction loops for the hard of hearing. Ask when booking.

For more on disabled living in Edinburgh, contact **Grapevine**, part of the Lothian Centre for Integrated Living.

Grapevine *Norton Park, 57 Albion Road, Calton Hill, EH7 5QY (475 2370/fax 475 2392/www.lothian cil.org.uk).* **Open** *Phone enquiries* 9.30am-4pm Mon-Fri.

Drugs

Despite confusion over cannabis's reclassification as a Class C drug early in 2004, both hard and soft drugs are illegal in Scotland, as they are in the rest of the UK.

Electricity

The UK electricity supply is 220-240 volt, 50-cycle AC rather than the 110-120 volt, 60-cycle AC used in the US. Foreign visitors will need to run appliances via an adaptor. TV and video employ different systems to the US.

Embassies & consulates

For a list of consular offices in Edinburgh, consult the *Yellow Pages*, or see www.edinburgh. gov.uk/cec/consulates/consulates.html. The majority of embassies and consulates (the US is an exception) do not accept personal callers without an appointment.

Australian Consulate *Forsyth House, 93 George Street, EH2 3ES (624 3333/www.australia.org.uk). Princes Street buses.* **Map** p326/p330 F6, p336 C1.
Canadian Honorary Consulate *Burness, Festival Square, EH3 9WJ (473 6320/www.cic.gc.ca). Bus 10, 11, 15, 15A, 16, 17, 22, 24, 30.* **Map** p326 E8, p336 A4.
Irish Consulate General *16 Randolph Crescent, EH3 7TT (0131 226 7711/http://foreign affairs.gov.ie). Bus 36, 37, 41, 47.* **Map** p325/p329 D6.
US Consulate General *3 Regent Terrace, Calton Hill, EH7 5BW (556 8315/after-hours emergencies 01224 857097/http:// londonusembassy.gov/scotland). Bus 1, 35.* **Open** *Personal callers* 1-5pm Tue, Thur. **Map** p331 L5.

Emergencies

In the event of a serious accident, fire or incident, call 999 and specify whether you require an ambulance, the fire service or the police. *See also p301* **Helplines**.

Gay & lesbian

Several campaigning groups maintain offices in Edinburgh, such as **Stonewall Scotland** (557 3679, www.stonewall scotland.org.uk) and the **Equality Network** (07020 933952, www.equality-network. org). **LGBT Youth Scotland** runs a weekly helpline (0845 113 0005, 7.30-9pm Tue; www. lgbtyouth.org.uk). Also here is **Remember When** (558 2820, www.rememberwhen.org.uk), an ongoing oral history project.

Among the special-interest groups in the city are the **Edinburgh Gay Women's Group** (www.stormpages. com/fabwymyn), which runs a social at Nexus from 8.30pm every Wednesday, and **Gay Dads Scotland** (www.gay dadsscotland.org.uk), which meets on the last Thursday of the month at the LGBT Centre.

Edinburgh Lesbian, Gay & Bisexual Centre
58a-60 Broughton Street, Broughton (556 9471). Bus 8, 13, 17. **Open** hours vary. **Map** p326 H4. Start here if you're looking for more information.

Lothian Gay & Lesbian Switchboard
Main line 556 4049/lesbian line 557 0751/www.lgls.co.uk. **Open** *Main line* 7.30-10pm daily. *Lesbian line* 7.30-10pm Mon, Thur. Advice and support. The Switchboard also runs Icebreakers, a social event held every other Wednesday at CC Blooms (*see p225*); call for dates.

Health

National Health Service (NHS) treatment is free to EU nationals, UK residents and those studying here. All can register with a doctor (commonly known as a general practitioner, or GP). There are no NHS charges for accident and emergency treatment, diagnosis and treatment of some communicable diseases (including STDs) and family planning. If you aren't eligible to see an NHS doctor, you will be charged the cost price for medicines prescribed by a private doctor.

If you don't fit into any of the above categories but want to find out if you still qualify for free treatment, contact **NHS Lothian Primary Care Services** on 537 8400, or see www.nhslothian.scot.nhs.uk.

Accident & emergency

Royal Infirmary of Edinburgh

51 Little France Crescent, Old Dalkeith Road, EH16 (536 1000). Bus 8, 18, 24, 32, 33, 38, 49. Edinburgh's 24-hour casualty department.

Complementary medicine

See p202 and 204.

Contraception & abortion

Caledonia Youth

5 Castle Terrace, South Edinburgh (229 3596/www.caledoniayouth.org). Bus 1, 10, 11, 15, 15A, 16, 17, 22, 24, 30, 34. **Open** noon-6pm Mon-Thur; noon-3.30pm Fri; noon-2.30pm Sat. **Map** p330 E8, p336 A3. Advice on contraception, abortion and sexual health for under-25s. Staff can offer referrals to NHS hospitals or private clinics.

Family Planning & Well Woman Services

18 Dean Terrace, Stockbridge (332 7941). Bus 24, 29, 42. **Open** *By appointment* 9.30am-7.30pm Mon-Thur; 9.30am-3.30pm Fri. *Drop-in clinic (under-25s)* 9.30am-noon Sat. **Map** p325 D4. Confidential advice, contraceptive provision, pregnancy tests and abortion referral.

Dental services

Western General Hospital Dental Clinic

Crewe Road South, Stockbridge (537 1338). Bus 19, 19A, 28, 29, 37, 37A, 38. **Open** 7-9pm Mon-Fri; also 10am-noon Sat, Sun. A walk-in emergency clinic, for tourists and Lothian residents only.

Hospitals

See above **Accident & emergency**.

Opticians

The **Alexandra Pavilion** offers a free walk-in service for emergency eye complaints. For dispensing opticians, *see p203.*

Princess Alexandra Eye Pavilion *Chalmers Street, South Edinburgh (536 1000). Bus 35.* **Open** 8.30am-5pm Mon-Fri. **Map** p330 G9.

Pharmacies

See p203.

STDs, HIV & AIDS

The **Genito-Urinary Medicine Clinic** (GUM), affiliated with the Royal Infirmary of Edinburgh, provides free, confidential advice and treatment of STDs, and offers HIV tests by appointment. The **Solas Centre** is the city's HIV and AIDS support resource.

Genito-Urinary Medicine Clinic *Lauriston Building, Lauriston Place, South Edinburgh (536 2103). Bus 35.* **Open** *Walk-in clinic (emergencies)* 9-10am Mon-Fri. *Appointments* call for details. **Map** p330 G9.
Waverley Care Solas HIV Support Centre *2-4 Abbeymount, Calton Hill (661 0982/www.waverley care.org). Bus 30, 35.* **Open** 11am-4pm Mon-Fri. **Map** p307 J4.

Help & advice

Drop-in centres

Advice Shop

South Bridge, Old Town (225 1255). Nicolson Street–North Bridge buses. **Open** 9.30am-4pm Mon, Wed, Thur; 10am-4pm Tue; 9.30am-3.30pm Fri. **Map** p331 J7, p336 F4. Advice on consumer problems and welfare benefits.

Citizens Advice Bureau

58 Dundas Street, New Town (557 1500/appointments 557 3681/ www.cas.org.uk). Bus 13, 23, 27. **Open** 9.30am-4pm Mon, Tue, Thur; 9.30am-12.30pm, 6.30-8pm Wed. **Map** p330 F4.

Free advice on legal, financial and personal matters. Aside from this city-centre branch, there are three other offices around Edinburgh.

Helplines

Alcoholics Anonymous *0845 769 7555/www.alcoholics-anonymous. org.uk.* **Open** 24hrs daily.
Childline *0800 1111/www.childline. org.uk.* **Open** 24hrs daily.
Drinkline *0800 917 8282.* **Open** 24hrs daily.
Edinburgh Women's Rape & Sexual Abuse Centre *556 9437.* **Open** hrs vary.
Edinburgh Women's Aid (Domestic Violence) *315 8111.* **Open** 10am-3pm Mon, Wed, Fri; 10am-7pm Thur; 10am-1pm Sat.
Gamblers Anonymous *08700 508880/www.gamblersanonymous. org.uk.* **Open** 9am-8pm daily.
Know the Score Drugs Helpline *0800 587 5879/www.knowthescore. info.* **Open** 24hrs daily.
National AIDS Helpline *0800 567123.* **Open** 24hrs daily.
NHS Helpline *0800 4546/www. nhsdirect.nhs.uk.* **Open** 24hrs daily.
Samaritans *National 08457 909090/local 221 9999/www. samaritans.org.* **Open** *National* 24hrs daily. *Local* 9am-10pm daily.
Victim Support *National 0845 303 0900/local 0845 603 9213/ www.victimsupportsco.demon.co.uk.* **Open** *National* 9am-9pm Mon-Fri; 9am-7pm Sat, Sun. *Local* 9am-4.30pm Mon-Thur; 9am-4pm Fri.

ID

ID is not widely required in the UK, but you will need a passport or drivers' licence (assuming it has a photocard) for changing money, collecting travellers' cheques and so on.

Insurance

Non-nationals should arrange baggage, trip-cancellation and medical insurance before departures. Medical centres will ask for details of your insurance company and your policy number; keep the details with you at all times.

Internet

Public internet access is abundant in Edinburgh. Many cafés and bars offer

Directory

free Wi-Fi internet access, and chain cafés such as Starbucks offer wireless access via a paid-for subscription. For more on Wi-Fi coverage, *see p170* **Totally unwired**. If you're not toting a laptop, a handful of internet cafés have computers available for rent.

easyInternetcafé *58 Rose Street, New Town (220 3577/www.easy internetcafe.com). Princes Street buses.* **Open** *7.30am-10.30pm daily.* **Map** *p326/p330 F6, p336 C1.*

Edinburgh Internet Café *98 West Bow, Old Town (226 5400/ www.edininternetcafe.com). Bus 2, 23, 27, 41, 42.* **Open** *10am-11pm daily.* **Map** *p330 G8, p336 D4.*

Wired Café *1a Brougham Place, South Edinburgh (659 7820/ www.wiredcafe.info). Bus 10, 11, 15, 15A, 16, 17, 23, 24, 27, 45.* **Open** *9am-9pm Mon-Fri; 10am-9pm Sat, Sun.* **Map** *p330 F9.*

Left luggage

Edinburgh Airport
0870 040 0007/www.edinburgh airport.com. **Open** *5am-11pm daily.* Left luggage facilities are located between the check-in area and the internationals arrivals home.

St Andrew Square Bus Station
There are lockers in the station.

Waverley Station
558 3829/www.excess-baggage.com. **Open** *7am-11pm daily.* The left luggage facilities here are operated by Excess Baggage.

Legal help

If a legal problem arises, contact your embassy, consulate or high commission (*see p300*). You can get advice from any **Citizens Advice Bureau** (for details, *see p301*) or one of the organisations listed below. If you need financial assistance, be sure to ask about Legal Aid eligibility. For leaflets explaining how the system works, write to the **Scottish Legal Aid Board**. Advice on problems concerning visas and immigration can be obtained from the **Immigration Advisory Service**.

Edinburgh & Lothians Race Equality Council *14 Forth Street, EH1 3LH (556 0441/www.elrec.org.uk).*

Immigration Advisory Service *115 Bath Street, Glasgow, G2 2SZ (0141 248 2956/www.iasuk.org).*

Law Society of Scotland *26 Drumsheugh Gardens, EH3 7YR (226 7411/www.lawscot.org.uk).*

Scottish Legal Aid Board *44 Drumsheugh Gardens, EH3 7SW (office 226 7061/helpline 0845 122 8686/www.slab.org.uk).*

Libraries

The **Central Library** (*see p84*) stocks a wide selection of publications, and has a large reference section (242 8060). You must live locally to join the lending library (242 8020).

The **National Library of Scotland** (*see p85*) is a deposit library. The Reading Rooms are open for reference and research; admission is by ticket to approved applicants.

University of Edinburgh Main Library
George Square, South Edinburgh (650 3384/www.lib.ed.ac.uk). Bus 2, 41, 42. **Open** *Term-time* 8.30am-10pm Mon-Thur; 9am-7pm Fri; 9am-5pm Sat; noon-7pm Sun. *Holiday time* 9am-5pm Mon, Tue, Thur, Fri; 9am-9pm Wed. **Map** *p330 H9.*
Students who aren't studying at the university may use it for reference purposes. Other users get research access for £5 a day, £15 a week, £30 a month and £60 for 3 months; full borrowing membership costs £60 for 3 months, £100 for 6 months and £160 for 12 months.

Lost property

Always inform the police if you lose anything, if only to validate insurance claims. A lost passport should also be reported at once to your embassy or consulate, if relevant (*see p300*). Below are the details of the lost property offices for items left on public transport.

Edinburgh Airport
344 3486/www.edinburghairport. com. **Open** *5am-11pm daily.* The lost property office at Edinburgh Airport is located in the international arrivals hall.

Lothian Buses
Annandale Street, Broughton (558 8858). Bus 7, 10, 12, 14, 16, 22, 25, 49. **Open** *10am-1.30pm Mon-Fri.* **Map** *p327 J3.*

Taxis
Edinburgh Police Headquarters, Fettes Avenue, Stockbridge (311 3141). Bus 19, 24, 29, 37, 38, 42, 47. **Open** *9am-5pm Mon-Fri.* **Map** *p325 A4.*
All property that has been left in a registered black cab, as well as in the street or in shops, gets sent here.

Waverley Station
558 3829/www.excess-baggage.com. **Open** *8am-5.30pm daily.* Waverley's lost property facilities are operated by Excess Baggage. For items lost in other stations or on trains, contact the individual station.

Media

Most of Scotland's newspapers, and much of its TV output, operate on a quasi-national basis pitched somewhere between the regional media and London's self-styled 'national' press. The attitudes on display both reflect and illuminate the current state of that nebulous beast known as Scottish identity. From the time-honoured east/west rivalry to the thorny question of the tabloid *Daily Record*'s Rangers affiliations, from Radio Scotland's Sony Award-winning output to the cranky couthiness of the *Sunday Post* letters page, the cultural divergences that impelled the campaign for devolution continue to pervade the media.

Newspapers

One effect of devolution has been the tartanisation of much of the London-based press, which now prints Scottish editions. London nationals such as the *Guardian* and Sunday sibling the *Observer* (left-leaning, arts-friendly), the *Times* and the *Sunday Times* (right-slanted, business-heavy), and the *Sun* and Sunday's *News of the World* (trashy, gossipy) are all widely sold, and London's flimsy *Metro* freesheet also publishes an Scottish edition. Listed below, though, are papers native to Scotland.

The Scotsman & Scotland on Sunday
www.scotsman.com & http:// scotlandonsunday.scotsman.com.
This Edinburgh-based broadsheet has gone a little downmarket in recent years, and has abandoned its traditional devolutionary bias. The editorial line tends to the right; arts and features have an east coast bias. *Scotland on Sunday* is its sister paper.

The Herald & Sunday Herald
www.theherald.co.uk & www.sundayherald.com.
This Glasgow-based broadsheet has the edge over the *Scotsman* in terms of news. Any Glaswegian bias in its features coverage complements the *Scotsman*'s east coast orientation. The *Sunday Herald* is the sister paper.

Daily Record & Sunday Mail
www.dailyrecord.co.uk & www.sundaymail.co.uk.
Published by the Mirror Group in Glasgow, Scotland's best-selling daily and its Sunday sibling are quite frothy, although sports coverage is strong and both papers have a campaigning instinct.

Evening News
http://edinburghnews.scotsman.com.
Edinburgh's daily evening tabloid. The latest headlines from around the world are combined with a strong local Edinburgh flavour.

Magazines

Tradition still has a place on Scottish magazine shelves. First published in 1739, **Scots Magazine** (www.scots magazine.com) has pretensions to being a Scottish *Reader's Digest*, while the similarly old-school **Scottish Field** (www.scottishfield.co.uk) offers lifestyle features. The country's thriving literary scene is reflected in the likes of the quarterly **Chapman** (www.chapman-pub.co.uk) and the biannual **Edinburgh Review** (www.englit.ed.ac.uk/ edinburghreview). But there are also style and satirical

magazines based in Scotland: **Is This Music?** (www.isthis music.com) is the country's leading music magazine, while the **Drouth** (www.thedrouth. com) offers a mix of cultural and satirical writing.

The city's most high-profile publication is **The List** (www. list.co.uk). Issued fortnightly on Thursdays (weekly during August), it contains full listings for Glasgow and Edinburgh on everything from major gigs to readings by local writers, and also publishes a generally comprehensive annual *Eating & Drinking Guide* to both cities (£5.95). More specialist listings are provided by **Scotsgay** (www. scotsgay.co.uk), distributed free each month in gay venues and available in full online.

Radio

Most UK national stations are accessible in Edinburgh, chief among them the five main BBC stations (www.bbc.co.uk/ radio): **Radio 1** (97.6-99.8 FM, youth-slanted pop), **Radio 2** (88-90.2 FM, adult pop and rock), **Radio 3** (90.2-92.4 FM, classical), **Radio 4** (92.4-94.6 FM, current affairs and culture) and **Radio 5 Live** (693 & 909 MW, news and sport).

However, several stations are unique to Scotland. **BBC Radio Scotland** (92.4-94.7 FM) commands respect for its mix of talk and music-based programming. **Forth 1** (97.3 FM, www.forthone.com) is a sort of Scottish Radio 1 with added commercials, while **Forth 2** (1548 AM, www. forth2.com) plays older music. **Xfm** (105.7-106.1 FM, www. xfmscotland.co.uk) offers indie music; **Real Radio** (100.3-101.1 FM, http://scotland.real radiofm.com) is a downmarket mix of music and chat; and **Talk 107** (107 FM, www. talk107.co.uk) is Scotland's only speech-based commercial radio network.

Television

Both the BBC and ITV in Scotland opt in and out of the UK-wide output, with BBC Scotland and the independent Scottish Television (STV) contributing regularly to their respective networks.

Money

Britain's currency is the pound sterling (£). One pound equals 100 pence (p). 1p and 2p coins are copper; 5p, 10p, 20p and 50p coins are silver; the £1 coin is gold; the £2 coin is silver with a gold surround.

Three Scottish banks – **Bank of Scotland**, the **Royal Bank of Scotland** and the **Clydesdale Bank** – issue their own paper notes. The colour of the notes varies slightly between the three, but an approximation is as follows: green £1; blue £5; brown £10; purple/pink £20; red or green £50; bold red £100.

The euro is not used in the UK but is accepted in some shops in tourist areas.

Banks

In general, banks are open 9am-4pm Mon-Fri, but some remain open later. ATMs, usually situated outside banks, give 24-hour access to cash; most will also allow you to draw money on a credit card tied to international networks such as Cirrus or Plus.

There are branches of the three Scottish clearing banks throughout the city. Customers of English banks should be able to draw money from their ATMs at no charge; check with your bank. Some English banks do maintain a limited presence in the city; main branches are listed below.

Barclays *1 St Andrew Square, New Town (08457 555555/ www.barclays.co.uk). Princes Street buses.* **Open** 9am-5pm Mon-Fri. **Map** p326 G5, p336 E1.

Directory

HSBC *76 Hanover Street,*
New Town (08457 404404/
www.hsbc.co.uk). Bus 13, 23, 27/
Princes Street buses. **Open** 9am-5pm
Mon-Fri; 9.30am-12.30pm Sat.
Map p326/p330 G6.
Lloyds TSB *28 Hanover Street,*
New Town (0845 300 0000/
www.lloydstsb.co.uk). Bus 13, 23, 27/
Princes Street buses. **Open** 9am-5pm
Mon, Tue, Fri; 10am-5pm Wed;
9am-6pm Thur; 10am-4pm Sat.
Map p326/p330 G6.
National Westminster
8 George Street, New Town (0845
366 1965/www.natwest.com). Princes
Street buses. **Open** 9am-5pm Mon,
Tue, Thur, Fri; 9.30am-5pm Wed;
9.30am-1pm Sat. **Map** p326/p330 G6,
p336 E1.

Bureaux de change

Bureaux de change charge fees
for cashing travellers' cheques
or exchanging foreign currency.
Commission rates vary greatly;
it pays to shop around. There
are bureaux de change at the
airport and Waverley Station;
others are scattered around in
areas popular with tourists.

Most banks offer currency-
exchange facilities; rates are
usually better than at bureaux
de change. Commission is often
charged for cashing travellers'
cheques in foreign currencies,
but not for sterling travellers'
cheques, provided you cash
them at a bank affiliated to the
issuing bank; get a list when
you buy your cheques.

When changing currency
or travellers' cheques, you
will need photo ID, such as a
passport or drivers' licence.

Lost/stolen
credit cards

Report lost or stolen credit
cards immediately both to the
police and the 24-hour phone
lines listed below. Inform your
bank by phone and in writing.
American Express
0800 587 6023/
www.americanexpress.com.
Diners Club *0870 190 0011/*
www.dinersclub.co.uk.
MasterCard *0800 964767/*
www.mastercard.com.
Visa *0800 891725/*
www.visa.com.

Money transfers

Western Union (0800
833833, www.westernunion.
co.uk) is the UK's most widely
used money transfer company,
but fees are high. Alternatively,
ask your own bank to find
out with which British banks
it's affiliated. You can then
nominate a branch to which
the money can be sent.

Opening hours

In general, business hours are
9.30am-5.30pm Mon-Fri. Most
shops are open 9am-5.30pm
Mon-Sat and 11am-5pm on
Sun. Many restaurants are
open all day; some stay open
well beyond 11pm. Officially,
closing time for pubs is 11pm,
but most pubs have licences to
sell alcohol until 1am. Many
shops, restaurants, pubs and
clubs operate longer hours
during the August festivals.

Police

If you've been the victim of
a crime, look under 'Police' in
the phone directory for the
nearest police station, or call
directory enquiries (*see p306*).
The **Police Information
Centre** in the Old Town
(*see p89*) is both a museum
and a working police centre.
For emergencies, *see p300*.

Postal services

The UK has a fairly reliable
postal service. If you have
a query on any aspect of
Royal Mail services, contact
Customer Services on 08457
740740. For business enquiries
contact the Royal Mail
Business Centre for Scotland
on 08457 950950.

Post offices are usually open
9am-5.30pm during the week
and 9am-noon on Saturdays,
although some post offices
shut for lunch and smaller
offices may close for one or
more afternoons each week.

Three central post offices, two
in the New Town and one in
the Old Town are listed below;
for others, call the **Royal Mail**
on 08457 223344 or check
www.royalmail.com. For
general customer services
enquiries, call 08457 740740;
for business enquiries, try
08457 950950.

You can buy individual
stamps at post offices, and
books of four or 12 first- or
second-class stamps at
newsagents and supermarkets
that display the appropriate
red sign. A first-class stamp
for a regular letter costs 32p;
second-class stamps are 23p.
It costs 44p to send a postcard
to another EU country, and
50p to send one to all other
countries. For details of other
rates, see www.royalmail.com.

Post offices
Frederick Street *40 Frederick
Street, New Town (08457 223344).
Bus 28, 37, 41, 42/Princes Street
buses.* **Open** 9am-5.30pm Mon,
Wed-Fri; 9.30am-5.30pm Tue;
9.30am-12.30pm Sat. **Map** p326/
p330 F6, p336 C1.
St James Centre *8-10 Kings Mall,
St James Centre, New Town (08457
223344). Princes Street buses.*
Open 9am-5.30pm Mon, Wed-Sat;
9.30am-5.30pm Tue. **Map** p326 H5.
St Mary's Street *46 St Mary's
Street, Old Town (08457 223344).
Nicolson Street–North Bridge buses.*
Open 9am-12.30pm, 1.30-5.30pm
Mon, Tue, Thur, Fri; 9am-1pm Wed;
9am-noon Sat. **Map** p331 J7.

Poste restante

If you intend to travel around
the UK during your stay,
friends from home can write
to you care of a post office,
where mail will be kept at the
enquiries desk for up to one
month. The envelope should
be marked 'Poste Restante' in
the top left-hand corner, with
your name displayed above
the address of the post office
where you want to collect your
mail. Take photo ID (a driving
licence or passport) when you
collect your post. The post
office at the St James Centre
(*see above*) offers this service.

Religion

Baptist

Charlotte Baptist Chapel
*204 Rose Street, New Town
(225 4812/www.charlottechapel.org).*
Princes Street buses. **Services**
11am, 6.30pm Sun. **Map** p330 E7,
p336 A1.

Buddhist

The **Portobello Buddhist Priory**
(27 Brighton Place, Portobello,
669 9622, www.portobellobuddhist.
org.uk) offers daily Zen Buddhist
meditation, with a resident monk
and lay followers. The **Edinburgh
Buddhist Centre** (30 Melville
Terrace, Marchmont, 662 6699, www.
edinburghbuddhistcentre.org.uk)
is run by the Friends of the Western
Buddhist Order and offers regular
classes and meditation sessions.
Other Buddhist groups in Edinburgh
have no central meeting place
and tend to share space with other
faiths or organisations.

Catholic

St Mary's Cathedral *61 York
Place, New Town (556 1798/www.
stmaryscathedral.co.uk). Playhouse
buses.* **Services** 10am, 12.45pm
Mon-Fri; 10am, 6pm (vigil mass) Sat;
9.30am, 11.30am, 6pm (vigil mass),
7.30pm Sun. **Confessions heard**
10.30am-12.30pm, 5-5.45pm Sat.
Map p326 H5.

Church of Scotland

St Giles' Cathedral *High Street
(225 4363/www.stgilescathedral.
org.uk). Bus 2, 23, 27, 41, 42, 45.*
Services 8am (Holy Communion),
10am (Holy Communion), 11.30am,
6pm, 8pm Sun. **Map** p330 H7,
p336 E4.

Episcopalian

St Mary's Episcopal Cathedral
*Palmerston Place, New Town (225
6293/www.cathedral.net). Bus 2, 3,
3A, 4, 12, 25, 26, 31, 33, 38, 44,
44A.* **Services** 7.30am, 1.05pm,
5.30pm Mon-Wed, Fri; 7.30am,
11.30am, 1.05pm, 5.30pm Thur;
7.30am Sat; 8am, 10.30am, 3.30pm
Sun. **Map** p329 C8.

Hindu

**Edinburgh Hindu Mandir &
Cultural Centre** *St Andrew Place,
Leith (440 0084). Bus 12, 16, 35.*
Meetings 2-4pm 2nd & 4th Sun of
mth. **Map** p324 Y4.

Islamic

Edinburgh Central Mosque
*50 Potterrow, South Edinburgh
(667 1777/www.discover-islam.com).
Bus 2, 41, 42.* **Prayer times** phone
for details. **Map** p331 J8.

Jewish

Synagogue Chambers
*4 Salisbury Road, South Edinburgh
(667 3144/www.ehcong.com).
Bus 2, 14, 30, 33.* **Services** times
vary; call for details. **Map** p331 L11.

Methodist

**Nicolson Square Methodist
Church** *25 Nicolson Square, South
Edinburgh (667 1465/www.nicsquare.
org.uk). Nicolson Street–North
Bridge buses.* **Services** 11am,
6.30pm Sun. **Map** p331 J8.

Quaker

Quaker Meeting House
*7 Victoria Terrace, Victoria Street,
Old Town (225 4825/http://quaker
scotland.gn.apc.org). Bus 2, 23, 27,
41, 42, 45.* **Meetings** 12.30pm Wed;
11am Sun. **Map** p330 G7, p336 D4.

Sikh

Guru Nanak Sikh Gurdwara
*1 Mill Lane, Leith (553 7207). Bus 1,
7, 10, 11, 14, 21, 32, 34.* **Services**
phone for details. **Map** p336 X3.

Safety & security

Violent crime is relatively rare
in central Edinburgh, but it
still pays to use common sense.
Keep your wallet and other
valuables out of sight; and
never leave bags, coats and
purses unattended.

Edinburgh's city centre is a
pretty safe and civilised place,
but the rather lairy pub culture
on the Cowgate and Lothian
Road can be a little unpleasant
at closing time. Ill-lit parks
such as the Meadows have
been the scene of (infrequent)
assaults down the years.
Women should avoid the Leith
backstreets, one of the region's
main red-light districts. Away
from the centre at Edinburgh's
various peripheral housing
schemes, things get a lot dicier;
these areas are best avoided.

Smoking

Smoking has been banned
in enclosed public spaces
across Scotland, including
all restaurants and pubs,
since early 2006. The sight of
smokers huddled around their
cigarettes on street corners is
now common around town.

Study

A good deal of Edinburgh's
character is defined by its big
student population. Most study
at one of four universities, of
which the most prestigious is
the **University of Edinburgh**
(Old College, South Bridge,
South Edinburgh, 650 1000,
www.ed.ac.uk). Founded in
1583, it's since been joined by
Heriot-Watt University
(Riccarton Campus, Currie, 449
5111, www.hw.ac.uk), **Napier
University** (Craiglockhart
Campus, 219 Colinton Road,
South Edinburgh, 0845 260
6040, www.napier.ac.uk) and
Queen Margaret University
(Corstorphine Campus,
Clerwood Terrace, West
Edinburgh, 317 3000, www.
qmuc.ac.uk). There's also the
well-regarded **Edinburgh
College of Art** (Lauriston
Place, South Edinburgh, 221
6000, www.eca.ac.uk).

For language courses, check
the *Yellow Pages*.

Telephones

The area code for Edinburgh
is 0131. From outside the UK,
dial the international access
code (011 if you're in the US),
then the country code (44 for
the UK), then the area code
omitting the first 0, then the
rest of the number. To reach
the **Edinburgh Convention
Bureau** (*see p299*) from the
US, for example, dial 011 44
131 473 3666; for **Edinburgh
Airport** (*see p296*), call 011
44 870 040 0007. Glasgow's
area code is 0141.

Dialling codes

Mobile phone numbers begin
077, 078 and 079. It's free to
call numbers prefixed 0800
or 0808. Calls to numbers
beginning 0845 are charged
at local rates; calls to 0870
numbers are charged at
national rates. Premium-rate
numbers begin 09.

International codes

Australia 00 61; Belgium 00 32; Canada 00 1; France 00 33; Germany 00 49; Ireland 00 353; Italy 00 39; Japan 00 81; Netherlands 00 31; New Zealand 00 64; Spain 00 34; USA 00 1.

Mobile phones

Mobile phones in the UK operate on either the 900 MHz or 1800 MHz GSM frequencies common throughout most of Europe. If you're travelling to the UK from Europe, your phone should be compatible; if you're travelling from the US, you'll need a tri-band handset. Either way, you should check that your phone is enabled for international roaming, and that your service provider at home has a reciprocal arrangement with a UK provider.

Operator services

Operator 100.
Speaking clock 123.
Automated alarm calls *55*.
Directory enquiries This service is now operated by a variety of different firms. The most reliable is BT (call 118 500); a similar service is available from other companies by calling 118 118, 118 247, or 118 800.

Public phones

Public payphones take coins, credit cards or prepaid phonecards (and sometimes all three). The minimum cost is 20p. BT phonecards are available from post offices and many newsagents in denominations of £2, £5, £10 and £20. Most public phones in the city centre also have now an integrated internet facility (see p283).

Time

Edinburgh operates on Greenwich Mean Time (GMT). Clocks go forward to run on British Summer Time (BST) at 1am on the last Saturday in March, and return to GMT on the last Saturday in October.

Tipping

Tipping 10-15% in taxis, restaurants, hairdressers and some bars (but not pubs) is normal. Some restaurants and bars add service automatically to all bills; always check to avoid paying twice.

Toilets

It's generally not acceptable to use the toilets of cafés or bars unless you're a customer or have a small and desperate child in tow. However, the department stores on and around Princes Street all have public lavatories, while the city maintains a decent number of public toilets around town. A number of them are listed below. Those at Tollcross, the Mound, Nicolson Square and Hamilton Place have disabled facilities; the Tollcross toilets also have baby-changing facilities.

Public toilets

Canonmills *Stockbridge*. **Open** 10am-8pm daily. **Map** p326 F3.
Castlehill *Old Town*.
Open *Summer* 10am-8pm daily. *Autumn-spring* 10am-6pm daily. **Map** p330 G7, p336 D4.
Hunter Square *Old Town*.
Open 10am-10pm daily.
Map p331 J7, p336 F4.
The Mound *Princes Street, New Town*. **Open** *Men* 10am-10pm daily. *Ladies* no facilities. *Disabled* 24hrs daily using National Key Scheme.
Map p326/p330 G6, p336 D2.
Nicolson Square *Old Town*. **Open** 10am-8pm daily. **Map** p331 J8.
Tollcross *Old Town*. **Open** 10am-8pm daily. **Map** p330 F9.
West Princes Street Gardens *Princes Street, New Town*.
Open *Summer* 8am-8pm daily.
Map p330 F7, p336 C2.

Tourist information

The **Edinburgh & Lothians Tourist Board** operates the main tourist office in the city, at the east end of Princes Street. As well as distributing a wealth of information on tours and attractions, staff can book hotels and event tickets (via Ticketmaster), car hire and coach trips. There's also internet access and a bureau de change. The information point at the airport has a smaller range of services, but can help with tours and hotels. There are other centres around the Lothians; see www. edinburgh.org for details.

If you're travelling via London, the **Scottish Tourist Board** office may be worth a visit. The range of services is similar to that offered at the office in Edinburgh.

Edinburgh & Scotland Information Centre *Above Princes Mall, 3 Princes Street, New Town, EH2 2QP (0845 225 5121/www.edinburgh.org). Princes Street buses.* **Open** *Apr, Oct* 9am-6pm Mon-Sat; 10am-6pm Sun. *May, June, Sept* 9am-7pm Mon-Sat; 10am-7pm Sun. *July, Aug* 9am-8pm Mon-Sat; 10am-8pm Sun. *Nov-Mar* 9am-5pm Mon-Sat; 10am-5pm Sun. **Map** p326/p330 H6, p336 F2.
Edinburgh Airport Tourist Information Desk
Edinburgh Airport (0870 040 0007/ www.edinburgh.org). **Open** *Apr-Oct* 6.30am-10.30pm daily. *Nov-Mar* 7am-9pm daily.
Scottish Tourist Board
19 Cockspur Street, London SW1Y 5BL (0845 225 5121/www.visit scotland.com). Piccadilly Circus tube. **Open** *May-Sept* 9.30am-6.30pm Mon-Fri; 10am-5pm Sat. *Oct-Apr* 10am-6pm Mon-Fri; noon-4pm Sat.

Visas & immigration

EU citizens do not require a visa to visit the UK; citizens of the USA, Canada, Australia, South Africa and New Zealand can also enter with only a passport for tourist visits of up to six months as long as they can show they can support themselves during their visit and plan to return. Use www. ukvisas.gov.uk to check your visa status well before you travel, or contact the British embassy, consulate or high commission in your own country. You can arrange visas online at www.fco.gov.uk. For work permits, see p307.

Home Office *Immigration & Nationality Bureau, Lunar House, 40 Wellesley Road, Croydon, Surrey CR9 1AT (0870 606 7766/ applications 0870 241 0645/ www.homeoffice.gov.uk).*

Weights & measures

As part of Europe, Scotland uses kilos and metres, but only nominally: natives still tend to think in Imperial measures.

When to go

There isn't really a best or a worst time to visit Edinburgh: it all depends on what you want from your visit. The slew of cultural festivals means August is the liveliest and most interesting month of the year. However, it's also the busiest: the pavements are awash with tourists and street performers, and there are queues virtually everywhere. Similarly, the Hogmanay celebrations draw hordes each year, but aren't to everyone's taste. For more on August's festivals, *see pp41-50*; for other special events, *see pp208-209*.

The legendarily changeable Scottish weather further complicates matters. Winters can be quite chilly and summers are generally pleasant, but the rain is a constant threat all year round. There's no guarantee of good weather at any time, but between the months of May and October, when the days get longer and you can finally get your thermals off, the city is probably at its best.

Public holidays

Edinburgh shares some public holidays with the whole of the UK and others with only the rest of Scotland, and even has one holiday of its own. Many shops remain open on public holidays, but public transport services are less frequent.

Virtually everything is closed on Christmas Day, and most businesses are shut on New Year's Day.

New Year Holidays
2007 Mon 1 Jan, Tue 2 Jan.
2008 Tue 1 Jan, Wed 2 Jan.
Easter Holidays
2007 Fri 6 Apr (Good Friday), Mon 9 Apr (Easter Monday).
2008 Fri 21 Mar (Good Friday), Mon 24 Mar (Easter Monday)
Spring Holiday
2007 Mon 16 Apr.
2008 Mon 21 Apr.
May Day
2007 Mon 7 May.
2008 Mon 5 May.
Victoria Day (Edinburgh only)
2007 Mon 21 May.
2008 Mon 19 May.
Autumn Holiday
2007 Mon 17 Sept.
2008 Mon 15 Sept.
Christmas Holidays
2007 Tue 25 Dec (Christmas Day), Wed 26 Dec (Boxing Day).
2008 Thur 25 Dec (Christmas Day), Fri 26 Dec (Boxing Day).

Women

Women travelling on their own face the usual hassles, but this is generally a safe city. Take the same precautions you'd take in any big city. Many of the city's black cab firms now give priority to lone women, whether booked by phone (recommended after midnight) or flagged in the street. *See p305* for general safety and security tips.

Working in Edinburgh

Finding temporary work in Edinburgh can tough, but if you speak English and are an EU citizen or the owner of a work permit, you should be able to find a job in catering or labouring, or in a bar, pub, café or shop. Graduates with an English or foreign-language degree could try teaching. For more, see *Summer Jobs in Britain* (available from www.vacationwork.co.uk).

To find work, check the *Scotsman* and other national newspapers, and in windows of newsagents. There's often temporary and unskilled work available: look in the *Yellow Pages* under 'Employment Agencies'. Restaurants and bars often advertise jobs in their windows.

Work permits

EEA citizens, residents of Gibraltar and certain categories of other overseas nationals (such as citizens of other Commonwealth countries aged 17-27) do not require a work permit. However, Citizens of non-European Economic Area (EEA) countries need a permit to work legally in the UK.

Climate

	Average high	Average low	Average rain
Jan	6°C (43°F)	1°C (34°F)	64mm (2.5in)
Feb	7°C (45°F)	1°C (34°F)	45mm (1.8in)
Mar	9°C (48°F)	2°C (36°F)	52mm (2.0in)
Apr	11°C (52°F)	3°C (37°F)	43mm (1.7in)
May	14°C (57°F)	6°C (43°F)	49mm (1.9in)
June	17°C (63°F)	9°C (48°F)	53mm (2.1in)
July	19°C (66°F)	11°C (52°F)	58mm (2.3in)
Aug	19°C (66°F)	10°C (50°F)	53mm (2.1in)
Sept	16°C (61°F)	9°C (48°F)	62mm (2.4in)
Oct	13°C (55°F)	6°C (43°F)	70mm (2.8in)
Nov	9°C (48°F)	3°C (37°F)	61mm (2.4in)
Dec	7°C (45°F)	1°C (34°F)	67mm (2.6in)

Directory

Further Reference

Books

Fiction

Kate Atkinson
One Good Turn
The fifth novel by York-born, Edinburgh-based Atkinson is set at the International Festival.

Iain Banks *Complicity*
A visceral, body-littered thriller, with spot-on characterisation of both the city and the protagonists.

Pat Barker *Regeneration*
During World War I, Wilfred Owen and Siegfried Sassoon met at Craiglockhart Hospital, where both were being treated for shellshock. Writing from the perspective of the hospital's psychiatrist, Barker skilfully blends fact and fiction.

Ron Butlin *Night Visits*
'Edinburgh at its grandest, coldest and hardest… as if nothing less than such a stony grip and iron inflexibility were needed to prevent unimaginable pain,' as the *TLS* put it.

Laura Hird *Born Free*
Family life on a modern Edinburgh housing estate. Beautifully observed and humorous to boot.

James Hogg *Confessions of a Justified Sinner*
An ironic jibe against religious bigotry in the 17th and 18th centuries, set in the turmoil of Edinburgh at that time.

Paul Johnston
The Bone Yard; Body Politic; Water of Death
Futuristic detective fiction set in a nightmare vision of Edinburgh as a city state with a year-round Festival, where the impoverished populace lives to serve the needs of the tourists. Some locals will tell you this book should be classified under non-fiction.

Alexander McCall Smith
The Sunday Philosophy Club; Friends, Lovers, Chocolate; 44 Scotland Street
The prolific Edinburgh University law professor's output includes a detective series set in the city and a collection of whimsical short stories about the residents of the 44 Scotland Street, first published in the *Scotsman*. Look out for a cameo from Ian Rankin.

Ian Rankin
Inspector Rebus novels
Hardbitten Detective Rebus inhabits a city that many of Edinburgh's inhabitants recognise as their own. The earlier novels are best for a strong sense of place.

JK Rowling *Harry Potter and the Philosopher's Stone; Harry Potter and the Chamber of Secrets*; et al
An unemployed Rowling headed to Edinburgh cafés to write the first book in the Harry Potter series. According to *Forbes* magazine in the US, she's now a billionaire.

Sir Walter Scott
The Heart of Midlothian
Scott's 1818 novel contains, among many other tales, an account of the Porteous lynching of 1736.

Robert Louis Stevenson
Edinburgh: Picturesque Notes; The Strange Case of Dr Jekyll and Mr Hyde
Stevenson's *Picturesque Notes* are perceptive, witty and the source of many subsequent opinions about Edinburgh. The inspiration for his famous tale of a murderous split personality, meanwhile, came from the double life of one of Edinburgh's more notorious citizens, cabinet-maker turned criminal Deacon Brodie.

Muriel Spark
The Prime of Miss Jean Brodie
Schoolteacher Jean Brodie makes a stand against the city's moral intransigence and small-minded conventionality. Practically the official Edinburgh novel.

Alan Warner *The Sopranos*
Spot-on story about a group of badly behaved teenage choir girls on a school trip in the capital.

Irvine Welsh *Trainspotting; Porno; Filth; The Acid House*
The first and best of Welsh's novels, *Trainspotting*, focuses on the culture of drugs, clubs and unemployment that many genteel Edinburgh residents do their best to ignore.

Non-fiction

Neil Ascherson *Stone Voices: The Search for Scotland*
Edinburgh-born Ascherson's unusual, insightful and beautifully written meditation on Scotland past and present.

George Bruce
Festival of the North
The story of the Edinburgh International Festival, from its conception and its birth in 1947 until 1975.

Donald Campbell
Edinburgh: A Cultural and Literary History
Part of the always-involving Cities of the Imagination series, Campbell's book takes a digressionary wander through Edinburgh's cultural past.

David Daitches
Edinburgh
A highly readable and academically sound history of the city.

Jan-Andrew Henderson
The Town Below the Ground: Edinburgh's Legendary Underground City
Everything you needed to know about the below-ground slums of the Old Town.

John Lamond & Robin Tucek *The Malt Whisky File*
Reviews of all the distilleries and nearly every malt that's sold, with useful tasting notes.

John Prebble
The King's Jaunt
Everything you could want to know about King George IV's agenda-setting visit of 1822.
James U Thomson
Edinburgh Curiosities
A look at the city's history that reveals its dark underbelly and quirky nature, with the stories of some of its more colourful characters and events.
AJ Youngson *The Making of Classical Edinburgh*
An exhaustive account, with superb photos and plans, of the building of the New Town.

Poetry

Robert Burns
Complete Poems and Songs
Widely regarded as Scotland's national poet, Rabbie Burns' works are known the world over. Among them are 'Auld Lang Syne' and 'To a Mouse'.
William Dunbar
Selected Poems
There's plenty to enjoy in the vibrant, bawdy poems of William Dunbar, poet, priest and member of James IV's court. 'To the Merchantis of Edinburgh' is a vivid (and less than flattering) depiction of 15th-century Edinburgh's sights, sounds and smells.
Robert Fergusson
Selected Poems
Born in Edinburgh in 1750, Fergusson died in poverty in the city's Bedlam just 24 years later. One of his most staunch admirers was Robert Burns, who paid for a memorial stone to mark his fellow poet's grave in the Canongate. 'Auld Reekie', his most famous poem, brings the squalid streets of 18th-century Edinburgh to life.
William McGonagall
Poetic Gems
Was he serious? Was it all one big prank? Decide for yourself in this selection of works by Edinburgh-born McGonagall, widely acknowledged to be one of the worst published poets in literary history.

Films

Chariots of Fire
(*David Puttnam, 1981*)
Based on the true story of the 1924 Olympics, where Edinburgh sportsman Eric Liddell ran for Britain, David Puttnam's film has spectacular shots of Salisbury Crags.
The Da Vinci Code
(*Ron Howard, 2006*)
Rosslyn Chapel, six miles south of Edinburgh, plays a key role in Ron Howard's blockbuster adaptation of Dan Brown's novel.
The Debt Collector
(*Anthony Neilson, 1999*)
Shot for the most part in Glasgow, this thriller – starring Billy Connoly – was nonetheless set in Edinburgh, and features several prominent and recognisable city locations.
The Prime of Miss Jean Brodie
(*Ronald Neame, 1969*)
God forbid they should ever remake it. Maggie Smith will forever be Edinburgh's best-known schoolmarm.
Shallow Grave
(*Danny Boyle, 1994*)
Darkly humorous feature about three Edinburgh yuppies who find themselves landed with a suitcase full of drug money and a dead body.
The 39 Steps
(*Alfred Hitchcock, 1935*)
Hitchcock's loose adaptation of John Buchan's novel introduced what would become one of his enduring themes: the innocent man framed by circumstantial evidence. Shots of Edinburgh are scarce but evocative; Ralph Thomas's 1959 remake featured the city more prominently.
Trainspotting
(*Danny Boyle, 1996*)
Based on Irvine Welsh's novel, this portrayal of the city's heroin culture is a pitch-black comedy. The film was shot mostly in Glasgow, but its opening sequences were filmed in Edinburgh.

Websites

Edinburgh City Council
www.edinburgh.gov.uk
That rare beast: a local government website that's well designed and easily browsed.
Edinburgh & Lothians Tourist Board
www.edinburgh.org
The 'official' guide to the city.
Edinburgh Festivals
www.edinburgh-festivals.com
An excellent resource, featuring searchable listings for all the cultural festivals held in August.
Edinburgh Galleries Association
www.edinburgh-galleries.co.uk
Listings information for Edinburgh's art scene.
Edinburgh's Hogmanay
www.edinburghshogmanay.org
Happy new year...
General Register Office
www.gro-scotland.gov.uk
Information on tracing your family history.
Historic Scotland
www.historic-scotland.gov.uk
The government body in charge of Scotland's historic monuments. There's details of events and attractions, though the search function is a bit cranky.
The List *www.list.co.uk*
The magazine's website is the best online resource for event listings in the city.
National Trust for Scotland *www.nts.org.uk*
Information on all NTS properties around the country.
Scotch Malt Whisky Society *www.smws.co.uk*
The SMWS site contains a useful malt whisky primer.
Scottish Executive
www.scotland.gov.uk
Useful information.
Scottish Parliament
www.scottish.parliament.uk
A user-friendly guide to the newish set-up in the city.
Scottish Tourist Board
www.visitscotland.com
The countrywide tourist agency.

Directory

Index

Note: page numbers in **bold** indicate section(s) giving key information on topic; *italics* indicate illustrations.

Advertisers' Index

Index

Glasgow Street Index

Place of interest and/or entertainment	☐
Hospital or college	☐
Railway station	☐
Parks	☐
River	☐
Motorway	═══
Main road	
Pedestrian road	
Airport	✈
Church	✚
Area name	LEITH
Hotels	➊
Restaurants & cafés	➊
Pubs & bars	➊

Maps

Scotland

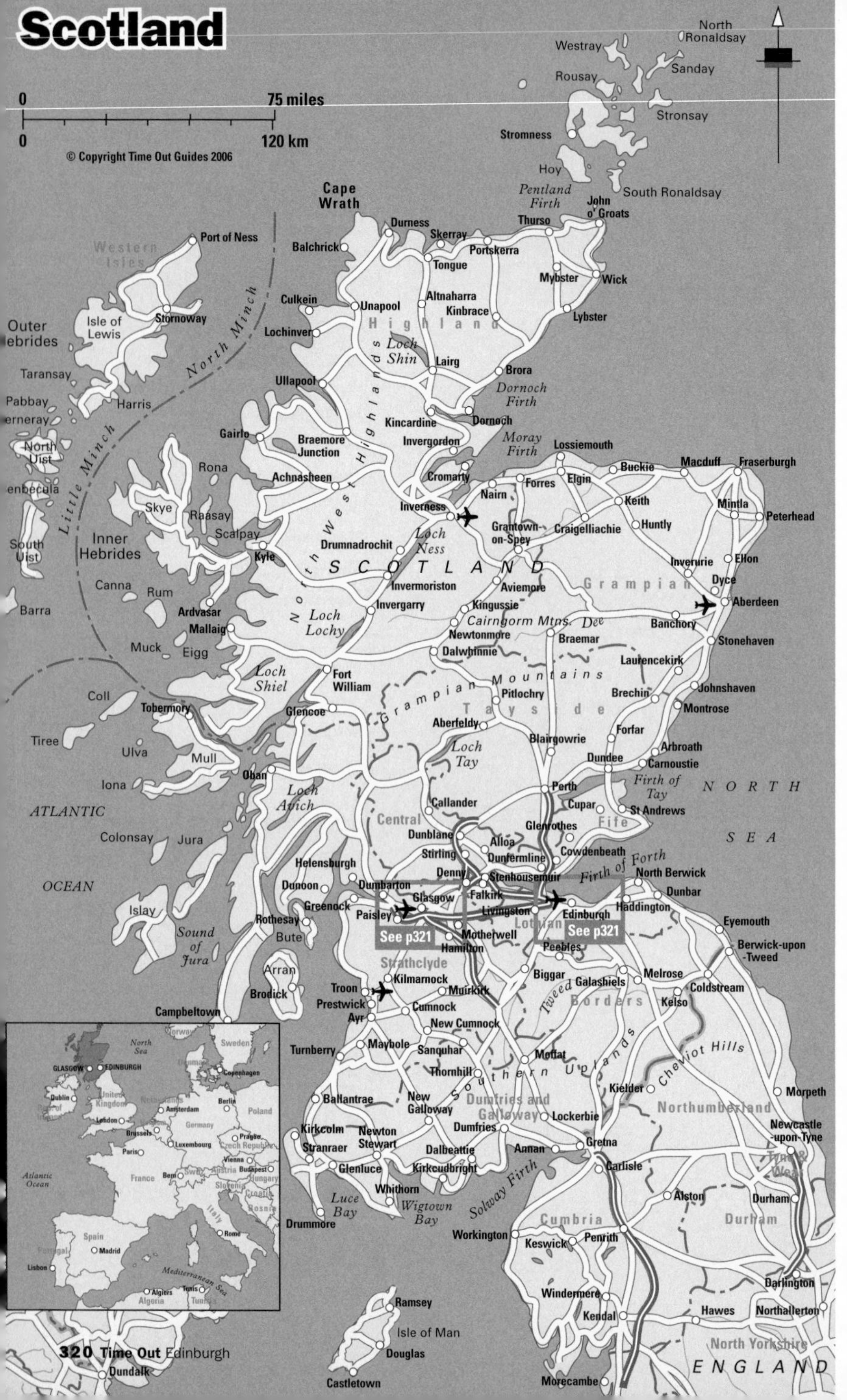
0
75 miles
0
120 km
© Copyright Time Out Guides 2006
North Ronaldsay
Westray
Sanday
Rousay
Stronsay
Stromness
Hoy
South Ronaldsay
Pentland Firth
John o' Groats
Thurso
Cape Wrath
Durness
Skerray
Portskerra
Balchrick
Tongue
Mybster
Wick
Port of Ness
Western Isles
Culkein
Unapool
Altnaharra
Kinbrace
Lybster
Outer Hebrides
Isle of Lewis
Stornoway
Lochinver
Highland
Loch Shin
Lairg
Brora
North Minch
Taransay
Ullapool
Dornoch Firth
Pabbay
Harris
Berneray
Kincardine
Dornoch
Gairloch
Braemore Junction
Invergordon
Moray Firth
Lossiemouth
North Uist
Little Minch
Rona
Cromarty
Buckie
Macduff
Fraserburgh
Benbecula
Achnasheen
Forres
Elgin
Nairn
Keith
Mintla
Peterhead
Skye
Raasay
Inverness
Grantown-on-Spey
Craigelliachie
Huntly
South Uist
Inner Hebrides
Scalpay
Loch Ness
Drumnadrochit
Kyle
North West Highlands
SCOTLAND
Inverurie
Ellon
Dyce
Invermoriston
Aviemore
Grampian
Canna
Rum
Barra
Ardvasar
Invergarry
Kingussie
Aberdeen
Mallaig
Loch Lochy
Cairngorm Mtns.
Dee
Banchory
Newtonmore
Muck
Eigg
Braemar
Stonehaven
Dalwhinnie
Laurencekirk
Loch Shiel
Fort William
Mountains
Johnshaven
Coll
Grampian
Pitlochry
Brechin
Tobermory
Glencoe
Tayside
Montrose
Aberfeldy
Forfar
Tiree
Ulva
Mull
Loch Tay
Blairgowrie
Arbroath
Dundee
Carnoustie
Iona
Oban
Firth of Tay
NORTH
ATLANTIC
Loch Awich
Perth
Callander
Cupar
St Andrews
Central
Glenrothes
Fife
Colonsay
Jura
Dunblane
Alloa
SEA
Stirling
Dunfermline
Cowdenbeath
Helensburgh
Firth of Forth
OCEAN
Denny
Stenhousemuir
North Berwick
Dunoon
Dumbarton
Falkirk
Dunbar
Glasgow
Greenock
Livingston
Haddington
Islay
Paisley
Edinburgh
Rothesay
Lothian
Eyemouth
Sound of Jura
Bute
See p321
Motherwell
See p321
Hamilton
Peebles
Berwick-upon-Tweed
Arran
Strathclyde
Biggar
Galashiels
Melrose
Troon
Kilmarnock
Tweed
Brodick
Borders
Coldstream
Prestwick
Muirkirk
Kelso
Campbeltown
Cumnock
Ayr
New Cumnock
Turnberry
Maybole
Sanquhar
Moffat
Cheviot Hills
Southern Uplands
Thornhill
Kielder
Morpeth
Ballantrae
New Galloway
Dumfries and Galloway
Lockerbie
Northumberland
Kirkcolm
Newton Stewart
Dumfries
Newcastle-upon-Tyne
Stranraer
Dalbeattie
Annan
Gretna
Tyne & Wear
Glenluce
Kirkcudbright
Carlisle
Whithorn
Solway Firth
Alston
Durham
Luce Bay
Wigtown Bay
Drummore
Cumbria
Durham
Workington
Keswick
Penrith
Darlington
Windermere
Ramsey
Isle of Man
Kendal
Hawes
Northallerton
Douglas
North Yorkshire
Dundalk
Castletown
Morecambe
ENGLAND
North Sea
Norway
Sweden
GLASGOW
EDINBURGH
Denmark
Copenhagen
Dublin
United Kingdom
Netherlands
Berlin
Rep. of Ireland
Amsterdam
Poland
London
Germany
Brussels
Prague
Luxembourg
Czech Republic
Paris
Vienna
Budapest
Atlantic Ocean
France
Bern
Switz.
Austria
Hungary
Slovenia
Croatia
Bosnia
Italy
Rome
Spain
Madrid
Portugal
Lisbon
Mediterranean Sea
Algiers
Tunis
Algeria
Tunisia

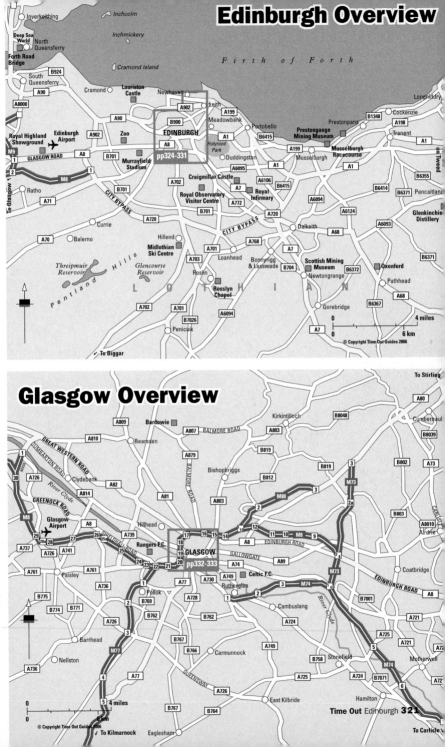

Edinburgh Overview

Glasgow Overview

Edinburgh by Area

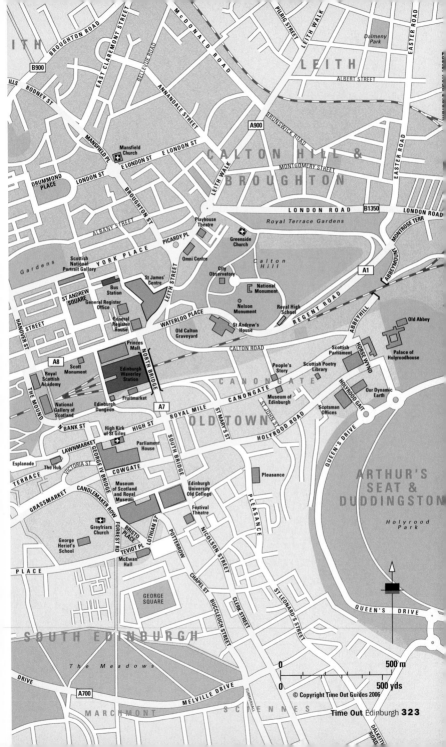

ITH

B900

ILLS

RODNEY ST

DRUMMOND
PLACE

Gardens

HANOVER STREET

BROUGHTON ROAD

EAST CLAREMONT STREET

MANSFIELD PL

Mansfield
Church

LONDON ST

BELLEVUE ROAD

ANNANDALE STREET

McDONALD ROAD

PIRIG STREET

LEITH WALK

Dalmeny
Park

EASTER ROAD

LEITH

ALBERT STREET

E LONDON ST

E LONDON ST

BROUGHTON ST

A900

BRUNSWICK ROAD

CALTON HILL &

BROUGHTON

EASTER ROAD

MONTGOMERY STREET

ALBANY STREET

Scottish
National
Portrait Gallery

ST ANDREW
SQUARE

General Register
Office

General
Register
House

YORK PLACE

PICARDY PL

Playhouse
Theatre

Omni Centre

LEITH STREET

St James'
Centre

Bus
Station

Princes
Mall

Greenside
Church

City
Observatory

LONDON ROAD

B1350

LONDON ROAD

Royal Terrace Gardens

MONTROSE TERR

Calton
Hill

National
Monument

Nelson
Monument

A1

ABBEYMOUNT

A8

Royal
Scottish
Academy

THE MOUND

National
Gallery of
Scotland

Scott
Monument

Edinburgh
Waverley Station

Fruitmarket

Edinburgh
Dungeon

WATERLOO PLACE

Old Calton
Graveyard

NORTH BRIDGE

St Andrew's
House

Royal High
School

REGENT ROAD

CALTON ROAD

People's
Story

Scottish
Parliament

Scottish Poetry
Library

HORSE WYND

Old Abbey

Palace of
Holyroodhouse

ABBEYHILL

BANK ST

High Kirk
of St Giles

HIGH ST

Museum
of Edinburgh

Scotsman
Offices

Our Dynamic
Earth

HOLYROOD GAIT

Esplanade

TERRACE

The Hub

Victoria St

LAWNMARKET

GEORGE IV BRIDGE

COWGATE

Parliament
House

SOUTH BRIDGE

CANONGATE

ROYAL MILE

A7

OLD TOWN

ST MARY'S ST

ST JOHN'S ST

CANONGATE

HOLYROOD ROAD

QUEEN'S DRIVE

ARTHUR'S
SEAT &
DUDDINGSTON

Holyrood
Park

GRASSMARKET

CANDLEMAKER ROW

Greyfriars
Church

George Heriot's
School

BRISTO
PLACE

FORREST RD

TEVIOT PL

Museum
of Scotland
and Royal
Museum

McEwan
Hall

Edinburgh
University
Old College

Festival
Theatre

LOTHIAN ST

POTTERROW

CHAPEL ST

Pleasance

PLEASANCE

NICOLSON STREET

ST LEONARD'S STREET

PLACE

GEORGE
SQUARE

BUCCLEUCH STREET

CLERK STREET

QUEEN'S DRIVE

SOUTH EDINBURGH

The Meadows

A700

MELVILLE DRIVE

MARCHMONT

SUMMERHALL

SCIENNES

0   500 m

0   500 yds

© Copyright Time Out Guides 2006

DALKEITH ROAD

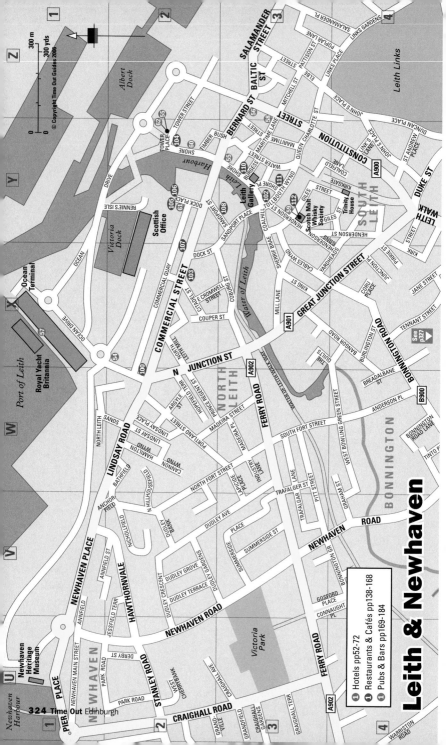

Leith & Newhaven

Z

300 m
300 yds

© Copyright Time Out Guides 2006.

Albert Dock

Victoria Dock

Scottish Office

Y

Ocean Terminal

Royal Yacht Britannia

Port of Leith

X

Newhaven Harbour

Newhaven Heritage Museum

W

V

Victoria Park

U

SALAMANDER STREET

BALTIC ST

BERNARD ST

CONSTITUTION STREET

DUKE ST

Leith Links

Leith Gallery

SOUTH LEITH

Trinity House

Scotch Malt Whisky Society

LEITH WALK

NORTH LEITH

COMMERCIAL STREET

JUNCTION ST

GREAT JUNCTION STREET

BONNINGTON ROAD

FERRY ROAD

BONNINGTON

NEWHAVEN ROAD

FERRY ROAD

NEWHAVEN PLACE

LINDSAY ROAD

HAWTHORNVALE

STANLEY ROAD

NEWHAVEN

PIER PLACE

CRAIGHALL ROAD

WARRISTON ROAD

Water of Leith

See p327

① Hotels pp52-72
① Restaurants & Cafés pp138-168
① Pubs & Bars pp169-184

324 Time Out Edinburgh

FERRY ROAD

Edinburgh
Academy

1

Inverleith
House

INVERLEITH PLACE

INVERLEITH PLACE LANE

ARBORETUM ROAD

KINNEAR ROAD

0   300 m
0   300 yds
© Copyright Time Out Guides 2006

EAST FETTES AVENUE

Inverleith
Park

Fettes
College

INVERLEITH PLACE

59

Royal Botanic
Garden

2

See
p326

ARBORETUM PLACE

INVERLEITH TERRACE

CARRINGTON ROAD

Inverleith
Pond

TEVIOTDALE PL

3

FETTES AVENUE

EAST FETTES AVENUE

NORTH PARK TERR

PORTGOWER PLACE

ARBORETUM AVENUE

REID TERRACE

H MILLER PL

BONILY PL

COLVILLE PL

SUMMERBANK

RINTOUL PL

BALLENTINE PL

GABRIEL'S RD

SAXE COBURG
PLACE

DEAN BANK LANE

STOCKBRIDGE

COMELY BANK RD

RAEBURN PLACE

ST BERNARDS ROW

MALTA TERR

DEANHAUGH ST

KERR ST

33

4

B900

COMELY BANK RD

COMELY BANK PLACE

COMELY BANK

BANK GROVE

COMELY BANK AVENUE

COMELY BANK PLACE

DEAN PARK ST

BEDFORD STREET

CHEYNE ST

RAEBURN ST

DEAN STREET

58

37

52

LESLIE PLACE

DEAN TERRACE

SAUNDERS ST

INDIA PLACE

LEARMONTH AVENUE

LEARMONTH GROVE

LEARMONTH PLACE

DEAN PARK MEWS

DEAN STREET

ST BERNARD'S
CRESCENT

CARLTON ST

DANUBE STREET

LEARMONTH GARDENS

SOUTH LEARMONTH GARDENS

ORCHARD BRAE

37 60

LEARMONTH TERRACE LANE

LEARMONTH TERRACE

DEAN PARK CRESCENT

ANN STREET

DOUNE TERR

5

MORAY

ORCHARD BRAE AVENUE

A90

OXFORD TERRACE

LENNOX ST

ETON TERRACE

QUEENSFERRY ROAD

BUCKINGHAM TERRACE

CLARENDON CRES

Water of Leith

PLACE

Dean
Cemetery

DEAN PATH

RAVELSTON
TERRACE

BELGRAVE PLACE

BELGRAVE CRESCENT LANE

BELGRAVE CRESCENT

AINSLIE
PLACE

ST COLME ST

Georgian
House

6

DEAN
BRIDGE

DEAN PATH

See
p329

D E A N

Time Out Edinburgh **325**

See p336

❶ Hotels pp52-72
❶ Restaurants & Cafés pp138-168
❶ Pubs & Bars pp169-184

St Marks Park

Warriston Cemetery

Water of Leith

WARRISTON GD
WARRISTON TERRACE
WARRISTON DRIVE
WARRISTON AVE
WARRISTON
EILDON TERRACE
EILDON STREET

INVERLEITH ROW

1 Glasshouses

Sports Ground

WARRISTON CRESCENT

WARRISTON ROAD

LOGIE GREEN ROAD

POWDERHALL ROAD

BEAVERBANK PLACE

BEAVERHALL ROAD

DUNEDIN STREET

B900

2 Royal Botanic Garden

INVERLEITH TERRACE
38
INVERLEITH TERR LANE

BROUGHTON ROAD

HERIOT HILL TERR

CLAREMONT GROVE

CLAREMONT BANK

CLAREMONT CRES
45

EAST CLAREMONT STREET

CLAREMONT GARDENS

MELGUND

BELLEVUE

CANONMILLS
57

RODNEY STREET

BELLEVUE TERR

GREEN STREET

S T O C K B R I D G E

AVONDALE
KEMP PL
BELL'S
GLENOGLE ROAD

BRANDON TERRACE

CANON LANE
CANON ST
EYRE CRESCENT
CANON ST
EYRE PLACE
LOGAN ST
PROSPECT BANK

MANSFIELD PL

BELLEVUE LANE
BELLEVUE PLACE
BELLEVUE CRESCENT

Mansfield Church ✚

B R O U G

See p325

Edinburgh Academy

PERTH ST

HENDERSON ROW
18

DUNDAS STREET

EYRE PLACE
39
EYRE TERRACE

ROYAL CRESCENT

SCOTLAND STREET

LANE WEST

SCOTLAND ST LANE EAST

BELLEVUE CRESCENT

DRUMMOND

LONDON STREET

E LONDON ST
36

SAXE COBURG PL
HAMILTON PLACE
CLARENCE ST
W SILVERM'LLS LANE
LLS LANE
EAST SILVERMILLS LANE

FETTES ROW

C'LAND ST NW LANE
C'LAND ST
19
DUNDONALD STREET

PLACE

BROUGHTON

BROUGHTON

4 **Theatre Workshop**

54
34
32 61
62

CIRCUS LANE

ROYAL

NW CIRCUS PLACE

CIRCUS

CUMBERLAND ST
C'LAND ST SW LANE
24
GREAT KING STREET

N'LAND ST NE LANE

NELSON ST

BARONY STREET

ALBANY ST LANE
64

ALBANY STREET
28

BROUGHTON MARKET
52

YORK LANE

YORK LANE

GLOUC PL

INDIA STREET

N E W

5

GLOUCESTER LANE

MORAY PLACE

JAMAICA ST N LANE
JAMAICA
JAMAICA ST S LANE

HOWE STREET

NORTHUMBERLAND STREET NW LANE
31
46
N'LAND ST SE LANE

T O W N

NORTHUMBERLAND STREET SW LANE
34
47
HERIOT ROW

ABERCROMBY PLACE

DUBLIN STREET

DUBLIN ST LANE SOUTH

Gardens

Scottish National Portrait Gallery
17

YORK PLACE

See p336

St James Centre

FORRES ST
WEMYSS PL

Q U E E N

QUEEN ST GDNS W

QUEEN ST GDNS E

S T R E E T

Queen Street

Gardens

33

ST ANDREW

CLYDE ST
MULTREES WALK
40

ELDER ST
ST JAMES PLACE
ST JAMES SQ

Bus Station
45

G

YOUNG ST LANE
24
YOUNG ST S LANE
29
23

NORTH CHARLOTTE ST

N CASTLE ST

YOUNG STREET

HILL STREET
HILL ST N LANE
HILL ST S LANE
38
33

GEORGE ST

FREDERICK STREET
28 32
44
30
36
37

THISTLE ST NW LA
THISTLE ST NE LA
51
THISTLE STREET
THISTLE ST SE LA
THISTLE ST SW LA

HANOVER ST

22
25
41

GEORGE STREET

25
14

SQUARE

General Register Office

W REGISTER ST
16
20
15
19
35

General Register House

7 **G**

326 Time Out Edinburgh

Albert Memorial

E

ROSE ST N LANE

GEORGE ST
29
32

ROSE ST N LANE
ROSE ST S LANE

F

Assembly Rooms
15

ROSE STREET
ROSE ST S LANE

ROSE

MEUSE LANE
SOUTH ST DAVID ST
SOUTH ST ANDREW ST

PRINCES STREET

Scott Monument

See p330

WAVERLEY BRIDGE

N BRIDGE

Princes Mall

Edinburgh Waverley Station

A8

Royal Scottish Academy

G

H

1 Hotels pp52-72
1 Restaurants & Cafés pp138-168
1 Pubs & Bars pp169-184

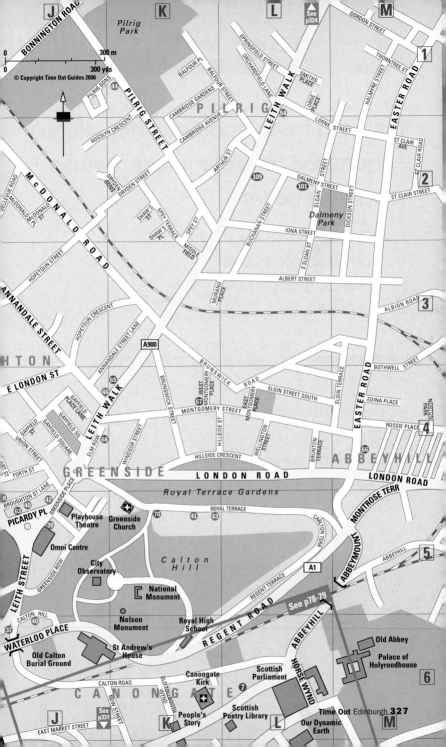

fast and fresh noodles · rice dishes · squeezed to order juices · wines · japanese beers

wagamama glasgow
97—103 west george st G2 1PB
0141 229 1468

opening hours mon to sat 12—11pm ı sunday 12—10pm

wagamama.com

uk ı ireland ı holland ı australia ı dubai ı antwerp ı auckland ı copenhagen ı istanbul

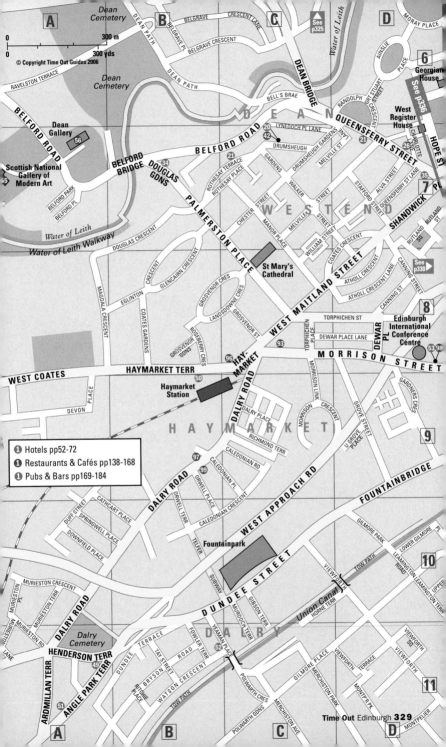

A Dean Cemetery
B
C See p325 Water of Leith
D MORAY PLACE

6 Georgian House

RAVELSTON TERRACE

Dean Cemetery

Dean Gallery 56

Scottish National Gallery of Modern Art

BELFORD ROAD

Water of Leith

Water of Leith Walkway

BELFORD BRIDGE

DOUGLAS GDNS

BELFORD PARK

BELFORD PL

BELFORD ROAD 21

DOUGLAS CRESCENT

MAGDALA CRESCENT

EGLINTON CRESCENT

COATES GARDENS

GLENCAIRN CRESCENT

GROSVENOR CRES

GROSVENOR ST

ROSEBERY GDNS

ROSEBERY CRES

LANDSDOWNE CRES

WEST COATES

DEVON PLACE

HAYMARKET TERR 50

Haymarket Station

DALRY ROAD

DUFF STREET

CATHCART PLACE

SPRINGWELL PLACE

DOWNFIELD PLACE

DALRY ROAD

ORWELL PLACE

ORWELL TERR

TELFER

CALEDONIAN CRESCENT

CALEDONIAN PL 99

CALEDONIAN RD 97

DALRY PLACE

RICHMOND TERR

MURIESTON CRESCENT

MURIESTON PL

MURIESTON TERR

MURIESTON RD

MURIESTON

DALRY ROAD

HENDERSON TERR

ARDMILLAN TERR 51

ANGLE PARK TERR

Dalry Cemetery

DUNDEE TERRACE

TAY STREET

BRYSON ROAD

RITCHIE PLACE

WATSON CRESCENT

TOW PATH

POLWARTH CRES

POLWARTH GDNS

MERCHISTON AVE

DEAN

DEAN PATH

DEAN CEMETERY

BELGRAVE PL

BELGRAVE CRESCENT

CRESCENT LANE

BELL'S BRAE

DEAN BRIDGE

QUEENSFERRY STREET

LYNEDOCH PL LANE 20 42

DRUMSHEUGH

ROTHESAY TERRACE

ROTHESAY PLACE

DRUMSHEUGH GARDENS

MELVILLE ST

CHESTER STREET

WALKER STREET

MELVILLE STREET

MANOR PLACE 34

PALMERSTON PLACE

St Mary's Cathedral

WEST END

WEST MAITLAND STREET

WILLIAM STREET

STAFFORD STREET

ALVA STREET

QUEENSFERRY ST LANE

COATES CRESCENT

ATHOLL CRESCENT

ATHOLL CRESCENT LANE

CANNING STREET

CANNING ST

RUTLAND STREET

RUTLAND SQ

SHANDWICK 7 PL

See p330 35

TORPHICHEN ST

TORPHICHEN PLACE

DEWAR PLACE LANE

DEWAR PL

93

MORRISON STREET

Edinburgh International Conference Centre 8

53 98

96 HAY-MARKET

HAYMARKET

MORRISON LINK

MORRISON CRESCENT

GROVE STREET

U GROVE PLACE

GARDNERS CRES

9

WEST APPROACH RD

FOUNTAINBRIDGE

VIEWFORTH

Fountainpark

DUNDEE STREET

GILMORE PARK

LOWER GILMORE

LEAMINGTON ROAD

LEAMINGTON TERRACE

UPPER

10

SUBWAY

GIBSON TERR

MURDOCH TERR

YEAMAN PLACE 52

FOWLER TERR

Union Canal

HORNE TERR

TOW PATH

GILMORE PLACE

VIEWFORTH PLACE

VIEWFORTH TERRACE

VIEWFORTH SQ

VIEWFORTH

MERCHISTON PARK

MONTPR PK

MONTPR PL

MONTPELIER

11

DALRY

MOORY PLACE

AINSLIE PLACE

RANDOLPH CRESCENT

GRT STUART STREET

CHARLOTTE

HOPE ST

West Register House

26

West End

❶ Hotels pp52-72
❶ Restaurants & Cafés pp138-168
❶ Pubs & Bars pp169-184

0   300 m
0   300 yds
© Copyright Time Out Guides 2006

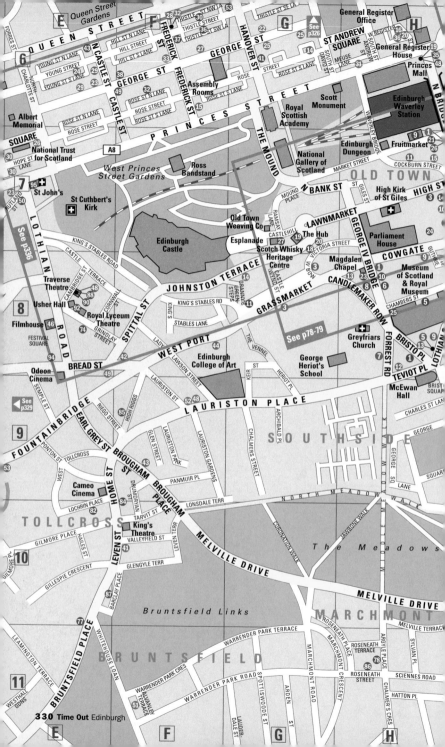